Desktop Data Analysis with SYSTAT®

Leland Wilkinson

Grant Blank

Christian Gruber

PRENTICE HALL, Upper Saddle River, New Jersey 07458

Library of Congress Cataloging-in-Publication Data

Wilkinson, Leland
    Desktop data analysis with SYSTAT / Leland Wilkinson, Grant Blank,
Christian Gruber.
        p. cm.
    Includes bibliological references (p.   -   ) and index.
    ISBN: 0-13-569310-1
    1. SYSTAT. 2. Mathematical statistics--Data processing.
I. Blank, Grant. II. Gruber, Christian. III. Title.
QA276.4.W58   1996
519.5'0285'53--dc20   96-11572
                                                                   CIP

Assistant Vice-President of Production
    and Manufacturing: **DAVID W. RICCARDI**
Editor-in-Chief: **JEROME GRANT**
Managing Editor: **LINDA BEHRENS**
Acquisitions Editor: **ANN HEATH**
Production Editor: **RICHARD DeLORENZO**
Cover Designer: **BRUCE KENSELAAR**
Prepress / Manufacturing Buyer: **ALAN FISCHER**
Editorial Assistant: **MINDY INCE**

©1996 by Prentice-Hall, Inc.
 Simon & Schuster / A Viacom Company
Upper Saddle River, NJ 07458

Printed in the United States of America

10 9 8 7 6 5 4 3 2 1

ISBN 0-13-569310-1

Prentice-Hall International (UK) Limited, London
Prentice-Hall of Australia Pty. Limited, Sydney
Prentice-Hall Canada Inc., Toronto
Prentice-Hall Hispanoamericana, S.A., Mexico
Prentice-Hall of India Private Limited, New Delhi
Prentice-Hall of Japan, Inc., Tokyo
Simon & Schuster Asia Pte. Ltd., Singapore
Editora Prentice-Hall do Brasil, Ltda., Rio de Janeiro

To Ruth, Denise, and Diane

Brief Contents

Contents

Part 2 Predicting Continuous Variables from Continuous Variables

Part 3 Predicting Continuous Variables from Categorical Variables

Part 4 Predicting Categorical Variables from Continuous Variables

Preface

You had one course in statistical methods in business school and now you must forecast ticket sales by prescreening films to selected test audiences.

You are an engineer who had introductory statistics 15 years ago and you have to model a process with time series methods.

You are a graduate student and want to learn something about multidimensional scaling to see if it is applicable to your dissertation.

You are a professor teaching multivariate data analysis and need a companion book to help students carry out computer analyses on their laptops at home.

You are an undergraduate student considering whether to major in statistics and you want to see how applied statisticians approach problems.

You are a professional statistician and want to see how SYSTAT handles analysis of variance designs.

You are someone who bought a copy of SYSTAT (or another statistical package) and produced six miles of printed and graphical output by tapping a few keys and you have no idea how to interpret it.

This should give you some idea of why we wrote *Desktop Data Analysis with SYSTAT*. This book should be useful to everyone from students with no more than a single statistics course to experienced researchers who need to know how to run SYSTAT to solve substantive problems.

This is not a statistics book. The world already has plenty of those and we wouldn't presume to approach the skills of people like David Moore, Frederick Mosteller, John Rice, John Tukey, Paul Velleman, and many others who have written outstanding introductions to statistics. Besides, you cannot learn statistics solely by running data through a computer. The best we can do is point you in the right directions and show you how we approach these problems. We want you to learn how to ask good questions.

This is not a cookbook. We try to present our thought processes on real data, but there is not a simple solution for each problem. We're hoping to indicate what we think of as good statistical practice. Many of the details of good statistical practice vary from statistician to statistician, but there are areas of agreement. Good data analysis, we believe, requires the use of a variety of statistical tools, both exploratory and confirmatory. We often make use of the synergy between exploratory and confirmatory statistics to illuminate different aspects of the data. Our approach is to integrate exploratory and confirmatory procedures at all stages of the data analysis process.

Background

A favorite statement in the preface of introductory statistics books is, "We presume only high-school algebra." That gives them a larger potential market. In our experience, students with only a high school algebra background can barely keep their head above water in statistics courses. Although this book is *not* aimed at mathematicians, we assume you've had at least a statistics course in college. If you haven't and you are using a statistical computer package on important data, we are scared about what you might do.

If you want to review your statistics before plunging ahead, we recommend Iman (1994), Siegel (1996), and Moore and McCabe (1995). Social scientists should look at Loether and McTavish (1993). Business people should consult Siegel (1996).

Style

We use real data examples everywhere. We do so for several reasons. The first is pragmatic. Mathematical approaches to statistics are not easy for many people to understand. Unfortunately, this does not stop people from needing or doing statistics. Examples can at least guide the mathematically challenged.

Second, research indicates that people who read technical writing learn more easily from examples than from abstract statements of principles (see Anderson et al. 1983). A major reason for this is that a good example motivates people to want to know the answer and how it was reached.

Looking at real data prepares people for real research. If someone asks a student to calculate a chi-square test or fit a regression, he or she can apply the formulas. But students usually have only vague ideas about what statistics are appropriate to their questions, or what methods will help reveal different structures in their data. We address these problems throughout the book. In practice, data analysis requires integrating a variety of statistical tools, both numerical and graphical. Integration cannot be learned in the abstract. The most effective way to learn it is in the context of actual data analysis on real datasets.

We gathered a wide variety of datasets from areas as diverse as anthropology, agriculture, criminal justice, economics, marketing, sociology, medicine, psychology, and ecology. If you are a teacher who needs additional datasets as well as a good summary of the reasons for using real data see Singer and Willett (1990).

If you find any datasets interesting, we encourage you to pursue further analysis; you will learn more about data analysis and graphics as well as about interesting substantive problems. To make it easy for you, we print all datasets and the commands that produced each output. The datasets are short; you can type them in yourself or you can find the datasets and commands on the SPSS website: http://www.spss.com.

We print the commands rather than showing you screen shots of menus and dialog boxes. SYSTAT runs identically either from commands or menus. Menu choices have the same names and dialog boxes offer the same options as commands. Printing the commands serves as a concise way to indicate the choices you would make on the menus and dialog boxes. This takes a lot less paper and we like to save trees.

The commands use SYSTAT version 6 syntax and options, and match the version 6 menus. Owners of previous versions can use this book effectively, although some syntax will be different. Some plots need high resolution graphics that are not available in version 4 or earlier. Version 5 commands for most chapters are available on the SPSS website.

We ran the output in both DOS and Windows version 6. The printing and formatting of your output may differ in minor ways.

Organization

A fundamental organizing principal of the book is the division of variables into two kinds: categorical and continuous. This is an oversimplification, but it has its benefits. Mainly, it helps classify many statistical methods, particularly ones which involve mixtures of categorical and continuous variables. While all classifications can be misleading, we think this one does more good than harm.

We classify variables, but we try to avoid classifying data. The distinction is important. A variable is a symbol in a mathematical model which represents a set of values (numbers or labels). Data are numbers or labels assigned to individual observations of some phenomenon. Whether data are appropriately modeled by one or more variables is both a statistical and scientific question. It cannot be answered without reference to the data *and* to the model. Velleman and Wilkinson (1993) argue that data typing, while appealing to some mathematicians, computer scientists, and social scientists (but few statisticians), defeats good data analysis. We need to know how data were selected, observed, collected, and how they look graphically and statistically before we can even guess at their type. We may want to analyze the same data quantitatively *and* qualitatively before making judgments (if at all) about their type.

This book does not have to be read from front to back like a novel. There are occasional dependencies, but most readers should be able to read the chapters corresponding to the data and statistical problems that they face. The book is divided into seven parts based on the type of variables being analyzed and the goals of the analyst. We recognize that many readers need to go further than we can carry them. The *Notes* sections at the end of chapters contain further reading.

The first four Parts of the book are titled *Predicting*. They cover methods which are useful when your goal is to predict values of a dependent variable from values of one or more independent variables. The basic organizing theme is a classification of the independent and dependent variables into qualitative or quantitative types. This yields a four-fold table corresponding to the first four parts of the book.

Part 5, titled *Analyzing Series*, discusses how to analyze time series data. Many of the techniques are similar to those found in the other chapters, but there are important differences.

Part 6, titled *Finding Groups or Patterns*, present methods for finding groups of observations or variables. These methods are based on associations rather than predictions.

The last section, *Special Topics*, covers statistical and graphical methods useful in all parts of the book. The final chapter, *Graphics*, highlights the rich graphical tools available in SYSTAT. Organized as a tutorial, it shows how sizes, shapes, contours, smoothers, overlays, and other graphics options can help you find and display patterns in your data.

Acknowledgments

We wish to thank Larry Basem, Rebecca M. Blank, Elisabeth Clemens, Jacob Cohen, Sheila Courington, Angela Cowser, Gerard Dallal, Nancy A. Denton, Mitchell L. Eggers, Marc Feldesman, Pat Fleury, Rebecca German, Mary Conklin Gomberg, David Grusky, Mary Ann Hill, Robert Lerner, Kathryn M. Neckerman, and Judith See for reading portions of earlier drafts. We received helpful advice from Edward Brent, Nancy A. Denton, Katherine Donato, Mitchell L. Eggers, Douglas S. Massey, Gary C. Mc-Donald, William L. Parish, James H. Steiger, and James Walker. SPSS Inc. and the Sociology Department at the University of Chicago provided valuable support. All controversial opinions and errors in this book are due to these well-intentioned contributors.

The Piet Hein grook, "On Problems," is reprinted with kind permission of Piet Hein as, DK-Middelfart © 1966.

We are grateful to Robert Lerner for permission to use the data on the Disability Rights Movement analyzed in Chapter 8.

This book was written, illustrated, and produced with SYSTAT and FrameMaker software on Apple Macintosh and Microsoft Windows. We would like to thank Pat Howe, Jenna Beck, Bob Gruen, Bonnie Shapiro, Yvonne Smith, and Bonnie Melton for typograpy design and Frame help.

Jack Noonan, President of SPSS, Vice Presidents Louise Rehling, Ed Hamburg, Mark Battaglia, and Sue Phelan, and COB Norman Nie have given SYSTAT a new home. The improvements in Version 6 reflect the wise management and depth of resources at SPSS.

Finally, we wish to thank our patient wives, Ruth VanDemark, Denise Carter-Blank, and Diane Gruber for their support throughout this long project. They did not type the manuscript.

References

Anderson, P. V., Brockmann, R. J. and Miller, C. R. (1983). *New Essays in Technical and Scientific Communication: Research, Theory, Practice*. Farmingdale, NY: Baywood Publishing Co.

Iman, R.L. (1994). *A Data-Based Approach to Statistics*. Belmont, CA: Duxbury Press.

Loether, H.J. and McTavish, D.G. (1993). *Descriptive and Inferential Statistics: An Introduction* (4th ed.).. Boston: Allyn and Bacon.

Moore, D.S. and McCabe, G. (1995). *The Basic Practice of Statistics*. New York: W.H. Freeman.

Siegel, A. (1996). *Statistics and Data Analysis: An Introduction* (2nd ed.). New York: John Wiley & Sons.

Siegel, A. (1996). *Practical Business Statistics* (3rd ed.). Chicago: Richard D. Irwin.

Singer, J. D. and Willett, J. B. (1990). Improving the teaching of applied statistics: Putting the data back into data analysis. *The American Statistician, 44,* 223-230.

Velleman, P. and Wilkinson, L. (1993). Nominal, ordinal, interval, and ratio typologies are misleading for classifying statistical methodology. *The American Statistician, 47,* 65-72.

Part 1

Predicting Categorical Variables from Categorical Variables

Chapter 1: Simple Tables

Chapter 2: Measuring Associations in Two-Way Tables

Chapter 3: Prediction Using Log-Linear Models

1

Simple Tables

What would a society look like if there were many more of one gender than another? If women were relatively scarce, men would have to compete for their affection. Personal competition might translate into a societywide legal and political system favorable to women, giving them superior rights over men. However, if there were a surplus of women the reverse could be true and the legal and political system might favor men (see Davis & van den Oever 1982, and Guttentag & Secord 1983). The relative number of men to women is called the sex ratio. To make this question concrete, we will look at how the sex ratio is related to a single legal issue: the right to leave an unhappy marriage by divorce. In societies with a surplus of women, we expect men to be able to initiate divorce more easily. We expect the reverse to be true in societies with a surplus of men.

As we investigate this question, we will follow the entire process of data analysis: starting with data input and checking, ending when we produce the tables used to test the hypothesis.

1.1 How to set up your data

We will use a sample of 90 societies drawn by Martin King Whyte from the 1,250 human cultures known to have existed (Whyte 1978a, 1978b, 1978c). Since most of the world's societies have no detailed population records, Whyte had to rely on general statements. For each society, Whyte gathered information on two variables, named SEXRATIO$ and DIVORCE$. The sex ratio was coded into three categories: A surplus of women (coded "Women+"), roughly identical numbers of men and women (coded "Same num") and a surplus of men (coded "Men+"). The ease with which divorce can be initiated is also coded into three categories. This gives us 90 sets of scores, one for each society in the sample.

Figure 1.1 shows the sex ratio category and the divorce category for each of the 90 societies. In this form, the data are often called **raw data**. The data in Figure 1.1 have been read into a SYSTAT file named SEXRATIO.SYS. There are several ways to read raw data into a SYSTAT file. You may read the raw data directly into a SYSTAT file using SYSTAT BASIC. You may type the data into a spreadsheet or database program and use SYSTAT's IMPORT command to read them into a SYSTAT file. Finally, you may enter the data in SYSTAT's Data Editor and save the file. If you are lucky someone else has already done the work for you. The names of the societies are stored in a variable called SOCIETY$. This variable, called a **case ID** variable or simply an **ID** variable, is important when we want to locate individual cases. Typical uses are to find the name of a case with unusual values and to correct errors or omissions in the input.

Figure 1.1
Sex Ratio—Divorce Dataset

SOCIETY$	DIVORCE$	SEXRATIO$
Nama Hott.	Men easy	Same num
Thonga	Rights =	Same num
Mbumdu	Rights =	Women+
Bemba	Men easy	Women+
Hadza	Rights =	Women+
Kikuyu	Rights =	Same num
Mbuti	Rights =	Women+
Banen	Rights =	Women+
Ibo	Rights =	Women+
Ashanti	Men easy	Women+
Wolof	Rights =	Women+
Massa	Rights =	Same num
Fur	Rights =	Same num
Shilluk	Rights =	Same num
Kaffa	Rights =	Same num
Konso	Rights =	Same num
Nubians	Men easy	Same num
Tuareg	Wom easy	Women+
Egyptians	Men easy	Women+
Babylon	Rights =	Same num
Turks	Rights =	Same num
Romans	Rights =	Same num
Irish	Rights =	Men+
Yurak	Rights =	Same num
Abkhaz	Rights =	Same num
Kurds	Men easy	Women+
Punjabi	Rights =	Same num
Toda	Rights =	Men+
Uttar Prad	Rights =	Same num
Kazak	Men easy	Same num
Lolo	Rights =	Same num

SOCIETY$	DIVORCE$	SEXRATIO$
Garo	Rights =	Same num
Burmese	Rights =	Same num
N Vietnam	Men easy	Same num
Khmer Camb	Rights =	Same num
Semang	Rights =	Same num
Andamanese	Rights =	Men+
Tanala	Men easy	Women+
Javanese	Rights =	Same num
Iban	Rights =	Women+
Toradja	Rights =	Same num
Alorese	Men easy	Same num
Aranda	Rights =	Same num
Kimam	Rights =	Same num
Kwoma	Wom easy	Men+
Lesu	Rights =	Same num
Siuai	Rights =	Men+
Pentacost	Rights =	Same num
Ajie	Rights =	Same num
Marquesans	Rights =	Men+
Gilbertese	Rights =	Same num
Truk	Rights =	Same num
Palauans	Rights =	Men+
Atayal	Rights =	Women+
Manchu	Men easy	Same num
Japanese	Rights =	Same num
Gilvak	Wom easy	Men+
Chukchee	Rights =	Women+
Aleut	Rights =	Women+
Montagnais	Men easy	Same num
Salteaux	Rights =	Same num
Kaska	Rights =	Men+
Haida	Rights =	Same num
Twana	Rights =	Women+
Pomo	Rights =	Same num
Paiute	Rights =	Same num
Kutenai	Rights =	Women+
Hidatsa	Rights =	Same num
Omaha	Rights =	Women+
Creek	Rights =	Same num
Comanche	Rights =	Same num
Zuni	Rights =	Same num
Papago	Men easy	Same num
Aztec	Rights =	Same num
Quiche	Wom easy	Same num
Bribri	Rights =	Same num
Goajiro	Rights =	Same num
Callinago	Men easy	Same num
Yanomamo	Rights =	Men+
Saramacca	Rights =	Same num
Cubeo	Rights =	Same num
Jivaro	Rights =	Same num

SOCIETY$	DIVORCE$	SEXRATIO$
Inca	Rights =	Same num
Siriono	Men easy	Same num
Trumai	Rights =	Same num
Tupinamba	Rights =	Same num
Shavante	Men easy	Women+
Cayua	Rights =	Same num
Abipon	Men easy	Women+
Tehuelche	Rights =	Women+

1.2 Summaries for one categorical variable

Data displayed like Figure 1.1 are hard to read and difficult to interpret. We need to summarize. One simple summary groups the scores into categories and counts the number of cases in each category. These data are already divided into categories, so we can use the XTAB command to produce output like Figure 1.2. This is usually called a **one-way table**, a univariate table or a frequency table.

Figure 1.2 contains a summary of the information in the variable SEXRATIO$. We used the PRINT / LIST command to request more readable list-format output. A similar table can be produced for DIVORCE$. We leave this as an exercise for the interested reader. In Figure 1.2, SYSTAT has printed five columns and five rows. The top two rows contain titles identifying the contents of each column. The titles are **Count**, **Cum Count**, **Pct**, **Cum Pct** and **SEXRATIO$**. We will discuss the contents of these columns in detail because they illustrate fundamental concepts you will need later to understand more complex work with categorical data.

Figure 1.2
One-Way Table
Summary of the Information in SEXRATIO$

```
XTAB
   USE SEXRATIO
   PRINT / LIST
   TABULATE SEXRATIO$
```

```
         Cum          Cum
Count   Count   Pct   Pct  SEXRATIO$
  10      10   11.1  11.1  Men+
  58      68   64.4  75.6  Same num
  22      90   24.4 100.0  Women+
```

SEXRATIO$. The rightmost column, headed by the variable name SEXRATIO$, lists every category of the variable. SEXRATIO$ has three categories: "Men+" which signifies a surplus of men, "Same num" indicating roughly identical numbers of men and women, and "Women+" standing for a surplus of women. SYSTAT has sorted the category names in alphabetic order. We chose category names carefully so that their alphabetic order corresponds to increasing sex ratio. If the categories had been coded as numbers (i.e., as "1" or "2" instead of "Men+" or "Same num") they would have been sorted in numeric order. We chose category names of 8 characters or less because that is all SYSTAT prints in some tables. In statistics, the same thing is often given several different names. The categories are also called values, codes, or outcomes of the variable, or the response categories.

Count. The leftmost column, labeled **Count**, is the count of the number of cases in each category. For example, the "Women+" category contained 22 cases. A list of the number of cases in each category like we see in this column is often called the **distribution** of cases. Since the number of cases in a category is called the frequency, the list is also called the frequency distribution of SEXRATIO$. Because it involves only one variable, it is sometimes labeled the univariate frequency distribution. From the frequency distribution we can see that the mode (the category containing the most cases) is the middle category, "Same num."

Cum Count. The second column in Figure 1.2, headed **Cum Count**, is the cumulative count of cases. This is the number of cases equal to or less than each category. The last row in this column gives the total number of cases available for this variable, 90 cases. A list like the second column is also known as the cumulative frequency distribution. Cumulative counts are not very useful for discrete data like these. They are important where cumulative information is valuable as in monthly sales or expenditure data.

Pct. The third column gives the percent of cases in each category. For example, 24.4% of the cases fall in the "Women+" category. This column gives the **percentage distribution**, sometimes called the percentage frequency distribution. This is often the most useful column. Since percentages express the categories as parts of 100, they simplify comparison of categories in the same table, as well as comparison between different tables. Interpretation often focuses on percentages.

Cum Pct. Finally, the fourth column gives the cumulative percentages. This is the percentage of cases equal to or less than each category. Because percents must always sum to 100% (except for rounding error), the last row in this column is always 100%. The data in this column are sometimes called the **cumulative percentage distribution** of cases for SEXRATIO$. Cumulative percentages are important for the same kind of data where cumulative counts are valuable.

The table in Figure 1.2 is an excellent summary in the sense that it has retained almost all the information in the raw data. This is why tables are such a popular means of presenting information: almost no information is lost when raw data are converted to a table. The information in Figure 1.2 can be interpreted as follows. The most striking information is that almost two-thirds of all societies (64%) have identical male-female ratios. Among the cases with unbalanced sex ratios, almost twice as many have a surplus of females than a surplus of males; 22 cases (24%) have more females, while only 10 cases (11%) have a surplus of males.

1.3 Checking your data

Producing one-way tables for all categorical variables is a common first step as you begin to work with a new dataset. They give you a good, basic idea of the distribution of cases. You can answer questions like: Which categories contain the bulk of the data? Are there categories that you think are important but have no cases? Or very few cases? Do some categories seem to have more cases than you expected? This can help prevent surprises later in the analysis.

One-way tables often display categories that should not exist. We might, for example, have found a category misspelled like "Womne+" in the SEXRATIO$ variable. You must go to the data and find cases with incorrect categories. The FIND command in the SYSTAT Data Editor Worksheet can help. The cause is usually a simple data entry error (as in this example where the 'n' and 'e' were transposed), but in statistics as elsewhere in life, Murphy's Law is alive and well: any mistake that can be made will be made. Too often you will find that the original source was in error and it contains invalid codes. The important point is that you must go back and check. Regardless of the source of the data, even if you collected them yourself (and you, being perfect, never make mistakes) or you received them from a trusted colleague or a trusted government agency, it is dangerous to assume that they are correct until you have checked them yourself. If your data are not clean, every later analysis will be faulty. Locating incorrect data is an important reason why your first statistical analysis should be to print a one-way table for every categorical variable in your dataset.

1.4 Graphical summaries for one categorical variable

While the numeric summary in Figure 1.2 is easier to understand than the raw data, it still requires reading and understanding several numbers. Even more simplification is sometimes useful. You can produce **bar graphs** that display the information from Figure 1.2 in a visual form. A bar graph is a diagram where the number of cases or the percentage is represented by the length of the bars. Figure 1.3 contains a bar graph of SEXRATIO$.

Figure 1.3
Categorical Data: A Bar Graph

```
USE SEXRATIO
BAR SEXRATIO$ / FILL=1
```

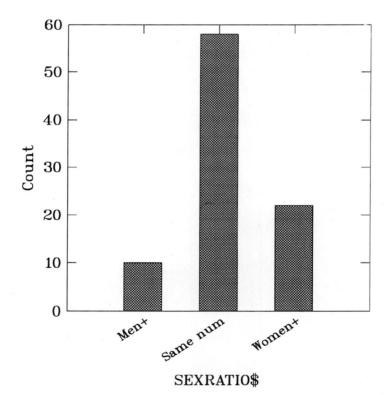

If you compare the graph to the table in Figure 1.2 you can see that the numeric information is identical—counts for each category of SEXRATIO$—but graphs are more visual. You would interpret the graph the same way that you would interpret the table: most societies contain identical numbers of men and women; of the societies with unequal sex ratios, about twice as many have a surplus of women.

The advantage of graphs compared to tables is that your eye can compare the length of the bars more easily than numbers. This helps viewers understand the overall features of a graph quickly. Graphs are valuable for presentations where you want the audience to grasp the central point easily. The advantages of visual displays also lend themselves readily to the display of continuous data, the subject of Part II of the book. For more information on visual graphics see Tufte (1983).

A disadvantage of graphs is that the bars for some categories may look the same length even if the counts differ slightly. Bar graphs summarize the substance of a table and small differences do not change the central message. When you need precise detail, use numbers not graphs.

For percentages, add the PERCENT option to the BAR command.

```
BAR SEXRATIO$ / PERCENT  LABEL
```

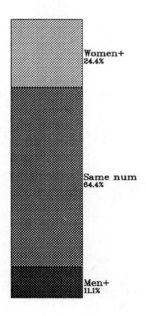

The interpretation of the graphs is always the same as the tables. Bar graphs are also called bar charts and the bars are sometimes horizontal rather than vertical.

1.5 Two-way tables

The bar graph in Figure 1.3 shows that about one-fourth of the societies in our sample have a surplus of women. From the graph or the one-way table that is all we can say. We can't say anything about the effect of a surplus of women on the ability of men or women to initiate a divorce. Even if we arrange the one-way tables for SEXRATIO$ and DIVORCE$ next to each other on the same page like Figure 1.4, we still can't say if a surplus of women means that men or women can divorce their spouses more easily. We would like to be able to explore that question and others like it. One-way tables are useful for describing and summarizing distributions of a single variable, but most research focuses on relationships between variables.

Figure 1.4
One-Way Tables

```
XTAB
    USE SEXRATIO
    PRINT / LIST
    TABULATE SEXRATIO$ DIVORCE$
```

```
          Cum          Cum
Count    Count   Pct   Pct  SEXRATIO$
   10       10  11.1  11.1  Men+
   58       68  64.4  75.6  Same num
   22       90  24.4 100.0  Women+

          Cum          Cum
Count    Count   Pct   Pct  DIVORCE$
   17       17  18.9  18.9  Men easy
   69       86  76.7  95.6  Rights =
    4       90   4.4 100.0  Wom easy
```

We need to subdivide each line in the SEXRATIO$ table into the societies where divorce is easier for men, the same for both sexes, and is easier for women. For example, among the 22 societies with a surplus of women, we want to know how many allowed women to divorce their husbands more easily, how many allowed equal rights for both spouses, and how many allowed men superior rights to divorce their wives. We want the answers to similar questions about the 58 societies with equal sex ratios and the 10 societies where there was a surplus of men. Figure 1.5 shows how easily we can construct a table to answer these questions.

Figure 1.5
Two-Way Table

```
XTAB
  USE SEXRATIO
  PRINT NONE / FREQ
  TABULATE SEXRATIO$ * DIVORCE$
```

```
Frequencies
  SEXRATIO$ (rows) by DIVORCE$ (columns)

            Men easy  Rights =  Wom easy     Total
          +---------------------------------+
  Men+    |    0         8         2     |     10
          |                              |
  Same num|   10        47         1     |     58
          |                              |
  Women+  |    7        14         1     |     22
          +---------------------------------+
  Total       17        69         4           90
```

The TABULATE command tells SYSTAT what table to construct; the categories of the variable before the asterisk (SEXRATIO$) become rows and the categories of the variable after the asterisk (DIVORCE$) become columns. In the resulting table, Figure 1.5, the 90 societies are divided by the three categories of sex ratio and further subdivided by the ease with which they allow men or women to initiate divorce. The labels at the left and on top of the table describe what's in each row and column. To the right and along the bottom of the table are the total counts for each row and column. This means, for example, that the totals for SEXRATIO$ on the right of the table are the same as the values in the COUNT column in the one-way table of SEXRATIO$. Thus the row and column totals in a two-way table reproduce the counts from the one-way tables for SEXRATIO$ and DIVORCE$. You can check this by looking at the tables in Figure 1.4.

Because the table is constructed from two variables, it is called a **two-way table.** Another name is a cross-classification table because the categories of the variables are "crossed" with each other. This is sometimes shortened to crosstabulation or, simply, crosstab. A third name is contingency table.

Each location where the categories cross is called a **cell**. A two-way table has a cell for every combination of the categories of the two variables; the table in Figure 1.5 has 9 cells. Inside each cell is the number of societies with that combination of characteristics. The number in each cell is usually called the **cell frequency** or cell count. For example, the column total in the last column (Wom easy) shows that our sample contained a total of 4 societies where women have easier access to divorce. As these 4 cases are crossed by the categories of SEXRATIO$ we see that: 1 society had a surplus of females, 1 had identical numbers of men and women, and 2 had a surplus of men.

A graph of these data can reveal patterns in the table more effectively than the numbers, particularly for large tables. Figure 1.6 shows two graphs of the table in Figure 1.5. The graph on the left, called a 3-D bar chart, uses altitude of the bars to represent count and the one on the right, called a mosaic, uses fill density. The 3-D bar chart is appealing to many nontechnical viewers, but it has the disadvantage of hiding small bars behind large. We tend to prefer mosaic plots for tables. The dot in the BAR command is required in order to signal that we we want SYSTAT to compute frequencies from the data and use them as a third variable for the plot. Otherwise, we would get a two-variable plot.

Figure 1.6
Graphs of Two-Way Tables

```
USE SEXRATIO
BEGIN
BAR .*SEXRATIO$*DIVORCE$/LOC=0,0 HEI=2IN WID=2IN ALT=2IN
BAR .*SEXRATIO$*DIVORCE$/TILE LOC=3IN,0 HEI=2IN WID=2IN,SURF=FILL
END
```

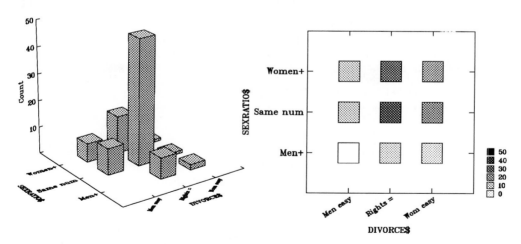

We could try to use the counts in the table to answer our questions about sex ratio and divorce. This won't work but, to explain exactly why, we need to trace the argument in detail. Notice that the left column of Figure 1.5 (Men easy) indicates that more societies with identical numbers of men and women allow men to more easily initiate divorce: 10 societies, compared to 7 societies with a female surplus and 0 societies with a male surplus. In other words, more societies with the same number of each sex give men easier divorce rights. This does not support our hypothesis. But have we disproved it? Is this the question we really wanted to answer? The row totals show that over half of the societies in the table have identical numbers of men and women. Even if the sex ratio had nothing to do with divorce, you expect to see more cases in the cells of the Same num row just because the sample contains more societies with identical numbers of men and women. Having different numbers of cases in the rows makes it hard to compare cell counts. This is why cell counts can't tell us much about our hypothesis.

1.6 Percentage tables

Because each row has a different number of cases, we can't easily compare the cell counts. To do the comparisons that test the effects of sex ratio on divorce, we need to "standardize" the rows, meaning convert the numbers to the form in which they would appear if they each had the same number of cases. The solution is simple: percents. This provides a standard basis because percents always add up to 100%. Figure 1.7 shows you the table converted to percents.

Figure 1.7
Percentage Table

```
XTAB
   USE SEXRATIO
   REM COMMAND BELOW TELLS SYSTAT TO PRINT ONLY ROW PERCENTS
   PRINT NONE / ROWPCT
   TABULATE SEXRATIO$ * DIVORCE$
```

```
Row percents
  SEXRATIO$ (rows) by DIVORCE$ (columns)

              Men easy  Rights =  Wom easy     Total        N
            +--------------------------------+
   Men+     |    .00     80.00     20.00      | 100.00       10
            |                                 |
   Same num |  17.24     81.03      1.72      | 100.00       58
            |                                 |
   Women+   |  31.82     63.64      4.55      | 100.00       22
            +--------------------------------+
   Total       18.89     76.67      4.44        100.00
      N          17        69         4                      90
```

The table in Figure 1.7 makes comparison much easier. Looking at the column where women can more easily initiate divorce (Wom easy), for example, we see that 4.55%

of societies with a surplus of women allow women to initiate divorce more easily compared to 20% of societies with a surplus of men. The evidence for societies where men can more easily initiate divorce is even stronger. In 31.82% of the societies with a surplus of women, men can initiate divorce more easily. By comparison, in societies with a surplus of men none allow men to initiate divorce more easily. These results support our theory. (Note that we print 2 decimal places so that you can unambiguously locate the results in Figure 1.7. If you were presenting to a professional audience and had only 90 cases, you would use fewer.)

The table in Figure 1.7 is called a **bivariate percentage distribution** because it allows you to compare the percentage distribution of one variable (e.g. DIVORCE$) within the different categories of a second variable, SEXRATIO$. Comparisons like this are fundamental to scientific research which attempts to develop and test theoretical statements about the relationship between variables and the conditions under which these relationships occur.

Tables, like almost everything else in statistics, have several names for each characteristic. The rows are also called stubs and the columns are sometimes labeled banners. Row and column totals may be called marginal totals because they occur in the table's margins. This is sometimes further shortened to marginals. This table had three rows and three columns. Tables are often characterized by the number of rows and columns, so this is a 3-by-3 table. It is often written, 3x3. This at least is constant: the number of rows is always written first, followed by the number of columns. Another common table, a 2x2 table, has two rows and two columns.

1.7 Customary table layout

Our theory explicitly states that the ratio of males to females influences divorce rights. In this sense, we say that divorce rights in a society *depend* on the sex ratio. DIVORCE$ is the **dependent variable** in this theory. Since ease of divorce does not influence the sex ratio, SEXRATIO$ does not depend on DIVORCE$. SEXRATIO$ is called the **independent variable**. The twin ideas of independent and dependent variables play an important role in coming chapters.

Many times in statistics the same thing has different names. Other names for the independent variable are exogenous variable, predictor variable, explanatory variable, treatment variable or, simply, the carrier. The dependent variable is sometimes called the response variable, endogenous variable, or criterion variable.

Independent and dependent variables also have a role in the customary layout of two-way tables. You can instruct SYSTAT to use either the row or the column variable as the dependent variable. In the most common layout, which we follow in this book, the dependent variable is always the column variable. This means the things you want to compare will be in the same column. This custom is not always observed, but your tables will be easier to read and interpret if you construct them in one consistent way.

Percentage tables are commonly used because they simplify comparisons across categories with unequal numbers of cases. When computing percentages the primary rule is:

> **Percentages sum to 100 % for each category of the independent variable.**

If you put the independent variable on the side of the table, like we did in Figure 1.7, then you want to request row percentages. When you set up a table this way, the appropriate comparisons are within the columns. For example, in Figure 1.5 we wanted to compare the number of societies where divorce was easier for males for different sex ratios. This proved impossible because the number of cases in each category of sex ratio differed so much. To remove this effect, we constructed another table by percentaging across (in the direction of the independent variable); Figure 1.7. Then we were able to do our comparisons down the columns of the table. The rule that emerges is:

> **Percentage in one direction (rows) and compare in the other direction (columns).**

SYSTAT also calculates column percentages. Usually either row or column percentages answers the questions that you ask. Which one you use depends on whether you have chosen to use rows or columns for the independent variable. If you follow the rules above, you may never use column percentages. An exception occurs when it is not clear which variable is dependent or independent, or when you can think of the data in both ways. Here you might compute both row and column percentages and examine each table.

A two-way table effectively displays the relationship between two variables. Sometimes, however, we want to summarize the relationship using a single number. There are many alternatives, and you will learn what they are and how to choose among them in the next chapter.

Notes

The data, from Whyte (1978a and 1978c), follow the Standard Cross-Cultural Sample designed by Murdock and White (1969). The sample is designed to fully represent the known variation in human culture while minimizing a form of spatial autocorrelation called "Galton's Problem" in anthropology (see Naroll, 1970). For further information consult Whyte (1978b) and the references given there. Following a practice common during the early 1970s, Whyte (1978b) refers to his variables by number rather than name. He calls SEXRATIO$ "IV 38" (meaning Independent Variable 38) and DI-VORCE$ is named "DV 35" (Dependent Variable 35). The sex ratio refers only to adults, and does not include children. Whyte's dataset contains 93 cases, but three societies with missing data for DIVORCE$ were omitted.

Checking your data

This is only an introduction to some of the problems of data checking. Chapter 7, section 7.1, discusses handling wild or incorrect data in more detail.

Further reading

For further information on analysis and design of percentage tables see Davis and Jacobs (1968), Loether and McTavish (1988), Rosenberg (1968), and Zeisel (1985). For more advanced analyses, see the references at the end of Chapter 2 and Chapter 3.

References

Davis, J. A. and Jacobs, A. M. (1968). Tabular presentation. *International Encyclopedia of the Social Sciences* (vol. 15, pp. 497-509). New York: Macmillan.

Davis, K. and van den Oever, P. (1982). The demographic basis of sex roles. *Population and Development Review, 3*, 495-511.

Guttentag, M. and Secord, P. F. (1983). *Too Many Women? The Sex Ratio Question.* Beverly Hills, CA: Sage Publications.

Loether, H. J. and McTavish, D. G. (1988). *Descriptive and Inferential Statistics*: *An Introduction* (3rd ed.). Boston: Allyn and Bacon.

Naroll, R. (1970). Galton's problem. In R. Naroll and R. Cohen (eds.), *A Handbook of Method in Cultural Anthropology* (pp. 974-989). Garden City: Natural History Press.

Murdock, G. P. and White, D. R. (1969). Standard cross-cultural sample. *Ethnology, 8*, 329-369.

Rosenberg, M. (1968). *The Logic of Survey Analysis*. New York: Basic Books.

Tufte, E. R. (1983). *The Visual Display of Quantitative Information*. Cheshire, CT: Graphics Press.

Whyte, M. K. (1978a). Cross-cultural codes dealing with the relative status of women. *Ethnology, 17*, 211-238.

Whyte, M. K. (1978b). *The Status of Women in Preindustrial Society*. Princeton, N.J.: Princeton University Press.

Whyte, M. K. (1978c). [Independent and control variables used in Whyte 1978b.] Unpublished raw data.

Zeisel, H. (1985). *Say it with Figures* (6th ed.). New York: Harper & Row.

2

Measuring Associations in Two-Way Tables

If the sex ratio influences relations between the sexes, then we expect to find that it has an important impact on how housework is divided. In Chapter 1 we outlined a theory that says relationships between men and women change as their relative proportions in the population change. Tables in Figure 2.1 further explore this theory and Figure 2.2 contains the data. The percentage table at the bottom of Figure 2.1 shows that men do no housework in 63.64% of the societies with a surplus of women (Women+). This is more than the 46% of societies with about the same number of men and women and 50% with a surplus of men. Clearly, if there is a surplus of women, men tend to do less housework than when the sex ratio is even or there is a surplus of men. This supports our hypothesis.

2.1 Four characteristics of an association

We can see a relationship between SEXRATIO$ and HOUSEWK$ because we can see that the percentage distribution of the dependent variable changes as we move from category to category of the independent variable. The statistical name for the relationship between two categorical variables is an **association**. We can describe the association between the two variables using a percentage table, like Figure 2.1, but we often want to summarize the association more concisely. When we consider how to summarize an association, there are four characteristics that we need to take into account:

1. Does an association *exist*?
2. The *strength* of the association.
3. The *direction* of the association.
4. The *pattern* of the association.

Each characteristic will be discussed in turn and later in the chapter we will develop several alternative measures for each. The first three characteristics can often be described by a single number.

Figure 2.1
Tables of Sex Ratio by Housework

```
XTAB
    USE HOUSEWK
    PRINT NONE / ROWPCT  FREQ
    TABULATE SEXRATIO$ * HOUSEWK$
```

```
Frequencies
   SEXRATIO$ (rows) by HOUSEWK$ (columns)

             Men none  Men some      Total
           +-------------------+
   Men+    |     5         5   |      10
           |                   |
   Same num|    26        31   |      57
           |                   |
   Women+  |    14         8   |      22
           +-------------------+
   Total        45        44          89


Row percents
   SEXRATIO$ (rows) by HOUSEWK$ (columns)

             Men none  Men some      Total      N
           +-------------------+
   Men+    |   50.00     50.00 |    100.00      10
           |                   |
   Same num|   45.61     54.39 |    100.00      57
           |                   |
   Women+  |   63.64     36.36 |    100.00      22
           +-------------------+
   Total       50.56     49.44      100.00
      N          45        44                  89
```

Existence

An association exists between two variables if the distribution of the dependent variable differs across at least some categories of the independent variable. The simplest way to see this is in percentage tables, like the lower table in Figure 2.1. In that table the percentages indicate that the distribution of housework done by men is likely to be different depending on whether the society has a surplus of women or not. The general rule is: *after computing percentages in the appropriate direction, if there is **any** difference in the percentage distributions then an association exists.* When we observe no association we say the two variables are **independent**, or statistically independent, of each other. Statistical independence has a precise technical definition and it is usually important in the context of whether a difference you observe in a sample is also likely to exist in the population. Later in this chapter we will show how you can test the hypothesis that two variables are statistically independent in the population.

Figure 2.2
Sex Ratio–Housework Data

SOCIETY$	SEXRATIO$	HOUSEWK$
Nama Hott.	Same num	Men some
Thonga	Same num	Men some
Mbumdu	Women+	Men none
Bemba	Women+	Men some
Hadza	Women+	Men some
Kikuyu	Same num	Men none
Mbuti	Women+	Men some
Banen	Women+	Men none
Ibo	Women+	Men some
Ashanti	Women+	Men none
Wolof	Women+	Men none
Massa	Same num	Men none
Fur	Same num	Men some
Shilluk	Same num	Men some
Kaffa	Same num	Men some
Konso	Same num	Men some
Nubians	Same num	Men none
Tuareg	Women+	Men none
Egyptians	Women+	Men none
Babylon	Same num	Men none
Turks	Same num	Men none
Romans	Same num	Men none
Irish	Men+	Men none
Yurak	Same num	Men none
Abkhaz	Same num	Men none
Kurds	Women+	Men none
Punjabi	Same num	Men some
Toda	Men+	Men some
Uttar Prad	Same num	Men some
Kazak	Same num	Men none
Lolo	Same num	Men none
Garo	Same num	Men some
Burmese	Same num	Men some
N Vietnam	Same num	Men some
Khmer Camb	Same num	Men none
Semang	Same num	Men none
Andamanese	Men+	Men some
Tanala	Women+	Men some
Javanese	Same num	Men none
Iban	Women+	Men some

22 Predicting Categorical Variables from Categorical Variables

SOCIETY$	SEXRATIO$	HOUSEWK$
Toradja	Same num	Men some
Alorese	Same num	Men some
Aranda	Same num	Men some
Kimam	Same num	Men some
Kwoma	Men+	Men none
Lesu	Same num	Men some
Siuai	Men+	Men some
Pentacost	Same num	Men some
Ajie	Same num	Men none
Marquesans	Men+	Men some
Gilbertese	Same num	Men some
Truk	Same num	Men some
Palauans	Men+	Men none
Atayal	Women+	Men none
Manchu	Same num	Men some
Japanese	Same num	Men some
Gilvak	Men+	Men none
Chukchee	Women+	Men none
Aleut	Women+	Men none
Montagnais	Same num	Men some
Salteaux	Same num	Men none
Kaska	Men+	Men none
Haida	Same num	Men some
Twana	Women+	Men none
Pomo	Same num	Men some
Paiute	Same num	Men none
Kutenai	Women+	Men none
Hidatsa	Same num	Men none
Omaha	Women+	Men some
Creek	Same num	Men none
Comanche	Same num	Men none
Zuni	Same num	Men none
Papago	Same num	Men none
Aztec	Same num	Men some
Quiche	Same num	Men some
Bribri	Same num	Men none
Goajiro	Same num	Men some
Callinago	Same num	Men none
Yanomamo	Men+	Men some
Saramacca	Same num	Men some
Cubeo	Same num	Men some
Jivaro	Same num	Men some
Inca	Same num	Men none
Siriono	Same num	Men some
Trumai	Same num	Men none
Tupinamba	Same num	Men none
Shavante	Women+	Men none
Abipon	Women+	Men some
Tehuelche	Women+	Men none

Despite the confusing similarity of names, the concept of statistical independence is completely different from the idea of independent or dependent variables. Independent and dependent are labels that help clarify which variable is the cause and which is the effect. Two variables which are statistically independent have no association regardless of which is independent and which is dependent.

Strength

Usually we are not satisfied to know only that an association exists. When we are evaluating a theory or hypothesis, a strong association gives stronger support for the theory than a weak association. One way to assess the strength of an association is to compare the row percentages. We did this implicitly when we compared the percentages in the columns of the table. For example, by subtracting 50.00% from 63.64% in the first column of Figure 2.1 we see that in 13.64% more societies with a surplus of women, men did no housework compared to societies with a surplus of men. Although this is a useful way to gain a preliminary understanding of whether an association exists, this approach has a major problem. There are a lot of percentages that we could subtract, producing a variety of different numbers. It is hard to know which to select and what they mean. There is an easier way. Later in the chapter we will show how a single number can summarize the strength of an association in an entire table.

Direction

When categories of the independent and dependent variables can be ordered from highest to lowest, then we can speak of the direction of association. If high values of one variable tend to be associated with high values of the other variable and the low values of each variable also tend to go together then the variables have a *positive* association. On the other hand, if high values of one variable tend to be associated with low values of the other and vice versa then the variables have a *negative* association. The association between SEXRATIO$ and DIVORCE$, reproduced from Chapter 1 in Figure 2.3, is an example of a negative association because in societies with a surplus of females it was easier for men to initiate a divorce while in societies with an oversupply of males it was easier for women to initiate divorce.

Pattern

The pattern of the association between two variables can take on many forms. Sometimes, there is a generally uniform progression in the percentages. As we move up (or down) one category of the independent variable, the concentration of the percentages tends to also move up (or down) one or more categories. This may be called a monotonic or *linear* association because we could draw a straight line through the concentration of cases on the dependent variable. Many theories suggest a linear association between the independent and dependent variables.

To help you see the pattern of the association, you may want to underline the highest percentage in each column. This is particularly helpful in revealing linear associations. For example, the association between SEXRATIO$ and DIVORCE$ in Figure 2.3 is clearly linear. We describe several other important patterns of association later in this chapter.

Figure 2.3
Example of a Negative Linear Association

```
XTAB
    USE SEXRATIO
    PRINT NONE / ROWPCT
    TABULATE SEXRATIO$ * DIVORCE$
```

```
Row percents
   SEXRATIO$ (rows) by DIVORCE$ (columns)

           Men easy  Rights =  Wom easy    Total       N
          +--------------------------------+
  Men+    |    .00     80.00     20.00   |  100.00      10
          |                              |
  Same num|  17.24     81.03      1.72   |  100.00      58
          |                              |
  Women+  |  31.82     63.64      4.55   |  100.00      22
          +--------------------------------+
  Total     18.89     76.67      4.44      100.00
      N        17        69         4                  90
```

2.2 Proportional reduction in error (PRE) measures of association

We want to simplify our work by summarizing an association with a single statistic. The following example illustrates how a summary statistic can be constructed. If we used SEXRATIO$ as an independent variable to predict how much HOUSEWK$ men are likely to do, our prediction would have two possible results.

1. The sex ratio may *not* be related to male housework. In this case knowing the sex ratio of the society does not improve our prediction of HOUSEWK$. In other words, we could predict the values of the dependent variable as well when we used no information about the independent variable as we could when we know the independent variable.

2. Alternatively, if the sex ratio *is* related to male housework, then our prediction of HOUSEWK$ improves if we know the sex ratio. Our ability to predict the values of the dependent variable improves when we know the value of the independent variable.

A statistic can be constructed by counting the number of errors in prediction (i.e. misclassifications) that we would make if we did not use the independent variable and comparing that to the number of misclassifications when using the independent variable to improve our predictions. If errors are not reduced by using the independent variable then it didn't improve the prediction and there is no association. The reduction in errors is a measure of the strength of association; the larger the reduction, the stronger the association. This can be expressed as the ratio:

$$\frac{\left(\begin{array}{c}\textit{Misclassifications without}\\ \textit{using independent variable}\end{array}\right) - \left(\begin{array}{c}\textit{Misclassifications using information}\\ \textit{from independent variable}\end{array}\right)}{\left(\begin{array}{c}\textit{Misclassifications without}\\ \textit{using independent variable}\end{array}\right)}$$

This ratio yields a proportion expressing how much prediction errors are reduced by knowledge of the independent variable. Measures of association which use this ratio are called **proportional reduction in error** statistics, usually abbreviated **PRE** statistics. Much of the rest of this chapter discusses PRE statistics appropriate for different tables. We begin by making these statistics concrete with an extended example of a PRE statistic called lambda.

2.3 Goodman and Kruskal's lambda

If you had no data on SEXRATIO$, how much housework would you predict males would do? To make the smallest number of errors you would predict the category of HOUSEWK$ that occurs most often in your data. This category is called the **mode** or the modal category. The table of frequencies in Figure 2.4 shows that there are more societies where men do no housework than societies where men do some; your best guess would predict Men none. This guess is correct for 45 cases, but it misclassifies the 44 societies where men did some housework. Thus, 44 is the number of misclassifications if (1) were true and we had no information about SEXRATIO$.

Figure 2.4
Frequency Table of Sex Ratio by Housework

```
XTAB
   USE HOUSEWK
   PRINT NONE / FREQ
   TABULATE SEXRATIO$ * HOUSEWK$
```

```
Frequencies
  SEXRATIO$ (rows) by HOUSEWK$ (columns)

            Men none  Men some     Total
          +--------------------+
  Men+    |    5         5     |    10
          |                    |
  Same num|   26        31     |    57
          |                    |
  Women+  |   14         8     |    22
          +--------------------+
  Total       45        44         89
```

Since we know the sex ratio for each society, how much does this improve our ability to predict whether men do housework? We again use the mode: for each category of the independent variable, predict the modal category of the dependent variable. In other words, again predict the modal category of HOUSEWK$ but make a separate prediction for each category of SEXRATIO$.

Since SEXRATIO$ has 3 categories, we make 3 predictions. If you know that a society falls in the bottom row of Figure 2.4, it has a surplus of women (Women+) and the best guess is that men do no housework. Using this guess, you correctly classify 14 societies, but you misclassify 8. Applying the same rule to societies with the "Same num" of men and women you guess "Men some". You are wrong 26 times. For the top row, societies with a surplus of males, you can predict either "Men none" or "Men some". It doesn't matter because you misclassify 5 societies either way.

Comparing the errors, you misclassified 44 societies when you did not use any information about the independent variable. Using the information from the independent variable, SEXRATIO$, you were wrong (8 + 26 + 5) or 39 times. The **lambda** measure of association, λ, measures how much your error rate decreases when you use the information from SEXRATIO$. For the Sex Ratio Housework table in Figure 2.4 the estimated value of lambda is calculated as:

$$\hat{\lambda} = \frac{44 - 39}{44} = \frac{5}{44} = 0.114$$

By knowing the sex ratio of the society, you reduced your error rate by 11.4%. Lambda tells you the proportion by which you can reduce your error in predicting the dependent variable if you know the independent variable. It is a good example of a **PRE** statistic.

Lambda is a measure of the existence and strength of an association. It gives you information about a particular pattern of association: using each category of the independent variable to predict the modal category of the dependent variable. This pattern of association can be easily seen in the percentage tables like those in Figure 2.3 and Figure 2.5.

Lambda varies in size between zero and 1.00. Lambda is 1.00 when, for each category of the independent variable, only one cell contains all the cases. In this case, knowing the value of the independent variable permits you to make perfect predictions of the dependent variable—a 100% reduction in error.

When two variables are statistically independent, lambda is zero.Unfortunately, the reverse is not true: a zero lambda does not mean two variables are independent. Zero only means that the extra information in independent variable did not help predict the *mode* of the dependent variable, and this can happen easily. For example, in the familiar table relating sex ratio to divorce in Figure 2.5, lambda is zero. Notice that there is a clear association evident in the row percentage table at the bottom of the figure, but lambda does not detect it. The problem is that most of the cases in the table fall in the Rights = column. When the distribution of the dependent variable is highly concentrated in a single category, the mode within each category of the independent variable is likely to be the same as the overall mode of the dependent variable. In such a table the modal categories for every row fall in the same column and lambda is zero.

Figure 2.5
Example of Lambda = 0.0.
The Association in the Table is Not Detected by Lambda

```
XTAB
   USE SEXRATIO
   PRINT NONE / FREQ  ROWP
   TABULATE SEXRATIO$ * DIVORCE$
```

```
Frequencies
 SEXRATIO$ (rows) by DIVORCE$ (columns)

              Men easy  Rights =  Wom easy     Total
            +----------------------------+
  Men+      |     0         8         2   |      10
            |                             |
  Same num  |    10        47         1   |      58
            |                             |
  Women+    |     7        14         1   |      22
            +----------------------------+
  Total          17        69         4          90


Row percents
 SEXRATIO$ (rows) by DIVORCE$ (columns)

              Men easy  Rights =  Wom easy     Total       N
            +----------------------------+
  Men+      |   .00      80.00     20.00  |    100.00      10
            |                             |
  Same num  |  17.24     81.03      1.72  |    100.00      58
            |                             |
  Women+    |  31.82     63.64      4.55  |    100.00      22
            +----------------------------+
  Total       18.89     76.67      4.44       100.00
      N         17        69         4                     90
```

For this table:

$$\hat{\lambda} = \frac{(69 - (8 + 47 + 14))}{69} = \frac{(69 - 69)}{69} = \frac{0}{69} = 0$$

Like all measures of association, lambda is sensitive to only one pattern of association. It measures the reduction in error that results from using the categories of an independent variable to predict the modal values of the dependent variable. If that pattern is missing, then lambda is zero. When this happens it does not mean that there is no association, only that lambda could not detect it. Other measures of association can often find other patterns and the other patterns may be quite strong.

SYSTAT prints the estimated value for lambda, as well as other measures of association, when you give the command PRINT LONG before the TABULATE command. Figure 2.6 gives the commands and the SYSTAT output for the Sex Ratio–Housework

Dataset. SYSTAT also prints the asymptotic standard errors of many measures of association. The standard error is, you may remember from elementary statistics, the standard deviation of a statistic. If the statistic is calculated from a large sample, the sampling distribution of the statistic is a normal distribution. (SYSTAT uses the word "asymptotic" to remind you that these estimates of the standard errors are only accurate if you have a large number of cases.) Normal distributions have the property that distance measured in standard errors is directly related to an important probability: approximately 95% of the time, the actual value in the population will be within plus or minus two standard errors of the estimate given by the statistic. Thus, the standard error can be used to test hypotheses and construct confidence intervals. A confidence interval is a range which we expect to contain the actual population value in a certain portion of the samples, often 95% of the samples. A confidence interval for lambda can be obtained from these formulas:

$$\text{Upper bound} = \quad + \ z * (\textit{Standard Error of } \hat{\lambda})$$
$$\text{Lower bound} = \quad - \ z * (\textit{Standard Error of } \hat{\lambda})$$

where z is chosen from the standard normal distribution, $\hat{\lambda}$ is the estimated value of lambda in the table you're looking at and *Standard Error* is the asymptotic standard error for lambda in the same table. For example, a 95% confidence interval for lambda from the table in Figure 2.6 is:

$$\text{Upper bound} = \textit{0.114 + 1.96* 0.162 = 0.432}$$
$$\text{Lower bound} = \textit{0.114 - 1.96* 0.162 = -0.204}$$

By this calculation the 95% confidence interval for lambda ranges from -0.204 to 0.432. Since lambda is always greater than or equal to zero, the 95% confidence interval ranges from 0.0 to 0.432. Remember that a 95% confidence interval does *not* mean that the population parameter has a 95% chance of being inside the interval. Rather, if repeated samples are drawn from the same population under identical conditions, the confidence interval contains the population parameter 95% of the time. Since the population value is unknown, there is no way for you to know whether any particular interval contains it.

Since the confidence interval for lambda includes zero, we cannot conclude that the association of SEXRATIO$ and HOUSEWK$ was different from zero. This confidence interval is wide, including any value of lambda from zero to 43%, because our sample contains only 89 cases. A larger number of cases, like the 1500 cases typically used in national polls, produces a much narrower confidence interval. These confidence limits are valid only for random samples, like we have here. The modifications for other kinds of samples are given in Goodman and Kruskal (1963, 1972).

SYSTAT prints a variety of other statistics in Figure 2.6. Each statistic measures association in a specific way and is, therefore, appropriate for certain kinds of data and inappropriate for others. How you can choose the measure of association that is most appropriate for your data and your theory is the subject of the remainder of this chapter.

2.4 Level of measurement

Several decades ago the pyschophysicist S.S. Stevens (1975) developed an approach to measurement which classified data according to the amount of information recorded about the cases. He called the amount of information the **level of measurement** and he suggested that variables could be classified into four levels: nominal, ordinal, interval and ratio variables. This classification has been criticized, but it helps highlight some properties of variables and it continues to be widely used. It is particularly useful for qualitative variables because some measures of association were developed specifically for variables classified according to these levels of measurement.

The categories in **nominal** variables have no inherent order. The names or numbers assigned to represent the categories are merely labels or names. Race, sex, political party are examples of nominal variables. Since there is no order to the categories, race, for example, could be presented in alphabetic order or according to similarity on the color wheel with no effect on its meaning. Nominal variables are often called qualitative because the categories have different qualities but cannot be arranged in quantitative order from high to low.

Figure 2.6
Measures of Association for a Two-Way Table

```
XTAB
    USE HOUSEWK
    PRINT MEDIUM
    TABULATE SEXRATIO$ * HOUSEWK$
```

```
Frequencies
  SEXRATIO$ (rows) by HOUSEWK$ (columns)

          Men none  Men some   Total
        +--------------------+
Men+    |    5         5    |    10
        |                   |
Same num|   26        31    |    57
        |                   |
Women+  |   14         8    |    22
        +--------------------+
Total        45        44        89
```

Test statistic	Value	DF	Prob
Pearson Chi-square	2.064	2.000	0.356
Likelihood ratio Chi-square	2.085	2.000	0.353

Coefficient	Value	Asymptotic Std Error
Phi	0.152	
Cramer V	0.152	
Contingency	0.151	
Goodman-Kruskal Gamma	-0.223	0.194
Kendall Tau-B	-0.115	0.101
Stuart Tau-C	-0.117	0.103
Spearman Rho	-0.119	0.105
Somers D (column dependent)	-0.113	0.100
Lambda (column dependent)	0.114	0.162
Uncertainty (column dependent)	0.017	0.023

If the categories can be arranged in an order, the variable is called **ordinal**. For example, the three categories of SEXRATIO$ are arranged in a particular order in the tables: the categories run from a scarcity of females (Men+) to a surplus (Women+). Other examples of ordinal variables are rankings of football teams, bond ratings, and job satisfaction scales. Because the categories can be arranged from highest to lowest, the association in ordinal variables (but not nominal variables) can be described in terms of direction. Although the categories are ordered, the distances between adjacent categories have no meaning and they do not need to be equal.

The categories of an **interval** variable are defined on a scale where the distance between categories is constant. Temperature measured on the Fahrenheit scale is a good example: the difference between two days with average temperatures of 10 degrees and

20 degrees is the same as the difference between two days with average temperatures of 90 degrees and 100 degrees.

Ratio variables have a definite zero. Zero on a ratio scale means that none of the quantity being measured is present. When measured on a Kelvin scale, temperature is a ratio variable. Other examples of ratio variables are years of education, weight in pounds, people's ages, or annual incomes in dollars. The name ratio means you can construct meaningful proportions or ratios between items. A $30,000 income is three times as much as a $10,000 income.

The statistical techniques used to analyze categorical data are generally appropriate for nominal and ordinal variables. The term categorical data usually refers only to nominal or ordinal data. Continuous data measured by interval and ratio variables are usually better analyzed with the techniques in later parts of this book.

Variables measuring sex ratios, divorce, and the amount of male housework have a natural order to their categories. But lambda does not use the order of the categories in its definition of an association. If you interchanged the rows or switched columns in the table in Figure 2.6, lambda would not change. This characteristic of lambda means that it can be used to measure association between nominal variables. In the next section, we will study some measures of association that use the order of the categories and are only appropriate for ordinal variables.

2.5 Measures of association for ordinal variables

Measures of association that use the ordering of categories differ in two major ways from measures of association for nominal variables. First, since the categories are ordered, the association between two variables has a direction indicated by the sign of the coefficient. A plus means a positive association and a minus indicates a negative or inverse association. The possible values of ordinal measures of association vary from -1.0, indicating a perfect negative association, through 0.0, meaning no association, up to 1.0, expressing a perfect positive association. Second, since the categories are ordered, the cases can be ranked according to whether they fall into a higher or lower category. Because you need at least two cases for a ranking, it is natural to think in terms of pairs of cases. A synonym for ranking is sort order.

Remember that SYSTAT sorts the categories of variables before it calculates measures of association. If you're using a character variable, be sure you've named the categories so that they sort in the correct order. If the categories are ordered differently, the values for ordinal measures of association will be wrong.

Measures of association assess how well you can predict one variable if you know the values of another variable. We use this idea to construct a measure of association: if we know the rank order of a pair of cases on one variable, how well can we predict the ranking on a second variable. If our knowledge of the ranking of a pair of cases on one variable does not help predict the rank order of the pair on a second variable, then the measure of association should be zero. If knowledge of the ranking is useful, then the association will be either positive or negative, depending on the direction.

Types of pairs

This simple concept becomes more complex in actual application because there turn out to be several different types of pairs of cases. In fact, there are five. Unfortunately, there is no way to avoid defining them because you sometimes need to estimate the number of pairs of each type in a two-way table in order to decide which measure of association is most appropriate.

Figure 2.7 contains five cases taken directly from the Sex Ratio–Housework Dataset in Figure 2.2. We will use these cases to illustrate the types of pairs.

Figure 2.7
Selected Cases from Sex Ratio–Housework Dataset

SOCIETY$	SEXRATIO$	HOUSEWK$
Nubians	Same num	Men none
Hadza	Women+	Men some
Nama Hott.	Same num	Men some
Mbumdu	Women+	Men none
Mbuti	Women+	Men some

1. **Concordant pairs** are ranked in the same order on both variables. Ranking refers to the order in which they would appear if we sorted the dataset. For example, look at the Nubians and the Hadza in Figure 2.7. The case containing Nubians would come before the Hadza if the data were sorted either by SEXRATIO$ or by HOUSEWK$; this is what we mean when we say the Nubians "rank higher" than the Hadza on both SEXRATIO$ and HOUSEWK$. That is, "Same num" sorts higher than "Women+" and "Men none" sorts before "Men some". Notice that working with pairs requires simultaneous comparisons of two cases and two variables. On the

two variables, a pair of cases is concordant if one case always ranks higher (or lower) than the other case.

2. **Discordant pairs** are ranked in the opposite order on both variables. For example, the Nama Hottentots are ranked higher than the Mbumdu on SEXRATIO$ but are ranked lower on HOUSEWK$. A pair of cases is discordant if one case ranks higher on one variable and lower on the second variable.

3. Pairs are **tied on both variables** when they have exactly the same values for the independent and dependent variables. For example, the Hadza and the Mbuti are tied on both variables.

4. Pairs are **tied on the independent variable** when they have the same value for the independent variable but different values for the dependent variable. In Figure 2.7, the Mbumdu and the Hadza are tied on the independent variable.

5. Pairs are **tied on the dependent variable** when they have the same value for the dependent variable but different values for the independent variable. The Nama Hottentot and the Hadza are tied on the dependent variable.

These five types are exhaustive and mutually exclusive, so any pair of cases in a table must be in one and only one of these categories and the sum of the pairs of all types is equal to the total number of pairs in the table.

Measures of association for ordinal variables

To construct a PRE measure of association for ordinal variables we need two rules for prediction: prediction ignoring the independent variable and prediction using information from the independent variable. When we don't know the independent variable we predict that the pairs of cases are randomly ordered on the dependent variable. If we know the independent variable we can use one of two prediction rules. If there are more concordant pairs, then we know that as values of one variable increase (or decrease) so do the values of the other variable. This is a positive association and we predict that the pair of cases has the same rank on the dependent variable as it does on the independent variable. If there are more discordant pairs, then we know that as the values of one variable increase, the values of the other tend to decrease. This is a negative association and we predict that the pair of cases has the opposite rank on the dependent variable as it does on the independent variable.

Ordinal PRE measures of association are simple ratios of the various types of pairs discussed in the previous section. The numerator of each ratio is always the same: the difference between the number of concordant pairs and the number of discordant pairs, or *Concordances - Discordances*. The ratios differ according to which pairs they count in the denominator. Changing the denominator changes the types of pairs included in the prediction.

Below we will discuss three ordinal PRE statistics; gamma, tau-*b*, and Somers' *d*, as well as several other ordinal measures of association. We print the formulas for each statistic so that you can see which pairs are included in the denominator. However, we do not work out the arithmetic required to calculate each statistic. After all, that's one of the reasons you use a computer and SYSTAT: so the computer can do the routine arithmetic and you have more time for the hard stuff, like thinking about what the results mean. We do not print formulas for standard errors because they are complicated and not particularly useful in helping you understand the statistic. If you need to work out a statistic by hand, check Loether and McTavish (1988, Chapter 7) or Bohrnstedt and Knoke (1994, Chapter 9) for calculator formulas and worked examples. Figure 2.8 reproduces the data from Figure 2.6 with the ordinal measures of association highlighted.

Goodman and Kruskal's gamma

Gamma is the most widely used and the simplest of the PRE statistics for ordinal tables. It counts only concordant and discordant pairs in its formula:

$$\hat{\gamma} = \frac{Concordances - Discordances}{Concordances + Discordances}$$

Figure 2.8 shows that gamma for the association between SEXRATIO\$ and HOUSE-WK\$ is -0.223. This is a negative association and it means that as SEXRATIO\$ increases, the amount of HOUSEWK\$ done by men declines. The absolute value of gamma is a PRE statistic. By using the independent variable we reduced the number of errors by 22.3%. Remember that we are only predicting the ranking of pairs and only counting pairs which are ranked differently on both variables (non-tied pairs).

Gamma is a symmetric measure of association. This means that it has the same value regardless of whether the independent variable is the row variable or the column variable. Since gamma does not include any tied pairs, it can be based on a small number of cases. In fact gamma could be 1.0 (or -1.0) based on only one pair, if all other pairs were tied on one or both variables. Because of this potential weakness of gamma, if your table contains few non-tied pairs you may prefer one of the other statistics that we discuss below. In 2x2 tables, gamma is called Yule's Q.

Figure 2.8
Measures of Association for a Two-Way Table

```
XTAB
   USE HOUSEWK
   PRINT MEDIUM
   TABULATE SEXRATIO$ * HOUSEWK$
```

```
Frequencies
  SEXRATIO$ (rows) by HOUSEWK$ (columns)

             Men none  Men some    Total
           +--------------------+
  Men+     |     5         5     |    10
           |                     |
  Same num |    26        31     |    57
           |                     |
  Women+   |    14         8     |    22
           +--------------------+
  Total         45        44         89
```

Test statistic	Value	DF	Prob
Pearson Chi-square	2.064	2.000	0.356
Likelihood ratio Chi-square	2.085	2.000	0.353

Coefficient	Value	Asymptotic Std Error
Phi	0.152	
Cramer V	0.152	
Contingency	0.151	
Goodman-Kruskal Gamma	-0.223	0.194
Kendall Tau-B	-0.115	0.101
Stuart Tau-C	-0.117	0.103
Spearman Rho	-0.119	0.105
Somers D (column dependent)	-0.113	0.100
Lambda (column dependent)	0.114	0.162
Uncertainty (column dependent)	0.017	0.023

SYSTAT prints the asymptotic standard error of gamma which can be used for hypothesis testing and to construct confidence intervals. The formula for confidence intervals is the same as that given for lambda above (except, of course, that you need to substitute SYSTAT's estimate of gamma for lambda). For hypothesis testing you can use the formula:

$$z = \frac{\hat{\gamma} - \gamma}{\text{standard error of } \hat{\gamma}}$$

where $\hat{\gamma}$ is the sample estimate of gamma from the SYSTAT output, γ is the population value under the null hypothesis, and the standard error of $\hat{\gamma}$ is the asymptotic standard error of gamma from the SYSTAT output. For large random samples, z has an approximately standard normal distribution. The most common null hypothesis is that $\gamma = 0$. In this case the formula simplifies to:

$$z = \frac{\hat{\gamma}}{\textit{standard error of } \hat{\gamma}}$$

z can be evaluated against the normal distribution in the usual way. If the computed z is in the critical region, the null hypothesis can be rejected. If not, fail to reject it.

Somers' *d*

Most theories distinguish independent and dependent variables. Since we are trying to measure the reduction in error by using information from an independent variable, we should include all pairs which rank differently on the independent variable. Some of these will be concordant, some will be discordant and some will be tied on the dependent variable. Gamma does not include this last group of pairs, but Somers' *d* does. Its formula is:

$$\hat{d} = \frac{\textit{Concordances} - \textit{Discordances}}{\textit{Concordances} + \textit{Discordances} + \textit{Dependent Ties}}$$

where *Dependent Ties* is the number of cases tied on the dependent variable. Notice that the SYSTAT output in Figure 2.8 says, (COLUMN DEPENDENT) to remind you that it always assumes that the dependent variable is the column variable. There are two Somers' *d*s which can be computed from any table, depending upon whether the row variable or the column variable is the dependent variable. Usually these two values are different, so be sure that your dependent variable is in the right place.

In Figure 2.8, Somers' $\hat{d}$ is -0.113. This is substantially smaller than the gamma for the same table, indicating that the table contains many ties on the dependent variable. Somers' *d* will always be smaller in absolute value than gamma, but not always half the size.

The asymptotic standard error for Somers' *d* can be used for hypothesis testing and to construct confidence intervals.

Kendall's tau-*b*

A third approach to association takes into account ties on one variable or the other but not both variables. Tau-*b* is calculated by:

$$\hat{\tau}_b = \frac{Concordances - Discordances}{\sqrt{(Conc + Disc + Dep\ Ties)\ (Conc + Disc + Indep\ Ties)}}$$

where concordances and discordances are abbreviated, *Dep Ties* is the number of cases tied on the dependent variable and *Indep Ties* is the number of cases tied on the independent variable. A PRE interpretation of tau-*b* is that if we do not have a clear independent or dependent variable then the proportion of correct predictions for concordance or discordance should be compared to the total pool of possible pairs for which a prediction can be made. This includes not only the concordant and discordant pairs used by gamma but also pairs tied on one or the other of the variables.

Tau-*b* in Figure 2.8 has an estimated value of -.115 and an estimated standard error of .101, showing, like the other measures of association, the nonsignificant positive association between SEXRATIO$ and HOUSEWK$ in the table. The asymptotic standard error for Tau-*b* can be used for hypothesis testing and to construct confidence intervals.

Tau-*b* can have values of +1.0 or -1.0 only in square tables (i.e. where the number of rows equals the number of columns). This weakness has lead to the development of a statistic which can attain +1.0 and -1.0 in nonsquare tables.

Stuart's tau-*c*

Tau-*c* was explicitly designed to be able to attain values of +1.0 and -1.0 for nonsquare tables. Its formula is:

$$\hat{\tau}_c = \frac{2m\ (Concordances - Discordances)}{N^2\ (m - 1)}$$

where N is the total number of cases in the table and m is the smaller of the number of rows or columns Unfortunately, there is no PRE interpretation of tau-*c*. This has discouraged its use because it is hard to interpret. Tau-*b* is much more frequently used. Although the standard error of tau-*c* is available, tau-*c* is most often used as a descriptive measure of the association between two variables.

Spearman's rho for ranked data

A special case of ordinal data occurs when each case can be given a unique rank. If there are N cases in the sample, they can be ranked from 1 to N. Typical examples of ranked data are the Fortune 500 or the 20 largest cities ranked by population. A measure of association designed specifically for this situation is Spearman's rho:

$$\hat{r}_s = 1 - \frac{\left(6 \sum_{i=1}^{W} D^2 \right)}{N(N^2 - 1)}$$

where N is the number of cases in the sample, and D is the difference between the ranks for each case. $\sum D^2$ is the squared differences between the ranks of each case summed over all cases in the sample.

Spearman's rho reaches its maximum value of 1.0 when the ranks of the two variables match exactly and its minimum of -1.0 when the ranks are exactly opposite. A rho of zero indicates no rank association between the variables. If two or more cases are tied for the same rank, the ranks that they could hold are averaged and the average is assigned to all tied cases. Spearman's rho does not estimate an easily understandable population parameter, but interested readers may consult Kruskal (1958) for a fairly complex interpretation. Rho has no PRE interpretation, but rho^2 can be interpreted as the proportional reduction in error in predicting ranks for the dependent variable using the ranks of the independent variable versus predicting that all values of the dependent variable have the mean rank.

Some examples above illustrate creating ranks from a continuous variable (e.g. city population). A better statistic for measuring association in continuous data is the Pearson correlation coefficient; see Section 7.1. The standard error of rho can be used for confidence intervals or hypothesis testing in the usual way.

2.6 Measures of association for nominal variables

Christmas trees are the most striking secular symbol of the Christmas celebration. However, not everyone puts up a tree at Christmas. Who puts up a Christmas tree and who does not? As part of his investigations of Christmas trees, gift exchanges, and other rituals of Christmas Theodore Caplow (1982, 1984) found that strong rules require certain families to put up Christmas trees; the rules are enforced so effectively that he describes compliance as "spectacular." Simply, Caplow believes that any family with children is required to put up a tree. Some of the statistical evidence that Caplow presents is in Figure 2.10 and the data input appears in Figure 2.9. Pay attention to the data input in Figure 2.9. The approach is to make each cell in the table into a case and create a variable (called COUNT in this case) that contains the count in the cell. This technique can be used for secondary analysis of virtually any published table.

The Christmas tree dataset contains two nominal variables, XMASTREE$ and CHILDREN$. We use these data to illustrate several measures of association for nominal variables. Both variables have only two categories, so the two-way tables that we examine are all 2-by-2 tables. Several measures of association have been developed solely for 2-by-2 tables. The measures of association for nominal variables are highlighted in Figure 2.11.

Figure 2.9
Middletown Christmas Tree Dataset

```
BASIC
SAVE XMASTREE
INPUT XMASTREE$ CHILDREN$ COUNT
RUN
"Tree" "Children" 76
"Tree" "No Child" 2
"No Tree" "Children" 4
"No Tree" "No Child" 11
~
```

The chi-square significance test

The title of this subsection refers to the "chi-square significance test" rather than to chi-square as a measure of association. This highlights that chi-square is not a measure of the association between two variables in the sense that we use the term elsewhere in this chapter. Chi-square is a statistic that indicates whether or not two variables are independent. Unlike the other measures of association the chi-square value gives us no information about the strength, direction, or pattern of the association.

Chi-square estimates are based on the relationship between the cell frequencies that we observe in a table like Figure 2.11 (called observed frequencies) and the cell frequencies that we expect to observe if the null hypothesis of no association were true (called expected frequencies). To understand the chi-square test you need to know how the expected frequencies are calculated.

Figure 2.10
Families with Children are Required to Put up Christmas Trees

```
XTAB
   USE XMASTREE
   FREQ COUNT
   PRINT NONE / FREQ ROWPCT
   TABULATE CHILDREN$ * XMASTREE$
```

```
Frequencies
  CHILDREN$ (rows) by XMASTREE$ (columns)

                No Tree      Tree      Total
             +---------------------+
   Children  |      4        76   |     80
             |                    |
   No Child  |     11         2   |     13
             +---------------------+
   Total           15         78        93


Row percents
  CHILDREN$ (rows) by XMASTREE$ (columns)

                No Tree      Tree      Total      N
             +---------------------+
   Children  |    5.00     95.00   |   100.00     80
             |                    |
   No Child  |   84.62     15.38   |   100.00     13
             +---------------------+
   Total         16.13     83.87       100.00
      N            15         78                   93
```

If the two variables in the table are statistically independent then the expected frequency for the cell in row_i and $column_j$ is:

$$\left(\begin{array}{c} expected\ frequency \\ of\ cell_{ij} \end{array} \right) = \frac{\left(\begin{array}{c} row\ total \\ for\ row_i \end{array} \right) \left(\begin{array}{c} column\ total \\ for\ column_j \end{array} \right)}{N}$$

where N is the size of the sample. For example, the expected frequency for $cell_{11}$ (the upper left cell) in Figure 2.11 is:

$$\frac{(80)\ (15)}{93} = 12.9$$

Figure 2.11
Measures of Association for Nominal Variables

```
XTAB
  USE XMASTREE
  FREQ COUNT
  PRINT MEDIUM
  TABULATE CHILDREN$ * XMASTREE$
```

```
Frequencies
 CHILDREN$ (rows) by XMASTREE$ (columns)

           No Tree    Tree    Total
         +-----------------+
Children |     4       76   |     80
         |                  |
No Child |    11        2   |     13
         +-----------------+
 Total         15       78        93
```

WARNING: More than one-fifth of fitted cells are sparse (frequency < 5).
         Significance tests computed on this table are suspect.

Test statistic	Value	DF	Prob
Pearson Chi-square	52.399	1.000	0.000
Likelihood ratio Chi-square	39.251	1.000	0.000
McNemar Symmetry Chi-square	48.563	1.000	0.000
Yates corrected Chi-square	46.679	1.000	0.000
Fisher exact test (two-tail)			0.000

Coefficient	Value	Asymptotic Std Error
Odds Ratio	0.010	
Ln(Odds)	-4.649	0.924
Phi	-0.751	
Cramer V	0.708	
Contingency	0.600	
Goodman-Kruskal Gamma	-0.981	0.017
Kendall Tau-B	-0.751	0.096
Stuart Tau-C	-0.383	0.096
Yule Q	-0.981	0.017
Yule Y	-0.822	0.075
Cohen Kappa	-0.257	0.080
Spearman Rho	-0.751	0.096
Somers D (column dependent)	-0.796	0.103
Lambda (column dependent)	0.600	0.152
Uncertainty (column dependent)	0.478	0.133

If XMASTREE$ and CHILDREN$ were independent and the table had the row and column totals that we see in Figure 2.11, we would expect 12.9 cases in the upper left cell. This is quite different from the 4 cases which we observe in that cell.

SYSTAT prints three different chi-square statistics, the PEARSON CHI-SQUARE, the LIKELIHOOD RATIO CHI-SQUARE, and the YATES CORRECTED CHI-SQUARE. All summarize the discrepancy between the observed and expected frequencies and all are distributed according to the χ^2 sampling distribution in large samples when the null hypothesis of no association (or independence) is true. In general, they are all quite similar.

Pearson chi-square: $$\chi^2 = \sum \frac{(Observed - Expected)^2}{Expected}$$

Likelihood ratio chi-square: $$L^2 = 2\sum (Observed)\, log\left(\frac{Observed}{Expected}\right)$$

Yates' corrected chi-square: $$\chi^2_c = \sum \frac{\left(|Observed - Expected| - \frac{1}{2}\right)^2}{Expected}$$

where the summation in all three equations is over all cells in the table.

The exact shape of the chi-square sampling distribution depends on the size of the table to which you compare it. The precise technical term for the size of table is the **degrees of freedom** in the table. In a table, the degrees of freedom is the number of cell frequencies which are free to vary, given that the row and column totals are fixed. The general formula for calculating the degrees of freedom in 2-way tables is:

$$df = (Number\ of\ rows - 1)\ (Number\ of\ columns - 1)$$

Thus, the 2x2 table in Figure 2.11 has (2 - 1) (2 - 1) = 1 degree of freedom. By contrast, the 3-by-3 table in Figure 2.5 has (3 - 1) (3 - 1) = 4 degrees of freedom.

The interpretation of degrees of freedom for a chi-square test can be illustrated as follows. Suppose you know the row and column totals for the Christmas tree dataset and you are given the cell frequency of 4 from the upper left cell Since the row total for the first row is 80, the total in the upper right cell must be (80 - 4 =) 76. Similarly, since the column total for the left column is 15, the total in the lower left cell must be (15 - 4 =) 11. Since you now know both the cell frequencies for both the upper right and lower left, you can use either to find the lower right cell frequency. This illustrates that, for any size table, if the row and column totals are known and you also know the cell frequencies in a block of (rows - 1) * (columns - 1) cells, then all the other cells are determined. The degrees of freedom, then, are the number of cells with cell frequencies that are "free to vary" in the sense that if those cells' frequencies were known, all other cell frequencies would also be known.

SYSTAT calculates the chi-square value for each estimate, the number of degrees of freedom, and the probability of obtaining that chi-square value if the null hypothesis of no association were true. You can see that the probability of obtaining the chi-square values for the table in Figure 2.11 is tiny, less than 0.0005. These variables are not independent. This result strongly supports Caplow's hypothesis that families with children have to put up a Christmas tree.

Comparing different chi-square estimators

The Pearson chi-square, the likelihood ratio chi-square, and the Yates' corrected chi-square all estimate the same theoretical sampling distribution of chi-square. The differences can be summarized as:

- The likelihood ratio chi-square has formal mathematical properties which are superior to those of the Pearson chi-square. It is the chi-square statistic for which maximum likelihood estimates give the minimum values.

- When applied to data, the Pearson chi-square and the likelihood ratio chi-square rarely differ enough to matter. As Bishop, Fienberg, and Holland (1975, p. 126) say, " ... the difference in numerical value ... is seldom large enough to be of practical importance."

- When the model is not correct, the Pearson chi-square and likelihood ratio chi-square estimates do not have the same behavior and may diverge considerably. This happens when you would reject the null hypothesis, so it rarely matters when testing for independence in two-way tables. This is evident in the table in Figure 2.11, where the two estimates are different.

- There is some controversy over how large a sample must be for these estimates to be good approximations of chi-square. A safe rule of thumb is that the total sample size be at least ten times the number of cells in the table (Fienberg 1980, p. 41). Alternative advice, from Cochran (1954), is that at least 80% of the cells should have expected frequencies exceeding 5.0 and the expected frequency in all cells should exceed 1.0. The warning that SYSTAT prints in tables like Figure 2.11 refers only to chi-square significance tests, not to significance tests based on other measures of association (gamma, lambda, etc.).

- Recent evidence suggests that smaller samples can be used. Larntz, in a 1978 Monte Carlo study, suggests a minimum expected cell frequency of greater than 1.0 is sufficient. The Pearson chi-square is a much closer approximation to chi-square than the likelihood ratio in cells with small observed counts. When the minimum expected frequency is between 1.0 and 4.0, Larntz finds that the Pearson chi-square "on average" approximates the chi-square distribution but the likelihood ratio chi-square is too large and it tends to show significant departures from independence where none exist.

- Yates' correction is defined only for 2-by-2 tables. In small samples the Pearson chi-square may be too large. The Yates' correction usually makes the estimated chi-square smaller and it will often be closer to the theoretical sampling distribution than the uncorrected Pearson chi-square. Conover (1974) recommends researchers use it only when they have fixed the row and column totals (as in an experiment) and either the two row totals are identical or the two column totals are identical.

Ironically, chi-square statistics have problems not only in small samples, but also in large samples. If the sample size is large enough, a chi-square test shows a significant relationship between almost any two variables. Unlike the problems of small samples this is not a mathematical issue, but it hampers the ability of the researcher with a large sample to separate statistical from substantive significance. For example, if you double each cell frequency in a table, the strength, direction, and pattern of the association (if any) do not change, but the chi-square test statistic doubles and becomes more significant. Some solutions to this large-sample trap are described in the next chapter in the discussion of Raftery's BIC.

The actual value of the chi-square statistic tells you only about the independence of the variables. It provides no information about the strength, direction, or pattern of the association. For example, the chi-square statistic may be significant if only one cell in a large table differs dramatically from independence. Since the estimated chi-square depends on sample size as well as the independence of the variables, you cannot compare chi-square values from different tables with different sample sizes. Finally, since chi-square is based only on expected versus observed cell counts, tables with very different associations can have the same estimated chi-square value.

The weaknesses of chi-square as a measure of association are widely known and several statistics have attempted to correct them. The corrections modify chi-square so that it is not influenced by sample size and so that it falls in the range from 0.0 to 1.0.

The phi coefficient

The most direct way to remove the influence of sample size is to divide chi-square by the sample size and take the square root:

$$\hat{\phi} = \sqrt{\frac{\chi^2}{N}}$$

where N is the sample size. The maximum value of phi is the square root of $k - 1$ where k is the smaller of the number of rows or columns. Thus, in tables with more than 2 rows or columns phi can exceed 1.0. A further problem is that phi has no PRE interpretation.

Two-by-two tables are a special case and SYSTAT calculates phi using a slightly different formula than the one given above. This formula allows phi to be negative with a lower bound of -1.0 and an upper bound of 1.0. Thus, in 2x2 tables, phi measures the direction of association and can be used to measure associations between ordinal variables. For nominal variables, drop the sign and use only the magnitude of phi. For a 2-by-2 table, phi is the same as the correlation coefficient. In 2-by-2 tables, phi can be interpreted as a measure of the degree to which the cases concentrate on the diagonal, a PRE interpretation.

Contingency coefficient

The contingency coefficient always lies between 0.0 and 1.0. Unfortunately, it can never reach 1.0, even in a table with a perfect association. Its maximum possible value depends on the number of rows and columns in the table. Its formula is:

$$\hat{C} = \sqrt{\frac{\chi^2}{\chi^2 + N}}$$

Like phi, the population parameter that $\hat{C}$ estimates is not clear and it has no PRE interpretation.

Cramer's *V*

This coefficient corrects a major deficiency of the previous two: it can achieve its maximum of 1.0 in a table of any size. The sample estimate is:

$$\hat{V} = \sqrt{\frac{\chi^2}{N(m-1)}}$$

where m is the smaller of the number of rows or columns. In 2-by-2 tables $\hat{V}$ is identical to $\hat{\phi}$ so SYSTAT only prints it for larger tables. Since $\hat{V}$ cannot be expressed in terms of probabilities or odds, it is difficult to know what it means.

Odds ratio

An odds ratio is the ratio of the frequencies of two categories. If a, b, c, and d are cell frequencies in a 2x2 table:

$$\begin{array}{|cc|} \hline a & b \\ c & d \\ \hline \end{array}$$

The odds ratio measure of association (not available in Version 5) is defined as the odds of being classified in column 1 instead of column 2 of the first row (a/b) divided by the same odds in the second row (c/d).

$$odds\ ratio = \frac{a}{b} \div \frac{c}{d}$$

When the odds ratio is greater (or less) than 1.0, a subject in row 1 is more (or less) likely to be classified in column 1 than a subject in row 2. An odds ratio of 1.0 means no association. The odds ratio has a range of 0 to infinity; farther from 1.0, in either direction, indicates a stronger association. Odds ratios of 0 or infinity occur when one cell in the table has zero frequency. In the Christmas tree data, the odds ratio of the first row is (4/76 =) 0.0526 and the second row is (11 / 2 =) 5.50. The ratio of these odds ratios is (0.0526 / 5.50 =) 0.010, indicating a strong association. The odds ratio of less than 1.0 indicates that households with no children (row 2) are more likely to have no Christmas tree (column 1) than households with children.

After a little algebra, the odds ratio can be expressed as (ad)/(bc). Since this is the ratio of the two diagonals in the 2x2 table, the odds ratio is sometimes called the cross-product ratio. Significance tests and confidence intervals for the odds ratio can be constructed using ln(odds), to which we now turn.

Ln(odds)

The log of the odds ratio (not available in Version 5) can be used for significance tests and to construct confidence intervals for the odds ratio. With a range between 0 and infinity, where 1.0 means no association, the odds ratio is extremely skewed to the right. By taking the natural logarithm, we create a new measure of association that is symmetric around zero, ranging from negative infinity to positive infinity. For the Christmas tree data, the value of ln(odds) is -4.649 with a standard error of 0.924. To construct an approximate 95% confidence interval, use the statistics plus or minus 2 times its standard error:

$$-4.649 \pm 2 \times 0.924 = -4.649 \pm 1.848$$

The resulting confidence interval is:

$$-6.497 < ln(odds) < -2.801$$

Since zero is not included in the confidence interval, we conclude that the ln(odds) for the Christmas tree data differs significantly from zero and that the odds ratio differs significantly from 1.0.

To construct a confidence interval for the odds ratio, take the antilogs of the ends of the ln(odds) interval. For the Christmas tree data:

$$e^{-6.497} < odds\ ratio < e^{-2.801}$$

$$0.00151 < odds\ ratio < 0.0607$$

You can do this within SYSTAT by using the SYSTAT calculator. For example, to find the upper limit of the Christmas tree data you would type CALC EXP(-2.801).

Yule's Q

One of the best known measures of *association* for 2x2 tables is Yule's Q. The formula is:

$$\hat{Q} = \frac{ad - cb}{ad + cb}$$

where the a, b, c, and d refer to the same cell frequencies as the odds ratio, above.

Q can be interpreted as a measure of diagonal concentration. In the Christmas tree dataset, the $\hat{Q}$ of -0.981 with a standard error of 0.017 indicates a strong, significant concentration. Notice that if any one of the four cells is zero, $\hat{Q}$ shows a perfect association of 1.0 or -1.0. For nominal data, like these, the sign of the coefficient would be dropped.

In ordinal data, the sign indicates direction of association. $\hat{Q}$ is identical to Goodman and Kruskal's gamma, so it has a PRE interpretation and can be used for ordinal data. See the discussion of gamma in Section 2.5 for more information.

Yule's *Y*

Yule's *Y* is closely related to Yule's *Q*, as you can see from the formula:

$$\hat{Y} = \frac{\sqrt{ad} - \sqrt{cb}}{\sqrt{ad} + \sqrt{cb}}$$

Y has many of the same properties as *Q*. It is symmetric, ranging between -1.0 and 1.0 and can be used for ordinal tables. Bishop, Fienberg and Holland (1975, p. 379) interpret *Y* as the difference between the probabilities in the diagonal and off-diagonal cells of a table where the row and column probabilities have been standardized to $\frac{1}{2}$. What this means in substantive or theoretical terms will be left as an exercise for the reader. This coefficient is sometimes called Yule's coefficient of colligation.

Fisher's exact test

In small samples for 2-by-2 tables when the Yates' corrected chi-square statistic may be unreliable you can use Fisher's exact test. The word "exact" has special meaning: if the null hypothesis of independence is true and the marginals of the table are fixed by the researcher (as in an experiment), then we could construct all possible arrangements of cell frequencies and calculate the probability of obtaining each. This distribution of probabilities constitutes the sampling distribution for the table. To obtain the p-value associated with the observed table we are interested in the tail of this distribution, so we just calculate the sum of the probabilities of obtaining the observed table and all less likely tables. Because it is time-consuming to compute, SYSTAT prints Fisher's exact test only when the total number of cases is less than 100. The formula is complicated and not particularly enlightening, so we do not print it here. Discussions with examples are in Blalock (1979, p. 287-291), and Walker and Lev (1953, p. 103-105).

Mantel-Haenszel chi-square

If you wish to test the null hypothesis of independence in a 2x2 table controlling for a third variable, you can use the Mantel-Haenszel chi-square. The third variable is called a **stratification variable** and the test is appropriate when each category of this variable is a separate population, called a **stratum**. An analysis that uses the data in each stratum, summarized across the entire table, is called a **stratified analysis**, also known as blocked analysis or matched analysis. The Mantel-Haenszel chi-square requires that the row and column marginals of each stratum be fixed. This restricts its use primarily to controlled experiments where the researcher determines the marginals before collecting data. Since it is a chi-square test, it has the problems common to other chi-square statistics in tables with small cell counts or large samples. SYSTAT requires that you specify the stratification variable first in the TABULATE command, yielding a k-by-2-by-2 table. For further information see Mantel and Haenszel (1959).

Uncertainty coefficient

The uncertainty coefficient is the proportional reduction in uncertainty of the dependent variable resulting from knowing the independent variable. The concept of uncertainty is based on information theory. Briefly, information theory attempts to measure the uncertainty associated with an observed probability distribution. The uncertainty coefficient is a PRE statistic with a range from 0 to 1. It is sometimes called the entropy statistic because uncertainty is measured by entropy. The formulas for entropy and the uncertainty coefficient are difficult to understand without a more detailed explanation of information theory than we have space to present. If you need to use information theory and the uncertainty coefficient seems appropriate, we suggest that you consult Theil (1970, 1972) for details.

McNemar symmetry chi-square

Sometimes you may want to define and test more narrowly defined null hypotheses than those we have examined above. In square tables you may want to know if the proportions in the off-diagonal cells are symmetric (that is, if the proportion in a cell is equal to the proportion in the cell on the equivalent location on the other side of the diagonal). By redefining the expected frequencies this hypothesis can be tested using a chi-square statistic. Bishop, Fienberg, and Holland (1975, p. 283) give this formula for the expected frequencies under the null hypothesis of symmetry:

$$\begin{pmatrix} observed \\ frequency \\ in\ cell_{ij} \end{pmatrix} = \frac{\begin{pmatrix} observed \\ frequency \\ in\ cell_{ij} \end{pmatrix} + \begin{pmatrix} observed \\ frequency \\ in\ cell_{ji} \end{pmatrix}}{2} \qquad for\ i \neq j$$

$$= \begin{pmatrix} observed \\ frequency \\ in\ cell_{ij} \end{pmatrix} \qquad for\ i = j$$

For example, the expected frequency for the upper right cell in Figure 2.11 is:

$$\frac{(76) + (11)}{2} = 43.5$$

These expected counts are then compared to the observed counts using the Pearson chi-square formula given above. This measure shares the strengths and weaknesses of the other chi-square estimators. Beware of small cell counts and large samples. In a 2-by-2 table like Figure 2.11, there is only one cell on each side of the diagonal and the meaning of symmetry is unambiguous, but in larger tables, several kinds of symmetry are possible. The McNemar symmetry chi-square does not distinguish between them, so that very different tables could have the same chi-square value. You can design tests for different kinds of symmetry using procedures described in Chapter 3, Section 3.9.

Cohen's kappa

Another coefficient that defines association narrowly is Cohen's kappa. Cohen is a psychologist who originally developed kappa to assess the degree of agreement between two raters who attempt to classify the same subject. Typical uses are to assess agreement between husbands and wives, or parents and children. Kappa is measured by:

$$\hat{\kappa} = \frac{\begin{pmatrix} Observed\ proportion \\ on\ main\ diagonal \end{pmatrix} - \begin{pmatrix} Expected\ proportion \\ on\ main\ diagonal \end{pmatrix}}{1 - \begin{pmatrix} Expected\ proportion \\ on\ main\ diagonal \end{pmatrix}}$$

where the observed and expected proportions on the main diagonal are just sums across the cells on the main diagonal. The expected proportion for a cell is calculated by dividing the expected cell frequency by the total number of cases. Kappa examines only the proportion of cases on the main diagonal (in SYSTAT the main diagonal always runs from the upper left cell to the lower right cell). Cases off the diagonal are never considered regardless of their location. SYSTAT only prints κ for square tables. Kappa ranges from -1.0 to 1.0. It has the value 0.0 when the level of agreement is exactly that expected by chance, 1.0 means complete agreement, and negative numbers indicate agreement is less than chance.

In the Christmas tree dataset in Figure 2.11, $\hat{\kappa}$ is -0.257, indicating less agreement than would be expected by chance. This makes sense because almost all cases are located in the two off-diagonal cells. However, the table is not really set up the way that kappa assumes it is. We should reverse the rows so that the No tree/No Child cell is in the upper left corner and the Tree/Children cell is in the lower right. This would yield a strongly positive kappa. The problem is that this table is not set up to test the sort of hypothesis that kappa was designed for. If the two variables had the same categories (as they would if we were measuring agreement between two raters) the problem would not arise. For more information see Cohen (1960).

2.7 Choosing a measure of association

We have discussed over twenty measures of association. The discussion included many comments on the suitability of different measures under diverse conditions. Because it is not easy to absorb all relevant distinctions, in this section we will lay out the major issues to consider when you choose a measure of association for your research.

In Section 2.1, we discussed four characteristics which describe an association between two variables.

1. Existence
2. Strength
3. Direction
4. Pattern

No measure of association can assess all these characteristics. The categories of nominal variables cannot be ordered so they have no direction. Some measures of association for nominal variables can only determine the existence of an association: chi-square statistics, for example. Others, like lambda, assess the strength of the association and are sensitive to particular patterns (but not others). All the measures of association for ordinal variables can be used to measure the existence, strength, direction, and pattern of association. They differ in that they are each sensitive to different patterns.

Necessary and sufficient conditions

The pattern of the data in a table can often be characterized by the distinction between *necessary* and *sufficient* conditions. If you wish to determine the effect of an independent variable on a dependent variable, then there are two situations that can occur. In one, cases occur in a certain category of the dependent variable *only* when they are in a given category of the independent variable. The independent variable category is a necessary (but not sufficient) condition for us to observe a case in the dependent variable category. In the other situation, cases may be found in the dependent variable category for other reasons but, whenever a case is in a certain category of the independent variable, then the case is always in the dependent variable category. The independent variable category is a sufficient (but not necessary) condition for us to observe a case in the dependent variable category.

How necessary or sufficient conditions may appear in a SYSTAT table is shown in the first two tables in Figure 2.12. The characteristic pattern of frequencies in these tables is a triangular arrangement of cells containing large cell frequencies and, above or below that triangle, a cell (or group of cells) with zero (or very small) frequencies. The third table illustrates how a condition that is both necessary and sufficient would appear. The characteristic pattern of frequencies in this table is that the bulk of the cases fall on the diagonal with small, sometimes zero, cell counts in the off-diagonal cells. These patterns are also visible in percentage tables.

The Christmas tree dataset illustrates both. Since couples with children usually have trees, we would say that having children is a sufficient reason for a tree. Since couples who do not have trees also do not have children, we could say that children are also a necessary condition for having a tree.

These issues are important for two reasons; one statistical, the other substantive. The statistical issue is that different measures of association are able to detect different patterns of association. One way to think about this is to ask, what pattern of association must be present for a given measure to reach 1.0, a perfect association? Some measures define a perfect association to be the linear pattern of a condition which is both necessary and sufficient. (phi and Cohen's kappa are examples.) Other measures allow the necessary but not sufficient or the sufficient but not necessary conditions to be a perfect association (for example, gamma). Some measures of association cannot be used to assess these patterns at all because they do not attempt to assess the pattern of the association, only its existence or strength. Examples are the Pearson and likelihood ratio chi-square statistics and the measures of association based on chi-square (phi, the contingency coefficient, and Cramer's *V*).

Figure 2.12
Necessary and Sufficient Conditions

A Necessary Condition

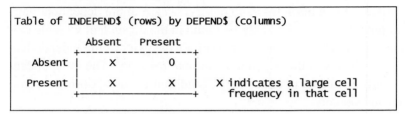

A Sufficient Condition

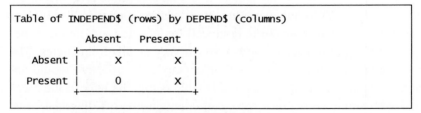

A Necessary and Sufficient Condition

```
Table of INDEPEND$ (rows) by DEPEND$ (columns)

            Absent    Present
          +--------------------+
 Absent   |    X         0     |
          |                    |
 Present  |    0         X     |
          +--------------------+
```

The substantive issue is that if your theory predicts a linear pattern of association, then you should use a coefficient which defines a linear association as a perfect association. That means a coefficient which uses the necessary and sufficient condition as its perfect association. On the other hand, if your theory predicts that the presence of some value on the independent variable is necessary but not sufficient (or sufficient but not necessary) for the presence of a dependent variable category, then you should use a coefficient with this definition of a perfect association. One reason gamma is such a popular measure of association is that it has exactly this definition of a perfect association.

For more details on these and other types of relationships between categorical variables, see Rosenberg (1968).

Effects of number of categories

The results of analyses depend greatly on the way categories are selected. This is true in two senses. First, consider the distribution of sex ratios in Figure 2.1. These data are the result of several processes, only one of which is the underlying sex ratio in a society. Many things like the precise delineation of boundaries (how many more men or women have to be present before there is a surplus?) or the wording of questions can become part of a variable. To some extent these are arbitrary, the result of the researchers' choices, and not the result of the underlying process being measured. Two researchers can study the same problem and obtain very different marginal frequencies. To the extent that their conclusions depend on measures of association that are sensitive to marginal distributions, the results may not be comparable. Even contradictory finding may be only an artifact of the specific techniques used in the study.

In general, as the number of categories increases, almost all measures of association tend to fall closer to their underlying continuous distributions. This is particularly true of lambda and gamma, but for different reasons. If there are only a few categories, lambda often equals zero, even though the variables are not independent. This happens when the mode of the dependent variable is so large that, when it is tabulated with an independent variable, all the modal categories still fall in the same column. For gamma, the problem is that it does not count ties. As the number of categories declines, the proportion of ties increases and gamma tends to overestimate the true association. With very few categories, tau-*b* or tau-*c* are better measures.

As a result of this problem, we recommend that you keep as many categories as possible for all variables. With one exception, this yields more accurate results. The exception is the chi-square measures, where small minimum expected frequencies cause problems. Small cell frequencies do not cause problems for measures of association not based on chi-square, nor do they cause problems for their standard errors. See Agresti (1976, 1990) for more information.

Summary of issues to consider

The important issues for you to consider are summarized below as numbered points:

1. **Table size.** Different measures of association are appropriate for 2x2 tables, larger square tables, and other rectangular tables.

2. **Level of measurement of the variables.** Nominal variables contain very limited information. They have no direction, strength is hard to measure (except for 2-by-2 tables using Yule's Q), and only a limited number of patterns can be assessed. Ordinal variables offer a wider variety of possibilities.

3. **Symmetry and asymmetry.** Symmetric measures of association do not change if the row and column variables are interchanged; an asymmetric coefficient changes. If your theory specifies a dependent variable, you need an asymmetric coefficient.

4. **PRE interpretation.** PRE measures of association may be easier to understand because they have a proportional reduction in error interpretation. Non-PRE measures do not and may be harder to interpret.

5. **Pattern of association.** Each statistic detects a specific pattern in the table. Consider your theoretical predictions of necessary, sufficient, or necessary and sufficient patterns. Many other patterns are possible. Pick a statistic which can detect the pattern that your theory expects. Some differences between various measures of association are summarized in Figure 2.13 for nominal scale variables and Figure 2.14 for ordinal scale variables.

Figure 2.13
Nominal Scale Measures of Association

	Limit Table Size	Symmetric or Asymmetric	Max Range	PRE?	Definition of Perfect Association	Notes
Chi-square (Pearson & likelihood ratio)	none	symmetric	0 to ∞	not PRE		No upper bound. Can only assess if association exists.
Fisher's exact test	2x2	symmetric	0 to 1	not PRE		Exact probability. Only assess existence. Printed if less than 100 cases.
Phi	2x2	symmetric	0 to 1	PRE	necessary and sufficient	Identical to correlation coefficient for a 2-by-2 table.
Phi	none	symmetric	0 to ∞	not PRE		No upper bound in large tables. Adjusts chi-square.
Contingency coefficient	none	symmetric	0 to <1	not PRE		Upper bound depends on table size. Adjusts chi-square.
Cramer's V	none	symmetric	0 to 1	not PRE		Identical to φ for 2-by-2 tables. Adjusts chi-square.
Odds ratio	2x2	asymmetric (col dep)	0 to ∞	not PRE		
Ln(odds)	2x2	asymmetric (col dep)	-∞ to ∞	Not PRE		Corrects odds ratio to allow hypothesis testing.
Yule's Q	2x2	symmetric	-1 to 1	PRE	necessary or sufficient	Identical to gamma. Only printed for 2-by-2 tables.
Yule's Y	2x2	symmetric	-1 to 1	not PRE		
Lambda	none	asymmetric (col dep)	0 to 1	PRE	all cases in modal category	
Uncertainty coefficient	none	asymmetric (col dep)	0 to 1	PRE		
McNemar symmetry chi-square	square	symmetric	0 to ∞	not PRE	identical cells off-diagonal	Tests symmetry of off-diagonal cells
Cohen's kappa	square	symmetric	-1 to 1	not PRE	zeros on off-diagonal	Tests agreement on main diagonal in square tables.

Figure 2.14
Ordinal Scale Measures of Association

	Limit Table Size	Symmetric or Asymmetric	Max Range	PRE?	Definition of Perfect Association	Notes
Gamma	none	symmetric	-1 to 1	PRE	necessary or sufficient	Only counts non-ties. Called Yule's Q for 2-by-2 tables. A popular measure.
Kendall's tau-*b*	square	symmetric	-1 to 1	PRE		Square tables only. Includes ties.
Stuart's tau-*c*	none	symmetric	-1 to 1	not PRE		Includes ties.
Somers' *d*	none	symmetric (col dep)	-1 to 1	PRE		Includes ties on dependent variable.
Spearman's rho	none	symmetric	-1 to 1	PRE for ranked data	identical ranks	

Recommendations

The issues discussed in the preceding pages need to be considered in terms of the circumstances of the particular table you are examining and the theory relevant to that table. Special circumstances may modify any general recommendation. Nonetheless, there are some general rules that may help you as a starting point for your work.

First, a complication of work with categorical data is that there are patterns that are easy to see in a percentage table for which no statistic exists. This underlines the fact that measures of association are not substitutes for close examination of appropriately percentaged tables. It is wise to look at any table from several points of view. Unless your theory explicitly assumes a particular definition of association you may overlook important aspects of the data by relying on a single measure.

Second, measures of association do not demonstrate the *relative* explanatory power of several independent variables. Many theories claim that one variable is a more important explanation of a specific dependent variable. You may be tempted to take the variable with the strongest association as the most important predictor or explanation. But since measures of association can be influenced by extraneous elements such as marginal distributions, and since each is sensitive to only a certain pattern of association, these comparisons can be misleading. In addition, the impact of one variable on another depends partly on its relationship to still other variables, many of which may be unmeasured. For these reasons, measures of association cannot usually establish explanatory importance.

Finally, some specific recommendations. In the next three paragraphs, we discuss appropriate measures of association when at least one variable is nominal, when both variables are ordinal and, lastly, several special cases.

If at least one variable in the table is *nominal*, consider only nominal measures of association. For 2-by-2 tables the most appropriate measure is either Yule's Q or phi (drop the sign in either case). One of the chi-square statistics or, if N < 100, Fisher's Exact test can be used to test for the existence of an association. In a larger table with no clear independent or dependent variable, chi-square tells you whether an association exists, which is about all you can say about this kind of table. In a larger table with a clear dependent variable, use lambda. This tells you the strength of the association, if lambda can find it. If lambda is zero, check the percentage table and chi-square statistics to see if there is any association in the table.

If both variables are *ordinal* you have more powerful statistics at your disposal. For 2x2 tables, Yule's Q or phi are still appropriate. For larger tables, if your theory claims that a certain pattern exists, be sure that the statistic you use can find that pattern. Be sensitive to the specific pattern of association implied by your theory. Remember that you can use measures for nominal variables (like lambda) on ordinal tables. This is useful if the pattern of association that lambda can detect matches your theory. Ordinal measures of association rely on the ordered relationship between the categories, so using them on nominal data usually yields a misleading value for the association. If you predict no pattern (a common circumstance) or no such statistic is available (also likely), you have the following choices. If you have no independent or dependent variable, use gamma. In the special case of a square table, tau-b may be better. If you have a clear dependent variable, Somer's d is appropriate.

There are several *special situations* defined by particular data or a particular hypothesis that you may want to test. If you have completely ranked data, use Spearman's rho. Multiple strata in an experimental design yielding 2-by-2 tables can be handled by the Mantel-Haenzel chi-square. If off-diagonal symmetry is important, the McNemar symmetry chi-square is appropriate. If you need to measure agreement in rankings of the same subject, choose Cohen's kappa.

This chapter has discussed several patterns of association which can be detected by different measures of association. If, however, your theory predicted a pattern for which no measure of association was available, the tools from this chapter would give you no way to detect it. In the next chapter we discuss how you can model many different patterns of association and test hypotheses.

Notes

Introduction

Whyte (1978) was unable to collect complete data on every case. The HOUSEWK$ variable has data on 89 of the 90 societies we used in Chapter 1.

Measures of association for nominal variables

Portions of Caplow's argument have been omitted to simplify the presentation. Particularly, he suggests that married and unmarried parents act differently, with unmarried parents falling somewhere between married parents and childless people. This complicates the statistical discussion so the 13 respondents who were unmarried parents have been omitted from the data used in this chapter. Three other cases reported in Caplow's Table 1 (1984) have also been omitted from this table because of apparent inconsistencies in the coding. They are an elderly married woman who was living with her married daughter while her husband was hospitalized. Her daughter had a Christmas tree but Caplow codes the respondent as not having a tree even though there is a tree in the household. This does not seem consistent with the coding of two similar cases where unmarried children are still living with their parents. They are coded by Caplow as having a tree because they reported a tree in the household. The coding of these cases appears to me to distort the message of the table. The rule Caplow proposes would lead us to expect trees. The effect of these changes is to strengthen the relationship reported in Figure 2.10. However, the relationship is strong and significant even without them.

Choosing a measure of association

Measures of association developed specifically for tables where one variable is ordered and the other is nominal are discussed in Agresti (1984, Section 9.3). The paragraph on relative explanatory power of variables follows Reynolds (1977).

Further reading

The discussion in this chapter owes much to the thorough, lucid discussion of bivariate tables and measures of association in Loether and McTavish (1988). In particular, their presentation of the four characteristics of an association was very helpful. We urge readers who feel that they need further information on this material to consult that book, especially Chapters 6, 7, and 16. See also Agresti (1990, 1996), Davis and Jacobs (1968), Rosenberg (1968), and Zeisel (1985).

References

Agresti, A. (1976). The effect of category choice on some ordinal measures of association. *Journal of the American Statistical Association, 71*, 49-55.

Agresti, A. (1984). *Analysis of Ordinal Categorical Data.* New York: John Wiley & Sons.

Agresti, A. (1990). *Categorical Data Analysis.* New York: John Wiley & Sons.

Agresti, A. (1996). *Introduction to Categorical Data Analysis.* New York: John Wiley & Sons.

Bishop, Y. M. M., Fienberg, S. E. and Holland, P. W. (1975). *Discrete Multivariate Analysis.* Cambridge, MA: MIT Press.

Blalock, H. M. (1979). *Social Statistics* (3rd ed.). New York: McGraw-Hill.

Bohrnstedt, G. W. and Knoke, D. (1994). *Statistics for Social Data Analysis* (3rd ed.). Itasca, IL: F. E. Peacock.

Cochran, W. G. (1954). Some methods of strengthening the common χ^2 tests. *Biometrics, 10*, 417-451.

Cohen, J. (1960). A coefficient for agreement for nominal scales. *Educational and Psychological Measurement, 20*, 37-46

Conover, W. J. (1974). Some reasons for not using the Yates' continuity correction on 2x2 contingency tables (with discussion). *Journal of the American Statistical Association, 69*, 374-382.

Caplow, T. (1982). Christmas gifts and kin networks. *American Sociological Review, 47*, 383-392.

Caplow, T. (1984). Rule enforcement without visible means: Christmas gift giving in Middletown. *American Journal of Sociology, 89*, 1306-1323.

Davis, J. A. and Jacobs, A. M. (1968). Tabular presentation. *International Encyclopedia of the Social Sciences.* (vol. 15, pp. 497-509). New York: Macmillan.

Fienberg, S. E. (1980). *The analysis of cross-classified categorical data* (2nd ed.). Cambridge, MA: MIT Press.

Goodman, L. A. and Kruskal, W. H. (1963). Measures of association for cross-classifications III: Approximate sampling theory. *Journal of the American Statistical Association, 58,* 310-364.

Goodman, L. A. and Kruskal, W. H. (1972). Measures of association for cross-classifications IV: Simplification of asymptotic variances. *Journal of the American Statistical Association, 67,* 415-421.

Kruskal, W. H. (1958). Ordinal measures of association. *Journal of the American Statistical Association, 53,* 814-861.

Larntz, K. (1978). Small sample comparisons of exact levels for chi-square goodness-of-fit statistics. *Journal of the American Statistical Association, 73,* 253-263.

Loether, H. J. and McTavish, D. G. (1993). *Descriptive and Inferential Statistics: An Introduction* (4th ed.). Boston: Allyn and Bacon.

Mantel, N. and Haenszel, W. (1959). Statistical aspects of the analysis of data from retrospective studies of disease. *Journal of the National Cancer Institute, 22,* 719-748.

Reynolds, H. T. (1977). *The Analysis of Cross-classifications.* New York: Free Press.

Rosenberg, M. (1968). *The Logic of Survey Analysis.* New York: Basic Books.

Stevens, S. S. (1975). *Psychophysics: Introduction to its Perceptual, Neural and Social Prospects.* New York: John Wiley & Sons.

Theil, H. (1970). On the estimation of relationships involving qualitative variables. *American Journal of Sociology, 76,* 103-154.

Theil, H. (1972). *Statistical Decomposition Analysis.* Amsterdam: North Holland.

Walker, H. M. & Lev, J. (1953). *Statistical Inference.* New York: Holt, Rinehart and Winston.

Whyte, M. K. (1978). *The Status of Women in Pre-industrial Society.* Princeton: Princeton University Press.

Zeisel, H. (1985). *Say it with Figures* (6th ed.). New York: Harper & Row.

3

Prediction Using
Log-Linear Models

Prisons rarely rehabilitate their inmates. Upon release many return to crime and are subsequently rearrested and imprisoned again. Many experienced criminologists and prison officials have believed that one reason many ex-convicts soon return to crime is that they lack income during the crucial first months after their release. Fewer ex-offenders would return to crime, they believed, if they had some financial support during those first months. To test this belief, the U.S. Department of Labor and the states of Texas and Georgia conducted a large-scale, randomized, controlled experiment. The experiment compared the rearrest rate—the percentage of ex-offenders rearrested for a crime within one year after release—for experimental groups who received income support payments with a control group of ex-convicts receiving no payments. Figure 3.1 gives some results of the experiment.

Figure 3.1 is not very encouraging; 57.25% of ex-offenders in the control group were rearrested and 56.47% in the payment groups. The difference is trivial and disappointing. A lot of money and time was spent on this experiment, and the results do not support the original belief that income support payments would reduce the rearrest rate.

The past two chapters illustrated the use of percentages, like this example, to analyze two-way tables. These give a clear answer for this table. If we need a formal test, we can use one of the measures of association or a chi-square goodness-of-fit test.

This works well for two-way tables, but many applications require use of three, four, five, or even more variables and, in multi-way tables, percentages become complicated and difficult to understand. For similar reasons the measures of association discussed in Chapter 2 also become less useful. We need a better summary of the pattern of associations when we have multi-way tables. Even in two-way tables we want to specify and test our own theoretical hypothesis, rather than relying the hypotheses built into the assumptions of measures of association. **Log-linear models** do just that. We can easily summarize a complex pattern of associations and we can design tests customized to the specific theory and data at hand. Rather than a simple global test for the presence of an association, we can distinguish many different patterns of association.

Figure 3.1
Percentage of Rearrests for Experimental and Control Groups

```
Frequencies
 GROUP$(rows) by REARREST$(columns)

                No        Yes        Total
           +-------------------+
 Control   |    165       221  |        386
           |                   |
 Payment   |    239       310  |        549
           +-------------------+
 Total          404       531           935

Row percents
 GROUP$ (rows) by REARREST$ (columns)

                No        Yes        Total        N
           +-------------------+
 Control   |   42.75     57.25 |       100.00     386
           |                   |
 Payment   |   43.53     56.47 |       100.00     549
           +-------------------+
 Total         43.21     56.79         100.00
    N          404       531                       935
```

On one level, log-linear models are very simple. We specify a model. By model, we mean the pattern of associations that we expect to find in the table. Using the model, SYSTAT calculates the expected cell counts that we should find in the data. This process is called *fitting the model* and the expected counts are called **fitted values.** We can then compare the fitted values to the observed counts in the table using a standard chi-square test. (Section 2.6 discusses chi-square tests.) If the model does not fit the data the expected pattern of associations will not be the same as the actual pattern of associations in the table. In this case, there will be a large discrepancy between the observed counts and the expected counts. The significant chi-square test will show that the observed and expected counts are different. If the model fits the data, the difference between the observed and fitted counts is small, and the chi-square test shows the differences not significant. It is worth emphasizing that the dependent variable is the observed counts, not the scores on some analytic dependent variable (e.g. REARREST$). The fitted counts are sometimes called the fitted values, predicted values, predicted counts, expected values, estimated values, expected counts, or the fit.

A note for version 5 users: Log-linear models have changed more than any other statistical procedure from version 5 to version 6. Almost everything in this chapter can be done with version 5, but the changes are significant. If you need to work with version 5 log-linear models, you may want to look at the version 5 command files on the SPSS website (http:\\www.spss.com).

3.1 Summarizing tabular relationships

The preceding section introduced the idea of a model without really saying what it was. Log-linear models attempt to duplicate the pattern of observed counts in a table. This is same as asking, "What variables and associations are necessary to match the observed counts in this table?" One very simple model is that one variable has no effect whatsoever on the observed counts. For example, in the next paragraphs we will test the model that the observed cell counts in the table in Figure 3.1 are solely the result of the differences in the numbers of ex-offenders assigned to the Control and Payment categories by the experimenters. This model says that only the GROUP$ variable is important, that we can duplicate the observed counts without using the REARREST$ variable at all. In SYSTAT's LOGLIN module (version 6) this model is written:

```
MODEL GROUP$*REARREST = GROUP$
```

The MODEL statement is written with the table on the left side of the equals sign. The order of the variables is irrelevant and they are separated by asterisks, *. To the right of the equals sign, we write the effect(s) we want to model.

In version 5, the MODEL command is part of the TABLES module. In TABLES you must first specify a table with the TABULATE command, then use the MODEL command to specify a log-linear model for the table. Since the table is specified in the TABULATE command, it is not restated in the version 5 MODEL command. Thus the version 5 MODEL command consists of only the specification to the right of the equals sign. All the models in this book use version 6 MODEL commands; version 5 readers can use them by simply reading only the portion to the right of the equals sign. In SYSTAT's TABLES module (version 5) this model is written:

```
MODEL GROUP$
```

This model says we want to know the effect that the variable GROUP$ has on the observed counts in the table, GROUP$*REARREST$. So we can describe the model by saying that it is a model of the GROUP$ **effect**. Other variables may also have effects on the observed counts and we show how to incorporate additional effects below. A synonym for effect is **term**. This is a model with one term, the variable GROUP$. We use the words term and effect interchangeably in the remainder of this chapter.

The model of the GROUP$ effect and the SYSTAT output are shown in Figure 3.2. Notice that the PRINT command requests tables of observed and expected counts, plus an overall chi-square test.

Figure 3.2
Model of GROUP$ Effect Only

```
LOGLIN
   USE EXCON01
   FREQ COUNT
   PRINT NONE / OBS CHISQ EXPECT
   MODEL GROUP$*REARREST$ = GROUP$
   ESTIMATE
```

Here is the SYSTAT output:

```
Observed Frequencies
========================================
GROUP$   |        REARREST$
         | No            Yes
---------+------------------------------
Control  |        165           221
Payment  |        239           310
---------+------------------------------
Pearson ChiSquare  17.3065  df   2  Probability  0.00017
    LR ChiSquare   17.3610  df   2  Probability  0.00017
    Raftery's BIC   3.6799

Expected Values
========================================
GROUP$   |        REARREST$
         | No            Yes
---------+------------------------------
Control  |     193.000        193.000
Payment  |     274.500        274.500
---------+------------------------------
```

Looking at the fitted counts in the second table, you can see that SYSTAT fit the row totals for GROUP$ exactly: the counts in each row add to the observed row totals. The model makes the simple assumption that an even proportion (i.e. 50%) of ex-convicts in each category of GROUP$ are rearrested. Comparing the fitted values to the observed frequencies in the first table in Figure 3.2, we can see that this is not quite accurate. In fact, looking back at the percentage table in Figure 3.1, we can see that about 57% of the ex-convicts in each group were rearrested.

Obviously, the model in Figure 3.2 does not fit the data very well. The likelihood ratio chi-square value shows that the expected cell counts (in the second table) deviate significantly from the observed counts (in the first table). Notice that SYSTAT reports we have two degrees of freedom. The table had three degrees of freedom, and we used one degree of freedom by fitting the model.

The results of fitting the previous model suggest that we need to add a term for REARREST$. This alternative model says that there is an unequal distribution of counts among the categories of both GROUP$ and REARREST$. This model is the same as the standard chi-square model of no association (or independence) discussed in Section 2.6. The SYSTAT commands and the output for the model are in Figure 3.3.

Figure 3.3
Model of GROUP$ and REARREST$ Effects

```
LOGLIN
    USE EXCON01
    FREQ COUNT
    PRINT NONE / OBS CHISQ EXPECT
    MODEL GROUP$*REARREST$ = GROUP$ + REARREST$
    ESTIMATE
```

Here is the output:

```
Observed Frequencies
═══════════════════════
GROUP$    |      REARREST$
          | No           Yes
----------+-------------------------
Control   |      165           221
Payment   |      239           310
----------+-------------------------
Pearson ChiSquare   0.0573  df   1  Probability  0.81083
    LR ChiSquare    0.0573  df   1  Probability  0.81080
    Raftery's BIC  -6.7832

Expected Values
═══════════════════════
GROUP$    |      REARREST$
          | No           Yes
----------+-------------------------
Control   |    166.785       219.215
Payment   |    237.215       311.785
----------+-------------------------
```

This time SYSTAT fit both the row totals for GROUP$ and the column totals for RE-ARREST$ exactly; the counts in each row and column add to the observed row and column totals. The result is that the fitted values generated by the model in the second table are very close to the observed values in the first table. The chi-square test shows that the difference between them is not significant. This model fits. This confirms what we already knew this from the percentages: REARREST$ and GROUP$ are not associated.

You are probably tired of variables which are not associated and can be modeled as easily with a percentage table as with a fancy log-linear model. Well, we began with a simple series of models to give you an understanding of the basics of log-linear analysis. If you are bored, just keep reading—things are about to become more exciting.

3.2 More complex models

The tables in the previous section omitted a third variable which has a major impact on the data. The additional variable is called WORK$, defined as whether or not the ex-convict was able to find work during his or her first year. After adding the new variable, the simple model of independence (i.e. no associations between the three variables) does not fit the observed data in this table. The data are contained in the file EXCON02:

Figure 3.4
Ex-Convict Transitional Aid Dataset (EXCON02)

GROUP$	WORK$	REARREST$	COUNT
Payment	Yes	No	187
Payment	Yes	Yes	58
Payment	No	No	52
Payment	No	Yes	252
Control	Yes	No	146
Control	Yes	Yes	77
Control	No	No	19
Control	No	Yes	144

Figure 3.5
Three-Variable Table and Model of Independence

```
LOGLIN
  USE EXCON02
  FREQ COUNT
  PRINT SHORT
  MODEL WORK$*GROUP$*REARREST$ = WORK$ + GROUP$ + REARREST$
  ESTIMATE
```

And the output:

```
Observed Frequencies
════════════════════

WORK$       GROUP$   |       REARREST$
                     | No            Yes
---------+---------+---------------------------
No          Control  |        19            144
            Payment  |        52            252
                     +
Yes         Control  |       146             77
            Payment  |       187             58
-------------------+-------------------------------
Pearson ChiSquare 314.7795  df    4  Probability  0.00000
     LR ChiSquare 343.4288  df    4  Probability  0.00000
     Raftery's BIC 316.0667

Expected Values
════════════════

WORK$       GROUP$   |       REARREST$
                     | No            Yes
---------+---------+---------------------------
No          Control  |    83.303        109.490
            Payment  |   118.481        155.726
                     +
Yes         Control  |    83.482        109.725
            Payment  |   118.734        156.059
-------------------+-------------------------------
```

If the independence model does not work, we infer that there must be some associations in the table. How do we go about finding them? How can we know when we've found one? How do we choose the best model? These questions are the subject of the remainder of this chapter.

Modeling associations: interaction effects

In general, the associations that you model are given by the substantive theory in the field where you are working and by the hypotheses that you intend to test with your data. For the ex-convict transition aid data, our dependent variable is REARREST$. We expect that convicts who work are less likely to be rearrested than those who do not find a job. This suggests that there may be an association between REARREST$ and

WORK\$. In log-linear models, associations are called **interaction effects**. Like association the word "interaction" refers to the relation between two or more variables. When variables influence each other we say they "interact." An interaction exists between two variables when as one variable changes the other also changes in a systematic way. For example, an interaction between WORK\$ and REARREST\$ implies that ex-offenders who work have a different probability of being rearrested than those who do not work. That is another way of saying that WORK\$ and REARREST\$ influence each other. Another example is the familiar chi-square independence model. This tests the null hypothesis that there is no interaction effect in a table; in other words, that the variables do not influence each other. Interactions are named using the variables involved, so an interaction involving WORK\$ and REARREST\$ is called a "WORK\$-by-REARREST\$" interaction. In the rest of this chapter we use the terms association and interaction interchangeably.

Interactions always involve at least two variables. So an interaction effect is a two-variable effect, in contrast to the one-variable effects that we have used in our models up to now. One-variable effects are sometimes called "main effects." (This terminology comes from analysis of variance. See Part III.) Three- and four-variable interactions are possible and even common in certain kinds of research. To tell SYSTAT to model an interaction, we separate the two variables by an asterisk (*). For example, the interaction term for the WORK\$-by-REARREST\$ interaction that we have been discussing is WORK\$*REARREST\$. The order of the variables does not matter, so WORK\$*REARREST\$ is the same as REARREST\$*WORK\$. The full version 6 SYSTAT model statement is:

```
MODEL WORK$*GROUP$*REARREST$ = WORK$ + GROUP$ + REARREST$ + WORK$*REARREST$
```

We test the model in Figure 3.6. We include the TABULATE command because the MODEL command only works if it follows a TABULATE command.

Figure 3.6
Adding a WORK$-by-REARREST$ Interaction to the Model of Independence

```
LOGLIN
    USE EXCON02
    FREQ COUNT
    PRINT NONE / OBS CHISQ
    MODEL WORK$*GROUP$*REARREST$ = WORK$ + GROUP$ + REARREST$,
                                    + WORK$*REARREST$
    ESTIMATE
```

Here is the SYSTAT output:

```
Observed Frequencies
════════════════════
WORK$       GROUP$    |      REARREST$
                      | No          Yes
---------+---------+--+------------------------
No          Control  |      19         144
            Payment  |      52         252
                     +
Yes         Control  |     146          77
            Payment  |     187          58
------------------+--+-------------------------
Pearson ChiSquare   24.8540  df   3  Probability 0.00002
      LR ChiSquare  24.9575  df   3  Probability 0.00002
     Raftery's BIC   4.4358

Expected Values
════════════════
WORK$       GROUP$    |      REARREST$
                      | No          Yes
---------+---------+--+------------------------
No          Control  |   29.311      163.482
            Payment  |   41.689      232.518
                     +
Yes         Control  |  137.474       55.733
            Payment  |  195.526       79.267
------------------+--+-------------------------
```

Even though the chi-square statistic for this model is much smaller than for the independence model, it still shows the model does not fit the data. Does this mean that there is no interaction between REARREST$ and WORK$? Not necessarily. We have to consider how the model has changed as we added the new interaction effect.

The hierarchy of models

As we add new effects, we measure their influence by looking at how the likelihood ratio chi-square changes. The table below compares the independence model with the model including the WORK$-by-REARREST$ interaction.

Model	Likelihood Ratio Chi-Square	Degrees of Freedom
GROUP$ + REARREST$ + WORK$	343.43	4
GROUP$ + REARREST$ + WORK$ + REARREST$*WORK$	24.85	3

Notice how the model with the interaction has a much smaller likelihood ratio chi-square statistic. It is still not significant but it has shrunk dramatically. This suggests a statistical test: when adding a new term, test its significance by comparing the difference in the two likelihood ratio chi-square statistics to a chi-square table. Use the difference in the degrees of freedom as the degrees of freedom for the test.

Thus, we can compare $343.43 - 24.85 = 318.58$ with $4 - 3 = 1$ degree of freedom to a chi-square table. This is highly significant. From this we conclude that there is a strong association between REARREST$ and WORK$.

We have just taken advantage of a general property of the likelihood ratio chi-square statistic. As we add terms to a model, the likelihood ratio chi-square never increases. The difference between the likelihood ratio chi-squares for two models also has a chi-square distribution with degrees of freedom equal to the difference in the degrees of freedom for the models. The test based on this property is called a **conditional goodness-of-fit test.** We will make frequent use of these conditional tests in the rest of this chapter. The Pearson chi-square does not have this property and cannot be used for these tests.

Notice that this requires that one model be a subset of the other model. The word "subset" refers to the terms in the two models. The model with more terms must include *all* the terms of the model with fewer terms plus the additional term(s) being tested. In this sense the smaller model is a subset of the larger model.

Testing the significance of terms requires creating models which differ from each other by one term and performing conditional tests which compare the likelihood ratio chi-squares. So to analyze the data in a table, you create a series of models each containing one more or fewer terms than the preceding model. We can order these models in a sequence ranging from models with few terms to models with many terms. This is called a **hierarchy** of models. The approach that we are describing is called hierarchical log-linear models. This is what we implicitly did in Section 3.1 on page 65, where we looked at two models:

```
MODEL  GROUP$*REARREST$  =  GROUP$
MODEL  GROUP$*REARREST$  =  GROUP$  +  REARREST$
```

SYSTAT can take advantage of this hierarchy in the MODEL statement. To emphasize the hierarchical nature of the models we consider SYSTAT uses the #-symbol to imply lower-order terms. Every higher-order term in the model (i.e. every interaction) automatically implies all the lower-order terms are included. So the following models are identical:

```
MODEL  WORK$*GROUP$*REARREST$  =  GROUP$  +  REARREST$  +  WORK$  +  REARREST$#WORK$
MODEL  WORK$*GROUP$*REARREST$  =  GROUP$  +  REARREST$  +  REARREST$#WORK$
MODEL  WORK$*GROUP$*REARREST$  =  WORK$  +  GROUP$  +  REARREST$#WORK$
MODEL  WORK$*GROUP$*REARREST$  =  GROUP$  +  REARREST$#WORK$
```

We will use this fact in future MODEL statements and include only the terms that SYSTAT requires in order to estimate the model. (In version 5, log-linear models are always hierarchical; the #-symbol is not used, only the asterisk, *. Thus, a version 5 interaction is written REARREST$*WORK$ and always includes all lower-order terms.)

This presentation emphasizes starting with simple terms and adding more complex interactions. Notice, however, that the hierarchy of models implies that you could just as easily begin with the most complex interaction term and successively work your way down to simpler models. These alternatives are compared in more detail in section Section 3.6 under *Stepwise model selection.*

Hierarchical models have the advantage of relatively simple interpretations that lead to simple, straightforward model selection strategies. It is possible to work with nonhierarchical log-linear models, and the commands for this are easy to specify in SYSTAT version 6. Nonhierarchical models tend to be more difficult to interpret. They arise in situations where data are not available for certain cells because they are too expensive or too difficult to collect. A simple example would be a 2x2x2 design where data were available for only 6 of the 8 cells. Nonhierarchical models are beyond the scope of this chapter.

Calculating fitted values

You may have noticed that log-linear models are simply a way of specifying expected values for the counts in the cells of a table. The fitted values are then compared to the observed values using a chi-square test. To understand why these fitted values are appropriate for tabular data, you need to know something about how they are calculated. It is not very complicated; like many good things, log-linear models consist of a few simple ideas pushed beyond the obvious.

A multi-way table can be thought of as a collection of smaller one-, two-, three-, or higher-way tables. Each of these smaller tables is called a **subtable**. Because of the limits of a two-dimensional page or screen, SYSTAT prints out three- and higher-way tables by printing a series of two-way subtables, for example in Figure 3.5. The idea of a subtable is crucial to understanding how SYSTAT calculates effects. In the next paragraphs we will show how SYSTAT calculates main effects and then how it calculates interactions.

Earlier in this section we saw that SYSTAT calculates a main effect (for example, GROUP\$ in Figure 3.2) by fitting the marginal totals exactly. To show how this works we use an example from the table of fitted values from the independence model GROUP\$ + REARREST\$ shown in Figure 3.3:

```
Expected Values
═══════════════
GROUP$       |      REARREST$
             | No            Yes
-------------+----------------------------
Control      |     166.785       219.215
Payment      |     237.215       311.785
-------------+----------------------------
```

For the upper left cell (REARREST\$ = No, GROUP\$ = Control) the fitted value is 166.785. To obtain this SYSTAT constructed two subtables. First, the subtable for GROUP\$, an ordinary one-way table:

```
              CUM           CUM
     COUNT   COUNT   PCT    PCT    GROUP$
      386     386    41.3   41.3   Control
      549     935    58.7   100.0  Payment
```

The category we are interested in, GROUP\$ = Control, contains 41.3% of the cases, or expressed as a proportion, 0.413. If we assign 41.3% of the cases in the fitted table to the row where GROUP$ = Control, we have fit that row exactly. We can fit the other row, GROUP$ = Payment exactly by assigning the remaining 58.7% of the cases it. Since the table of fitted values has exactly the same number of cases in each row as the table of observed values, we say we fit the marginal totals exactly.

The subtable for the column variable, REARREST$, is another one-way table:

```
              CUM           CUM
   COUNT    COUNT    PCT    PCT  REARREST$
    404      404    43.2   43.2  No
    531      935    56.8  100.0  Yes
```

The proportion of cases in the category we want, REARREST$ = No, is 0.432. We assign that proportion to the appropriate column. We assign 56.8% of the cases to the other column and we have fitted the column marginal totals exactly.

If the independence model is correct, we can fit the cell frequencies simply using the marginal proportions and the total number of cases in the table. To find the fitted proportion of cases in any given cell, multiply the proportion of cases in the row by the proportion of cases in the column. Multiply this by the total number of cases in the table to obtain the fitted count for the cell. Thus our fitted value for the cell REARREST$ = No, GROUP$ = Control can be calculated by: 0.413 * 0.432 * 935 = 166.81. Allowing for rounding error (SYSTAT uses over 15 digits in these calculations while we only used 3), this is exactly the fitted number of cases in the upper right cell, above. To be sure you understand this, we suggest you use the other row and column proportions in the subtables and calculate the other fitted counts in the table. The general formula for two-way tables is:

$$\begin{pmatrix} Fitted\ count \\ for\ cell_{ij} \end{pmatrix} = \begin{pmatrix} Proportion \\ in\ row_i \end{pmatrix} \begin{pmatrix} Proportion \\ in\ column_j \end{pmatrix} \begin{pmatrix} Total\ number \\ in\ table \end{pmatrix}$$

The main effects calculations are similar in three-, four-, or higher-way tables. The difference is instead of two one-way subtables, SYSTAT creates three, four, or more subtables to find the three, four, or more proportions that are multiplied together with the total number of cases to obtain the fitted value.

Let's summarize the process for calculating main effects. First, for each main effect in the model, SYSTAT forms the subtable for that variable to find the proportion of cases in each category of the variable. Second, fitted values for each cell are calculated by multiplying the proportions from all the categories involved in that cell with the total number of cases in the table.

Interaction effects are an extension of main effects, only the subtables are different. A main effect has only one variable, but an interaction consists of two or more variables. Thus, instead of fitting a one-way table exactly, fitting an interaction requires fitting a two- or higher-way table exactly.

For our example, we use the model from Figure 3.6:

```
MODEL GROUP$*WORK$*REARREST$ = GROUP$ + WORK$#REARREST$
```

Below are the fitted values from this model.

```
Expected Values
═══════════════════════════════════════════════════════
WORK$       GROUP$    |       REARREST$
                      | No          Yes
------------+---------+-----------------------------
No          Control   |   29.311     163.482
            Payment   |   41.689     232.518
                      +
Yes         Control   |  137.474      55.733
            Payment   |  195.526      79.267
------------------------+-----------------------------
```

We again fit the upper left cell: WORK$ = No, GROUP$ = Control, REARREST$ = No. The model requires that we fit the main effect for GROUP$ and the interaction effect, WORK$ # REARREST$. Our model has two terms, so to calculate the fitted value, we need to know the proportions for them: the main effect for GROUP$ = Control and the interaction effect for WORK$ = No, REARREST$ = No. From the previous example, we know that the proportion of cases in the main effect category GROUP$ = Control is 0.413. For the interaction effect, we need to construct the subtable for WORK$-by-REARREST$. This is just the ordinary two-way percentage table:

```
TABLE OF     WORK$    (ROWS) BY REARREST$    (COLUMNS)

              No       Yes       TOTAL      N
          +-------------------+
No        |  7.59    42.35     | 49.95      467
          |                    |
Yes       | 35.61    14.44     | 50.05      468
          +-------------------+
TOTAL       43.21    56.79      100.00
    N         404      531                  935
```

This percentage table shows that the proportion of cases in the cell with the two categories that we need, WORK\$ = No, REARREST\$ = No, is 0.0759. Thus we calculate the fitted value for the upper left cell as 0.413 * 0.0759 * 935 = 29.31.This is the exact fitted value SYSTAT printed for the cell. Other fitted values can be calculated from the other proportions in the main effect and interaction effect subtables. Three- and higher-way interactions simply involve constructing a three-or-higher-way subtable.

Notice that interactions automatically fit the marginal proportions for the corresponding main effects exactly. This is one sense in which log-linear models are hierarchical: the interaction effect WORK\$#REARREST\$ contains the main effects for WORK\$ and REARREST\$. Thus, when we specify an interaction, the main effects are redundant and, when we use the #-notation, SYSTAT does not require that we type them.

Degrees of freedom for log-linear models

There is no single formula for calculating degrees of freedom; it depends on the number of variables in the model and the number of categories in each variable; see Haberman (1978) for details. The formula for most models where all variables have only 2 categories is

$$\begin{pmatrix} Degrees\ of\ freedom \\ for\ \chi^2\ test \end{pmatrix} = \begin{pmatrix} Number\ of \\ cells\ in\ table \end{pmatrix} - 1 - \begin{pmatrix} Number\ of \\ terms\ in\ model \end{pmatrix}$$

where the number of terms in the model includes terms which are redundant in the SYSTAT model specification. Thus the model GROUP\$ + WORK\$#REARREST\$ requires subtracting four degrees of freedom: one for GROUP\$, one for the WORK\$#REARREST\$ interaction, one for the WORK\$ main effect, and one for the REARREST\$ main effect. The number of cells in the table is usually calculated as the product of the number of categories in each variable.

3.3 Parameter estimates

We have been assessing the significance of our models by looking at an overall chi-square test. An alternative is to estimate the effects of variables and associations directly. Since log-linear models predict the log of the cell frequencies, we want to look at which variables and associations improve our prediction of the log cell frequencies. One way to do this is to estimate a parameter for the effect of each variable and association. If the parameter is large compared to its standard error, then the association significantly improves our prediction. If we represent the parameters we want to estimate with the Greek letter lambda, λ, and G stands for GROUP\$ and R stands for REARREST\$ we can write the model as:

$$log(F_{ij}) = \theta + \lambda_i^G + \lambda_j^R + \lambda_{ij}^{GR}$$

where $log(F_{ij})$ is the natural log of the expected cell frequency and θ (theta) is an overall mean effect. λ's represent the effects of the variables and associations, i identifies the row, j identifies the column. For example, λ_1^G is the parameter of row 1 of the GROUP\$ variable. The lambdas sum to zero over the categories of the row and column variables. In words, this model says the log of each expected cell frequency is equal to the sum of an overall mean effect, plus a row effect, plus a column effect, plus a cell effect.

Instruct SYSTAT to produce estimates of the lambdas by using PRINT LONG or by specifying the LAMBDA option on the PRINT command. The commands are in Figure 3.7.

Looking at the upper table of the output the left cell, where GROUP\$ = Control, REARREST\$ = No, has an observed frequency of 165. The table of lambdas contains the parameter estimates to calculate the expected count. We construct the expected count by using the parameters for this cell:

$$log(F) = \theta + \lambda_c^G + \lambda_n^R + \lambda_{cn}^{GR}$$

where λ_c^G is the lambda for the main effect GROUP\$ = Control, λ_n^R is the lambda for REARREST\$ = No, and λ_{cn}^{GR} is the lambda for the interaction GROUP\$ = Control, REARREST\$ = No. If we substitute the numbers from Figure 3.7 we have:

```
log(F)= 5.429 + (-.177) + (-.138) + (-.008)
      = 5.106
```

By taking the natural antilog of 5.106, we find the expected frequency to be:

```
F = 165.009
```

Figure 3.7
Log-Linear Model Parameters

```
LOGLIN
    USE EXCON02
    FREQ COUNT
    PRINT SHORT / OBS LAMBDA
    MODEL GROUP$**REARREST$ = GROUP$ # REARREST$
    ESTIMATE
```

The output is:

```
Observed Frequencies
======================================
GROUP$    |        REARREST$
          | No          Yes
----------+---------------------------
Control   |        165         221
Payment   |        239         310
----------+---------------------------
Log-Linear Effects (Lambda)
======================================

        THETA
    -------------
        5.429
    -------------


        GROUP$
    Control     Payment
    ---------------------------
       -0.177        0.177
    ---------------------------


        REARREST$
    No          Yes
    ---------------------------
       -0.138        0.138
    ---------------------------


GROUP$    |        REARREST$
          | No          Yes
----------+---------------------------
Control   |       -0.008        0.008
Payment   |        0.008       -0.008
----------+---------------------------
```

Within rounding error (we only used 3 digits to the right of the decimal and SYSTAT used over 15) we matched the observed value perfectly. Similar calculations can be done for the other 3 cells in the table. We invite interested readers to try them. The size of a parameter does not tell us if it is significant. For that, we need to know the standard error of the parameter.

3.4 Standardized parameter estimates

SYSTAT calculates the standard errors of the parameters, but we're not usually interested in standard errors alone. To assess the significance of parameters we need the ratio of the parameter divided by its standard error, called the **standardized parameter estimate**. For large samples they have an approximate standard normal distribution. Thus they can be used to form the usual critical ratio. To test the null hypothesis that a parameter is significantly different than zero the rule of thumb is that the ratio of the parameter to its standard error must be greater than plus-or-minus 2. Instruct SYSTAT to print the parameters divided by their standard errors using PRINT SHORT or the RATIO option of the PRINT command (See Figure 3.8).

Starting at the top of the table, the value for theta is large, and so are the values in the GROUP$ and the REARREST$ tables. But notice that every number in the GROUP$*REARREST interaction is much less than plus-or-minus 2. We conclude that GROUP$ and REARREST$ are significant and that the GROUP$*REARREST$ interaction is not significant. This is the same conclusion that we reached using the chi-square tests in Figures 3.2 and 3.3: GROUP$ and REARREST$ are not associated. Theta is always included in the model but is not usually of any substantive significance.

A note about regression coefficients. If you know regression you may be thinking something like, "These parameters look like regression coefficients. Why spend so much time on chi-square tests when you can just look for significant parameters?" The answer is that log-linear model parameters are not as easy to interpret. Instead of a single regression coefficient for each variable, log-linear models estimate a separate parameter for each category of every variable plus additional parameters for every cell in an interaction. As a result the parameters are much more complex than regression coefficients, and assessment of the statistical significance of individual parameters is similarly more complex. This makes log-linear model parameters much harder to interpret. Although parameter estimates are useful for many purposes, assessing the fit of log-linear models generally requires examination of chi-square tests and various other measures. We will spend the rest of Chapter 3 showing you how to specify different models and how to decide how well your models fit the data.

Figure 3.8
Parameters Divided by Their Standard Errors

```
LOGLIN
    USE EXCON02
    FREQ COUNT
    PRINT SHORT / OBS CHISQ RATIO
    MODEL GROUP$*REARREST$ = GROUP$ # REARREST$
    ESTIMATE
```

The output is:

```
Observed Frequencies
========================
GROUP$    |       REARREST$
          |  No          Yes
----------+-------------------------
Control   |      165          221
Payment   |      239          310
----------+-------------------------
Pearson ChiSquare   0.0000  df   0  Probability      .
      LR ChiSquare  -0.0000  df   0  Probability      .
     Raftery's BIC  -0.0000

Lambda / SE(Lambda)
========================

         THETA
    -------------
        5.429
    -------------

        GROUP$
    Control     Payment
    -------------------------
       -5.285        5.285
    -------------------------

       REARREST$
    No        Yes
    -------------------------
       -4.117        4.117
    -------------------------

GROUP$    |       REARREST$
          |  No          Yes
----------+-------------------------
Control   |     -0.239        0.239
Payment   |      0.239       -0.239
----------+-------------------------
```

3.5 Comparing SYSTAT to texts about log-linear models

If you are familiar with or are reading other texts on log-linear models, you may be puzzled as to how they connect with SYSTAT. There are two issues here. First is the question of which techniques are available in SYSTAT. SYSTAT calculates goodness-of-fit tests, but not parameter estimates or odds ratios. We restricted this presentation to the techniques available in SYSTAT.

Second, most texts use a mathematical notation to define models, whereas we have used standard SYSTAT variable names. There are two reasons to choose this approach. First, Leland Wilkinson designed SYSTAT so that models in all SYSTAT procedures use a similar command, the MODEL statement. The consistency makes it easy to use and understand models anywhere in SYSTAT. Keeping this book consistent with SYSTAT has the same advantage. Second, we find variable names to be easier to understand than the notations employed by other authors. However, we want you to be able to make the connections easily from the material in this chapter to other texts. The table in Figure 3.9 compares a typical SYSTAT MODEL command with the same model as described by other authors.

SYSTAT omits portions of the full model whenever this does not cause confusion. Log-linear models have no dependent variable in the sense that we use the term elsewhere in this book. Instead we are trying to predict the natural logarithm of the cell count from a model of the associations in the table. Even though the notation differs from author to author, all log-linear models predict the same thing and, thus, SYSTAT version 5 omits it from the MODEL statement. In version 6, where log-linear models and crosstabs are separate, SYSTAT needs to be told which table to apply the effects, so the MODEL statement contains the table to the left of the equals sign. The constant term (represented by μ or θ in the table) is the overall mean of the log cell counts. SYSTAT always assumes that it exists, so it is also omitted from the MODEL statement. What we have left are the main effects (like GROUP$) and interaction effects (i.e. GROUP$*REARREST$) and these must be specified because they differ from model to model.

Figure 3.9
Comparison of SYSTAT to other Log-Linear Model Notations

SYSTAT version 5	GROUP$ + REARREST$ + GROUP$*REARREST
SYSTAT version 6	GROUP$*REARREST = GROUP$ + REARREST+ GROUP$*REARREST
Agresti (1983, 1990)	$\log m_{ij} = \mu + \lambda_i^G + \lambda_j^R + \lambda_{ij}^{GR}$
Fienberg (1980); Bishop, Fienberg & Holland (1975)	$\log m_{ij} = \mu + \mu_{1\,(i)} + \mu_{2\,(i)} + \mu_{12}$
Goodman (1971)	$\xi_{ij} = \theta + \lambda_i^A + \lambda_j^B + \lambda_{ij}^{AB}$
Haberman (1978)	$\log m_{ij} = \lambda + \lambda_i^A + \lambda_j^B + \lambda_{ij}^{AB}$
Knoke & Burke (1980)	$G_{ij} = \theta + \lambda_i^G + \lambda_j^R + \lambda_{ij}^{GR}$

Goodman often expresses his models in their multiplicative form rather than the additive form used by SYSTAT. The above model in multiplicative form is:

$$F_{ij} = \eta \tau_i^A \tau_j^B \tau_{ij}^{AB}$$

where $\xi_{ij} = \log(F_{ij})$, $\theta = \log \eta$, $\lambda_i^A = \log\left(\tau_i^A\right)$, etc. As you can see, the multiplicative form can be converted to the additive form by taking logs of both sides of the equation. This is the source of the name, log-linear. These models are linear in their log form. Recognizing the clumsiness of these notations, Goodman also introduced the most stripped down notation possible. He represents variables by the first letter of their name. For example, G stands for GROUP$. Individual terms are enclosed in curly brackets, like {G}, and interaction effects are denoted by including all variables in the interaction inside the curly brackets. Thus {GR} is the GROUP$-by-REARREST$ interaction. Since models are hierarchical and every higher-order term automatically implies all lower-order terms, Goodman writes only the higher-order terms. In this compressed notation, the above model is:

{GR}

Agresti (1990) uses a similar notation but encloses the terms in parentheses. The simplicity of this notation is appealing and we will use it in future summary tables. We will not dwell on notation further because, for us, the form in which the model is written is less important than the effects that are in the model and how they are substantively interpreted. SYSTAT handles the details of estimating the expected counts and calculating the chi-square test.

3.6 Choosing a model

The best model is often the simplest model that fits the data. Simple models are also called parsimonious. Simple models have as few terms as possible. Since models are hierarchical, the terms will be low-order terms rather than high-order terms.

We can use the hierarchy of models to help us choose a simple model. There are two basic hierarchical approaches: if you have relatively few variables in the model, you can explore all possible models. Otherwise, you can use a stepwise approach. We illustrate both approaches and, in addition, discuss three nonhierarchical tools: substantive theory, sampling issues, and analysis of the residuals from a model. A variety of other approaches are possible. See Fienberg (1980) and Agresti (1990) for a summary and further references. We close this section with a summary and some recommendations.

All possible models

When we have only three variables, there are very few models that can be fitted. In this case, an alternative is to fit all models and summarize the results in a single table. We use the compressed format described in the previous section. This means, for example, that the model {G} {W} {R} is the independence model (in SYSTAT: MODEL WORK$*GROUP$*REARREST$ = WORK$ + GROUP$ + REARREST$). {WR} represents the WORK$-by-REARREST$ interaction and indicates that WORK$ and REARREST$ are associated. Figure 3.10 lists the symbols corresponding to several possible models for a three-way table. The models are ordered from simple to complex from the top to the bottom of the table.

Figure 3.10
One Hierarchy of Log-Linear Models
Ex-Convict Transition Aid Dataset

Model	Interpretation
{G} {W} {R}	All variables are independent. The independence model.
{G} {WR}	Only WORK$ and REARREST$ are associated. GROUP$ is independent of both WORK$ and REARREST$.
{GR} {WR}	Only GROUP$ and WORK$ are independent.
{WG} {WR} {GR}	Each pair of variables is associated. No 3-variable interaction.
{WGR}	All pairs are associated and there is a 3-variable interaction.

The last model, containing the three-way interaction {WGR}, is a special case. This model fits *any* three-way table perfectly. It is called the **saturated model**. This means that the model has so many parameters that it forces all the expected values to exactly equal the observed values. As a result, the chi-square statistic equals zero, and there are zero degrees of freedom.

Using the notation from Figure 3.10, Figure 3.11 contains the likelihood ratio chi-square statistic and the degrees of freedom for the results of fitting several log-linear models to the ex-convict transition aid dataset. The smaller the chi-square, the better the fit. This is important and sometimes causes confusion. The testing strategy for log-linear models is the opposite of that used for testing independence in two-way tables. In two-way tables, you want to find an association and reject the hypothesis of independence. To do this you want a large chi-square value and a significant *p*-value. In log-linear models, you want to find a model that fits. A model that fits has a small chi-square and a nonsignificant *p*-value.

Figure 3.11
Goodness-of-Fit Tests for Log-Linear Models
GROUP\$ = G, WORK\$ = W, and REARREST\$ = R

Model	Likelihood Ratio Chi-Square	Degrees of Freedom	*p*-value
{W}{G}{R}	343.43	4	.000
{W}{GR}	343.37	3	.000
{R}{GW}	327.71	3	.000
{G}{WR}	24.96	3	.000
{GW}{GR}	327.66	2	.000
{GR}{WR}	24.90	2	.000
{GW}{WR}	9.24	2	.010
{GW}{WR}{GR}	0.06	1	.813
{WGR}	0.00	0	undefined

The models are ordered in the hierarchy we discussed above, the simplest models at the top and the most complex models at the bottom. Starting from the top the first model, {G}{W}{R}, is the familiar independence model for a three-way table.

The next three models each fit a single interaction term. The model {G} {WR}, which includes the WORK\$-by-REARREST\$ interaction, fits strikingly better than the others. The {GR} interaction seems to have almost no effect. This is consistent with our earlier conclusion that assignment to the control group or payment group makes no difference in an ex-offender's rearrest probability.

The next three models fit two interaction terms. The two models without the {WR} term do not fit well at all. The best fitting model of the three includes both {WR} and {WG}. This model says that GROUP\$ and REARREST\$ are independent, controlling for WORK\$, but the other two pairs of variables are associated.

The second to last model, {GW}{WR}{GR}, fits all two-way interactions. It is not significant and, compared to the bottom model, {WGR}, it shows a significant decrease in the conditional goodness-of-fit from adding the {GR} term. Thus once we include the other two interaction terms in the model, the GROUP-by-REARREST\$ interaction is also significant.

Figure 3.11 suggests that the model, {GW}{WR}{GR}, which allows associations between all pairs of variables, is the best fitting model since it is the only model where the likelihood ratio chi-square is greater than the conventional 5% level. An argument can also be made, using reasons we discuss in Section 3.5, that the model where {G} and {R} are independent, {GW}{GR}, may be a better model.

Looking at all possible models is a very effective way to choose a best-fitting model. The problem is that as the number of variables increases, the number of possible models enlarges very quickly. In a four-variable table, for example, there are 112 different hierarchical log-linear models that are more complex than the independence model. SYSTAT can easily fit these models; in version 6 the PRINT option HTERM will give most of these in a single command. The problem is that you, the data analyst, would have to interpret them and they are not all easy to interpret. When you have more than 3 variables it is no longer practical to look at all possible models; you can use either a bottom-up or a top-down approach to finding a best fitting model.

Stepwise model selection

Goodman (1971) suggests a stepwise approach to model selection.This is a very general approach so that even though we apply it to a four-way table, you can easily extend it to tables with five or more variables.

We begin with an initial screening to find the general location of the best fitting model. To do this we test the goodness-of-fit of three models:

1. All two-variable interactions are zero.
1. All three-variable interactions are zero.
1. The four-variable interaction is zero.

Notice that because of the hierarchical nature of the models, if model (1) is true (i.e. fits the data), then models (2) and (3) must be true. Similarly, if model (2) is true, then model (3) must be true. Fitting these three models quickly limits the number of potential models we must consider, eliminating much work. We use the data that Goodman used from a detergent brand preference experiment (Ries and Smith 1963). The BRAND data file, shown in Figure 3.12, contains degree of water softness (SOFTNESS$), brand preference of either brand X or M (BRAND$), indication of a prior user of brand M (PRIORUSE$), and water temperature (TEMP$). In these various stepwise analyses we ignore the distinction between independent and dependent variables.

Figure 3.12
Detergent Brand Preference Dataset

SOFTNESS$	BRAND$	PRIORUSE$	TEMP$	COUNT
Soft	X	M	High	19
Soft	X	M	Low	57
Soft	X	"Not M"	High	29
Soft	X	"Not M"	Low	63
Soft	M	M	High	29
Soft	M	M	Low	49
Soft	M	"Not M"	High	27
Soft	M	"Not M"	Low	53
Medium	X	M	High	23
Medium	X	M	Low	47
Medium	X	"Not M"	High	33
Medium	X	"Not M"	Low	66
Medium	M	M	High	47
Medium	M	M	Low	55
Medium	M	"Not M"	High	23
Medium	M	"Not M"	Low	50
Hard	X	M	High	24
Hard	X	M	Low	37
Hard	X	"Not M"	High	42
Hard	X	"Not M"	Low	68
Hard	M	M	High	43
Hard	M	M	Low	52
Hard	M	"Not M"	High	30
Hard	M	"Not M"	Low	42

To test the three models (1-3) we need the goodness-of-fit statistics for three SYSTAT models: the independence model, the model with all two-variable interactions, the model with all three-variable interactions. Model (3) is, of course, the saturated model and we know exactly what it looks like. This output is shown in Figure 3.13.

Figure 3.13
Detergent Brand Preference Study
SYSTAT Output for Initial Screening

```
LOGLIN
    USE BRAND
    FREQ COUNT
    PRINT NONE / CHISQ
    MODEL SOFTNESS$*PRIORUSE$*BRAND$*TEMP$ =,
        SOFTNESS$ + PRIORUSE$ + BRAND$ + TEMP$
    ESTIMATE
```

```
Pearson ChiSquare   43.9022   df  18  Probability  0.00060
     LR ChiSquare   42.9287   df  18  Probability  0.00082
    Raftery's BIC  -81.5544
```

```
    MODEL SOFTNESS$*PRIORUSE$*BRAND$*TEMP$ = SOFTNESS$..TEMP$^2
    ESTIMATE
```

```
Pearson ChiSquare    9.8706   df   9  Probability  0.36106
     LR ChiSquare    9.8462   df   9  Probability  0.36308
    Raftery's BIC  -52.3953
```

```
    MODEL SOFTNESS$*PRIORUSE$*BRAND$*TEMP$ = SOFTNESS$..TEMP$^3
    ESTIMATE
```

```
Pearson ChiSquare    0.7379   df   2  Probability  0.69146
     LR ChiSquare    0.7373   df   2  Probability  0.69166
    Raftery's BIC  -13.0941
```

This is easier to see in a summary table, like Figure 3.14. We begin by choosing a significance level, like 0.05. Notice that the independence model ({S}{P}{B}{T}) does not fit the data, while the model with all two-variable interactions and the model with all three-variable interactions both fit the data. This tells us that the true model is somewhere between the independence model and the model with all two-variable interactions.

Figure 3.14
Initial Screening for Stepwise Model Selection
Variables: SOFTNESS$ (S), PRIORUSE$ (P), BRAND$ (B), and TEMP$ (T)

Model	Likelihood Ratio Chi-Square	Degrees of Freedom	*p*-value
{S}{P}{B}{T}	42.93	18	.001
{SP}{SB}{ST}{PB}{PT}{BT}	9.85	9	.363
{SPB}{SPT}{{PBT}{SBT}	0.74	2	.692
{SPBT}	0.00	0	undefined

Using a *forward selection* approach, we begin with the independence model since that is the most complex model to show significant lack of fit. The basic strategy is to sequentially add the term which seems to have the largest impact. In step 1, we form a table like Figure 3.15 containing all models with a single two-variable interaction. The SYSTAT output required to create the table has been omitted. Looking at Figure 3.15, the model with the {PB} interaction fits best; it is the only model with a nonsignificant p-value. Further, the difference between that model and the independence model is (42.93 - 22.35 =) 20.58 with one degree of freedom which is significant at our chosen level of 0.05. We add the {PB} term to the model.

Figure 3.15
Step 1 of Stepwise Model Selection
Variables: SOFTNESS$ (S), PRIORUSE$ (P), BRAND$ (B) and TEMP$ (T)

Model	Likelihood Ratio Chi-Square	Degrees of Freedom	*p*-value
{S}{P}{B}{T}	42.93	18	.001
{S}{P}{BT}	39.57	17	.002
{S}{B}{PT}	41.68	17	.001
{S}{T}{PB}	22.35	17	.172
{P}{B}{ST}	36.83	'16	.002
{P}{T}{SB}	42.53	16	.000
{B}{T}{SP}	41.85	16	.000

In step 2, we form a table in Figure 3.16 which contains all models with the {PB} interaction and a second two-variable interaction. Looking at these models, the {BT} interaction is the most significant. Further, the difference between the model with both the {PB} and the {BT} interactions and the model with only {PB} is 22.43 -

17.99 = 4.45 with one degree of freedom is significant at our chosen level of 0.05. We add the {BT} term to the model.

Figure 3.16
Step 2 of Stepwise Model Selection
Variables: SOFTNESS$ (S), PRIORUSE$ (P), BRAND$ (B) and TEMP$ (T)

Model	Likelihood Ratio Chi-Square	Degrees of Freedom	p-value
{S}{T}{PB}	22.35	17	.172
{S}{PB}{BT}	17.99	16	.325
{S}{PB}{PT}	21.09	16	.175
{T}{PB}{SP}	21.27	15	.128
{T}{PB}{SB}	21.95	'15	.109
{PB}{ST}	16.25	15	.366

In step 3, we form a table in Figure 3.17 which contains all models which include the {PB}{BT} terms and a third two-variable interaction. Looking at these models, the {ST} interaction is the most significant. Further, the difference between the model with the {PB}{BT}{ST} terms and the model with only {PB}{BT} is 17.99 - 11.89 = 6.10 with two degrees of freedom, which is significant at our chosen level of 0.05. We add the {ST} term to the model.

Figure 3.17
Step 3 of Stepwise Model Selection
Variables: SOFTNESS$ (S), PRIORUSE$ (P), BRAND$ (B) and TEMP$ (T)

Model	Likelihood Ratio Chi-Square	Degrees of Freedom	p-value
{S}{PB}{BT}	17.99	16	.325
{S}{PB}{BT}{PT}	17.29	15	.302
{PB}{BT}{SP}	16.91	14	.261
{PB}{BT}{SB}	17.59	14	.226
{PB}{BT}{ST}	11.89	'14	.615

In step 4, we form a table in Figure 3.18 containing all models which include the {PB}{BT}{ST} terms and a fourth two-variable interaction. Looking at these models, none of the fourth interaction terms makes a significant reduction in the goodness-of-fit statistic. So we cannot add any further two-variable terms to the model. The forward selection process leads us to the {PB} {BT} {ST} model as the best model.

Figure 3.18
Step 4 of Stepwise Model Selection
Variables: SOFTNESS\$ (S), PRIORUSE\$ (P), BRAND\$ (B) and TEMP\$ (T)

Model	Likelihood Ratio Chi-Square	Degrees of Freedom	p-value
{PB}{BT}{ST}	11.89	14	.615
{PB}{BT}{ST}{PT}	11.19	13	.595
{PB}{BT}{ST}{SB}	11.54	12	.483
{PB}{BT}{ST}{SP}	10.80	12	.546

A summary of the procedure for forward selection is as follows. Begin with the most complex model which does *not* fit the data. In the brand preference data, this was the independence model (see Figure 3.14). Add higher-order interactions as described below until no further interactions are significant. In the brand preference data the independence model did not include any interactions, so we added two-variable interactions.

1. Add the higher-order interaction which has the most significant conditional goodness-of-fit given that it does not exceed the significance level that was preselected. (We preselected a significance level of 0.05 in this case.)

2. Add the next most significant interaction using the conditional goodness-of-fit test involving the model from the prior step.

3. An optional step which we did not choose to employ in the brand preference example is to delete any higher-order interactions which are no longer significant.

4. Repeat steps 2 and 3 until no more terms can be added or dropped.

The alternative approach, *backward elimination*, begins with the simplest model which fits the data. In our case this is the model with all two-variable interactions (see Figure 3.14). Backward elimination does the opposite of forward selection. On each step, it removes the least significant term from the model until all the remaining terms are significant.

For reasons of space we do not display the entire set of tables needed to carry out the backward elimination procedure on these data. Instead, we show the first step, summarize the results of other steps, and invite you to construct the tables yourself. We begin with the model including all two-variable interactions. Construct a table which contains models each of which omits one of the interactions. SYSTAT provides a simple way to produce these models as part of the output from the model of all two-variable interactions by using the PRINT statement HTERM option.

Figure 3.19
Backward Elimination Using HTERM Option

```
LOGLIN
   USE BRAND01
   FREQ COUNT
   PRINT NONE / CHISQ HTERM
   MODEL SOFTNESS$*BRAND$*PRIORUSE$*TEMP$ = SOFTNESS$...TEMP$^2
   ESTIMATE
```

Term tested hierarchically	The model without the term ln(MLE)	Chi-Sq	df	p-value	Removal of term from model Chi-Sq	df	p-value
Pearson ChiSquare 9.8706 df 9 Probability 0.36106							
LR ChiSquare 9.8462 df 9 Probability 0.36308							
Raftery's BIC -52.3953							
SOFTNESS$. . .	-75.105	17.80	17	0.4019	7.95	8	0.4384
BRAND$	-83.461	34.51	14	0.0017	24.66	5	0.0002
PRIORUSE$. . .	-83.230	34.05	14	0.0020	24.20	5	0.0002
TEMP$.	-113.311	94.21	14	0.0000	84.36	5	0.0000
SOFTNESS$ * BRAND$ . . .	-71.238	10.06	11	0.5248	0.22	2	0.8978
SOFTNESS$ * PRIORUSE$. .	-71.633	10.85	11	0.4558	1.00	2	0.6050
BRAND$ * PRIORUSE$. .	-81.077	29.74	10	0.0009	19.89	1	0.0000
SOFTNESS$ * TEMP$. . . .	-74.178	15.94	11	0.1433	6.10	2	0.0475
BRAND$ * TEMP$. . . .	-73.000	13.58	10	0.1928	3.74	1	0.0532
PRIORUSE$ * TEMP$. . . .	-71.500	10.59	10	0.3907	0.74	1	0.3897

The table of hierarchical terms contains three major components. On the left is a column of terms. These identify the rows of the table. In the center are a set of likelihood ratio chi-squares that test the goodness-of-fit of the model without the term. The terms are hierarchical, meaning that if a lower-order effect is removed, all higher-order effects containing it are also removed. For example, the first line tests the model without any terms containing SOFTNESS$. In this model there are four such terms: {S}, {SB}, {SP}, and {ST}. The model being tested in this line contains only {PT}{PB}{TB} and their lower-order interactions. On the right is a conditional goodness-of-fit test of the difference between the original model and the reduced model.

In backward elimination we want to eliminate the one term that contributes least to the model, so we look at the lines containing two-variable interactions. The conditional goodness-of-fit test shows that the {SB} terms has the smallest chi-square, 0.22. This suggests that we eliminate the {SB} term and continue with the model:

$$\{SP\}\{ST\}\{PT\}\{PB\}\{TB\}$$

We summarize the remaining steps. On the second step we drop {PT}, leaving us with the model: {SP}{ST}{PB}{TB}. The next step deletes {SP}, so the remaining terms are {ST}{PB}{TB}. Removing any of these terms will cause a significant increase in the chi-square statistic, so none can be deleted. The final model from backward elimination is the same as the model chosen by forward selection.

The table of hierarchical terms, Figure 3.19, suggests something else, outside the scope of backward elimination but useful enough that it is worth pausing to discuss it. Notice in the first line of the table, testing SOFTNESS$, the conditional test is not significant. This suggests that models without any terms containing softness fit the data. This is not consistent with the results for forward or backward stepping, but it is certainly substantively interesting and worth further exploration. Our point here is that the HTERM table can be used to eliminate large numbers of models very quickly and help you focus on smaller, more manageable subsets. In addition to the stepwise procedures, this gives you yet another method to assist your search for a simple, well-fitting model.

Backward elimination can be summarized as follows. Begin with the simplest model which fits the data. Then eliminate the highest-order interaction terms until removal of any remaining terms would significantly increase the chi-square value.

1. Find the least significant effect in the model, if its significance level exceeds a preselected level (often 0.05) using the conditional goodness-of-fit test.

2. Construct a new model without the effect from (1).

3. Optionally, add any terms which significantly improve the fit of the model.

4. Repeat (1), (2), and (3) until no more terms can be added or deleted.

In general, backward elimination is believed to be a better approach. When effects combine synergistically to create important patterns in the data, these tend to show up only in the higher-order interactions. Since forward selection tends to look at fewer high-order interaction terms, it is more likely to miss these terms. Backward elimination tends to retain more terms than forward selection. If this happens the final model will be more complex. This is often thought to be a disadvantage because we seek a model that is simple to interpret, showing us the most important features of the data without overfitting.

There are several disadvantages associated with stepwise procedures. In this example, both forward selection and backward elimination gave the same model, but they often lead to different "best" models. When you look at a large number of models, interpret the significance levels of the goodness-of-fit tests with great caution. They do not reflect the number of models being tested. Finally, alternative approaches may lead to yet other "best" models. We describe such an approach in Section 3.7 using Raftery's BIC. This approach leads us to a different "best" model: a model which is arguably more reasonable than the model we found here. The point is, stepwise procedures should not be used as automatic devices for finding the appropriate log-linear model. At best they reduce the number of models which the analyst has to study. But they offer no guarantee that one of the models they point to is the simplest or most substantively interesting. Other models may exist that also provide an acceptable fit to the data, and the most appropriate model is better selected using substantive theory rather than a blind statistical rule.

Using standardized parameter estimates

An alternative approach builds on the stepwise procedures just discussed. Goodman (1971) suggests fitting the saturated model and examining the standardized parameter estimates. Select all the terms with at least one standardized parameter estimate greater than, say, than plus-or-minus 2. Fit this model. If it fits, then try to simplify it using backward elimination. If it does not fit, add terms using forward selection. Figure 3.20 shows the result of applying this to the brand preference data.

Figure 3.20
Standardized Parameter Estimates for Model Selection

```
LOGLIN
    USE BRAND01
    FREQ COUNT
    PRINT NONE / RATIO
    MODEL SOFTNESS$*BRAND$*PRIORUSE$*TEMP$ =,
          SOFTNESS$ # BRAND$ # PRIORUSE$ # TEMP$
    ESTIMATE
```

Lambda / SE(Lambda)

THETA
3.675

SOFTNESS$

Hard	Medium	Soft
0.528	0.469	−0.972

BRAND$

M	X
0.453	−0.453

PRIORUSE$

M	Not M
−1.258	1.258

TEMP$

High	Low
−8.495	8.495

SOFTNESS$	BRAND$	
	M	X
Hard	−0.045	0.045
Medium	0.294	−0.294
Soft	−0.245	0.245

SOFTNESS$	PRIORUSE$	
	M	Not M
Hard	−0.682	0.682
Medium	1.183	−1.183
Soft	−0.496	0.496

```
BRAND$    |      PRIORUSE$
          | M              Not M
----------+--------------------------
M         |      4.669         -4.669
X         |     -4.669          4.669
----------+--------------------------


SOFTNESS$ |      TEMP$
          | High       Low
----------+--------------------------
Hard      |      2.246         -2.246
Medium    |     -0.148          0.148
Soft      |     -2.038          2.038
----------+--------------------------


BRAND$    |      TEMP$
          | High       Low
----------+--------------------------
M         |      1.905         -1.905
X         |     -1.905          1.905
----------+--------------------------


PRIORUSE$ |      TEMP$
          | High       Low
----------+--------------------------
M         |      0.769         -0.769
Not M     |     -0.769          0.769
----------+--------------------------


SOFTNESS$ BRAND$   |      PRIORUSE$
                   | M              Not M
----------+--------+--------------------------
Hard      M        |      1.292         -1.292
          X        |     -1.292          1.292
                   +
Medium    M        |      0.672         -0.672
          X        |     -0.672          0.672
                   +
Soft      M        |     -1.914          1.914
          X        |      1.914         -1.914
----------+--------+--------------------------


SOFTNESS$ BRAND$   |      TEMP$
                   | High       Low
----------+--------+--------------------------
Hard      M        |     -0.331          0.331
          X        |      0.331         -0.331
                   +
Medium    M        |     -0.102          0.102
          X        |      0.102         -0.102
                   +
Soft      M        |      0.421         -0.421
          X        |     -0.421          0.421
----------+--------+--------------------------
```

```
SOFTNESS$  PRIORUSE$ |        TEMP$
                     | High        Low
---------+---------+---------------------------
Hard       M         |      -0.030       0.030
           Not M     |       0.030      -0.030
                   +
Medium     M         |       1.033      -1.033
           Not M     |      -1.033       1.033
                   +
Soft       M         |      -0.982       0.982
           Not M     |       0.982      -0.982
-------------------+---------------------------

BRAND$     PRIORUSE$ |        TEMP$
                     | High        Low
---------+---------+---------------------------
M          M         |       1.501      -1.501
           Not M     |      -1.501       1.501
                   +
X          M         |      -1.501       1.501
           Not M     |       1.501      -1.501
-------------------+---------------------------

SOFTNESS$  BRAND$   PRIORUSE$ |       TEMP$
                             | High        Low
---------+---------+---------+------------------------
Hard       M         M        |      -0.815       0.815
                     Not M    |       0.815      -0.815
                            +
           X         M        |       0.815      -0.815
                     Not M    |      -0.815       0.815
---------+---------+---------+------------------------
Medium     M         M        |       0.626      -0.626
                     Not M    |      -0.626       0.626
                            +
           X         M        |      -0.626       0.626
                     Not M    |       0.626      -0.626
---------+---------+---------+------------------------
Soft       M         M        |       0.179      -0.179
                     Not M    |      -0.179       0.179
                            +
           X         M        |      -0.179       0.179
                     Not M    |       0.179      -0.179
-------------------+---------+------------------------
```

The terms with large standardized parameter estimates are {T}, {BP}, and {ST}. These point to the model {BP}{ST}. Both stepwise procedures suggested a model including these terms plus the {BT} effect. Since the standardized parameter estimate for {BT} is 1.9, very close to 2.0, the results in this case are similar to the other stepwise approaches. There is no guarantee that the results from these different procedures will be so similar. Goodman (1971) points out that a weakness of this approach is that the size of the standardized parameter estimates depends on which other parameters are in the model. The standardized parameter estimate for the term {AB} may be very different depending on whether the term {ABC} is included in the model or not.

Terms required by sample design

Many samples are designed so that certain marginal totals are fixed. Any model of such data should include the terms needed to assure that the expected values are identical to the observed values in those marginals. For example, suppose that the sample for the brand preference data had been drawn so that the number of users of the two brands, X and M, and whether they had been prior users was fixed in the design. Then every model should include the {BP} term, regardless of its statistical significance, because it is required in order that the fitted and observed values match for the BRAND$ and PRIORUSE$ marginal totals. This implies that the least complex model we would examine would not be the independence model, but the model {S}{T}{BP}, and that every model would include the {BP} interaction.

Using substantive theory

Most researchers do not do log-linear models for the thrill of reading chi-square statistics, they do them to answer substantive questions. Whenever possible we want to choose models that help find these answers. The stepwise approach is often mechanistic and not sensitive to substantive theoretical hypotheses. Substantive issues often suggest that many models are not very interesting and can be ignored. This can greatly simplify the task of selecting a model.

The key question is, where to begin? One approach, similar to forward selection, suggests that we start with a simple model. On statistical grounds we often begin with a model claiming that none of the variables in the table are associated. This is the independence model. If this model fits, you need look no further because the hierarchical nature of log-linear models guarantees that every more complex model also fits. But the simplest theoretically sensible model is often not the independence model. Let's look at an example. In the ex-convict transitional aid dataset our models assessed the influence of the independent variables (GROUP$ and WORK$) on the dependent variable (REARREST$). This suggests that we begin with a model saying that the independent variables have no association with the dependent variable. That is, we want a model saying that the observed frequencies can be fit by assuming that there is no difference in REARREST$ across GROUP$ and WORK$. This is:

```
MODEL WORK$*GROUP$*REARREST$ = REARREST$ + GROUP#WORK$
```

This is called the **baseline model**, meaning the starting point, the simplest model that we examine. This is an appropriate baseline model only when we do not care whether the GROUP\$-by-WORK\$ interaction is significant, that is, when we're not interested in associations among the independent variables. We are only interested in associations of one or more independent variables with the dependent variable. If this model fits, we know that we can explain the pattern of frequencies in the table without referring to any associations between the independent and dependent variables. This would be a strong argument that the independent variables have no influence on the dependent variable. If this model does not fit (it does not, see Figure 3.11, page 86), then we can explore the associations {WR} and {GR} and the three-variable interaction {WGR}. This would involve examining five models rather than the nine models used when we looked at all possible models, a substantial reduction.

Similarly, if we were only interested in brand preference in the detergent brand preference data, our baseline model would be that none of the independent variables had any effect on brand preference: {STP}{B}. We could then explore the two- and three-way interactions which include BRAND\$. This would be considerably fewer than the models in the stepwise selection process above and it would focus on the hypotheses that we really care about.

The further point is that careful consideration of the theoretical hypotheses that you intend to test may significantly reduce the amount of work that you need to do to explore the associations in a table.

Analysis of residuals

When we fit a model we almost never find any cells where the model fits the observed frequencies exactly. This is why we say that a model is only a summary of the relationship between the variables. A summary is not the whole relationship. It leaves something out. If we have a good theory and the summary is a good one, the part left out is small compared to the summary, and the goodness-of-fit test shows that the model fits the data. Thus, in statistical language, the summary is the model which has been fitted to the data. The part left out is the *residual*. We can examine the residuals in each cell because, for each cell, we have the relationship:

$$observed\ count = fitted\ count + residual$$

This is a fundamental relationship in data analysis. We will use it to emphasize different aspects of data analysis. Here the point is to notice that the residuals can be used to make a cell-by-cell comparison of the observed and expected counts. The model may fit some cells poorly and this lack of fit may give us insight into the associations in a table. In the extreme case, remember that the chi-square can be significant when only one cell deviates widely from the model. Similarly, if the pattern of positive and negative residuals is systematic, this often suggests other associations to include in the model. The most important thing to remember about residuals is that they contain structure which has not yet been incorporated into a model.

SYSTAT can print 6 statistics that can be considered to be residuals from the model. The simplest are the observed minus expected counts, called differences. Then there are 4 kinds of standardized cell residuals: standardized residuals, Pearson residuals, likelihood ratio residuals, and Freeman-Tukey residuals. Finally, it can supply the contribution of each cell to the model's log likelihood. All these residuals are related and they tend to show similar things. For each, extreme values — either positive or negative — indicate that a cell is not well fit by the model. We describe each statistic in turn.

Keep in mind that most of what we say depends on asymptotic theory, meaning it works best when there are large numbers of cases in each cell. Be careful when evaluating residuals from cells with small N's because asymptotic theory will be least helpful.

The SYSTAT manual often uses the word "deviates" or "deviations" for these residuals. This is commonly used in contingency tables where the residuals can be thought of as deviations from the observed cell frequency. We use both words, but we use residuals most often because it makes clear the link between these statistics and the residuals from other statistical procedures and the link to analysis of residuals. Many standard analysis of residuals procedures may bear fruit here.

Differences. These simple residuals are calculated for each cell using the formula:

$$residual = observed\ count - fitted\ count$$

SYSTAT version 5 calls these residuals "differences" and you can obtain them by requesting the DIFFERENCE option on the SAVE or the MODEL commands. SYSTAT version 6 uses the word "deviations"; request them using the FITTED option on the SAVE command or the DEVIATIONS option on the PRINT command. These simple residuals are difficult to interpret because cell counts are often widely different. The size of the residual may depend more on the number of cases in the cell than on how well the model fits.

Standardized residuals. By correcting for the number of cases in the cell, we obtain more easily interpretable residuals, **standardized residuals**. For each cell:

$$standardized\ residual\ =\ \frac{(observed\ count - fitted\ count)}{\sqrt{fitted\ count}}$$

SYSTAT version 5 gives standardized residuals if you add the RESIDUAL option to the MODEL or SAVE commands. In version 6, give the FITTED option on the SAVE command or the STAND option on the PRINT command.

Pearson chi-square components.[1] The contribution of each cell to the overall Pearson chi-square is the square of the standardized residual. Since it is squared, it will always be positive. Compared to standardized residuals, squaring increases the impact of large deviations from the observed frequencies. These show up more strongly. In version 6, give the FITTED option on the SAVE command or the PEARSON option on the PRINT command.

Likelihood ratio chi-square components.[2] These are contribution of each cell to the likelihood ratio chi-square statistic. In general, they will display patterns very similar to the Pearson chi-square components. In version 6, give the FITTED option on the SAVE command or the LRDEV option on the PRINT command.

Freeman-Tukey deviates standardize the cells by attempting to stabilize the variance.[3] The formula is not particularly intuitive so we will not describe it here (see Bishop, Fienberg, & Holland 1975 for details). When the data are from a Poisson distribution, Freeman-Tukey deviates are approximately normally distributed with mean 0 and variance 1. The Poisson distribution typically arises from data that are counts or incidences of events. Number of deaths from horse-kicks in the Prussian army is famous Poisson-distributed data. In version 6, give the FITTED option on the SAVE command or the FTDEV option on the PRINT command.

Log-likelihood components.[4] SYSTAT estimates the parameters of a log-linear model by a maximum likelihood method; for mathematical reasons the actual quantity estimated is the log of the likelihood function, called the log-likelihood. Each cell contributes to the overall log-likelihood of the model. Models which fit well have a small overall log-likelihood. Thus cells with large contributions to the log-likelihood

---

1. Version 5 cannot produce the components of the Pearson chi-square statistic.
2. Version 5 cannot produce the components of the likelihood ratio chi-square statistic.
3. Version 5 cannot produce Freeman-Tukey deviates.
4. Version 5 cannot produce the components of the log-likelihood.

are not being fit well by the model. Thus, although the contributions to the log-likelihood are not, strictly speaking, residuals, they often behave like residuals. Since the
log-likelihood of the model varies from table to table, there is no overall standard
against which you can compare individual cell contributions to assess their significance. In version 6, give the FITTED option on the SAVE command or the LOGLIKE
option on the PRINT command.

We use the ex-convict transitional aid dataset to show how we can use information in
the residuals improve our understanding of the associations in the table. We will use
the standardized residuals for this analysis; use of the other kinds of residuals yields
similar results. In the rest of this chapter, when we use the word residual we mean the
standardized residuals. We begin with the familiar baseline model, {GW}{R}.
Figure 3.21 shows the residuals and the chi-square tests for that model.

Figure 3.21
Standardized Residuals from Baseline Model: {GW}{R}

```
LOGLIN
    USE EXCON02
    FREQ COUNT
    PRINT NONE / CHISQ STAND
    SAVE BASELINE / FITTED
    MODEL WORK$*GROUP$*REARREST$ = GROUP$*WORK$ + REARREST$
    ESTIMATE
```

The output is:

```
Pearson ChiSquare 305.0885  df   3  Probability  0.00000
     LR ChiSquare 327.7127  df   3  Probability  0.00000
    Raftery's BIC 307.1910

Estimates have been saved.

Standardized Deviates = (Obs-Exp)/sqrt(Exp)

WORK$      GROUP$   |      REARREST$
                    | No          Yes
----------+---------+--------------------------
No         Control  |     -6.128       5.345
           Payment  |     -6.924       6.039
                    +
Yes        Control  |      5.058      -4.411
           Payment  |      7.886      -6.879
--------------------+--------------------------
```

To interpret the residuals in Figure 3.21, notice that when the model *under*estimates the
number of cases in a cell, the observed count is larger than the fitted count and the residual is positive. Alternatively, when the model *over*estimates the count in a cell, the

observed count is smaller than the fitted count and the residual is negative. The first table of residuals is for WORK$ = No. Notice that the pattern of signs in the table is:

−	+
−	+

and this pattern repeats in the second table, where WORK$ = Yes, except the positive and negative signs are reversed. We describe this pattern as follows: In the first table, where WORK$ = No, the model overestimates the number of cases in the REARREST$ = No cell but underestimates the count when REARREST$ = Yes. In the second table, where WORK$ = Yes, it does the opposite, underestimating the REARREST$ = No cell but overestimating when REARREST$ = Yes. The interpretation of this pattern is simple: having controlled for {GW}{G} in the model, the effect of WORK$ on REARREST$ differs from level to level. This describes an interaction between WORK$ and REARREST$. Because the pattern is the same for both levels of GROUP$, we infer that the interaction does not involve GROUP$.

This suggests we add the {WR} term to the model and look at residuals again. We do this in Figure 3.22.

Figure 3.22
Standardized Residuals from Model: {GW}{WR}

```
SAVE RESID2 / FITTED
MODEL WORK$*REARREST$*GROUP$ = GROUP$#WORK$ + WORK$#REARREST$
ESTIMATE:
```

```
Pearson ChiSquare    9.1463  df   2  Probability  0.01033
    LR ChiSquare     9.2413  df   2  Probability  0.00985
   Raftery's BIC    -4.4398

Estimates have been saved.

Standardized Deviates = (Obs-Exp)/sqrt(Exp)
```

WORK$	GROUP$		REARREST$	
			No	Yes
No	Control		−1.161	0.492
	Payment		0.850	−0.360
Yes	Control		−1.006	1.580
	Payment		0.960	−1.507

Notice that the residuals are much smaller, showing this model fits much better. Notice again the pattern of plus and minus signs. In the first table, where WORK$ = No, we see — + + —. The pattern repeats in the second table. This suggests an interaction between GROUP$ and REARREST$. Since the pattern is the same for both levels of WORK$, it is not involved in the interaction. We will not show the output from the model including the {GR} term, but we know from Figure 3.10 that the likelihood ratio chi-square is 0.06.

If the model is correct, the standardized residuals are normally distributed with a mean of 0. The average variance of the standardized residuals equals the degrees of freedom in the model divided by the number of cells in the table. The number of cells is always greater than the degrees of freedom, so the average variance is smaller than 1.0. This means that standardized residuals have a smaller variance than a standard normal distribution, and residuals larger than plus-or-minus two (or 1.96) have no special meaning.

We noted above that the chi-square statistic can be significant if only one cell deviates sharply from the model. Examination of the residuals is the only way to see potential problems on a cell-by-cell basis. Looking at the table printed by SYSTAT is one option, but a graphic approach is often a useful supplement. If the model fits the standardized residuals are approximately normally distributed. In our ex-convict transitional aid dataset, this means that the 8 residuals should (approximately) resemble 8 observations from a normal distribution with a zero mean. (However, with only 8 cases and 2 degrees of freedom, we need to be cautious.) A plot of the residuals in order against the expected values from a normal distribution the result should be a straight line from the lower left corner toward the upper right. Deviations from the line, particularly one or two points which are dramatically higher or lower than expected, are evidence that the model does not fit certain cells. This plot is called a **normal probability plot** (or a theoretical quantile-quantile plot or a rankit plot). Statistically, it is a plot of the empirical cumulative distribution function of the residuals against the cumulative distribution which would have resulted had the residuals been drawn as a sample from a normal distribution.

We can save the standardized residuals and use SYSTAT's graphics to print a normal probability plot. Figure 3.23 shows the SYSTAT commands and the normal probability plot of the residuals from the baseline {WG}{R} model.

Figure 3.23 does not show a straight line. There are two separate clusters, each containing four cell residuals. If you look back at the residuals tables in Figure 3.21, where you can see which cell is represented by which point, you can see that these two groups are another indication of the very strong interaction between WORK$ and REAR-

REST$. After fitting the {WR} interaction and saving residuals, the GRAPH module gives us the plot reproduced in Figure 3.24.

Figure 3.23
Normal Probability Plot of Residuals from Model: {WG}{R}

```
USE BASELINE
PPLOT RESIDUAL / XFORMAT=0   YFORMAT=0
```

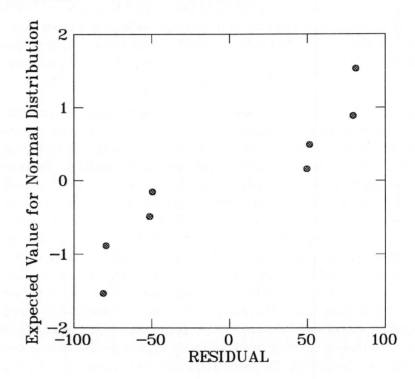

Figure 3.24
Normal Probability Plot of Standardized Residuals from Model: {WG}{WR}

```
USE RESID2
PPLOT RESIDUAL / XFORMAT=0   YFORMAT=0
```

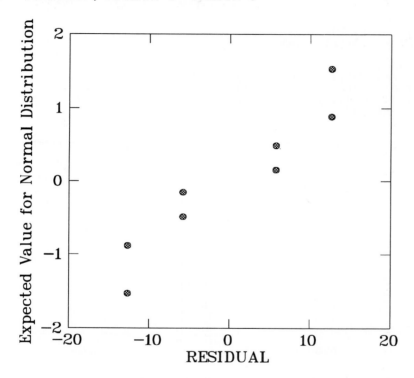

The plot in Figure 3.24 looks very good; it is about as close to a straight line as we ever see in a sample of eight cases. This is a strong suggestion that the {WG}{WR} model fits well. There is one more normal probability plot that we can run: from the {WG}{WR}{GR} model. We leave this as exercise for the interested reader.

One important question is, How can you know whether any deviation from a straight line is significant enough to warrant attention? The easy way is to create 10 variables from a normal distribution with the same number of cases as in your sample and plot them in 10 normal probability plots.

Use the SYSTAT ZRN function in a short program like this. Use the REPEAT command to create 8 cases because our dataset contains 8 cases.

Figure 3.25
Normal Probability Plots Data Sampled from a Normal Distribution

```
BASIC
   SAVE RANDOM
   REPEAT 8
   DIM RANDOM(10)
   FOR I = 1 TO 10
      LET RANDOM(I) = ZRN
   NEXT
   USE RANDOM
   PPLOT RANDOM(1) / SYM=1   SIZE=2   FILL
   PPLOT RANDOM(2) / SYM=1   SIZE=2   FILL
   PPLOT RANDOM(3) / SYM=1   SIZE=2   FILL
   PPLOT RANDOM(4) / SYM=1   SIZE=2   FILL
```

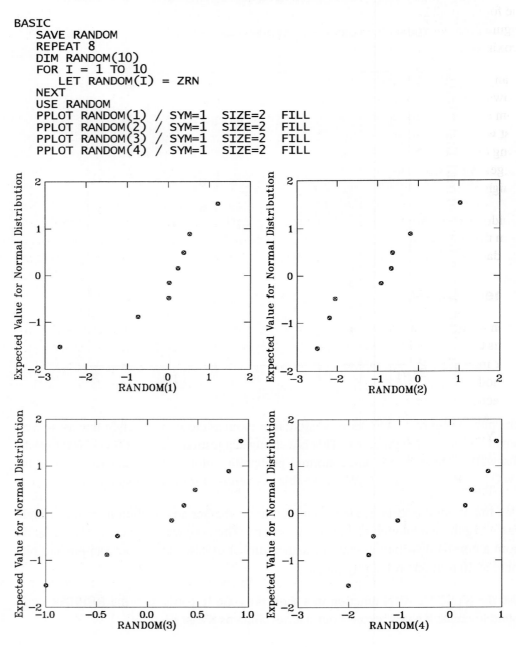

This will give you some idea of how much deviation from a straight line you can expect in samples the size of yours drawn from a true normal distribution. Figure 3.25 shows the four normal probability plots from the program above. Comparing Figure 3.24 and Figure 3.25 we can conclude that the residuals from the {WG}{WR} model are approximately normally distributed.

If anything, the normal probability plot from the ex-convict transitional aid dataset shows a straighter line than the samples from a normal distribution. Samples of size 8 from a normal distribution are unstable. We need larger sample sizes for stability. The best way to learn how to interpret normal probability plots is to make your own plots, using different sample sizes. To give you an idea of how a larger sample behaves, we suggest you create ten samples of 100 cases each and plot them. They will look much straighter.

Residuals play an important role in many aspects of modern data analysis and we use them throughout the book. Several other kinds of residuals can be defined for categorical data. See Bishop, Fienberg, and Holland (1975, Section 4.4) for more information.

General considerations in model selection

When we have a choice of several models we usually choose the simplest model. This means the model with fewer terms or the model with simpler terms (i.e. fewer or lower-order interactions). When comparing models with the same number of terms, choose the model with the simplest terms. For example, if one model includes a three-variable interaction and the other doesn't, we usually prefer the model with no three-variable term. An exception is a complex model that has a more natural substantive interpretation. You can always present more than one model, particularly if each model has an important theoretical interpretation.

Our approach to model-building emphasizes sequential examination of a number of different models. This fits well with many research situations where we have specific hypotheses in mind, but we usually do not have strong ideas about most of the structure of the data. We use the data themselves to find the appropriate model. There are two important parts of this kind of stepwise approach to understanding data. First, the goal is one (or more) final model(s) which fit the data and answer questions posed by our hypotheses. But this is only part of the way we come to understand the data. The process we follow to develop and refine the model is a second vital part. The point of the process is not just the final model. Rather, it is *through the process* of refining the model that we understand what the data say.

Regardless of how you arrive at your final models, it is important to emphasize that they should include the interactions that are fixed by your sampling design, and address the theoretical hypotheses of interest.

As the model-building proceeds, later models are increasingly based on information gathered by examining earlier models. This creates a problem. The degrees of freedom printed by SYSTAT (or any other package) are increasingly misleading because we used information in the data to suggest the models. We use the p-value to protect us from the probability of finding a significant effect when none exists, but if the degrees of freedom are wrong, the p-value is incorrect. This means that the probability of finding a significant effect when none exists (i.e. a Type I error) is greater than the p-value suggests.

Our sequential examination of model after model also increases the probability that one or more of the interactions that we find is simply due to chance. This is particularly true since, in our search for the one model which includes all correct effects, we often include all the significant terms that we encounter. We can easily include too many terms in the model.

There is no easy way to control the Type I error rate. One solution is to increase the sample size, but this is often not possible. A more common solution is to reduce the Type I p-value from the conventional 5% level to somewhere between 10% to 30%. This is the primary reason, in our discussion of all possible models in Section 3.6, we said that the {WG}{WR} model with a chi-square of 9.24 and a p-value of 0.010 provided the "best" fit to the ex-convict transitional aid data even though adding the {GR} term resulted in a significant further reduction in the goodness-of-fit.

The dilemma is a result of our strategy of building the model on same dataset used to test the fit of the model. Since we have only one dataset we inevitably build a structural model which fits not only the structure of the dataset but also its quirks. The only way to obtain a trustworthy estimate of the departure of the data from the model is to use a different dataset to assess the fit after we have chosen a structural model. This approach is called **cross-validation**.

For more information consult Bishop, Fienberg, and Holland's (1976, Chapter 9) excellent discussion of the problems of model selection. Portions of this section are paraphrases of their material. See also Agresti (1990, Chapter 7).

3.7 How good is the fit?

You often want a single number to summarize how well a model fits the data. The traditional method is to use the likelihood ratio chi-square and that works effectively so long as the total number of cases in the table is no larger than the sample size used by national surveys, around 1500 cases. Some research, however, requires a much larger dataset: census data on national populations can run into millions of cases and many tables contain tens of thousands of cases. As we pointed out in Section 2.6, the size of the estimated chi-square is directly related to the number of cases in the table. The result is a large-sample trap; in large samples almost any interaction is significant and virtually the only model which fits the data is the saturated model. This is unacceptable even if nonsaturated models fit the data, because it results in complicated models which tend to be substantively uninterpretable, containing many effects which may be statistically significant but are substantively irrelevant.Three approaches that attempt to overcome these problems are the index of dissimilarity, an analog to PRE statistics, and, most important, Raftery's *BIC*.

The index of dissimilarity

The **index of dissimilarity** (Δ) has an appealingly simple interpretation. It is the percentage of cases which would have to be relocated to make the observed and expected counts equal. Its formula is:

$$\Delta \,=\, 100 \, \triangleright \frac{\Sigma |residual|}{2N}$$

where *N* is the total number of cases in the table and the sum is over all cells in the table. The *residual* is just the observed count minus the fitted count. SYSTAT version 5 calls this the DIFFERENCE, version 6 calls it the DEVIATE. Residuals are important in a variety of contexts and are discussed in detail in Section 3.6, above.

For the model {GW}{WR} in Figure 3.24, the index of dissimilarity is Δ = 3.948. We would have to move only about 4% of the cases in the table in order to make the expected frequencies fit the observed count. This is an excellent fit. Δ is often reported as a proportion, rather than a percentage. Just divide the percentage by 100 to find the proportion. In this example, $\Delta = .039$.

An alternative measure of fit: The PRE analog

Another alternative measure of the fit of a model is analogous to the PRE (proportional reduction in error) statistics discussed in Section 2.2. Since log-linear models are based on a goodness-of-fit statistic, we use the proportional reduction in lack of fit rather than the proportional reduction in errors. This statistic is constructed exactly like other PRE statistics. We compare our baseline model to other, more complex models. The likelihood ratio chi-square (L^2) of the baseline model gives the total amount of lack of fit that we need to remove to fit the data. When the proportion of that lack of fit accounted for by an alternative model is high, say above 90%, then the alternative model may provide a satisfactory fit even though strict statistical tests indicate a significant lack of correspondence between observed and expected values. The PRE analog is the ratio:

$$\frac{\left(L^2 \text{ of baseline model} \right) - \left(L^2 \text{ of alternative model} \right)}{\left(L^2 \text{ of baseline model} \right)}$$

This ratio yields a proportion which shows how far we reduced the lack of fit by fitting the alternative model. As an example, we apply this statistic to the ex-convict transitional aid dataset, even though the sample is small. The choice of a baseline model is crucial. The independence model is one common baseline model. Many times, however, your data or your theory suggest an alternative baseline. In our example, we use the model {WG}{R}, which says that the two independent variables have no association with REARREST\$. The alternative model that we use is {WG}{WR}, which says that there are associations between WORK\$ and GROUP\$, and WORK\$ and REARREST\$, but no association between GROUP\$ and REARREST\$. Using the likelihood ratio statistics from Figure 3.11 we find that:

$$\frac{(327.71 - 9.24)}{327.71} = 0.972$$

Thus our alternative captures over 97% of the lack of fit in the baseline model. The proportion explained is large enough to conclude that this alternative provides an acceptable fit to the data even though there is still a significant lack of fit in the table.

The likelihood ratio chi-square is not the same as the residual used to calculate the index of dissimilarity, Δ. Thus, the PRE analog is usually close to Δ, but not identical. For practical purposes, these two statistics are interchangeable. The PRE analog is sometimes called R^2 in analogy to the statistic used in regression.

Raftery's *BIC*

Since the problems with chi-square are due both to sample size and to number of interactions in the model, we want a statistic which adjusts for both. Adrian Raftery (1985, 1986) introduced such a statistic, called the Bayesian information criterion, or *BIC*.

BIC is based on the idea that as we compare models we prefer the model which is more likely to have produced the observed frequencies in the table. For example, we can compare the saturated model with an alternative model and ask, which model is more likely to have produced the observed frequencies? Notice that this approach differs from the traditional hypothesis testing approach which attempts to reject false models. Rather than accepting or rejecting models, we presume that the structure in the data are correct and we look for the model most likely to have produced that pattern. This is a Bayesian approach to model selection. In the context of Bayesian statistics the best model has the greatest "posterior odds," given the data. Odds are calculated from the ratio:

$$B = \frac{Probability \ (alternative \ model \ is \ the \ true \ model)}{Probability \ (saturated \ model \ is \ the \ true \ model)}$$

If this ratio is greater than 1, the alternative model is more likely to be true (i.e. have produced the observed frequencies) than the saturated model. When two alternative models have B greater than 1, the model with the largest B is most likely to be true. Raftery applied these ideas to log-linear models, showing that in large samples:

$$-2 \log B = L^2 - df \log N$$

where L^2 is the likelihood ratio chi-square statistic, df is the degrees of freedom for the alternative model, and N is the total number of cases in the table. From this we define *BIC* as:

$$BIC = L^2 - df \log N$$

When the alternative model is more probable, the ratio B is greater than 1, $\log B$ is positive, and $-2 \log B$ is negative so *BIC* is negative. Therefore, if *BIC* is negative we conclude that the alternative model is preferable to the saturated model. The more probable the alternative model, the larger the ratio B and the smaller $-2 \log B$. When comparing several alternative models we prefer the model with the lowest *BIC* value. Using similar reasoning, if *BIC* is positive the saturated model is more likely.

BIC provides a consistent model selection procedure in the sense that in large samples it has a high probability of choosing the correct model. It adjusts the chi-square for both the complexity of the model (measured by the degrees of freedom) and the size of the sample. All things being equal, *BIC* leads you to choose a simpler model over a more complex model. This is important because simpler models are often easier to interpret and, hence, substantively preferable. Since the size of the adjustment is proportional to sample size, in large samples complicated models (which have few degrees of freedom) tend not to be very probable. This offers us a way out of the large sample trap, where every added effect tends to significantly lower the chi-square even though it may be substantively irrelevant. Finally, *BIC* gives us a firm basis for preferring one model over another. This avoids the subjective decisions inherent in other procedures like the PRE analog and the index of dissimilarity. For our data from Figure 3.11 we can compare the model {WG}{WR} and the model {WG}{WR}{GR} with the saturated model {WGR}:

$$\text{Model \{WG\}\{WR\}} \quad BIC = 9.24 - 2 \log 935 = -4.44$$
$$\text{Model \{WG\}\{WR\}\{GR\}} \quad BIC = 0.06 - 1 \log 935 = -6.78$$

Both models fit better than the saturated model. *BIC* suggests we prefer the first model, including all two-variable interactions, over the second model which includes only the {WG}{WR} interactions.

Detergent brand preference revisited

An extended example using *BIC* in model selection will make some of these points clearer. Figure 3.26 contains a partial summary table of models considered in the detergent brand preference dataset introduced in Section 3.6.

Figure 3.26
Raftery's *BIC* in Model Selection

Model	Likelihood Ratio Chi-Square	Degrees of Freedom	*p*-value	BIC	PRE
{S}{P}{B}{T}	42.9	18	.01	-81.6	—
{S}{T}{PB}	22.4	17	.17	-95.2	47.8
{S}{PB}{BT}	18.0	16	.33	-92.7	58.0
{ST}{PB}	16.3	15	.37	-87.5	62.0
{PB}{BT}{ST}	11.9	14	.62	-84.9	72.3
{PB}{BT}{ST}{PT}	11.2	13	.60	-78.7	73.9

Several stepwise procedures suggested {PB}{BT}{ST} as the best model. The minimum *BIC* points toward a simpler model, {S}{T}{PB}. This model suggests that the {ST} and {BT} interactions contribute little to the pattern of frequencies in the table. The PRE column supports this interpretation since the {PB} interaction alone accounts for almost 50% of the lack of fit in the independence model.

To understand how *BIC* adjusts the chi-square, compare the two models {S}{PB}{BT} and {ST}{PB}. Both models explore the effect of adding a single interaction to the model with the smallest *BIC* value. The {ST}{PB} model has a smaller chi-square (16.3 compared to 18.0) and a larger PRE (62% compared to 58%), yet *BIC* prefers the other model. The reason is that the {ST} interaction adds a variable, SOFTNESS$, with 3 rather than 2 categories. This reduces the degrees of freedom by 2 rather than 1. Thus by including information about sample size and number of parameters, *BIC* takes into account the complexity of individual interaction terms. A more complex interaction must account for proportionately more of the structure of the data to be worth including in the final model. This strategy of preferring simplicity is faithful to the spirit of most research. The *p*-values suggest that all of these models fit the data relatively well.

No single statistic should be used to the exclusion of all others. *BIC* is most useful analyzing large samples where the chi-square statistic indicates that only the most complicated models fit the table. *BIC* may point to simpler models that explain the central features of the data. In small samples, *BIC* has little effect on model selection. The chi-square statistic is more appropriate when your goal is to find a single true model including all high order interactions. In any case, attention to multiple measures of the fit always improves your understanding of the models under consideration.

3.8 Cells with no cases

Sometimes a table contains zero cells. This can occur as a result of two situations: sampling zeros and structural zeros. **Sampling zeros** occur when the sample size is small so that some combinations of categories do not occur in the table. For example, some teenagers become widows but there are so few that an ordinary sample is unlikely to find any. In large, multidimensional tables it is difficult to obtain a sample large enough to avoid all the sampling zeros. When a table has more than one sampling zero, some interaction terms cannot be fitted. Unfortunately, it is often very difficult to see which terms are affected. The signal is that the fitted values for some of the cells containing zeros are negative (see Fienberg 1980, p. 140). If you see a negative fitted value, remove the offending term from the model.

If you need further information, consult Fienberg (1980, Chapter 8). Often, textbooks advise researchers to eliminate sampling zeros by collapsing categories. Fienberg cautions, "...when the categories for a given variable are truly meaningful, collapsing of categories is not necessarily a good procedure, especially given the availability of the methods just described."

Sampling zeros may cause problems for the algorithms that calculate parameter estimates. You may need to increase the default number of iterations; use the ITER option on the ESTIMATE command. You can use the DELTA option on the MODEL statement to add a small constant (Goodman (1970) recommends 1/2) to each cell in the saturated model. This can be useful to match results other researchers have obtained. In nonsaturated models adding a small constant tends to make the test statistics conservative. Agresti (1990 p. 250) recommends, "performing a sensitivity analysis. Repeat the analysis by adding constants of various sizes, in order to gauge the effect on parameter estimates and goodness-of-fit statistics." A large number of zero or very small cells causes problems for chi-square estimates (see Section 2.6 for a full discussion).

The second case occurs when some combinations of categories are logical impossibilities. These are called **structural zeros**. Examples occur in studies of medical problems, e.g., a table of gender by type of operation has structural zeros for male hysterectomies and female prostrate operations. SYSTAT will predict a positive count for the zero cells, unless you tell it otherwise. Use the ZERO command to tell SYSTAT not to include the zero cells in its estimates. Structural zeros do not cause problems for parameter estimates because once you declare them they are omitted from all calculations. An example is in Figure 3.26. These data are from a study of health problems causing concern for teenagers (Brunswick 1971). Since males do not have menstrual problems, two cells in the table are zero. Notice that SYSTAT has adjusted the degrees of freedom by subtracting two for the zero cells. Fienberg (1980, Chapter 8) also discusses structural zeros.

Figure 3.27
Teen Health Problems Dataset (ZERO01)

SEX$	AGE$	PROBLEM$	COUNT
Female	12-15	General	19
Female	12-15	Menstrul	4
Female	12-15	Nothing	71
Female	12-15	Sex,repr	9
Male	12-15	General	42
Male	12-15	Menstrul	0
Male	12-15	Nothing	57
Male	12-15	Sex,repr	4
Female	16-17	General	10
Female	16-17	Menstrul	8
Female	16-17	Nothing	31
Female	16-17	Sex,repr	7
Male	16-17	General	7
Male	16-17	Menstrul	0
Male	16-17	Nothing	20
Male	16-17	Sex,repr	2

3.9 Designing tests for specific hypotheses

The American Dream has always been that through hard work, frugal living, and talent people could become whatever they wanted. Family background and wealth were not as important as sheer drive and skill. This idea has always been controversial and even its defenders agree that racial and ethnic minorities and women have not had the same opportunities for upward mobility as white males. We can't settle the debates over the extent of upward mobility in American society, but using log-linear models we can test some hypotheses about how easily people change their social status.

Researchers in mobility use some of the most sophisticated log-linear models (e.g., Grusky and Hauser 1984). In fact, much of the development of log-linear models is due to the needs of research in mobility (for example, Goodman 1961, 1965). We will look specifically at occupational mobility, how people change occupations between two points in time. We started with a question about the extent to which family background and wealth made a difference in status. One way to look at this question is to compare father's occupation with son's first occupation. Figure 3.26 contains a cross-tab of father's occupation with son's first full-time civilian occupation in a form known as a **mobility table.**

Figure 3.28
Handling Structural Zeros: The ZERO Statement

```
LOGLIN
    USE ZERO01
    FREQ COUNT
    PRINT NONE / OBSFREQ CHISQ EXPECT
    MODEL AGE$*SEX$*PROBLEM$ = AGE$ + SEX$ + PROBLEM$
    ZERO EMPTY
    ESTIMATE
```

```
Observed Frequencies
═══════════════════════
AGE$        SEX$     |                 PROBLEM$
                     | General    Menstrul   Nothing    Sex,repr
---------+---------+------------------------------------------------
12-15       Female   |    19          4         71          9
            Male     |    42         *0         57          4
                    +
16-17       Female   |    10          8         31          7
            Male     |     7         *0         20          2
------------------+----------------------------------------------
          *  indicates structural zero cells
Pearson ChiSquare   30.5358  df   8  Probability  0.00017
    LR ChiSquare    28.2428  df   8  Probability  0.00043
    Raftery's BIC  -17.1438

Expected Values
═══════════════════
AGE$        SEX$     |                 PROBLEM$
                     | General    Menstrul   Nothing    Sex,repr
---------+---------+------------------------------------------------
12-15       Female   |   29.093      8.495     66.764      8.206
            Male     |   26.124     *7.628     59.951      7.368
                    +
16-17       Female   |   12.004      3.505     27.548      3.386
            Male     |   10.779     *3.147     24.737      3.040
------------------+----------------------------------------------
          *  indicates structural zero cells
```

At the beginning of this chapter, we promised that log-linear models could be used to test specific hypotheses about the cells in tables. The goal of this section is to show you how you can design a model to test practically any hypothesis that you can dream up about the cells in a table. Along the way, we will illustrate how you can test several common hypotheses.

Figure 3.29
1973 U. S. Mobility Table
Father's Occupation by Son's First Occupation

```
Frequencies
 FATH_OCC (rows) by SON_OCC (columns)
```

	1	2	3	4	5	Total
1	1414	521	302	643	40	2920
2	724	524	254	703	48	2253
3	798	648	856	1676	108	4086
4	756	914	771	3325	237	6003
5	409	357	441	1611	1832	4650
Total	4101	2964	2624	7958	2265	19912

```
where the categories are:

1 = Upper Nonmanual:  professionals, managers and non-retail salespersons
2 = Lower Nonmanual:  proprietors, clerical workers, retail salespersons
3 = Upper Manual:     craftspeople (skilled workers and foremen)
4 = Lower Manual:     laborers, service workers, unskilled craftspeople
5 = Farm:             farmers, farm managers and farm laborers
```

A simple design matrix

The crucial technique for testing hypotheses is a **design matrix**. It is a table containing the same number of rows and columns as the table you will analyze. The values in the cells of the design matrix indicate which rows, columns, and cells are to be compared to test the hypothesis. The term "design matrix" comes from analysis of variance, where tests of hypotheses are often the result of a designed experiment. An analysis of variance design matrix is similar to a log-linear model design matrix. Below is an example of the simplest kind of design matrix for the mobility table in Figure 3.26:

```
1  1  1  1  1
2  2  2  2  2
3  3  3  3  3
4  4  4  4  4
5  5  5  5  5
```

The matrix contains the numbers 1 through 5, arranged in rows. The actual values are not important, they are mere indicators telling SYSTAT what is to be compared. Each row in this design matrix been given a different number to indicate that each row is different from the others. Within each row the columns have same value. For example, in the first row, they are 1s. Thus, this matrix says, when the row totals are controlled, the columns do not differ. This design matrix tests the hypothesis that each row has a different row total, but, within each row, the columns have no effect on the pattern of counts in the table. This is the hypothesis that only the row variable (here FATH_OCC) has an effect. We tested a hypothesis of this kind on different data in Figure 3.29. Another simple design matrix is:

$$
\begin{array}{ccccc}
1 & 2 & 3 & 4 & 5 \\
1 & 2 & 3 & 4 & 5 \\
1 & 2 & 3 & 4 & 5 \\
1 & 2 & 3 & 4 & 5 \\
1 & 2 & 3 & 4 & 5
\end{array}
$$

In this design matrix we assigned the columns different numbers, but within each column, the rows are the same. It could be used to test the hypothesis that each column has a different column total, but, within each column, the rows have no effect on the table. You may recognize this as the hypothesis that only the column variable (here SON_OCC) has an effect. If you are familiar with analysis of variance design matrices you may recognize that each design matrix has created a set of dummy variables.

If we put these two design matrices together in the same model, we could test the hypothesis that only the rows and columns of the table have an effect on the counts—that there is no association between the two variables. This is the familiar model of independence. In a mobility table, independence is the same as saying that there is no association at all between son's occupation and father's occupation. It is a test of an extreme form of the ideal of equal opportunity.

To test this hypothesis, we read each design matrix into a SYSTAT file as a variable. Figure 3.30 creates a SYSTAT dataset and Figure 3.31 tests the hypothesis of independence for the mobility data from Figure 3.26. Notice that the design matrices above are, respectively, the FATH_OCC and SON_OCC variables read into a SYSTAT file in Figure 3.30. All the independent variables that we have seen in this chapter are, in fact, design matrices. We just called them by a different name. In SYSTAT (but not necessarily in other packages), design matrices need to be variables. For the rest of this chapter we are going to depart from our usual practice of not showing data input. In order for you to construct your own design matrices, you need to know what they look like in their raw form. The easiest way to show you this is to show small programs that read the design matrices into SYSTAT files. You can input your design matrices any way you like (in the SYSTAT Editor, in a spreadsheet, etc.).

Figure 3.30
Data Input for U. S. Mobility Data

```
basic
save mobil01
 input fath_occ son_occ count
 run
 1 1 1414
 1 2 521
 1 3 302
 1 4 643
 1 5 40
 2 1 724
 2 2 524
 2 3 254
 2 4 703
 2 5 48
 3 1 798
 3 2 648
 3 3 856
 3 4 1676
 3 5 108
 4 1 756
 4 2 914
 4 3 771
 4 4 3325
 4 5 237
 5 1 409
 5 2 357
 5 3 441
 5 4 1611
 5 5 1832
 ~
```

Since the independence model does not fit the data, we conclude that there are associations in the table. We asked SYSTAT to print a table of residuals because the residuals show patterns which we use to generate design matrices that test additional hypotheses about mobility.

There are three important things to remember about design matrices. First, a design matrix is a duplicate of the table with integers used to indicate what groups of cells you want to compare. The actual numbers are irrelevant, but positive integers beginning with 1 are customary. Second, the hypothesis tested by a design matrix is that cells with the same integer are the same (i.e. have the same count), while cells with different numbers are different. Third, when there are several design matrices in the model (except in classroom exercises, there always are), the second point is modified to be *controlling for the other terms in the model*, cells with the same number are the same, while cells with different numbers are different.

Figure 3.31
Test of Independence Model

```
LOGLIN
    USE MOBIL01
    FREQ COUNT
    PRINT NONE / OBSFREQ CHISQ STAND
    MODEL FATH_OCC*SON_OCC = FATH_OCC + SON_OCC
    ESTIMATE
```

The SYSTAT output is:

```
Observed Frequencies
═══════════════════════════════════════════════════════════════════════
FATH_OCC |                         SON_OCC
         | 1           2           3           4           5
---------+-------------------------------------------------------------
1        |     1414         521         302         643          40
2        |      724         524         254         703          48
3        |      798         648         856        1676         108
4        |      756         914         771        3325         237
5        |      409         357         441        1611        1832
---------+-------------------------------------------------------------
Pearson ChiSquare7166.7709  df  16  Probability  0.00000
     LR ChiSquare6170.1301  df  16  Probability  0.00000
     Raftery's BIC6011.7449

Standardized Deviates = (Obs-Exp)/sqrt(Exp)
═══════════════════════════════════════════════════════════════════════
FATH_OCC |                         SON_OCC
         | 1           2           3           4           5
---------+-------------------------------------------------------------
1        |   33.136       4.141      -4.221     -15.339     -16.030
2        |   12.069      10.300      -2.490      -6.579     -13.010
3        |   -1.501       1.613      13.685       1.064     -16.549
4        |  -13.661       0.683      -0.714      18.902     -17.062
5        |  -17.730     -12.740      -6.939      -5.739      56.658
---------+-------------------------------------------------------------
```

Design matrices which indicate rows and columns are usually not interesting because every table already has variables indicating rows and columns. We began this way because rows and columns are easy categories to understand; the next hypotheses has more complex categories. In hierarchical fashion we will add new terms to our model.

Testing a specific hypothesis: uniform inheritance

Looking at the residuals in Figure 3.31, we notice that the three largest residuals are all on the main diagonal and they are all positive. The expected counts underestimate the number of cases that we observed. The diagonal cells contain sons who remained in the same occupational categories as their fathers who were immobile. Thus, the residuals suggest that there are more immobile sons than the independence model predicts.

An alternative model is that there are two groups of people, called movers and stayers. The stayers remain in the same occupational category as their fathers, so they show up on the main diagonal. For now we assume that the proportion of stayers is the same in all categories. This corresponds to assuming that the processes of socialization are equally effective for all occupational groups. An alternate hypothesis that accounts for uniform inheritance is that barriers between classes are all the same size. The movers are sons whose occupational category is different from their fathers; they are the cases off the diagonal. For now we assume that all movers change categories at random. This corresponds to assuming that, net of marginal effects, the movers are equally distributed to all other categories.

Because we assumed that the proportion of stayers is uniform in all categories, we call this model the *uniform inheritance* model. The design matrix for the model is input into SYSTAT in Figure 3.32. Notice how that matrix embodies our assumptions about movers and stayers. Notice also the use of the backslash (\) to read more than one case per line with the INPUT command. The MERGE command adds the new variable (UNIFORM) to the dataset.

Figure 3.32
Design Matrix for Uniform Inheritance

```
BASIC
   NEW
   SAVE TEMP1
   INPUT UNIFORM \
   RUN
   2  1  1  1  1
   1  2  1  1  1
   1  1  2  1  1
   1  1  1  2  1
   1  1  1  1  2
   ~
SAVE MOBIL02
MERGE TEMP1 MOBIL01
```

The model of uniform inheritance is fit in Figure 3.33. Several things in the output may look strange and you need to know why they are there. First, the table specified on the left of the equals sign in the MODEL statement must include every variable used in the model, including UNIFORM, and this gives us $2 * 15 * 5 = 50$ cells but only $5 * 5 = 25$ cells are filled, the rest are zero. This accounts for the zero cells in the observed frequencies and in the residuals table. Ignore the zero cells; they mean nothing. Second, we only want to model the cells which actually occur in the mobility table. So we use the ZERO EMPTY command to tell SYSTAT not to fit the model to the zero cells (Version 5 use the ZERO option on the MODEL command). For more information on zero cells see Section 3.8 on page 116. The chi-square results show that the model is not significant, but the conditional goodness-of-fit test yields a chi-square value of $6170.13 - 2567.66 = 3602.47$ on $16 - 15 = 1$ degree of freedom, indicating that the additional term for uniform inheritance is spectacularly significant. BIC is a huge positive number, 2419.17, indicating that the saturated model is much better than the model we fit. Clearly we need to add additional structure to our model to fit the pattern of counts.

Figure 3.33
Uniform Inheritance Model

```
LOGLIN
    USE MOBIL02
    FREQ COUNT
    PRINT NONE / OBSFREQ CHISQ STAND
    MODEL UNIFORM*FATH_OCC*SON_OCC = FATH_OCC + SON_OCC + UNIFORM
    ZERO EMPTY
    ESTIMATE
```

Observed Frequencies

UNIFORM	FATH_OCC	SON_OCC 1	2	3	4
1	1	*0	521	302	643
	2	724	*0	254	703
	3	798	648	*0	1676
	4	756	914	771	*0
	5	409	357	441	1611
2	1	1414	*0	*0	*0
	2	*0	524	*0	*0
	3	*0	*0	856	*0
	4	*0	*0	*0	3325
	5	*0	*0	*0	*0

UNIFORM	FATH_OCC	SON_OCC 5
1	1	40
	2	48
	3	108
	4	237
	5	*0
2	1	*0
	2	*0
	3	*0
	4	*0
	5	1832

 * indicates structural zero cells

```
Pearson ChiSquare2460.7937   df  15  Probability  0.00000
    LR ChiSquare2567.6581    df  15  Probability  0.00000
    Raftery's BIC2419.1719

Standardized Deviates = (Obs-Exp)/sqrt(Exp)
=========================================================
UNIFORM    FATH_OCC |                    SON_OCC
                    | 1           2          3          4
---------+----------+------------------------------------------------
1          1        |   *-21.827      8.747      1.629     -5.941
           2        |    16.625    *-17.157      1.764      1.205
           3        |     1.723       3.676   *-20.816     11.066
           4        |    -2.414      11.975     13.500   *-37.513
           5        |   -15.901     -11.740     -2.992      2.811

                    +
2          1        |     4.641    *-30.559   *-26.859   *-46.164
           2        |   *-32.150     -8.934   *-24.425   *-41.980
           3        |   *-44.380   *-38.361     -8.328   *-57.950
           4        |   *-46.532   *-40.221   *-35.351     -6.036
           5        |   *-48.075   *-41.554   *-36.523   *-62.774
---------+----------+------------------------------------------------
UNIFORM    FATH_OCC | SON_OCC
                    | 5
---------+----------+--------------
1          1        |   -12.404
           2        |   -10.191
           3        |   -13.193
           4        |    -7.866
           5        |   *-20.479

                    +
2          1        |   *-24.393
           2        |   *-22.183
           3        |   *-30.621
           4        |   *-32.106
           5        |    22.059
---------+----------+--------------
         *  indicates structural zero cells
```

Nesting models: a one-step diagonals model

Although the residuals on the main diagonal continue to be large, let's turn our attention to the off-diagonal residuals. There we see a pattern of positive residuals (indicating underestimates) close to the diagonal and negative values (overestimates) in cells farther away. This suggests that long jumps in status, say from lower manual (category 4) to upper nonmanual (1) or vice versa, are less frequent than are short jumps, for example from lower manual (4) to upper manual (3). One test of this observation is the design matrix in Figure 3.34, called a **one-step diagonals** model. This model claims that moving one step is much easier than moving two or more steps in status. It retains the assumption that moving one step is the same for all occupational groups. Further it assumes that one step up in status is the same as one step down.

The output from fitting the one-step model is in Figure 3.35. The conditional goodness-of-fit test shows that $2567.66 - 1955.96 = 611.70$ on $15 - 14 = 1$ degrees of freedom: the additional effect of moving one step is highly significant. *BIC* is still very large, over 1800, indicating that we're not doing very well and there is much more structure in the residuals.

Figure 3.34
Design Matrix for One-Step Diagonals Model

```
BASIC
   NEW
   SAVE  TEMP2
   INPUT ONE_STEP \
   RUN
   3   2   1   1   1
   2   3   2   1   1
   1   2   3   2   1
   1   1   2   3   2
   1   1   1   2   3
   ~
   SAVE MOBIL03
   MERGE MOBIL02 TEMP2
```

Notice something very important about these last two models: they are *hierarchical* or nested. The design matrix for the one-step diagonals model includes all the effects in the uniform inheritance model plus one, the effect for moving one step off the main diagonal. You need to be careful about this because it is easy to construct a design matrix which breaks the hierarchy, and then the conditional goodness-of-fit tests are not accurate. To avoid this problem, remember that once you have established a category in the design matrix you can subdivide that category as often as you like and continue to use the conditional tests. For example, in moving from the uniform inheritance model to the one-step diagonals model, we subdivided the off-diagonal category into two categories. What you cannot do is introduce a new category which includes cells from more than one higher-level category. As long as you continue to subdivide existing categories the hierarchy is maintained and the conditional goodness-of-fit tests are an accurate measure of how well each additional category fits the data.

Figure 3.35
Output from One-Step Diagonals Model

```
LOGLIN
    USE MOBIL03
    FREQ COUNT
    PRINT NONE / CHISQ STAND
    MODEL ONE_STEP*FATH_OCC*SON_OCC = FATH_OCC + SON_OCC + ONE_STEP
    ZERO EMPTY
    ESTIMATE
```

```
Pearson ChiSquare1905.6844   df  14   Probability  0.00000
     LR ChiSquare1955.9659   df  14   Probability  0.00000
     Raftery's BIC1817.3788

Standardized Deviates = (Obs-Exp)/sqrt(Exp)
===========================================================================
ONE_STEP  FATH_OCC |                          SON_OCC
                   | 1          2          3          4
---------+---------+-------------------------------------------------------
1         1        |   *-20.671    *-17.084     5.201      0.969
          2        |   *-18.435    *-15.236   *-13.352     9.500
          3        |     7.378    *-20.496    *-17.961    *-29.846
          4        |     0.361     17.913    *-19.783    *-32.874
          5        |   -13.080     -7.430      1.777     *-33.450
                   +
2         1        |   *-26.368      2.116    *-19.097    *-31.733
          2        |     7.271    *-19.435     -2.118     *-28.301
          3        |   *-31.634     -1.358    *-22.911      5.952
          4        |   *-34.844    *-28.796     5.317     *-41.933
          5        |   *-35.455    *-29.302   *-25.678     -4.914
                   +
3         1        |    -0.008    *-31.080    *-27.237    *-45.259
          2        |   *-33.539     -8.814    *-24.291    *-40.364
          3        |   *-45.118    *-37.287     -6.480    *-54.298
          4        |   *-49.695    *-41.070    *-35.991     -4.210
          5        |   *-50.567    *-41.791    *-36.623    *-60.856
-------------------+-------------------------------------------------------
ONE_STEP  FATH_OCC | SON_OCC
                   | 5
---------+---------+-------------
1         1        |   -10.786
          2        |    -8.295
          3        |    -9.873
          4        |   *-18.109
          5        |   *-18.427
                   +
2         1        |   *-17.481
          2        |   *-15.590
          3        |   *-20.973
          4        |   -12.841
          5        |   *-23.506
                   +
3         1        |   *-24.932
          2        |   *-22.235
          3        |   *-29.912
          4        |   *-32.946
          5        |    21.123
-------------------+-------------
       *   indicates structural zero cells
```

Fitting a single cell: farmers

The largest residual in the last model is farmers on the main diagonal (category 5). The positive residual suggests that farmers are not nearly as mobile as other groups. We can model this fact by fitting a category for farmer immobility. Notice that this continues our hierarchical model by subdividing the diagonal (coded as 3s in the design matrix from Figure 3.34) into two groups (coded as 3 and 4 in the next design matrix). We call this the *one-step diagonals plus farm* model. Notice also that this illustrates how log-linear techniques can model a single cell in a table. The design matrix is input in Figure 3.36 and the output is in Figure 3.37.

Figure 3.36
One-Step Diagonals Plus Farm Design Matrix

```
BASIC
    NEW
    SAVE TEMP3
    INPUT FARM \
    RUN
    3 2 1 1 1
    2 3 2 1 1
    1 2 3 2 1
    1 1 2 3 2
    1 1 1 2 4
    ~
    NEW
    SAVE MOBIL04
    MERGE MOBIL03 TEMP3
```

Figure 3.37
Output from One-Step Plus Farm Model

```
LOGLIN
    USE MOBIL04
    FREQ COUNT
    MODEL FARM*FATH_OCC*SON_OCC = FATH_OCC + SON_OCC + FARM
    ZERO EMPTY
    ESTIMATE
    RUN
```

```
Pearson ChiSquare 465.8821  df  13  Probability  0.00000
     LR ChiSquare 463.0335  df  13  Probability  0.00000
     Raftery's BIC 334.3455
```

Standardized Deviates = (Obs-Exp)/sqrt(Exp)

FARM	FATH_OCC	SON_OCC 1	2	3	4
1	1	*-22.797	*-18.674	1.406	-5.331
	2	*-19.906	*-16.305	*-14.573	3.997
	3	3.983	*-21.566	*-19.274	*-32.524
	4	-6.242	11.012	*-22.543	*-38.041
	5	-8.067	-2.520	6.382	*-30.458
2	1	*-28.759	-1.442	*-21.054	*-35.528
	2	3.720	*-20.570	-4.568	*-31.022
	3	*-33.213	-3.388	*-24.315	-0.183
	4	*-38.846	*-31.821	-1.329	*-47.990
	5	*-31.104	*-25.478	*-22.771	3.502
3	1	5.518	*-28.625	*-25.583	*-43.170
	2	*-30.513	-4.029	*-22.338	*-37.694
	3	*-40.357	*-33.058	-0.572	*-49.856
	4	*-47.202	*-38.665	*-34.556	-1.290
	5	*-37.794	*-30.958	*-27.668	*-46.689
4	1	*-106.203	*-86.995	*-77.750	*-131.199
	2	*-92.732	*-75.961	*-67.888	*-114.558
	3	*-122.650	*-100.468	*-89.791	*-151.518
	4	*-143.452	*-117.507	*-105.020	*-177.216
	5	*-114.859	*-94.086	*-84.087	*-141.893

FARM	FATH_OCC	SON_OCC 5
1	1	-3.787
	2	-0.947
	3	.197
	4	*-11.475
	5	*-9.188
2	1	*-10.717
	2	*-9.358
	3	*-12.377
	4	1.896
	5	*-11.591
3	1	*-13.022
	2	*-11.370
	3	*-15.039
	4	*-17.590
	5	*-14.084
4	1	*-39.576
	2	*-34.556
	3	*-45.705
	4	*-53.457
	5	0.000

```
     *  indicates structural zero cells
```

The conditional test of $1955.96 - 463.03 = 1492.93$ on 1 degree of freedom shows that fitting this single cell improves the fit remarkably. *BIC* is still positive, indicating that the saturated model is preferable and there is a great deal more structure here that we can fit. Two unusual items in this model deserve comment. First, as you begin to fit more zero cells you may need to increase the number of iterations. Second, when you fit a single cell, you fit it exactly. This means that the residual is zero. The table for FARM = 4 contains a zero in cell (5,5) because the farm cell has a zero residual.

Even though much more can be said about these data we are going stop fitting models. For further information on models for these data, consult the models fit by Featherman and Hauser (1978) and Hout (1983).

The point of this section was to illustrate how to design tests of virtually any hypothesis. A test identical to the special chi-square tests discussed in Chapter 2, the McNemar symmetry chi-square or Cohen's kappa, is easy to design. Log-linear models are flexible; design matrices that test for complex forms of symmetry or agreement are easy to develop. Studying how we fit the models in this Section should give you the information that you need to design tests for hypotheses relevant to your own data.

3.10 Concluding comments

Log-linear models are a flexible tool for modeling categorical data.They have been used in a broad variety of circumstances. In this chapter we have used log-linear models to examine the results of a public policy experiment, consumer brand preferences, health concerns of teenagers, and intergenerational mobility. Other applications include Markov models (Brent & Sykes 1979), interaction patterns of dyads (Larntz & Weisberg 1976), and causal analysis of surveys (Goodman 1979).

Log-linear models have two weaknesses. Almost any model, not just log-linear models, gives misleading results if you omit important variables from the model. In practical research, you often encounter situations of significant associations becoming insignificant or insignificant associations becoming significant when the effects of a third variable are controlled. Everitt (1977, p. 34-36) has a good discussion of the bias that can occur if relevant variables are not controlled.

The second weakness is that they have no clear dependent variable. This can be partially overcome by the technique, introduced in Section 3.6 under "Use of substantive theory," of constructing a baseline model with no interactions between the independent variables and the dependent variable (i.e. {GW}{R} for the ex-convict transitional aid dataset). However, if you have a strong dependent variable, consider using an alternative approach which explicitly specifies a dependent variable: logit models. For a comparison of log-linear and logit models, see Agresti (1990).

A primary goal of this chapter was to suggest how the log-linear capabilities of SYS-TAT can be used to fit a variety of data using a wide range of models. Further, the chapter shows how models can be selected and evaluated and how the statistical output of SYSTAT can be translated into substantively meaningful interpretations. We hope that presenting these methods enables researchers to perform more informative and useful statistical analyses.

Notes

The data from the transitional aid research project used in this chapter are from Zeisel (1982a, p. 385). The project is more complex than presented here, including four experimental conditions, two control groups, and a large number of background variables. The data in this chapter are from Texas, but the Georgia data are not substantively different and the results for all four experimental groups are also substantively identical. The full project is documented in Rossi, Berk, and Lenihan (1980) and Berk, Lenihan, and Rossi (1980). Zeisel disagrees with the conclusions of the experimenters. His comments (1982a), the response of Rossi, Berk, and Lenihan (1982), and Zeisel's conclusions (1982b) are well worth reading for the light they shed on the difference between experimental and nonexperimental research.

Comparing SYSTAT to texts about log-linear models

Actually, the absence of the constant term in SYSTAT's model specification means that SYSTAT cannot fit the model where equal proportions would be found in each cell. Since this model is rarely of interest to researchers, its omission has little practical impact.

Choosing a model

The detergent brand preference data are also analyzed by Fienberg (1980).

How good is the fit?

Parts of this discussion draw on an unpublished paper on *BIC* by Eric D. Nordmoe.

Cells with no cases

The teen health problems dataset is also analyzed by Grizzle and Williams (1972), and Fienberg (1980).

Further reading

None of the texts on log-linear models are both complete and accessible. Agresti (1990) is complete, clear, and often summarizes the literature to offer practical advice to the researcher. Unfortunately, it may be too terse for many readers. Despite this it is indispensable reading for anyone doing serious work with log-linear models. The standard reference is Bishop, Fienberg, and Holland (1975) but large parts of it are in-accessible to nonmathematicians. Considerably less complete but more accessible are Fienberg (1980), or Knoke and Burke (1980). Unfortunately neither book presents the material as systematically as it could, so each is sometimes confusing.

References

Agresti, A. (1984). *Analysis of Ordinal Categorical Data.* New York: John Wiley & Sons.

Agresti, A. (1990). *Categorical Data Analysis.* New York: John Wiley & Sons.

Bishop, Y. M. M., Fienberg, S. E. & Holland, P. W. (1975). *Discrete multivariate analysis.* Cambridge, MA: MIT Press.

Brent, E. E. & Sykes, R. E. (1979). A mathematical model of symbolic interaction between police and suspects. *Behavioral Science, 24,* 388-402.

Brunswick, A. F. (1971). Adolescent health, sex and fertility, *American Journal of Public Health, 61,* 711-720.

Cochran, W. G. (1954). Some methods of strengthening the common chi-square tests. *Biometrics, 10,* 417-451.

Everitt, B. S. (1977). *The Analysis of Contingency Tables.* London: Chapman and Hall.

Featherman, D. L. & Hauser, R. M. (1978). *Opportunity and Change*. New York: Academic Press.

Fienberg, S. E. (1980). *The Analysis of Cross-classified Categorical Data* (2nd ed.). Cambridge, MA: MIT Press.

Goodman, L. A. (1961). Statistical methods for the mover-stayer model. *Journal of the American Statistical Association, 56*, 841-868.

Goodman, L. A. (1965). On the statistical analysis of mobility tables. *American Journal of Sociology, 70*, 564-585.

Goodman, L. A. (1970). The multivariate analysis of qualitative data: Interactions among multiple classifications. *Journal of the American Statistical Association, 65*, 226-256.

Goodman, L. A. (1971). The analysis of multidimensional contingency tables: Stepwise procedures and direct estimation methods for building models for multiple classifications. *Technometrics, 13*, 33-61.

Goodman, L. A. (1979). A brief guide to the causal analysis of data from surveys. *American Journal of Sociology, 84*, 1078-1095.

Goodman, L. A. (1981). Criteria for determining whether certain categories in a cross-classification table should be combined, with special reference to occupational categories in an occupational mobility table. *American Journal of Sociology, 87*, 612-650.

Grizzle, J. E. & Williams, O. (1972). Log-linear models and tests of independence for contingency tables. *Biometrics, 28*, 137-156.

Grusky, D. B. & Hauser, R. M. 1984. Comparative social mobility revisited: Models of convergence and divergence in 16 countries. *American Sociological Review, 49*, 19-38.

Haberman, S. J. (1978). *Analysis of Qualitative Data*. New York: Academic Press.

Hout, M. (1983). *Mobility Tables*. Sage University Paper series on Quantitative Applications in the Social Sciences, 07-031. Beverly Hills and London: Sage Publications.

Knoke, D. & Burke, P. J. (1980). *Log-Linear Models*. Sage University Paper series on Quantitative Applications in the Social Sciences. Beverly Hills and London: Sage Publications.

Larntz, K. & Weisberg, S. (1976). Multiplicative models for dyad formation. *Journal of the American Statistical Association, 71*, 455-461.

Raftery, A. E. (1986). A note on Bayes factors for log-linear contingency table models with vague prior information. *Journal of the Royal Statistical Society, Series B, 48,* 249-250.

Raftery, A. E. (1986). Choosing models for cross-classifications. *American Sociological Review, 56,* 145-6.

Reynolds, H. T. (1977). *The Analysis of Cross-classifications.* New York: Free Press.

Ries, P. N. & Smith, H. (1963). The use of chi-square for preference testing in multidimensional problems. *Chemical Engineering Progress, 59,* 39-43.

Rossi, P. H., Berk, R. A., & Lenihan, K. J. (1980). *Money, Work and Crime: Experimental Evidence.* New York: Academic Press.

Rossi, P. H., Berk, R. A., & Lenihan, K. J. (1982). Saying it wrong with figures: A comment on Zeisel. *American Journal of Sociology, 88,* 390-393.

Zeisel, H. (1982a). Disagreement over the evaluation of a controlled experiment. *American Journal of Sociology, 88,* 378-389.

Zeisel, H. (1982b). Hans Zeisel concludes the debate. *American Journal of Sociology, 88,* 394-396.

Part 2

Predicting Continuous Variables from Continuous Variables

4

Simple Linear Relationships

The United States is a nation of immigrants. Much of the history of American politics, social life, and the economy can be told in terms of the distinctive roles played by different immigrant groups at different times. Significant parts of this story (blacks are an important exception) describe how different groups became acculturated to life in the United States, were accepted by older immigrants, and gradually moved toward full participation in American society and politics. During the past 20 years two new ethnic groups have migrated to the United States in unprecedented numbers: Hispanics and Asians. Do the processes of acculturation and assimilation work for them like they did for the Irish or Germans?

Figure 4.2 shows an answer to this question for Hispanics. A sensitive indicator of successful acceptance is the extent to which the new immigrants live in neighborhoods alongside older established groups. We measure this by an index of the extent to which Hispanics live in integrated neighborhoods with non-Hispanic whites, HOUSINT. One measure of acculturation is the proportion of Hispanics who report being able to speak English well, SPEAKENG. For a random sample of 30 large metropolitan areas, we have plotted HOUSINT against SPEAKENG. This data in the HOUSE1 data file, shown in Figure 4.1, includes the following variables:

CITY$ Name of central city in metro area

HOUSINT   Index of Hispanic housing integration

SPEAKENG   Proportion of Hispanics able to speak English well

Figure 4.1
Housing Integration Data (HOUSE1)

CITY$	HOUSINT	SPEAKENG
Anaheim	.610	.714
Atlanta	.736	.907
Boston	.653	.755
Buffalo	.751	.866
Chicago	.499	.676
Cincinnati	.799	.973
Dallas-FortW	.619	.779
Dayton	.837	.971
Denver-Bould	.649	.929
El Paso	.229	.707
Fresno	.469	.759
Gary-Hammond	.538	.818
Greensboro	.765	.954
Indianapolis	.824	.950
Los Angeles	.347	.657
Memphis	.524	.980
Miami	.341	.567
Mpls-St.Paul	.870	.944
New Orleans	.708	.885
New York	.330	.690
Newark	.481	.647
Oklahoma C.	.810	.893
Paterson	.368	.576
Philadelphia	.500	.771
Sacramento	.691	.868
St. Louis	.804	.958
San Antonio	.276	.837
San Francisc	.582	.838
San Jose	.547	.857
WashingtonDC	.705	.835

These data indicate a pattern: the higher the proportion of Hispanics who speak English well, the more likely they are to live near whites. The level of acculturation seems to influence the acceptance of Hispanic immigrants. This is one answer to the questions we asked above.

Figure 4.2
Housing Integration Scatterplot

```
USE HOUSE1
PLOT HOUSINT * SPEAKENG / SYMBOL=1 SIZE=1.5
```

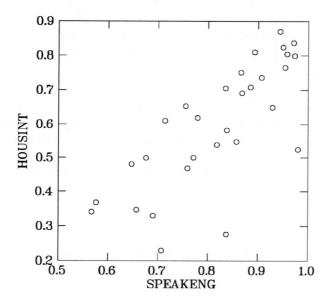

If a scatterplot shows a relationship between the variables, we often want to summarize it algebraically. One of the most convenient summaries is a straight line. In the remainder of this chapter, we use SYSTAT to find a line summarizing the relationship between SPEAKENG and HOUSINT. In the process, we discuss the statistics printed by SYSTAT and how to use them. Finally, we show you how to tell if the line is a good summary.

4.1 Summarizing linear relationships

Let's try to use a straight line to summarize the data in the scatterplot in Figure 4.2. If the symbols x and y represent variables, a straight line has a simple form which you may remember from high school algebra:

$$y = mx + b$$

where:

$$
\begin{aligned}
y &= \text{variable on the vertical axis} \\
x &= \text{variable on the horizontal axis} \\
b &= \text{intercept of the line with the vertical axis when } x = 0. \\
m &= \text{slope of the line (change in } y \text{ units / change in } x \text{ units)}
\end{aligned}
$$

The intercept (b) is the value of y when $x = 0$. It is sometimes called the y-intercept because it is the place where the line crosses (or intercepts) the y-axis. The slope (m) is the change in y for every one-unit change in x. It is sometimes described as rise over run.

The process of calculating the equation of a line for sample data is called fitting a line. Figure 4.3 shows a summary line superimposed on the scatterplot of the housing integration dataset. This line is called the fitted line or the regression line.

The statistical way to represent a regression line is slightly different from the algebraic form:

$$
y = \beta_0 + \beta_1 x
$$

The only change here is that b is replaced by β_0 and m is replaced by β_1.

If all possible pairs of points (y_i, x_i) do not fall on a straight line relating y to x, then we need to *estimate* the values of y from the values of x using a straight line. To denote that we are estimating, we change our notation and substitute b's for the β's:

$$
\hat{y} = b_0 + b_1 x
$$

where:

- $\hat{y}$ is called the **predicted variable** (or "y hat"). It will not always have the same values as the observed values of y for each x in the data.

- b_0 is called the **constant**. It is identical to the y-intercept. In our example it is a negative value: -0.345.

- b_1 is the **coefficient** for x. It is the slope: the average number of units that y changes for every one-unit change in x. In our example, every one percent increase in the proportion of Hispanics who speak English well results in an increase of 1.149 in the index of housing integration.

- The variables, x and y, have a particular relationship in the equation. We think of housing integration as being dependent on the proportion of Hispanics who speak

English in the sense that if the level of English-speaking Hispanics were higher or lower then the amount of housing integration would also be higher or lower. According to this theory, additional English-speaking is not caused by housing integration and is therefore independent of it. Thus, we call SPEAKENG (x) the **independent variable**, and housing integration (y) is the **dependent variable**. In plots, the convention is to place the independent variable (x) on the horizontal axis and the dependent variable (y) on the vertical axis.

Figure 4.3
Housing Integration Data with Regression Line

```
USE HOUSE1
PLOT HOUSINT * SPEAKENG / SYMBOL=1 SIZE=1.5 SMOOTH=LINEAR SHORT
```

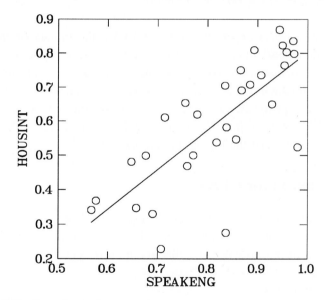

The equation of the line above is:

$$\hat{y} = -0.346 + 1.149x$$

We can rewrite the equation of the line drawn for the Hispanic integration data in SYS-TAT form:

HOUSINT = –0.346 + 1.149 * SPEAKENG

Many times in statistics the same thing has different names. Other names for the independent variable are exogenous variable, predictor variable, explanatory variable, treatment variable or, simply, the carrier. The dependent variable is sometimes called the response variable, endogenous variable, or criterion variable.

4.2 Choosing a regression line

We obtained the equation of the regression line in Figure 4.3 from SYSTAT's REGRESS module with the following commands:

```
REGRESS
   USE HOUSE1
   MODEL HOUSINT = CONSTANT + SPEAKENG
   ESTIMATE
```

The MODEL command is crucial. It tells SYSTAT the names of the independent (SPEAKENG) and dependent (HOUSINT) variables for which you want to calculate a regression line. The format of the MODEL command is similar to the equation of a line: dependent variable on the left side of the equals sign, independent variable and constant on the right side. Except for the lack of a coefficient for the independent variable, it is identical to the equation of a line. The ESTIMATE command tells SYSTAT to calculate and print the equation of the line and associated statistics.

SYSTAT's equation for a line

The resulting output is in Figure 4.4. There is a great deal of important information in the output, but for now we will highlight only those parts of the output which are relevant to the equation of the line. We will discuss the rest later.

Figure 4.4
Housing Integration Regression Coefficient Estimates

```
REGRESS
    USE HOUSE1
    MODEL HOUSINT = CONSTANT + SPEAKENG
    ESTIMATE
```

Dep Var: HOUSINT N: 30 Multiple R: 0.764 Squared multiple R: 0.584

Adjusted squared multiple R: 0.569   Standard error of estimate: 0.120

Effect	Coefficient	Std Error	Std Coef	Tolerance	t	P(2 Tail)
CONSTANT	-0.346	0.152	0.0	.	2.277	0.031
SPEAKENG	1.149	0.183	0.764	1.000	6.267	0.000

Analysis of Variance

Source	Sum-of-Squares	DF	Mean-Square	F-Ratio	P
Regression	0.568	1	0.568	39.271	0.000
Residual	0.405	28	0.014		

In the first line you see:

- **Dep Var**. This is the name of the dependent variable, HOUSINT.
- **N**. The number of cases used to estimate the regression line, in this instance, 30 cases.

The third, fourth, and fifth lines of output contain the table of statistics for the variables, one line for each variable in the equation. Here notice the first two columns and the fourth column:

- **Effect.** The column labeled "Effect" contains the names of the two independent variables in our model, CONSTANT and SPEAKENG.
- **Coefficient**. The regression coefficients are estimates of the amount of increase or decrease in the dependent variable for a one-unit change in the independent variable. In the Hispanic integration data, every additional one percent of Hispanics who speak English well results in an increase of 1.149 in the index of housing integration. The coefficient for the constant is the y-intercept: the point at which the regression line crosses the y-axis when the values of x equal zero. Here the constant is –0.346.
- **Std. Coeff.** Regression coefficients provide a clear interpretation of the relationship between two variables when the units of measurement (called the **metric**) are unambiguous. However, they may be difficult to interpret when the metric of

the variables is not clear. Many variables, particularly in the social sciences, have no natural or agreed-on unit of measure. Examples include such variables as industrialization, socioeconomic status, alienation, attraction, or religiosity. Furthermore, when variables are measured in widely varying units, the comparative importance of the variables is difficult to assess. An example is a regression model which included as independent variables number of children (with a range of from 0 to, say, 12 children) and yearly household income (with a range of $0 to, say, $500,000).

The **standardized regression coefficient** provides a way to retain the original metric but still be able to compare variables on a common scale. It is calculated by:

$$\tilde{b} = b\frac{s_x}{s_y},$$

where s_x is the standard deviation of the independent variable and s_y is the standard deviation of the dependent variable.

Multiplying by the ratio of standard deviations changes the metric so that a standardized coefficient is measured in units of standard deviations. Interpret a standardized coefficient as the number of standard deviations that the dependent variable changes when an independent variable changes by one standard deviation. Thus, in the housing integration data, every time SPEAKENG changes by one standard deviation, the index of Hispanics living in integrated neighborhoods with whites changes by 0.764 standard deviations.

Ordinary regression coefficients are sometimes called *un*standardized or **raw coefficients** when they need to be distinguished from standardized coefficients. Standardized coefficients are also called beta coefficients or **beta weights** (an unfortunate confusion of terminology, since we usually use Greek to refer to population parameters in statistics).   Standardized coefficients play an important role in path analysis and are discussed in more detail in Section 7.2.

The name, standardized coefficient, comes from the fact that this coefficient is the same as the ordinary regression coefficient which would be calculated if a variable had been converted to a standardized variable. (You may want to be reminded that a **standardized variable** is constructed by calculating the mean and standard deviation of a variable and then, for each case, subtracting the mean and dividing by the standard deviation. The new variable has a mean of zero and a standard deviation of one. This handles the problems of unclear or varying metrics, but at the cost of losing any information contained in the original scale. Another name for standardized variables is *Z* scores.) You should be familiar with both the standardized and unstandardized approaches to writing up the results of regression models since both are widespread.

How did SYSTAT find this line?

There are many ways to find a line that summarizes the relation between two variables. What makes the line that SYSTAT estimated a good choice? If we plot the data and the summary (like Figure 4.3), a good summary line is one that is as close as possible to the points on the plot. But this poses a dilemma: moving the line closer to some points usually increases its distance from others. One way to resolve this dilemma is to calculate the overall distance of the line from all points and then fit the line in such a way that the overall distance is as small as possible. We calculate the distance from the line to each point by measuring the vertical distance between each point and the line (see Figure 4.5). The vertical distances are called residuals.

The most common measure of the overall distance to the line is obtained by squaring the residuals (this makes them all positive) and finding the sum. The regression line that makes the sum of the squared residuals as small as possible is called the least squares line. This is the line that SYSTAT estimated in Figure 4.4.

The least squares method has valuable advantages. First, it is a very general method that can fit complicated linear and curved relationships to both continuous and categorical data. Second, the statistical properties of the least squares line are optimal for many types of models and data. Third, the mathematics of least squares yield relatively simple formulas which make the slope and constant easy to compute.

least squares also has weaknesses. First, the least squares line is highly sensitive to outliers, that is, wild values that are much larger or smaller than all others. This is one reason why this book devotes so much attention to plots of the data: to look for outliers that distort the results. Second, least squares cannot estimate coefficients accurately when the model has several independent variables and they are correlated. Both this problem, called collinearity (or multicollinearity), and the problem of outliers are discussed in Section 6.1.

Sometimes you do not need to do any calculations to find a line. For many purposes, you can choose a line simply by looking at a scatterplot like Figure 4.2 and drawing the line that seems to pass through the middle of the points. Particularly for preliminary purposes, this may be all you need. This method is used so often that it has a name, the black thread method (see Mosteller et al. 1985).

Figure 4.5
Data, Regression Line, and Residuals

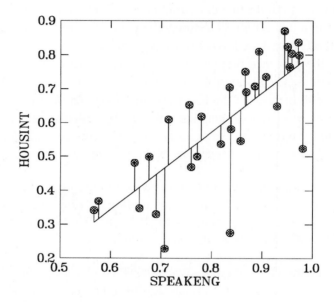

4.3 Measuring how well the line fits the data

If the fitted line is a summary of the relationship between the independent and dependent variables, is it a good summary? This section shows you how to answer that question in several ways. The section begins by showing you how a type of plot called a residuals plot can help you answer that question. In addition, SYSTAT prints several statistics designed to measure how well the line fits the data. We will show you how to interpret them and tell you which ones are best. The section closes by describing statistics you can use to assess the significance of the overall model.

Residuals and residuals plots

Looking at Figure 4.5, notice that few of the data points fall exactly on the line. This is the reason that we said that the line was only a summary of the relationship between the proportion of Hispanics who speak English well and level of Hispanic housing integration. A summary is not the whole relationship; it leaves something out. In statistical language, the summary is a line which has been fitted to the data. It is also referred to as the fitted line or, simply, the fit. The part left out is the residual. More concisely, we have the relationship:

observed data = fit + residual

This is a fundamental relationship in data analysis. A good fit implies that the residuals are relatively small. Thus, the residuals can be used to measure how well the line fits the data. Another use for the residuals is to find relationships and patterns that are not yet incorporated in the model. Later in this chapter and in the next we illustrate various techniques for finding information in the residuals.

Figure 4.5 illustrates the relationship between the observed data, the fit and the residuals in graphical form. The fitted line is represented by the regression line. For each case, we can use the equation of the fitted line to calculate a prediction for HOUSINT. The prediction is called the fitted value. Fitted values are sometimes called predicted values, estimated values, or the fit. SYSTAT stores fitted values in a variable named ESTIMATE. Fitted values are calculated from the regression equation, in this example:

$$\text{fit} = -0.346 + 1.149 \text{ SPEAKENG}$$

For example, for Oklahoma City, SPEAKENG = 0.893 and HOUSINT = 0.810. Substituting the 0.893 for SPEAKENG in the above equation, we find the fitted value:

$$
\begin{aligned}
\text{fitted value} \quad &= \quad -0.346 + 1.149 * 0.893 \\
&= \quad 0.681
\end{aligned}
$$

For each prediction, a residual can be calculated as the difference between the actual and fitted values. For Oklahoma City, the residual is:

$$
\begin{aligned}
\text{residual} \quad &= \quad \text{data} - \text{fit} \\
&= \quad \text{HOUSINT} - \text{ESTIMATE} \\
&= \quad 0.810 - 0.681 \\
&= \quad 0.129
\end{aligned}
$$

Figure 4.6 shows you the commands that would save the residuals. It does not show the output from the regression but it prints the original data, the fitted values and the residuals. If you have quick graphs turned on when you save residuals, SYSTAT will print an informative plot called a "Residuals plot." We do not show the plot here, but we will examine it in detail in Figure 4.13 and the following pages.

In Figure 4.5, the residual for Oklahoma City is represented by the vertical line drawn between the regression line and the data point. Although the Oklahoma City results in Figure 4.6 match exactly the results we calculated by hand, this will not always be true. SYSTAT carries out all its internal calculations using about 15 digits of accuracy while we only used the three digits that it printed. When you need more accuracy on the printout, use the FORMAT command to request SYSTAT print more digits.

A crucial question in any analysis is, "How good is the model?" A good model has several characteristics:

1. The residuals are small relative to the fit. This means that the model is a good summary of the data.

2. The fit is not distorted by outliers. One or more outliers are very common and, when they lie far enough beyond the other data points, the least squares fit may summarize no more than the relation between the outlier(s) and the rest of the data. Less severe distortions are more frequent but equally unwanted.

3. Because we fit a straight line to the data, we want to be sure that the actual relationship in the data is not a curve or some other non-straight-line relation.

We can check for all of these possibilities by printing a residuals plot. Using the original plot in Figure 4.2, we leave the independent variable on the horizontal axis and replace the vertical axis with the residuals. SYSTAT calculates and saves residuals if, before you give the ESTIMATE command, you use the SAVE command.

```
REGRESS
   USE HOUSE1
   MODEL HOUSINT = CONSTANT + SPEAKENG
   SAVE HOUSE2 / DATA  RESIDUAL
   ESTIMATE
```

Figure 4.6
Original Data, Fitted Values and Residuals

```
REGRESS
    USE HOUSE1
    MODEL HOUSINT = CONSTANT + SPEAKENG
    SAVE HOUSE2 / DATA  RESIDUAL
    ESTIMATE

FORMAT 3
LIST CITY$ HOUSINT SPEAKENG ESTIMATE RESIDUAL
```

Case number	CITY$	HOUSINT	SPEAKENG	ESTIMATE	RESIDUAL
1	Anaheim	0.610	0.714	0.475	0.135
2	Atlanta	0.736	0.907	0.697	0.039
3	Boston	0.653	0.755	0.522	0.131
4	Buffalo	0.751	0.866	0.650	0.101
5	Chicago	0.499	0.676	0.431	0.068
6	Cincinnati	0.799	0.973	0.773	0.026
7	Dallas-FortW	0.619	0.779	0.550	0.069
8	Dayton	0.837	0.971	0.770	0.067
9	Denver-Bould	0.649	0.929	0.722	-0.073
10	El Paso	0.229	0.707	0.467	-0.238
11	Fresno	0.469	0.759	0.527	-0.058
12	Gary-Hammond	0.538	0.818	0.595	-0.057
13	Greensboro	0.765	0.954	0.751	0.014
14	Indianapolis	0.824	0.950	0.746	0.078
15	Los Angeles	0.347	0.657	0.410	-0.063
16	Memphis	0.524	0.980	0.781	-0.257
17	Miami	0.341	0.567	0.306	0.035
18	Mpls-St.Paul	0.870	0.944	0.739	0.131
19	New Orleans	0.708	0.885	0.672	0.036
20	New York	0.330	0.690	0.447	-0.117
21	Newark	0.481	0.647	0.398	0.083
22	Oklahoma C.	0.810	0.893	0.681	0.129
23	Paterson	0.368	0.576	0.316	0.052
24	Philadelphia	0.500	0.771	0.541	-0.041
25	Sacramento	0.691	0.868	0.652	0.039
26	St. Louis	0.804	0.958	0.755	0.049
27	San Antonio	0.276	0.837	0.616	-0.340
28	San Francisc	0.582	0.838	0.618	-0.036
29	San Jose	0.547	0.857	0.639	-0.092
30	WashingtonDC	0.705	0.835	0.614	0.091

Notice that we saved both the original data and the residuals. You usually want to do this so you can plot other variables against the residuals. The plot uses SYMBOL = 1 to print open circles because they let you see when points overlap. We also used a YLIMIT command to draw a line where the residual equals 0. This is the special place on the plot where the fitted values and the observed data are identical. It provides a visual reference. For residuals above the line the fitted values are less than the data so we are underfitting; below the line the fit is larger, it overpredicts. Figure 4.7 shows the residuals plot for the housing integration regression.

Figure 4.7
Residuals Plot: Residuals vs. Independent Variable

```
USE HOUSE3
PLOT RESIDUAL * SPEAKENG / SYMBOL=1 SIZE=1.5 YLIMIT=0,-9999
```

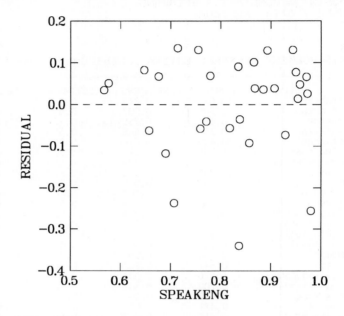

Looking across the residual plot, notice that there is no systematic pattern in the residuals: the points seem to be scattered without any tendency to drift up or down or to curve. All trend up or down has been taken out of the residuals and is in the regression line. Three points stand out lower than the main body of the data; we will shortly investigate what cities they represent and why they stand out. All in all this is a good-looking residuals plot. At least as a first try, it suggests that our model, that the level of acculturation influences whether immigrant groups live near established groups, is working.

Plotting residuals versus the dependent variable is not the only way to examine residuals. Other kinds of residuals plots are sensitive to a variety of conditions that can tell you how well your model fits the data. In Section 4.7 we look at other residuals plots to show you how you can use them to find and correct flaws in your model.

Summary statistics for the model

In the previous section, we answered the question of how well the fitted line summarizes the relationship between the independent and dependent variables by plotting the fitted line and the data simultaneously on a single plot and by looking at residuals (see Figure 4.5 and Figure 4.7). Another answer to this question uses a single number to measure the goodness of the fit. Because such a number measures how well the fitted line summarizes the data it is called a summary statistic. REGRESS provides several summary statistics; we describe them following Figure 4.8.

Figure 4.8
Summary Statistics for a Model

```
REGRESS
   USE HOUSE1
   MODEL HOUSINT = CONSTANT + SPEAKENG
   ESTIMATE
```

Dep Var: HOUSINT N: 30 Multiple R: 0.764 Squared multiple R: 0.584

Adjusted squared multiple R: 0.569   Standard error of estimate: 0.120

Effect	Coefficient	Std Error	Std Coef	Tolerance	t	P(2 Tail)
CONSTANT	−0.346	0.152	0.0	.	2.277	0.031
SPEAKENG	1.149	0.183	0.764	1.000	6.267	0.000

Analysis of Variance

Source	Sum-of-Squares	DF	Mean-Square	F-Ratio	P
Regression	0.568	1	0.568	39.271	0.000
Residual	0.405	28	0.014		

Summary statistics are widely used because they are concise. They are single numbers which are easy to report in a publication and some have very useful interpretations. Below we describe the statistics printed by SYSTAT.

- **Multiple R.** Printed in the middle of the first line of output, this coefficient is one measure of the strength of the relationship between the data and the fitted values. In the housing integration regression, it is .764. In simple regressions, multiple R can be interpreted as the slope that the line would have if both variables were measured in units that had the same standard deviation. In this case, it is the same as the standardized coefficient. It ranges between zero and one. The squared multiple R, discussed in the next paragraph, can be more easily interpreted and, for that reason, is more widely used. The multiple R is printed mostly for historical reasons.

- **Squared Multiple R.** On the right side of the first line of the output SYSTAT prints a more useful measure of how well a model fits the data is the squared multiple R, also called the multiple R-square the coefficient of determination, or simply the R^2. This is a superior statistic because it has a simple interpretation that can be readily extended to the case where the regression equation has multiple independent variables. The multiple R-square indicates the proportion of variance in the dependent variable which can be accounted for or explained by the independent variable(s) in the regression model. Expressed differently, it is the ratio of the variance of the dependent variable accounted for by the model over the total variance of the dependent variable. It ranges from 0 to 1.0, but is often multiplied by 100 and used as a percent. A zero multiple R-square indicates that the model explains none of the variance in the dependent variable, while 100% means that all of the variance has been explained. In this example, the independent variable, SPEAKENG, explains 58.4% of the variance in HOUSINT.

The multiple R-square is a member of the family of statistics called proportional reduction in error (PRE) measures. PRE measures are ratios which express by what proportion you can reduce the errors in predicting the values of the dependent variable by use of the independent variable(s). (See Section 4.5 for details on PRE statistics.)

- **Adjusted Squared Multiple R.** When a regression model is based on relatively few cases, the multiple R-square tends to be an optimistic estimate of how well the model fits the underlying population. The model usually does not fit the population as well as it fits the sample from which it was calculated. The adjusted R-square corrects the multiple R-square to more closely reflect the fit of the model in the population. Here the adjusted R-square is 56.9%. If you must use only one number to summarize the fit of a regression model, the adjusted R-square is the best choice.

All these statistics share a common problem. Like the fitted line, they are misleading if outliers, curvature, or other forms of nonlinearity are present in the data. Thus, they should never be used without being checked by residuals plots.

- **Standard Error of Estimate.** The square root of the residual mean square in the ANOVA table is called the standard error of estimate. Like the multiple R-square, it is a measure of the accuracy with which the regression equation predicts the dependent variable from the independent variable(s), but it has no PRE interpretation. Its lower bound is zero, but it has no upper bound.

The most common use for the standard error of estimate is in circumstances when the multiple R-square statistic is large, say over 97%, and changes caused by new parameters do not have much effect on that statistic. This frequently happens in time series and panel regressions when the time trend alone may account for well over 95% of the variance in the dependent variable. Then reductions in the standard error of estimate are an appropriate way to measure the impact of adding new variables to the model.

The analysis of variance table

The analysis of variance (ANOVA) table provides a test of the overall significance of the regression model. This is the same as testing whether the multiple R-square is significantly different from zero. Notice that it is different from the tests that individual regression coefficients are different from zero because it is a simultaneous test of the equation as a whole. Sometimes, especially when the regression equation contains several independent variables which are being estimated by relatively few data points, t-tests may show that some coefficients are significantly different from zero even though the regression equation as a whole is not. The solution is to remove some of the independent variables with nonsignificant coefficients. Looking at the ANOVA table warns you if this problem exists.

To interpret the ANOVA table you need to know something about how it is constructed. Our explanation here will be brief because the ANOVA table is not a central part of regression. If you need more than a summary, see Section 8.2. Analysis of variance begins by calculating the total sum of squares about the mean (sum-of-squares, for short) of the dependent variable. You may want to be reminded that the sum-of-squares is constructed by subtracting the mean from each value in the dataset, squaring each result, and adding all the squared values. The total sum-of-squares is divided (partitioned is the technical term used in ANOVA) into two parts. (1) The portion accounted for by the regression model is called the regression sum-of-squares. (2) The remaining portion, left over after the regression has been calculated, is called the residual sum-of-squares. This gives us the following formula:

$$\begin{pmatrix} Total \\ sum\text{-}of\text{-}squares \end{pmatrix} = \begin{pmatrix} Regression \\ sum\text{-}of\text{-}squares \end{pmatrix} + \begin{pmatrix} Residual \\ sum\text{-}of\text{-}squares \end{pmatrix}$$

The analysis of variance table displays these sums-of-squares under the heading SUM-OF-SQUARES. In our data the regression sum-of-squares is 0.568, the residual sum-of-squares is 0.405. The total sum-of-squares is not reported because it is just the sum of the others.

Using a similar strategy the degrees of freedom in the data are partitioned as well. Degrees of freedom is a mathematical concept. The basic idea is this: In general, the more parameters in a mathematical model, the better it fits a given dataset. At the limit, the model will fit every point exactly. To construct a line which passes through every point in a dataset, you would need at most one parameter in the model for each point in the dataset. Thus the total number of points is the upper limit on the number of parameters needed to fit the data exactly. Degrees of freedom are used in the ANOVA table to correct for the fact that a model should always fit better if it has more parameters.

To keep track of the number of parameters estimated in a regression model, one degree of freedom is assigned to the model for each parameter. The remaining degrees of freedom are assigned to the residual. Since the Hispanic housing integration model estimates the CONSTANT and SPEAKENG you might think that the model had 2 degrees of freedom. However, the degree of freedom for the CONSTANT is not included in either the model or the total. So the Hispanic integration model has one degree of freedom because it estimates one parameter, the coefficient for SPEAKENG. The remaining degrees of freedom in the dataset, 28, are assigned to the residual. This is reported in the DF column.

The sum-of-squares divided by the degrees of freedom gives the mean square, reported in the MEAN-SQUARE column. If the data meet the regression assumptions (discussed in Section 4.5), the ratio of the regression mean-square to the residual mean-square is distributed as an F statistic with p and $N - p$ degrees of freedom. N is the total number of cases used to estimate the regression and p is the number of predictors in the regression (including the constant). This ratio is 39.271 for the Hispanic integration regression. This F-ratio is the actual test statistic assessing whether the overall model is significant. The probability associated with the F-ratio is reported in the P column. If it is small, you can reject the hypothesis that the multiple R-square equals zero. The conventional definition of small is that we reject the null hypothesis if the probability is less than .05. If the probability is above .05, fail to reject. This convention may be different in different disciplines and research specialties. In the Hispanic housing integration example, the probability is 0.000, so we can safely assume that the multiple R^2 is not equal to zero.

The *R*-square and the adjusted *R*-square are widely used regression summary statistics. For other types of analysis (see Section 8.2) the analysis of variance table is important, and it is explained in more detail in those chapters. In regression you are usually much more interested in the effects of individual variables than in the model as a whole. Significance tests of the overall model are not as important as the size and significance of the individual coefficients. This is the subject that we examine in the next section.

4.4 Testing hypotheses about the coefficients

We have used regression to describe the relation between acculturation and integration into American society. Description of observed data is one typical use of regression. Frequently, your data are a sample and you want to draw conclusions about the population from evidence contained in your sample. For example, we want to draw conclusions about the experience of Hispanics in all large cities from our sample of 30. This section describes how you can answer a variety of questions about the population coefficients.

Following Figure 4.9 we describe those portions of the output needed to test hypotheses about the coefficients in the population.

Figure 4.9
Are Coefficients Different from Zero?

```
REGRESS
    USE HOUSE1
    MODEL HOUSINT = CONSTANT + SPEAKENG
    ESTIMATE
```

Dep Var: HOUSINT N: 30 Multiple R: 0.764 Squared multiple R: 0.584						
Adjusted squared multiple R: 0.569 Standard error of estimate: 0.120						
Effect	Coefficient	Std Error	Std Coef	Tolerance	t	P(2 Tail)
CONSTANT	−0.346	0.152	0.0	.	2.277	0.031
SPEAKENG	1.149	0.183	0.764	1.000	6.267	0.000

Analysis of Variance					
Source	Sum-of-Squares	DF	Mean-Square	F-Ratio	P
Regression	0.568	1	0.568	39.271	0.000
Residual	0.405	28	0.014		

Is the coefficient different from zero?

Standard Error. The key statistic needed to test hypotheses about a regression coefficient is the standard error of the coefficient. This appears in the column titled "Std Error". The standard error is the estimated standard deviation of the coefficients; it estimates the variability of the coefficients. In the Hispanic integration regression, the standard errors are 0.152 for the constant and 0.183 for SPEAKENG. To test the plausibility of any hypothesized value, we calculate:

$$critical\ ratio = \frac{calculated\ statistic - hypothesized\ value}{std\ error\ of\ the\ statistic}$$

When the null hypothesis is true, the critical ratio is near zero: a good rule of thumb is between −2 and +2. When the hypothesized value is not the population value, then the ratio is far from zero. Since we almost never know the population standard deviation of the statistic, the formula above uses the estimated standard error and, instead of comparing the critical ratio to values from the standard normal distribution, we compare it to values from a t-distribution with degrees of freedom determined by the sample size.

The usual significance test is a test of the null hypothesis that the coefficient of the population regression line is zero against the alternative that it is different from zero. In effect, this test answers the question of whether there is a relation between an independent variable and the dependent variable in the population. Since SYSTAT prints both the coefficient and its standard error, the critical ratio calculation is simple. For example, for SPEAKENG it is:

$$t = \frac{b_1}{s_{b_1}} = \frac{1.149}{0.183} = 6.267$$

SYSTAT automatically calculates the critical ratio for this null hypothesis and prints it in the column labeled **"t"**. The name comes from the fact that SYSTAT compares the test statistic in this column to a t-distribution. In the housing integration example, the t values are −2.277 and 6.267 for the CONSTANT and SPEAKENG, respectively. Both of these are well beyond the range of −2 through +2.

The rule of thumb serves for many purposes, but you often want to be more precise in tables prepared for journals, technical reports, or presentations to professional audiences. Then you need to know the exact probability that the coefficients in your sample would occur if the null hypothesis were true, that is, if the regression coefficients in the population were really zero.

SYSTAT reports the exact probability in the column labeled **P(2-Tail)**. These p-values are the basis for the asterisks on written reports and technical papers. As you see in Figure 4.9, this probability for SPEAKENG is so small that we can confidently reject the null hypothesis that the slope of the regression line is zero. This confirms the graphical analyses that we conducted in Figure 4.2 and Figure 4.3. In the social sciences, the significance of the CONSTANT is rarely tested, but this is less true in physical or biological sciences. Since the standardized coefficients are multiples of the unstandardized coefficients, the tests of hypotheses are identical for both. The p-value printed by SYSTAT is a 2-tailed test. For a 1-tailed p-value, multiply the printed value by 2.

Testing other null hypotheses about coefficients

Sometimes you want to test other null hypotheses; for example, that the true regression coefficient in the population is, say, 1.0. GLM (MGLH) gives us the capability to test hypotheses about the coefficients interactively without having to construct a critical ratio or consult a table of the t distribution. These tests are constructed using two special SYSTAT matrices. The A matrix tells which coefficient to test and the D matrix specifies the value for the null hypothesis. If you need to perform such a test, consult the GLM chapter in the SYSTAT manual for detailed explanations and an example. This discussion is meant to alert you that such a test is easy to conduct and show you how the output looks. To test the hypothesis that the true coefficient for SPEAKENG is 1.0, after ESTIMATEing the parameters, give the commands:

```
HYPOTHESIS
SPECIFY [SPEAKENG = 1.0]
TEST
```

The output is in Figure 4.10. As part of the output SYSTAT prints an "A matrix" and a "Null hypothesis value for D." These are part of SYSTAT's ability to test a wide range of complex hypotheses and they are beyond the scope of this chapter; see the SYSTAT manual for details. We are concerned with the overall F-test. The F-test indicates that we cannot reject this null hypothesis. Of course, since we don't really care whether the coefficient for SPEAKENG is 1.0, this test has no substantive meaning in this case; it illustrates how to conduct the test and how to read the output.

Confidence intervals for the regression coefficients

You are often more interested in the size of a coefficient than in whether or not it is zero. For example, a very small coefficient, even if statistically significant, may be theoretically unimportant. A confidence interval for the coefficient can give you this information. The endpoints for the confidence interval can be calculated by:

Figure 4.10
Test of Null Hypothesis: SPEAKENG = 1.0

```
REGRESS
   USE HOUSE1
   MODEL HOUSINT = CONSTANT + SPEAKENG
   ESTIMATE

   HYPOTHESIS
   SPECIFY [SPEAKENG = 1.0]
   TEST
```

```
HYPOTHESIS.

A MATRIX

                    1            2

                 0.000       -1.000

NULL HYPOTHESIS VALUE FOR D

                  -1.000

TEST OF HYPOTHESIS

     SOURCE       SS       DF       MS          F          P

   HYPOTHESIS    0.010      1      0.010      0.663      0.422
       ERROR     0.405     28      0.014
```

$$\begin{pmatrix} Confidence \\ interval \end{pmatrix} = \begin{pmatrix} Estimated \\ coefficient \end{pmatrix} \pm \begin{pmatrix} Multiple\ of\ the\ standard \\ error\ of\ the\ coefficient \end{pmatrix}$$

To construct a confidence interval for SPEAKENG, use the t-distribution to choose a multiple of the standard error. A common choice is 2 because it corresponds, roughly, to a 95% confidence interval. Again, if you publish or report your results to a professional audience you may need to be more precise. In this case, find the exact 2-tailed t-value for $(N - p)$ degrees of freedom from a table at the back of almost any statistics book. N is the number of cases used to calculate the regression. 30 cases are reported on the SYSTAT output. p is the number of predictors in the regression equation, including the constant. Here, p is 2. For $(30 - 2) = 28$ degrees of freedom the 2-tailed t-value is 2.048. We calculate the confidence interval as:

$$\text{lower bound} = 1.149 - 2.048 * 0.183 = 0.774$$
$$\text{upper bound} = 1.149 + 2.048 * 0.183 = 1.524$$

The 95% confidence interval for SPEAKENG is from 0.774 to 1.524. Remember that a 95% confidence interval does not mean that the population parameter has a 95% chance of being inside the interval. Rather, if repeated samples are drawn from the same population under identical conditions, the confidence interval contains the population parameter 95% of the time. Since the population value is unknown, there is no way for you to know whether any particular interval contains it.

If you know the value of the population standard deviation, make two changes in this procedure. First, substitute the population standard deviation for the estimated standard error of the coefficient. Second, choose a multiple from the tables of the normal distribution with mean zero and variance one (often 1.96, a value which corresponds to a 95% confidence interval). In most cases you do not know the population standard deviation, so you will follow the procedure outlined earlier.

4.5 Assumptions of regression models

If you are like most researchers, you usually work with a sample, not the entire population. In order to conduct the significance tests for the model and the coefficients, you have to make some assumptions about how your observed data are related to the population. Regression coefficients estimated from a single sample typically differ from the population values and their values vary from sample to sample. To use these estimates to make inferences about the population values, for example, to test whether the population values are significantly different from zero, we need the sampling distributions of the regression coefficients. When the regression model meets the assumptions, then the sampling distribution of the regression coefficients is normal.

The following assumptions are needed:

The model is correct

This is the most critical assumption. Basically it says that the theoretical model embodied in the equation is correct. In the terminology of regression, we assume that the model is correctly specified. If this assumption is not met, we say that the model is misspecified. There are three parts to this assumption:

- That the functional form of the relation between the independent and independent variables is a straight line. We checked this using the plots, especially the residuals plot, Figure 4.7.

- That every relevant independent variable has been included in the model.

- That no irrelevant independent variables have been included.

These last two issues are complex because there is no simple way to know if every relevant variable is in the model. For reasons that we explain in the next chapter, the mere fact that a coefficient is nonsignificant does not mean that the variable has no effect on the dependent variable and vice versa. When important variables are omitted, the estimated coefficients are not accurate estimates of the population coefficients. This is called **omitted variable bias**.

Omitted variables are not a problem if your regression is based on data collected in an experiment. If the randomization procedures in the experiment were effective, then you can be sure that only variables included in the experiment influence the outcome. You can find irrelevant independent variables by looking at the significance tests. The issue of linearity is still important but that is relatively easy to check with a residuals plot. The next part of the book deals with experimental data.

Like the Hispanic housing integration dataset, most regressions are run on observed data. In this situation omitted variables are a common, serious problem. We can be sure, for example, that many things affect Hispanic integration into American society and culture. Thus, on theoretical grounds alone, despite the good-looking residuals plot, we know a model with one independent variable is too simple and we need additional variables. We would say that the model used in the Hispanic integration regression has been *misspecified*. Which additional variables are needed is a question that we deal with in the next chapter. Much of the remainder of this chapter, and the other chapters in this part of the book, can be read as an extended commentary on ways of determining which variables belong in the model and which do not.

The following assumptions involve the residuals:

The variance of the residuals is constant

This assumption implies that the variance of the residuals must be constant across the entire range of the independent variable. This assumption is required because we calculate only one estimate of the standard error of each coefficient. If the variance is not constant then a single estimate has to be wrong, and the significance tests and confidence intervals are also wrong. For the Hispanic integration regression, the fact that the residuals in Figure 4.7 form a band of constant width across the entire range of SPEAKENG indicates that the data meet this assumption. Other names for constant variance are stability of variance and homoscedasticity. If the variance of the residuals is not constant the residuals are termed heteroscedastic. Section 6.4 discuses the diagnosis and correction of heteroscedasticity in depth.

The residuals are independent

Each of the residuals must not be correlated with any other residuals. Correlated residuals are said to be autocorrelated. If there is autocorrelation, the parameter estimates are still accurate but the standard errors usually underestimate the true standard errors. This leads to Type I errors: a coefficient appears to be statistically significant when in fact it is not. This is a common problem in time series data, particularly economic data like unemployment, sales, or productivity data. The special techniques appropriate for handling autocorrelated residuals are discussed in Section 16.2.

The residuals are normally distributed

When the residuals are normally distributed, the sampling distribution of the coefficients is also normally distributed and, if the residuals are also homoscedastic, we can use the t-distribution to construct significance tests and confidence intervals. If the residuals are not normally distributed, the t- and F-tests are not accurate. Graphical tests of this assumption are described below in Section 4.7. The normal distribution is also called the Gaussian distribution.

Do the assumptions really matter?

Some researchers believe that they don't have to worry about assumptions because regression "...gets the right answer under any reasonable practical circumstances, even if a great many of the classical assumptions are violated" (Achen, 1973, p. 37). An opposing perspective is represented by Bibby (1977), who feels that violations of the assumptions can render parameter estimates almost useless. This is a controversial point, but there is research that sheds light on some of the issues.

Any general statement that researchers need not be concerned with regression assumptions is simply wrong. A single outlier, one case out of a multithousand case dataset, is sufficient to make regression results misleading. If the outlier is large enough, the coefficient estimates do nothing more than summarize the relation between the outlier and the rest of the data. Large outliers (often due to simple coding or data entry errors) are not unusual. Be warned.

Specification error is also very damaging. Certain kinds of specification error can be corrected. Nonlinearity can usually be handled by techniques discussed in Section 6.2 and Section 22.3. Omitted variables, on the other hand, are very difficult to handle, partly because you often do not know what variable you have omitted, and partly because, even when you know the variable, measuring it may be difficult. Omitted variables can have strong effects on coefficient estimates. Every practicing data analyst has seen variables become nonsignificant or nonsignificant variables become significant as other variables are added to the model. We will see some examples in the next chapter. A major obstacle is that, since the omitted variables are often unknown, you may not even know that omitted variable bias exists.

Heteroscedasticity is easy to see in residuals plots, and formal tests are discussed in Section 6.4. It does not change the coefficient estimates, but it inflates their standard errors and it may conceal more serious problems like nonlinearity. It can usually be corrected with techniques described in Section 6.2 or Section 22.3. A summary of the research on heteroscedasticity is in Bohrnstedt and Carter (1971).

The research on the effects of nonnormality indicates that the distribution of the residuals has little effect on the t values, given a sufficiently large sample size (see Bartlett 1935, Boneau 1960, and Bohrnstedt and Carter 1971). This is true only if there are no outliers: outliers are always damaging. Remember also that without independent observations a large number of cases does not mean a large sample.

For more detailed information consult Bohrnstedt and Carter (1971), Kmenta (1971) and the summary in Lewis-Beck (1980); see also Section 6.2 and Section 22.3, below.

4.6 Statistics from the residuals

SYSTAT calculates several statistics from the residuals which can help you understand your model and diagnose certain problems. In addition, you may need to calculate a confidence interval for a new case. These statistics are discussed below.

Detecting influential cases

Serious problems arise in a regression when the coefficient estimates depend on a small number of observations. This can occur when one or a few cases are substantially different from the rest of the data, that is, when there are outliers in the data. One or a few influential cases damage the coefficient estimates because: (1) if they are far enough away the regression may only estimate the line between the outlier(s) and the rest of the data; (2) even when they are closer, outliers tilt the regression line or inflate the standard errors of the coefficients so that the line is no longer an accurate summary of the bulk of the data. Even when cases do not look very different, the researcher may know that a few observations were made under unusual circumstances, such as strikes or wars, and may want to know the extent to which the results depend on these few points. When a data point or a small group of points are so important that they significantly change the parameter estimates, they are called influential cases.

SYSTAT provides several ways to identify influential cases. We have used several graphical methods in Figure 4.1 and Figure 4.7 and we look at other plots in Section 4.7. Plots are extremely useful, but their value diminishes as datasets become large; in large datasets, even with very detailed resolution, so many cases are overprinted that plots become largely unreadable.

As an alternative we can examine the residuals directly. But a large residual does not indicate an influential case. Therefore, for diagnostic purposes, the residuals need to be modified to enhance our ability to detect problem data. For this purpose, SYSTAT calculates three statistics which can be used to assess the influence of individual cases. These are the Studentized residuals, leverage, and Cook's D. They are automatically saved in the dataset created by the SAVE command in REGRESS. Routine examination of these statistics as part of the diagnostic phase of model construction will help you find many errors and data problems. In addition, SYSTAT calls your attention to cases which may be excessively influential by printing the case number of any case with a large Studentized residual, a large leverage, or a large Cook's D. We see this in later examples. Section 6.1 and the references there provide a more thorough discussion of influential observations.

Figure 4.11 prints the additional variables SYSTAT saves when you request that it save the results of a regression. We save the data along with the residuals so that we have variables like CITY$, HOUSINT, and SPEAKENG. You usually want to do this because then you can more easily identify unusual cases.

Studentized residuals

If we divide each residual by its estimated standard error the result is called a Studentized residual. The division puts all residuals on an approximately equal footing. If the regression assumptions hold (see Section 4.5), since we have estimated the standard error, the distribution of Studentized residuals will behave approximately like a t-distribution with $N - p - 2$ degrees of freedom, where N is the total sample size and p is the number of predictors (including the constant). In large samples, we can use the usual rule of thumb and expect about 5% of the Studentized residuals to exceed ± 2.0. If more than 5% exceed ± 2.0, you may have influential cases. Notice that one case in the STUDENT column in Figure 4.11, San Antonio, has a Studentized residual of less than -3.3. This happens about once in 1,000 cases, so we need to find out why.

When you save residuals, SYSTAT looks at the t-distribution and prints a warning for cases where a t-value appears that should occur in less than 1% of the data, a level corresponding to about 1 in 100 cases in a standard normal distribution. Figure 4.12 highlights the output that SYSTAT produces when you save residuals. If you have quick graphs turned on when you save residuals, SYSTAT will display a residuals plot; see Figure 4.13. You notice that SYSTAT warns you about an excessive Studentized residual in case 27, San Antonio. (We looked up the city name on the printout in Figure 4.11.) In a dataset of 30 cases, one case with a Studentized residual less than 3.3 is unlikely, so San Antonio really stands out and we definitely need to pay attention. The large residual, a potential outlier, is warning us about a problem in how well our regression model fits the data.

Leverage

Leverage measures the distance of an individual case from the average of the independent variable. An case with a high leverage value is a long way from the center. The average value for leverage is p/N, where p is the number of predictors including the constant and N is the number of cases. If the standard regression assumptions hold, then roughly 5% of the cases will have leverage exceeding $2p/N$. Examine cases with high leverage values as potentially influential cases. In the housing integration data, we calculate $2p/N = 2*2/30 = .267$ and the LEVERAGE column in Figure 4.11 shows no cases exceeding this value. When you save residuals, SYSTAT warns you of cases exceeding the 1% level, a more stringent criterion. The absence of warnings suggests that the independent variable has no unusually large values.

Figure 4.11
Residuals and Influence Statistics Saved by REGRESS

```
USE HOUSE2
LIST CITY$ HOUSINT SPEAKENG ESTIMATE RESIDUAL,
     STUDENT COOK LEVERAGE SEPRED
```

Case number	CITY$	HOUSINT	SPEAKENG	ESTIMATE	RESIDUAL	STUDENT	COOK	LEVERAGE	SEPRED
1	Anaheim	0.610	0.714	0.475	0.135	1.163	0.042	0.059	0.029
2	Atlanta	0.736	0.907	0.697	0.039	0.328	0.003	0.051	0.027
3	Boston	0.653	0.755	0.522	0.131	1.116	0.028	0.043	0.025
4	Buffalo	0.751	0.866	0.650	0.101	0.854	0.015	0.039	0.024
5	Chicago	0.499	0.676	0.431	0.068	0.579	0.015	0.081	0.034
6	Cincinnati	0.799	0.973	0.773	0.026	0.225	0.003	0.089	0.036
7	Dallas-FortW	0.619	0.779	0.550	0.069	0.579	0.007	0.037	0.023
8	Dayton	0.837	0.971	0.770	0.067	0.572	0.016	0.087	0.036
9	Denver-Bould	0.649	0.929	0.722	-0.073	-0.621	0.013	0.062	0.030
10	El Paso	0.229	0.707	0.467	-0.238	-2.175	0.139	0.062	0.030
11	Fresno	0.469	0.759	0.527	-0.058	-0.484	0.005	0.042	0.025
12	Gary-Hammond	0.538	0.818	0.595	-0.057	-0.472	0.004	0.033	0.022
13	Greensboro	0.765	0.954	0.751	0.014	0.120	0.001	0.076	0.033
14	Indianapolis	0.824	0.950	0.746	0.078	0.664	0.018	0.073	0.033
15	Los Angeles	0.347	0.657	0.410	-0.063	-0.539	0.015	0.094	0.037
16	Memphis	0.524	0.980	0.781	-0.257	-2.430	0.260	0.094	0.037
17	Miami	0.341	0.567	0.306	0.035	0.315	0.011	0.181	0.051
18	Mpls-St.Paul	0.870	0.944	0.739	0.131	1.131	0.048	0.070	0.032
19	New Orleans	0.708	0.885	0.672	0.036	0.304	0.002	0.044	0.025
20	New York	0.330	0.690	0.447	-0.117	-1.014	0.040	0.072	0.032
21	Newark	0.481	0.647	0.398	0.083	0.721	0.030	0.102	0.038
22	Oklahoma C.	0.810	0.893	0.681	0.129	1.104	0.029	0.046	0.026
23	Paterson	0.368	0.576	0.316	0.052	0.464	0.023	0.170	0.050
24	Philadelphia	0.500	0.771	0.541	-0.041	-0.338	0.002	0.039	0.024
25	Sacramento	0.691	0.868	0.652	0.039	0.325	0.002	0.039	0.024
26	St. Louis	0.804	0.958	0.755	0.049	0.414	0.008	0.078	0.034
27	San Antonio	0.276	0.837	0.616	-0.340	-3.370	0.146	0.034	0.022
28	San Francisc	0.582	0.838	0.618	-0.036	-0.296	0.002	0.034	0.022
29	San Jose	0.547	0.857	0.639	-0.092	-0.777	0.012	0.037	0.023
30	WashingtonDC	0.705	0.835	0.614	0.091	0.763	0.010	0.034	0.022

Cook's distance

The Studentized residuals measure the vertical distance of residuals from the regression line. Leverage measures the horizontal distance of the cases from the center of the independent variable. Cook's D combines both of these characteristics, measuring a combination of vertical and horizontal distance. It is the closest single measure to what we mean by an influential case: that is, a point both far away from the regression line and far out in the tail of the independent variable is most likely to have a significant influence on the parameter estimates. Under the usual regression assumptions, Cook's D has an F-distribution with 1 and $N - p - 1$ degrees of freedom. (N is the number of cases and p is the number of parameters including the constant.) Looking at the COOK column of the Hispanic housing integration residuals in Figure 4.11, you will see that no case has a large Cook's D. When you save residuals, SYSTAT prints a warning for an influential point if Cook's D exceeds the expected 99% level. Therefore we conclude that no observations were unusually influential. For more details see Cook (1979) and Section 6.1.

Figure 4.12
Output When Saving Residuals

```
REGRESS
    USE HOUSE1
    MODEL HOUSINT = CONSTANT + SPEAKENG
    SAVE HOUSE2 / DATA  RESIDUAL
    ESTIMATE
```

```
Dep Var: HOUSINT N: 30 Multiple R:  0.764 Squared multiple R:  0.584

Adjusted squared multiple R:  0.569    Standard error of estimate:      0.120

Effect          Coefficient     Std Error    Std Coef Tolerance     t    P(2 Tail)

CONSTANT           -0.346          0.152        0.0        .      2.277    0.031
SPEAKENG            1.149          0.183        0.764    1.000    6.267    0.000

                          Analysis of Variance

Source          Sum-of-Squares   DF   Mean-Square    F-Ratio      P

Regression            0.568       1      0.568       39.271     0.000
Residual              0.405      28      0.014

***WARNING***
Case            27 is an outlier        (Studentized REsidual =      -3.370)

Durbin-Watson D Statistic     1.579
First Order Autocorrelation   0.178

Residuals have been saved.
```

What to do when you find an influential case

If you find cases with a large Cook's D, a large leverage, or a large Studentized residual, you may have one or more influential cases. Keep in mind that these three statistics illuminate different aspects of the data, so they do not necessarily identify the same cases. Potential influential cases must be checked carefully. They often result from data entry errors or cases which are unusual and not representative of the data. If possible they should be corrected. For a detailed discussion of your options, read the discussion in Section 6.1.

Confidence interval for a single new case

SYSTAT calculates another statistic from the residuals that can help you calculate the value of the dependent variable for a single new case. For example, we may know (or want to assume) the proportion of Hispanics who speak English well in a city not in our sample and want to know what proportion of Hispanics can be expected to live near whites. To obtain the confidence interval for a single new case at existing values of the independent variable(s) you can use the variable SEPRED that is saved by REGRESS. Use the same approach that we used to obtain a confidence interval for regression co-efficients (see Section 4.4). The formulas are:

$$\text{Upper bound} = \text{ESTIMATE} + t * \text{SEPRED}$$
$$\text{Lower bound} = \text{ESTIMATE} - t * \text{SEPRED}$$

where t is chosen from the t-distribution with $N - p$ degrees of freedom. N is the number of cases in the regression, p is the number of predictors including the constant. For example, if in another city the proportion of Hispanics who spoke English well was .755 (i.e. a new case replicating the situation in Boston), a 95% confidence interval for the new predicted value would be:

$$\text{Upper bound} = 0.522 + 2.048 * 0.025 = 0.573$$
$$\text{Lower bound} = 0.522 - 2.048 * 0.025 = 0.471$$

Note that this is not a simultaneous confidence band for the entire line, nor is it a confidence interval for the situation where more than one new observations are made at some existing values of the independent variables. Since this statistic requires that you draw an additional observation at an existing value of the dependent variable, it is not very useful for observed data. It is more commonly used in experimental work when the experimenter has control over the values of the independent variable.

4.7 What can the residuals tell us?

We introduced the idea of residuals with the formula:

$$data = fit + residual$$

We looked to the residuals for evidence to answer the question, how good is the fit? Now we are going to introduce a second, more important use of the residuals. The formula above was developed by John Tukey in a series of papers and books, notably *Exploratory Data Analysis* (1977). It emphasizes that the residuals are not errors in prediction. Rather, *the residuals are the location of other structure which has not yet been accounted for in the model.* This concept has had a major impact on data analysis. It emphasizes that fitting a model and looking at statistical output can show you only what you more or less anticipated was there. You do not learn enough until you remove the effects of everything that you know influences the data and then plot what remains, the residuals. Here you may find the utterly unanticipated. This focuses attention on looking at the residuals in a variety of ways, each of which highlights potential sources of additional structure in the data. The result is a data analysis process which consists of fitting a model, looking at residuals, fitting a new model based on the results of the residual analysis, examining the new residuals, etc. Good data analysis is iterative.

Most of the techniques for examining the residuals are graphical, easy to do, easy to understand, and are usually very revealing when something is wrong. The principal ways of plotting the residuals are:

1. Against the fitted values of the dependent variable.

2. Against the actual values of the independent variable.

3. Against other variables not in the equation.

4. In time sequence if there is a known order.

5. Against categorical variables if they seem important.

6. In a probability plot against a standard normal distribution.

We will look at each of these plots in turn, discussing the information they contain and how to interpret them. Remember that this list does not exhaust the possibilities for examination of residuals. In general, residuals should be plotted in any way which seems useful for the problem at hand. The plots below are basic and should be routinely performed for every analysis, but they are only a starting point for a full analysis.

Plots against the fitted values

Figure 4.13 shows the plot of the residuals versus the fitted values for the housing integration regression. This is the plot produced by quick graph whenever you save residuals. It is similar to the plot that we saw earlier, in Figure 4.7, with SPEAKENG on the horizontal axis replaced by the estimated values. SYSAT draws a horizontal line where the residuals = 0 because this is the location where the predicted values are identical to the actual values. The plot shows the residuals spread out in an approximately horizontal band across the entire range of the estimated values.   The plot supports our model, that the level of acculturation influences the extent to which Hispanics live with whites.

Figure 4.13
Quick Graph Produced When Saving Residuals

Plot of Residuals against Predicted Values

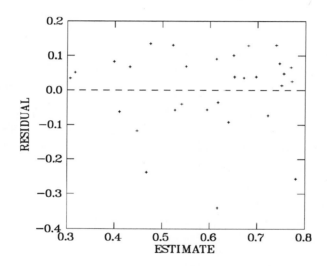

There is an important limitation to what this plot and the others discussed below can tell us. Although the plot suggests that our model is correct, it cannot prove the model correct. In somewhat the same sense as a null hypothesis, residual plots can only fail to invalidate the model. As we shall see soon, residual plots with no visible structure do not guarantee that no further structure exists to be discovered. Plots indicating that the model is invalid may look like those in Figure 4.14.

Figure 4.14
Some Problems Revealed by Residual Plots

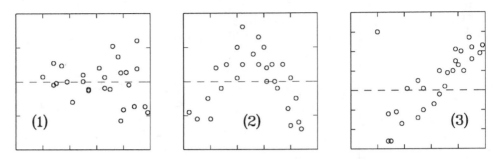

1. The variance is not constant. This indicates a need for weighted least squares or a transformation of the dependent variable. See Section 6.4 and Section 22.4.

2. The model is incorrect. Any clustering of cases, slope, curvature or other deviations from a generally horizontal pattern indicates specification error. Specification errors takes many forms and corrections are also varied. For example, another variable may need to be added to the model, a variable already in the model may need to be transformed (e.g. squared) and entered in both the original and transformed form, a variable already in the model may need to be replaced by a nonlinear function of itself (e.g. logs), or the dependent variable may need to be transformed. See Section 22.2 for more on transformations.

3. An outlier is distorting the regression line. Why the outlier exists needs to be investigated; it may need to be fixed or removed. It may also indicate that one or more variables have been omitted.

Highlighting influential points

A quick graph is valuable because SYSTAT produces it with no work on your part. Often, however, you may want to produce a modified residuals plot to highlight important information. One visual highlight uses SYSTAT's SIZE option to control the size of the plotting symbols. For example, a plot using the values of Cook's D for the size would make influential points large and easy to see. Since this highlights the influence of the points it is sometimes called an **influence plot**. We only care about the relative size of the symbols and Cook's D is small, so we multiply it by 15 to make the symbols larger and more visible.

Figure 4.15
Influence Plot
Residuals Plot Where Symbol Size Measures Influence

```
USE HOUSE2
LET COOK15 = COOK * 15
PLOT RESIDUAL * ESTIMATE / SIZE=COOK15 SYM=1 SIZE=1.5 YLIM=0,-99
```

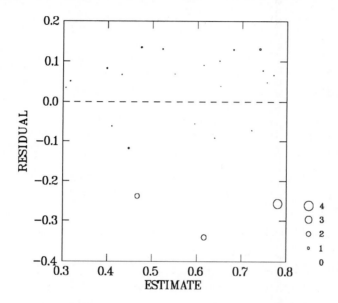

Figure 4.15 contains the resulting plot of the fit versus the residuals. This plot suggests we may have at least one outlier, in the lower right, and perhaps two others in the lower middle and the lower left. Let's investigate what's going on. To help our investigation, we need an easy way to find out what points correspond to which city.

Figure 4.16
Adding an ID Variable

```
BASIC
   NEW
   INPUT CITY$ ID$
   RUN
'Anaheim      '   'a'
'Atlanta      '   'A'
'Boston       '   'B'
'Buffalo      '   'b'
'Chicago      '   'C'
'Cincinnati   '   '('
'Dallas-FortW '   'D'
'Dayton       '   'd'
'Denver-Bould '   'v'
'El Paso      '   'E'
'Fresno       '   'f'
'Gary-Hammond '   'G'
'Greensboro   '   'g'
'Indianapolis '   'I'
'Los Angeles  '   'L'
'Memphis      '   'F'
'Miami        '   'M'
'Mpls-St.Paul '   'm'
'New Orleans  '   'N'
'New York     '   'Y'
'Newark       '   'n'
'Oklahoma C.  '   'O'
'Paterson     '   '%'
'Philadelphia '   'P'
'Sacramento   '   '$'
'St. Louis    '   '^'
'San Antonio  '   '@'
'San Francisc '   'S'
'San Jose     '   'J'
'WashingtonDC '   'W'
~
   SORT CITY$
   save ADDID
   RUN

   USE HOUSE2
   SORT CITY$

   SAVE HOUSE3
   MERGE HOUSE2 ADDID / CITY$
```

Figure 4.16 shows how to add an ID$ variable. It would have been simpler if we had anticipated this issue and created the ID$ variable when we originally read the data into SYSTAT, then we wouldn't have had to add it later. Any character variable can be used to designate the plotting symbols, but you can distinguish points more easily if the variable has a unique value for each case. That's why we created a separate variable solely for this purpose.

We rerun the influence plot using SYMBOL=ID$ in Figure 4.17. The YLIMIT=0,-99 option tells SYSTAT to draw a reference line where the residuals are zero. SYSTAT recognizes 3-character abbreviations for the names of the options.

The influential point on the lower right, the F, is Memphis and the influential point on the lower left, the E, is El Paso. What is going on with these cities? Both stand out because their housing is less integrated than we expect, given the proportion of Hispanics who speak English. El Paso is directly on the Mexican border and it has one of the largest proportions of Hispanics in the United States. Notice that the city on the plot between El Paso and Memphis is San Antonio. (Test your understanding of regression outliers and influence: San Antonio (designated by the @) has about the same influence as El Paso even though it is farther from the line. Why isn't it more influential?) Both San Antonio and El Paso have exceptionally high proportions of Hispanics and they have had them for centuries. This suggests our model does not fit well for cities with a high proportion of Hispanics.

Memphis is different. It is an outlier because of a quirk of American culture and the choices offered by the 1980 census. The 1980 census asked everyone whether they were "of Spanish/Hispanic origin or descent." Among the choices was "Yes, Mexican-Amer." Post-census surveys showed that in some cities in the south where few Hispanics live, a number of blacks were not sure what the census meant by "Spanish/Hispanic origin," but they were very sure that they were American. The only place in the 1980 census anyone could answer that they were "American" was by checking "Yes, Mexican-Amer." This was not a problem in cities with a large Mexican Hispanic population, like Los Angeles or El Paso, because blacks there know who is Hispanic and know that they are not Mexican. The result is that in certain cities a large, but unknown, number of blacks coded themselves as Hispanic. Memphis shows up with more segregated housing than we expect because blacks tend to be more segregated than Hispanics. (This information comes from a study of racial identity in the United States by Denton and Massey, 1989.)

From these plots, we conclude that we have omitted several important variables from our model of housing integration. The major theme of the next chapter is what variables to add and how to go about adding them.

Figure 4.17
Influence Plot
Residuals Plot Using ID Variable Where Symbol Size Measures Influence

```
USE HOUSE3
LET COOK15 = COOK * 15
PLOT RESIDUAL * ESTIMATE / SIZE=COOK15 SYMBOL=ID$, YLIM=0,-99
```

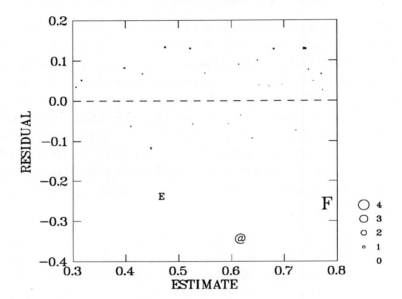

Plots versus the independent variable(s)

Here again look for evidence of problems in your model. Figure 4.18 plots the residuals against the independent variable. This is another good-looking plot. The residuals form an approximately horizontal band across the entire range of SPEAKENG. We see our three familiar outliers and influential cases, El Paso, San Antonio, and Memphis. Since the Hispanic integration regression has only a single independent variable, this plot essentially duplicates the information in the plot of RESIDUAL * ESTIMATE, Figure 4.14. Plots like Figure 4.18 are much more informative when there are more than one independent variable. The problems that we may see in this plot are the same as those in the plots of the residuals against the estimated values in the previous paragraph, illustrated in Figure 4.14. These are:

- Nonconstant variance.

- Deviations from horizontal band indicating an incorrect model.

- Outliers distorting the regression coefficients.

The remedies are the same as for the problems shown in earlier plots.

Figure 4.18
Residuals Plot: Residuals vs. Independent Variable

```
USE HOUSE5
PLOT RESIDUAL * SPEAKENG / SYMBOL=ID$ SIZE=1.5 YLIMIT=0,-9999
```

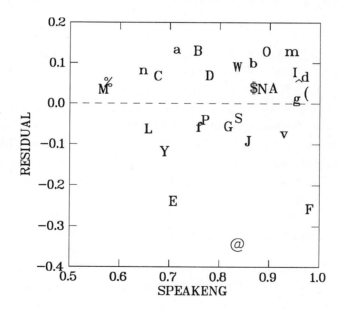

Plots of variables not in the model

The Hispanic housing integration results may stem from a variety of factors. For example, the arrival of new immigrants lowers the average proportion who speak English well. Previous analysis of residuals has suggested some, and your own ideas about your neighborhood or community and why you chose to live there as well as other research may suggest still other variables. This process of theoretically considering which forces influence the dependent variable is a vital part of any data analyst's task. New variables can be added to the dataset and plotted against the residuals. Any pattern of systematic structure in the plot may be evidence that an additional variable should be included in the model.

Other variables

In general, your knowledge of the particular problem you are studying often suggests that you should study other types of residuals plots and other variables. Draper and Smith note, "Residuals should be plotted in any reasonable way that occurs to the experimenter or statistician, based on specialist knowledge of the problem under study". (1981, p. 150). In the next chapter we will take up the issue of other variables when we take an in-depth look at multiple regression.

Sequential plots

The housing integration data in our example were collected in the 1980 census so they are a cross section in time. Many datasets, however, have some time-related order. Cases are often collected in a certain order. For example, experiments are usually run repeatedly in a sequence, or sample surveys are conducted over a period of days and weeks. In many circumstances, a pattern related to time- or sequential-order is unwanted because it can obscure or confound the effects of other variables. This is a particularly nasty problem for data gathered from an experiment because it usually indicates that the randomization procedures were defective. Sequence effects are an important source of **lurking** variables, that is, variables that have powerful effects not considered in the original model (Joiner 1981). If your data were collected in some sequence, a sequential plot of the residuals in the order in which they were collected is very important.

In a sequential plot, like other residuals plots, you hope to see no indication that there is a time trend in the residuals. This would be indicated by a horizontal band of residuals with no apparent tendency to curve, go up or down, or change width. If we were to see any of the patterns in Figure 4.19 we would conclude that there was some sort of time effect.

Figure 4.19
Examples of Nonrandom Patterns in Sequential Plots

```
USE PROBPAT
   PLOT A * B / SIZE=2  SYM=1  HEIGHT=2in  WIDTH=2in  SCALE=0,
               YLABEL='Residual'  YLIMIT=60,-999,
               XLABEL='Time'  XFORMAT=1  YFORMAT=1  LOC=0,2.5
   WRITE '(1)' / LOC=1.5in,.5in

   PLOT C * BB / SIZE=2  SYM=1  HEIGHT=2in  WIDTH=2in  SCALE=0,
               YLABEL='Residual'  YLIMIT=40,-999,
               XLABEL 'Time'  LOC=3,2.5
   WRITE '(2)' / LOC=1.5in,1.5in

   PLOT D * B / SIZE=2  SYM=2  HEIGHT=2in  WIDTH=2in  SCALE=0,
               YLABEL='Residual'  YLIMIT=10,-999,
               XLABEL='Time'  LOC=3IN,-.5IN
   WRITE '(3)' / LOC=.5in,1.5in
```

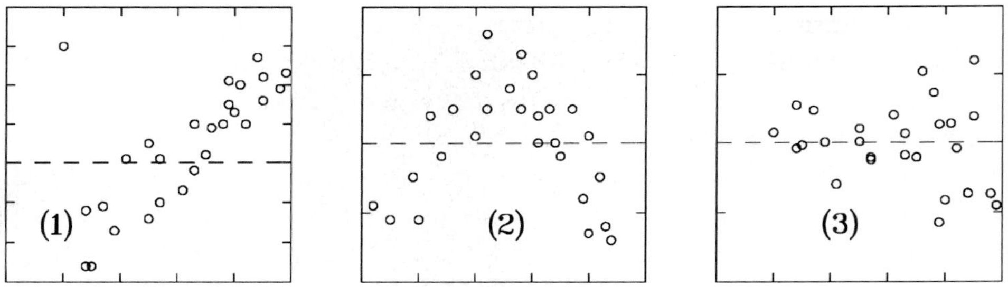

The plots in Figure 4.19 could indicate:

1. A linear time effect. What this means depends on the data. If the data are experimental, it suggests that later trials behave somewhat differently than earlier. This may occur for many reasons; a typical reason might be a flaw in the data collection: the experimenter was becoming more skilled or some measuring instruments were slowly drifting out of calibration. In observational data, it may indicate a flaw in the theory which may need to be revised to take into account the influence of other variables which are changing over time. A simple way to remove this effect is to include a linear time variable (i.e. CASENUM). A better approach is to explain what is happening with a variable chosen for theoretical reasons.

2. A nonlinear time effect. Again, what this means depends on the data. The possibility of both flaws in the data collection and a theoretically significant result should be investigated. A simple revision is to include both a linear and a quadratic variable in time in the model. This is not always theoretically sensible, however.

3. Variance not constant over time. This may indicate a need for weighted least squares or a robust regression procedure. A transformation (see Section 22.1) may also control this situation.

Plots for categorical variables

The apparent difference between the results for the South (exemplified by Memphis) compared to other regions suggests that we look more closely at the regions. This situation, where a categorical variable may be important in a regression model, is usually handled by including a dummy variable in the model. We discuss the modeling aspects of this situation in the next chapter. Here we focus on how residuals plots can show the effects of a categorical variable.

Figure 4.20 is a **grouped box-and-whiskers plot** of the Hispanic integration residuals. Usually, the name is shortened to **grouped box plot**. If you are unfamiliar with box plots see Section 8.1 or the SYSTAT manual for a description of the symbols and their interpretation. The groups are the four regions, Northeast, Midwest, South, and West, and the data are the residuals from the Hispanic integration regression. To create the regions, we added a variable called REGION$ to our dataset. This variable assigns each case (or city) to one of the four region categories. Since the process of adding another variable is the same as adding the ID$ variable, we do not show it here. The main message is very clear: the residuals from the West and the Midwest are different and the residuals from cities in the South have a larger variance than the other regions.

Once again, the plot tells us that additional variables are necessary to adequately model housing integration. Of course, region itself does not cause anything. Through region we are seeing the effects of other variables which differentially influence Hispanics in different regions. For example, some cities in the Midwest have only experienced significant Hispanic immigration in recent years while Western cities have had Hispanic populations for centuries. Regional differences could be showing us differences in the years of Hispanic presence.

Figure 4.20
Grouped Box Plot: Residuals Grouped by Region

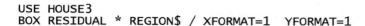

```
USE HOUSE3
BOX RESIDUAL * REGION$ / XFORMAT=1   YFORMAT=1
```

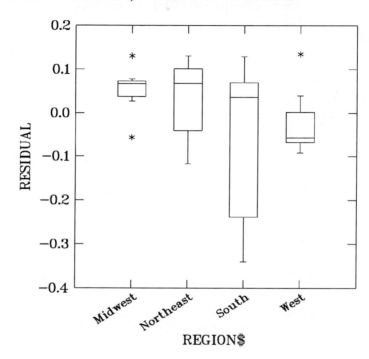

Are the residuals normally distributed?

To do hypothesis tests and construct confidence intervals for the coefficients from a least squares regression you need to assume that the residuals are a sample from a normal distribution (see Section 4.5). In our example, this means that the 30 residuals should (approximately) resemble 30 observations from a normal distribution with a zero mean. A plot of the residuals against the expected values from a normal distribution is shown in Figure 4.21. This is called a **normal probability plot** (or a theoretical quantile-quantile plot or a rankit plot). Statistically, this is a plot of the empirical cumulative distribution function of the residuals against the cumulative distribution which would have resulted had the residuals been drawn as a sample of size 30 from a normal distribution. If the residuals are normally distributed, they form a straight line from the lower left to the upper right of the plot. To more easily see any deviation from linearity, we instructed SYSTAT to draw the line.

Figure 4.21
Normal Probability Plot of Residuals

```
USE HOUSE3
PPLOT RESIDUAL / SYM=1 SIZE=1.5 SMOOTH=LINEAR XFORMAT=1 YFORMAT=1
```

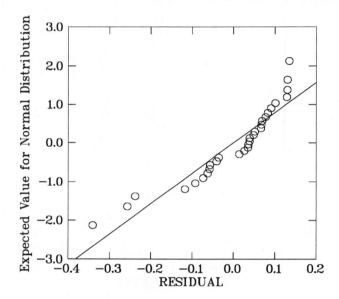

If the assumption of normality is correct, then the points in Figure 4.21 should fall approximately on a straight line slanting from the lower left to the upper right. How can you know whether any deviation from a straight line is worrisome? The easy way is to generate eight or ten plots from samples of the same size as your data from a normal distribution and construct normal probability plots with them. You can create data from a normal distribution using the SYSTAT ZRN function (see Figure 4.22.)

Figure 4.22
Normal Probability Plots of Four Samples from a Normal Distribution

```
BASIC
  NEW
  SAVE RANDOM
  REPEAT=30
  DIM RANDOM(8)
  FOR I = 1 TO 8
     LET RANDOM(I) = ZRN
     NEXT
  RUN

  USE RANDOM
  PPLOT RANDOM(1..4) / SYMBOL=1 FILL SMOOTH=LINEAR
```

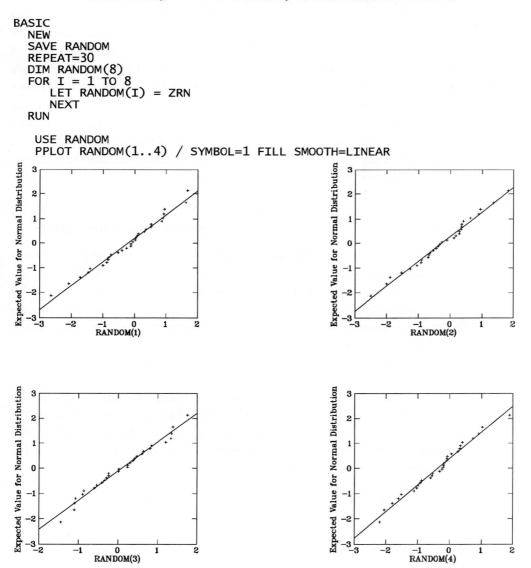

This gives you some idea of how much deviation from a straight line you can expect in samples the size of yours from exactly normally distributed data. Figure 4.22 shows the first four normal probability plots. Comparing Figure 4.21 and Figure 4.22 we can conclude that the housing integration residuals look different from data drawn from true normal distribution. Specifically, the small residuals in the lower left of Figure 4.21 and the large residuals in the upper right are above the line. The residuals in the middle are all below the line. The plots in Figure 4.22 show generally random deviations above and below the line. This is yet more confirmation of the message that there is additional structure to be removed from the residuals before they are random. The best training in interpreting normal probability plots comes from making your own plots, using different sample sizes. For more detail on assessing the distributional assumptions about data see Chambers et al. (1983, Chapter 6).

4.8 Summary: The characteristics of a relationship

Regression is the most complex statistical procedure in wide use. Its complexity stems in part from the fact that much of the standard output from regression software (e.g. coefficient estimates or summary statistics) can easily be inaccurate and misleading. To employ regression effectively requires not only that you can read and interpret the output, but also that you know what may go wrong and how to check it. Of course, when you find something wrong, you have to know how to fix it and we have only introduced the question, "What can you do?" Section 6.1 covers it in depth.

This chapter has introduced a large number of statistics, interpretations, and plots. We can reduce some of the complexity by showing you how they can all fit together into a few categories. In a broad sense, regression methods are used to describe relationships between variables. When we describe a relationship using regression there are five characteristics that we need to take into account:

1. Does the relationship *exist?*

2. The *strength* of the relationship.

3. The *size* of the relationship.

4. The *direction* of the relationship.

5. The *pattern* of the relationship.

We will discuss each characteristic in turn, with particular emphasis on which statistics and plots can be used to describe that characteristic.

Existence

The existence of a relationship between a dependent variable and one or more independent variables is assessed by two statistics. The p-value from the analysis of variance table tells us whether the fit of the overall model is significantly different from chance. The t-tests and associated p-values of individual coefficients tell us whether a relationship exists between each independent variable and the dependent variable.

Strength

Regression workers are rarely satisfied to show that relationships exist. A strong relationship gives more support for a theory than a weak one. In regression, a strong model is one which predicts the dependent variable accurately, with a small error. To measure the strength of a model we can examine the multiple R, the multiple R-squared, the adjusted multiple R-squared and the standard error of the mean. The adjusted multiple R-squared is the best all-purpose summary of strength.

Size

You are often more interested in the size of the regression coefficients than in testing whether they differ from zero. In this case, examine the coefficient estimates.

Direction

Most theories do not predict the actual size of the coefficient, they predict the direction of the relation, whether it is positive or negative. The sign of the coefficient gives this information.

Pattern

This is most subtle, yet vital attribute of any relationship. It has fundamental implications for the accuracy of all of the statistics that SYSTAT prints. Researchers often fail to deal with this effectively because so many patterns have to be taken into account. Plots and statistics based on the residuals give information about the pattern of the relationship. We have used them to assess:

- Is the relationship linear?

- Do plots show apparent outliers?

- Do Cook's D, the standardized residuals, or leverage indicate influential cases?

- Are the residuals curved, or otherwise irregular in shape or direction? In other words, should other variables be added to the model?

- Do the residuals form a horizontal band across the entire range of the dependent variable; that is, are the residuals homoscedastic?

- Are the residuals normally distributed?

The foregoing discussion of different patterns of a relationship emphasizes the importance of close examination of your data. We suggest you begin analysis with a simple model and carefully examine the residuals. The residuals indicate complications or point you toward additional variables. Effective use of regression requires this iterative approach. We illustrate it in detail in Section 5.4 where we introduce additional independent variables into our model.

Notes

The housing integration dataset is a sample adapted from a dataset constructed from 1980 census data. The dataset was made available to us courtesy of Douglas S. Massey and Nancy A. Denton. It has been used in a variety of published work (e.g. Denton and Massey 1988, 1989; Massey and Denton 1987, 1988a, 1988b, 1989). In order to make the dataset more accessible, we have described it without using technical jargon. The disadvantage is that those who know the 1980 census may not understand which of several alternatives we have chosen. For a complete description of the data, see one of the articles cited above, but a brief technical description is in order here. The cases are based on Standard Metropolitan Statistical Areas (SMSAs) as defined in 1980 by the Bureau of the Census. Our dependent variable, HOUSINT, is the P^* index popularized by Lieberson (1980, 1981). It can be interpreted as the probability of residential contact between Hispanics and whites within census tracts of SMSAs. We used the word neighborhoods as a non-technical name for census tracts. Whites are defined as non-Hispanic whites and are called Anglos in the Massey-Denton papers. Our independent variable, SPEAKENG, is the proportion of Hispanics who reported being able to speak English well from the 1980 census.

As you read the analysis in this chapter, keep in mind that Hispanics are an ethnic group, not a race. An ethnic group (e.g. Irish, German, English; or Chinese, Japanese, Korean) is defined by culture; a race (black, white, asian, American indian) is defined by biology. Hispanics are members of all races. Thus there are black Hispanics, white Hispanics, asian Hispanics, and indian Hispanics.

P^* has a possible range from 0 to 1. All proportions or percents have similar limited ranges. This sometimes creates a problem because cases tend to bunch up near the ceiling and the floor, producing relationships that are often curved. One technique to remove curvature is to mathematically transform these variables into a form that has no ceiling or floor. (See Section 22.3 for a more complete discussion of transformations.) A standard transformation is called a logit, the log of the ratio of proportions. The logit of HOUSINT is calculated as:

```
LET LHOUSINT = LOG (HOUSINT / (1 - HOUSINT))
```

Substituting this new variable into the model we have been working with in this chapter gives us:

```
MODEL LHOUSINT = CONSTANT + SPEAKENG
```

From the new model, we obtained new output:

```
DEP VAR:LHOUSINT      N:      30  MULTIPLE R: 0.761  SQUARED MULTIPLE R: 0.580
ADJUSTED SQUARED MULTIPLE R:   .565     STANDARD ERROR OF ESTIMATE:         0.550

VARIABLE        COEFFICIENT    STD ERROR    STD COEF  TOLERANCE     t     P(2 TAIL)

CONSTANT          -3.825         0.693        0.000       .      -5.516    0.000
SPEAKENG           5.210         0.838        0.761     1.000     6.216    0.000


                    ANALYSIS OF VARIANCE

SOURCE       SUM-OF-SQUARES   DF   MEAN-SQUARE      F-RATIO       P

REGRESSION        11.682       1      11.682        38.645      0.000
RESIDUAL           8.464      28       0.302
```

Compared to the output from the regression on untransformed data, e.g. Figure 4.4, this regression is very similar. The significance levels and signs of the coefficients remain the same. Unlike P^* the transformed data can be negative, so the negative coefficient for the constant is less bothersome. However, the constant is only important if SPEAKENG is zero and the smallest value in the data is above 0.5. Since no American cities have a proportion of Hispanic English speakers anywhere near zero and it is questionable to extend a relationship beyond the range of the data, this is not an important issue in this regression. The issue is important if zero is a meaningful value in your data. The summary statistics indicate the transformed data do not fit quite as well; both the R-square and F-ratio are slightly smaller. In this case, the logit transformation is a technical correction which makes no practical difference. Interested readers will find further confirmation of this using the appropriate residuals plots. Because of its technical superiority, we will use the logit of housing integration as our dependent variable in the next chapter.

Do the assumptions really matter?

To be fair to Achen, the quotation that regression "gets the right answer" is in the context of his discussion of the consistency of least squares regression. In our view, this is not particularly helpful. In order to prove consistency, you have to assume, among other things, that the model is correctly specified and that there are no outliers. In other words, the really problematic issues that researchers confront when they face real data are assumed away.

Confidence interval for a single case

To find a simultaneous confidence band for a bivariate regression, you need to correct SEPRED for the number of cases in the regression. This involves some minor addition and subtraction. The formula is in Draper and Smith (1981, p. 48, Section 1.7.2). Confidence surfaces cannot be found using SEPRED.

Further reading

Vast numbers of books have been written about regression, so you can easily find one. But you probably want a good book. Picky, picky, picky. Among introductory statistics texts you can find good basic introductions to regression in Agresti and Findley (1986), and Bohrnstedt and Knoke (1994). Tufte (1974) is also good. Like most introductory texts, these books focus on interpreting the statistics produced by regression and they go very lightly over plotting and other diagnostics that would help you find pathological data that distort the statistics. It's important that you take this into account as you read. Among advanced books the more accessible are Atkinson (1985), Chambers et al. (1983), and Cleveland (1994). For other advanced books on multiple regression, see the notes at the end of the next chapter; for information on specific problems with your data see the notes at the end of the Problems with your Data chapter.

References

Achen, C. H. (1982). *Interpreting and Using Regression.* Sage University Paper Series on Quantitative Applications in the Social Sciences, series 07-029. Beverly Hills and London: Sage Publications.

Agresti, A. and Findley, B. (1986). *Statistical Methods for the Social Sciences.* San Francisco: Dellen.

Atkinson, A. C. (1985). *Plots, Transformations, and Regression.* New York: Oxford University Press.

Bartlett, M. S. (1935). The effect of non-normality on the *t*-distribution. *Proceedings of the Cambridge Philosophical Society, 31*, 223.

Beckman, R. J. and Cook, R. D. (1983). Outlier..........S (with discussion). *Technometrics, 25*, 119-163.

Bibby, J. (1977). The general linear model: a cautionary tale. In C. A. O'Muircheartaigh and C. Payne (eds.), *The Analysis of Survey Data: Model Fitting* (pp. 35-79). New York: John Wiley & Sons.

Bohrnstedt, G. W. and Knoke, D. (1994). *Statistics for Social Data Analysis* (3rd ed.). Itasca, IL: F. E. Peacock.

Bohrnstedt, G. W. and Carter, T. M. (1971). Robustness in regression analysis. In H. Costner (ed.), *Sociological Methodology,* 118-146. San Francisco: Jossey-Bass.

Boneau, C. A. (1960). The effects of violations of assumptions underlying the *t* test. *Psychological Bulletin, 57*, 49-64.

Chambers, J. M., Cleveland, W. S., Kleiner, B., and Tukey, P. A. (1983). *Graphical Methods for Data Analysis.* Boston: Duxbury.

Cleveland, W. S. (1994). *The Elements of Graphing Data* (rev. ed.). Summit, NJ: Hobart Press.

Cook, R. D. (1979). Influential observations in linear regression. *Journal of the American Statistical Association, 74*, 169-174.

Denton, N. A. and Massey, D. S. (1988). Residential segregation of blacks, Hispanics, and asians by socioeconomic status and generation. *Social Science Quarterly, 69*, 797-817.

Denton, N. A. and Massey, D. S. (1989). Racial identity among Caribbean Hispanics: The effect of double minority status on residential segregation. *American Sociological Review, 54,* 790-808.

Draper, N. and Smith, H. (1981). *Applied Regression Analysis* (2nd ed.). New York: John Wiley & Sons.

Freedman, D., Pisani, R., and Purves, R. (1978). *Statistics.* New York: Norton.

Joiner, B. L. (1981). Lurking variables: Some examples. *The American Statistician, 35,* 227-233.

Kmenta, J. (1971). *Elements of Econometrics.* New York: Macmillan.

Lewis-Beck, M. S. (1980). *Applied Regression.* Sage University Paper Series on Quantitative Applications in the Social Sciences, series 07-022. Beverly Hills and London: Sage Publications.

Lieberson, S. (1980). *A Piece of the Pie: Blacks and White Immigrants since 1880.* Berkeley: University of California Press.

Lieberson, S. (1981). An asymmetric approach to segregation. In C. Peach, V. Robinson, and S. Smith (eds.), *Ethnic Segregation in Cities*, 61-82. Croom Helm.

Massey, D. S. and Denton, N. A. (1987). Trends in the residential segregation of Hispanics, blacks, and asians, 1970-1980. *American Sociological Review, 52,* 802-825.

Massey, D. S. and Denton, N. A. (1988a). The dimensions of residential segregation. *Social Forces, 67,* 281-315.

Massey, D. S. and Denton, N. A. (1988b). Suburbanization and segregation in U. S. metropolitan areas. *American Journal of Sociology, 94,* 592-626.

Massey, D. S. and Denton, N. A. (1989). Hypersegregation in U. S. metropolitan areas: Black and Hispanic segregation along five dimensions. *Demography, 26,* 373-391.

Mosteller, F., Siegel, A., Trapido, E., and Youtz, C. (1985). Fitting straight lines by eye. In D. C. Hoaglin, F. Mosteller, and J. W. Tukey (eds.), *Exploring Data Tables, Trends, and Shapes*, 225-240. New York: John Wiley & Sons.

Mosteller, F., and Tukey, J. W. (1977). *Data Analysis and Regression.* Reading, MA: Addison-Wesley.

Tufte, E. R. (1974). *Data Analysis for Politics and Policy.* Englewood Cliffs, NJ: Prentice-Hall.

Tukey, J. W. (1977). *Exploratory Data Analysis.* Reading, MA: Addison-Wesley.

5

Multiple Regression

At the end of Chapter 4 our hero, the residuals plot, seemed to be telling us that the integration of Hispanics into U. S. society and culture was influenced by more than just Hispanic acculturation. This is going to make our model more complex. Instead of a single independent variable, the proportion of Hispanics able to speak English well (SPEAKENG), we will have at least two and perhaps more independent variables. A regression which uses multiple independent variables is called a **multiple regression**. This chapter discusses several different multiple regression models that we can use to predict the extent to which Hispanics have found housing in areas integrated with whites. As we build these models we will introduce a variety of different techniques to assist you in your interpretation and use of regression with multiple independent variables.

We want to add new independent variables to improve our prediction of LHOUSINT, an index of Hispanic housing integration. As we add new variables, we will follow a procedure broadly similar to the procedure we used in the last chapter. We begin with plots to give us preliminary evidence that the variables are linearly related and there are no outliers. If the plots look good, we run the regression. Finally, we look at residuals to confirm linearity, lack of outliers or influential points, and that our model meets key regression assumptions. The process may be repeated several times as we add or remove variables.

What variables should we add to our model? Let's look at a residuals plot again to see what it suggests. We reproduce the commands and the plot in Figure 5.1.

In the last chapter we noticed one influential point, E = El Paso, had an unusually high proportion of Hispanics compared to other cities. This was also true for San Antonio, the at-sign (@) on the plot, a city even farther from the regression line than El Paso.

This suggests that a variable measuring proportion of Hispanics in a city may be important.

When we looked into possible explanations for the other influential point, Memphis (*F*), we discovered a problem in the wording of the 1980 census questionnaire which caused many non-Hispanic blacks in southern cities to be coded Hispanic. Since we know that blacks are more segregated than Hispanics, this would explain why the regression model over predicts LHOUSINT for Memphis. If blacks in general are less integrated then perhaps black Hispanics are also less integrated. This suggests that we should add the proportion of black Hispanics to our model.

Figure 5.1
Residuals Plot Using SIZE and SYMBOL Options

```
USE HOUSE3
LET COOK15 = COOK * 15
PLOT RESIDUAL * ESTIMATE / SIZE=COOK15 SYMBOL=ID$ YLIMIT=0,-99
```

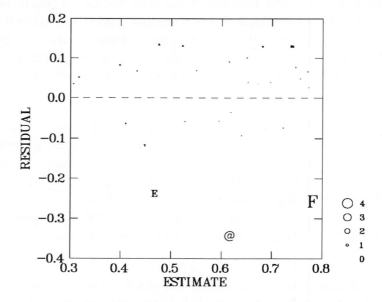

We also have to decide what to do about Memphis itself, since it is clearly an outlier. Nationally, black Hispanics are less than 4% of the Hispanic population; in Memphis the census reports more than 48% black Hispanics, a figure that no one believes. There are ways of estimating the true proportion of black Hispanics but they are complex and well beyond the scope of this chapter. If this were a research paper we would do the corrections, but for the purposes of teaching multiple regression we will drop Memphis from the sample. See Section 5.1 for more information on handling outliers.

Based on further analysis of plots and theoretical considerations we could add still other variables to our regression. However, since our goal in this chapter is not theory building, but rather to discuss multiple regression, we will begin simply and think about the implications of adding these two new variables. We invite interested readers to consider what other variables they would add and why.

The important point here is the process: We carefully analyzed various residuals plots (including some in the last chapter). We compared negative residuals to positive residuals and small residuals to large residuals. We observed several patterns, for example cities with large residuals have high proportions of Hispanics. Thinking about the patterns suggested some new variables. Residuals analysis like this is an vital part of regression and we are going into such detail to show you how it is done.

The census also contains data on the proportion of Hispanics in a metropolitan area and the proportion of black Hispanics. These variables, PHISP, the proportion of Hispanics in city, and PBHISP, the proportion of black Hispanics in city, are added to our original data in Figure 5.2.

5.1 Preliminary plots

Most of the plots we examine prior to a multiple regression are similar to those that we used in the bivariate regression in the last chapter. With only two variables, a single plot could display the entire regression. Now we are considering several independent variables and we need to keep several plots in mind in order to understand how the regression is working. We again look for evidence of irregular behavior, unusual data points, or intriguing relationships which can help guide our choice of models and fitting procedures. We also look for evidence of problems which may occur when we try to submit the data to SYSTAT's REGRESS procedure.

Figure 5.2
Adding New Variables to the Housing Integration Dataset

```
BASIC
  SAVE NEWVAR
  INPUT CITY$ PHISP PBHISP
  RUN
  'Anaheim      '    .148    .003
  'Atlanta      '    .012    .208
  'Boston       '    .024    .089
  'Buffalo      '    .013    .062
  'Chicago      '    .082    .022
  'Cincinnati   '    .006    .184
  'Dallas-FortW'    .084    .009
  'Dayton       '    .006    .136
  'Denver-Bould'    .109    .008
  'El Paso      '    .647    .003
  'Fresno       '    .292    .004
  'Gary-Hammond'    .072    .021
  'Greensboro   '    .006    .224
  'Indianapolis'    .008    .099
  'Los Angeles  '    .276    .008
  'Miami        '    .358    .018
  'Mpls-St.Paul'    .011    .031
  'New Orleans  '    .041    .093
  'New York     '    .165    .066
  'Newark       '    .068    .048
  'Oklahoma C.  '    .024    .037
  'Paterson     '    .139    .029
  'Philadelphia'    .025    .071
  'Sacramento   '    .100    .011
  'San Antonio  '    .468    .002
  'San Francisc'    .108    .017
  'San Jose     '    .175    .004
  'St. Louis    '    .009    .123
  'WashingtonDC'    .031    .079
  ~

  MERGE NEWVAR HOUSE3 / CITY$
  IF CITY$='Memphis' THEN DELETE
  SAVE HOUSE4
  RUN
```

Simple plots

The initial plotting is very simple: look at a plot for each pair of variables, both independent and dependent. These plots give you information similar to that yielded by the single plot in a bivariate regression. We discussed this in the last chapter, but here is a review of what to look for:

- Do the relationships appear linear or curved?

- Are there apparent outliers?

- Do the variances look constant?

- Do the data cluster in interesting patterns?

As in a bivariate regression, these plots tell you what to be alert for and what possible problems may occur when you fit a model and examine the residuals. However, unlike a bivariate regression, in a multivariate regression the simple plots cannot give us definitive answers because multivariate relationships often involve several variables at once. For example, a point which appears as an outlier on a scatterplot will often be the result of high values of other variables not in that plot.

Plots of independent variables versus independent variables

The plots of all pairs of independent variables are in Figure 5.3. These plots are sometimes called the **design configuration plots**. The name comes from the case where the values of the independent variables have been set by an experimental design and has been extended to nonexperimental data. The format of the plots is called a **scatterplot matrix** or, in SYSTAT-ese, a **SPLOM**. It is also called a casement plot. To read the SPLOM find a column variable (e.g. PHISP) and a row variable (e.g. PBHISP). The intersection is the scatterplot of the column variable on the horizontal axis and the row variable on the vertical axis. Each plot in the SPLOM is scaled separately, using exactly the same techniques as the PLOT command. If you need to see fine details, use the PLOT command to look at individual plots.

Our primary concerns when we look at a SPLOM of the independent variables are:

- To find potentially influential cases on the periphery of the point swarm. Especially important may be cases which seem separated from the main body of the points.

- To see the patterns generated by the points. Here we hope to see random patterns, indicating that the independent variables are unrelated to each other. We are rarely so lucky. Any apparent relationship between independent variables is evidence of collinearity which may damage the parameter estimates and inflate the standard errors.

Figure 5.3
Scatterplot Matrix of Independent Variables

```
USE HOUSE4
SPLOM SPEAKENG PHISP PBHISP / SYMBOL=1 SIZE=1.5 DENSITY=HIST
```

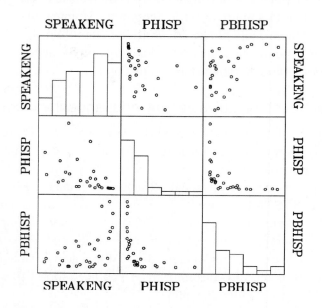

Looking at the SPLOM in Figure 5.3, the plot of SPEAKENG versus PHISP shows a pair of outliers in the upper portion of the plot. These are San Antonio and El Paso, the two cities that in Figure 5.1 suggested we add the variable measuring proportion Hispanic. There are no other visible outliers. The plot of PHISP and PBHISP shows a strange pattern: the points seem squashed against the left side and the bottom. What does this mean? If we think about these variables, we realize that both are proportions, ranging from 0 to 1. Further, there are many cities with few Hispanics and few black Hispanics. Some cities have proportions less than 0.01. This is why the points are squashed against the side and bottom.

This is a problem for our regressions because proportions have absolute limits at 0 and 1.0. Near these values, regardless of how other variables change, proportions can change very little. These are called ceiling and floor effects and they often cause curved relationships like we see in Figure 5.3. Proportions are sometimes called "limited range variables" because they cannot stray out of a fixed range. We can resolve the problem of limited range by a mathematical operation called a **transformation**. Transformations are more fully explained in Chapter 22. For now, the important thing you should know about transformations is that they can make some nonlinear relations into linear ones. In particular, a transformation called an **arcsine** transformation often changes a limited range proportion into an unrestricted range variable. This often linearizes relationships between proportions and other variables. The name is usually abbreviated as **arcsin** transformation. We will insert the following LET statements before the generating the next SPLOM:

```
LET APHISP  = ASN(SQR(PHISP))
LET APBHISP = ASN(SQR(PBHISP))
```

Figure 5.4 reprints the SPLOM with the new variables. We also added DENSITY=HIST to tell SYSTAT to print histograms in the cells of the diagonal of Figure 5.4.

You may ask, "SPEAKENG is a proportion too. If the arcsin transformation is appropriate for proportions, why don't we also transform it?" The answer is that the arcsin transformation mostly affects proportions below 0.1 and above 0.9. If you look at the distribution of SPEAKENG (e.g. use a stem-and-leaf plot, see Chapter 7) you will find that it doesn't have such extreme values. A transformation wouldn't make any difference in the regression. Further, a disadvantage of transformations is that the units often become uninterpretable. Most people have an intuitive understanding of a proportion, but what is the arcsin of the square root of a proportion? Instead of interpreting the coefficient (e.g. "as x changes by 1%, y changes by n%") we are reduced to interpreting the sign, whether the coefficient is positive or negative. For this reason, when the transformed units are hard to understand and when a transformation will not help make a relation linear, we sometimes prefer to stay with the original scale.

Now APHISP and APBHISP look much better. They are still negatively related but not squashed against the sides of the plot. SPEAKENG and PBHISP are also positively related but it doesn't look like a very strong relationship. Both of these plots may indicate collinearity problems. Again, we want to warn you not to read too much into these plots. Looking at two independent variables at a time is a good start, but it is not enough.

Independent variables versus the dependent variable

Unlike the plots in the last section where we looked at only independent variables, when we look at plots using the dependent variable, we are looking for evidence of a relationship. The three plots of the transformed independent variables against the de-

pendent variable are in Figure 5.5. You may want to repeat this plot using the untransformed variables to see the effects of the arcsinE transform.

Figure 5.4
Scatterplot Matrix of Transformed Independent Variables

```
USE HOUSE4
LET APHISP  = ASN(SQR(PHISP))
LET APBHISP = ASN(SQR(PBHISP))
SPLOM SPEAKENG APHISP APBHISP / SYMBOL=1 SIZE=1.5 DENSITY=HIST
RUN
```

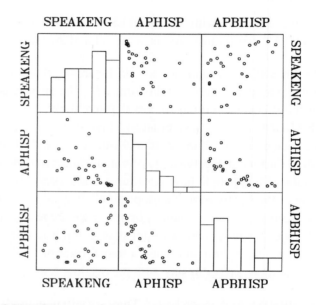

We asked for **LOWESS smoothing** or SMOOTH = LOWESS to highlight any nonlinearity in the relationships. LOWESS stands for LOcally WEighted Scatterplot
Smoothing. It finds a line based on a weighted average of nearby points. It has two
valuable properties: Since it is based on local groups of points the slope changes according to local nonlinearities. Thus it shows where a relationship deviates from linearity. Second, it is robust, meaning that it is not excessively influenced by outliers.
LOWESS is an outstanding tool for finding nonlinearities; you will see it in many plots
in this book. Its only disadvantage is that it requires a lot of computations and may be
time consuming. We recommend that you use it routinely in the plots supporting your
regressions. (For a more complete discussion, see Section 6.2)

Figure 5.5
Preliminary Plots for Multiple Regression
Plots of Independent Variables vs. the Dependent Variable

```
USE HOUSE7
SPLOM LHOUSINT*SPEAKENG APHISP APBHISP/ SMOOTH=LOWESS SHORT,
                                        SYMBOL=1 SIZE=1.5
```

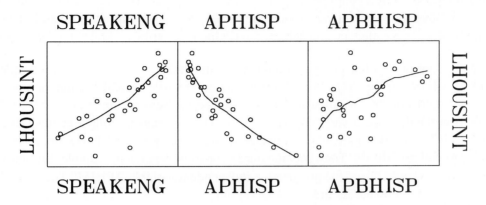

In these plots we see the relationship between LHOUSINT and SPEAKENG that we studied in the last chapter. We also see a strong linear relationship between LHOUS-INT and APHISP. You can check for yourself that the relation between LHOUSINT and APHISP is much more linear after the transformation than before. APBHISP seems to have a weaker relation to LHOUSINT, probably not linear. We see no evidence of outliers (except for our old friends, El Paso and San Antonio) and the variance seems constant. These plots, in short, show little evidence of any pattern that would distort the regression.

When multiple independent variables are included in the model then both the relationships between the independent variables as well as their individual relations to the dependent variable influence the size and direction of the regression coefficients. The scatterplots in Figure 5.5 only display the individual relations of each independent variable to the dependent variable. They do not take into account the relationships between independent variables, so they can be misleading. We need to plot independent and dependent variables taking into account relationships among the independent variables. The next section describes a type of plot to handle this problem.

Partial residuals plots

In the last chapter we fit one variable (SPEAKENG) in our model of housing integration and we would like to know what other variables, if any, should be added. This is a common situation. Good analysis often takes place in stages, and plots are an excellent tool to help us decide what to do in the next stage. The scatterplots that we examined in the previous section could be misleading because they do not take into account the effects of other independent variables in the model. We can do this using a **partial residuals plot**, also called an adjusted residuals plot, or a partial residuals leverage plot.

Creating a partial residuals plot is simple. We remove the effects of our current independent variable(s) (i.e. SPEAKENG) from the other variables and examine a plot of the resulting residuals. Specifically, here is what we do. Remove the effect of SPEAKENG from the dependent variable LHOUSINT. The residuals no longer contain all of LHOUSINT, only that part which remains after removing SPEAKENG, hence their name **partial residuals**. They become our new partial dependent variable. Similarly, remove SPEAKENG from the prospective independent variable APHISP. These residuals become our new partial independent variable.

SYSTAT makes this easy with the PARTIAL option to the SAVE command:

```
REGRESS
   USE HOUSE4
   MODEL LHOUSINT = CONSTANT + SPEAKENG + APHISP
   SAVE HOUSRES1 / PARTIAL
   ESTIMATE
```

The PARTIAL option puts out all possible partial residuals, removing in turn the effect of each independent variable. For our model, with only two independent variables, the process occurs only twice and the output file contains four residual variables:

```
YPARTIAL(1):  residuals of LHOUSINT = CONSTANT + APHISP
XPARTIAL(1):  residuals of SPEAKENG = CONSTANT + APHISP
YPARTIAL(2):  residuals of LHOUSINT = CONSTANT + SPEAKENG
XPARTIAL(2):  residuals of APHISP   = CONSTANT + SPEAKENG
```

YPARTIAL(2) contains the residuals after removing the effect of SPEAKENG from LHOUSINT. XPARTIAL(2) contains residuals after removing SPEAKENG from APHISP.

If you had more than one independent variable, you would remove the effects of all of them to create the various partial residuals. Other names for partial residuals are adjusted variables, or adjusted residuals.

A plot of the partial dependent variable against the partial independent variable is called a partial residuals plot. Compared to the standard statistical output from multiple regression, partial residuals plots have the same strengths as other plots. Their special importance stems from the fact that, since we have removed the effects of all other independent variables from both variables in the partial residuals plot, *we can interpret the plot exactly as if we were working with a simple bivariate regression.* Like a simple scatterplot in a bivariate regression, a partial residuals plot provides a *visual image of the coefficient* from the multiple regression. In addition to looking for outliers, nonlinearity, constant variance, etc. we use partial residuals plots to help judge whether the effects of prospective independent variables are important, and that helps us decide whether to keep them in the model.

Figure 5.6
Partial Residuals Plot
LHOUSINT vs. APHISP after Removing Effect of CONSTANT + SPEAKENG

```
REGRESS
   USE HOUSE4
   MODEL LHOUSINT = CONSTANT + SPEAKENG + APHISP
   SAVE HOUSRES1 / PARTIAL
   ESTIMATE

   USE HOUSRES1
   PLOT YPARTIAL(2) * XPARTIAL(2) / SYMBOL=1 SIZE=1.5 SMOOTH=LOWESS,
        SHORT YLABEL='Partial LHOUSINT' XLABEL='Partial APHISP'
```

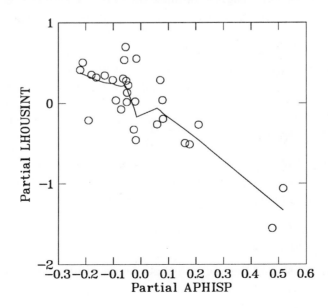

Figure 5.6 shows the partial residuals plot for LHOUSINT and APHISP. The plot shows a strong relationship, meaning that APHISP and LHOUSINT are closely related after the exclusion of SPEAKENG. The two points in the lower right corner of the plot are our old friends, El Paso and San Antonio, the cities which suggested that we include this variable in the first place. Although they are outliers they continue the line already established by the other points, suggesting that their values are the result of the same forces that influenced the other cities. This justifies retaining them in the dataset.

Figure 5.7 shows a similar partial residuals plot for LHOUSINT and APBHISP, with a curved relationship. The curve may be due to two points in the lower left corner. There seems to be little relation between LHOUSINT and APHISP on the right half of the plot. Compared to the partial residuals plot of LHOUSINT and APHISP the points seem more loosely clustered about the line, suggesting that the relationship is weaker.

5.2 Multiple regression output

The previous section completed the preliminary plots for this model and now we are ready to do another regression. Using the results from the partial residuals plots, we decide to add APHISP to the model that we developed in Chapter 4. Our model is:

$$LHOUSINT = b_0 + b_1 SPEAKENG + b_2 APHISP$$

In SYSTAT, give these commands to produce the output shown in Figure 5.8. We do not show the quick graph in order to show a different residuals plot in Figure 5.9.

Notice support for the partial residuals plot: APHISP has a significant effect on LHOUSINT. The negative coefficient suggests that the larger the proportion of Hispanics in the city, the less likely they are to find housing integrated with whites.

Comparing Figure 5.8 with the simple regression in the notes at the end of Chapter 4, we notice several changes.

- The adjusted R-square has jumped from 58% to 88% and the ANOVA table shows that it continues to be highly significant.
- The standard error of estimate has halved, from .550 to .300.
- The coefficient for SPEAKENG has dropped from 5.210 to about 3.199, but it remains highly statistically significant.
- SYSTAT warns us that El Paso (case 10) is a potential high leverage point.

Figure 5.7
Partial Residuals Plot
LHOUSINT vs. APBHISP after Removing Effect of CONSTANT + SPEAKENG

```
REGRESS
    USE HOUSE4
    MODEL LHOUSINT = CONSTANT + SPEAKENG + APBHISP
    SAVE HOUSRES2 / PARTIAL
    ESTIMATE

    USE HOUSRES2
    PLOT YPARTIAL(2) * XPARTIAL(2) / SYMBOL=1 SIZE=1.5 SMOOTH=LOWESS,
         SHORT YLABEL='Partial LHOUSINT' XLABEL='Partial APBHISP'
```

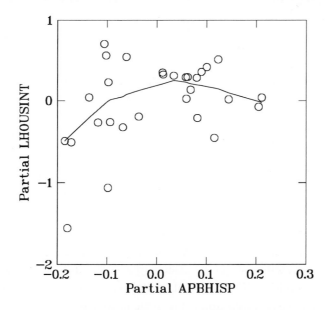

A look at the residuals plot in Figure 5.9 confirms these results. The plot shows there are somewhat more large residuals than we would expect from a dataset of this size. We may want to look closely at the characteristics of these points to try to find a common reason. The distribution of the residuals seems to have fatter tails than a true normal distribution (check this with a stem-and-leaf plot). The variance looks stable. The LOWESS line shows only a gentle curvature. A first guess is that it is caused by the several large residuals, another reason for looking closely at them. You may want to check these suggestions for yourself by doing some additional plots; a normal probability plot is another obvious plot.

Figure 5.8
Output from Model: LHOUSINT = CONSTANT + SPEAKENG + APHISP

```
REGRESS
   USE HOUSE4
   MODEL LHOUSINT = CONSTANT + SPEAKENG + APHISP
   SAVE HOUSRES3 / DATA RESIDUAL
   ESTIMATE
```

Dep Var: LHOUSINT N: 29 Multiple R: 0.940 Squared multiple R: 0.883

Adjusted squared multiple R: 0.874   Standard error of estimate: 0.300

Effect	Coefficient	Std Error	Std Coef	Tolerance	t	P(2 Tail)
CONSTANT	−1.452	0.546	0.0	.	2.660	0.013
SPEAKENG	3.199	0.589	0.454	0.644	5.430	0.000
APHISP	−2.297	0.323	−0.595	0.644	7.117	0.000

Analysis of Variance

Source	Sum-of-Squares	DF	Mean-Square	F-Ratio	P
Regression	17.678	2	8.839	97.972	0.000
Residual	2.346	26	0.090		

Durbin-Watson D Statistic   1.899
First Order Autocorrelation −0.009

Residuals have been saved.

The addition of another variable has worked so that, at least from a technical point of view, we have substantially improved our ability to predict LHOUSINT. What can the regression coefficients tell us about the effects of acculturation and size of the minority population on assimilation? The simplest interpretation of, for example, the SPEAK-ENG coefficient is that every additional 1% in the proportion of Hispanics able to speak English well yields a gain in housing integration; adding about 3.199 to our index of Hispanic housing integration. Unfortunately, this simple interpretation is almost certainly wrong.

Figure 5.9
Residuals Plot
Model: LHOUSINT = CONSTANT + SPEAKENG + APHISP

```
USE HOUSRES3
PLOT RESIDUAL * ESTIMATE / SYM=1 SIZE=1.5 SMOOTH=LOWESS SHORT,
                          SPIKE=0 FILL YLIM=0,-999
```

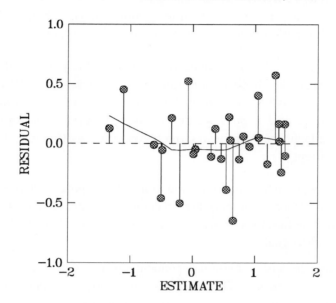

5.3 Interpreting multiple regression coefficients

The tipoff that the simple interpretation is wrong comes when you notice that the coefficient for SPEAKENG changed from 5.210 to 3.199 as we added APHISP to the model. (Compare Figure 5.8 with the bivariate regression at the end of Chapter 4.) This change of over two standard deviations occurred merely because we added another variable to the model. Further, there was no indication from the results of the bivariate regression model that anything like this could occur. This is not uncommon. The point is that in multiple regression, the size of any coefficient depends not only on the sample and the values of the variable but also on which other variables are in the model. In fact, the other variables in a model may often be more important in determining the size of a coefficient than the values of the variable itself. This is a tricky problem.

Some researchers respond to these problems by saying that they don't look at the size of the coefficient, only at whether it is significant or not. This too is a house built upon sand. Every one of the effects that we discussed in the preceding paragraph distorts not only the estimated coefficients but also the estimates of the standard errors.

The conditions that we have been describing were called specification error in the discussion of the assumptions of regression in Section 4.4. This should give you a better sense of why specification error is so insidious and so important.

The importance of these problems depends, in part, on the purpose of the regression. Specification error makes it difficult to interpret the regression coefficients and their standard errors, but it is less significant for other aspects of regression. Thus, if your purpose is only to be able to predict a dependent variable (sometimes called forecasting) rather than attach a substantive interpretation to the coefficients, then these issues may not be important.

However, in many practical and policy situations our purpose is to assess how the various independent variables influence the dependent variable. Here these issues are very important. In such situations we need to recognize that there is a crucial difference between two alternative goals:

1. Changing the values of a single independent variable when the other independent variables are free to change. This often describes policy-oriented research in natural settings where researchers have no control over most variables.

2. Changing a single independent variable when the other independent variables cannot change. This often describes designed experiments.

If the independent variables are basically unrelated to each other, then the second alternative may be feasible. However, this is rare in the social sciences and economics. In most situations, the regression model will be able to predict what will happen only in the former case. Changing one variable while holding the others constant will almost certainly interfere with the underlying pattern of variation and covariation which originally produced the regression results, thus making the original coefficient estimates no longer accurate. The point is this: The regression works only to the extent that the independent and dependent variables together continue to be driven by the same fundamental forces that were acting when the data were collected. If we interfere with these forces, the results of a regression will most likely change and the direction and magnitude of that change will not be predictable from the original regression results. In most policy situations, this is a real danger.

This problem is particularly serious in situations where we have no way to measure a variable directly. Intelligence, acculturation, socioeconomic status, and economic growth are examples of variables which can only be measured indirectly, by finding one or more other variables which we believe to be closely related to them. These variables are called **proxy variables**. The coefficients of proxy variables are very difficult, possibly impossible, to interpret.

There is an important difference between experimental and observational studies. In an observational study, regardless of how the variables are selected, the researcher can never be sure that there are not other independent variables related to the dependent variable in the population sampled. These may be unknown to the researcher, difficult to measure, or thought to be unimportant. To the extent that these variables are correlated with the variables observed (to some degree, they always will be), the coefficients of the variables in the model will overestimate (or underestimate, if the correlation is negative) the actual effects of the observed variables. Since the inaccuracies in the coefficient estimates depend on variables which have not been measured, it is hard to judge how much inaccuracy is present. In an experimental study, if the randomization has been properly employed, then unknown variables will not influence the model.

Regression is probably the most powerful single technique we have for analyzing data. But it will not give you accurate results if you do not take into account the ways in which its results may be misleading and biased. It is strongest when used carefully in conjunction with other techniques, especially graphical methods. The above paragraphs are a summary of some, but by no means all of the weaknesses of the coefficient estimates. If you want to read more, consult Mosteller and Tukey (1977, Chapter 13), Snedecor and Cochran (1967, Section 13.6), and Tukey (1973, 1974), from which much of this material was drawn.

5.4 Adding variables to the model

After adding a new variable to the model, you will want to know if there have been significant changes in the relationship between the new model and the variables still not included in the model. Frequently, you will find important changes. To examine this possibility, create a new set of partial residuals plots for each of the other variables not in the model. We used the commands shown in Figure 5.10 to create a new partial AP-BHISP variable and plot it.

Figure 5.10
Partial Residuals Plot
Adjusted for CONSTANT + SPEAKENG + APHISP

```
REGRESS
   USE HOUSE4
   MODEL LHOUSINT = CONSTANT + APBHISP + SPEAKENG + APHISP
   SAVE HOUSRES4 / PARTIAL
   ESTIMATE

   USE HOUSRES4
   PLOT YPARTIAL(1) * XPARTIAL(1) / SYMBOL=1 SIZE=1.5 SMOOTH=LINEAR,
        SHORT YLABEL='Partial LHOUSINT' XLABEL='Partial APBHISP'
```

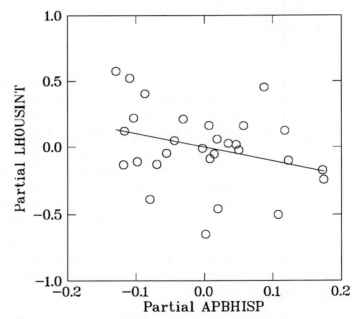

The new partial residuals plot is in Figure 5.10. Notice the relationship. We saw a positive relationship between LHOUSINT and APBHISP in all previous plots (see Figure 5.5 and Figure 5.7) but, once we control for the influence of both SPEAKENG and APHISP, the proportion of Hispanics living in neighborhoods with whites seems negatively related to APBHISP. This is consistent with our original hypothesis that black Hispanics, like blacks generally, would be more segregated than nonblack Hispanics. With APBHISP our model is:

```
LHOUSINT =   CONSTANT + SPEAKENG + APHISP + APBHISP
```

The REGRESS output from that model is in Figure 5.11.

Figure 5.11
Output from Model: LHOUSINT = CONSTANT + SPEAKENG + APHISP + APBHISP

```
Dep Var: LHOUSINT N: 29 Multiple R:  0.946 Squared multiple R:  0.895

Adjusted squared multiple R:  0.882     Standard error of estimate:     0.291

Effect          Coefficient    Std Error    Std Coef Tolerance    t   P(2 Tail)

CONSTANT          -1.179         0.553         0.0         .      -2.133   0.043
SPEAKENG           3.293         0.573         0.467     0.638     5.749   0.000
APHISP            -2.730         0.406        -0.707     0.381    -6.723   0.000
APBHISP           -1.032         0.619        -0.162     0.447    -1.667   0.108

                        Analysis of Variance

Source          Sum-of-Squares    DF   Mean-Square    F-Ratio       P

Regression          17.912         3     5.971        70.707     0.000
Residual             2.111        25     0.084
```

Comparing this output to the previous model in Figure 5.8, notice:

- The adjusted R-squared has increased slightly, from 88% to 89%.

- The coefficients for SPEAKENG and APHISP remain almost unchanged. This is consistent with plots of those variables against APBHISP; we saw a generally random scatter of points.

- The negative coefficient of APBHISP suggests that cities with a large proportion of black Hispanics tend to have less integrated housing. This coefficient is not significant at the conventional 5% level.

In general, these are positive results, but the fact is that the estimated coefficient for APBHISP is not significant at the conventional level. If APBHISP has important theoretical significance, we would probably leave it in the model. If we were building our model with less of an eye toward theory, we would probably not add it to our model. The various residuals plots are not reproduced here for reasons of space. We suggest that you run them yourself to confirm that this is a good model. You will still see some outliers. What do they suggest to you about other variables to add to the model?

Some researchers would have approached this model differently than we have. They would have simply put all the variables in a model and let the regression determine which were significant and which were not. This seems so much easier; why didn't we do it? This approach has a very serious problem. There are hints about the problem in our discussion of partial residuals plots; now we can make them explicit. We stressed looking at partial residuals plots because simple plots can be very misleading. Without looking at partial residuals plots, you have no way to check that the SYSTAT regression output is correct. The output could be completely misleading, for example, because of a single outlier or serious curvature that didn't show up in the simple plots, and you would never know it. Although there are other ways to check these possibilities, they are much more difficult to use than plots and eyeballs. The output from regression is only as accurate as the input: garbage in, garbage out.

5.5 Why are regression coefficients nonsignificant?

The SYSTAT regression output apparently contradicts the evidence we saw in the plots. The partial residuals plot in Figure 5.10 suggested that APBHISP had a negative slope but the output said it was not significant at the 5% level. APBHISP had a positive slope in earlier partial residuals plots. What is going on here? The general issue is, why is a regression coefficient significant or not significant? The straightforward reason is that there may be no relationship between the independent variable and the dependent variable. At times, for theoretical or other reasons, you will doubt this. There are several reasons why a coefficient may be nonsignificant even though the independent and dependent variables are in fact related. Here is a partial list:

1. Specification error in the model (e.g omitted variable bias)
2. Collinearity
3. Sample size too small
4. Restricted variation in the independent variable

Specification error is always a possible problem in observational studies. As we said at the beginning of the chapter, there are undoubtedly many factors that influence housing integration, and we've not included most in this model. Another source of specification error would be if the relationship between the independent and dependent variables were not linear, but curved. This sort of specification error would show up in the plots, so we can eliminate it, at least in this case.

Collinearity is a problem when the independent variables are not statistically independent, but are related to each other. It is too complex to discuss in this paragraph; refer to Section 6.3.

The sample in the housing integration regression is small. This could easily make the APBHISP coefficient nonsignificant. We could add more cities to our sample, but it wouldn't be easy or cheap. A massive amount of data reduction is required to summarize the census data into a single case for each metropolitan area. In other research, new cases can sometimes be added more readily.

A characteristic of regression is that as the variation of an independent variable declines, the standard error of its regression coefficient increases. In this regression, the variation in APBHISP is quite small. After the arcsin transformation it ranges from 0.045 to 0.493. and, even if we had more cities, it would not be likely to increase very much. In some studies, the researcher can find cases with more extreme values of an independent variable.

The point is, a nonsignificant coefficient may indicate a nonsignificant relationship, but it may also result from something entirely different. You need to be aware of the other possibilities so you know when to take them into account.

5.6 Dummy variables

This part of the book emphasizes the analysis of continuous variables, but we occasionally want to use regression to analyze data with several distinct categories. The categories are different subgroups of the data which we think display different behavioral patterns. Typical examples of such subgroups of data are males and females, different sources of data (i.e. if the data came from several machines or factories), or different regions of the country.

In SYSTAT there are two ways you can use categorical variables in regression. One makes use of the SYSTAT CATEGORY statement and is generally called analysis of covariance. This is discussed in Chapter 12. The second makes use of **dummy variables**. A dummy variable is a variable which is coded 1 to indicate the presence of an attribute and 0 to indicate its absence. Dummy variables are used in two situations: a simple case where you have only two categories, and a complex case with more than two categories. The theoretical and methodological implications of these two situations are different so we will discuss them separately.

The simple case is the most common. Our discussion of the simple, two-category case uses data from the housing integration example. There are two competing explanations of how new immigrants influence integration. The acculturation argument claims that new immigrants find housing near friends and relatives in the immigrant ghettos and barrios. This argument suggests that new immigrants tend to lower the average level of housing integration. The housing stock argument claims that although this may be true for small or moderate numbers of new immigrants, large numbers tend to overwhelm the available housing in immigrant areas, forcing new immigrants to look for housing in other areas. This would tend to raise the average level of housing integration.

To test these competing explanations using dummy variables we would create a new variable, NEWIMM, to indicate the presence of large numbers of new Hispanic immigrants. NEWIMM has two categories, coded 0 and 1. A case where NEWIMM = 1 means that the city has a large proportion of new Hispanic immigrants and NEWIMM = 0 means a small proportion. Which category is coded 0 and which is coded 1 is not important from a technical point of view—this coding could have been reversed—but switching the coding will reverse the sign of the coefficient and this may make the output less intuitively clear. In Figure 5.12, we enter the data and run the regression. Since our goal is to describe the use and interpretation of dummy variables, we will proceed without the usual preliminary plots. If you were doing the plots, a good starting point would be a grouped box plot: see Section 4.7 and Figure 4.20.

The coefficient for NEWIMM is significant and positive. It suggests that on average in the nine cities with a large proportion of new Hispanic immigrants more Hispanics live in neighborhoods integrated with whites compared to the other 20 cities. This supports the housing stock explanation.

Figure 5.12
Adding a Dummy Variable for New Immigrants

```
BASIC
   SAVE NEWVAR2
   INPUT CITY$ NEWIMM
   RUN
'Anaheim    '    1
'Atlanta    '    0
'Boston     '    1
'Buffalo    '    0
'Chicago    '    1
'Cincinnati '    0
'Dallas-FortW'   1
'Dayton     '    0
'Denver-Bould'   1
'El Paso    '    0
'Fresno     '    0
'Gary-Hammond'   0
'Greensboro '    0
'Indianapolis'   0
'Los Angeles'    0
'Miami      '    0
'Mpls-St.Paul'   1
'New Orleans'    0
'New York   '    0
'Newark     '    0
'Oklahoma C.'    1
'Paterson   '    1
'Philadelphia'   0
'Sacramento '    0
'San Antonio'    0
'San Francisc'   0
'San Jose   '    0
'St. Louis  '    0
'WashingtonDC'   1
~

   SAVE HOUSE5
   MERGE HOUSE4 NEWVAR2 / CITY$


REGRESS
   USE HOUSE5
   MODEL LHOUSINT = CONSTANT + SPEAKENG + APHISP + NEWIMM
   ESTIMATE
```

The output:

```
Dep Var: LHOUSINT N: 29 Multiple R:  0.950 Squared multiple R:  0.902

Adjusted squared multiple R:  0.891     Standard error of estimate:       0.280

Effect        Coefficient   Std Error    Std Coef Tolerance    t    P(2 Tail)

CONSTANT         -1.896        0.546        0.0        .      -3.475    0.002
SPEAKENG          3.566        0.573        0.506    0.591     6.229    0.000
APHISP           -2.091        0.314       -0.542    0.589    -6.652    0.000
NEWIMM            0.265        0.119        0.148    0.897     2.237    0.034

                        Analysis of Variance

Source           Sum-of-Squares   DF   Mean-Square    F-Ratio       P

Regression           18.069        3      6.023       77.037      0.000
Residual              1.955       25      0.078
```

Suppose, however, we wanted to know how the model changed for different cities. Then we could use the following procedure. The model estimated by REGRESS is:

```
LHOUSINT = -1.896 + 3.556 SPEAKENG - 2.091 APHISP + .265 NEWIMM
```

In the cities with high proportions of new immigrants NEWIMM = 1, so we can rewrite the above model as:

```
LHOUSINT = -1.896 + 3.556 SPEAKENG - 2.091 APHISP + .265 * 1
         = (-1.896 + .265) + 3.556 SPEAKENG - 2.091 APHISP
         = -1.631 + 3.556 SPEAKENG - 2.091 APHISP
```

In cities with low proportions of new immigrants NEWIMM = 0:

```
LHOUSINT = -1.896 + 3.556 SPEAKENG - 2.091 APHISP + .265 * 0
         = -1.896 + 3.556 SPEAKENG - 2.091 APHISP
```

Thus, by using this dummy variable we created two separate models: one predicting the proportion of Hispanics who live in neighborhoods with whites in cities with a large proportion of new Hispanic immigrants and a different one for cities with a small proportion of Hispanic immigrants. Notice that the two models have the same coefficients for SPEAKENG and APHISP, they differ only in their constants. This is crucial. Dummy variables are used to investigate the situation where the data can be divided into discrete categories and we think that the *coefficients are the same for all categories* but that the *constants are different*. Thus, the fitted values from a regression model with a dummy variable form two parallel lines (since the coefficients are the same, the lines are parallel) with different constants.

In the second, complex case dummy variables are used when the categorical variable that you want to test has more than two categories. The technical changes here are straightforward: instead of one dummy variable, you create several new variables, one for each category. What makes this situation complicated is the interpretation of the co-efficients and the theoretical implications of the results. We will begin by showing how to create several dummy variables from one categorical variable, and then discuss the interpretation of the results and the theoretical implications.

Suppose, for example, we had reason to believe that the REGION in which the city was located influenced LHOUSINT. If REGION were coded:

> 1 = Northeast
> 3 = Midwest
> 3 = South
> 4 = West

Then we could create four new variables coding the city as:

NOR_EAST	1 means city is in the Northeast, 0 if not
MIDWEST	1 means city is in the Midwest, 0 if not
SOUTH	1 means city is in the South, 0 if not
WEST	1 means city is in the West, 0 if not

We could then enter any three of the four dummy variables into our model. We can only enter three because all the information about REGION is contained in any subset of three variables. That is, for a case if NOR_EAST, SOUTH, and WEST are coded as 0, we know that MIDWEST must be coded as 1. This would be the way the four variables were coded for Chicago, for example. Similarly, if another case has NOR_EAST coded as 1 and MIDWEST and SOUTH coded as 0, then WEST must also be coded as 0 (Boston is an example). The general rule for dummy variables is: if a variable has n categories, you may enter any n - 1 dummy variables in your regression model. We followed this rule in the simple case above when, although we had two categories of cities, we only entered one variable: NEWIMM. By convention the categories are mutually exclusive and exhaustive.

Here is an example which, for reasons of space, we present without the output. Suppose that we wanted to test the effect of REGION on LHOUSINT. If we decide to omit NOR_EAST, then the model statement would be:

```
MODEL LHOUSINT = CONSTANT + MIDWEST + SOUTH + WEST +,
                 SPEAKENG + APHISP
```

For cases where the city was in the Northeast (like Boston), the fitted value would simply be:

```
LHOUSINT = CONSTANT + SPEAKENG + APHISP
```

because MIDWEST, SOUTH, and WEST are all 0 for those cases. For cases of midwestern cities (like Gary, Indiana), the fitted value would be:

```
LHOUSINT = CONSTANT + MIDWEST + SPEAKENG + APHISP
```

The t-test for MIDWEST compares cities in the Midwest with cities in the Northeast. Had we chosen a different category to omit, the test for MIDWEST would have been compared to that category.

The category that you choose to omit is important and should be chosen carefully. The t-test associated with a given dummy variable is the difference between the means of cases from only two categories of the dependent variable. The first mean is the mean of all cases included in the category coded as 1. The second mean is the mean of the cases in the category which was omitted from the model. Any continuous variables in the model are automatically taken into account in this test. Thus, the t-tests for dummy variables are only significant when the omitted category is significantly different from the categories included in the model. For this reason the omitted category is essential to interpret the effects of dummy variables and, if at all possible, you should choose a theoretically significant category to omit. If you can't find a theoretically meaningful category, pick the category with the largest number of cases.

In many cases, the t-tests that SYSTAT prints automatically are not appropriate because they test the significance of only one coefficient. Often we have created several dummy variables from a single conceptual variable. In this situation, the appropriate significance test is a *simultaneous* test of whether the coefficients of all dummy variables are zero. For example, if we believed that REGION was a single concept, we would need to test the hypothesis that the coefficients of all three dummy variables were zero. Following the ESTIMATE statement we would give these commands:

```
HYPOTHESIS
EFFECT = MIDWEST & SOUTH & WEST
TEST
```

The resulting F-statistic is the appropriate simultaneous test.

The crucial point to grasp is that you should not interpret the t-tests for dummy variables in the same way that you interpret t-tests for continuous variables. The appropriate interpretation depends on whether the dummy variables can be interpreted alone or whether they are only meaningful simultaneously, as a single conceptual unit. In neither case is the interpretation the same as that for continuous variables.

A single conceptual variable is often used to create several dummy variables in exploratory research. The researchers who use this strategy do not really believe that the conceptual variable causes changes in the dependent variable. Rather they use the conceptual variable as a proxy for other causal variables. For example, no one believes that "region" by itself causes anything. But there are significant historical, cultural, climatic, economic, social, and other differences between regions. We may want to know if any of them has an effect. We can use REGION as a crude measure for these differences. If REGION is significant, we would search for a continuous variable that accounts for the differences that we see. One way to do this is to put likely continuous variables into the model, looking for one that makes the effect of REGION disappear.

It is important to keep the relationship between your theory and your dummy variables clearly in mind. Ask yourself if the categories of your variable really cause changes in the dependent variable in the same sense as the continuous variables in your model. If they don't, perhaps you should find a continuous variable that more closely measures the theoretical concepts you're trying to test. If you use a dummy variable, make sure that each category of your dummy variable makes theoretical sense. For example, if you intend to test the common theory that for many social, cultural, economic, and political variables "the South is always different," then creating a set of dummy variables from REGION would not be an appropriate test. Instead, you should create a single dummy variable to test South versus non-South.

This section has discussed categorical variables in regression. Specifically, we've shown how you can use dummy variables to model a situation where the coefficients are the same, but the constants are different. Another situation arises when the coefficients are different but the constant is the same. You can also model a third case where both the coefficient and the constant are different. These latter cases are substantially more complex. These issues and others are discussed in Hanushek and Jackson (1977).

5.7 Choosing a model

In much of the past two chapters we have been talking about models, and we have suggested a variety of criteria by which a model could be chosen. It is appropriate to bring these together and summarize them.

Use of theory

What variables help explain the proportion of Hispanics who live in integrated neighborhoods? Certainly the proportion who speak English, the overall proportion of Hispanics in the city, and the proportion of new Hispanic immigrants which are in our model. Other plausible variables include the number of new jobs available, and how much inexpensive housing is available for immigrants. Perhaps the level of housing integration differs according to the average income and education of the Hispanic population. This is a shortened list that can easily grow much longer. Just which variables to use is a serious problem. It is largely unresolvable without relying on previous theoretical and empirical work. Even in small studies, the number of potentially informative models and their associated plots, regressions, and datasets quickly becomes unmanageably huge. For practical purposes, theory must guide and limit the number of relationships and models examined.

One particularly fruitful approach is to develop two or more different theoretical explanations of the same phenomenon. Regression models of each of the theories often suggest that one theory is preferable to the other(s). If you show that a particular model is significant, keep in mind that your argument will be much stronger if you can also show that alternative models do not work. Particularly in the social sciences, theory is not usually strong enough to support this approach and most research is more exploratory in nature. It attempts to elaborate or refine an existing theory and the conditions under which it is true.

A sound general approach to model building is to start with the simplest relationships and slowly add more complexity to the model. An example of this is the analysis that we have done over the last two chapters with the housing integration dataset.

Model building is rarely straightforward. Typically the results from early versions of your model will compel you to rethink part of your theory. Similarly, as your theory changes, you will often want to change your model. Adding new variables to the dataset, as we did when we saw the residuals plot in Figure 5.1, is common. This iterative relationship between theory-building and statistical model-building is character-istic of good research.

Finally, as you examine the output from regressions and plots keep the data in mind. Remember where they came from, how many cases there are, the variance of the variables, whether the variables are proxies or direct measurements of a theoretical phenomenon, the source of the measurements, whether or not multiple measurements of the variables were made, the quality of the data measuring different variables and the specification of the model. If you would like to read further discussion of the role of theory in research see Blalock (1970), Campbell and Stanley (1963) and Stinchcombe (1968).

Analysis of residuals

This book has emphasized the analysis of residuals as the most effective way to discover flaws in a model and suggest alternatives. Rather than repeat the techniques developed in previous sections we refer you to the following sections:

4.6   Statistics from the residuals
4.7   What can the residuals tell us? (residuals plots)
5.1   Preliminary plots (partial residuals plots)

Plots and statistics can help you answer crucial questions about the model.

- Are there apparent outliers?
- Are there influential points?
- Do the relationships look linear or are they curved or bent?
- Do the data cluster in interesting patterns?
- Are the residuals sequentially correlated?
- Do the variances appear constant?
- Do variables not currently in the model appear related?
- Are the residuals normally distributed?
- Does the design configuration appear balanced?

Stepwise regression

A variety of possible models can be calculated from the same set of variables. Sometimes you may find it useful to let your computer sort through these models in some automated fashion to select the best model according to some criteria. Stepwise regression is a procedure for selecting the best model based on including only the variables which meet a certain significance level for entry into the model but do not meet another significance level for removal. In REGRESS these two significance levels are called ALPHA-TO-ENTER and ALPHA-TO-REMOVE. REGRESS allows a variable to enter the equation only if the significance level of the variable is less than ALPHA-TO-ENTER. It removes a variable if its' significance level rises above the level of ALPHA-TO-REMOVE. In contrast to ordinary regression where REGRESS simply calculates the coefficients of the model that you specified, in stepwise regression REGRESS adds or deletes variables until it arrives at a single best model.

The stepwise procedure that REGRESS follows works like this. First, if a constant was included in the MODEL statement, the constant is added to the model. Second, the variables are scanned to find the one with the smallest p-value. If that level is greater than ALPHA-TO-ENTER the procedure ends with no variables in the model. Otherwise, the variable is added to the model. Third, the remaining variables not in the model are scanned to select variable with the smallest significance level. Again, if that level is less than ALPHA-TO-ENTER, the variable is added to the model. Otherwise, the procedure terminates. Fourth, from this point the variables already in the model are examined to see if any have a significance level greater than ALPHA-TO-REMOVE. If any meet this criterion, they are removed from the model one by one until all remaining variables have significance levels below ALPHA-TO-REMOVE. Then the variables not in the model (including any which were removed in the previous step) are examined to find a variable to add to the model. This process of removing and adding variables continues until no more variables meet the removal or entry criteria.

This process has several advantages. It is fast. The steps are printed, so you can see how the variables were added and deleted and how the multiple R-square changed at each step. This may teach you something about how your variables are related. It is so easy that it is very appealing when you have many variables and want a quick, best model.

The process also has many disadvantages. When you have many variables, the results will frequently be misleading. Commonly, several different models, often with different variables, have about the same Multiple R-square. Stepwise regression, however, gives you only one model and does not show you alternatives. Like all regression procedures, it is sensitive to outliers and to collinearity. Particularly, the presence of collinearity can lead to very confusing results. There is no guarantee that it will produce the model with the highest R-square; the SYSTAT manual contains an example. For a further summary of its problems see the references in the SYSTAT manual.

Stepwise regression gives you a model which is the best model according to the procedure described above. This may or may not be the model that you want. Sensible judgment is still needed in initial selection of variables. You want to use it after you have examined the preliminary plots. Like all least squares procedures, stepwise regression is not effective in the presence of outliers, curvature, unstable variances, etc. Data must be clean first. It is most useful when you use it repeatedly on different sets of variables. After you have found several initial models, it may be particularly helpful to substitute more theoretically meaningful or more interpretable variables in the models. SYSTAT provides an INTERACTIVE option to give you more control over the steps. Use it to explore alternative models.

Stepwise regression has a bad reputation because it has been used in a mindless fashion without paying attention to its weaknesses. Used carefully, it is a valuable tool. Careful use implies attention to the correct specification of the model, to analysis of influential cases, to preliminary plotting, to partial residuals plots, to residuals plots, and to all the other sometimes tedious and time-consuming issues that we have been discussing in the past two chapters. There is no rest for the righteous researcher.

Omitting the constant

Many users are suprised to find that when they omit the term CONSTANT from a SYSTAT regression model, the R-square often approaches 1.0. While it would be nice to have a magical technique like this to make any results significant, we cannot condone the practice. Kvaalseth (1985) discusses a number of R-square measures when the constant is omitted from the model. First, remember that the standard formula for R-square is

$$R^2 = 1 - (\text{residual sum of squares})/(\text{total sum of squares about mean of } Y)$$

When the constant is omitted, the default formula used by SYSTAT (and SAS®) is the one Kvaalseth recommends, namely,

$$R^2 = 1 - \text{(residual sum of squares)/(total sum of squares about zero)}$$

These formulas make clear why SYSTAT's R-square usually increases when the constant is omitted; if the intercept is nonzero when included, then the total sum of squares about zero is larger than the total sum of squares about the mean of the dependent variable. This makes the second term in the equation smaller. Kvaalseth mentions a number of methods proposed to correct this difference, but each has its problems. The simple fact is, if you expect that the constant is nonzero, *never* omit it from the model. The only time you should be playing with a zero intercept is when you have prior knowledge that the intercept *must* be zero. This can be true if you are working in the physical sciences with established models or in certain types of psychometric scaling, but it is rare.

5.8 Purposes of regression

Now that the last two chapters have introduced regression analysis, it is useful to stand back and think about the purposes for which this tool can be used. Regression is a very general method which is used for a variety of problems. Here is a summary of the purposes that regression can serve.

- To summarize a relation, a use illustrated in the housing integration example when we found that when the average proportion of Hispanics who speak English increases by 1%, then the proportion of Hispanics who live in neighborhoods integrated with whites increases by 0.7%.

- To remove the effect of a variable which might confuse the analysis. This is the point of seasonal adjustments made to economic data because the seasonal effects are often so large that, if not removed, they would obscure the underlying trend and make analysis very difficult.

- To contribute to attempts at causal analysis is a popular use for regression. While causation usually cannot be settled by use of regression, it can support or fail to support causal arguments. In the housing integration example, the argument that housing integration increases when there are large numbers of new immigrants was supported by the results of the regression model.

- Prediction or forecasting is a common use of regression. For example, we have only 30 large cities in our housing integration dataset. You could use the coefficients from the regression equation and information on the proportion of Hispanics who speak English and the proportion of Hispanics to predict the index of housing integration in other cities.

- You may want to measure the size of an effect through a regression coefficient. An extreme example of this is an attempt to discover a mathematical or empirical law. As we discussed above, this use has many difficulties when there are multiple causes and when noncausal variables are associated with other causal variables. See Mosteller and Tukey (1977, Chapter 13), Section 5.3, and Section 5.5, above, for discussion of these problems.

- You may want to remove the effects of one variable on a dependent variable so that you can study the relation between the dependent variable and some third variable. For example, you may want to remove the effects of income on marital satisfaction and then see what is left to be explained by number of children.

Whenever you confront a problem like one of these, consider using regression to help you solve it.

Notes

The additional data PHISP, PBHISP, and NEWIMM were made available to us courtesy of Douglas S. Massey and Nancy A. Denton. They are adapted from a much larger dataset assembled from the 1980 census. For a complete description see the sources cited at the end of Chapter 4. The object of the regressions presented here is to teach the use of multiple regression, not to do a complete analysis of these data. Much more can be done with these data and, if you are interested in some possibilities, consult the articles cited in the notes at the end of the previous chapter.

Dummy variables. The housing stock argument describes an inherently nonlinear process. Integration decreases until some critical level or tipping point is reached and new immigrants, unable to find housing in Hispanic barrios, spill out into other neighborhoods. The nonlinearity cannot be modelled by a linear regression and, since it is probably nonmonotonic, it cannot be corrected by a transformation. New immigrants were defined as Hispanics who entered the United States during the decade between 1970-1980. The point at which the ethnic enclave fills up varies city to city and it is not clearly specified in previous work. So we chose the cutpoints empirically by looking at partial residuals plots of partial LHOUSINT plotted against the partial proportion of new Hispanic immigrants. Cities where new immigrants composed over 55% of their Hispanic population were assigned to NEWIMM = 1. For cities with 55% or less new immigrants, NEWIMM = 0.

This introduction to dummy variables has not covered all of the aspects of dummy variables. The type of coding we've discussed is called "dummy variable coding." It is the simplest coding system. Other coding is possible and, in analysis of variance, SYSTAT uses a coding system called "effects coding." The SYSTAT manual's discussion of categorical variables is different in several respects because of this difference in coding. An excellent discussion of dummy variables is in Hanushek and Jackson (1977), see also Draper and Smith (1981).

Further reading

Too many books discuss multiple regression; the crucial problem for a reader is finding one worth reading. Small computers have changed the way regression is done by making extensive diagnostics and plots feasible. Many excellent older discussions of regression statistics and their interpretation, for example Hanushek and Jackson (1977), Kerlinger and Pedhazur (1973), Snedecor and Cochane (1967), and Tufte (1974), show their age by their lack of attention to these crucial issues. Be aware of this if you read them. Good modern discussions are in Atkinson (1985), Draper and Smith (1981), Mosteller and Tukey (1977). For good discussions of plots and other diagnostics see Atkinson (1985), Chambers et al. (1983), Chatterjee and Hadi (1988), and Cleveland (1993, 1994). The SYSTAT manual, particularly the chapter titled *Cognitive Science and Graphic Design*, contains a valuable summary of the ways people interpret visual aspects of plots, see also Tufte's (1983, 1990) outstanding books. For more basic references on regression, see the notes at the end of Chapter 4; for references on specific diagnostic tools, see the notes at the end of Chapter 7.

References

Atkinson, A. C. (1985). *Plots, Transformations, and Regression.* New York: Oxford University Press.

Belsley, D. A, Kuh E., and Welsh, R. E. (1980). *Regression Diagnostics: Identifying Influential Fata and Sources of Collinearity.* New York: John Wiley & Sons.

Blalock, H. M. (1970). *An Introduction to Social Research.* Englewood Cliffs, NJ: Prentice-Hall.

Campbell D. T., and Stanley, J. C. (1963). *Experimental and Quasi-experimental Designs for Research*. Chicago: Rand McNally.

Chambers, J. M., Cleveland, W. S., Kleiner, B., and Tukey, P. A. (1983). *Graphical Methods for Data Analysis*. Boston: Duxbury.

Chatterjee, S. and Hadi, A. S. (1988). *Sensitivity Analysis in Linear Regression*. New York: John Wiley & Sons.

Cleveland, W. S. (1979). Robust locally weighted regression and smoothing scatterplots. *Journal of the American Statistical Association, 74*, 829-836.

Cleveland, W. S. (1981). LOWESS: A program for smoothing scatterplots by robust locally weighted regression. *The American Statistician, 35*, 54.

Cleveland, W. S. (1993). *Visualizing Data*. Summit, NJ: Hobart Press.

Cleveland, W. S. (1994). *The Elements of Graphing Data* (rev. ed.) Summit, NJ: Hobart Press.

Draper, N. and Smith, H. (1981). *Applied Regression Analysis* (2nd ed.). New York: John Wiley & Sons.

Hanushek, E. A. and Jackson, J. E. (1977). *Statistical Methods for Social Scientists*. New York: Academic Press.

Kerlinger, F. N. and Pedhazur, E. J. (1973). *Multiple Regression in Behavioral Research*. New York: Holt, Rinehart & Winston.

Kvaaalseth, T.O. (1985). Cautionary note about R^2. *The American Statistician, 39*, 279-285.

Mosteller, F. and Tukey, J. W. (1977). *Data Analysis and Regression*. Reading, MA: Addison-Wesley.

Snedecor, G. W. and Cochran, W. G. (1967). *Statistical Methods*. Ames, IA: Iowa State University Press.

Stinchcombe, A. L. (1968). *Construction of Social Theories*. New York: Harcourt, Brace and World.

Tufte, E. R. (1974). *Data Analysis for Politics and Policy*. Englewood Cliffs, NJ: Prentice Hall.

Tufte, E. R. (1983). *The Visual Display of Quantitative Information*. Cheshire, CT: Graphics Press.

Tufte, E. R. (1990). *Envisioning Information*. Cheshire, CT: Graphics Press.

6

Problems With Your Data

ON PROBLEMS

Our choicest plans
    have fallen through,
our airiest castles
    tumbled over,
because of lines
    we neatly drew
and later neatly
    stumbled over.

Piet Hein

This chapter is about what you can do after you stumble. Sometimes you can pick your-self and your model up. We discuss five major problems and what you can do about them.

1. Outliers
2. Non-linearity
3. Collinearity
4. Heteroscedasticity
5. Too much data

The first problem is, how do you know that you've got a problem? This is the problem of diagnosis. Diagnosis requires the ability to identify symptoms. Each section opens with a discussion of how to identify the problem. If you don't have a problem, great! But if you do, you want to know what to do about it. The second part of each section discusses a variety of possible solutions.

6.1 Outliers

Identification of outliers is crucial to the effective use of regression. A single outlier can distort the predicted values, parameter estimates, standard errors, and the hypothesis tests—in short, everything important in the regression model.

We discuss three kinds of outliers: large residuals, high leverage points, and influential points. These represent three ways in which cases can be surprising or discrepant and may distort the regression output. The diagnosis subsection focuses on techniques to make discrepant points stand out from the mass of the data. We will show you how to test single points. We use the word outlier as a generic name for any wild value. Wild values are also called discordant observations, rogue values, contaminants, mavericks, and similar names. Residuals, high leverage points, and influential points are not always the same; large residuals may not be influential and high leverage points may not be large residuals. It is important to check for all three.

Diagnosis

Film-making is a notoriously uncertain business but it could be less uncertain if some reliable way could be found to predict how well a movie will do at the box office. A little thought will convince you that there are a large number of influences affecting the popularity of a film: for example, the time of year it is released, the stars, the plot, the soundtrack, and the effectiveness of its advertising campaign. Most of these are not easily measured but one measurable variable is a simple count of the number of theaters showing the movie. Other things being equal, we expect the more theaters showing the film, the higher the box office gross receipts. We plotted the relationship between box office gross and number of screens in Figure 6.1. Figure 6.2 lists the reported box office receipts and the number of screens showing the film (some theaters have more than one screen) for the first weekend that the film was released.

Figure 6.1
Film Box Office Dataset
Box Office Gross vs. Number of Screens

```
USE FILM1
PLOT BOXOFF * SCREENS / SYM=1  SIZE=1.5  XMIN=900  XMAX=1600,
                       YMIN=0   YMAX=16000
```

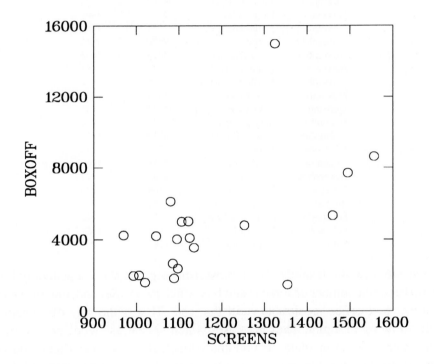

Figure 6.2
Film Box Office Dataset
Gross for First Weekend in Wide Release
October 1985—February 1986

MONTH$	FILM$	BOXOFF	SCREENS
October	Commando	7700	1495
October	Jagged Edge	4094	1125
November	Death Wish 3	5319	1460
November	Live&Die L.A	3551	1135
November	Target	2670	1085
November	Once Bitten	4025	1095
November	Rainbow Brit	1847	1088
November	KSolomon Min	5005	1122
November	Starchaser	1614	1020
December	Rocky IV	14993	1325
December	Santa Claus	4235	970
December	Spies LikeUs	8614	1556
December	Jewel of Nil	4983	1106
December	Clue	2014	1006
December	101 Dalmaton	2389	1097
January	Iron Eagle	6104	1080
January	My Chauffeur	4781	1253
February	Murphy's Rom	4195	1046
February	Youngblood	1483	1354
February	Eliminators	1987	993

The scatterplot has two features. First, most films seem to show a generally linear relationship between number of screens and box office gross. Second, one film had strikingly higher box office receipts than all the rest. This is the way discrepant points typically show up in a plot. They are cases which appear as "wild" points, separated from the main body of the data. If you know much about popular films, you will not be surprised to learn that this is the movie *Rocky IV*. Plots, like this scatterplot, are one of the best tools available for identifying unusual values. This is one reason we stressed looking at preliminary plots of all two-way relationships in your data before running regressions.

Now we have a choice. Because *Rocky IV* is clearly not part of the linear relationship in the scatterplot, we could omit it from later analyses. Alternatively, we could leave it until we have the results of other diagnostics. Deleting a case has implications that we describe below in the section, *What can you do?* Until considering these issues we will leave it in. The results of the regression appear in Figure 6.3 (we omitted the quick graph of residuals).

Figure 6.3
Output from Model: BOXOFF = CONSTANT + SCREENS

```
REGRESS
    USE FILM1
    MODEL BOXOFF = CONSTANT + SCREENS
    SAVE FILM2 / DATA RESIDUAL
    ESTIMATE
```

```
Dep Var: BOXOFF N: 20 Multiple R:  0.551 Squared multiple R:  0.303

Adjusted squared multiple R:  0.265    Standard error of estimate:    2691.392

Effect          Coefficient    Std Error    Std Coef Tolerance    t    P(2 Tail)

CONSTANT         -6980.348      4172.359       0.0        .      -1.673    0.112
SCREENS              9.876         3.527       0.551    1.000     2.800    0.012

                       Analysis of Variance

Source           Sum-of-Squares   DF  Mean-Square    F-Ratio      P

Regression        5.67903E+07      1  5.67903E+07     7.840     0.012
Residual          1.30385E+08     18  7243593.445

Durbin-Watson D Statistic      2.065
First Order Autocorrelation   -0.035
Residuals have been saved.
```

Because outliers can cause severe problems, SYSTAT warns you if it finds any. When SYSTAT saves residuals, for each case it calculates and saves three statistics: Studentized residuals, leverage, and Cook's distance. It prints a warning about cases with unusual values to alert you to potential problems. These three statistics identify three kinds of outliers: large residuals, high leverage points, and influential points.

Studentized residuals

Residuals measure the vertical distance above or below the regression line. Studentized residuals are the residuals divided by an estimate of their standard error. A residual may be an outlier if it has a large Studentized residual. If the residuals are normally distributed, the Studentized residuals are distributed according to a t-distribution. The rule of thumb is that in large samples about 5% of the Studentized residuals are greater than +2 or less than -2. SYSTAT looks at the t-distribution and prints a warning when the t-value exceeds the expected 99% level, about ±3. Cases 10 and 19 have high Studentized residuals. Looking back at Figure 6.2, you can see that case 10 is *Rocky IV* and case 19 is *Youngblood*. The Studentized residual of 5.8 for *Rocky IV* is so improbable that it should never appear in a dataset of 20 cases. This certainly confirms our initial impression that *Rocky IV* doesn't belong with these data.

Leverage

Leverage measures the horizontal distance of an individual case from the average of the independent variable(s). The dependent variable has no effect on leverage. A high leverage point is a case that is a long way from the center. The average value of leverage is p/N where p is the number of predictors (including the constant) and N is the number of cases. Cases with high leverage values should be examined as potential influential cases. SYSTAT prints its warning for cases exceeding the expected 99% level for leverage. The lack of warnings suggests that there are no extraordinarily large values for the independent variables.

Cook's distance

Cook's D combines vertical and horizontal distance. It is the closest single measure to what we mean by an influential case: a point both far away from the regression line and far out in the tail of the independent variable(s) which has significant influence on the parameter estimates. Compare D to an F-distribution with 1 and $N - p - 1$ degrees of freedom. (N = number of cases, p = number of parameters including the constant.) SYSTAT prints a warning for an influential point if Cook's D exceeds the expected 99% level. No points in our film box office dataset are influential by this standard. Note that Cook's D measures influence on the parameter values, not their standard errors.

Comparing residuals, leverage, and influence

The Studentized residuals measure the vertical distance from the regression line. Leverage measures the horizontal distance from the center of the independent variables. Cook's D combines the two. Large residuals, high leverage points, and influential observations are interrelated as illustrated by Figure 6.4.

Figure 6.4
Comparison of Large Residuals, High Leverage, and Influential Points

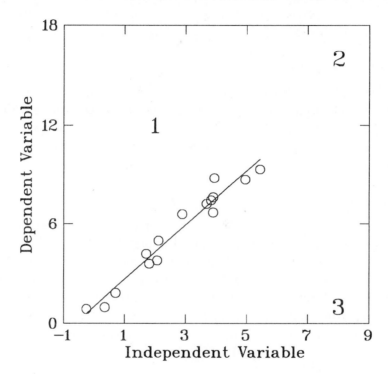

1. This point is a large residual near the mean of the independent variable(s). Near the mean, leverage will be small. However, it will have a large influence; it won't affect the slope parameters but it will change the constant (intercept). It may also affect the standard errors of the coefficients.

2. A point like this has a small residual because it is located near the line. Because it is a long way away from the center of the independent variable, it has a large leverage. Its location close to the line means that even though it has unusually large values for both the independent and dependent variable, it has a small influence.

3. Finally, this is a large residual, far from the center of the independent and dependent variables. This point is highly influential and has a large leverage.

SYSTAT's warnings about Studentized residuals, high leverage, and high influence cannot find every outlier. In particular, multivariate outliers may not show up. Nor is every case highlighted by the warnings truly an outlier; on average, at the 99% level, one case out of 100 will be reported as a potential outlier. These messages mean exactly what they say: they are *warnings* that something needs further investigation. The rest of this section illustrates other techniques you can use to make outliers stand out from the rest of the data.

Diagnostics saved in a file

The dataset created by the SAVE command contains three statistics to help you diagnose outliers: Studentized residuals, leverage, and Cook's *D*. The residuals and the predicted values are also saved, as well as the standard error of the predicted values. Several plots help you extract information from these diagnostic data. These plots are discussed below.

Stem-and-leaf plots

One simple approach is to look at stem-and-leaf plots of several residual statistics. Stem-and-leaf plots show the distribution of a variable. They look like a histogram, but they provide more information. SYSTAT prints the median, the hinges (the 25th and 75th percentiles), and the extremes, as well as the actual values in the leaves of the plot. Exceptionally large or small values are flagged as "outside values." For exact definitions of these statistics and more complete information on interpreting stem-and-leaf plots, see the SYSTAT manual. Notice that stem-and-leaf plots are designed for character graphics, thus they are part of the descriptive statistics module, STATS.

Figure 6.5 contains the stem-and-leaf plots for leverage, the Studentized residuals, and Cook's *D* statistic. Since the largest Cook's *D* is less than 1.0, no case has unusual influence on the regression. Leverage also shows no problems. However, the Studentized residuals show a potential problem. Studentized residuals indicate a potential outlier when they exceed ±3.0. The smallest Studentized residual is less than -2.1, which is not unusual in a sample of 20 observations drawn from a standard normal distribution, but the largest Studentized residual is excessive: over 5.8.

Figure 6.5
Stem-and-Leaf Plots of Residual Statistics

```
STATS
    USE FILM2
    STEM LEVERAGE COOK STUDENT
```

```
Stem and Leaf Plot of variable:     LEVERAGE, N = 20
          Minimum:           0.052
          Lower hinge:           0.060
          Median:           0.070
          Upper hinge:           0.106
          Maximum:           0.305
              5 H 234799
              6    1124
              7 M 6
              8    8
              9    06
             10 H 47
             11    9
      * * * Outside Values * * *
             19    3
             23    0
             30    5

Stem and Leaf Plot of variable:       COOK, N = 20
          Minimum:           0.000
          Lower hinge:           0.002
          Median:           0.006
          Upper hinge:           0.023
          Maximum:           0.600
              0 H 000112344
              0 M 5679
              1
              1    67
              2 H
              2    89
      * * * Outside Values * * *
              9    2
             22    5
             60    0

Stem and Leaf Plot of variable:     STUDENT, N = 20
          Minimum:          -2.108
          Lower hinge:          -0.475
          Median:          -0.132
          Upper hinge:           0.328
          Maximum:           5.828
             -2    1
      * * * Outside Values * * *
             -0    8
             -0    7
             -0 H 55
             -0    33322
             -0 M 00
              0    00
              0 H 333
              0
              0    6
              0    9
      * * * Outside Values * * *
              5    8
```

The results of examining leverage and the Studentized residuals suggest that we may have as many as five points that are outliers or influential points. To find out which points these are, we need to print the data, like we have done in Figure 6.6. There we see that the films with high leverage are *Commando* (Case 1), *Death Wish 3* (Case 3), and *Spies LikeUs* (Case 12). The large Studentized residuals are *Rocky IV* (Case 10) and *Youngblood* (Case 19). We will investigate why each of these points seems unusual in the next section, *What can you do?*

In addition to the residuals statistics, you can identify unusual points using a plot of the residuals versus the fitted values, a residuals plot.

Residuals plots

Residuals plots highlight many different data problems, including the outliers that we focus on here. This plot of the residuals versus the fitted values appears in Figure 6.7. SYSTAT produces a similar plot using quick graph whenever you save residuals. Figure 6.7 shows the horizontal band of points that we hope to find in a good-looking residuals plot, but it also shows a large positive residual and a large negative residual separated from the horizontal band. If you check the residuals printed in Figure 6.6, you will find that the positive residual is *Rocky IV* and the negative residual is *Youngblood*.

You can highlight important information in a residuals plot using SYSTAT's SIZE option to control the size of the plotting symbols. For example, a plot using Cook's *D* for the size makes influential points large and easy to see. This plot is so useful that it has been named an "influence plot". Since we only care about the relative, not absolute, size of the symbols and Cook's *D* is small, we multiply it by 15 to make the symbols larger. The IF-statement makes tiny values of COOK15 readable.

The output is in Figure 6.8. Two aspects of this plot simplify identification of influential cases. First, the SYSTAT option SYMBOL = FILM$ uses the first letter of the FILM$ as the plotting symbol. This makes it easy to find the case corresponding to each point. Second, since the size of the plotting symbols is governed by the values of Cook's *D*, the largest symbols show the cases with the most influence on the regression. The large R indicates *Rocky IV*.

Figure 6.6
Printout of Influence, Leverage, and Outlier Statistics

```
USE FILM2
LIST FILM$ BOXOFF SCREENS RESIDUAL LEVERAGE STUDENT COOK
```

Case number	FILM$	BOXOFF	SCREENS	RESIDUAL	LEVERAGE	STUDENT	COOK
1	Commando	7700	1495	-84.459	0.231	-0.035	0.000
2	Jagged Edge	4094	1125	-36.293	0.054	-0.013	0.000
3	Death Wish 3	5319	1460	-2119.794	0.194	-0.871	0.093
4	Live&Die L.A	3551	1135	-678.054	0.052	-0.252	0.002
5	Target	2670	1085	-1065.248	0.063	-0.399	0.006
6	Once Bitten	4025	1095	190.991	0.060	0.071	0.000
7	Rainbow Brit	1847	1088	-1917.876	0.062	-0.726	0.018
8	KSolomon Min	5005	1122	904.336	0.054	0.337	0.003
9	Starchaser	1614	1020	-1479.299	0.089	-0.565	0.016
10	Rocky IV	14993	1325	8887.483	0.091	5.828	0.600
11	Santa Claus	4235	970	1635.507	0.119	0.637	0.028
12	Spies LikeUs	8614	1556	227.098	0.305	0.098	0.002
13	Jewel of Nil	4983	1106	1040.354	0.057	0.389	0.005
14	Clue	2014	1006	-941.034	0.097	-0.359	0.007
15	101 Dalmaton	2389	1097	-1464.761	0.059	-0.550	0.010
16	Iron Eagle	6104	1080	2418.133	0.064	0.925	0.030
17	My Chauffeur	4781	1253	-613.436	0.062	-0.229	0.002
18	Murphy's Rom	4195	1046	844.921	0.077	0.318	0.004
19	Youngblood	1483	1354	-4908.925	0.108	-2.108	0.225
20	Eliminators	1987	993	-839.644	0.104	-0.321	0.006

A useful enhancement to the plot above would be to plot STUDENT * ESTIMATE instead of RESIDUAL * ESTIMATE. The vertical axis of this plot would be in units of standard deviations, which may be more meaningful for some data. Similar plots could be produced using Studentized residuals and leverage to control the size of the plotting symbols. We leave these plots for the interested reader.

In summary, outliers and influential points can be identified in the following ways. Prior to model fitting, preliminary scatterplots provide effective tools. After fitting a model, as it saves residuals, SYSTAT will warn you if Cook's D, leverage, or Studentized residuals are unusually large. Influence statistics (Cook's D, leverage, and Studentized residuals) should be routinely checked as well as residuals plots. You want to check all these tools; they have different strengths, highlight different aspects of the data, and they can show different outliers.

Figure 6.7
Residuals Plot

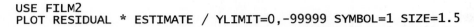

USE FILM2
PLOT RESIDUAL * ESTIMATE / YLIMIT=0,-99999 SYMBOL=1 SIZE=1.5

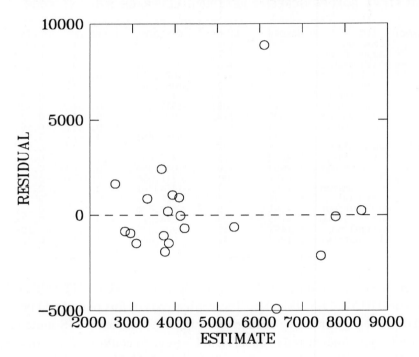

If you have multiple independent variables, you may want to use several special plots discussed in Section 5.1. Prior to the regression a scatterplot matrix (SPLOM) will display relationships between several variables simultaneously. During the regression, adjusted variable plots show the relationship between the dependent variable and any independent variable net of the effects of all other independent variables. Residuals plots are also important in multiple regression. Finally, the residuals may be plotted against any variable not yet in the model. Any evidence of a systematic pattern may indicate that the variable should be added to the model.

Figure 6.8
Influence Plot

```
USE FILM2
REM Make points larger and easier to see
   LET COOK15 = COOK * 15
   IF COOK15 < 1.0 THEN LET COOK15 = 1.0
PLOT RESIDUAL * ESTIMATE / YLIM=0,-9999 SYMBOL=FILM$ SIZE=COOK15
```

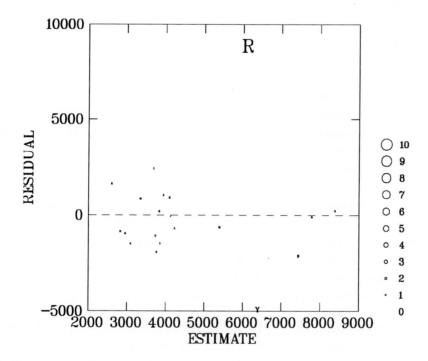

What can you do?

An outlier or an influential observation may occur for many reasons. What you can do about it depends on why it occurred.

The single most frequent source of outliers and influential observations is an error in coding or data input. Transposition, duplicate records, records out of order, off-by-one-column, and related problems are common errors and may account for as many as 90-95% of the outliers you identify. These are the first possibilities to check when a deviant case is identified. After checking the five outliers identified in the film box office dataset we find that the values for *Commando*, *Death Wish 3*, *Spies LikeUs* and

Rocky IV are correct. The fifth outlier, *Youngblood*, is an error. Two digits were in fact transposed, and the correct value is not $1.483 million, but $4.183 million. Dealing with outliers produced by coding errors, like *Youngblood*, is easy because they can be fixed. We have not reproduced the regression with the correct value for *Youngblood* but we invite you to run it and confirm that *Youngblood* is no longer an outlier. Much more difficult to handle are outliers, like *Rocky IV*, which are not the result of a coding error and will not disappear so easily. Here are some useful approaches.

One possibility is that the input may be correct, but the original source of the data may be in error. This is a common cause of deviant points in published data; typesetters make errors too. Deciding that the original source is wrong is not an easy decision to make and requires careful judgment. Here are some ideas that may help. If data have been published in several locations, you can check if the deviant point(s) appear everywhere. If other researchers have analyzed the data, you can ask them what they did. Do not be surprised if they answer, unhelpfully, that they either (1) never noticed the point(s); or (2) threw them away without bothering to check why they were deviant. Many data are part of a series (e.g. census data or economic time series) and you can check adjacent points to see if they agree with the apparent deviant point. See the Notes on section 7.4, page 288 for errors of this type in the military spending dataset. Some data are revised periodically (e.g. government economic data) so you may be able to check for a revision. None of these suggestions will guarantee you an answer, but they will help you decide how plausible the deviant point(s) are. It is risky to simply assume that all outliers and influential points are errors.

Some deviant points are accurate. If they appear at an extreme value of the dependent variable, this may mean that the true relation between the independent and dependent variables is curved. Or it may imply that the variance of the dependent variable is not stable. Or you may have omitted an important variable from the model. All of these possibilities imply that the influential point is accurate and that some effort should be made to find the actual cause of its excessive magnitude. Additional data, gathered in the same region as the influential point, may pay valuable dividends. For example, in the box office dataset, we could gather data on other unusually popular films like the *Indiana Jones* or *Star Trek* series to see if the relationship between extremely popular movies and number of screens is different from run-of-the-mill films. In their discussion of industrial data, Daniel and Wood (1980, p. 29) point out that if the influential point ". . .is a high-yield point or a particularly desirable property of a product, knowledge of its cause may be more valuable than all the rest of the data. In many cases [the search for a cause] . . . has led to the discovery of important variables that had not previously been considered. Numerous patents have resulted . . ."

Least squares regression is extremely sensitive to outliers, and a set of regression techniques, called *robust* regression, have been developed to produce parameter estimates less sensitive to the effects of extreme cases. The SYSTAT manual describes a technique called "least absolute values regression" as part of the NONLIN module. A robust technique that is particularly easy to apply in SYSTAT is *LOWESS* (see Section 7.3). It gives you a visual image, on the scatterplot, of how the regression line would look if any deviant point(s) had minimum influence and it shows nonlinearities as well.

The last resort would be to discard the influential cases. This step may be taken if you have good reason to believe that the points are errors. If the points seem to be accurate, you may want to discard them and report that your model does not fit some small subset of the data. Reporting that some data have been discarded is important in scientific work. It is probably appropriate to delete *Rocky IV*; apparently extremely popular films do not follow the same relationship between box office gross and number of screens as ordinary films. If you follow this alternative, you may want to report two equations; one with and one without the influential observations. This is cumbersome but it preserves the information contained in the influential cases for future researchers. This is an especially attractive alternative if your current regression work is part of an ongoing research project and you, or a colleague, may have the opportunity to return to study the circumstances that produced the influential cases.

Once we correct *Youngblood* and delete *Rocky IV*, we still face the question of what do to about the three potential outliers identified by leverage. If we look at the residuals plot after the corrections, Figure 6.9, we notice an unusual pattern. Fourteen points cluster in a circular pattern on the left and the remaining 5 form a tail to the right. The three right-most points are the three high leverage points. This pattern suggests that the entire relationship between box office and screens may be due only to those five points in the tail. Is the significant regression simply an artifact, due to part of the data? This is a real possibility. The only way to resolve this question would be to gather more data. We could easily do this, but a particularly severe problem is that our source, *Variety*, does not report information on films grossing less than $1 million. If we couldn't find another source, any additional data would be truncated as well. We have no clear answer to this problem and we let the interested reader try different solutions.

Figure 6.9
Influence Plot after Outlier Correction

```
REGRESS
    USE FILM2
    IF FILM$ = 'Youngblood' THEN LET BOXOFF=4183
    IF FILM$ = 'Rocky IV' THEN DELETE
    MODEL BOXOFF = CONSTANT + SCREENS
        SAVE FILM3 / DATA  RESIDUAL
        ESTIMATE

    USE FILM3
    REM Make points easier to see
        LET COOK15 = COOK * 15
        IF COOK15 < 1.0 THEN LET COOK15 = 1.0
    PLOT RESIDUAL * ESTIMATE / YLIMIT=0,-9999 SYMBOL=FILM$,
                               SIZE=COOK15 XFORMAT=0 YFORMAT=0
```

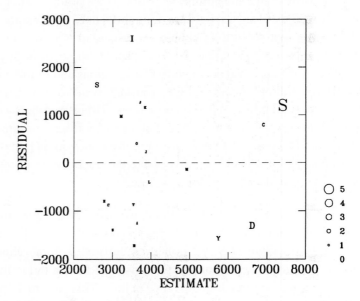

As you deal with outliers and influential points, keep in mind a final attribute: *outliers nest*. That means correcting one set of outliers and influential points alters the regression line, and the new line often uncovers other outliers and influential points. You may go through the cycle of finding and correcting outliers and influential points, and then rerunning the regression, several times before you have a completely clean dataset. Furthermore, the choices that you may have to make may be very uncomfortable. For example, the plot in Figure 6.9 suggests that if we deleted the 5 cases in the tail, we would have no relationship left to explain.

Outlier problems were the subject of exchanges in the *American Sociological Review* in October 1986 (Kahn and Udry 1986, Jasso 1986) and June 1986 (Weede 1986, Muller 1986). The fact that these debates occurred highlights the significance of responsible handling of apparent outliers. Neither Muller nor Jasso mentioned the apparent outliers in their original papers; it is not clear that they realized their data contained possible outliers until Kahn and Udry, and Weede pointed it out. The Jasso outliers are particularly serious since the removal of 8 cases (from 2,500) causes the signs of important regression coefficients to reverse. These 8 cases are very influential and, when they are included, the estimated regression coefficients reflect the relation between them and the other 2,500 cases, not the relationships in the mass of the data. When 8 of 2,500 cases are this influential, the regression is seriously distorted. This suggests the following warning: If you intend to keep apparent outliers in your dataset and not mention that they exist, many of your colleagues may be suspicious of your results and your data analytic skills.

The entire subject of outliers and influential cases is difficult and complex. These few pages have only been able to introduce some of the simpler issues. For more information see Atkinson (1985), Barnett and Lewis (1978), Beckman and Cook (1983), Chatterjee and Hadi (1988), and Cook and Weisberg (1982).

6.2 Nonlinearity

Everyone knows that taxes have increased dramatically during the last 20 years. The big federal tax increases have not been in income tax but in the social security tax. It has more than tripled. What caused this huge increase? Robert Lerner (1984) developed an explanation of the increase in one of the four social security funds: the Disability Insurance fund. He suggests that a social movement among the disabled, the Handicapped Persons' Rights movement, made disability more acceptable, less of a stigma, and that people in touch with the movement became more willing to label themselves disabled. Hence, many more people applied to the federal government for disability payments, and federal disability payments increased 8-fold in about 10 years. Lerner investigated his theory using dataset in Figure 6.10, quarterly data from 1968-1977.

Figure 6.10
Lerner Disability Dataset

```
BASIC
    rem Lerner disability dataset
    rem
    rem Variables:
    rem PROTEST  Number of protests reported
    rem LEGIS    Number of times legislation was mentioned
    rem LAWSUIT  Number of lawsuits reported
    rem IDEOLOGY Number of times social movement ideology mentioned
    rem IWORD    Number of ideological words
    rem NUMART   Total number of articles in which disability
                 mentioned
    rem APPLY    Number of applications for Social Security
                 disability payments
    INPUT PROTEST LEGIS LAWSUIT IDEOLOGY IWORD NUMART APPLY
    RUN
0 0   0  0   0  5  183064
0 0   1  0   0  8  186861
0 1   0  1   1  9  184156
0 2   0  2  16 13  165690
1 0   1  1   4 14  180584
0 0   0  0   0  7  185785
0 0   0  0   0 12  180824
0 0   0  0   0  6  177978
0 0   0  0   0  7  199292
0 5   1  3  13 12  221832
0 0   0  1   0  3  231848
0 0   0  0   1 12  216866
0 0   0  0   0  8  233963
0 1   2  2   1 19  243404
0 0   0  0   0  7  233473
0 1   2  2   6 22  213096
0 2   0  3  13 17  240718
0 1   0  1   3 11  237005
0 1   0  1   1 21  241657
2 1   1  3   5 29  288075
0 0   0  2   2 14  268420
1 1   0  3   4 24  267000
0 0   0  0   1 20  273236
0 0   0  3   1 15  258833
3 2   1  7   4 30  361259
0 9   0 12  32 34  343648
0 2   1  3   8 10  321556
0 7   0 10   8 24  304688
1 2   0  5  10 31  326598
0 10  0 13  15 37  330948
0 2   1  2   8 21  326441
1 8   0 12  35 33  300301
1 6   1 10  14 28  305385
1 8   0 12  43 26  311072
0 12  3 17  58 33  319420
0 4   0  8  30 18  292420
0 6   2 11  27 13  321850
8 15  0 25  64 37  319437
0 3   4  9   8 25  316969
0 14  1 15  29 24  277116
```

```
SAVE LER01 / ,
    'Lerner disability dataset',
    ' ',
    'APPLY      Number of applications for Social Security',
    '           disability payments',
    'SUMNEWS    Sum of reported movement activity',
    ' ',

REM sum newspaper reports of Disability Rights movement activity
LET SUMNEWS = PROTEST + LEGIS + LAWSUIT + IDEOLOGY + IWORD + NUMART
DROP PROTEST LEGIS LAWSUIT IDEOLOGY IWORD NUMART
RUN
```

According to one of Lerner's crucial hypothesis, the activities of the Handicapped Persons' Rights movement encouraged people to apply for federal disability payments. This relation between number of disability payment applications (APPLY) and a variable composed of the sum of newspaper reports of several kinds of Handicapped Persons' movement activity (SUMNEWS) is plotted in Figure 6.11. It looks like a strong relation, but something is wrong. The relation is not a straight line, but a shallow concave curve. If we were to run a regression on these data, the coefficient estimates would not be accurate because regressions estimate the equation of a straight line, not a curve. Since the underlying relation is not a straight line, it is called a nonlinear relation. The condition is called **nonlinearity**.

Diagnosis

In order to diagnose nonlinearity, we have to know that it is there. Several techniques make it easier to see.

Look at a plot

The simplest technique is to look at a scatterplot of the data, as in our plot of APPLY vs. SUMNEWS. Any nonlinearity will show up as some form of a curve. The nonlinearity that we see in Figure 6.11, a curve which is concave to the right, is common and relatively easy to correct. As we have emphasized, plots of all pairs of variables in a regression are the easiest way to see a variety of problems, like curvature, that may cause misleading or inaccurate results.

Figure 6.11
Social Security Disability Payment Applications (APPLY) vs.
Handicapped Persons' Rights Movement Activities (SUMNEWS)

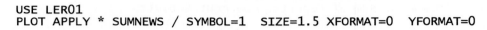

```
USE LER01
PLOT APPLY * SUMNEWS / SYMBOL=1  SIZE=1.5 XFORMAT=0  YFORMAT=0
```

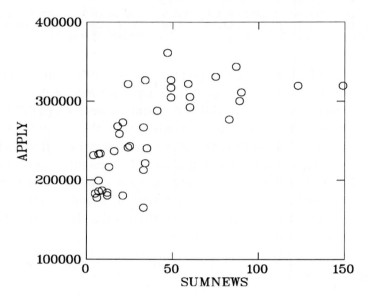

Look at residuals

Sometimes you may not be sure whether a plot shows curvature or not. For example, shallow curves are often hard to see. In these conditions you may want to create a plot which gives nonlinearity more emphasis. Removing the linear pattern from the data highlights any nonlinearity. Remove the linear pattern by doing a regression. Save the residuals and look at the quick graph. If the underlying relation between the two variables is only a linear relation, the regression will have removed all the systematic pattern. What remains will be random error. Thus the residuals will form an approximately horizontal band across the width of the plot.

The regression in Figure 6.12 and the quick graph in Figure 6.13 illustrate this process. As you can see, the residuals form a very odd pattern, definitely not random. There are also two influential points, the two on the extreme right of the residuals plot. Notice that the coefficient for SUMNEWS is highly significant with a t-statistic over five.

Some people assume that statistically significant coefficient estimates imply that the regression is O.K. Life is never this simple. The coefficient estimates are the result of a statistical estimation procedure which will almost always produce some result. You can never know whether a result accurately reflects the underlying relation between variables by looking only at the regression statistics; you have to look at the residuals. Any pattern in the residuals that is not a horizontal band or some other, more complex curve is a warning that you will have to deal with nonlinearity. Since you will be plotting the residuals anyway, you can easily check for a nonlinear pattern as you look for outliers and other potential problems.

Figure 6.12
Output from MODEL: APPLY = CONSTANT + SUMNEWS

```
REGRESS
    USE LER01
    MODEL APPLY = CONSTANT + SUMNEWS
    SAVE RES / DATA  RESIDUAL
    ESTIMATE
```

```
Dep Var: APPLY N: 40 Multiple R:  0.680 Squared multiple R:  0.462

Adjusted squared multiple R:  0.448    Standard error of estimate:    41780.206

Effect          Coefficient    Std Error    Std Coef Tolerance    t    P(2 Tail)

CONSTANT        215531.659    10180.634         0.0         .    21.171    0.000
SUMNEWS           1128.345      197.359         0.680    1.000    5.717    0.000

                        Analysis of Variance

Source          Sum-of-Squares   DF  Mean-Square    F-Ratio      P

Regression        5.70574E+10     1  5.70574E+10    32.687      0.000
Residual          6.63323E+10    38  1.74559E+09

Durbin-Watson D Statistic     1.072
First Order Autocorrelation   0.445

Residuals have been saved.
```

LOWESS: Scatterplot smoothing

An alternative to a regression is to create a smooth curve through the scatterplot and examine it for curvature. William Cleveland developed this idea (1979, 1981, 1994) into a technique called LOWESS (*LO*cally *WE*ighted *S*catterplot *S*moothing). The curve created by LOWESS has two valuable characteristics. First, it passes through the center of the local data. By local data we mean that LOWESS uses only a small region of the data as it calculates each smoothed point. This makes it sensitive to changes in the slope of points in local areas of the plot, revealing nonlinearities. Second, LOW-ESS weights its calculations to minimize the effects of points far from the local center. Thus even when outliers are in the local region they have little influence on the smoothed line. For these reasons, superimposing a LOWESS smooth curve on a plot can be very revealing. The LOWESS smoothed values have been superimposed on the plot of APPLY versus SUMNEWS in Figure 6.14. The curvature is so obvious in these data that LOWESS adds little to our understanding. This will not be true for plots that we look at later in this section.

Figure 6.13
SYSTAT Quick Graph Residuals Plot
Model: APPLY = CONSTANT + SUMNEWS

Plot of Residuals against Predicted Values

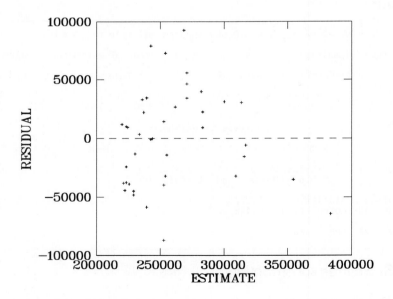

There are three graphical tools for detecting nonlinearity: examining a scatterplot, a residuals plot, and the LOWESS smoothed curve in a scatterplot or residuals plot. As a general rule of thumb, the scatterplot is the least sensitive of these tools. The residuals plot is more sensitive and LOWESS is the most sensitive. LOWESS is particularly useful because it can detect forms of nonlinearity other than simple curves, such as ceiling or threshold effects and other complex curves. LOWESS shows nonlinearity effectively in a residuals plot.

Figure 6.14
Disability Payment Applications vs. Handicapped Persons' Rights Movement
Activity Scatterplot with LOWESS Smoothed Curve

```
USE LER01
PLOT APPLY * SUMNEWS / SMOOTH=LOWESS SHORT SYMBOL=1 SIZE=1.5,
                       XFORMAT=0 YFORMAT=0
```

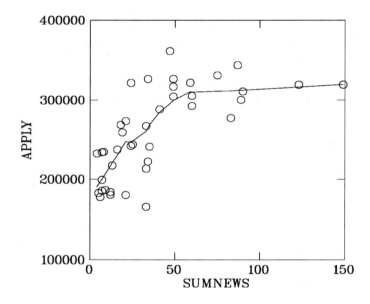

What can you do?

Like outliers and influential points, nonlinearity is not a statistical problem. It is a data problem which causes the least squares estimates of the regression coefficients to be misleading. Regression coefficients are the best estimates (i.e. produce the smallest squared residuals) of a *linear* relation. Thus the general fix for nonlinearity is to *transform* the nonlinear relation between APPLY and SUMNEWS into a linear relation.

Transformations are general-purpose statistical tools. Chapter 22 covers broader applications of transformations, while this section focuses on using transformations to correct nonlinearity. Even if you need to use a transformation only to correct nonlinearity,

Chapter 22 is worth reading because it covers a wider range of nonlinearities, but the discussion of nonlinearity is more abstract, without the detailed example presented in this chapter. Transformations are sometimes called reëxpressions.

How do we transform data? We begin by examining what kind of data we have in the independent variable. SUMNEWS is a count of the number of newspaper reports of Handicapped Persons' Rights movement activity. Counts have the property that they are always positive (or zero). For mathematical reasons that are beyond the scope of this book, they can often, but not always, be effectively transformed using square roots. The square root of SUMNEWS, called SSUMNEWS, has been plotted with APPLY in Figure 6.15. Compared to Figure 6.14, this looks better; the relation between the square root of SUMNEWS and APPLY looks much closer to linear. As we hoped, the square root transformation removed the curve, but another problem is now evident: the right side of the plot looks different from the left. The left side is a straight line sloping upward to the right until SSUMNEWS is about 7 or 8, then the LOWESS line suddenly bends and becomes almost horizontal out to the right edge of the plot.

Seeing this, we could try several possibilities. One possibility would be to use a stronger transformation to try to further straighten the relation, like a logarithm. The effect of a square root transformation is to pull in the stretched-out right tail while stretching out a bunched-up left tail. This is why we chose to use the square root of SUMNEWS: because the right side was very stretched-out. The log transformation would have the same effect, only stronger. It would pull in the right tail farther and stretch out the left side even more. (See Section 22.2 for more information on the strength of different transformations, especially Figure 22.3, the Ladder of Transformations.)

We do not show the plot of APPLY against the log of SUMNEWS, though you may find it helpful to explore the effect of this and other transformations on these data. In general, the skewness on the right is too strong; stronger transformations do not straighten out the right side, but they begin to cause a bend in the data on the left. This makes the model more complex, so, in the interest of simplicity, we will stop with the square root. A further reason for stopping here is theoretical. This looks like a ceiling effect. The newspaper reports of the activity of the Handicapped Persons' Rights movement has an impact on applications for disability payments only up to a certain point. This corresponds to the upward-sloping portion of Figure 6.15. After that point, further increases in newspaper reports seem to have little influence. This corresponds to the horizontal portion of the relation. The horizontal portion is the ceiling. It represents the upper limit of the effect of newspaper reports.

Figure 6.15
Scatterplot with LOWESS after Square Root Transformation

```
USE LER01
LET SSUMNEWS = SQR(SUMNEWS)
PLOT APPLY * SSUMNEWS / SMOOTH=LOWESS SHORT SYMBOL=1  SIZE=1.5
```

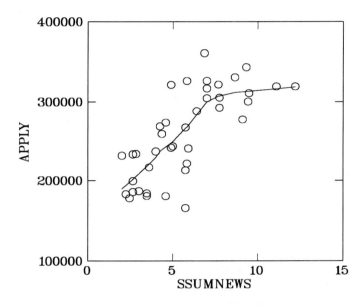

Ceiling effects like this are part of a common class of nonlinear patterns which are called **piecewise linear**. This means that the relation between variables is linear in pieces, but that the slope and intercept are different for each piece. To develop a model of this pattern, we need some way to estimate the ceiling at which SSUMNEWS ceases to have an effect. We can estimate the ceiling using SYSTAT's NONLIN module.

The NONLIN model that we will use is:

$$APPLY = b_0 + b_1 \text{ SSUMNEWS} + b_2 (\text{SSUMNEWS} - x) (\text{SSUMNEWS} > x)$$

This model may look a little strange. To understand how it can estimate a different slope and constant for each of the pieces, you need to understand a little about NON-LIN. You will want to read the complete explanation in the NONLIN chapter of the SYSTAT manual but this is a brief summary. The MODEL statement is an algebraic expression of variables and parameters. When NONLIN encounters a name which is not among the variables in the file that you are USEing, it assumes that it is a parameter.

This model instructs NONLIN to compute estimates for b_0 (the constant), b_1 (a slope parameter), b_2 (another slope parameter) and x (the discontinuity point where the slope and intercept change). The last part of the expression (SSUMNEWS > x) is 1 if SSUM-NEWS exceeds x and 0 otherwise. This is the discontinuity point. An estimate of its location is one of our most important goals. If (SSUMNEWS > x) is 0, then the regression equation looks like this:

$$\text{APPLY} = b_0 + b_1\text{SSUMNEWS}$$

If (SSUMNEWS > x) is 1, then with a little algebra and collecting terms, the regression looks like this for large values of SSUMNEWS:

$$\text{APPLY} = (b_0 - b_2\, x) + (b_1 + b_2)\text{SSUMNEWS}$$

Our single MODEL is thus two regressions, depending on the value of SSUMNEWS.

On the ESTIMATE command, the START option gives NONLIN a set of starting values for the four parameters; $b_0 = 170000$, $b_1 = 25000$, $b_2 = -25000$ and $x = 7$. NONLIN operates by repeatedly reading the data. Each time it reads the dataset it calculates estimates of the parameters and a value for the "loss function." The loss function is the function that it is minimizing. By default, the loss function is least squares, the same function used by REGRESS. Thus the value of the loss function is the same as the residual sum of squares from a regression. Each pass through the data is called an iteration and NONLIN attempts to make the loss function smaller with each iteration. When the loss stops shrinking, NONLIN prints the current estimates of its parameters. Many passes through the data are time-consuming, but the time can be reduced if we give NONLIN a good guess as to where to start looking for the minimum. Our initial guess is called the **starting values**. We found them by using a black thread and a ruler on the LOWESS plot in Figure 6.15. Very high tech. The output appears in Figure 6.16.

Figure 6.16
Piecewise Linear Regression Model

```
NONLIN
    USE LER01
    LET SSUMNEWS = SQR(SUMNEWS)
    MODEL APPLY = B0 + B1 * SSUMNEWS +,
                  B2 * (SSUMNEWS - X) * (SSUMNEWS > X)
    SAVE LER02 / RESIDUAL  DATA
    ESTIMATE / START = 170000 25000 -25000 7
```

```
 Iteration
 No.    Loss        B0           B1           B2           X
  0 .111683D+12 .170000D+06 .250000D+05-.250000D+05 .700000D+01
  1 .488177D+11 .138456D+06 .228188D+05-.200931D+05 .731372D+01
  2 .487940D+11 .138456D+06 .228188D+05-.200931D+05 .739033D+01
  3 .487940D+11 .138456D+06 .228188D+05-.200931D+05 .739033D+01
  4 .487940D+11 .138456D+06 .228188D+05-.200931D+05 .739033D+01

Dependent variable is APPLY

     Source   Sum-of-Squares   DF   Mean-Square
 Regression      2.77484E+12    4   6.93709E+11
   Residual      4.87940E+10   36   1.35539E+09


      Total      2.82363E+12   40
Mean corrected  1.23390E+11   39

        Raw  R-square  (1-Residual/Total)      =       0.983
Mean corrected R-square (1-Residual/Corrected) =       0.605
        R-square (observed vs predicted)       =       0.605

                                             Wald Confidence Interval
Parameter        Estimate      A.S.E.    Param/ASE    Lower < 95%> Upper
B0             138455.630   20763.647       6.668   96345.001   180566.259
B1              22818.767    4313.918       5.290   14069.736    31567.798
B2             -20093.080    9372.394      -2.144  -39101.177    -1084.982
X                   7.390       1.188       6.222    4.981          9.799

Data, estimates and residuals have been saved.
```

The discontinuity point, x is estimated at 7.390. Below that point, the model is:

$$APPLY = 138,455.630 + 22,818.767 * SSUMNEWS$$

There are 10 cases with values of SSUMNEWS above 7.390. For them, the model is:

$$
\begin{aligned}
APPLY &= [138,455.630 - (7.390 * -20,093.080)] + \\
&\quad [22,818.767 + (-20,093.080)] * SSUMNEWS \\
&= 286,943.491 + 2,725.687 * SSUMNEWS
\end{aligned}
$$

This is very close to the starting values that we found on the plot. NONLIN gives us three different summary statistics. They are:

Raw R-square (1-Residual/Total). This is the appropriate R-square for models without a constant term and it is usually large. It compares the residual sum-of-squares to the total sum-of-squares. The total sum-of-squares is calculated about the line where the dependent variable equals zero. Thus adding or subtracting a constant from the dependent variable to make it closer to zero will increase the raw R-square. Since adding or subtracting such a constant is usually substantively irrelevant, this is a significant disadvantage.

Mean corrected R-square (1-Residual/Corrected). This R-square is appropriate for models with a constant term. The calculation is similar to that for the raw R-square except the denominator uses the total sum-of-squares calculated about the line formed by the mean of the dependent variable; in this sense it is "corrected" for the mean. It will always be less than the raw R-square, except when the mean of the dependent variable equals zero.

R-square (observed vs predicted). This is the square of the Pearson correlation between the observed and predicted values. For ordinary linear regression with a constant term, this value will be the same as the mean corrected one above. For nonlinear models, this measure best represents how closely the fitted values approximate the actual values on a standard scale.

A fourth summary statistic is frequently used: the square root of the residual mean-square. The residual mean-square measures the overall error in your model. You can use the square root of the residual mean-square as an estimate of the average error of prediction. It is the same as the standard error of the estimate SYSTAT prints for an ordinary regression. In Figure 6.16 we would take the square root of 1.35539E+9 which is 36,815. The advantage of this statistic is that it is expressed in the same metric as the dependent variable. If the metric of the dependent variable is meaningful and is not just an arbitrary scale, then this can be meaningful way to tell how well you can predict. The question you want to ask is, "If my average prediction has an error this large, am I concerned?"

The NONLIN results are displayed in Figure 6.16. Compare these results with the original regression in Figure 6.12 and you can see that, after the transformation to square roots and the piecewise regression, the summary statistics look *much* better—comparing the "squared multiple R" to the "R-square (observed vs predicted)" we find an increase of almost 15%. The residuals look better, too, although there is still an outlier.

Generally, you cannot expect this magnitude of improvement when you correct for nonlinearity. The rule of thumb is that transformations will give you at most an additional 10% higher R-square and the residuals will look much better. The major gain here came when we realized that the relation between APPLY and SSUMNEWS was not a simple linear relation, but was piecewise linear. As in this case, changing the *form* of the model will often result in major improvements in the fit.

The quick graph from NONLIN is in Figure 6.17. Instead of a residuals plot like REGRESS, NONLIN graphs the independent variable (SSUMNEWS) versus the dependent variable (APPLY). It plots both the data points and the fitted line. Notice the clear elbow where the regression shifts to a different slope. If your model has two independent variables, NONLIN will do a 3-D plot of the independent variables against the dependent variable. Since there are two independent variables the fitted values will be a 2-dimensional surface instead of a line.

Figure 6.17
Quick Graph from Piecewise Linear Regression

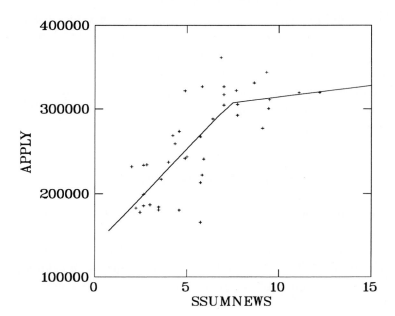

Notice how the techniques that we have developed work together to help you fit the model. The need for a transformation was easy to see in the scatterplots and in the residuals plot after the initial regression. After transformation, LOWESS made the need for a change in the form of the model easy to see. It also helped us get good starting values. Finally, NONLIN estimated the piecewise linear model. Notice that we could have fit a more complicated curve using the same piecewise method: break the curve into pieces and fit each piece separately.

This has been a complicated example, a transformation followed by a piecewise linear model. Often, life will be simpler. Transformations alone will solve many data analysis problems. They are useful for clarifying relations in almost all kinds of data. We have used them on counts but they are also useful for fractions and proportions (data ranging from 0 to 1), ranks, balances (numbers which may be positive or negative) and measures of size or magnitude (data which are inherently positive). Transformations and their uses are thoroughly discussed in Chapter 22. Consult that chapter for references and further reading.

Working with nonlinearity is not easy. It is time-consuming and typically requires a large number of trial-and-error approaches to find a reasonable solution. For example, the analysis for this chapter required four days work and generated over a hundred pages of plots, REGRESS, and NONLIN models. Among the many things we found during this work, we discovered that without accurate starting values the model would converge to a local minimum with a smaller R-square. We would not have discovered this if we had not tried several starting values and checked the results using the quasi-Newton and simplex algorithms in addition to the default modified Gauss-Newton method. The danger of a local minimum is one of the problems of nonlinear regression. There are a variety of other issues that you should be aware of; the SYSTAT manual contains a brief discussion.

6.3 Collinearity

Cities show large differences in average death rates. In fact the highest death rate is over 40% greater than the lowest. Many people (particularly residents of cities with high death rates) may want to know what causes these differences. One potential cause is the well-known toxic effect of air pollution. This seems like a natural problem for regression. The concentrations of different pollutants are clearly continuous variables, as is the death rate (called the mortality rate). Data on three major air pollutants for the

60 largest cities have been assembled in Figure 6.18. and the regression results appear in Figure 6.19. We omit the quick graph for all the output in this section. To remove nonlinearity, we use the logarithms of the three pollutants. See Section 6.2 and Chapter 22 for more information on removing nonlinearity.

Figure 6.18
Air Pollution Dataset

```
BASIC
  NEW
  INPUT CITY$ HC SO2 NOX MORT
  RUN
'Akron      OH'  21   59   15   921.870
'Albany     NY'   8   39   10   997.875
'Allentown PA'    6   33    6   962.354
'Atlanta    GA'  18   24    8   982.291
'Baltimore MD'   43  206   38  1071.289
'BirminghamAL'   30   72   32  1030.380
'Boston     MA'  21   62   32   934.700
'BridgeportCN'    6    4    4   899.529
'Buffalo    NY'  18   37   12  1001.902
'Canton     OH'  12   20    7   912.347
'ChattanoogTN'   18   27    8  1017.613
'Chicago    IL'  88  278   63  1024.885
'CincinnatiOH'   26  146   26   970.467
'Cleveland OH'   31   64   21   985.950
'Columbus   OH'  23   15    9   958.839
'Dallas     TX'   1    1    1   860.101
'Dayton     OH'   6   16    4   936.234
'Denver     CO'  17   28    8   871.766
'Detroit    MI'  52  124   35   959.221
'Flint      MI'  11   11    4   941.181
'Ft Worth   TX'   1    1    1   891.708
'Grand RapdMI'    5   10    3   871.338
'GreensboroNC'    8    5    3   971.122
'Hartford   CN'   7   10    3   887.466
'Houston    TX'   6    1    5   952.529
'IndianaplsIN'   13   33    7   968.665
'KansasCityMO'    7    4    4   919.729
'Lancaster PA'   11   32    7   844.053
'LosAngelesCA'  648  130  319   861.833
'LouisvilleKY'   38  193   37   989.265
'Memphis    TN'  15   34   18  1006.490
'Miami      FL'   3    1    1   861.439
'Milwaukee WI'   33  125   23   929.150
'MinneapolsMN'   20   26   11   857.622
'Nashville TN'   17   78   14   961.009
'New Haven CN'    4    8    3   923.234
'New OrleanLA'   20    1   17  1113.156
'New York   NY'  41  108   26   994.648
'PhiladelphPA'   29  161   32  1015.023
'PittsburghPA'   45  263   59   991.290
'Portland   OR'  56   44   21   893.991
'ProvidenceRI'    6   18    4   938.500
'Reading    PA'  11   89   11   946.185
'Richmond   VA'  12   48    9  1025.502
'Rochester NY'    7   18    4   874.281
'San Diego CA'  144   20   66   839.709
'San Jose  CA'  105    3   32   790.733
```

```
'SanFrancisCA' 311  86 171  911.701
'Seattle  WA'  20  20   7  899.264
'SpringfeldMA'  5  20   4  904.155
'St. Louis MO'  31  68  15  953.560
'Syracuse  NY'  8  25   5  950.672
'Toledo    OH'  11  25   7  972.464
'Utica     NY'  5  11   2  912.202
'WashingtonDC'  65 102  28  967.803
'Wichita   KS'  4   1   2  823.764
'WilmingtonDL'  14  42  11 1003.502
'Worcester MA'  7   8   3  895.696
'York      PA'  8  49   8  911.817
'YoungstownOH'  14  39  13  954.442
~
    SORT CITY$
    SAVE AIR01 /,
    'Air Pollution Dataset',
    ' ',
    'Variables:',
    'CITY$ Name of city',
    'HC      Hydrocarbons, HC.'
    'SO2     Sulfur dioxide, SO2.',
    'NOX     Oxides of nitrogen, NOx. ',
    'MORT    Mortality rate in deaths per 100,000 people age-adjusted.',
    ' '

    LET LOGHC  = LOG(HC)
    LET LOGSO2 = LOG(SO2)
    LET LOGNOX = LOG(NOX)
    RUN
```

The regression results are surprising. If air pollution increases the mortality rate, then all the regression coefficients will be negative, but this is true only for hydrocarbons (LOGHC). The coefficient for sulfur dioxide is nonsignificant. Further, the positive coefficients seem to say that the more oxides of nitrogen (LOGNOX) and the more sulfur dioxide (LOGSO2) in the air, the lower the mortality rate. This is hard to believe because it contradicts previous scientific evidence and theories. Does it mean that your mom would be healthier if you bought her a sulfur dioxide generator next Christmas? No. The nonsignificance of LOGSO2 and the unexpected positive coefficients of other toxic pollutants warn us of a serious problem.

The problem is called **collinearity**. It arises when two or more independent variables are "highly" correlated with each other. Such highly correlated variables are called **collinear variables**. Intuitively, the damaging effects of collinear data can be understood by realizing that, since they are highly correlated, the information that each collinear variable provides in a regression model is not very different from that provided by the others. It is very difficult, therefore, to estimate the separate influence of such variables on the dependent variable.

Figure 6.19
Predicting Mortality Rates from Air Pollution Data

```
REGRESS
    USE AIR01
    MODEL MORT = CONSTANT + LOGHC + LOGSO2 + LOGNOX
    ESTIMATE
```

Dep Var: MORT N: 60 Multiple R: 0.525 Squared multiple R: 0.275						
Adjusted squared multiple R: 0.236 Standard error of estimate: 54.361						
Effect	Coefficient	Std Error	Std Coef	Tolerance	t	P(2 Tail)
CONSTANT	924.965	21.449	0.0	.	43.125	0.000
LOGHC	−57.300	19.419	−1.083	0.096	−2.951	0.005
LOGSO2	11.762	7.165	0.283	0.435	1.642	0.106
LOGNOX	58.336	21.751	1.111	0.075	2.682	0.010

Analysis of Variance

Source	Sum-of-Squares	DF	Mean-Square	F-Ratio	P
Regression	62822.545	3	20940.848	7.086	0.000
Residual	165485.099	56	2955.091		

Specifically, the damage is that the standard errors of collinear variables are inflated. This means that the sampling variability is large and the information available to estimate the population coefficients is not precise. While this does not bias the coefficient estimates, the inflated standard errors mean that the estimated coefficients may not be very close to the population coefficients and their size, sign, and significance tests may not be accurate. This is why we see the unexpected positive signs in the coefficients for LOGNOX and LOGSO2 in Figure 6.19.

Collinearity is also called multicollinearity (a term which we avoid because it is redundant) or ill conditioning. A collinear relation between several variables is also sometimes called a dependency or a dependent relation. We do not use this nomenclature because it is too easy to confuse with dependent and independent variables.

Diagnosis

One way to think about collinearity is to recall that when two variables correlate highly, one can be used to predict the other with a high degree of accuracy. This is the idea behind **tolerance**. Tolerance measures the presence of collinearity by the calculation:

$$\text{Tolerance} = 1 - R^2$$

where R-square is the amount of the variance in an independent variable explained by the other independent variables in the model. Tolerance ranges from zero to one. Low tolerance near zero indicates that most of the variance in an independent variable is explained by the other independent variables in the equation. High tolerance near one means that the variable is generally not associated with the other independent variables in the equation. SYSTAT prints the tolerance for each variable in the model in the column astutely titled TOLERANCE. In Figure 6.19 tolerance shows that over 90% of the variance in LOGHC and LOGNOX and over 50% in LOGSO2 can be explained by other independent variables. A related statistic is called the variance inflation factor or VIF, defined as 1 - tolerance.

Tolerance has the following characteristics. When there is only one variable in the model, none of the variance in that variable can be explained by other variables so its' tolerance will always be 1.0. Look at any of the examples in Chapter 4. When a model contains two variables, tolerance is one minus the square of the simple correlation between them, so it will be identical for both variables, see Figure 5.2. If there are more than two independent variables in the model the tolerance of each variable will differ depending on how much of the variance of each variable can be explained by the other independent variables.

Tolerance is a good warning and it has the valuable advantage that SYSTAT prints it without additional effort by the user, but it has two weaknesses which make it unreliable as a general tool for diagnosing collinearity. First, there is no meaningful boundary which can be used to distinguish values of tolerance which are too low from those which are acceptable. Second, it is unable to distinguish between several different sets of collinearities among the independent variables, so you cannot use it to find what is collinear with what.

A method often used to diagnose collinearity is to examine the correlation matrix of the independent variables. This too is unreliable because, like tolerance, correlation coefficients have no meaningful boundary that can distinguish damaging collinearity and they are unable to distinguish between several different sets of collinearities. The most serious problem is, "…the absence of high correlations cannot be viewed as evidence of no problem. It is clearly possible for three or more variates to be collinear while no two of the variates taken alone are highly correlated. The correlation matrix is wholly incapable of diagnosing such a situation" (Belsley, Kuh, and Welsh 1980 p. 92). SYSTAT handles these problems with other collinearity diagnostics.

Condition indices and variance proportions

The state-of-the-art procedure that we will use was developed by Belsley, Kuh, and Welsch (1980). It consists of two related steps: (1) detecting the presence of collinear variables; and (2) assessing which coefficient estimates have been damaged and the extent of the damage.

To use this procedure we need more information about the regression model. The PRINT LONG command provides the results displayed in Figure 6.20. In addition to the usual regression output, SYSTAT has also printed EIGENVALUES OF UNIT SCALED X'X, CONDITION INDICES and VARIANCE PROPORTIONS.

Eigenvalues tell us how independent each variable is. If all eigenvalues were 1.000 all independent variables would be completely statistically independent of each other. When one or more eigenvalues are greater than 1.000, some independent variables are correlated and collinearity is a potential problem. Thus, we want to pay special attention to column 1, which contains the largest eigenvalue.

Condition indices are the most useful indicator of collinearity. They are defined as the square root of the ratio of the largest eigenvalue divided by the eigenvalue of each column. They are valuable because, unlike tolerance, correlations, or eigenvalues, they have an explicit diagnostic boundary. Above that boundary, collinearity is harming the regression; below that boundary, collinearity is not harmful. Belsley, Kuh, and Welsh suggest that condition indices of over 15 suggest a potential problem and condition indices of over 30 indicate a serious problem. The condition index of 22.483 in column 4 of Figure 6.20 confirms that we have a problem.

Now that we have identified a collinearity problem, we would like to know which coefficient estimates have been damaged. The **variance proportions** provide this information. They are, as their name suggests, proportions; the numbers in each row sum to 1.0. The columns measure the independence of each variable. If each variable were completely independent, then each column would contain a single 1.000 and a set of 0.000s. If several variables are collinear, most of their variance will show up in a single column. Thus one column may contain several large variance proportions. To find collinear variables we look at the column which corresponds to the condition index showing collinearity damage. In Figure 6.20 this is the column with a condition index of 22.483, column 4. Here LOGHC has 0.950 of its variance and LOGNOX has 0.958. This indicates that both LOGHC and LOGNOX are seriously degraded by collinearity.

Figure 6.20
SYSTAT Collinearity Diagnostics

```
REGRESS
    USE AIR01
    PRINT=LONG
    MODEL MORT = CONSTANT + LOGHC + LOGSO2 + LOGNOX
    ESTIMATE
```

Eigenvalues of unit scaled X'X

1	2	3	4
3.800	0.124	0.069	0.008

Condition indices

1	2	3	4
1.000	5.538	7.418	22.483

Variance proportions

	1	2	3	4
CONSTANT	0.007	0.622	0.027	0.345
LOGHC	0.001	0.006	0.042	0.950
LOGSO2	0.005	0.011	0.799	0.185
LOGNOX	0.001	0.026	0.015	0.958

Dep Var: MORT N: 60 Multiple R: 0.525 Squared multiple R: 0.275

Adjusted squared multiple R: 0.236   Standard error of estimate: 54.361

Effect	Coefficient	Std Error	Std Coef	Tolerance	t	P(2 Tail)
CONSTANT	924.965	21.449	0.0	.	43.125	0.000
LOGHC	-57.300	19.419	-1.083	0.096	-2.951	0.005
LOGSO2	11.762	7.165	0.283	0.435	1.642	0.106
LOGNOX	58.336	21.751	1.111	0.075	2.682	0.010

Correlation matrix of regression coefficients

	CONSTANT	LOGHC	LOGSO2	LOGNOX
CONSTANT	1.000			
LOGHC	-0.600	1.000		
LOGSO2	-0.475	0.246	1.000	
LOGNOX	0.471	-0.915	-0.512	1.000

Analysis of Variance

Source	Sum-of-Squares	DF	Mean-Square	F-Ratio	P
Regression	62822.545	3	20940.848	7.086	0.000
Residual	165485.099	56	2955.091		

Auxiliary regressions

Collinearity is a mathematically complex problem and, under many conditions, the condition indices cannot tell us every variable involved in a collinear relationship. To confirm which variables are involved requires forming an **auxiliary regression** for each collinear relationship. The auxiliary regression output (omitting the quick graph) for our air pollution model is shown in Figure 6.21. This regression uses the variable with the largest condition index as the dependent variable (LOGNOX) and the other independent variables (CONSTANT, LOGHC, and LOGSO2) as predictors. In the auxiliary regressions our primary concern is to identify variables which are significant predictors of the dependent variable. Figure 6.21 confirms the involvement of LOGHC but the significant t-statistics for both LOGSO2 and the CONSTANT indicate that they too are involved. We conclude that the all three coefficient estimates in our original regression in Figure 6.20 have been significantly influenced by collinearity. Based on this evidence of collinearity damage, we would have to say that the positive coefficients of LOGSO2 and LOGNOX may be the result of collinearity and do not contradict previous research on the toxicity of various airborne pollutants.

Figure 6.21
Auxiliary Regression to Assess the Impact of Collinearity

```
REGRESS
    USE AIR01
    MODEL LOGNOX = CONSTANT + LOGHC + LOGSO2
    ESTIMATE
```

Here is the output:

```
Dep Var: LOGNOX N: 60 Multiple R:  0.962 Squared multiple R:  0.925

Adjusted squared multiple R:  0.922    Standard error of estimate:      0.331

Effect        Coefficient    Std Error     Std Coef Tolerance     t    P(2 Tail)

CONSTANT        -0.464        0.115        0.0        .       -4.029    0.000
LOGHC            0.817        0.048        0.811      0.589   17.108    0.000
LOGSO2           0.169        0.037        0.213      0.589    4.498    0.000

                        Analysis of Variance

Source        Sum-of-Squares   DF   Mean-Square    F-Ratio       P

Regression         76.521       2      38.260      349.139     0.000
Residual            6.246      57       0.110
```

Multiple collinear relations

One collinear relationship is relatively simple. Diagnosis becomes more difficult when a regression includes several collinear relationships. Air pollution is not the only variable influencing mortality rates. Prior research indicates that poverty and crowded housing also increase mortality. We measure poverty by the percent of families below the poverty line (POOR). Since we can't measure crowding directly, we use number of people per household (POP_HH) as our measure. Figure 6.22 adds the data for those variables and Figure 6.23 gives the regression results. Both POOR and POP_HH are significant and their signs are positive; as expected, they increase the mortality rate. But notice the collinearity diagnostics: Condition index 5 is 28.846 and condition index 6 is 65.962. Apparently we have two collinear relationships. Associated with the largest condition index, column 6, are the CONSTANT and POP_HH. Associated with the second largest condition index, column 5, are LOGNOX and LOGHC. Clearly we need to look at results of auxiliary regressions.

One procedure for forming auxiliary regressions with multiple collinear relations is the following. (1) Construct one auxiliary regression for each large condition index. Since we have two large condition indices, we use two auxiliary regressions. (2) Choose as dependent variable for each auxiliary regressions the variable which has the largest variance proportion for that condition index. Our dependent variables with be the CONSTANT (condition index of 0.990) and LOGNOX (condition index 0.943). (3) The independent variables in the auxiliary regressions are all the remaining independent variables in the model. We never use the original dependent variable, MORT, in an auxiliary regression. There are other ways to construct auxiliary regressions; in particular, the theory and variables in a given dataset may suggest a natural set of dependent variables. If you lack other criteria, this procedure is simple and chooses dependent variables which are certain to be strongly involved in the underlying collinearity.

Figure 6.22
Additional Quality of Life Variables

```
BASIC
    NEW
    INPUT CITY$ POOR POP_HH
    RUN
'Akron      OH'    11.7    3.34
'Albany     NY'    14.4    3.14
'Allentown PA'     12.4    3.21
'Atlanta    GA'    20.6    3.41
'Baltimore MD'     14.3    3.44
'BirminghamAL'     25.5    3.45
'Boston     MA'    11.3    3.23
'BridgeportCN'     10.5    3.29
'Buffalo    NY'    12.6    3.31
'Canton     OH'    13.2    3.36
'ChattanoogTN'     24.2    3.39
'Chicago    IL'    10.7    3.20
'CincinnatiOH'     15.1    3.21
'Cleveland OH'     11.4    3.29
'Columbus   OH'    13.9    3.26
'Dallas     TX'    16.1    3.22
'Dayton     OH'    12.0    3.35
'Denver     CO'    12.7    3.15
'Detroit    MI'    13.6    3.44
'Flint      MI'    12.4    3.53
'Ft Worth   TX'    18.5    3.22
'Grand RapdMI'     12.3    3.37
'GreensboroNC'     19.5    3.45
'Hartford   CN'     9.5    3.25
'Houston    TX'    17.9    3.35
'IndianaplsIN'     13.2    3.23
'KansasCityMO'     13.9    3.10
'Lancaster PA'     12.0    3.38
'LosAngelesCA'     12.3    2.99
'LouisvilleKY'     17.7    3.37
'Memphis    TN'    26.4    3.49
'Miami      FL'    22.4    2.98
'Milwaukee WI'      9.4    3.26
'MinneapolsMN'      9.8    3.28
'Nashville TN'     24.1    3.32
'New Haven CN'     12.2    3.16
'New OrleanLA'     24.2    3.36
'New York   NY'    12.4    3.03
'PhiladelphPA'     13.2    3.32
'PittsburghPA'     13.8    3.32
'Portland   OR'    13.5    2.99
'ProvidenceRI'     15.7    3.19
'Reading    PA'    14.1    3.08
'Richmond   VA'    17.5    3.32
'Rochester NY'     10.8    3.21
'St. Louis MO'     15.3    3.23
'San Diego CA'     14.0    3.11
'SanFrancisCA'     12.0    2.92
'San Jose   CA'     9.7    3.36
'Seattle    WA'    10.1    3.02
'SpringfeldMA'     12.3    3.21
'Syracuse   NY'    11.1    3.34
'Toledo     OH'    13.6    3.22
'Utica      NY'    13.5    3.28
'WashingtonDC'     10.3    3.25
'Wichita    KS'    13.2    3.27
```

```
'WilmingtonDL'   10.9   3.39
'Worcester MA'   14.0   3.25
'York    PA'     14.5   3.22
'YoungstownOH'   13.0   3.48
~
    SORT CITY$
    SAVE TEMP
    RUN

    SAVE AIR02
    MERGE AIR01 TEMP / CITY$
```

Figure 6.23
Multiple Collinear Relationships

```
REGRESS
    USE AIR02
    PRINT LONG
    MODEL MORT = CONSTANT + POP_HH + POOR,
            + LOGHC + LOGSO2 + LOGNOX
    ESTIMATE
```

Eigenvalues of unit scaled X'X

	1	2	3	4	5
	5.599	0.277	0.072	0.044	0.007

	6
	0.001

Condition indices

	1	2	3	4	5
	1.000	4.495	8.791	11.324	28.846

	6
	65.962

Variance proportions

	1	2	3	4	5
CONSTANT	0.000	0.001	0.000	0.010	0.007
POP_HH	0.000	0.001	0.001	0.011	0.007
POOR	0.002	0.068	0.052	0.747	0.131
LOGHC	0.000	0.006	0.035	0.015	0.943
LOGSO2	0.002	0.033	0.594	0.126	0.238
LOGNOX	0.000	0.012	0.024	0.006	0.956

	6
CONSTANT	0.981
POP_HH	0.981
POOR	0.000
LOGHC	0.001
LOGSO2	0.007
LOGNOX	0.003

```
Dep Var: MORT N: 60 Multiple R:  0.703 Squared multiple R:  0.495
Adjusted squared multiple R:  0.448    Standard error of estimate:      46.228

Effect        Coefficient   Std Error    Std Coef Tolerance    t    P(2 Tail)

CONSTANT        572.520      119.774        0.0        .       4.780    0.000
POP_HH           71.981       35.761        0.199    0.954     2.013    0.049
POOR              6.393        1.544        0.428    0.878     4.140    0.000
LOGHC           -38.942       17.144       -0.736    0.089    -2.271    0.027
LOGSO2           16.882        6.362        0.406    0.399     2.654    0.010
LOGNOX           39.811       19.360        0.758    0.069     2.056    0.045


Correlation matrix of regression coefficients

                 CONSTANT      POP_HH         POOR        LOGHC       LOGSO2
   CONSTANT        1.000
   POP_HH         -0.961        1.000
   POOR           -0.116       -0.116        1.000
   LOGHC          -0.104       -0.047        0.268        1.000
   LOGSO2          0.012       -0.144        0.264        0.299       1.000
   LOGNOX          0.018        0.117       -0.283       -0.919      -0.553


                  LOGNOX
   LOGNOX         1.000

                      Analysis of Variance

Source        Sum-of-Squares   DF   Mean-Square    F-Ratio      P

Regression      112907.812      5    22581.562     10.567     0.000
Residual        115399.832     54     2137.034
```

The results of the auxiliary regressions in appear in Figure 6.24. The regression using the constant (a variable called CON) as the dependent variable shows that POP_HH and, surprisingly, LOGHC are both involved in a collinearity. The regression on LOG-NOX indicates that not only are the other pollutants, LOGHC and LOGSO2, collinear but also POP_HH and POOR.

Figure 6.24
Auxiliary Regressions for Multiple Collinearities

```
REGRESS
    USE AIR02
    REM Create a constant--a column of 1s
    LET CON=1
    MODEL CON = POP_HH + POOR + LOGHC + LOGSO2
    ESTIMATE:
```

```
Model contains no constant

Dep Var: CON N: 60 Multiple R:  0.999 Squared multiple R:  0.998

Adjusted squared multiple R:  0.997     Standard error of estimate:     0.052
```

Effect	Coefficient	Std Error	Std Coef	Tolerance	t	P(2 Tail)
POP_HH	0.288	0.010	0.948	0.045	30.082	0.000
POOR	0.001	0.002	0.021	0.074	0.872	0.387
LOGHC	0.013	0.007	0.037	0.092	1.702	0.094
LOGSO2	-0.001	0.006	-0.004	0.102	-0.199	0.843

Analysis of Variance

Source	Sum-of-Squares	DF	Mean-Square	F-Ratio	P
Regression	59.851	4	14.963	5623.168	0.000
Residual	0.149	56	0.003		

```
    MODEL LOGNOX = POP_HH + POOR + LOGHC + LOGSO2
    ESTIMATE
```

Here is the output:

```
Model contains no constant

Dep Var: LOGNOX N: 60 Multiple R:  0.993 Squared multiple R:  0.986

Adjusted squared multiple R:  0.985     Standard error of estimate:     0.319
```

Effect	Coefficient	Std Error	Std Coef	Tolerance	t	P(2 Tail)
POP_HH	-0.248	0.059	-0.314	0.045	-4.194	0.000
POOR	0.022	0.010	0.129	0.074	2.205	0.032
LOGHC	0.813	0.045	0.933	0.092	17.871	0.000
LOGSO2	0.182	0.037	0.246	0.102	4.967	0.000

Analysis of Variance

Source	Sum-of-Squares	DF	Mean-Square	F-Ratio	P
Regression	401.019	4	100.255	984.408	0.000
Residual	5.703	56	0.102		

We conclude that the data underlying our model of mortality rates contain two strong collinear relationships. Every variable in the model is involved in one or both of these collinearities and each is degraded to some degree. POP_HH appears to be most strongly damaged because it is heavily involved in the stronger of the two collinearities and also in the weaker. This may be why is only significant at the 0.049 level in Figure 6.23. LOGHC is also seriously affected because of its involvement in both collinearities. This illustrates a critical methodological problem in the study of air pollution: Everything correlates highly. Even our original pollutants, HC, SO2 and NOX, are strongly related with other pollutants like lead, particulates, and carbon monoxide. As a result it is difficult to demonstrate the causes and effects of specific pollutants.

The general question is: when, exactly, is collinearity a problem? There is no clear agreement on this issue. We offer the following as a tentative rule of thumb. If the auxiliary regressions show that a variable is involved in a collinear relation and the coefficient estimates for that variable are either nonsignificant or in an unexpected direction then that variable probably has a collinearity problem. The coefficient estimates and significance tests should be reported only if accompanied by a warning to the readers that they have been damaged by collinearity and may be meaningless. Along with other summary statistics from a regression, like the adjusted R-square, it is also a good idea to report the largest condition index. Keep in mind that nonsignificant results and unexpected signs are often not the result of collinearity, but are evidence that the data do not support the theory.

What can you do?

Like outliers and influential observations, and nonlinearity, collinearity has to do with specific characteristics of the data. Collinearity is a data problem, not a statistical problem. Since the basic problem of collinearity is that the information contained in collinear variables cannot be separated for the purposes of constructing coefficient estimates, the corrective measures focus on obtaining new or better information.

The most straightforward solution is to obtain more data points. In an experiment, you can sometimes gather more data. This is particularly true if the data were gathered sequentially. If you are able to do this, you will need to consider the effects of the additional data on your assumption of randomness and check to be sure that there is no difference between the data you gathered first and the data gathered later. In nonexperimental settings, you can sometimes find extensions of your data. Particularly you may be able to extend time series data to another period earlier or later. But obtaining additional cases is often costly (in terms of collection costs or time, especially if you have to wait for new cases to occur) and frequently impossible.

A more common solution is to combine the collinear variables into a single variable. There are several ways to find a combination. If the variables are measured on equivalent scales and they are positively related, the simplest combination is to add them. If the scales are not equivalent, you can find the principal components of the collinear variables and use the factor scores from the first principal component as a single combined variable. SYSTAT calculates and saves factor scores in the FACTOR procedure. A new variable constructed from the sum of several variables or from factor scores is interpretable and produces interpretable coefficients only if the variables are conceptually similar. Since the air pollution variables are conceptually similar and are measured on equivalent scales, we chose the simple approach and computed a new variable:

```
LET LGPOLUTE = LOG(HC + SO2 + NOX)
```

Figure 6.25 shows the results from the new regression. As you can see, the tolerances are all very high, indicating that collinearity is no longer a problem.

A final alternative is to include in your model only one of the collinear variables. This works best when your variables are involved in only one collinear relation. Stepwise regression may be used to select a variable for inclusion or you may want to pick one on theoretical grounds. We have not included an example from the air pollution dataset, though you may want to try one. Models using any one of the three air pollution variables fit almost equally well.

When you are trying to decide what to do about collinearity, consider the following:

- Are there theoretical reasons for preferring to keep one of the collinear variables in your model?
- Some people don't like to delete variables which have very different theoretical meanings because the omission of certain variables may make the model appear not to have considered important theoretical perspectives. In this case you may want to combine the variables.
- If the variables are measured on different scales, you can rescale them to standard units (divide by the standard deviation and subtract the mean) before combining or you may need to combine them using principal components (see SYSTAT's FACTOR procedure).

Figure 6.25
Regression Demonstrating the Reduced Effects of Collinearity

```
REGRESS
   USE AIR02
   LET LGPOLUTE = LOG(HC + SO2 + NOX)
   MODEL MORT = CONSTANT + POP_HH + POOR + LGPOLUTE
   ESTIMATE
```

```
Dep Var: MORT N: 60 Multiple R:  0.610 Squared multiple R:  0.372

Adjusted squared multiple R:  0.338    Standard error of estimate:     50.619

Effect        Coefficient    Std Error    Std Coef Tolerance    t    P(2 Tail)

CONSTANT       488.463       131.768       0.0         .       3.707   0.000
POP_HH          81.656        38.573       0.226     0.983     2.117   0.039
POOR             6.789         1.609       0.454     0.970     4.221   0.000
LGPOLUTE        21.183         5.476       0.417     0.968     3.868   0.000

                        Analysis of Variance

Source          Sum-of-Squares   DF   Mean-Square    F-Ratio      P

Regression          84819.563     3    28273.188      11.034     0.000
Residual           143488.081    56     2562.287
```

- Remember that outliers and influential points may influence the apparent correlation between variables. Before you start combining or deleting variables, be sure that the apparent collinearity is real and not due to a few wild points.
- If your goal is to accurately predict the values of the dependent variable and you are not concerned with which variables you use, then remember that collinearity does not interfere with the accuracy of the fitted values. It only effects the coefficient estimates and their standard errors.

Collinearity is a serious problem in a wide variety of datasets. While the diagnostics can tell you if collinearity is a problem and which parameter estimates are degraded, the solutions above will not be acceptable under many circumstances. There are times when you may just have to live with the fact that collinearity will prevent you from finding a reliable estimate of an important parameter. For a summary of some alternatives, see Judge et al. (1985).

6.4 Heteroscedasticity

Some people oppose military spending because they claim it harms the national economy by reducing economic growth. The problem is acute in less developed countries where the size of the economy may not be large to begin with. We have gathered data on the size of the national economy (measured by 1980 gross domestic product) and the military budget (also for 1980) for 60 countries in Latin America, South Asia and Sub-Saharan Africa in Figure 6.26. Since we know that many variables besides military spending influence the size of an economy, we included some of the most influential. The more workers who produce goods, the greater the size of the economy. POP80 measures this. If workers have more machinery, they will be more productive; so the level of investment in factories and machinery is included. Finally, the government spends money on many nonmilitary items and this spending should be part of the model. The point is, we need a multiple regression model to test the effects of military spending. If the hypothesis that military spending reduces the size of the national economy is true, then we expect to see a significant negative relation between the size of the military budget and the size of the economy, controlling for the other variables.

Figure 6.26
Military Spending Dataset

```
BASIC
    INPUT COUNTRY$ GDP80 MIL80 POP80 GDI80 GOVT80 EXCG80,
          DEFLBASE DEFL80
    RUN
"Argentina     " 111800    1628  27740   27700    14800    1837.16  .07   200.
"Bangladesh    " 69210     156   88513   6196     4916.4   15.47    .416  1.051
"Bolivia       " 19161     106   5570    2154     2614     24.51    .331  2.58
"Botswana      " 359.1     33    901     157.9    64.5     0.776    1     1.92
"Brazil        " 481000    1550  118332  113200   42600    52.714   .328  8.93
"Cameroon      " 1063700   82    8444    234200   71800    209.21   1.127 1.637
"Chad          " 52000     22    4455    6200     9300     211.3    .686  1.406
"Chile         " 362634.6  1456  11104   86728.9  46009.3  39       7.139 21.084
"Colombia      " 229294    302   25892   52746.9  17675.3  47.28    .424  2.933
"Congo         " 200800    61    1605    82700    30600    211.3    1     1.84
"Costa Rica    " 9647.8    0     2279    2753.3   1276.4   8.57     .445  1.913
"Ecuador       " 147202    208   8354    41828    23308    25       1     1.913
"El Salvador   " 4714.4    54    4540    707.2    683.2    2.5      .704  1.897
"Ethiopia      " 4947.3    447   31065   498.8    409.5    2.07     .777  1.322
"Gabon         " 191100    74    657     96500    42200    211.3    .519  2.261
"Gambia, The   " 286.4     0     591     103.7    81.2     1.721    1.134 1.571
"Ghana         " 5475.2    50    11500   464.3    1223.5   8.5      1     7.487
"Guatemala     " 3106.9    101   7262    535.4    222.7    1        .644  1.636
"Honduras      " 2067      45    3691    446      297      2        .685  1.567
"India         " 552800    4451  674984  118400   69300    7.893    .629  1.458
"Ivory Coast   " 1835400   125   8262    486400   325800   211.3    1.582 1.911
"Jamaica       " 1850.8    20    2172    212.5    456.5    1.781    .825  2.12
"Kenya         " 37478     300   16642   9572     7466     7.42     1.189 1.666
"Lesotho       " 109.8     0     1341    28.3     30.4     0.778    .627  1.782
"Liberia       " 491.4     26    1873    129.4    61       1        .61   1.386
```

"Malawi "	577.6	55	6037	94.8	55.5	0.812	.782	1.682
"Mali "	262000	39	6699	39300	58500	422.6	.74	1.581
"Mauritania "	14612	30	1523	5392	4559	45.916	.718	1.488
"Mexico "	841854.5	756	69393	235974.1	74957.5	22.951	.555	2.818
"Mozambique "	47687	160	12084	4188	6486	36	.568	1.671
"Nicaragua "	21891.6	70	2672	3364.1	4106.6	10.05	2.364	2.364
"Niger "	142200	17	5532	38700	13100	211.3	.676	1.903
"Nigeria "	32581	2288	82603	7325	3600	0.547	1.267	1.707
"Panama "	1714.7	18	1835	415.1	265.4	1	.698	1.42
"Paraguay "	360383	69	2982	110061	22308	126	1.147	1.783
"Peru "	483826	457	16610	72353	68926	288.653	.611	8.149
"Senegal "	290900	64	5703	40200	65100	211.3	.681	1.358
"Sierra Leone"	454.9	14	3474	74.3	43.6	1.05	.736	1.853
"South Africa"	18933.7	2320	28723	5779.9	2402.6	0.778	.59	1.938
"Sri Lanka "	20920	41	14738	7065	1786.7	16.534	.583	1.855
"Sudan "	5191.2	200	18681	864.5	596.4	0.5	2.538	1.982
"Swaziland "	152	13	618	47	22.7	0.778	.746	1.831
"Tanzania "	13216	250	18534	2509	1798.9	8.195	.564	1.692
"Togo "	170900	23	2578	47700	28300	211.3	1.143	1.437
"Uruguay "	34727	260	2908	6993	4268	9.16	3.42	9.267
"Venezuela "	76612	755	14930	22122	12664	4.293	.545	1.827
"Zambia "	1369.7	516	5647	205	275.2	0.789	.908	1.98
"Zimbabwe "	1317.6	478	6894	298.7	390.4	0.643	.667	1.788

~

```
    SAVE MIL01 /,
    'MILITARY EXPENDITURE DATASET',
    '     COUNTRY$  Name of country',
    '     GDP80     Gross Domestic Product, constant market prices',
    '     MIL80     Military expenditures 1980 prices--USA dollars',
    '     POP80     Population--mid-year',
    '     GDI80     Gross Domestic Investment constant market prices',
    '     GOVT80    Government expenditures, constant market prices',
    '     DEFL80    Implicit GDP deflator index',
    '     DEFLBASE  Implicit GDP deflator index for base year of',
    '               price index',
    '     EXCG80    Exchange rate between local currency and US$',
    ' ,   All data are from 1980 unless otherwise stated',

    REM Use price indexes to convert to 1980 prices
        LET GDP80  = GDP80  * DEFL80 / DEFLBASE
        LET GDI80  = GDI80  * DEFL80 / DEFLBASE
        LET GOVT80 = GOVT80 * DEFL80 / DEFLBASE
    REM Use exchange rate to convert to USA dollars
        LET GDP80  = GDP80  / EXCG80
        LET GDI80  = GDI80  / EXCG80
        LET GOVT80 = GOVT80 / EXCG80
    REM MIL80 is already expressed in 1980 USA dollars
    REM Remove military spending from other govt expenditures
        LET GOVT80 = GOVT80 - MIL80
    RUN
```

The results of the regression of GDP80 on MIL80 and the other variables are in Figure 6.27 and the quick graph is in Figure 6.28. The regression coefficient for MIL80 is negative but not significant which seems to disconfirm the hypothesis that military spending has an important impact on growth. However, a supporter of the hypothesis could immediately point out two problems. First, the large number of influential points and outliers suggests that the model does not fit.

Figure 6.27
Gross Domestic Product Regressed on Military Spending

```
REGRESS
   USE MIL01
   MODEL GDP80 = CONSTANT + MIL80 + POP80 + GDI80 + GOVT80
   SAVE MIL02 / DATA   RESIDUAL
   ESTIMATE
```

The output is:

```
Dep Var: GDP80 N: 48 Multiple R:  0.996 Squared multiple R:  0.992

Adjusted squared multiple R:  0.992    Standard error of estimate:    4978.538

Effect         Coefficient    Std Error    Std Coef Tolerance    t    P(2 Tail)

CONSTANT         293.808       829.611        0.0        .       0.354    0.725
MIL80             -1.217         1.861       -0.018    0.226   -0.654    0.517
POP80              0.046         0.013        0.083    0.339    3.633    0.001
GDI80              3.331         0.241        0.828    0.049   13.799    0.000
GOVT80             1.487         0.660        0.142    0.044    2.254    0.029

                     Analysis of Variance

Source          Sum-of-Squares   DF  Mean-Square    F-Ratio      P

Regression       1.40224E+11      4  3.50560E+10   1414.355    0.000
Residual         1.06579E+09     43  2.47858E+07

Durbin-Watson D Statistic     2.061
First Order Autocorrelation  -0.031

Residuals have been saved.
```

You can see the second problem by looking at the residuals plot in Figure 6.28. The data concentrate on the left side of the plot and they seem to spread out in a fan-shaped pattern toward the right.

This pattern suggests that the small residuals have a smaller variance than the larger residuals. The statistical virtues of least squares regression are based, in part, on the assumption that the variance of the residuals is constant across their entire range. When this is true, the residuals are said to be **homoscedastic**. When the variance is not constant the residuals are **heteroscedastic**. The plot in Figure 6.28 is an example of heteroscedastic residuals. Strictly speaking, heteroscedasticity inflates the standard errors but does not influence the parameter estimates. In practice, however, heteroscedasticity often conceals other problems such as nonlinearity so it deserves careful attention.

Like many other topics covered in this book, the overview of heteroscedasticity presented here can be complicated by a variety of factors. The best general discussion of types of heteroscedasticity and the various solutions is Judge et al. (1985, Chapter 11).

Figure 6.28
Quick Graph Residuals Plot

Plot of Residuals against Predicted Values

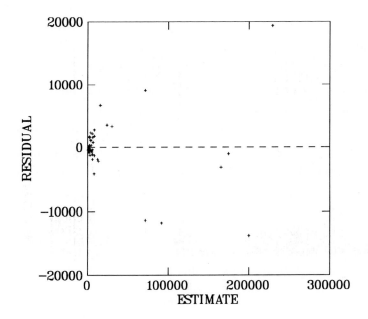

Diagnosis

Figure 6.28 shows typical heteroscedasticity. As the estimated values become larger, the variance of the residuals (measured by the vertical distance between the largest and smallest residuals at each point) increases. A visual check of the residuals is the simplest way to diagnose heteroscedasticity. If the plot appears to show that the size of the residuals is related to the size of the fitted values, then you may want to do a more formal check. One of the best of the formal tests is the Goldfeld-Quandt test.

The Goldfeld-Quandt test

The **Goldfeld-Quandt test** (Goldfeld and Quandt, 1965) is a formal test of whether the residuals are heteroscedastic:

1. Sort the cases according to the variable which seems related to the variance to the residuals. We looked at plots of the residuals against several independent variables and chose MIL80 as the variable to sort. The plots indicate that several other variables are also related to the variance of the residuals and could have been chosen.

2. Omit the middle cases, perhaps up to 20 percent, leaving two equal-sized groups of cases, one group corresponding to the low values of the chosen variable and the other group corresponding to high values. For small samples (less than 30 cases) no cases need to be eliminated. We chose to omit 8 cases from the military spending data.

3. Run separate regressions on the two groups and calculate the ratio of their residual sum-of-squares. As the numerator use the residual sum-of-squares from the cases with large variances; the denominator will be cases with small variances.

4. This ratio is distributed as an F statistic with $(N - d - 2p)/2$ degrees of freedom in both the numerator and denominator. N is the total number of cases, d is the number of omitted cases, and p is the number of predictors in the model including the constant.

5. The null hypothesis is that there is no difference between the variance of the residuals from the two groups. If the ratio of the sums-of-squares is larger than the tabulated F value, reject the assumption that the residuals have a constant variance.

The data for Goldfeld-Quandt test are in Figure 6.29. We would compute the F-statistic as:

$$\frac{1014980000.}{2060686.924} = 492.54$$

The ratio is so large (almost 500) that you needn't bother looking it up in an F table. These data are extremely heteroscedastic. The usefulness of the Goldfeld-Quandt test depends on your ability to rank the cases in terms of increasing variance.

Figure 6.29
Goldfeld-Quandt Test for Heteroscedasticity

```
BASIC
    USE MIL01
    SORT MIL80
    SAVE TEMP
    RUN

    REM Create dataset of large-variance countries.
    REM 20 cases: sorted cases 29 through 48.
    USE TEMP
    SAVE TEMPLGE
    IF CASE < 29 THEN DELETE
    LET SIZE$ = 'Large Var.'
    RUN

    REM Create dataset of small-variance countries.
    REM 20 cases: sorted cases 1 through 20.
    NEW
    USE TEMP
    SAVE TEMPSML
    IF CASE > 20 THEN DELETE
    LET SIZE$ = 'Small Var.'
    RUN

    REM Create combined dataset.
    SAVE MIL03
    APPEND TEMPLGE TEMPSML

REGRESS
    REM Large- and small-variance groups
    USE MIL03
    BY SIZE$
    MODEL GDP80 = CONSTANT + MIL80 + POP80 + GDI80 + GOVT80
    ESTIMATE
```

The output is:

```
The following results are for:
   SIZE$        = Large Var.

Dep Var: GDP80 N: 20 Multiple R:  0.995 Squared multiple R:  0.991

Adjusted squared multiple R:  0.988     Standard error of estimate:     8225.889

Effect          Coefficient   Std Error    Std Coef Tolerance      t    P(2 Tail)

CONSTANT         1151.474     2658.061        0.0       .        0.433    0.671
MIL80              -1.732        3.360      -0.025    0.271     -0.515    0.614
POP80               0.048        0.022       0.095    0.349      2.222    0.042
GDI80               3.341        0.405       0.835    0.062      8.243    0.000
GOVT80              1.447        1.109       0.138    0.057      1.305    0.212

                     Analysis of Variance

Source          Sum-of-Squares   DF   Mean-Square     F-Ratio       P

Regression       1.05859E+11    4   2.64648E+10     391.113      0.000
Residual         1.01498E+09   15   6.76652E+07
-------------------------------------------------------------------------


The following results are for:
   SIZE$        = Small Var.

Dep Var: GDP80 N: 20 Multiple R:  0.979 Squared multiple R:  0.958

Adjusted squared multiple R:  0.947     Standard error of estimate:      370.647

Effect          Coefficient   Std Error    Std Coef Tolerance      t    P(2 Tail)

CONSTANT         -187.004      173.952        0.0       .       -1.075    0.299
MIL80               4.743        5.126       0.055    0.779      0.925    0.370
POP80               0.040        0.028       0.091    0.670      1.415    0.178
GDI80               1.845        0.259       0.443    0.728      7.137    0.000
GOVT80              3.713        0.371       0.623    0.726     10.021    0.000

                     Analysis of Variance

Source          Sum-of-Squares   DF   Mean-Square     F-Ratio       P

Regression       4.69583E+07    4   1.17396E+07      85.454      0.000
Residual        2060686.924    15    137379.128
```

There are various other less common forms of heteroscedasticity than the "fan" shape we see here. No single "best test" can find all forms. You should always do a simple graphical check (like the residuals plot in Figure 6.28). If you see some indication of heteroscedasticity, then do a formal test. Be aware that a significant test statistic may indicate heteroscedasticity or it may indicate that the model is misspecified: variables may be omitted or the functional form of the model may be incorrect. This means tests for heteroscedasticity lack power and you will need to consider possible misspecification when you interpret the results of the test. An outstanding discussion of these and related issues is in Judge et al. (1985).

What can you do?

First, consider whether the model is correctly specified. Like many other data problems in regression, heteroscedasticity may often be corrected by adding omitted variables or changing the functional form of the model. If you reject this alternative then you need to consider how you can correct the heteroscedasticity.

The fundamental problem of heteroscedasticity is that residuals associated with high variance cases strongly influence the regression. The logic goes like this: cases with a large variance usually have large residuals and, since the residuals are squared, a large residual can become very influential. An appropriate correction reduces the influence of the large-variance cases and increases the influence of the small-variance cases. We will describe an approach that weights each case to equalize their influence. The weighting procedure divides each case by an estimate of its variance; large-variance cases are divided by a large number and their influence is proportionately reduced, while small-variance residuals are divided by a small number and their influence becomes proportionately larger. The name of this procedure is **weighted least squares**.

The procedure for weighted least squares is simple, the difficult problem is obtaining estimates of the variance of each residual to be used as weights. In the remainder of this section we will demonstrate two examples illustrating different ways of obtaining estimates of the variances of the residuals. In closing, we will summarize a general strategy for heteroscedasticity correction.

To estimate the variance of the residuals, the crucial problem is to decide on the form of the variance. The form of the variance determines the method used to obtain weights. One common form is that the variance is proportional to the square of the fitted values. Here you can obtain the appropriate weights by dividing each case by the squared estimates from an ordinary regression. Figure 6.30 illustrates how this assumption would be implemented using the military spending dataset.

Notice that the actual correction divides each variable in the model (don't forget the constant) by the *square root* of the weight. Did the correction work? Figure 6.31 has the quick graph residuals plot with the answer.

Figure 6.30
Heteroscedasticity Correction
Assuming Variance Is Proportional to Square of Fitted Values

```
BASIC
   NEW
   USE MIL02
   SAVE MIL05
   LET WEIGHT = ESTIMATE * ESTIMATE
   LET WGDP80  = GDP80   / SQR(WEIGHT)
   LET WCON    = 1 / SQR(WEIGHT)
   LET WMIL80  = MIL80   / SQR(WEIGHT)
   LET WPOP80  = POP80   / SQR(WEIGHT)
   LET WGDI80  = GDI80   / SQR(WEIGHT)
   LET WGOVT80 = GOVT80 / SQR(WEIGHT)
   DROP WEIGHT ESTIMATE
   RUN

REGRESS
   USE MIL05
   MODEL WGDP80 = WCON + WMIL80 + WPOP80 + WGDI80 + WGOVT80
   SAVE MIL06 / DATA   RESIDUAL
   ESTIMATE
```

Model contains no constant

Dep Var: WGDP80 N: 48 Multiple R: 0.982 Squared multiple R: 0.964

Adjusted squared multiple R: 0.961   Standard error of estimate: 0.207

Effect	Coefficient	Std Error	Std Coef	Tolerance	t	P(2 Tail)
WCON	-216.440	81.388	-0.104	0.548	-2.659	0.011
WMIL80	2.669	0.837	0.132	0.485	3.188	0.003
WPOP80	0.081	0.014	0.250	0.468	5.936	0.000
WGDI80	2.370	0.284	0.474	0.258	8.358	0.000
WGOVT80	2.984	0.449	0.363	0.278	6.638	0.000

Analysis of Variance

Source	Sum-of-Squares	DF	Mean-Square	F-Ratio	P
Regression	49.708	5	9.942	232.117	0.000
Residual	1.842	43	0.043		

WARNING

Case	2 has large leverage	(Leverage =	0.400)
Case	14 has large leverage	(Leverage =	0.565)
Case	47 has large leverage	(Leverage =	0.665)

Durbin-Watson D Statistic   2.097
First Order Autocorrelation -0.098

Residuals have been saved.

Figure 6.31
Residuals Plot Following Heteroscedasticity Correction

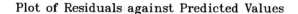

Plot of Residuals against Predicted Values

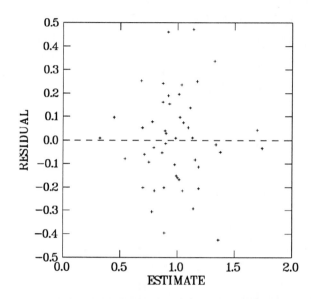

This is a fine-looking residuals plot; the heteroscedasticity has been removed. Comparing the original regression in Figure 6.27 with Figure 6.30, you will notice that the significance levels of the coefficients have improved and there are fewer apparent outliers. In general, Figure 6.30 looks like a much better model. The only problem is substantive: the sign of the coefficient for MIL80 has reversed and military spending appears to be positively related to economic growth. We leave this problem to interested readers.

A second common form of heteroscedasticity is that the variance is constant within groups and varies between groups. Here there are two possibilities. The easiest approach is to use groups which are already part of the data. Practically any categorical variable is a candidate for use as a grouping variable (e.g. REGION$ in our data). The important criterion is that the variance must be constant within categories and vary between categories. A second approach is to sort the data according to their expected variance, then divide the sorted cases into equal-sized groups.

In both cases, run separate regressions on each group. The appropriate weight for the cases in each group is the residual sum-of-squares from the regression for that group divided by $(N_i - p)$. N_i is the number of cases in group i and p is the number of parameters in the regression, including the constant. Figure 6.32 we sort the military spending dataset and divide it into four equal-sized groups. We chose this approach to show you how the groups could be created. When you divide data into groups, remember that smaller groups are usually better because smaller groups are more likely to have homogenous variances. However, you don't want the groups to be so small that the regression estimates become unstable. We chose four groups because, since we are fitting five parameters in the military spending regression, that gave us over two cases per parameter in the regressions used to find the weights.

Figure 6.32
Heteroscedasticity Correction Using Grouped Data

```
BASIC
    USE MIL01
    REM Assume variance proportional to GDI80.
    SORT GDI80
    SAVE MIL07
    RUN

    NEW
    USE MIL07
    SAVE MIL08
            IF CASE <= 12                    THEN LET GROUP = 1
    ELSE IF CASE > 12 AND CASE <= 24 THEN LET GROUP = 2
    ELSE IF CASE > 24 AND CASE <= 36 THEN LET GROUP = 3
    ELSE                                     LET GROUP = 4
    RUN

REGRESS
    USE MIL08
    REM Find weights.
    BY GROUP
    MODEL GDP80 = CONSTANT + MIL80 + POP80 + GDI80 + GOVT80
    ESTIMATE
```

Here is the output:

```
The following results are for:
   GROUP        =        1.000

Dep Var: GDP80 N: 12 Multiple R:  0.958 Squared multiple R:  0.918

Adjusted squared multiple R:  0.871    Standard error of estimate:      266.584

Effect          Coefficient    Std Error     Std Coef Tolerance    t    P(2 Tail)

CONSTANT         -235.989      249.719         0.0        .      -0.945    0.376
MIL80               4.784        6.876         0.133    0.321     0.696    0.509
POP80               0.068        0.054         0.182    0.566     1.262    0.247
GDI80               2.533        1.507         0.317    0.330     1.680    0.137
GOVT80              2.759        0.606         0.623    0.629     4.554    0.003
                        Analysis of Variance

Source          Sum-of-Squares   DF  Mean-Square    F-Ratio        P

Regression       5552139.141      4  1388034.785     19.531      0.001
Residual          497468.441      7    71066.920
-----------------------------------------------------------------------------


The following results are for:
   GROUP        =        2.000

Dep Var: GDP80 N: 12 Multiple R:  0.929 Squared multiple R:  0.863

Adjusted squared multiple R:  0.784    Standard error of estimate:      711.066

Effect          Coefficient    Std Error     Std Coef Tolerance    t    P(2 Tail)

CONSTANT        -1147.680      946.455         0.0        .      -1.213    0.265
MIL80               3.405        1.705         0.376    0.554     1.997    0.086
POP80               0.095        0.036         0.507    0.527     2.628    0.034
GDI80               3.252        1.427         0.362    0.779     2.279    0.057
GOVT80              4.077        0.763         0.837    0.800     5.344    0.001
                        Analysis of Variance

Source          Sum-of-Squares   DF  Mean-Square    F-Ratio        P

Regression       2.22165E+07      4  5554131.529     10.985      0.004
Residual         3539303.674      7   505614.811
```

```
The following results are for:
   GROUP       =       3.000

Dep Var: GDP80 N: 12 Multiple R:  0.749 Squared multiple R:  0.561

Adjusted squared multiple R:  0.311    Standard error of estimate:    2036.200

Effect          Coefficient     Std Error     Std Coef Tolerance     t    P(2 Tail)

CONSTANT          -491.890      3752.954        0.0         .      -0.131    0.899
MIL80                5.700         8.448        0.317     0.284     0.675    0.522
POP80                0.087         0.032        0.846     0.645     2.713    0.030
GDI80                3.814         2.930        0.552     0.348     1.301    0.234
GOVT80              -1.142         4.200       -0.146     0.218    -0.272    0.794

                         Analysis of Variance

Source          Sum-of-Squares   DF   Mean-Square    F-Ratio       P

Regression        3.71272E+07     4   9281798.827     2.239      0.166
Residual          2.90228E+07     7   4146111.760
------------------------------------------------------------------------------

The following results are for:
   GROUP       =       4.000

Dep Var: GDP80 N: 12 Multiple R:  0.993 Squared multiple R:  0.986

Adjusted squared multiple R:  0.978    Standard error of estimate:   11950.708

Effect          Coefficient     Std Error     Std Coef Tolerance     t    P(2 Tail)

CONSTANT          -495.802      6495.862        0.0         .      -0.076    0.941
MIL80               -0.956         5.350       -0.015     0.294    -0.179    0.863
POP80                0.044         0.034        0.102     0.317     1.285    0.240
GDI80                3.348         0.591        0.828     0.093     5.668    0.001
GOVT80               1.485         1.623        0.139     0.086     0.915    0.391

                         Analysis of Variance

Source          Sum-of-Squares   DF   Mean-Square    F-Ratio       P

Regression        7.09099E+10     4   1.77275E+10   124.125      0.000
Residual          9.99736E+08     7   1.42819E+08
```

```
BASIC
   USE MIL08
   SAVE MIL09
   REM (N - p) = 7 for all groups.
        IF GROUP = 1 THEN LET WEIGHT =  497468.441 / 7
   ELSE IF GROUP = 2 THEN LET WEIGHT = 3539303.674/ 7
   ELSE IF GROUP = 3 THEN LET WEIGHT = .290228E08  / 7
   ELSE                  LET WEIGHT = .999736E09  / 7

   LET WGDP80  = GDP80  / SQR(WEIGHT)
   LET WCON    = 1      / SQR(WEIGHT)
   LET WMIL80  = MIL80  / SQR(WEIGHT)
   LET WPOP80  = POP80  / SQR(WEIGHT)
   LET WGDI80  = GDI80  / SQR(WEIGHT)
   LET WGOVT80 = GOVT80 / SQR(WEIGHT)
   RUN

REGRESS
   USE MIL09
   MODEL WGDP80 = WCON + WMIL80 + WPOP80 + WGDI80 + WGOVT80
   SAVE MIL10 / DATA  RESIDUAL
   ESTIMATE
```

The output is:

```
Model contains no constant

Dep Var: WGDP80 N: 48 Multiple R:  0.989 Squared multiple R:  0.979

Adjusted squared multiple R:  0.977    Standard error of estimate:      0.988

Effect          Coefficient    Std Error    Std Coef Tolerance    t   P(2 Tail)

WCON             -171.955        93.600       -0.054    0.570   -1.837    0.073
WMIL80              2.767         1.154        0.079    0.455    2.398    0.021
WPOP80              0.058         0.014        0.133    0.455    4.014    0.000
WGDI80              2.579         0.200        0.572    0.254   12.926    0.000
WGOVT80             2.932         0.394        0.352    0.222    7.434    0.000

                        Analysis of Variance

Source          Sum-of-Squares   DF   Mean-Square    F-Ratio       P

Regression           1921.612     5     384.322      393.353     0.000
Residual               42.013    43       0.977
***WARNING***
Case      11 has large leverage  (Leverage =      0.455)
Case      17 has large leverage  (Leverage =      0.399)
Case      20 has large leverage  (Leverage =      0.562)
Case      21 is an outlier       (Studentized Residual =       2.768)
Case      26 has large leverage  (Leverage =      0.321)
Case      45 has large leverage  (Leverage =      0.424)
Case      45 is an outlier       (Studentized Residual =      -3.056)
Case      48 has large leverage  (Leverage =      0.320)
Case      48 is an outlier       (Studentized Residual =       2.987)

Durbin-Watson D Statistic     2.185
First Order Autocorrelation  -0.152

Residuals have been saved.
```

Figure 6.33
Residuals Plot Following Heteroscedasticity Correction

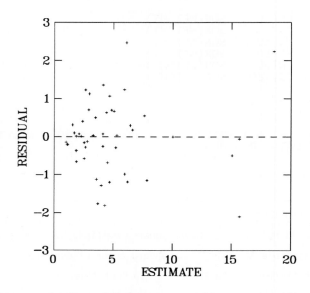

Again, after the heteroscedasticity correction, the model looks much better. To check the success of the correction, the quick graph residuals plot is printed in Figure 6.33. This plot doesn't look as good as the plot from the previous correction. It looks like the residuals are still heteroscedastic. If you do the Goldfield-Quandt test on these data, the F-statistic is significant.

So, this correction didn't work. This will also happen to you from time to time. Here are things to consider when the correction doesn't work. The most likely problem is that we have chosen the wrong form for the variance. In this case, the heteroscedasticity may not be related to the groups and we need to consider that heteroscedasticity may be related to the expected value, as in the first example. Perhaps we chose the wrong groups (we may need more or fewer) or the variable we chose to sort the data was wrong. If we were using a categorical variable to determine the groups, maybe we chose the wrong variable. Remember that the model itself may be misspecified. Correct this and you may not need a heteroscedasticity correction.

Finally, an alternative approach for correcting "fan" shaped heteroscedasticity is to log the dependent and independent variables. This simple method is easy to interpret and works well if the model generating the errors is multiplicative. See Section 22.4.

In general, this is the strategy to follow to diagnose and correct heteroscedasticity.

1. Check the residuals plot for evidence of heteroscedasticity.
2. If the residuals show that heteroscedasticity is likely, you may want to do a formal test like the Goldfeld-Quandt test.
3. If the test is negative, you are probably safe staying with the simple linear model. Don't trust the test if your eyes say otherwise, however. It won't hurt to do the transformation or weighted least squares anyway.
4. If the test is significant, determine the functional form of the heteroscedasticity.
5. Obtain weights appropriate to the functional form.
6. Divide every variable in the model (including the constant) by the square root of the weights.
7. Run the weighted regression.

If your model is correctly specified and the form of heteroscedasticity that you assumed is the correct form for your data, the regression coefficients will have the correct variance and the significance tests will be appropriate

6.5 Too much data

The title of this section is facetious but the point is simple. You may have noticed that all the examples in this book use small datasets and you may be thinking something like, "These ideas are fine if you only have 50 cases, but what about my 1,000 cases? What about 10,000 cases? 100,000? Or more?" Many things change as datasets become large. For one, graphical techniques become less useful because, even with very fine resolution, so many points tend to overprint at the same location that plots become hard to interpret. Most noticeably, each pass through a large dataset takes a long time, and slowness discourages exploration of different approaches and flexibility.

These are serious problems. Data analysis is most effective when it is most flexible and it thrives on multiple views of the same data. If you really have 1,000 or 10,000 cases, the first thing to realize is that beginning the analysis with the entire dataset may not be the best strategy. It is time consuming and you will be unable to use many of the most effective analysis techniques. You almost certainly learn more if you start your work with subsamples: perhaps a subsample of 300 and a sub-subsample of 100; if you have 10,000 cases, the appropriate subsamples may be 500 and 125. The size of the subsamples can be designed to step up by a factor of 3, 5, or 10 to successively larger datasets. Figure 6.33 shows how to take both exact and approximate random samples. Begin the analysis with the smallest subsample and when you have learned as much as you can from that subsample, move up to the next larger subsample. If you encounter a problem with a larger sample, you can always step down to a smaller sample to figure out what's happening. Data often come in a particular order so be sure to take a random sample of the entire file and don't just grab the first 100 cases. Keep in mind that if some infrequently occurring process is of special interest, you may need to oversample it to have enough cases in your subsample. Working with small subsamples will speed up analysis and encourage flexible exploration of the data.

Figure 6.34
Exact and Approximate Random Samples

```
REM Pick an approximate random sample of one-tenth from a file
BASIC
    USE DATA
    SAVE NEWDATA
    IF URN > 0.1 THEN DELETE
    RUN
    REM To vary the sample size, change the 0.1 proportion to another
    REM number between 0 and 1.0

REM Pick an approximate random sample of one-fifth, keep both
REM selected and deselected cases in the same file.  The INCLUDE
REM variable can be used with the SELECT command to select
REM the random subsample for cross-validation
    USE DATA
    SAVE NEWDATA
    IF URN > 0.2 THEN LET INCLUDE = 0
    ELSE LET INCLUDE = 1
    RUN

REM Pick an exact random sample of size ns from a file of size nf
    USE DATA
    SAVE NEWDATA
    HOLD
    IF CASE = 1 THEN LET NUMFILE = nf
    IF CASE = 1 THEN LET NUMSAMP = ns
    LET RAND = URN
    IF RAND > NUMSAMP / NUMFILE THEN DELETE
    ELSE LET NUMSAMP = NUMSAMP - 1
    LET NUMFILE = NUMFILE - 1
    DROP NUMFILE NUMSAMP RAND
    RUN
    REM Replace nf with the number of cases in the original file
    REM Replace ns with the number of cases you want in your sample
```

Subsamples are an effective way to use a desktop computer to complement a mainframe for very large datasets. You may need a mainframe to analyze your 200,000 or 1,000,000-case dataset, but you can take advantage of the flexible, graphical approach of a desktop machine to analyze subsamples of 500 and 2,500.

Subsamples can also be used to assess the stability of your results. You can directly compare coefficients estimated from different subsamples or use the jackknife; see Mosteller and Tukey (1977, Chapter 8) and the references there.

Besides the issue of data analytic strategy, there are other ways you can speed up analysis when you are working with large amounts of data. The most significant technique is to compute your regressions using the sum-of-squares-and-cross-products (SSCP) matrix rather than the data. The SYSTAT manual explains the procedure for creating a SSCP matrix for use in regression. The regression coefficients will be identical regardless of which method you use. Regressions using the SSCP matrix will be *very* fast, but you will not be able to do residuals analysis, so this will not be appropriate in many circumstances.

During a regression calculation, SYSTAT spends much of its time reading data. Minimize this by minimizing the amount of data read. If your dataset contains many variables not needed in your current analyses, creating a smaller dataset without those variables will improve speed. One approach creates a masterfile containing all your variables while extracting the variables used for analysis into smaller workfiles.

When you analyze large amounts of data, the probability of getting the observed results by chance becomes very small. This means that almost *any* coefficient estimate will be statistically significant. In large samples you may find correlations of 0.01 statistically different from zero, but they are not substantively different from zero. In regression you should be looking at the values of the regression coefficients themselves rather than at p-values. Thus statistical significance and substantive significance are no longer identical.

You need to review the literature in your field to find out what coefficients are considered meaningful. For example, in some areas in psychology a pearson correlation of less than 0.3 is generally considered meaningless. In some areas of biology, correlations of less than 0.6 are usually thought "too small". The point is that in large samples p-values will no longer be a useful way to decide whether you have found an effect;

you will have to depend on what other investigators working in the same field have found to know whether your analyses are substantively useful.

Notes

Outliers

The BOXOFF data are printed weekly in *Variety* magazine. Two issues, dated 10/2/85 and 10/16/85, did not contain box office data. The *Variety* data are truncated, only including films which grossed over $1 million. Since we don't know about the other films this distorts the relation between BOXOFF and SCREENS. We have attempted to reduce this distortion by including only films playing at over 950 screens. The relation that the regression summarizes only applies to films grossing over $1 million and playing at over 950 screens on their opening weekend. BOXOFF has been modified for films released before Friday. For films released on Thursday, 15% of the box office gross was subtracted. For films released on Wednesday, 25% of the box office was subtracted. We invite interested readers to gather additional cases and analyze the larger dataset. Readers should keep in mind that our primary goal in this section is to illustrate the use of diagnostics for identifying outliers and influential cases, not to exhaustively analyze the relation between box office success and number of screens.

Some researchers use a normal probability plot to show outliers. We do not present one here because normal probability plots are primarily useful for assessing the extent to which the residuals are normally distributed. The information they provide about outliers is duplicated by the other graphics discussed in this section. Residuals containing outliers are not normally distributed. Recall from the discussion in Section 4.7 that normally distributed residuals appear as a straight line sloping from the lower left to the upper right in the normal probability plot. Outliers appear as points widely separated from that line. We leave the production of normal probability plots to the interested reader.

The plot in Figure 6.4 and the accompanying discussion follows Chatterjee and Hadi (1988, section 4.4.2.).

Nonlinearity

We used only a portion of the Lerner disability dataset here. Twenty-four cases were deleted to reduce the size of the dataset and simplify the analysis. The analysis developed here is not the last word on these data. Remaining issues include: how to handle the outlier in the eighth case (the point where ID$ = H); and in what other ways can the activity of the Disability Rights movement be summarized. We are grateful to Robert Lerner for permission to use these previously unpublished data.

Collinearity

We adapted the air pollution dataset from McDonald and Ayers (1978) which also contains more detailed descriptions of the variables. We wish to thank Gary C. McDonald for suggesting this dataset and for discussions about regression diagnostics. The air pollution dataset has been analyzed before. See Henderson and Velleman (1981) for a summary of prior work. Our aim is to illustrate how collinearity can be diagnosed and corrected, not to discover the final model for the data. A great deal more can be said about these data. The simplest extension of our analyses would attempt to deal with several outliers and influential points. You will find that the fit of the model can be significantly improved by extending it to take these points into account. We leave this problem as an exercise for the reader. A fine case study illustrating the use of regression diagnostics applied to a well-known air pollution dataset is Gibbons and McDonald (1983).

Heteroscedasticity

The military spending dataset includes only countries classified by the World Bank as developing economies in Sub-Saharan Africa, Latin America and South Asia. The World Bank excludes the High-Income Oil Exporters. See page xxxiv in World Bank (1983).

The source of most of the data is World Bank (1983). GDP80, GOVT80, GDI80, DEFLBASE, DEFL80, and EXCG80 come from the individual country tables in Economic Data Sheet 1. For countries where the base year for constant prices is before 1970, we calculated DEFLBASE from Economic Data Sheet 1 in World Bank (1980). GDP80, GOVT80 and GDI80 are expressed in constant market prices (not constant factor cost or current market prices). Sivard (1983), Table II, is the source for MIL80. Interested readers can gather additional data from these sources to extend the dataset.

International data have more problems than most. The numbers may not be accurately reported by individual countries. In order to obtain comparable data, we converted each currency to common units (U.S. dollars), and this conversion depends on the accuracy of exchange rates. But exchange rates may be held artificially high or low by government policy. In some cases, ". . .an alternate conversion factor is used when the official exchange rate is judged to diverge by an exceptionally large margin." (World Bank 1985, p. 231). Unfortunately the World Bank does not give the countries, years, or the alternate conversion factors used.

Here are the changes made for these data. Sivard (1983) reports Guyana MIL80 as $101 million but 1979 is reported as $16 million (Sivard 1982, p. 27) and 1982 is $22 million (Sivard 1985, p. 35). Further, Guatemala is reported to have the following military spending: 1979, $85 million; 1980, $20 million; and 1982, $93 million. My judgement is that Guatemala and Guyana 1980 military spending data were interchanged in Sivard (1983). The GNP and area data also seem to have been interchanged, making Guatemala appear much smaller in 1983 and Guyana much larger—for that one year only. I switched these data to make 1980 consistent with other years. For Uganda, EXCG80 = 7.424 which causes GDP80 to be exceptionally large. Further, the 1981 exchange rate is 50.238. This suggested that EXCG80 is too low and it was changed to 20.0. For Ghana, EXCG80 = 2.75 and this again makes GDP much too large. The exchange rate was changed to 8.5. Finally, Argentina EXCG80 = 176.117 which is probably too low. Changing it to 200.00 makes it more compatible with World Bank estimates.

Further reading

The problems discussed in this chapter have many solutions beyond those we discussed. Most other solutions require considerably more mathematical and statistical expertise than many of our readers possess.

Outliers and influential points

See Chatterjee and Hadi (1988), Beckman and Cook (1983), Cook and Weisberg (1982), and their references. Chatterjee and Hadi have a particularly good discussion of the distinction between outliers, leverage, and influential points, and when they are not the same.

Nonlinearity

For further information on piecewise linearity, see Neter, Wasserman, and Kutner (1990). An excellent discussion of using plots and LOWESS is in Chambers et al. (1983). For information on use of transformations to correct nonlinearity, see Chapter 22 and the references there, especially Tukey (1977), Mosteller and Tukey (1977).

Collinearity

The basic source on modern collinearity diagnostics is Belsley, Kuh, and Welsh (1980). An outstanding summary with valuable additional references is Judge et al. (1985).

Heteroscedasticity

A fine summary of current knowledge about heteroscedasticity is Judge et al. (1985). Some researchers use ratio variables (e.g. GDP per capita) in this kind of cross-national research. This eliminates one form of heteroscedasticity but it is controversial; see Schuessler (1974).

References

Atkinson, A. C. (1985). *Plots, Transformations, and Regression.* New York: Oxford University Press.

Barnett, V. and Lewis, T. (1978). *Outliers in Statistical Data.* New York: John Wiley & Sons.

Beckman, R. J. and Cook, R. D. (1983). Outlier..........S (with discussion). *Technometrics, 25,* 119-163.

Belsley, D. A, Kuh E., and Welsh, R. E. (1980). *Regression Diagnostics: Identifying Influential Data and Sources of Collinearity.* New York: John Wiley & Sons.

Bohrnstedt, G. W. and Carter, T. M. (1971). Robustness in regression analysis. In H. Costner (ed.), *Sociological Methodology 1971* (pp. 118-146). San Francisco: Jossey-Bass.

Chambers, J. M., Cleveland, W. S., Kleiner, B., and Tukey, P. A. (1983). *Graphical Methods for Data Analysis*. Boston: Duxbury.

Chatterjee, S. and Hadi, A. S. (1988). *Sensitivity Analysis in Linear Regression*. New York: John Wiley & Sons.

Cleveland, W. S. (1979). Robust locally weighted regression and smoothing scatterplots. *Journal of the American Statistical Association, 74*, 829-836.

Cleveland, W. S. (1981). LOWESS: A program for smoothing scatterplots by robust locally weighted regression. *The American Statistician, 35*, 54.

Cleveland, W. S. (1994). *The Elements of Graphing Data* (rev. ed.) Summit, NJ: Hobart Press.

Cook, R. D. (1979). Influential observations in linear regression. *Journal of the American Statistical Association, 74*, 169-174.

Cook, R. D. and Weisberg, S. (1982). *Residuals and Influence in Regression*. New York: Chapman and Hall.

Daniel, C. and Wood, F. S. (1980). *Fitting Equations to Data* (2nd ed.). New York: John Wiley & Sons.

Draper, N. and Smith, H. (1981). *Applied Regression Analysis* (2nd ed.). New York: John Wiley & Sons.

Gibbons, D. I. and McDonald, G. C. (1983). Illustrating regression diagnostics with an air pollution and mortality model. *Computational Statistics & Data Analysis, 1*, 201-220.

Goldfeld, S. M. and Quandt, R. E. (1965). Some tests for heteroskedasticity. *Journal of the American Statistical Association, 60*, 539-547.

Hein, P. (1966). *Grooks*. New York: Doubleday.

Henderson, H. V. and Velleman, P. F. (1981). Building multiple regression models interactively. *Biometrics, 37*, 391-411.

Jasso, G. (1986). Is it outlier deletion or is it sample truncation? Notes on science and sexuality. *American Sociological Review, 51*, 738-742.

Judge, G. G., Griffiths, W. E., Hill, R. C. and Lee, T. (1985). *The Theory and Practice of Econometrics* (2nd ed.). New York: John Wiley & Sons.

Kahn, J. R. and Udry, J. R. (1986). Marital coital frequency: Unnoticed outliers and unspecified interactions lead to erroneous conclusions. *American Sociological Review, 51*, 734-737

Lerner, R. (1984). *The Rise in Applications for Social Security Benefits.* Unpublished doctoral dissertation, University of Chicago, Chicago, Illinois.

McDonald, G. C. and Ayers, J. A. (1978). Some applications of "Chernoff Faces." In P. C. C. Wang (Ed.), *Graphical Representation of Multivariate Data* (pp. 183-197). New York: Academic Press.

McDonald, G. C. and Schwing, R. C. (1973). Instabilities of regression estimates relating air pollution to mortality. *Technometrics, 15,* 463-481.

Mosteller, F., and Tukey, J. W. (1977). *Data Analysis and Regression.* Reading, MA: Addison-Wesley.

Muller, E. N. (1986). Income inequality and political violence: The effect of influential cases. *American Sociological Review, 51,* 441-445.

Neter, J., Wasserman, W, and Kutner, M. (1990). *Applied Linear Statistical Models* (3rd ed.). Homewood, IL: Irwin.

Schuessler, K. (1974). Analysis of ratio variables. *American Journal of Sociology, 80,* 379-396.

Sivard, R. L. (1982). *World Military and Social Expenditures 1982.* Washington, DC: World Priorities.

Sivard, R. L. (1983). *World Military and Social Expenditures 1983.* Washington, DC: World Priorities.

Sivard, R. L. (1985). *World Military andSocial Expenditures 1985.* Washington, DC: World Priorities.

Snedecor, G. W., and Cochran, W. G. (1967). *Statistical Methods.* Ames, IA: Iowa State University Press.

Tufte, E. R. (1983). *The Visual Display of Quantitative Information.* Cheshire, CT: Graphics Press.

Tukey, J. W. (1973). The zig-zag climb from initial observation to successful improvement. In W. E. Coffman (Ed.), *Frontiers of Educational Measurement and Information* (pp. 113-120). Boston: Houghton Mifflin.

Tukey, J. W. (1974). Instead of Gauss-Markov least squares, what? In R. P. Gupta (ed.), *Applied Statistics* (pp. 351-372). Proceedings of a conference at Dalhousie University, Halifax, Nova Scotia, May 2-4. North-Holland Publishing Co.

Tukey, J. W. (1977). *Exploratory Data Analysis.* Reading, MA: Addison-Wesley.

Turner, R. H. (1969). The theme of contemporary social movements. *British Journal of Sociology, 20*, 390-405.

Weede, E. (1986). Income inequality and political violence reconsidered. *American Sociological Review, 51*, 438-441.

World Bank (1980). *WorldTables* (2nd ed.). Baltimore, MD: Johns Hopkins Press.

World Bank (1983). *World Tables* (3rd ed.). Baltimore, MD: Johns Hopkins Press.

World Bank (1985). *World Development Report, 1985*. Baltimore, MD: Johns Hopkins Press.

7
Regression Modeling

This chapter discusses three topics. The first two topics show how regression can handle a wider variety of situations. The third topic introduces a complex modeling technique that is not regression-based:

1. Correlation and partial correlation
2. Path models
3. Introduction to covariance structure models

7.1 Correlation and partial correlation

Like the Civil Rights movement's efforts for blacks or the Feminist movement's efforts for women, the Handicapped Persons' Rights movement focussed on changing society's response to the handicapped by removing barriers to their full participation in jobs and social life. Handicapped persons should not be pitied, the movement argued; rather, like other minority groups, they deserved a sense of dignity and a sense of self-worth as a matter of right (see Turner 1969). Lerner (1984) suggested that, as knowledge of the movement spread, one effect would be to remove the stigma associated with being disabled and make people more willing to "come out of the closet" with their handicaps, thereby increasing the number of people willing to call themselves disabled.

We used some of the Lerner data in the discussion of nonlinearity in Section 7.2. The SYSTAT command file in Figure 7.1 reads additional variables into a SYSTAT data file and merges that file with the original data from Chapter 7.

Correlations

Lerner's first question was, "Is there any relationship between these variables or should I look for another dissertation topic?" We've answered this question for many datasets by looking at scatterplots. Even though scatterplots are a rich source of information, they take a lot of space and it is sometimes more appropriate to present only a summary of what the scatterplot would show. One presentation is an array of correlation coefficients. The array (called a matrix) of correlations for these variables is presented in Figure 7.2.

In the Pearson correlation matrix at the top of Figure 7.2, each row refers to a different variable. The columns also refer to variables. The number at the intersection of a given row and column is the correlation coefficient between the variables printed in the row and column headings. Correlation coefficients measure the relationship between pairs of variables. They vary between -1 and +1. -1 is a perfect inverse association (when one variable goes up the other goes down) while +1 is a perfect positive association (both variables go up or down together). The correlation of a variable with itself is always 1.0.

The correlation matrix in Figure 7.2 shows exactly what Lerner hoped to see: high correlations between all the variables, indicating strong relationships that he could work with for his dissertation.

Along with the correlation matrix, SYSTAT prints a scatterplot matrix. The rows and columns of the scatterplot matrix contain the same variables in the same order as the correlation matrix. Instead of correlation coefficients, the cells of the scatterplot matrix contain small plots of the relationship between the row variable and the column variable. In short, a scatterplot matrix is a visual correlation matrix. You can produce scatterplot matrices using the SPLOM command.

Figure 7.1
Combined Lerner Disability Dataset

```
BASIC
    NEW
    SAVE LER03 /,
    "   Second Lerner disability dataset",
    " ",
    "NORGS    Number of social movement organizations",
    "DISMAJ   % of Americans reporting a major disabling impairment"

    INPUT NORGS DISMAJ \
    RUN
6       8.7       6       8.825
6       8.95      6       9.075
6       9.1       6.5     9.125
7       9.05      7.5     8.975
8       8.9       8.75    9
9.5     9.1       10.25   9.2
11      9.3       12      9.375
13      9.45      14      9.525
15      9.6       15.5    9.75
16      9.9       16.5    10.05
17      10.2      18.5    10.3
20      10.4      21.5    10.5
23      10.6      23.25   10.65
23.5    10.7      23.75   10.75
24      10.8      24.75   10.8
25.5    10.8      26.25   10.8
27      10.8      27.25   10.7
27.5    10.6      27.75   10.5
28      10.4      27.75   10.45
27.5    10.5      27.25   10.55
~

NEW
    REM Merge disability data into one dataset
    MERGE LER02 LER03

    SAVE LER04
    REM LSUMNEWS has a linear relation to NORGS, DISMAJ, and APPLY
    LET LSUMNEWS = LOG(SUMNEWS)
    RUN
```

Figure 7.2
Matrix of Correlation Coefficients

```
CORR
   USE LER04
   PEARSON LSUMNEWS DISMAJ APPLY NORGS / PROB
```

Pearson correlation matrix

	LSUMNEWS	DISMAJ	APPLY	NORGS
LSUMNEWS	1.000			
DISMAJ	0.785	1.000		
APPLY	0.751	0.930	1.000	
NORGS	0.816	0.960	0.926	1.000

Bartlett Chi-square statistic: 211.688 DF=6 Prob= 0.000

Matrix of Probabilities

	LSUMNEWS	DISMAJ	APPLY	NORGS
LSUMNEWS	0.0			
DISMAJ	0.000	0.0		
APPLY	0.000	0.000	0.0	
NORGS	0.000	0.000	0.000	0.0

Number of observations: 40

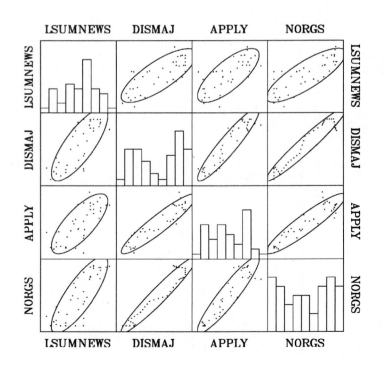

Characteristics of correlation coefficients

In Chapter 2 we described coefficients that summarize the relation between two variables by four characteristics: direction, strength, existence, and pattern. Direction is the simplest. The sign of the coefficient describes the direction. A positive correlation says that as the values of one variable increase (or decrease), the values of the other variable do likewise. A negative correlation means that as the values of one variable increase (or decrease), the values of the other variable do the opposite.

Strength is measured by the size of the correlation coefficient. The most intuitively meaningful interpretation of strength uses the square of the correlation coefficient. The square has a proportional reduction in error (PRE) interpretation because it is the same as the R-square of a bivariate regression. That is, it displays the proportion of variance in one variable that is explained by the other. Alternatively, the correlation can be interpreted like the standardized regression coefficient from a bivariate regression. (A bivariate regression, you may recall, has only one independent variable and one dependent variable.) That is, it is the slope of the line corrected so that it does not depend on the units of measurement. (Refer to Section 4.2 for details on standardized regression coefficients, Section 4.3 for information on the multiple R-square, and Section 2.2 for details on PRE measures.)

Existence is measured by tests of statistical significance. To obtain significance tests for the coefficients in a correlation matrix, add the option PROB or BPROB to the PEARSON statement. The p values testing significance are in the matrix of probabilities at the bottom of Figure 7.2. Interpreting the p values, however, is not as straightforward as it seems. The p values are based on the assumption that you are looking at only one coefficient. If you looked at 100 correlation coefficients from variables created with the SYSTAT random number generator, on average 5 correlations would be significant at the customary 5% level. Since most correlation matrices contain many coefficients, you may have trouble knowing when the significant correlations you observe are not artifacts of random chance. To help you know if you are looking at relationships stronger than chance SYSTAT prints the Bartlett chi-square test of the hypothesis that some of the individual coefficients are significant. If this global test isn't significant, don't bother with the individual p values. Even when the Bartlett test is significant, the individual p values are not the true probabilities associated with each coefficient. The BPROB option asks SYSTAT to print the Bonferroni-adjusted probabilities. These guarantee that the probability of erroneously finding a significant relation is less than the critical value you select.

Correlation coefficients handle one pattern: linearity. The coefficients accurately reflect the relation between two variables only if it is linear. If your data contain nonlinearities, correlations are misleading. You can use the scatterplot matrix to verify linearity. If you construct SPLOMs you can add LOWESS smoothing to the plot to help your eye see nonlinear portions; see Section 6.2. Notice that we created LSUMNEWS (the log of SUMNEWS) in order to make a linear relation.

Unlike regression, correlation does not distinguish independent or dependent variables, so the correlation of X with Y is the same as the correlation of Y with X. Because of this correlation coefficients are said to be a "symmetric" measure of association. This allows SYSTAT to save space and only print half of the correlation matrix, called the "lower triangle" because of its triangular shape.

Pearson correlations are named after Karl Pearson, an early statistician. For technical reasons they are also called Pearson product-moment correlations. They are appropriate when both variables are continuous. Other kinds of correlation coefficients are appropriate for other kinds of data, and SYSTAT provides several in the CORR procedure. Spearman correlations, appropriate when both variables are ranks, are widely used (see Chapter 2). Many other measures of similarity or dissimilarity are often expressed in the form of a matrix of coefficients. See Section 23.3 and Section 23.4 and the SYSTAT manual's instructions for the CORR procedure.

Partial correlations

One important question that Lerner wanted to test was whether the Handicapped Persons' Rights movement exerted direct influence on the number of applications for disability insurance applications, or whether the key mechanism was through publicity about the movement in the public media, or both. This is a classic statistical question: Which of several possible alternatives is true? The correlation matrix in Figure 7.2 cannot answer this question. It shows that both number of organizations (NORGS) and newspaper publicity (LSUMNEWS) are strongly related to disability applications (APPLY). However, they are also strongly related to each other (the correlation is .816). The problem is that these three variables are all changing simultaneously, and this makes it difficult to tell which variable is influencing the others.

We could solve this problem if we were able somehow to control the two independent variables, NORGS and LSUMNEWS. Suppose that the number of organizations could be fixed at a single number. If we increased the amount of newspaper publicity, would there be corresponding increases in the number of disability applications? Or, suppose the amount of publicity were held constant. If the number of organizations expanded, would the number of disability applications grow also? While we cannot conduct such experiments in real life, we can use regression to remove the effects of one variable and continue to see the effects of other variables. If we do the regressions:

$$Y = \text{CONSTANT} + X, \qquad \text{and}$$

$$Z = \text{CONSTANT} + X,$$

the residuals from the first regression are that part of Y which remains after removing the effects of X and, from the second regression, the residuals are the portion of Z which remains after controlling for X. In effect, we have statistically controlled for the effects of X on both Y and Z. The correlation between the residuals from the two models will be the correlation between Y and Z after controlling for or removing the effects of X. This is called a **partial correlation**. (The strange name comes from an archaic way of saying, "controlling for" which was "partialling out the effects of.") This is exactly what we want and there is an easy way to get it in SYSTAT. Simply put the variables for which you want the partial correlations on the left side of the equals sign in the MODEL statement and the variable you want to control on the right side. Use the PRINT LONG command before you ESTIMATE your model, and the RESIDUAL CORRELATION MATRIX on the printout will be the correlation matrix that you want.

Lerner answered his question by computing the partial correlation between LSUM-NEWS and APPLY holding NORGS constant and comparing that to the partial correlation between NORGS and APPLY holding LSUMNEWS constant. Figure 7.3 shows the MODEL statements and part of the output.

Figure 7.3
Partial Correlations

```
REGRESS
    USE LER04
    MODEL APPLY LSUMNEWS = CONSTANT + NORGS
        PRINT=MEDIUM
        ESTIMATE
```

Number of cases processed: 40
Dependent variable means

	APPLY	LSUMNEWS
	259819.200	3.283

Regression coefficients $B = (X'X)^{-1} X'Y$

	APPLY	LSUMNEWS
CONSTANT	149386.033	1.645
NORGS	6388.036	0.095

Standardized regression coefficients

	APPLY	LSUMNEWS
CONSTANT	0.0	0.0
NORGS	0.926	0.816

Total sum of product matrix

	APPLY	LSUMNEWS
APPLY	1.23390E+11	
LSUMNEWS	1559786.103	34.962

Residual sum of product matrix $E'E = Y'Y-Y'XB$

	APPLY	LSUMNEWS
APPLY	1.76763E+10	
LSUMNEWS	-8454.065	11.697

Residual covariance matrix $S_{Y.X}$

	APPLY	LSUMNEWS
APPLY	4.65166E+08	
LSUMNEWS	-222.475	0.308

```
Residual correlation matrix  R
                            Y.X
                      APPLY    LSUMNEWS

    APPLY             1.000

    LSUMNEWS         -0.019      1.000


Multiple correlations
                      APPLY    LSUMNEWS
                      0.926      0.816

Squared multiple correlations
                      APPLY    LSUMNEWS
                      0.857      0.665
```

Adjusted $R^2 = 1-(1-R^2)*(N-1)/DF$, where N = 40, and DF = 38

```
                      APPLY    LSUMNEWS
                      0.853      0.657

          (Additional output omitted)
```

MODEL APPLY NORGS = CONSTANT + LSUMNEWS
ESTIMATE

```
Number of cases processed: 40
Dependent variable means

                      APPLY       NORGS
               259819.200        17.287
```

Regression coefficients $B = (X'X)^{-1}X'Y$

```
                      APPLY       NORGS

    CONSTANT     113353.569       -5.765

    LSUMNEWS      44614.067        7.022
```

Standardized regression coefficients

```
                      APPLY       NORGS

    CONSTANT          0.0         0.0

    LSUMNEWS          0.751       0.816
```

```
Total sum of product matrix

                        APPLY         NORGS

    APPLY           1.23390E+11

    NORGS           1.65486E+07      2590.569


Residual sum of product matrix   E'E = Y'Y-Y'XB

                        APPLY         NORGS

    APPLY           5.38013E+10

    NORGS           5596050.041       866.728


Residual covariance matrix   S
                             Y.X
                        APPLY         NORGS

    APPLY           1.41582E+09

    NORGS            147264.475        22.809


Residual correlation matrix   R
                              Y.X
                        APPLY         NORGS

    APPLY              1.000

    NORGS              0.819          1.000


Multiple correlations

                        APPLY         NORGS

                        0.751         0.816


Squared multiple correlations

                        APPLY         NORGS

                        0.564         0.665


           2          2
Adjusted R = 1-(1-R )*(N-1)/DF, where N = 40, and DF = 38
                        APPLY         NORGS

                        0.552         0.657

            (Additional output omitted)
```

It is easy to get lost in all this output, so we simplify matters by constructing a small summary table, Figure 7.4.

Figure 7.4
Table of Correlations and Partial Correlations

Variables	Correlation From Figure 7.2	Partial Correlation From Figure 7.3	Control Variable
APPLY and NORGS	.926	.819	LSUMNEWS
APPLY and LSUMEWS	.751	-.019	NORGS

Figure 7.4 shows clearly that controlling for LSUMNEWS has little effect on the correlation between APPLY and NORGS. However, the partial correlation between APPLY and LSUMNEWS holding NORGS constant drops to -.019. In effect, when we control for NORGS, the relationship between APPLY and LSUMNEWS vanishes. From this analysis Lerner concluded that the activities of the Handicapped Persons' Rights movement organizations are the key component producing both publicity for the movement and applications for disability insurance payments.

From this example you should be able to see how easily you can control for more than one variable; just add the other control variables to the list on the right side of the equals sign in the MODEL statement. If you need to compute an entire matrix of partial correlation coefficients, just place the variables on the left side of the equals sign.

Partial correlations are named by the number of variables controlled. When the effects of only one variable are controlled, like in Figure 7.3, they are called **first-order partial correlations** or first order correlations. When the effects of two variables are controlled, the coefficients would be **second-order partial correlations**. Ordinary correlation coefficients, where no variables are controlled, are called **zero-order correlations**.

Partial correlations are one way to examine the relations between groups of variables. But they are relatively simple, and you may have a more complex model that you want to test. An approach that can handle more complex models is called **path analysis**.

7.2 Path models

Lerner developed and tested an explicit model of the impact of the Handicapped Persons' Rights movement on disability insurance applications. One way to diagram this model is Figure 7.5. The arrows in Figure 7.5 indicate that Lerner saw an explicit causal link between the event on the left side of the arrow and the event on the right side. For example, rising social movement activity *causes* a rising number of people willing to call themselves disabled. The diagram is a shorthand, visual way of stating a (modest) theory. This is a theory that we can test using a variant of multiple regression known as **path analysis**. Other names for path analysis are structural equation modeling or causal modeling.

Figure 7.5
Model of Rising Social Security Disability Insurance Costs
Used by Lerner (1984)

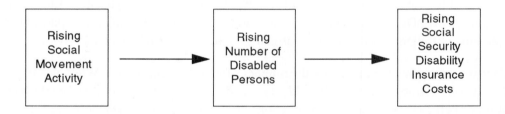

Causes play an important role in path analysis. There is a lot of controversy about the concept of causation, and we do not intend to take sides or to review the controversy. Even though the word is sometimes avoided, much of the work in the physical and social sciences deals with causes and effects. For example, one important area of research, policy research, is explicitly concerned with causes: how social, political, and economic events can be altered to achieve policy goals. In other areas, questions of why an event has occurred often carry an implicit question of causality. For further discussions of these issues, see Miller (1971), Nagel (1965), and Wold (1970).

Path analysis is not a method for discovering causes. It is applied to a causal model, called a **path model**, which has been constructed from theory and logical analysis by the researcher. It can *test* whether a model is consistent with the data, but it cannot prove that any particular model is the true model. Often more than one causal model will be consistent with the same data.

Path diagrams

To turn Figure 7.5 into a path model requires several steps. Obviously, we cannot measure a concept such as "social movement activity" directly, so we need to find an indicator; that is, a variable which we can measure and which is an accurate reflection of the level of activity of the Handicapped Persons' Rights movement. Measurement is a complex problem, well beyond the scope of this book (for more information see Duncan (1975, 1984)). Lerner collected data on a variety of measures and tested several models, one of which is diagramed in Figure 7.6.

Figure 7.6
Path Diagram of Lerner Model

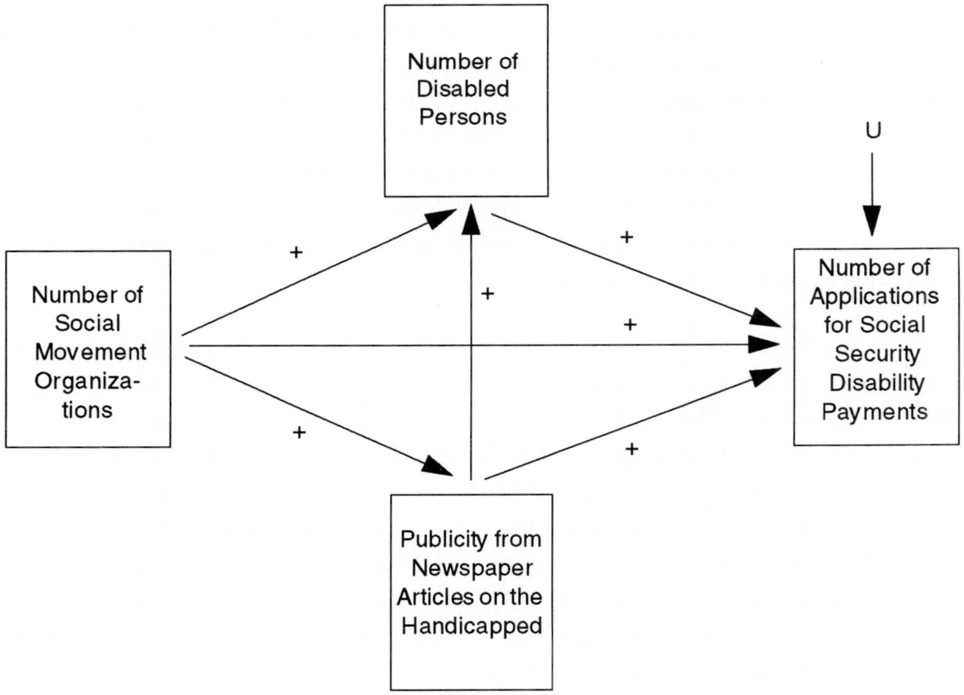

Figure 7.6 is called a **path diagram**, or an arrow diagram or a causal diagram. It is a condensed statement of a theory. Each of the arrows represents a specific hypothesis that we will later test against the data. Path diagrams clarify the relationships you ex-

pect to find, thereby helping you construct a path model and communicate it to other people. Good path diagrams have several characteristics.

- Variables on the left in the diagram are causally prior to those on the right. Thus, the right most variable is the dependent variable.

- The direction of the arrows visually displays the causal relationships that the researcher will test.

- The actual variables measured are included in the diagram (not unmeasured, theoretical variables).

- Small plus or minus signs indicate whether we expect the causal relations to be positive or negative.

The path model in Figure 7.6 contains a variable U which is connected only to the dependent variable. This variable is called a **residual variable**. After we have subtracted all the influences on disability payment applications that are accounted for in the model, it represents the unexplained residue that remains. No arrows connect the residual variable with any other variable in the model (other than the dependent variable, of course). This makes explicit the assumption that the residual variable is unrelated to the other variables in the model. You will recall that this is one of the assumptions about the error term in a multiple regression model and, in this sense, the residual variable corresponds roughly to the error term.

The model in Figure 7.6 is called **recursive**. That means all the causal arrows run in one direction, so that once a path passes through a variable, it will never again return to the same variable. Thus the variables in a recursive model have an unambiguous causal order. This is an assumption of the model. It assumes variable X_1 influences X_2 but that X_2 does not affect X_1. We will not know if X_1 actually influences X_2 until we have done an empirical test; the point here is that the causal flow is in only one direction, not both simultaneously. This assumption is also called "weak causal ordering." It is particularly convincing when the variables involved are relatively unchanging attributes of people (like race or gender) and less stable attitudes (like voting intentions) or variables for which there is a clear time order. (We know that this use of recursive has exactly the opposite meaning from its use standard English, where it means a procedure which repeats itself. And, no, we don't know why. You will have to live with the ambiguity.) The analysis of **nonrecursive** path models (where causal flows travel from X_1 to X_2 and from X_2 to X_1) is more complex and beyond the scope of this chapter. Section 7.3 introduces RAMONA, a SYSTAT procedure capable of analyzing complex recursive and nonrecursive models. If you need to analyze nonrecursive models, see Berry (1984), Blalock (1971), Duncan (1975), or the references at the end of this chapter.

Path analysis has developed an extensive vocabulary to describe relationships between variables. Much of this is beyond the scope of this book, but several concepts are fundamental. The path diagram in Figure 7.7 illustrates direct and indirect effects, intervening variables, how to calculate positive and negative effects, and spurious causation. All except for spurious causation exist in the path diagram in Figure 7.6, but they are easier to see in a more abstract form.

Diagram (A) shows a bivariate relationship between X_1 and Y. Here X_1 (the independent variable) has a **direct effect** on Y (the dependent variable).

Diagram (B) adds another variable, X_2, between X_1 and Y, creating a chain of causes and effects. According to the theory illustrated in this diagram, X_1 only influences Y via its influence on X_2, an **intervening variable**. X_1 is said to have an **indirect effect** on Y because it is connected to Y only through the intervening variable. Increases in X_1 increase the level of X_2, but the higher levels of X_2 decrease the level of Y. Thus, the higher the value of X_1, the lower the level of Y. The sign of the indirect effect of X_1 on Y can be calculated by multiplying the signs of the paths. A positive (+) number times a negative (-) is negative, so the indirect effect of X_1 on Y is negative.

Diagram (C) illustrates how both direct and indirect effects can simultaneously influence Y. The indirect effect through X_2 is still negative, but the direct effect is positive. The diagram does not contain enough information to tell which effect is stronger. Below we will show you how to estimate the strengths of direct and indirect effects so that you can tell which are more influential.

Diagram (D) shows a common situation: a relation between and Y may be observed (say, in a correlation coefficient or a scatterplot) even though there is no causal connection. This is called a **spurious relation** because the observed influence of on Y is due entirely to the impact that has on both variables. The possibility of spurious relations is one basis for the familiar warning, *correlation is not causation.*

To estimate the path model in Figure 7.8 we will use the same Lerner disability dataset we used to illustrate correlation and partial correlation in the last section.

Figure 7.7
Simple Path Diagrams

A. Direct Effects

B. Indirect Effects Through An Intervening Variable

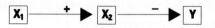

C. Direct and Indirect Effects

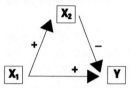

D. Spurious Cause

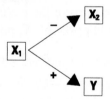

Structural equations

To estimate the direct and indirect effects, we translate the arrows in the path model into a set of **structural equations**. These equations are constructed directly from the paths pictured in the path diagram. In essence, every variable that is the target of an arrow is a dependent variable in a regression model. For each dependent variable, all the variables on the other end of the arrows are independent variables in the model. Since the Lerner path model has three variables with arrows pointing to them, we need three variables and three models. To make this easier to see, we have rewritten Figure 7.7 using SYSTAT variable names: NORGS (N), DISMAJ (D), LSUMNEWS (S), and APPLY (A). The structural equations are printed below the revised model in Figure 7.8.

Our goal is to estimate of the strength of each path. The estimate is called the **path coefficient** and, by convention, it is designated by a P with two subscripts. The subscripts refer to the variables on each end of the path; the first subscript denotes the dependent variable while the second subscript represents the independent variable. Thus is the path coefficient for the arrow connecting NORGS to DISMAJ. Each structural equation includes a path coefficient for each variable that the model says is a cause of each dependent variable. The residual variables are treated differently, as we describe below.

You can use either the standardized or unstandardized regression coefficients in a path model. Standardized coefficients were used exclusively in the early literature on path models; path coefficients are another name for standardized coefficients (see Wright 1960 for their advantages), although the term is often used loosely to describe any coefficient measuring the strength of a path. The standardized regression coefficients printed by SYSTAT in the column labeled, STD COEFF. Use of unstandardized coefficients has become more common recently, and they have mathematical advantages (Duncan 1975). Unstandardized coefficients are sometimes called structural coefficients. (Don't you just love how statisticians think up about a million different names for the same thing?) As far as we're concerned, the best basis of the decision is substantive: which communicates your point better. If the units in which your data are reported are important, unstandardized coefficients are better. If they aren't, standardized coefficients are probably clearer since they're expressed in units of standard deviations. You can always report both. We report standardized (i.e. path) coefficients here.

Figure 7.8
Path Diagram—Lerner Model Using SYSTAT Variable Names

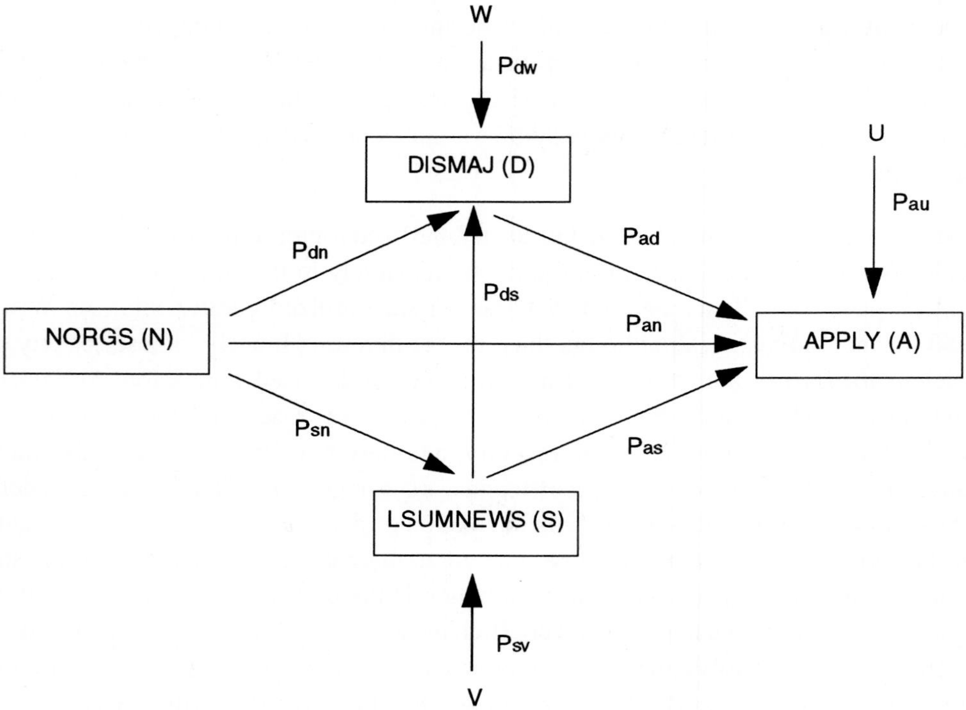

Estimating coefficients

Once we know the structural equations, we can easily estimate the coefficients by ordinary multiple regression. Simply regress each dependent variable on the independent variables in the structural equations. The SYSTAT MODEL statements required to estimate the coefficients for our model and the output from them are in Figure 7.9.

Figure 7.9
Regressions to Obtain Path Coefficients

```
REGRESS
    USE LER04
    MODEL APPLY = CONSTANT + LSUMNEWS + DISMAJ + NORGS
    ESTIMATE
```

Dep Var: APPLY N: 40 Multiple R: 0.938 Squared multiple R: 0.879

Adjusted squared multiple R: 0.869   Standard error of estimate: 20372.063

Effect	Coefficient	Std Error	Std Coef	Tolerance	t	P(2 Tail)
CONSTANT	−189476.729	133179.638	0.0	.	−1.423	0.163
LSUMNEWS	−939.536	5957.148	−0.016	0.335	−0.158	0.876
DISMAJ	40437.109	15768.009	0.530	0.079	2.565	0.015
NORGS	2967.161	1526.492	0.430	0.069	1.944	0.060

Analysis of Variance

Source	Sum-of-Squares	DF	Mean-Square	F-Ratio	P
Regression	1.08449E+11	3	3.61496E+10	87.103	0.000
Residual	1.49408E+10	36	4.15021E+08		

```
    MODEL DISMAJ = CONSTANT + LSUMNEWS + NORGS
    ESTIMATE
```

Dep Var: DISMAJ N: 40 Multiple R: 0.960 Squared multiple R: 0.921

Adjusted squared multiple R: 0.917   Standard error of estimate: 0.212

Effect	Coefficient	Std Error	Std Coef	Tolerance	t	P(2 Tail)
CONSTANT	8.409	0.129	0.0	.	64.947	0.000
LSUMNEWS	0.005	0.062	0.007	0.335	0.086	0.932
NORGS	0.086	0.007	0.954	0.335	11.961	0.000

Analysis of Variance

Source	Sum-of-Squares	DF	Mean-Square	F-Ratio	P
Regression	19.518	2	9.759	216.317	0.000
Residual	1.669	37	0.045		

```
MODEL  LSUMNEWS  =  CONSTANT  +  NORGS
ESTIMATE
```

```
Dep Var: LSUMNEWS N: 40 Multiple R:  0.816 Squared multiple R:  0.665

Adjusted squared multiple R:  0.657     Standard error of estimate:      0.555
t
Effect          Coefficient    Std Error    Std Coef Tolerance    t   P(2 Tail)

CONSTANT            1.645         0.208        0.0       .       7.912   0.000
NORGS               0.095         0.011        0.816   1.000     8.694   0.000

                        Analysis of Variance

Source          Sum-of-Squares   DF  Mean-Square    F-Ratio       P

Regression          23.265        1      23.265      75.578     0.000
Residual            11.697       38       0.308
```

From the first model in Figure 7.9, we obtain the following estimated coefficients:

Path	Path Coefficient	Unstandardized Coefficient	Standard Error	*t* value
P_{as}	-.016	-939.5	5,957.1	-.16
P_{ad}	.530	40,437.1	15,768.0	2.57
P_{an}	.430	2,967.2	1,526.5	1.94

Notice that the P_{as} path is not significant at the 5% level and the P_{an} path is only marginally significant. Tolerance in the second model shows that we may have a collinearity problem between NORGS and LSUMNEWS. (You can confirm this using the more sophisticated collinearity diagnostics described in Chapter 7.) Since collinearity is not our primary concern in this part of the book, we leave further analysis of collinearity as an exercise for interested readers. The collinearity suggests that NORGS and LSUM-NEWS are measuring about the same thing. A theoretical explanation is beyond the scope of this chapter but, methodologically, we note that every coefficient for LSUM-NEWS is nonsignificant. For purposes of this chapter, we drop the nonsignificant paths from further consideration in this model. Before you conclude that a nonsignificant coefficient means no relation exists, we urge you to read Chapter 5, section 5.5 on why regression coefficients are nonsignificant. The path coefficient from the residual variable to the dependent variable is the square root of $(1 - R^2)$ for that model. In this case, is the square root of $(1 - .879)$, which is .348. Figure 7.10 presents the estimated path coefficients for all significant paths.

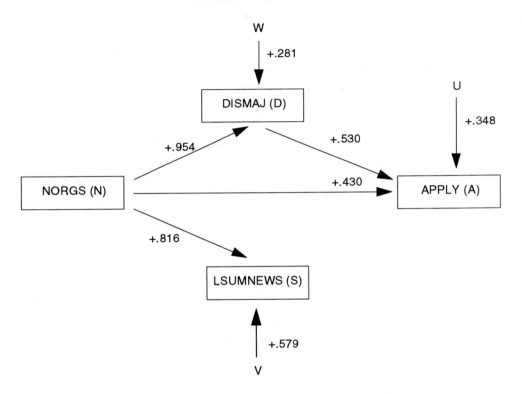

Figure 7.10
Numerical Estimates of Path Coefficients
Nonsignificant Paths Omitted

Assumptions of path models

The use of regression for each equation in the path analysis means that path analysis requires the standard regression assumptions but path analysis introduces additional complexity. Specifically, we assume:

1. The model is correct. That is, that the relations between variables are linear and additive and that all relevant variables have been included.

2. The variance of the residuals is constant.

3. The residuals from different structural equations are not correlated, nor are they correlated with any variables in the system.

4. The residuals are normally distributed.

In the context of path models, the first assumption is particularly troublesome. Assuming correctness requires assuming not only that all relevant variables are present, but also that the causal paths have been correctly drawn. The assumption that the causal paths are correct is an additional complexity beyond what we have to assume in ordinary regression. We have to assume that we specified the correct causal order between the variables. In our case, for example, we assumed that the number of social movement organizations (NORGS) affects the number of Americans claiming a major disability (DISMAJ) but not vice versa. Two issues combine to make this assumption troublesome. First, the size, direction, and significance of the coefficient estimates depend on the causal order. Second, no statistical method tests causal order. Given a specific causal order, the t-tests of the coefficient estimates test whether a specific path is significant and the ANOVA tests whether the overall regression is significant. Neither tests causal order. From the point of view of the statistics, this a pure assumption. The causal order must be justified on nonstatistical grounds (cf. Davis 1985).

This may be clearer in a concrete example. Suppose, instead of the model in Figure 7.8, we drew a model with a different causal order. For example, suppose our new model were different in only one path. Instead of an arrow saying that increases in the number of news stories about the handicapped (LSUMNEWS) increased the number of Americans claiming a major disability (DISMAJ), we might hypothesize the opposite causal order: increases in the number of Americans with a major disability increase the number of news stories about handicapped. We could test the significance, direction, and strength of the coefficients for both the model in Figure 7.8 and the new model. We could not test which one was the correct model. Lerner chose his model based on other considerations. He noted that the enormous rise in social security disability applications occurred at a time when there was no reason to believe that the number of disabled Americans changed at all. Thus, his theory is based on understanding why large numbers of people were more willing to claim they were disabled even though their physical condition did not change. This is the sense in which the causal order he specified is an assumption.

The third assumption, that the residuals are not correlated among themselves or with other variables in the system, may be relaxed under certain circumstances. However, this requires techniques beyond the scope of this section. RAMONA, another SYSTAT procedure, can handle this problem and a variety of others. See Section 7.3, below, for a brief introduction.

The other assumptions can be tested using the methods outlined in Chapter 4. Problems like nonlinearity or collinearity can be handled with the methods from Chapter 7. This means that effective use of path models requires the usual regression diagnostic work with scatterplots, residuals plots, SPLOMs, and other tools. For reasons of space, we have not shown any of those preliminaries here.

Comparing paths and effects

The path analysis is useful as a scientific tool because the path coefficients can be used to test hypotheses derived from theory. We have already done that implicitly when we decided to delete the nonsignificant paths from Figure 7.10. The nonsignificance, we decided, tended to disprove the hypotheses that publicity from newspaper articles (LSUMNEWS) was related to either number of disabled persons (DISMAJ) or applications for disability payment (APPLY). Because the path coefficients are standardized, we can compare different coefficients. In some research, the strength of different paths has been crucial. For example, there is a long scientific controversy over the importance of home versus school effects in studies of student achievement (e.g. Coleman 1972, 1975). The strongest path in our model is between NORGS and DISMAJ (+.954). This supports Lerner's hypothesis that the Handicapped Persons' Rights movement made more people willing to say that they were physically impaired.

The effect NORGS on DISMAJ is over twice as strong as the effect NORGS on APPLY (+.430). This raises the question of how the number of organizations has its effect. Is the direct effect from NORGS to APPLY stronger or is the indirect effect from NORGS through DISMAJ to APPLY more important? Indirect effects can be calculated by multiplying the appropriate path coefficients. Thus, the indirect effect of NORGS on APPLY is simply the product of the direct effect of NORGS on DISMAJ (.954) times the direct effect of DISMAJ on APPLY (.530), or 0.504. Since 0.504 is larger than 0.430 (the direct effect of NORGS on APPLY), the indirect effect of NORGS is more important than the direct effect. The total effect of a variable is just the sum of all its direct and indirect effects. Here, the total effect of NORGS on APPLY is 0.504 + 0.430 = 0.934. This total effect can be compared to the total effect of other variables to find which has stronger or weaker influences on the dependent variable.

This has been a simple example. Usually there is more than one path through which a variable has an indirect effect. Then we would have calculated indirect effects for every indirect path and added these indirect effects to obtain the total indirect effect for a variable. For example, if the direct effect of LSUMNEWS on DISMAJ had been significant, we would have calculated the indirect effect of NORGS on APPLY by adding the indirect effect of NORGS through DISMAJ on APPLY to the indirect effect of NORGS through LSUMNEWS through DISMAJ on APPLY. In complex path models, this can involve a lot of arithmetic.

The overall fit of a path model can be measured with the same coefficient used in multiple regression, the R-squared. In Figure 7.9, the R-squared shows that we have explained 87.9% of the variance in APPLY with our model.

Path analysis is primarily a method to help the researcher untangle the relations among independent variables. However, it is not a panacea. It requires that the researcher impose a causal model on the data. It imposes a restrictive set of assumptions which, when seriously violated, may lead to erroneous conclusions.

This section has introduced only the simple essentials of path analysis. For more information consult Blalock (1971) or Duncan (1975). The path models discussed in this section are a member of a large family of related techniques called structural models.

7.3 Introduction to covariance structure models

RAMONA is a SYSTAT procedure written by Michael Browne and specially designed for path analysis and the related, more complex statistical procedures called causal modeling, confirmatory factor analysis, linear structural equation modeling, structural modeling, or covariance structure models. Covariance structure modeling is like path analysis in the sense that it represents a causal system by using several structural equations. An advantage of covariance structure models is that they permit explicit modeling of situations where multiple, observable indicators are used to measure an underlying, unobservable concept. Thus, a measurement model can be explicitly incorporated into the development, evaluation, and interpretation of structural models.

The name, covariance structure, comes from the fact that these models estimate the parameters of the structural equations to reproduce, as closely as possible, an observed covariance matrix. In this sense they are different from regression models which attempt to reproduce the values of individual cases, not the covariance matrix. Covariance structure models can work from either a variance-covariance matrix or a correlation matrix. In the remainder of this section, unless we explicitly say otherwise the word covariance refers to either.

We're not going to discuss covariance structure models in detail in this chapter. We'll show you how to set up the Lerner disability model and talk briefly about the output. It will not be a complete discussion. This is a broad, complex area. If you need more than a summary, we refer you to the references at the end of the chapter. For more complete information on RAMONA, see the SYSTAT manual.

Keep in mind that covariance structure models, like regression, assume linear relationships and are sensitive to outliers and influential points. The apparatus of plots, influence statistics, and LOWESS smoothing described in Chapters 4, 5, and 7 is an indispensable part of structural models. Check your data and the bivariate relationships before you start modeling. Further, like path models, covariance structure models assume that you have the correct specification. The equations should accurately represent the causal mechanisms that produced the observed values of the dependent variables and, thus, the variance-covariance matrix.

There are several terms that you need to know in order to understand even the basics of covariance structure modeling.

- **Exogenous variable.** A variable which is always an independent variable; that is, in the path diagram all arrows point away from this variable. Since it is not explained by other variables in the theory it is also called a predetermined variable. An example is NORGS.

- **Endogenous variable.** A variable which is a dependent variable at least once; that is, in the path diagram at least one arrow points toward it. It is also called a jointly dependent variable. Examples are DISMAJ, LSUMNEWS, and APPLY.

- **Manifest variable.** A variable which is measured directly. All variables in this book are manifest variables. Manifest variables are contrasted to latent variables.

- **Latent variable.** A variable which is not observed. Only one or more indicators of the variable are observed. The value of latent variables is that they allow us to explicitly incorporate the characteristics of the measurement process into our theoretical model. An alternative name comes from the idea that we never observe actual concepts themselves, only indicators. A variable representing such an unobserved concept can be called a conceptual variable.

- These four concepts combine to describe a variable as a manifest exogenous variable (e.g. NORGS), a manifest endogenous variable (e.g. DISMAJ), a latent exogenous variable, or a latent endogenous variable.

Figure 7.11
Structural Model of Lerner Disability Dataset

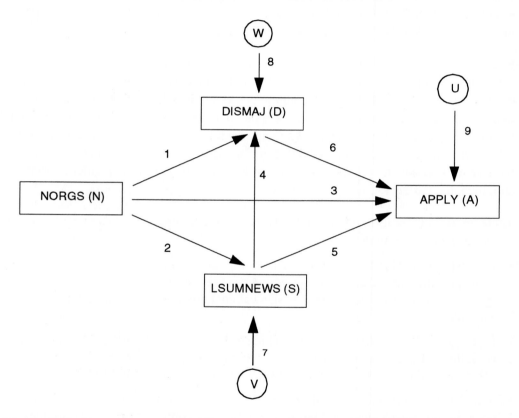

Figure 7.11 displays the model that we will fit. It looks similar to the model in Figure 7.8, but the differences are significant. First, instead of denoting the paths by P_{ij} they are numbered. These numbers are a bookkeeping measure, designed to simplify keeping track of what parameters are connected to which variables. Numbers, rather than P's, are used because in some models there are theoretical reasons for believing that more than one path has the same coefficient. This can be easily indicated by giving them the same number. Second, the residual variables U, V, and W are enclosed in circles. Circles represent latent variables. U, V, and W are latent error variables in our

model. Third, the other variables (e.g. NORGS and DISMAJ) are enclosed in boxes. The boxes indicate manifest variables.

A major strength of RAMONA is its language; you can unambiguously describe the model that you want to test directly from the path diagram. The RAMONA commands in Figure 7.12 begin with a few annotated lines describing the variables and the model. The core commands describe the paths in our model. These begin following the MODEL line and are denoted by dashes and arrows, <-, pointing from the independent variables to the dependent variable for each path.

Figure 7.12
RAMONA Commands to Fit Lerner Disability Model

```
RAMONA
   PRINT=MEDIUM
   USE LER04
   MANIFEST NORGS DISMAJ LSUMNEWS APPLY
   LATENT U V W
   MODEL ,
      DISMAJ    <- NORGS LSUMNEWS W        ,
      LSUMNEWS <- NORGS V                   ,
      APPLY     <- DISMAJ NORGS LSUMNEWS U ,
      U <-> U(0,1)  ,
      V <-> V(0,1)  ,
      W <-> W(0,1)
      ESTIMATE / METHOD=MWL DISP=CORR
```

Most of the RAMONA statements in Figure 7.12 are explained by the annotations, but several deserve comment.

1. We listed the manifest and latent variables explicitly. Had we not done so RAMONA would have assumed that variable names which appeared in the input file were manifest variables, like NORGS and LSUMNEWS. Names not in the input file are assumed to be latent variables, e.g. U, V, and W.

2. The lines following the word MODEL describe the 9 paths we want to estimate. For a full description of the language used to express these paths, see the RAMONARAMONA chapter in the manual. The MODEL contains 2 kinds of variables and 3 kinds of paths; see the next 5 items, below.

3. Most paths in the model command have the simple form: var1 <- var2, where var1 is a dependent variable and var2 is an independent variable. Thus, the statement DISMAJ <- NORGS describes a path from the manifest exogeneous variable NORGS to the manifest endogeneous variable DISMAJ. We have included several

independent variables in the same path.

4. Unlike regression-based path analysis, we specify the residual variances explicitly in the MODEL statement. Thus we see paths like DISMAJ <- U, where U represents the unpredicted part of DISMAJ. The path that will be estimated will be the residual variance for DISMAJ.

5. The bottom three lines of the MODEL statement contain double-headed arrows with the same variable on each side of the arrows, e.g. U <-> U(0,1). The double-headed arrows tell SYSTAT about variances that we want to include in our model. The ordered pair of numbers in parentheses gives, respectively, the variance number and the value of the variance. The variance number tells RAMONA that all variances with the same number are to have the same value. The value of the variance tells RAMONA that we want to fix the variance at 1.0. This is a reasonable choice, since we are working from a correlation matrix.

6. By default RAMONA estimates parameter values using a maximum likelihood procedure. More specifically, it uses ordinary least squares (that is, ordinary regression) to obtain starting values for the coefficient estimates and then proceeds to use maximum likelihood. We specified METHOD=MWL on the ESTIMATE command just to be clear that we would get maximum likelihood estimates. Starting values tell RAMONA where it should start work; they are important because they speed up the estimation process. Since we already know the least squares we could have told RAMONA what starting values to use, and this would have shortened the estimation process.

7. The final option on the ESTIMATE command, DISP=CORR, tells SYSTAT to use the correlation matrix to estimate the paths.

The output from this model is in Figure 7.13. Since this is an introduction to structural modeling, we will not comment on all aspects of the output. Read the RAMONA manual for a full description of the output.

Figure 7.13
RAMONA Output from Lerner Model

```
There are 4 manifest variables in the model. They are:
      APPLY NORGS DISMAJ LSUMNEWS

There are 3 latent variables in the model. They are:
      W V U

RAMONA options in effect are:
    Display              Corr
    Method               MWL
    Start                Rough
    Convg                0.000100
    Maximum iterations   100
    Number of cases      determined when data are read
    Restart              No
    Confidence Interval  90.000000
Variances and covariances of exogenous manifest variables were omitted
from the job specification and have been added by RAMONA.

Number of manifest variables        =     4
Total number of variables in the system  =   11.
Computing mean vector and covariance matrix...
Computing kurtosis coefficients

                 Overall kurtosis =      -2.568
                       Normalised =      -1.172
                         Relative =       0.893

                      Individual
           Variable    kurtoses    Normalised    Relative
        QUARTER        -1.269        -1.638        0.577
        LAWSUIT        -1.532        -1.977        0.489
        PROTEST        -1.599        -2.064        0.467
        LEGIS          -0.868        -1.121        0.711

                     Details of Iterations
   Iter    Method   Discr. Funct.  Max.R.Cos.   Max.Const.   NRP  NBD
  -------  -------  -------------  -----------  -----------  ---------
      0     OLS       0.049610                   0.000000
    1(0)    OLS       0.004178      0.620749      0.041405    0    0
    1(1)    OLS       0.013787      0.622122      0.012291    0    0
    2(0)    OLS       0.000846      0.655342      0.023159    0    0
    3(0)    OLS       0.000021      0.990451      0.004863    0    0
    4(0)    OLS       0.000000      0.0           0.000071    0    0
    4(0)    MWL       0.000000      0.0           0.000071    0    0
    5(0)    MWL       0.000000      0.0           0.000000    0    0

Iterative procedure complete.

Convergence limit for residual cosines = 0.000100 on 2 consecutive
iterations.

Convergence limit for variance constraint violations =  5.00000E-07
Value of the maximum variance constraint violation =  1.60450E-08
```

Sample Correlation Matrix :

	APPLY	NORGS	DISMAJ	LSUMNEWS
APPLY	1.000			
NORGS	0.926	1.000		
DISMAJ	0.930	0.960	1.000	
LSUMNEWS	0.751	0.816	0.785	1.000

Number of cases = 40.

Reproduced Correlation Matrix :

	APPLY	NORGS	DISMAJ	LSUMNEWS
APPLY	1.000			
NORGS	0.926	1.000		
DISMAJ	0.930	0.960	1.000	
LSUMNEWS	0.751	0.816	0.785	1.000

Residual Matrix (correlations) :

	APPLY	NORGS	DISMAJ	LSUMNEWS
APPLY	-0.000			
NORGS	0.000	0.0		
DISMAJ	-0.000	0.000	-0.000	
LSUMNEWS	-0.000	0.0	0.0	-0.000

Value of the maximum absolute residual =   0.000.

ML Estimates of Free Parameters in Dependence Relationships

	Path	Param #	Point Estimate	90.00% Conf. Int. Lower	Upper	Standard Error	T Value
DISMAJ	<- NORGS	1	0.954	0.848	1.061	0.065	14.72
DISMAJ	<- LSUMNEWS	2	0.007	-0.121	0.135	0.078	0.09
DISMAJ	<- W	3	0.281	0.210	0.352	0.043	6.51
LSUMNEWS	<- NORGS	4	0.816	0.728	0.904	0.054	15.23
LSUMNEWS	<- V	5	0.578	0.454	0.703	0.076	7.66
APPLY	<- DISMAJ	6	0.530	0.207	0.853	0.197	2.70
APPLY	<- NORGS	7	0.430	0.082	0.778	0.211	2.03
APPLY	<- LSUMNEWS	8	-0.016	-0.174	0.143	0.096	-0.16
APPLY	<- U	9	0.348	0.262	0.434	0.052	6.66

Scaled Standard Deviations (nuisance parameters)

Variable	Estimate
APPLY	1.000
DISMAJ	1.000
LSUMNEWS	1.000
NORGS	1.000

```
Values of Fixed Parameters in Variance/Covariance Relationships

           Path                   Value
------------------------   ------------
U            <->U                 1.000
V            <->V                 1.000
W            <->W                 1.000
NORGS        <->NORGS             1.000

                Equality Constraints on Variances

                                            Lagrange        Standard
           Constraint           Value      Multiplier         Error
--------------------------      -----      ----------       --------
APPLY      <-> APPLY           1.0000        -0.000          -0.000
DISMAJ     <-> DISMAJ          1.0000         0.000           0.000
LSUMNEWS   <-> LSUMNEWS        1.0000         0.000          -0.000


Maximum Likelihood Discrepancy Function

 Measures of fit of the model
 ---------------------------
 Sample Discrepancy Function Value           : 0.000   (2.805723E-14)

 Multiplier for obtaining test statistic  =     39.000
 Degrees of freedom                       = 0
 Effective number of parameters           = 10
```

The output has eight major parts and we will comment briefly on each in turn. The co-efficient estimates are near the bottom of the output, so we comment on them last.

The output begins by printing the names of the four manifest and three latent variables. Use this as a check to be sure that you have not misspelled any variable names and the correct variables are being used.

Second, the output displays the RAMONA options we have chosen, either explicitly on the ESTIMATE statement or by default.

Third, the output shows us the overall kurtosis and the kurtosis of each manifest variable. Kurtosis is a measure of the peakedness of a distribution; a normal distribution has a kurtosis of 0.0. Negative kurtosis means that the tails of the variable are shorter than a normal distribution; positive kurtosis indicates that the tails are longer. Kurtosis is only printed if the input was a standard SYSTAT cases-by-variables file and not a correlation or covariance matrix. We feel it is more useful to do a SPLOM of your variables in the model and examine the pairwise scatterplots *and* the histograms rather than to try do diagnose problems by examining kurtosis statistics.

Fourth, the output gives the details of each iteration.   To understand this procedure, you need to know three concepts: discrepancy function, starting values, and iterations. Technical details of these concepts and the mathematics underlying them are in the SYSTAT manual.

- The estimation begins by using a **discrepancy function**. This is another name for the quantity that we use to determine how good our fit is; in NONLIN it is called the "loss function." Just like regression, where a good fit has the smallest possible residuals, a good fit has a discrepancy function that is as small as possible. In the least squares estimation procedure, the discrepancy function is the sum of the squared deviations of the observed values of the dependent variable from the estimated values. We want to find coefficient estimates that make these squared values smallest, or least. Thus, this discrepancy function is called ordinary least squares, abbreviated OLS; the same discrepancy function used by REGRESS. RAMONA begins by using OLS because it is fast and easy to calculate.   Then it switches to the estimation method that we specified, MWL, for the final estimate. Iteration method is in the column labeled "Method."

- To find the minimum values, RAMONA starts with initial estimates of the coefficients (called **starting values**). Good starting values are very important because they shorten the estimation process and make it more accurate. We could have supplied our own starting values or allowed RAMONA to determine them. We let RAMONA have its way. See the SYSTAT manual for how to supply starting values.

- RAMONA uses a mathematical procedure to change the coefficient estimates so that the value of the discrepancy function becomes smaller. This requires several steps, sometimes hundreds. Each step is called an **iteration**. The iteration process ends when either the discrepancy function is almost zero or when RAMONA can no longer find a way to make it smaller from one iteration to another. For each iteration, RAMONA prints the iteration number (column "Iter" on the output) and the value of the discrepancy function (column "Discr. Funct." on the output).

- The other iterations statistics are discussed in the SYSTAT manual and are beyond the scope of this book.

- When RAMONA stops iterating it prints several statistics on the final result. First, it tells you if the iteration process was complete; that is, did the discrepancy function reach its minimum? If not, then it reached the maximum allowed number of iterations. This may indicate that you need to respecify your model, or give better starting values, or increase the number of iterations using the ITER parameter on the ESTIMATE command. Then it prints the convergence limit for variance constraint violations and the value of the maximum variance constraint violation. Both these should be very small numbers.

Following the details of the iteration RAMONA prints several correlation matrices. If you specified DISP=COV on the ESTIMATE command or input a variance-covariance matrix, these will be variance-covariance matrices.

- The Sample Correlation Matrix is the matrix of Pearson product-moment correlations used as input.

- The Reproduced Correlation Matrix is the correlation matrix reproduced using the coefficient estimates in the model.

- The Residual Matrix is the difference between the sample correlation matrix and the reproduced correlation matrix. You can use this to find correlations that have not been accurately reproduced by your model. This may suggest parameters that you should add to the model.

Next we come to the moment we've all been waiting for: the estimates of the parameters. The content of the columns is self-explanatory. Each of the 9 paths has an associated point estimate of the path coefficient. Point estimates are the covariance structure model equivalent of a regression coefficient estimate. In this case, where our covariance structure model is identical to the path model in Figure 7.10, the parameter estimates should be, and are, identical to the coefficients. Unlike regression, we specified the residual variances in the MODEL statement, so they are printed here as parameter estimates. Notice the ease with which you can read the coefficients and connect them to the appropriate paths in the path diagrams. SYSTAT also prints a 90% confidence interval for the coefficient estimates. To obtain another interval, like a 95% confidence interval, specify CONFI=0.95 on the ESTIMATE statement.

Following the parameter estimates, RAMONA prints the scaled standard deviations, values of fixed parameters, and the equality constraints on the variances. These are discussed in the SYSTAT manual.

The final portion of the output gives a series of measures of fit of the model. These are discussed in detail below.

Goodness-of-fit statistics

Typically your output will include several measures of the goodness-of-fit of the model. The model above had zero degrees of freedom, which means several measures cannot be calculated, so a sample of RAMONA output from another model is printed below.

```
Measures of fit of the model
----------------------------
Sample Discrepancy Function Value          : 0.581  (5.811892E-01)
Population discrepancy function value, Fo
Bias adjusted point estimate        : 0.427
90.000 percent confidence interval         :(0.104,1.005)

Root mean square error of approximation
Steiger-Lind : RMSEA = SQRT(Fo/DF)
Point estimate                  : 0.267
90.000 percent confidence interval         :(0.132,0.409)

Expected cross-validation index
Point estimate (modified aic)         : 1.350
90.000 percent confidence interval         :(1.027,1.928)
CVI (modified AIC) for the saturated model    : 1.077

Test statistic:                 : 22.666
Exceedance probabilities:-
Ho: perfect fit (RMSEA = 0.0)           : 0.001
Ho: close fit   (RMSEA <=     0.050)      : 0.002

Multiplier for obtaining test statistic  =    39.000
Degrees of freedom            = 6
Effective number of parameters       = 15
```

All the fit statistics are explained in the RAMONA manual. We will discuss one statistic that is particularly useful. The **root mean square error of approximation** can be interpreted as the root mean square standardized difference between the elements of the observed and estimated covariance matrix, adjusted for model complexity. It has a potential range from 0 to infinity, with zero indicating a perfect fit. In practice, values below .10 indicate a reasonably good fit, and below .05 an outstanding fit. RAMONA prints an approximate confidence interval for this statistic.

The important issue to remember about the root mean square error of approximation is that it has been adjusted for model complexity. This is important because the more parameters estimated, the better the fit of the model; more complex models inevitably fit better. We need fit indices that correct for this problem. As Steiger (1990, p. 178) says, "We want goodness of fit which is a result of a special match of model to data, rather than an inevitable consequence of model complexity." In basic terms, if you add a path to your model and the RMSEA does not get smaller, think twice before keeping it in the model, no matter how much you love it. More complex models won't necessarily impress your colleagues, unless they don't care to replicate your work.

Cautions about Latent Variables

In our model, the latent variables are exogenous errors. Most structural equation models include non-error latent variables. For example, we could have an explanatory variable called NEWS that was measured by five different measures of media attention to the disability issue. We could then replace our LSUMNEWS variable with this latent variable. In addition, we would then have five new paths from NEWS to these manifest media variables.

Adding such latent variables to a path diagram quickly gets us into slippery territory. First of all, the estimation of the model becomes problematic. Iterations do not always converge, and there are potential numerical instabilities. Second, it becomes much more difficult to specify a model which does not have redundant parameters or is otherwise ill-defined. Complexity increases exponentially when variables are added to these models because each new variable offers the possibility of many new paths. We cannot emphasize too strongly the advantages to keeping these models simple. Skeptics can always offer rival causal hypotheses, but you should resist the temptation to put everything into the hopper at once and expect the program to solve your problems. We are not experts in causal modeling, but our experience has convinced us that the theoretical benefits of latent variables do not necessarily outweigh the practical pitfalls.

Why RAMONA?

Several other programs provide capabilities similar to RAMONA. Why use it? RAMONA has three advantages. First, the alternatives are considerably more difficult to use. Some are so difficult that one is tempted to suggest that the major design goals of the software included providing a user interface that maximized the possibility of user error and minimized the ability of users to discover their errors. RAMONA has a simple, direct user interface that makes model specification easy and accurate while providing an unpretentious but powerful modeling language that can handle the most complex models. It won't just speed up your work by allowing you to describe your model to the computer twice as fast. For most models it will be faster by a factor of 10. The more complex the model, the bigger the advantage of RAMONA.

A second advantage is that RAMONA is simplicity. You give it the paths and it returns estimates of the coefficients, their standard errors, and several measures of the fit of the model. The alternative approaches require you to learn several matrices and the relations between them. This is very messy to learn or teach, and far too complicated. If you gained something from it, complexity wouldn't be a problem. The problem is, the complications are so *unnecessary*.

Third, RAMONA comes free with SYSTAT. This is particularly important for teaching or any situation where cost is an issue.

Covariance structure models are a valuable addition to the methodological capabilities of a discipline. They are, however, controversial and difficult to use. Anyone who intends to use them should read the controversy generated by Freedman (1987) and Kaplan (1990). These articles discuss some of the problems that need to be solved to use covariance structure models fruitfully. It is important to have some sense of how the different sides of these arguments are defined by their participants and what sides different people take. The technical and political landmines seem to be more frequent in covariance structure models than in many other methodologies. We can only warn the potential user to evaluate the arguments and people carefully.

Notes

Correlation

If you look at a LOWESS smoothed plot of LSUMNEWS against APPLY you will find that the log transformation brought the relation closer to linearity, but that there is still a distinct nonlinearity present. For our current purposes this is not important but if we presented our work as research findings about the Disabled Persons' Rights movement, it would be unacceptable. We would need to find a better way to fix the nonlinearity. There are several possibilities; for example, we could use the stepwise approach described in Chapter 7. We leave this as a problem for interested readers.

We are grateful to Robert Lerner for permission to use the previously unpublished data printed in Figure 7.1. They were originally collected by Lerner (1984) as part of his dissertation research.

Path models

There are a variety of issues arising during use of path models that we did not discuss. It is worth indicating some of them so that readers have some sense of how much further they may want to go. We did not discuss partitioning the R-squared into unique causal components (Duncan (1975) says don't bother), model identification, instrumental variables (aka indirect least squares), two-stage least squares, measurement error, or specification error, to mention only a few.

We estimate path coefficients using ordinary regression. Reading other books, you will quickly find that there are at least two other methods. Path coefficients can also be estimated directly from a correlation matrix. This technique can be done easily by hand and it was important when computers were expensive and not very accessible. We do not discuss it partly because the availability of fast computers and software like SYSTAT makes it unnecessary. More important, the output from regression is considerably richer and more informative.

The collinear relation between NORGS and LSUMNEWS can be handled in several ways. We invite interested readers to pursue this issue. Lerner (1984, p. 95-96) offers several reasons for omitting SUMNEWS from the model entirely. See the notes on Section 7.1, above, on persistent nonlinearity between LSUMNEWS and APPLY.

The diagrams in Figure 7.7 were inspired by similar figures in Bohrnstedt and Knoke (1988) and Saris and Stronkhorst (1984).

Further reading

The best overall introduction to path analysis is Duncan (1975). Blalock (1971) is also helpful. A valuable text that approaches path analysis from a different perspective is Heise (1975). All these books use techniques that were important before fast computers became widely available, so they use techniques that are no longer really necessary.

Introductory and intermediate level readings on covariance structure modeling are not easy to find because many issues and common problems are not discussed. With this warning in mind, the best, most accessible books are James et al. (1985) and McDonald (1985).

References

Berry, W. D. (1984). *Nonrecursive Causal Models*. Sage University Paper series on Quantitative Applications in the Social Sciences, series no. 07-037. Beverly Hills and London: Sage Publications.

Blalock, H. M. (1971). *Causal Models in the Social Sciences*. Chicago: Aldine-Atherton.

Bohrnstedt, G. W. and Knoke, D. (1988). *Statistics for Social Data Analysis* (2nd ed.). Itasca, IL: F. E. Peacock.

Coleman, J. S. (1972). The evaluation of equality of educational opportunity. In F. Mosteller and D. P. Moynihan (eds.), *On Equality of Educational Opportunity* (pp. 146-167). New York: Random House.

Coleman, J. S. (1975). Methods and results in the IEA studies of efforts of school in learning. *Review of Educational Research, 45*, 335-386.

Cudeck, R. (forthcoming). The analysis of correlation matrices using covariance structure models. *Journal of Educational Statistics*.

Davis, J. A. (1985). *The Logic of Causal Order*. Sage University Paper series on Quantitative Applications in the Social Sciences, series no. 07-055. Beverly Hills and London: Sage Publications.

Duncan, O. D. (1984). *Notes on Social Measurement*. New York: Russell Sage Foundation.

Duncan, O. D. (1975). *Introduction to Structural Equation Models*. New York: Academic Press.

Freedman, D. A. (1987). As others see us: A case study in path analysis. *Journal of Educational Statistics, 12*, 101-128.

Heise, D. (1975). *Causal Analysis*. New York, Wiley.

James, L.R., Muliak, S.A., and Brett, J.M. (1982). *Causal Analysis: Assumptions, Models, and Data*. Beverly Hills, CA: Sage Publications.

Kaplan, D. (1990). Evaluating and modifying covariance structure models: A review and recommendation. *Multivariate Behavioral Research, 24*, 137-156.

Lerner, R. (1984). *The rise in applications for social security benefits*. Unpublished doctoral dissertation, University of Chicago, Chicago, Illinois.

McDonald, R.P. (1985). *Factor Analysis and Related Methods*. Hillsdale, NJ: Lawrence Erlbaum Associates.

Miller, A. D. (1971). Logic of causal analysis: From experimental to nonexperimental designs. In H. M. Blalock (ed.), *Causal Models in the Social Sciences* (pp. 2294). Chicago: Aldine.

Nagel, E. (1965). Types of causal explanation in science. In D. Lerner (ed.), *Cause and Effect* (pp. 11-32). New York: Free Press.

Saris, W. E. and Stronkhorst, L. H. (1984). *Causal Modeling in Nonexperimental Research*. Amsterdam, The Netherlands: Sociometric Research Foundation.

Steiger, J. H. (1990). Structural model evaluation and modification: An interval estimation approach. *Multivariate Behavioral Research, 24*, 173-180.

Turner, R. H. (1969). The theme of contemporary social movements. *British Journal of Sociology, 20*, 390-405.

Wold, H. O. A. (1970). Causal inference from observational data: A review of ends and means. In M. Wittrock and D. Wiley (eds.), *The Evaluation of Instruction: Issues and Problems* (pp. 351-390). New York: Holt, Rinehart and Winston.

Wright, S. (1960). Path coefficients and path regressions: Alternative or complementary concepts? *Biometrics, 16*, 189-202.

Part 3

Predicting Continuous Variables from Categorical Variables

8

One-Way Analysis of Variance

Figure 8.1 shows the proportion of the total article area devoted to graphs in 50 articles printed in each of 47 different scientific journals. These data are adapted from Cleveland (1984), reprinted in Chambers, Cleveland, Kleiner, and Tukey (1983). You may wish to see Stellman (1985) and Cleveland (1985) for more comments on this research.

We have classified the type of journal into four categories of scientific discipline. Cleveland originally used three—Natural, Mathematical, and Social. By adding Life sciences, we can examine the classification in more detail. Furthermore, we have classified two of the experimental psychology journals (*Journal of Experimental Psychology* and *Perception and Psychophysics*) into the Life sciences group because this more accurately fits their content. This type of laboratory psychology is not a social science because it does not involve interaction between subjects. The data also support this classification, as we shall see.

8.1 Displaying the data

Let's summarize our data by looking at AREA and TYPE graphically. Figure 8.2 shows how to make a "dit plot" showing the scores in each TYPE. This is a type of dot plot which looks like histograms, or stem-and-leaf diagrams without numbers.

Figure 8.1
Proportions of Area in Scientific Articles Devoted to Graphs

CASE	TYPE$	AREA
1	Life	0.207
2	Life	0.157
3	Life	0.106
4	Life	0.091
5	Life	0.082
6	Life	0.089
7	Life	0.127
8	Life	0.034
9	Life	0.068
10	Life	0.084
11	Mathematics	0.059
12	Mathematics	0.034
13	Mathematics	0.105
14	Mathematics	0.019
15	Mathematics	0.114
16	Mathematics	0.025
17	Mathematics	0.045
18	Mathematics	0.057
19	Mathematics	0.014
20	Mathematics	0.067
21	Mathematics	0.139
22	Mathematics	0.070
23	Mathematics	0.023
24	Physical	0.055
25	Physical	0.063
26	Physical	0.200
27	Physical	0.122
28	Physical	0.089
29	Physical	0.158
30	Physical	0.264
31	Physical	0.310
32	Physical	0.066
33	Physical	0.164
34	Physical	0.199
35	Physical	0.149
36	Physical	0.097
37	Physical	0.108
38	Physical	0.098
39	Social	0.045
40	Social	0.041
41	Social	0.014
42	Social	0.038
43	Social	0.034
44	Social	0.032
45	Social	0.014
46	Social	0.014
47	Social	0.038

Figure 8.2
Area Proportions by Type of Discipline

```
USE AREAS
DENSITY AREA*TYPE$ / DIT,TRANSPOSE
```

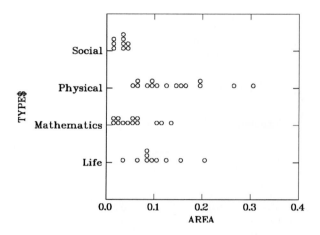

Do graph areas differ among disciplines? It is difficult to say at this point. The social sciences appear to have least space devoted to graphs and the physical sciences the most, but the spreads are so different that it is hard to generalize.

Let's do a plot which reveals location and spread a little better, albeit at the risk of losing the detail that plotting the raw data provides. Figure 8.3 shows the commands and output for a schematic plot (box plot) of the data. This graphical technique is one of a number developed by John Tukey for work in exploratory data analysis (Tukey, 1977).

Figure 8.3
Box Plot of Area Proportions by Type

```
USE AREAS
DENSITY AREA*TYPE$ / BOX,TRANSPOSE
```

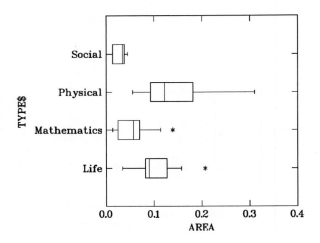

The various features of the box plot show the median (center line), the range (ends of the whiskers or special symbols), and the upper and lower quartiles or hinges (edges of the box) of the data in each group. Figure 8.4 shows how.

Figure 8.4
Key for Box Plots

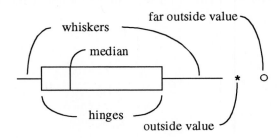

First, some definitions: The **median** splits each ordered batch of numbers in half, and the **hinges** split the remaining halves in half again. The median of the batch is marked by the center vertical line in the box. The lower and upper hinges comprise the edges of the central box. Thus, the box outlines the extent of the central half of the data in each group.

Hspread is comparable to the interquartile range or midrange. It is the absolute value of the difference between the values of the two hinges.

The **inner fences** are defined as follows:

$$\text{lower fence} = \text{lower hinge} - (1.5\text{Hspread})$$
$$\text{upper fence} = \text{upper hinge} + (1.5\text{Hspread})$$

The **outer fences** are defined as follows:

$$\text{lower fence} = \text{lower hinge} - (3\text{Hspread})$$
$$\text{upper fence} = \text{upper hinge} + (3\text{Hspread})$$

Values outside the inner fences are plotted with asterisks. Values outside the outer fences are plotted with empty circles.

Why not plot means and standard deviations (or error bars) instead of boxes? First of all, the summary features of box plots are based on ranks rather than sums. This makes these displays relatively less susceptible to the influence of a few extreme values. Second, box plots reveal skewness (nonsymmetry) in the data. Error bars (whether based on standard deviations or ranges) are symmetric about the mean and can be extremely misleading when the data are not symmetric.

Notice, for example, that our data are positively skewed in all four TYPEs. That is, the data look bunched up at the lower values and strung out on the higher: medians are lower in the boxes and whiskers appear longer on the right than they do on the left. Notice also that the ranges of each TYPE seem different. For example, the Hspread box of the social sciences is less than half the size of the others.

Because these data are skewed and because the ranges increase with the medians (or means), these data are good candidates for a transformation. We often use a logarithmic transformation to normalize skewed data like these, but when we have proportions, another transformation works better. It is called the arcsine transformation, although it involves a square root as well. Figure 8.5 shows how to make a new variable, PAREA, with this transformation. Notice how the box plots on this transformed variable are more comparable and how the outliers are gone.

Using a transformation like this may seem mysterious. If so, you should read Section 22.2. The goal of a transformation is to make the data look more appropriate for a statistical model.

Figure 8.5
Box Plot of Arc Sined Area Proportions by Type

```
LET PAREA=ASN(SQR(AREA))
DENSITY PAREA*TYPE$ / BOX,TRANSPOSE
```

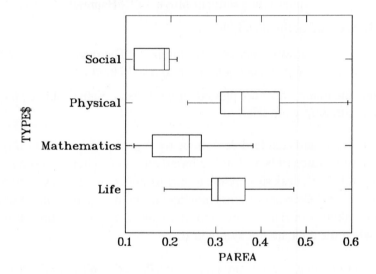

8.2 Constructing and understanding the model

A classical statistical procedure for analyzing data which have a quantitative dependent variable and a categorical independent variable is **analysis of variance** (ANOVA). analysis of variance seems like a misnomer. As mentioned above, our concern will be the analysis of *means*. We will not be focusing on means in isolation, however, but rather on how they vary among one another. We will compare this variance of means to the background variance of the data on which the means are based.

ANOVA techniques have been used for many decades. Over time some specialized terms have become conventional. For instance, a categorical independent variable (e.g., our TYPE) is often called a "factor" and the groups created by a categorical independent variable (Social, Physical, etc.) are often called "levels." Particular ANOVA models are identified by the number of factors (categorical independent variables) involved. This chapter concerns a single factor (TYPE), or a **one-way ANOVA** model.

Figure 8.6 shows the graphical form of the normal ANOVA model. We have superimposed normal curves on two dit plots of the transformed graph area proportions. In the left plot, the means of the normal curves are positioned at the overall mean of PAREA. In the right, the means are at the respective sample means of each TYPE. The standard deviations are the same for all eight curves. They are taken from the pooled within-groups standard deviation (i.e. averaged across the groups).

With our ANOVA, we will test whether the left plot (the null model where all means are the same) is a plausible model for explaining our samples. If not, then something like the right plot (the alternative model where each TYPE is sampled from a different population) would be more plausible. The validity of our ANOVA conclusions depends on how well our normal curves approximate the real data.

Figure 8.6
Graphical Model of One-Way ANOVA on Graph Data

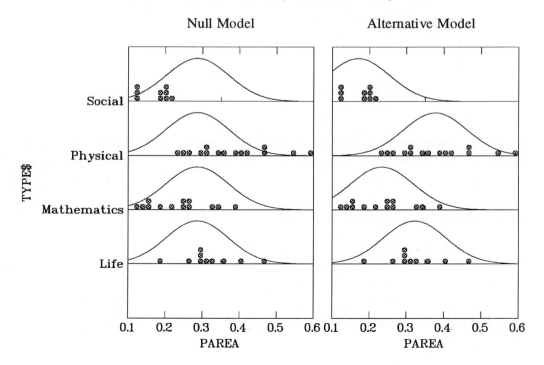

Figure 8.7 shows the commands that specify a one-way ANOVA on our data. The CATEGORY statement informs the program that TYPE is a categorical factor variable.

The MODEL command specifies our model—that the systematic part of PAREA can be predicted by the overall mean (CONSTANT) plus an additional effect for TYPE. This effect is either positive or negative. It is the difference between each mean (Life, Mathematics, etc.) and the overall grand mean of the areas. This set of commands constitutes a one-way ANOVA and will generate an ANOVA table.

Figure 8.7
ANOVA on Graph Area Data

```
GLM
USE AREAS
CATEGORY TYPE$
MODEL PAREA = CONSTANT + TYPE$
SAVE GRESID / MODEL
ESTIMATE
```

```
Categorical values encountered during processing are:
TYPE$ (4 levels)
   Life, Mathematics, Physical, Social

Dep Var: PAREA N: 47 Multiple R:  0.701 Squared multiple R:  0.491
```

		Analysis of Variance			
Source	Sum-of-Squares	DF	Mean-Square	F-Ratio	P
TYPE$	0.294	3	0.098	13.810	0.000
Error	0.305	43	0.007		

The SAVE command saves the residuals from our analysis. Adding the MODEL option causes the design (model) variables to be added to the residual file. We'll examine these new variables later.

Describing the variance in a model

ANOVA procedures compare differences in means. For our study we will be comparing the mean transformed area proportions. While ANOVA procedures can involve lots of calculations, the basic units involved in these calculations begin and end as variability—i.e., simple differences among data points and their means. Figure 8.8 labels the differences between grouped dependent variable scores that are involved in these calculations.

Figure 8.8
One Data Point's Contribution to Variance

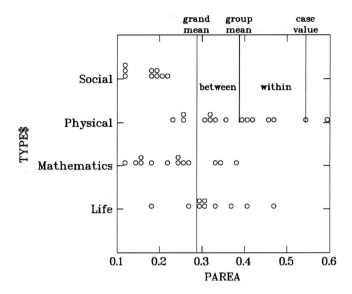

The baseline of all differences is the **grand mean** of scores—for our data the average transformed proportion of area is about .29 as shown by the long vertical line in Figure 8.8. ANOVA techniques compute the variability of each dependent value score from this base. We have selected a case from the Physical sciences group to illustrate how this variability is decomposed. The difference between this case and the grand mean of all areas is the contribution of the case to the total variability of all cases around the mean. One-way ANOVA partitions this total variability from the grand mean into two components: **within** and **between** variability.

Within-group variability is computed by referencing the appropriate group mean. The mean for the Physical sciences is about .38, as shown in the graph. Since our sample case comes from that group, its contribution to within-group variability comes from its the difference between .54 and .38.

Between-group variability is computed from the differences between group means and the grand mean. For our case, the relevant difference is between .38 and .29.

Sums of squares

So far we have discussed one data point's contribution to total variability, arising from within and between level variation. Now we want to include the information drawn from all the values. A straightforward procedure would simply figure the appropriate "between" and "within" differences for each data point and then add them up across all the data points to yield three summary quantities: sum of within-group differences, sum of between-group differences, and the sum of total differences. ANOVA works with squares, however. Each difference is squared before summing.

Why go to the trouble of squaring the differences? There are a number of reasons. First, raw differences can be positive and negative and thus would cancel each other if summed. This would conceal variability. Second, squaring and summing differences leads to a convenient quantity known as **variance**. Variance is the average of squared differences from a mean. For normally distributed data, sums of squared differences and ratios of variances have simple mathematical distributions which allow us to test a variety of useful hypotheses.

There are three sums of squares used in one-way ANOVA: sum of squares within levels (SS_W), sum of squares between levels (SS_B), and Total sum of squares (SS_T). They have a simple relation:

$$SS_T = SS_B + SS_W$$

Looking back at Figure 8.8, you can see that the breaking down of the total sum of squares into between- and within-groups components mirrors the breakdown of a single score's variability in the ANOVA model.

The fit of the model: The coefficient of determination

The sum of squares values provide the basis for a simple statistic which summarizes the goodness-of-fit of our model, the SQUARED MULTIPLE R value in the upper right corner of the table in Figure 8.7. This value, called the **coefficient of determination**, simply tells what proportion of the total variability contained in our data has been accounted for by the factor (TYPE) we included in our model: it is the ratio of sum of squares between levels to the total sum of squares,

$$
\begin{aligned}
R^2 \quad &= \quad SS_B \, / \, SS_T \\
&= \quad SS_B \, / \, (SS_B + SS_W) \\
&= \quad .294 \, / \, (.294 + .305) \quad = \quad .491
\end{aligned}
$$

In other words, almost half of the variation among transformed graph area proportions may be attributed to the effects of TYPE of discipline.

Testing the significance of the fit of the model

While the coefficient of determination provides a statistic that summarizes the fit of our model, we usually want a test of the likelihood that a fit this good or better could occur with normally distributed random data. The test for the model R^2 which we discussed in Section 4.3 can be used for this purpose. Let's look at that test a different way, however, using ANOVA terminology. For ANOVA, we can view this test as based on the ratio of variance between groups (like regression model variance) to variance within groups (like error variance). If the data are independent and normally distributed within cells, then this ratio with be distributed as an F statistic.

Degrees of freedom

To get our two variances for the ratio, we need to understand something about **degrees of freedom**. If you know the mean of some set of scores (say, 10) and you are given all but one of the scores that comprise it (say three scores of which you are told one is 12 and another is 4), then you may be certain that the third score can take only one value (i.e., 14). The same logic applies to the summary quantities in the analysis of variance. Knowing the grand mean (average) of all the areas and any 46 of the areas allows us to determine the remaining area. Thus, the sum of squares total (which is based on knowing the grand mean) has only 46 degrees of freedom (df_T=46). Similarly, knowing the grand mean and three of the four means for the factor levels of TYPE allows us to determine the fourth factor level mean. Thus, the sum of squares among the four factor means has only 3 degrees of freedom between levels (df_B=3). The 43 remaining degrees of freedom (i.e., 47 total minus 1 for the grand mean and 3 for factor level means equals 43) are those left to describe the variability of individual area proportions, that is 43 degrees of freedom remain for the sum of squares within levels (df_W=43).

Mean squares and the *F* ratio test of fit

Sums of squares divided by degrees of freedom are called **mean squares**. These are the variances we need for our F test. **Mean square between** (MS_B) is SS_B/df_B. **Mean square within** (MS_W) is SS_W/df_W. The F test involves forming the simple ratio of MS_B/MS_W.

Why does the ratio of MS_B/MS_W test our model? Imagine for a moment that we were to draw four random samples of size 12 from a common population of journals sharing a typical area proportion. Under these conditions, we would expect MS_W to be an estimate of the variance of all the areas (σ^2), because they all come from one group. We would not expect the sample means of each of these four samples to be identical, however. How much would we expect them to vary over repeated samples like this? The variance of the sample means is proportional (by $1/n$) to the population variance of the items themselves ($\sigma^2/12$). MS_B is equivalent to 12 times this variance of means because we summed group variation over all 12 cases in each group. Thus, if a null hypothesis that the groups are the same were true, the statistic $F=MS_B/MS_W$ would be expected to have a value around 1. This situation is graphically represented in the left panel of Figure 8.6.

Now consider an alternative. Assume that the four groups have common variance but different population means and we sample from them as before. This time, MS_W should still estimate σ^2 because it is computed around each group's sample mean. MS_B, however, now contains variation due to the separation between means as well as the variance within the groups. In this case, the F statistic will be tend to be larger than 1. The F statistic is itself a **likelihood ratio**. That is, when F is much larger than 1, the likelihood is high that the group means are really different. This situation is shown in the right panel of Figure 8.6.

Figure 8.9 shows the F distribution for the degrees of freedom in our example (3 for the numerator and 43 for the denominator) as well as one to the right with 9 and 43 degrees of freedom (as if we had done the same experiment with 10 TYPEs). We included the second curve to show you how the shape of F can vary depending on degrees of freedom. The value of F in our output is 13.81. The area under the (3,43) curve to the right of that point is off the graph and, the printout shows, is less than .001. We may reject at the .05 level the null hypothesis that the groups have equivalent means.

Figure 8.9
_F_ Distributions with (3,43) and (9,43) Degrees of Freedom

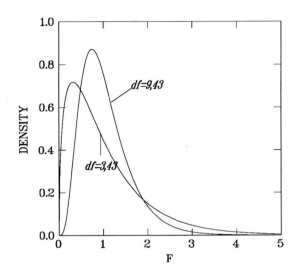

8.3 Checking assumptions: Can we believe our model?

Our results above are preliminary because they are based on some untested assumptions. We have seen that the F test is a ratio of variances. More explicitly, it is a comparison of the variance thought to be systematic (the variation between level means) to variance thought to be unsystematic (the variation among data points within levels). As with the F test associated with regression models, the ANOVA F test requires us to assume that the within-cell errors are independent, normally distributed with zero means and constant variance.

How can we test these assumptions? We will follow the same procedure we used for regression—analyze the residuals. What are the residuals from our model estimates? They are the distribution of scores in each group with the sample group mean subtracted out. After all, the model was:

PAREA = CONSTANT + TYPE

The variation in the data unpredicted by this model is the variation within cells. Remember, that's what we used for our error term. If we look at that variation, we can assess graphically whether the errors are normally distributed.

The two variables ESTIMATE and RESIDUAL were saved when we did the analysis. ESTIMATE contains the means of our levels, or in other words the variability due to the modeled factor. RESIDUAL contains within level variability, or in other words the part that we want to behave like a normal random variable. Figure 8.10 plots RESIDUAL against the ESTIMATE and is a common beginning for the investigation of residuals. It is the same residual plot we used for regression diagnostics.

Figure 8.10
Residual Plot for Graph Areas ANOVA

```
USE GRESID
PLOT RESIDUAL*ESTIMATE/SYMBOL=1
```

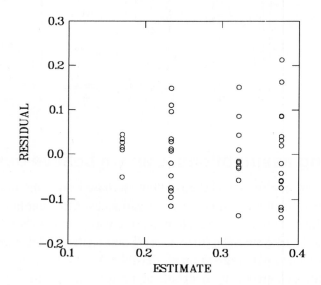

It is not coincidental that this looks somewhat like the dit plot in Figure 8.2 (transposed). RESIDUALs are simply PAREA with group means (i.e., ESTIMATE) subtracted. Thus each level's mean on this new variable is zero, so that the strips for each level become centered around this common value. Our question is whether these four strips appear to approximate what we would expect to see if four random samples were drawn from a single population which had a mean of zero and a normal distribution. Let's examine each of these assumptions.

Are the RESIDUALs normally distributed?

As in regression, we can get a sharper picture of the distribution of the residuals by pooling them across all levels of the predictor variable(s). A familiar display of a normal distribution is the "bell shaped curve" seen when such a distribution is plotted as a histogram. SYSTAT provides a useful variation on the histogram called a **stem-and-leaf display**. Figure 8.11 show this display for the RESIDUALs from the ANOVA of TYPE on PAREA. The "stem" is the vertical string of single digits on the left of the display, the first digit that significantly discriminates between values on the variable (in the case of our present residuals it is the dollar digit). To the right of each stem are the "leaves" which show each score as the single digit occurring in its next place value after the stem digit (for our display it is the tens of cents place). The display shows the shape of the distribution and also recreates each score that it comprises.

We have added a new variable to the GRESID file. This variable, NORMAL, is a random sample of 47 values from a normal distribution. Notice that, while still somewhat irregular, it is relatively symmetric and does not show the OUTSIDE VALUES warning. It's often useful to add a normal variable to your residual file for this type of comparison. You'll be surprised at how ragged real random variables can be, especially in small samples.

The M's and H's are the medians and hinges of the batches, the same values displayed as the middle and edges of the box plots in Figure 8.3.

Figure 8.11
Stem-and-leaf Display of RESIDUALS from ANOVA on PAREA

```
STATS
USE GRESID
LET NORMAL=ZRN
STEM RESIDUAL
STEM NORMAL
```

```
Stem and Leaf Plot of variable: NORMAL
  Minimum:          -2.194
  Lower hinge:      -0.595
  Median:            0.020
  Upper hinge:       0.618
  Maximum:           1.832

        -2   10
        -1   8765
        -1
        -0 H 98766655
        -0   433222110
         0 M 0012222344
         0 H 56678889
         1   02333
         1   8
```

```
Stem and Leaf Plot of variable: RESIDUAL
  Minimum:          -0.140
  Lower hinge:      -0.055
  Median:            0.007
  Upper hinge:       0.037
  Maximum:           0.213

        -1   4
        -1   32
        -1   11
        -0   98
        -0   776
        -0 H 5555544
        -0   3222
        -0   11
         0 M 000111
         0 H 2223333
         0   44
         0
         0   8889
         1   1
         1
         1   45
         1   6
  * * * Outside Values * * *
         2   1
```

Figure 8.12 shows the same values plotted as histograms. A normal curve has been superimposed on top. We tend to prefer the stem-and-leaf diagrams or dit plots because they show you every data value. Even when the number of bars is chosen relatively intelligently, as in SYSTAT, the histogram can lull you into thinking the data are smoother than they really are. Nevertheless, you can sense a slight skewness in the RESIDUAL values.

Figure 8.12
Histogram of RESIDUALS from ANOVA on PAREA

```
BEGIN
DEN RESIDUAL
DEN RESIDUAL / NORMAL AXES=NONE SC=NONE XLAB=' ' YLAB=' '
END

BEGIN
DEN NORMAL
DEN NORMAL / NORMAL AXES=NONE SC=NONE XLAB=' ' YLAB=' '
END
```

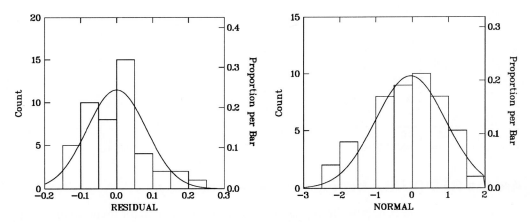

Finally, Figure 8.13 shows another way to test for normality: a probability plot. This graph plots the ordered values of a variable against the ordered values from a normal distribution. If the data are distributed perfectly normally (which cannot happen with random data), they will plot along a straight line. If they are sampled from a normal distribution, they will plot roughly along a straight line. As before, it is handy to have a sample of normal random values sitting around for comparison. We've done this in Figure 8.13. Many statisticians prefer these probability plots to histograms with super-imposed normal curves. In our experience, it is often more difficult to see departures from normality (such as the skewness in our residuals) with the probability plot.

Figure 8.13
Probability Plot of RESIDUALS from ANOVA on PAREA

```
PPLOT RESIDUAL / SYMBOL=1
PPLOT NORMAL / SYMBOL=1
```

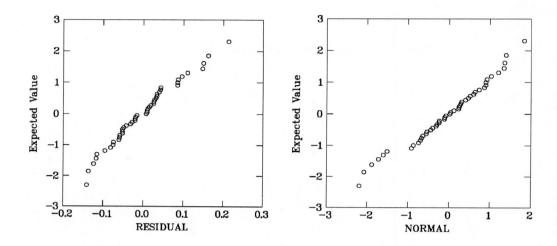

Are the RESIDUALs homogeneous by factor levels?

Our second question concerns the spread of values within each factor level. In order for our F tests to be meaningful, we must assume that the residuals within each level or group have the same variance. Box plots give a compact summary comparison of the variability in levels. Figure 8.3 does this for the raw data. Figure 8.14 does this for the residuals and our normal sample variable. Before making the plots, we merge the residuals and the raw data so that we can use the other variables in the data file. Using our random normal data helps us to see that the differences between the box widths are probably due to sample error. We shouldn't be too worried about them.

Figure 8.14
Box Plot of Residuals for PAREA ANOVA

```
MERGE AREAS GRESID
SAVE GRALL
RUN
USE GRALL
DENSITY RESIDUAL*TYPE$ / BOX
DENSITY NORMAL*TYPE$ / BOX
```

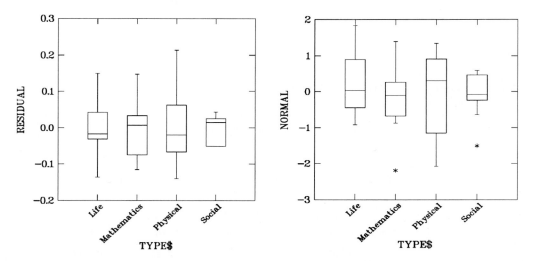

There are also some statistical tests for homogeneity of variances. Bartlett's (1937) test and Levene's (1960) test are popular. Bartlett's (1937) test is the most widely used test for homogeneity of variances but it has sensitivity problems. Bartlett's test compares the arithmetic and geometric means of sample variances. The more discrepant the sample variances, the more the arithmetic mean will dominate the geometric means in the ratio **mean squared error** divided by **geometric mean squared error**. Bartlett has shown that this comparison follows a chi-square distribution in large samples.

Unfortunately, the Bartlett test is sensitive not only to nonhomogeneity of variances, but also to nonnormality of variances. In fact it is much more sensitive to nonnormality than is the F test we are interested in protecting.   Levene's test is an easily applied alternative to the Bartlett test and is less sensitive to nonnormality in the residuals – for this reason it is sometimes called a more "robust" test. The appropriate occasion for its use is when 1) the residuals are only very roughly normally distributed (enough that you think the F-test will not be too badly distorted but think that the Bartlett test will be distorted) and 2) there appears some reason to continue questioning whether the residuals are homogeneously distributed. Levene's test is simply a one-way ANOVA on the absolute values of the residuals. Figure 8.15 shows the commands that apply Levene's test to the RESIDUALs of our areas data. The heterogeneity of variance does not appear to be significant.

Figure 8.15
Levene's Test for Homogeneity of Variances for PAREA

```
USE GRALL
LET LEVENE=ABS(RESIDUAL)
SAVE GRALL
GLM
CATEGORY TYPE$
MODEL LEVENE = CONSTANT + TYPE$
ESTIMATE
```

```
Categorical values encountered during processing are:
TYPE$ (4 levels)
    Life, Mathematics, Physical, Social


Dep Var: LEVENE N: 47 Multiple R:  0.371 Squared multiple R:  0.138


                          Analysis of Variance

Source              Sum-of-Squares   DF  Mean-Square     F-Ratio      P

TYPE$                        0.015   3         0.005       2.288    0.092

Error                        0.094   43        0.002
```

Are RESIDUAL values independent?

You recall that our assumption in testing an ANOVA is that the RESIDUALs be a good approximation of random draws from a normal population. The key here is "random draws". The selection of one value should offer no information about the expected value of any other value. In an experimental study this assumption is met by assigning study entities to treatments by random lot, a procedure which justifies this assumption. Joiner (1981), however, shows how these biases can be introduced even into well-planned experiments.

If we suspect that the order in which the data were collected is related to the values we recorded, then we should look for "autocorrelation" in our residuals. This doesn't seem plausible for the graph areas data, but we will show you how to examine this possibility for other data you might analyze. In Figure 8.16, we have used SERIES to produce an autocorrelation plot of the residuals. This is the same plot we use in the time series chapters to examine autocorrelations in time series. None of the autocorrelations is large here. If you suspected a problem and found large autocorrelations, however, you should proceed to examine the autocorrelations within each group's residuals separately to locate the source of the problem.

Figure 8.16
Autocorrelation Plot of Residuals from Graph Areas ANOVA

SERIES
ACF RESIDUAL

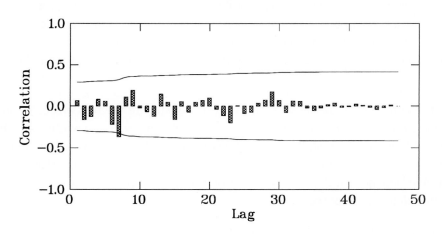

Transforming to achieve normality

Our diagnostic plots have indicated that the transformed graph area proportions meet the assumptions required for the ANOVA. You may have heard that ANOVA procedures are "robust to violation of the assumptions of the model" (e.g., Box, 1954; Sheffe, 1959; Boneau, 1960). So why have we done so many graphic analyses to test the assumptions?

Too often the reassurances are taken so globally that residuals analysis gets skipped. To counteract this we need to be aware of some issues. First, the older studies on robustness included the stipulation "for sufficiently large samples," but did not make clear that "sufficiently large" in practical applications should be translated to "greater than 1,000 cases." Second, the older studies were produced in the precomputer age and had to limit the number and variety of potential violations they investigated. Some recent work suggests that there are alternate forms of nonnormal distributions – for example, severely skewed ones—which seriously distort ANOVA results (Bradley, 1980; Wike and Church, 1982).

For these and for more pragmatic reasons, we do not favor relying on ANOVAs' forgiving nature. The example data set for this chapter shows why. Had we done the analysis on the untransformed areas, the F value would have been 10.60 instead of 13.81. That is still significant, but sometimes the difference can be between significant and nonsignificant results. It can work either way. Failing to meet distributional assumptions by avoiding a transformation can cause nonsignificant results to become significant, or vice versa. You go to considerable trouble to collect your data. They will always have a story to tell. You owe it to yourself to listen, even if it takes some care and attention to find and screen out the noise. It has been our aim to give you graphically oriented strategies which will make this work far more transparent and effective than has been the historical case.

It might also help to think back to why we use statistics in the first place. We turn to tests such as the F test because a sample of data helps us to draw conclusions about a larger population of interest. A statistical test merely helps us evaluate how much risk we are taking in making the inference from the sample to the larger population. A conclusion that depends on the values of just one or a few cases or that misspecifies the population defeats our purpose.

If we can't transform to achieve normality

Sometimes we can't find a nonlinear transformation which normalizes our data. Outliers may be present, or we may have a mixture of different distributions. In this case, we can look for more robust ANOVA procedures which are not influenced as much by outliers. We could treat dependent value scores as simple ranks, for example, and use procedures which do not require normally distributed variables. The original box plot performed at the beginning of this chapter is such an alternative, as it analyzes medians rather than means. You may also check the SYSTAT manual for the Kruskal-Wallace test, which provides a procedure analogous to a One-way ANOVA and requires only ranked dependent variable values. Unfortunately these alternatives lose power as they relax assumptions. In comparison to metric ANOVAs they will sometimes fail to detect significant differences in data where such differences exist.

In other cases, particularly where variances do appear correlated with their means but cannot be corrected with a simple transformation, you might want to try a weighted least squares regression approach to ANOVA. This method is beyond the scope of this book. If you need to pursue it, however, you can get an initial introduction to weighted least squares regression in Section 6.4. From there you will need to proceed to a text that gives a more extended treatment of the regression approach to ANOVA; Neter, Wasserman & Kutner (1990) are particularly lucid.

8.4 The ANOVA algebraic model

We've been using the same techniques found in the ordinary regression model, but so far there's been no equation. Let's look at one now. We want to express area proportion (y) as a function of type of journal (x). One way to do this is:

$$y = \mu_1 x_1 + \mu_2 x_2 + \mu_3 x_3 + \mu_4 x_4 + \varepsilon$$

where μ_j is the mean of a group and x_j is a variable which is 0 or 1. Here are the equations for the four groups:

$$y_1 = \mu_1 1 + \mu_2 0 + \mu_3 0 + \mu_4 0 + \varepsilon$$
$$y_2 = \mu_1 0 + \mu_2 1 + \mu_3 0 + \mu_4 0 + \varepsilon$$
$$y_3 = \mu_1 0 + \mu_2 0 + \mu_3 1 + \mu_4 0 + \varepsilon$$
$$y_4 = \mu_1 0 + \mu_2 0 + \mu_3 0 + \mu_4 1 + \varepsilon$$

Because of the zeros, these reduce to:

$$y_1 = \mu_1 + \varepsilon$$
$$y_2 = \mu_2 + \varepsilon$$
$$y_3 = \mu_3 + \varepsilon$$
$$y_4 = \mu_4 + \varepsilon$$

Or, simply

$$y_j = \mu_j + \varepsilon$$

Each observation, in other words, is simply a function of its group mean plus random error. This is called the **means model**, and is available with the MEANS option of the MODEL statement in GLM. It is attractive because each parameter is simply a group (cell) mean.

There is another way to express the ANOVA model, however, which is closer to the usual regression model with a constant:

$$y = \mu + \alpha_1 x_1 + \alpha_2 x_2 + \alpha_3 x_3 + \varepsilon$$

where μ is a grand mean for the constant, x_j is a variable which is 0 or 1 or -1, and α_j is an effect for each group. This is called the **effects model**. Here are the equations for the four groups:

$$y_1 = \mu + \alpha_1 1 + \alpha_2 0 + \alpha_3 0 + \varepsilon$$
$$y_2 = \mu + \alpha_1 0 + \alpha_2 1 + \alpha_3 0 + \varepsilon$$
$$y_3 = \mu + \alpha_1 0 + \alpha_2 0 + \alpha_3 1 + \varepsilon$$
$$y_4 = \mu - \alpha_1 1 - \alpha_2 1 - \alpha_3 1 + \varepsilon$$

Or,

$$y_j = \mu + \alpha_j + \varepsilon$$

Now, most students find this confusing. Where did the fourth alpha (α) go? You may remember that we have only three degrees of freedom for TYPE in our model, so we can have only four parameters altogether. Consequently, we constrain the fourth effect (α_4) to be minus the sum of the other three. This way, all the effects add to zero.

If you look in your GRESID file that we saved when we did the ANOVA, you'll see the MODEL variables (1, 0, or -1) that we asked for. Using these artificial (dummy) variables, we could compute an ANOVA with a regular regression program.

8.5 Interpreting results and testing hypotheses

The original F test printed in the ANOVA table is an "omnibus" test. It tells us only that something is going on with PAREA and that it has something to do with TYPE. Often we wish to know more about specific contrasts among means.

Some researchers follow up an ANOVA with some t-tests on means. They use a different error term for each test, based on the two groups being compared. A valid ANOVA rests on the assumption that all the groups share common error variance, however, so using separate error terms is a waste of time and power. Instead, we will compute contrasts on means and compare them to the same pooled mean square error (MSE) used in the ANOVA.

Single degree of freedom tests

Suppose we wish to determine whether the social science journals devote significantly less space to graphs than do the natural science journals. This is a single degree of freedom hypothesis because we are comparing only two things—social and natural sciences. Remember, degrees of freedom for such hypotheses are one less than the number of entities being compared.

Comparisons

SYSTAT lets you make such an explicit comparison among means in a convenient way with a CONTRAST statement. A **contrast** is a set of weights which add to zero and which compare one or more levels of a factor against the remaining levels. Figure 8.17 shows the commands and the output which test this hypothesis. The result is highly significant. Don't worry at this time about the "A MATRIX." It is explained in the SYSTAT manual, but you don't need to know how it works to be able to do analyses with the CONTRAST statement. Do notice, however, that the numbers in the contrast signify that the social science mean area proportion is being contrasted with the sum of the other three journal types' means. We would have gotten the same result if the signs had been reversed (-1 -1 -1 3), because the contrast is all that counts, not its direction.

Figure 8.17
Contrast of Social vs. Natural Sciences

```
HYPOTHESIS
EFFECT = TYPE$
CONTRAST [1 1 1 -3]
TEST
```

Test for effect called:	TYPE$			
A Matrix				
	1	2	3	4
	0.0	4.000	4.000	4.000
Test of Hypothesis				

Source	SS	DF	MS	F	P
Hypothesis	0.144	1	0.144	20.237	0.000
Error	0.305	43	0.007		

What other single degree of freedom hypotheses could we test? We could contrast mathematics with the applied sciences (-1 3 -1 -1). We could compare physical and life sciences (-1 0 1 0). Notice that this latter contrast leaves out mathematics and social sciences. Notice also that we usually weight the contrasts so that they add to zero. This is not always done, but it makes them more interpretable.

We can test as many of these hypotheses as we like. You can simply repeat the instructions (or menu actions) represented in Figure 8.17. After doing a lot of them, however, we might be suspected of hunting for one that makes our data look most impressive or significant. How can we protect ourselves from the dangers of a fishing expedition?

Tests for trend

When the levels of a factor fall on an ordered scale, it can be useful to test whether there is a trend across the levels. Our data do not fit an ordered scale, but if they did, the CONTRAST statement could be used to do these trend contrasts. See Section 9.4 for an example.

Bonferroni procedure for multiple contrasts

On occasions when you do wish to make more than one contrast among means, a slightly modified use of the CONTRAST method can be appropriate. The Bonferroni procedure (sometimes called the Fisher-Bonferroni method) simply requires that you reset your mental criteria for a significant finding at a level which adjusts for the multiple comparisons. The new level is the criterion you have decided to be appropriate for your study, divided by the number of contrasts you wish to test. Say for instance you wish to make four separate contrasts and have established that a difference between means at an overall level of $p < .01$ is required to assure appropriate protection against finding significant results in random data (known as a "Type I error"). Setting your mental criterion for a significant finding at the level of .01 divided by 4 or .0025 will permit you to distinguish among means at the appropriate level. Applying this Bonferroni criterion limits the chance of finding at least one significant difference in four contrasts on random data to less than .01. On these occasions you may have to change SYSTAT's default output format in order to see enough significant digits to make your decision. For example, FORMAT=5 would allow you to see 5 digits to the right of the decimal and so evaluate small probability values.

The Bonferroni procedure is useful for its simplicity and its power. It can be used for complex hypotheses involving combinations of means in linear contrast statements and is appropriate with factors containing unequal numbers of cases per level. It can also be a strong asset in making comparisons among simple pairs of means: on occasions where the number of comparisons you wish to make is small relative to the number of possible pairwise differences between means.

If you make too many comparisons, however, the Bonferroni procedure will become insensitive, failing to detect really significant differences at the chosen level of significance (known as a "Type II error"). This trade-off also means that you must be scrupulous in formulating the contrasts you wish to make prior to inspecting the data. Using prior knowledge of the data (i.e., the pattern or rank order of means) to select a limited set of likely contrasts will destroy the meaning of even the adjusted criterion p value.

Multiple comparison procedures

Let's go one step further. There are times when you do not have just a few explicitly testable expectations for your data. For example, you may be evaluating a number of similar products and merely want to determine if any one performs significantly better than each of the others. In this case we wish to compare differences among all possible pairs of level means.

The area of multiple comparisons involves some controversy among statisticians. In some texts you will find the varied approaches discussed and savored like vintage wines. If you have trained in this older school, you need to be aware of recent work with these procedures. Neither the Newman-Keuls nor especially the classical Duncan multiple range test meets its stated protection levels against finding significant results in random data (Type I errors). And others, like the Scheffé test, do not have adequate power (protection against failing to find significant results on real differences, called Type II errors) when they are applied to the all possible pairs multiple comparison problem.

Even though you may see Duncan or Newman-Keuls tests still appearing in reputable journals, do not assume they are acceptable for scientific research. It takes a long time for applied journals to adopt findings in the theoretical literature. For example, Day and Quinn (1989) used random data to simulate typical patterns of equal means experimenters might encounter. They show that the experimentwise error rate (chance, in percent, of falsely finding at least one significant difference among all pairs of random means) can be as high as 13 percent for Newman-Keuls and 22 percent for Duncan when the experimenter thinks it is .05! The reason these differences were not discovered in earlier simulations is that no one thought to look at several groups of equal means simultaneously. For further information, you should consult Scheffé (1959), Einot & Gabriel (1970), Begun & Gabriel (1981), Day and Quinn (1989), Hsu (1990) or the *Encyclopedia of Statistical Sciences* (1982) entries for "Multiple Comparison Procedures" and "Multiple Range and Associated Tests."

In recent references, the Tukey HSD test generally emerges as a favored alternative. It is easy to apply, has adequate power, and requires no special supplemental procedures. Here's how it works. Samples of a given size drawn from a normal population will show varied means. When repeated samples are drawn, the means will be distributed over a range; i.e., there will be an expected difference between the largest and smallest sample means. The expected difference will vary with the number of samples drawn and with the size of samples. The distribution of these sample ranges is called the **Studentized range**. The Tukey HSD simply compares the range of means in our study to a theoretical one composed of the same number of same-sized samples drawn from a single normal population. When sample groups differ in size, a conservative correction can be applied, which results in the so-called Tukey-Kramer test.

Figure 8.18 shows the application of the TUKEY procedure to our journal graph area data. Post-hoc tests are part of the HYPOTHESIS testing procedure in GLM. The results are printed as a pairwise triangular matrix. First come the differences between means. The largest absolute difference (-.207) is between the Social and Physical sciences and the smallest (.055) is between the Life and Physical sciences. The probabilities for each pair are listed below. They follow here (but not always) the pattern of mean differences. Using $p=.05$ as a conventional level, we can say that the only pairs which significantly differ are Social vs. Life, Mathematics vs. Physical, and Social vs. Physical.

Figure 8.18
Tukey Test of All Possible Pairs of Means

```
HYPOTHESIS
POST TYPE$ / TUKEY
TEST
```

```
COL/
ROW TYPE$
  1  Life
  2  Mathematics
  3  Physical
  4  Social
Using least squares means.
Post Hoc test of PAREA
---------------------------------------------------------------------------

Using model MSE of 0.007 with 43 DF.
Matrix of pairwise mean differences:

                       1           2           3           4
            1        0.0

            2       -0.088       0.0

            3        0.055       0.143       0.0

            4       -0.152      -0.064      -0.207       0.0


Tukey HSD Multiple Comparisons.
Matrix of pairwise comparison probabilities:

                       1           2           3           4
            1        1.000

            2        0.077       1.000

            3        0.385       0.000       1.000

            4        0.002       0.314       0.000       1.000
```

Notes

Box and stem-and-leaf plots

We described medians as middle or 50th percentile "values" and hinges as quartile or 25th and 75th percentile "values." This is only roughly true, as it often happens that the exact location of one or more of these "values" falls between two actual data points. For example, a sample of 12 cases may not have data points at the 25th, 50th, or 75th percentile. Moreover, quartiles (which are counted in from the ends of distributions) and hinges (which are counted out from the median) are not truly identical and will have slightly different values for some data. Those who have devised these plots have created conventions for assigning values to medians and hinges in these situations. If you are interested, Velleman and Hoaglin (1983) give a particularly clear account.

t tests

When a one-way analysis of variance contains only two levels, the probability value for the ordinary F test is equivalent to that for a t test. In fact, an F statistic with 1 and n degrees of freedom is equivalent to the square of a t statistic with n degrees of freedom. If you want to learn more about t tests, especially when variances differ among groups, consult the SYSTAT manual.

References

Bartlett, M.S. (1937). Some examples of statistical methods of research in agriculture and applied biology. *Journal of the Royal Statistical Society, Supplement 4*, 137-183.

Box, G.E.P., Hunter, W.G., and Hunter, J.S. (1978). *Statistics for Experimenters: An Introduction to Design, Data Analysis, and Model Building.* New York: John Wiley & Sons, Inc.

Chambers, J.M., Cleveland, W.S., Kleiner, B., and Tukey, P.A. (1983). *Graphical Methods for Data Analysis*. Belmont, CA: Wadsworth.

Cleveland, W.S. (1984). Graphs in scientific publications. *The American Statistician, 38*, 261-269.

Cleveland, W.S. (1985). Reply. *The American Statistician, 39*, 239.

Joiner, B. F. (1981) Lurking variables: Some examples. *The American Statistician, 35,* 227-233.

Levene, H. (1960). Robust tests for equality of variance. In I. Olkin (Ed.), *Contributions to Probability and Statistics.* Palo Alto, CA: Stanford University Press, 278-292.

Neter, J., Wasserman, W., and Kutner, M. (1990). *Applied Linear Statistical Models,* 3rd ed. Homewood, Illinois: Richard E. Irwin, Inc.

Stellman, S.D. (1985). Comment on "Graphs in scientific publications." *The American Statistician, 39,* 238.

9

Multi-Way ANOVA

Experimental studies frequently involve categorical and continuous data—for example, blood pressure is measured among patients given one of three drugs; productivity is measured among workers given new training materials and a control sample given the traditional materials; bar press rates of rats are measured under varied reinforcement protocols, etc. Each of these three examples would constitute a one-way ANOVA with a continuous dependent measure (blood pressure, productivity, bar press rate) predicted by a single categorical factor (drug, material, reinforcement schedule). The different treatments are the levels on the factor.

Experimental studies usually involve more than one factor, however. For example, different patients suffering from three different diseases are given one of the four drugs; new and experienced workers are given the different training materials; the type (e.g., food versus water) as well as the schedule of the reinforcement is varied among the rats, etc. These additional attributes (disease type, level of experience, reinforcement type) constitute separate factors.

Winer (1972) has long been a popular reference for ANOVA materials. Let's take a look at his example for the simplest form of multi-way ANOVA. The SYSTAT results and Winer's differ slightly because SYSTAT uses a more recently developed algorithm for computing the estimates. We'll learn how to get beyond the complex calculator formulas in Winer to the essence of the multi-way ANOVA model.

Figure 9.1 displays the data. In contrast to the data in the last chapter, we now have two categorical variables. METHOD denotes two different approaches to calibrating dials and BACK denotes four different levels of background illumination under which the experiment was conducted.

The dependent measure is ACCURACY, representing the accuracy of calibration for each observation. The design of this experiment is a complete one: all four BACK conditions were sampled under both METHOD conditions. Notice, however, that the numbers of subjects in the cells are not equal.

Figure 9.1
DIALS Data

CASE	METHOD	BACK	ACCURACY
1	1	1	3
2	1	1	4
3	1	1	6
4	1	1	7
5	1	2	5
6	1	2	6
7	1	2	6
8	1	2	7
9	1	2	7
10	1	3	4
11	1	3	6
12	1	3	8
13	1	3	8
14	1	4	8
15	1	4	10
16	1	4	10
17	1	4	7
18	1	4	11
19	2	1	2
20	2	1	3
21	2	1	4
22	2	2	3
23	2	2	5
24	2	2	6
25	2	2	3
26	2	3	9
27	2	3	12
28	2	3	12
29	2	3	8
30	2	4	9
31	2	4	7
32	2	4	12
33	2	4	11

9.1 ANOVA models for multiple factors

Constructing models

We need to consider two alternatives: an additive model and a multiplicative model. An additive model includes two or more factors to explain variation in the dependent variable. The model accounts for variation by summing effects from each factor. This means a prediction for a level of any factor is the same regardless of the levels chosen for other factors. A multiplicative model includes cross products between factors as well. That is, variation in the dependent variable is explained (at least in part) by products of factors. This model is more complex that the additive, but it allows for **interactions** among factors. In a multiplicative model, a prediction for a level of any factor depends on the levels chosen for other factors.

Additive (no interaction) models

One might have two simple, separable expectations for the outcome of this experiment: that one method is better than the other, and that a brighter background is better than a dimmer one. Figure 9.2 uses box plots to illustrate these expectations.

The left plot shows how ACCURACY varies by level of METHOD, the graphical equivalent to a one-way ANOVA. There is not much support here for any claims about the method one uses overall. The right plot shows how ACCURACY varies by the background, the graphical equivalent to second one-way ANOVA. Notice that the METHOD plot contains no information about BACK and the BACK plot contains no information on the METHOD factor.

Additive ANOVA incorporates these two factors into a single model like this:

```
MODEL ACCURACY = CONSTANT + METHOD + BACK
```

It is easy to see why this is called an **additive model**—the factors (categorical variables) are combined with a plus sign. There are no multiplications. Another term for this is a **main effects model** with METHOD and BACK taken to be main effect terms.

Figure 9.2
Box Plots for ACCURACY by Levels of Two Factors

```
USE DIALS
CATEGORY METHOD, BACK
BOX ACCURACY*METHOD, BACK
```

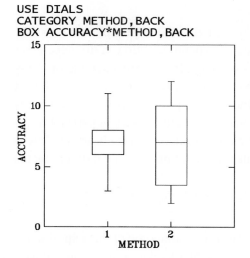 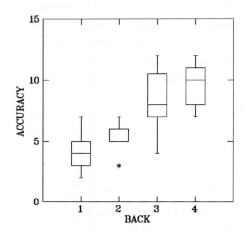

Multiplicative (interaction) models

If we analyze these data with an additive model, we risk ignoring the influence of one factor on the other. There may be no influence, but we should not prejudge this situation. Let's look at an alternative. Figure 9.3 shows ACCURACY by BACK box plots for each METHOD separately.

The left plot shows how ACCURACY varies by level of METHOD, the graphical equivalent to a one-way ANOVA. There is not much support here for any claims about the method one uses overall. The right plot shows how ACCURACY varies by the background, the graphical equivalent to second one-way ANOVA. Notice that the METHOD plot contains no information about BACK and the BACK plot contains no information on the METHOD factor.

Additive ANOVA incorporates these two factors into a single model like this:

```
MODEL ACCURACY = CONSTANT + METHOD + BACK
```

It is easy to see why this is called an **additive model**—the factors (categorical variables) are combined with a plus sign. There are no multiplications. Another term for this is a **main effects model** with METHOD and BACK taken to be main effect terms.

Figure 9.3
Box Plots of ACCURACY by METHOD

BOX ACCURACY*BACK / GROUP=METHOD

1   2

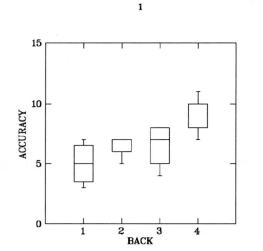
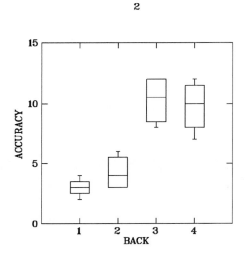

Box plots for additive models will show parallel lines if we connect the medians (center line of box) for each level of the factors. These two profiles of boxes do not appear to be parallel. The relation of ACCURACY to BACK is different for METHOD 1 than METHOD 2. We need a different model for these data.

Often researchers use a single line graph display with different symbols for the means of the groups. Unfortunately, these profile plots do not reveal the variability within each group the way box plots do. In many cases, trivial differences can be made to look dramatic. Nevertheless, these line graphs reveal clearly the nonparallelism that defines an interaction. Figure 9.4 shows one of these plots for Winer's data. We use the DOT (categorical plot) command, which displays means within category values.

Another way to reveal interaction is to display the means in a three-dimensional ribbon graph. In the ANOVA model, the continuous variable ACCURACY is a function of the categorical variables METHOD and BACK. A lattice can be constructed of the profiles connecting the combinations of treatments. If this lattice reveals a twisted surface, an interaction model would likely be needed to describe the systematic variability in the data. Figure 9.5 shows this to be the case. Notice how the ribbons are not parallel.

Figure 9.4
Profile Plot of Winer Data

DOT ACCURACY*BACK / GROUP=METHOD OVERLAY SYMBOL=1,4 SIZE=2,2

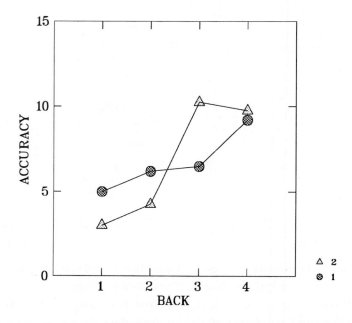

When results on one factor vary by levels on another factor, we say that there is an **interaction** between the two factors. The lines connecting cell means on a given factor level may diverge from the parallel in a number of ways: the lines may cross, or they may diverge or converge. But the presence of any type of interaction is sufficient to call the simple additive (parallel lines) model into question. Now a mathematical definition of parallelism is an ideal case we would not expect to see in real data. For statistical analysis we are interested in knowing how far off we are—that is, we want a test to tell us how likely it is that the variability in cell means at levels of factors (i.e., the departure from the parallel, the interaction) would occur in random data.

The algebraic interaction model includes the two independent sources shown in our additive model, plus a new element that estimates differences in cell means above and beyond differences in factor level means. Such a model is specified like this:

MODEL ACCURACY = CONSTANT + METHOD + BACK + METHOD*BACK

Figure 9.5
Three-Dimensional Plot of Winer Data Means

```
LINE ACCURACY*BACK*METHOD / TRANSPOSE ZGRID AXIS=CORNER
```

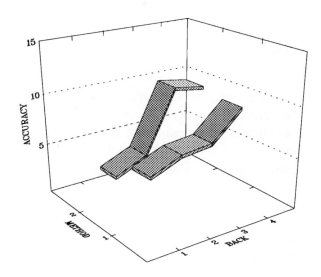

The last term of our new model, METHOD*BACK, is called an **interaction term**, and estimates the new information we desire: the variability of cell means that is distinct from the variability introduced by factor level means. Now we have a **multiplicative model**, as indicated by the multiplication sign between the METHOD and BACK factors in the interaction term.

An interaction is not a correlation. Some people think that variables that "interact" are, in ordinary language, "correlated." In experimental designs, factors are usually uncorrelated because we apply all combinations of treatments an equal number of times. Even in the Winer data, where the different numbers of cases within the groups make the factors somewhat correlated, the interaction has nothing to do with correlation. Interactions are more like a "synergy" between factors: the effect of one factor on the dependent variable appears enhanced at some levels of another factor, or dampened at other levels of the other factor.

What an interaction means to a given researcher with a particular set of data depends on the research context. In some research, interactions can be a nuisance or even troublesome: piecemeal findings that force us to qualify our conclusions. In other situations interactions are like gold: the expected outcome that supports the hypothesis under examination. For example, a drug may have one effect on blood pressure in males and a different effect in females. Years ago, this gender interaction was frequently ignored in pharmacological research. As a result, doctors prescribed the same drug to males and females. Now, gender interactions are routinely examined in experimental designs.

Estimating models

Figure 9.6 shows the commands and output that estimate two different models for these data: the one additive and the other containing a multiplicative interaction term. These two ANOVA tables contain more rows of entries than the one-way ANOVA table discussed in the previous chapter. There are also a few differences in interpretation that need explanation. Note that SYSTAT offers a shorthand method for requesting the full model in the lower panel of Figure 9.6. You can simply type

    ANOVA ACCURACY

instead of

    MODEL ACCURACY = CONSTANT + METHOD + BACK + METHOD*BACK

The output will be the same.

The sum of squares, degrees of freedom, and mean squares for the terms METHOD and BACK—called "main effect" terms—are computed and interpreted just as they would be for a one-way ANOVA on each given factor. That is, for each factor separately, differences are computed between the grand mean and factor level means, then squared and summed for every case in the data. The two-level METHOD factor requires the estimation of one mean beyond the grand mean and so requires only one degree of freedom, while the four-level BACK factor requires the estimation of three means beyond the grand mean and so three degrees of freedom. Mean squares are also straightforward, namely sum of squares divided by degrees of freedom for each term.

The METHOD*BACK row in the multiplicative model expresses a new set of differences. Here we are interested in how cell means differ from those predicted by factor level means. Consequently, the computed differences are those between each case's cell mean and that predicted by the means of its factor levels. Note that this is not the same as the difference between cell means and the grand mean; that difference subsumes all three of the kinds of difference we have been working to attribute to the separate terms of our model.

Figure 9.6
Additive and Multiplicative Two-Way ANOVAs

```
GLM
USE DIALS
REM ADDITIVE MODEL
CATEGORY METHOD BACK
MODEL ACCURACY=CONSTANT + METHOD + BACK
ESTIMATE
```

```
Categorical values encountered during processing are:
METHOD (2 levels)
        1,      2
BACK (4 levels)
        1,      2,      3,      4

Dep Var: ACCURACY N: 33 Multiple R:  0.754 Squared multiple R:  0.568
```

Analysis of Variance

Source	Sum-of-Squares	DF	Mean-Square	F-Ratio	P
METHOD	0.113	1	0.113	0.028	0.869
BACK	150.592	3	50.197	12.239	0.000
Error	114.841	28	4.101		

```
REM INTERACTION MODEL
  CATEGORY METHOD,BACK
  MODEL ACCURACY=CONSTANT+METHOD+BACK+METHOD*BACK
  SAVE DIALSRES / MODEL
  ESTIMATE
```

```
Categorical values encountered during processing are:
METHOD (2 levels)
        1,      2
BACK (4 levels)
        1,      2,      3,      4

Dep Var: ACCURACY N: 33 Multiple R:  0.856 Squared multiple R:  0.734
```

Analysis of Variance

Source	Sum-of-Squares	DF	Mean-Square	F-Ratio	P
METHOD	0.062	1	0.062	0.022	0.884
BACK	158.951	3	52.984	18.696	0.000
METHOD*BACK	43.991	3	14.664	5.174	0.006
Error	70.850	25	2.834		

```
Durbin-Watson D Statistic    2.252
First Order Autocorrelation  -0.165
Residuals have been saved.
```

Degrees of freedom for interaction terms are also slightly different. If we know the grand mean and the factor level means, then the model need not estimate every cell level mean; cell level means are constrained since their combinations must reproduce the corresponding factor level means. In fact, just as an interaction is a multiplicative term, so an interaction degrees of freedom reduces to the multiplication of degrees of freedom for the associated factors. Our factors have one and three degrees of freedom, so estimating the differences for the METHOD*BACK interaction requires one times three, or three degrees of freedom. After this, the mean squares are again simply the sum of squares divided by the associated degrees of freedom.

Note that these differences all refer to variability "between" means. Taken together these three elements—the sum of squares due to METHOD plus the sum of squares due to BACK plus the sum of squares due to METHOD*BACK—constitute the sum of squares between groups for our model. As our multi-way ANOVA has more than one term, the sum of squares between groups has been broken into more parts or components, but its overall interpretation is the same as discussed for the one-way example. It tells how much of all the variability in dependent variable scores is accounted for by the differences in means specified in our model.

The final differences are in the entries for the ERROR row. In the one-way example we referred to this as the variability "within." Just as in the one-way example, the sum of squares ERROR refers to the differences that remain after all systematic differences due to means have been removed.

The source of this variability is a bit simpler to understand for our multiplicative model than for the additive one. For this complete model—the one containing all the main effects and interactions—the estimate produces an analysis for cell means. In this case, variability "within" is simply the variability of dependent variable scores "within cells." In contrast, our additive model is incomplete—that is, one that does not include all the possible main and interaction effects—and the analysis stops short of estimating cell means.

In either model, the error term is derived the same way as in ordinary linear regression: through residual variation. This means that the ERROR for the *additive* model contains *interaction* sum of squares because we left the interaction term out of the model. Notice that the size of the error sum of squares for the additive model is comparable to the sum of the interaction model's error and interaction sum of squares. Because of this systematic variation in the error of the additive model, we could say that it misspecifies the data.

Degrees of freedom are all those not taken by the model (33 total minus 1 for the CONSTANT minus 1 for METHOD minus 3 for BACK leaves 28 for the ERROR term for the additive model and minus 3 more for the METHOD*BACK term leaves 25 for the ERROR term in the multiplicative model). And mean squares are sum of squares divided by degrees of freedom.

Testing models

We saw in one-way ANOVA that the total sum of squares can be partitioned into between and within components:

$$SS_T = SS_B + SS_W$$

Now we have broken it down into more elements:

$$SS_T = SS_{METHOD} + SS_{BACK} + SS_{METHOD*BACK} + SS_W$$

Since SS_T is a fixed quantity for a given set of data, there is only one place the additional explained variability can come from: the sum of squares within (ERROR) term. Thus adding terms to our model simultaneously increases the SS_B and decreases the SS_W (ERROR).

You can see the result of this by comparing the MULTIPLE R-SQUARE between our two models. As in one-way ANOVA, this statistic (also known as the coefficient of determination) summarizes how much variance is described by the model we estimate.

$$
\begin{aligned}
\text{R-SQUARE} \quad &= SS_B / SS_T \\
&= SS_B / (SS_B + SS_W)
\end{aligned}
$$

for the additive model SSB has two elements:

$$
\begin{aligned}
\text{R-SQUARE} \quad &= (SS_{METHOD} + SS_{BACK}) / ((SS_{METHOD} + SS_{BACK}) + SS_W) \\
&= (.113 + 150.592) / ((.113 + 150.592) + 114.841) \\
&= 150.705 / 265.546 \\
&= .568
\end{aligned}
$$

The additive model accounts for about 57% of the total variability in ACCURACY. The multiplicative model has one additional element:

$$
\begin{aligned}
\text{R-SQUARE} \quad &= (SS_{\text{METHOD}} + SS_{\text{BACK}} + SS_{\text{METHOD*BACK}})\, / \\
&\quad ((SS_{\text{METHOD}} + SS_{\text{BACK}} + SS_{\text{METHOD*BACK}}) + SS_{\text{W}}) \\
&= (.062 + 158.951 + 43.991)\, / \,((.062 + 158.951 + 43.991) + 70.850) \\
&= 203.004\, / \,273.854 \\
&= .741
\end{aligned}
$$

The multiplicative model accounts for about 74% of the variance in the data—a substantial improvement. (The missing cases in the data have made our model less than perfectly orthogonal, so that some of the "independent" terms overlap a bit. Consequently, our hand calculations describe slightly too much variance—74% versus SYSTAT's 73%. SYSTAT's estimates are the correct ones, of course.)

Does it seem that we are getting something for nothing—that just throwing in factors and interaction terms automatically produces a better fitting model? Yes, but... The MULTIPLE R-SQUARE does increase. For the F test there is a catch, however.

The F test is a ratio of mean squares, not sum of squares:

$$
F = MS_{\text{B}}\, /\, MS_{\text{W}}
$$

In this case we must consider not just the transfer of sum of squares into the model, but also the associated degrees of freedom. Consider what would happen if we were to transfer only a small amount of variability into the model (include a factor that showed only slight differences among its associated means) but at the cost of many degrees of freedom (e.g., a factor that has many levels). In the end our new ERROR mean square (i.e., MS_{W}) would be a slightly smaller sum of squares divided by a much smaller degrees of freedom. The result: a larger mean square error for the denominator of our F ratio and so a test that is substantially less able to discriminate significant differences. The DIALS dataset is different, however. Here an additional term, the METHOD*BACK interaction, carries a substantial sum of squares at the cost of but one degree of freedom.

You can see the impact of including the METHOD*BACK term by comparing the results of our additive and multiplicative models for the DIALS data. The BACK term that accounts for the virtually same mean square in both models nevertheless shows a larger F ratio and smaller probability of random occurrence in the multiplicative model. The interaction term has removed substantial variability from the ERROR term at the cost of few degrees of freedom, so the F test is more sensitive. Of course, if the interaction were not substantial, adding it to the model would not change the significance of the main effects the way it did here.

Selecting a best model

Most discussions of the analysis of variance assume the interaction model is always appropriate and present only the full, or complete factorial ANOVA table (lower panel of Figure 9.6). There are two reasons for doing this. First, we need the full model to test the significance of the interaction anyway, so we might as well do it straightaway. Second, for most factorial data, interactions really exist and it is important to model them.

It is possible, however, that an interaction does not exist in the experimental design and population we are sampling from. In these rare cases, adding the interaction is *overfitting* the model. We would be subtracting random error from the ERROR term and pretending it is systematic. The point of modeling is to fit a model that is appropriate to the data.

The submodels problem: loaves and fishes

Given this distinction between systematic and random variation, you may be wondering whether we should leave the BACK main effect in our model. The results in Figure 9.6 suggest that an appropriate model for these data could be:

$$\text{MODEL ACCURACY} = \text{CONSTANT} + \text{BACK} + \text{METHOD} * \text{BACK}$$

Should we go ahead and fit this model with the ESTIMATE command and publish the resulting incomplete ANOVA table? You can try it. The statistics will be similar to those for the complete model. This approach seems to turn everything Winer says about these data upside down. Some researchers would abhor including a factor in an interaction term when it isn't included as a main effect. Mathematically, however, there is nothing to prevent it.

Let's pursue this logic further. If we add more factors to a fully crossed design, the number of terms increases by a power of two. Consider:

$$\text{MODEL Y} = \text{CONSTANT} + A + B + A * B$$
$$\text{MODEL Y} = \text{CONSTANT} + A + B + C + A * B + A * C + B * C + A * B * C$$

and so on.

In general, there are $m = 2^k - 1$ terms (excluding the constant) in a complete model for k factors. For 3 factors, $m = 7$, for 4, $m = 15$. And for each of these complete models, there are $2^m - 1$ submodels. For 3 factors, there are already 127 submodels! Fortunately, the fully factorial design requires so many subjects (different ones in every cell) that researchers are usually discouraged from doing more than a three-way design.

We could use SYSTAT's stepwise regression option to do stepwise ANOVA. Only the "significant" terms would be included in the final model. There are problems with this approach—ones shared with stepwise regression itself. In modeling that is guided by the data, there is always the risk of being lured by random quirks. Nevertheless, estimating the full model with all the interactions on four or more factors is almost certainly going to result in overfitting. If you are doing ANOVA for purely exploratory or predictive purposes and intend to replicate your results, stepwise ANOVA is worth considering. Just use STEP instead of ESTIMATE in SYSTAT.

There are several approaches to limiting our choices of submodels and, therefore, protecting ourselves a bit from a fishing expedition. We have already seen one: consider only the k submodels, each omitting one of the main effects or interactions. This is what Winer and other conventional texts do when they present a full ANOVA table.

Another approach has been popular. Interaction terms express complex relations among factors and are often difficult to interpret, particularly for the three- and higher-way interaction terms that arise in complex study designs. For this reason experimenters seldom hold any real expectations for most of the interactions that might potentially arise in these models. And so the prevalent desire for most interaction terms in a model is that "they should go away." With this in mind, data analysts first specify a complete model that includes all the possible main and interaction effects. Thereafter, terms are examined beginning with the most complex interactions and proceeding down through increasingly simpler terms. Each term examined is dropped from the model if it appears to have no significant effect until the point is reached where the first significant effect is encountered. At that time the model is frozen. In some statistical packages this process is automated. Those that produce a "Type 1" sum of squares show a test on each term based on the sequence of terms in the MODEL statement. Terms to the right are not included in the hypothesis sum of squares. The error term is based on the full model that includes all the terms, however.

We think this is a dangerous procedure. First of all, using Type 1 sum of squares results in two different models: one for the hypothesis and one for the error. A single model is not being tested. Second, Fabian (1991) shows that even in the simplest two-way design, testing the interaction first and proceeding to an additive model if the interaction F statistic is not significant can lead to incorrect decisions when contrasting cell means using the model. If you choose an interaction model, you should stick with it even if the interaction is not significant.

Sometimes you may see research in which the analyst attempts to finesse this problem by limiting the hypotheses of the study. Since higher order interactions are hard to interpret, it is rare for researchers to have hypotheses for them. Consequently one might simply exclude from the first model all terms at this level of complexity. In the next chapter you will see that this logic for ignoring interaction terms underlies many of the classical experimental designs such as randomized blocks, Latin squares, fractional factorials. The risk here is obvious: the effects of any unestimated (and so unexamined) interactions that happen to occur in the data will remain and continue to lurk in the ERROR term. There they will simultaneously reduce the sensitivity of the tests on terms that are of interest and violate the assumptions under which the tests are performed.

You may be wondering what our position is on this matter. We'll do our best to evade the question. It depends. We are trying to point out that ANOVA is a particular type of regression model. Some researchers want to put blinders on when using it. Many mistakenly think, for example, that regression is for correlational (associative) data and ANOVA is for experimental (causal) data. Or they mistakenly think that regression is exploratory and ANOVA confirmatory. Some researchers who abhor adding product variables or polynomials to a regression model don't realize that adding interactions is a similar operation. In summary, for experimental designs involving a few factors and a sufficient number of subjects, fitting the full interaction model is preferable. For situations where prediction from the model is a goal and tests on cell means are not desired, the submodel/stepwise approach can make sense.

Protecting the experimentwise error rate

Any time you see an ANOVA table with more than one or two tests of significance, an alarm should go off in your head. Researchers who are sensitive to the warnings about experimentwise error rate when doing too many *t* tests or other tests of significance forget that the same warnings apply to the *F* tests in a single ANOVA table. If an ANOVA table contained 20 independent *F* tests on random data, then one of them would be expected to be significant at the .05 level by chance. This is an unlikely scenario because in factorial designs the *F* tests are correlated (they share the same error term). Thus, it is possible that even more than one *F* statistic would be expected to be significant at the conventional level by chance.

This problem is not discussed in most ANOVA textbooks, except for those covering industrial design for quality control. In that field, normal probability plots are used to locate "significant" effects. The SYSTAT manual gives an example under "Single Degree of Freedom Designs." A simpler protection method is to use a Bonferroni procedure. First count the number of tests and divide the criterion p value by this number to get a protected p value.

The Bonferroni procedure will lack power on designs with many factors, however. For the DIALS study, with only two factors and three terms, the Bonferroni procedure is reasonable. If we wish to set our risk of mistaking random differences for systematic effects at $p = .05$, then evaluating our three-term model will require a p of .05/3 or .017. The ANOVA table for the multiplicative model in Figure 9.6 shows two of three terms have high F ratios and low probabilities. The interaction term METHOD*BACK has a clearly significant effect and must be included in a model for these data. By our conventional decision process we retain this term as well as the two simpler main effect terms that involve the interacting factors. Thus we retain the whole of the multiplicative model as it was originally specified and dispense with the additive model in further analysis.

Interpreting the ANOVA

In interpreting effects, it helps to follow the same "complex to simple" logic we sometimes use to decide whether a term belongs in a model. That is, we interpret only the most complex term that has been retained in our model—in our case the METHOD*BACK interaction term. It is easy to see why this must be so if you recall what each term expresses. The significant main-effect METHOD term expresses a difference in ACCURACY due to METHOD, regardless of the level of BACK. But the significant term for the interaction between these two factors makes it clear that this is a misleading statement. As we saw in the original box plots, and confirmed in our F tests, the change in ACCURACY with levels of ILLUMINATION depends on the kind of METHOD involved: there is an increase in accuracy for levels of illumination with METHOD=1 but a strong split between the two lower levels of illumination and the two higher levels of illumination with METHOD = 2.

9.2 Checking assumptions

Now we want to check that our full model meets the required assumptions for using F tests: normal distribution of errors, homogeneous variance about all levels of the estimate, a proper inclusion of all (and only) the systematic effects that affect the dependent variable, and independence of the errors across cells. As usual, we will examine the residuals to test these assumptions. In Figure 9.6 we prepared for this by using a SAVE statement to get a new file containing the ESTIMATE and RESIDUAL variables. These two variables are just the same as in a one-way analysis. The ESTIMATE contains the values that are due to our model: for the multiplicative model these are the means for the individual cells of cases. The RESIDUAL contains what is left: the amount and direction that each case's actual dependent value differs from the mean that has been estimated for it. Figure 9.7 shows a standard residual plot of the RESIDUALs on the ESTIMATEs. Since our model contained eight cell means our plot has eight vertical strips, one for each cell, ordered by the size of mean ACCURACY.

There appear to be no grounds for concern about the homogeneity of the residuals. From group to group the spread of values is comparable. Nor do there appear to be any extreme values. Since the steps for evaluating residuals from multi-way ANOVAs are the same as for our one-way example, we will not repeat them here. You should try the procedures in Chapter 9 on these residuals as an exercise. For the Levene test of homogeneity of residuals, remember that the ANOVA on the absolute value of the residuals must involve the factorial structure. Your MODEL should be the same as the one used for the original analysis, except the dependent variable should be the absolute value of RESIDUAL.

9.3 Understanding the design matrix

Let's look at the dummy variables SYSTAT constructed to analyze Winer's DIALS data. Figure 9.8 shows the design variables contained in the file DIALSRES that was produced when we used the option SAVE DIALSRES / MODEL in Figure 9.6. The variables $X(1)$ through $X(7)$ are composed of the elements -1, 0 and 1. We have included the original categorical variables METHOD and BACK for reference and have put bold titles over the columns containing the design matrix and have highlighted the cells. We have omitted the CONSTANT in Figure 9.8. It is simply a column of 1's.

Figure 9.7
Residual Plot for Multiplicative Preliminary ANOVA

```
USE DIALSRES
PLOT RESIDUAL*ESTIMATE / SYMBOL=1
```

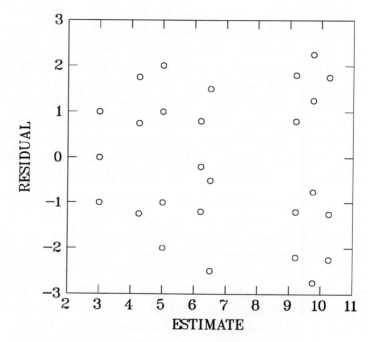

How did these get constructed? The M1 and B1 and B2 variables were each done the same way as the dummy variables for the one-way design in Chapter 9. M1 has the value 1 for any case in METHOD 1, and -1 for any case in METHOD 2. B1, B2, and B3 work similarly. The interaction variables M1B1 through M1B3 are simply the products of the respective marginal variables M1 and B1, B2, B3.

Figure 9.8
Design Matrix for DIALS DATA

CASE	METHOD	BACK	M1 X(1)	B1 X(2)	B2 X(3)	B3 X(4)	M1B1 X(5)	M1B2 X(6)	M1B3 X(7)
1	1	1	1	1	0	0	1	0	0
2	1	1	1	1	0	0	1	0	0
3	1	1	1	1	0	0	1	0	0
4	1	1	1	1	0	0	1	0	0
5	1	2	1	0	1	0	0	1	0
6	1	2	1	0	1	0	0	1	0
7	1	2	1	0	1	0	0	1	0
8	1	2	1	0	1	0	0	1	0
9	1	2	1	0	1	0	0	1	0
10	1	3	1	0	0	1	0	0	1
11	1	3	1	0	0	1	0	0	1
12	1	3	1	0	0	1	0	0	1
13	1	3	1	0	0	1	0	0	1
14	1	4	1	-1	-1	-1	-1	-1	-1
15	1	4	1	-1	-1	-1	-1	-1	-1
16	1	4	1	-1	-1	-1	-1	-1	-1
17	1	4	1	-1	-1	-1	-1	-1	-1
18	1	4	1	-1	-1	-1	-1	-1	-1
19	2	1	-1	1	0	0	-1	0	0
20	2	1	-1	1	0	0	-1	0	0
21	2	1	-1	1	0	0	-1	0	0
22	2	2	-1	0	1	0	0	-1	0
23	2	2	-1	0	1	0	0	-1	0
24	2	2	-1	0	1	0	0	-1	0
25	2	2	-1	0	1	0	0	-1	0
26	2	3	-1	0	0	1	0	0	-1
27	2	3	-1	0	0	1	0	0	-1
28	2	3	-1	0	0	1	0	0	-1
29	2	3	-1	0	0	1	0	0	-1
30	2	4	-1	-1	-1	-1	1	1	1
31	2	4	-1	-1	-1	-1	1	1	1
32	2	4	-1	-1	-1	-1	1	1	1
33	2	4	-1	-1	-1	-1	1	1	1

If we had specified PRINT=LONG before estimating our model, we would have seen the regression coefficients for each of these design variables. They would have looked like this for the DIALS data:

```
ESTIMATES OF EFFECTS   B = (X'X)
X'Y)

                   ACCURACY

   CONSTANT            6.769

    METHOD     1      -0.044

      BACK     1      -2.769

      BACK     2      -1.544

      BACK     3       1.606

    METHOD     1
      BACK     1       1.044

    METHOD     1
      BACK     2       1.019

    METHOD     1
      BACK     3      -1.831
```

The value for the CONSTANT (6.769) is the overall grand mean of the ACCURACY scores. The value for METHOD 1 (-.044) is the amount the mean for the first METH-OD (ignoring BACK) is below the grand mean. This implies that the second METHOD is the same amount *above* the grand mean, so it is not estimated separately. The same interpretation applies to the effects for BACK. Finally, the values for the interactions are the amounts that the cell means differ from those that would be predicted by an additive model. If the additive model fit the cell means of these data perfectly, these values would be zero. Now, the tests in the lower ANOVA table in Figure 9.4   are equivalent to the hypotheses that each respective block of effects (coefficients) are simultaneously equal to zero. Each has the same degrees of freedom as the number of design variables.

This design matrix has been constructed using the **effects model**. Chapter 9 outlines this model algebraically and contrasts it with the **means model**. We also pointed out there that many people find the effects model difficult to understand, even though it is the default coding for SYSTAT and most least squares ANOVA programs. Indeed, if you have found this section difficult, you should not worry too much. The GLM commands for contrasting means will do all the algebraic work for you anyway.

9.4 Analyzing patterns of means

Does the arrangement of means in our results conform to our expectations? In the previous chapter we used box plots, single degree of freedom tests and multiple comparison procedures to answer this question. You have already seen that box plots can be just as useful with multi-way ANOVAs as they were for one-way ANOVAs; single degree of freedom tests and multiple comparison procedures will also prove useful.

Main effects

With a one-way ANOVA we were able to contrast differences in means on a single factor by using SYSTAT's CONTRAST statement. In a multi-way ANOVA we can also use the CONTRAST statement, but only when we wish to contrast between levels on a single factor. The means we are contrasting are often called **marginal means**. They are computed for the levels of a factor by ignoring the other factor(s). We are going to show you how to compute these main effect hypotheses on the DIALS data, but we will see that they are misleading because there is a substantial interaction between BACK and METHOD. Before we compute simple hypotheses on BACK separately for the two different levels of METHOD, however, let's see how hypotheses on main effects are handled when there is no interaction.

Comparisons

For example if we wanted to contrast BACK=1 against BACK=4 regardless of the METHOD used, we would use the statements:

```
HYPOTHESIS
EFFECT=BACK
CONTRAST [-1 0 0 1]
TEST
```

The only difference from the one-way case is the EFFECT=BACK statement, which tells SYSTAT where to place the contrast.

Tests of trend

When the levels of a factor are ordered, it is often meaningful to test them for the type of trend they represent. This can be done with a set of weights called **orthogonal polynomials**. For example, the BACK factor represents intensity of background illumination. We can ask what happens to accuracy if we increase background illumination. Does accuracy increase? Or, does accuracy decrease and then increase? Or, does it increase, decrease, and increase again?

The lower three panels of Figure 9.9 shows these hypotheses as smooth functions, which were plotted from polynomial equations. We can test one fewer polynomials than levels of our factor. Thus, with only four levels, we cannot test the possibility represented by the top two curves in Figure 9.9. It's another degrees of freedom problem. If you think a bit, you will see that you can test only as many polynomials as there are degrees of freedom in the factor because each bend (plus the ends) must be represented by a data point.

Figure 9.9
Orthogonal Polynomials

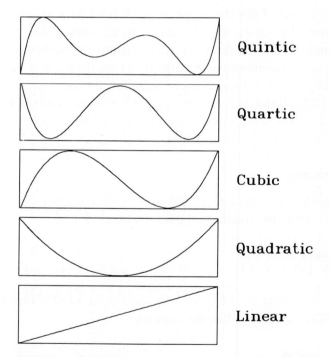

Quintic

Quartic

Cubic

Quadratic

Linear

Many ANOVA books, like Winer's, include tables of integer values for these polynomials. You can use them with the CONTRAST statement to test for trend. Here is an example of a linear trend:

```
HYPOTHESIS
EFFECT=BACK
CONTRAST [-3 -1 1 3]
TEST
```

Here is a quadratic:

```
HYPOTHESIS
EFFECT=BACK
CONTRAST [2 -1 -1 2]
TEST
```

Notice how the pattern of contrasts follows the quadratic curve in Figure 9.9. The end points are high (2) and the middle two are low (-1).

SYSTAT will compute the polynomial values automatically if you do it this way:

```
HYPOTHESIS
EFFECT=BACK
CONTRAST=POLYNOMIAL / ORDER=2
TEST
```

Whatever number you choose for the ORDER option will be the degree of the polynomial. If you forget the ORDER option, SYSTAT will compute all the polynomials and the resulting F value will be identical to the BACK main effect because the polynomials together soak up all the sum of squares for the factor. If you want to test several single degree of freedom polynomials, use a separate HYPOTHESIS paragraph for each.

Simple effects

The CONTRAST statement works with main effects on factors taken one at a time, but when there is an interaction between two or more factors we need to contrast cell means within levels of the interacting factor(s). The presence of the interaction effect means that there can be no simple statement about BACK ignoring METHOD. When an interaction is present, we need to use a method that allows us to refer to individual cells defined by levels on two or more factors. SYSTAT allows us to do this in several ways, but the SPECIFY statement is the easiest.

Figure 9.10 shows the test of the first level of BACK against the fourth within METHOD=1 and METHOD=2 separately. The syntax of the algebraic statement is very flexible. The following two statements are equivalent:

```
METHOD[1]BACK[1]=METHOD[1]BACK[4]
METHOD[1]BACK[1]-METHOD[1]BACK[4]=0
```

Figure 9.10
Contrasting Cell Means of Winer DIALS Data

```
HYPOTHESIS
SPECIFY [METHOD[1]BACK[1]=METHOD[1]BACK[4]]
TEST
```

|Hypothesis estimate|=   4.200 SE=   1.129

Hypothesis.

A Matrix

	1	2	3	4	5
	0.0	0.0	−2.000	−1.000	−1.000

	6	7	8
	−2.000	−1.000	−1.000

Null hypothesis value for D
                0.0

Null hypothesis contrast AB−D
                4.200

Inverse contrast $A(X'X)^{-1}A'$
                0.450

Test of Hypothesis

Source	SS	DF	MS	F	P
Hypothesis	39.200	1	39.200	13.832	0.001
Error	70.850	25	2.834		

```
HYPOTHESIS
SPECIFY [METHOD[2]BACK[1]=METHOD[2]BACK[4]]
TEST
```

|Hypothesis estimate|=	4.200 SE=	1.129

Hypothesis.

A Matrix

1	2	3	4	5
0.0	0.0	-2.000	-1.000	-1.000

6	7	8
-2.000	-1.000	-1.000

Null hypothesis value for D
    0.0

Null hypothesis contrast AB-D
    4.200

Inverse contrast $A(X'X)^{-1}A'$
    0.450

Test of Hypothesis

Source	SS	DF	MS	F	P
Hypothesis	39.200	1	39.200	13.832	0.001
Error	70.850	25	2.834		

If you are comparing these results to Winer's you will find that he expresses his test in terms of a t distribution. This is simply a special case of the F distribution, however, and can be easily translated. The square root of SYSTAT's F of 13.832 equals 3.719, which is within rounding error of Winer's t value of 3.73. (The rounding error is introduced by Winer's use of hand-figured means; SYSTAT's answer is more precise.) In any event you can check in any set of statistical tables that, at equivalent degrees of freedom, probability values for a t of 3.719 (or 3.73) and an F of 13.832 are identical and that t's are indeed the square roots of Fs.

You can use a similar approach to test the linear hypothesis mentioned in the last section: is there a linear increase in ACCURACY across equally spaced values of BACK illumination? The respective contrasts for the SPECIFY statements are:

```
  -3*METHOD[1]BACK[1]  -  1*METHOD[1]BACK[2],
  + 1*METHOD[1]BACK[3]  + 3*METHOD[1]BACK[4]=0
```

and

```
  -3*METHOD[2]BACK[1]  -  1*METHOD[2]BACK[2],
  + 1*METHOD[2]BACK[3]  + 3*METHOD[2]BACK[4]=0
```

If you do these, you will find that they are both highly significant.

Multiple comparison procedures in multifactor studies

Sometimes we have no prior hypotheses concerning contrasts among means. We simply want to compare all possible means on a factor to see which pairs are significantly different. We pay dearly for this lack of forethought because we must condition the p values on the number of tests we must do to get all pairs. It is better to do a smaller number of planned comparisons than to use multiple comparison methods involving all pairs. Nevertheless, it is even worse to select a small number of "planned" comparisons by looking at the data. Either decide in advance that you want to investigate only a few comparisons, or protect yourself by using a multiple comparison method.

The multiple comparison method for all possible pairs of means that is most highly regarded among statisticians is Tukey's HSD procedure. SYSTAT offers the Tukey/ Kramer version, which is appropriately conservative for cases with unequal cell sizes and is exactly Tukey's method when cell sizes are equal. The usual way to apply it is to use the HYPOTHESIS paragraph:

```
HYPOTHESIS
POST BACK / TUKEY
TEST
```

There's a catch. As with the planned comparisons, we have to do these on the simple effects, not the main effects because the interaction is significant. Thus, Figure 9.11 shows a different post-hoc command:

```
POST METHOD*BACK / TUKEY.
```

This compares all possible cells within the design. We are wasting a little power by comparing cells under METHOD=1 with those under METHOD=2, but overall, the same comparisons in Figure 9.10 are significant here.

Sometimes we wish to make comparisons only with a control group. If BACK=1 were our control, we could do this with the DUNNETT option:

```
POST BACK / DUNNETT,CONTROL=1
```

Unfortunately, this can be done only if the interaction is not significant, which is not the case here. All we could do would be to split the design into two one-way ANOVAs (one for each METHOD) and then do the DUNNETT test.

Figure 9.11
Tukey/Kramer HSD Test on Cell Means of Winer DIALS Data

```
HYPOTHESIS
POST METHOD*BACK / TUKEY
TEST
```

```
COL/
ROW METHOD      BACK
  1   1           1
  2   1           2
  3   1           3
  4   1           4
  5   2           1
  6   2           2
  7   2           3
  8   2           4
Using least squares means.
Post Hoc test of ACCURACY
------------------------------------------------------------------------

Using model MSE of 2.834 with 25 DF.
Matrix of pairwise mean differences:
```

	1	2	3	4	5
1	0.0				
2	1.200	0.0			
3	1.500	0.300	0.0		
4	4.200	3.000	2.700	0.0	
5	−2.000	−3.200	−3.500	−6.200	0.0
6	−0.750	−1.950	−2.250	−4.950	1.250
7	5.250	4.050	3.750	1.050	7.250
8	4.750	3.550	3.250	0.550	6.750

	6	7	8
6	0.0		
7	6.000	0.0	
8	5.500	−0.500	0.0

```
Tukey HSD Multiple Comparisons.
Matrix of pairwise comparison probabilities:
```

	1	2	3	4	5
1	1.000				
2	0.959	1.000			
3	0.905	1.000	1.000		
4	0.019	0.135	0.288	1.000	
5	0.771	0.201	0.162	0.001	1.000
6	0.998	0.671	0.569	0.004	0.974
7	0.004	0.026	0.069	0.980	0.000
8	0.010	0.070	0.160	1.000	0.001

	6	7	8
6	1.000		
7	0.001	1.000	
8	0.002	1.000	1.000

9.5 Unequal numbers of cases

Winer's DIALS data do not contain an equal number of subjects in every cell. In comparing the initial additive model to the one containing an interaction term we saw some very small changes in the sum of squares and mean squares for the main effect terms. For example, some of the variance that was contained in the BACK term in the additive model has disappeared into other terms in the interaction model. Yet the size of the change was negligible. These are the kinds of slight perturbations that can be expected (and accepted) when cell counts differ by a few cases.

When the differences are severe, these kinds of changes become pronounced and difficult to manage. Dropping or adding terms will change not only the sum of squares ERROR term, but also the sum of squares for any or all of the simpler effects retained in the model. Main effect and interaction terms that appear significant in one model will become nonsignificant in another model that adds or drops a single term containing a different factor. This problem occurs in multiple regression models with correlated predictors.

In addition, when cell counts are unbalanced across rows or columns, the total sum of squares will not be equal to the sum of the within and between. This confuses users who were trained to do ANOVA on calculators, because the usual old formulas are not appropriate for unbalanced designs.

SYSTAT produces the least squares estimates of effects that are appropriate for unbalanced designs. If you decide to test submodels, however, as we discussed early in this chapter, you must keep in mind that you will run into problems with overlapping variance. We feel that unless you are a professional statistician who knows about these problems, it is safer to stay with the full model and use the default F statistics in the SYSTAT ANOVA table in these cases.

9.6 Missing cells

The extreme example of an unbalanced design is one with one or more missing cells. In this case, the full model cannot be estimated. In fact, if you try to use the ordinary MODEL statement with data which are missing cells, you will get an error message:

```
ERROR: A MATRIX IN YOUR SYSTEM IS SINGULAR
```

In this case, you must use the MEANS option on your MODEL statement to handle missing cells. There are several examples in the SYSTAT manual.

Missing cells designs go beyond the scope of this book. Nevertheless, there are some examples you can compute if you keep in mind some basic rules. First, estimate a cell means model with the MEANS option to MODEL. SYSTAT will automatically code the design matrix with the cell means method and delete columns which represent empty cells. It will print an ANOVA table for the reduced model. Then, you must compute tests of main effects and interactions separately with the SPECIFY statement in the HYPOTHESIS paragraph.

For main effects, you must compute a contrast for each degree of freedom. Each contrast should be summed over all other factors which contain nonmissing cells for the selected contrast. For example, let's assume we have a a 4 (A) by 2 (B) design. Here are three typical contrasts on the cell means which test the A main effect. Notice that they sum over B:

A1B1	A2B1	A3B1	A4B1	A1B2	A2B2	A3B2	A4B2
1	-1	0	0	1	-1	0	0
0	1	-1	0	0	1	-1	0
0	0	1	-1	0	0	1	-1

For each single degree of freedom contrast, you need to use a separate algebraic statement after SPECIFY. Here is an example which implements the above contrasts. Notice that the zero terms are omitted and that signs of the terms involving the A factor are the same as in the above matrix:

$$A[1]B[1] - A[2]B[1] + A[1]B[2] - A[2]B[2] = 0$$
$$A[2]B[1] - A[3]B[1] + A[2]B[2] - A[3]B[2] = 0$$
$$A[3]B[1] - A[4]B[1] + A[3]B[2] - A[4]B[2] = 0$$

Now, if this design is missing cell $A[3]B[1]$, delete it from the complete set along with the other cell it is being contrasted against. This leaves a reduced set containing only the complementary subscripts:

$$A[1]B[1] - A[2]B[1] + A[1]B[2] - A[2]B[2] = 0$$
$$A[2]B[2] - A[3]B[2] = 0$$
$$A[3]B[2] - A[4]B[2] = 0$$

or, if you wish,

$$A[1]B[1] + A[1]B[2] = A[2]B[1] - A[2]B[2]$$
$$A[2]B[2] = A[3]B[2]$$
$$A[3]B[2] = A[4]B[2]$$

The contrasts for B look like this:

A1B1	A2B1	A3B1	A4B1	A1B2	A2B2	A3B2	A4B2
1	1	1	1	-1	-1	-1	-1

and the full set of SPECIFY statements looks like this:

$$A[1]B[1] + A[2]B[1] + A[3]B[1] + A[4]B[1] - A[1]B[2] - A[2]B[2] - A[3]B[2] - A[4]B[2] = 0$$

Missing cell $A[3]B[1]$ leaves us with a reduced set like this:

$$A[1]B[1] + A[2]B[1] + A[4]B[1] - A[1]B[2] - A[2]B[2] - A[4]B[2] = 0$$

or, if you wish,

$$A[1]B[1] + A[2]B[1] + A[4]B[1] = A[1]B[2] + A[2]B[2] + A[4]B[2]$$

Finally, for interactions you need contrasts of contrasts. These must be computed across other factors which contain nonmissing cells as well. Here are interaction contrasts:

A1B1	A2B1	A3B1	A4B1	A1B2	A2B2	A3B2	A4B2
1	-1	0	0	-1	1	0	0
0	1	-1	0	0	-1	1	0
0	0	1	-1	0	0	-1	1

and the corresponding SPECIFY statements:

$$A[1]B[1] - A[2]B[1] - A[1]B[2] + A[2]B[2] = 0$$
$$A[2]B[1] - A[3]B[1] - A[2]B[2] + A[3]B[2] = 0$$
$$A[3]B[1] - A[4]B[1] - A[3]B[2] + A[4]B[2] = 0$$

Missing cell A[3]B[1] leaves us with a reduced set like this:

$$A[1]B[1] - A[2]B[1] - A[1]B[2] + A[2]B[2] = 0$$
$$A[1]B[1] - A[2]B[1] - A[1]B[4] + A[2]B[4] = 0$$

or, if you wish,

$$A[1]B[1] + A[2]B[2] = A[2]B[1] + A[1]B[2]$$
$$A[1]B[1] + A[2]B[4] = A[2]B[1] + A[1]B[4]$$

Notice that we lost one degree of freedom for the interaction. We must pay a price for losing one cell. In general, each lost cell costs a degree of freedom. Furthermore, the subscripts have become permuted. We had to look around to find a combination of four nonmissing cells to contrast for each degree of freedom of the interaction. It's like searching on a checkerboard for patterns of four cells. This permutation problem is what makes missing cells designs so difficult even for professional statisticians. There are automatic algorithms for computing "Type IV" sums of squares, which is what we are doing here by hand, but they are not always correct for every design. If you are uncertain and must analyze missing cells designs, it is worth consulting a professional statistician.

Figure 9.12 shows how to analyze the DIALS data after we eliminate the cell for METHOD[1]BACK[4]. We use the BASIC procedure to delete this cell and then hand the new dataset over to GLM. The overall ANOVA table informs us that there are cells missing. We then must construct the specific hypotheses for the main effects and interactions. If you need to do a missing cell analysis with SYSTAT and are uncomfortable with the theory, you can hand this example to a statistician for guidance.

Figure 9.12
ANOVA of Winer DIALS Data with Cell (1,4) Missing

```
BASIC
    USE DIALS
    SAVE MISDIALS
    IF METHOD=1 AND BACK=4 THEN DELETE
    RUN

GLM
    USE MISDIALS
    MODEL ACCURACY=METHOD*BACK/MEANS
    CATEGORY METHOD,BACK
    ESTIMATE

HYPOTHESIS
    NOTE 'TEST OF METHOD'
    SPECIFY [METHOD[1]BACK[1] + METHOD[1]BACK[2] +,
            METHOD[1]BACK[3] =, METHOD[2]BACK[1] +,
            METHOD[2]BACK[2] + METHOD[2]BACK[3]]
    TEST

HYPOTHESIS
    NOTE 'TEST OF BACK'
    SPECIFY [METHOD[1]BACK[1] + METHOD[2]BACK[1] =.
            METHOD[1]BACK[2] + METHOD[2]BACK[2];
            METHOD[1]BACK[2] + METHOD[2]BACK[2] =,
            METHOD[1]BACK[3] + METHOD[2]BACK[3];
            METHOD[2]BACK[3] = METHOD[2]BACK[4]]
    TEST

HYPOTHESIS
    NOTE 'TEST OF METHOD*BACK'
    SPECIFY [METHOD[1]BACK[1] - METHOD[2]BACK[1] =,
            METHOD[1]BACK[2] -METHOD[2]BACK[2];
            METHOD[1]BACK[2] - METHOD[2]BACK[2] =,
            METHOD[1]BACK[3] - METHOD[2]BACK[3]]
    TEST
```

```
Categorical values encountered during processing are:
METHOD (2 levels)
        1,        2
BACK (4 levels)
        1,        2,        3,        4

Number of cases processed: 28
Means Model


Dep Var: ACCURACY N: 28 Multiple R:  0.856 Squared multiple R:  0.733

Ho: All means equal.

                    Unweighted Means Model

                    Analysis of Variance


Source      Sum-of-Squares   DF  Mean-Square    F-Ratio      P
Model           164.914       6     27.486        9.612     0.000
Error            60.050      21      2.860
------------------------------------------------------------------------


                        TEST OF METHOD
Contrasting using unweighted means.
Hypothesis.

A Matrix

                    1           2           3         4         5
                 -1.000      -1.000      -1.000     1.000     1.000


                    6           7
                 1.000       0.0

Null hypothesis value for D
                 0.0

Test of Hypothesis

       Source        SS        DF       MS          F            P

    Hypothesis     0.026       1      0.026       0.009        0.925
    Error         60.050      21      2.860
```

```
Contrasting using unweighted means.
Hypothesis.

A Matrix

                    1        2        3        4        5
        1        -1.000    1.000    0.0     -1.000    1.000

        2         0.0     -1.000    1.000    0.0     -1.000

        3         0.0      0.0      0.0      0.0      0.0


                    6        7
        1         0.0      0.0

        2         1.000    0.0

        3        -1.000    1.000

D Matrix

        1         0.0

        2         0.0

        3         0.0

Test of Hypothesis

        Source      SS       DF       MS            F            P

      Hypothesis   86.831    3      28.944        10.122        0.000
      Error        60.050   21       2.860
    --------------------------------------------------------------------

                        TEST OF METHOD*BACK
Contrasting using unweighted means.
Hypothesis.

A Matrix

                    1        2        3        4        5
        1        -1.000    1.000    0.0      1.000   -1.000

        2         0.0     -1.000    1.000    0.0      1.000
```

Further reading

Neter, Wasserman & Kutner (1985) provide the best integration of one-way and multi-way ANOVA. More elementary introductions are Bowerman and O'Connell (1990) and Keppel (1991).

References

Bowerman, B.L., and O'Connell, R.T. (1990). *Linear Statistical Models: An Applied Approach.* Boston: PWS-Kent.

Keppel, G. (1991). *Design and Analysis: A Researcher's Handbook.* Englewood Cliffs, NJ: Prentice-Hall.

Neter, J., Wasserman, W., and Kutner, M. (1985). *Applied Linear Statistical Models* (2nd ed.). Homewood, IL: Richard E. Irwin, Inc.

Winer, B.J. (1971). *Statistical Principles in Experimental Design* (2nd ed.). New York: McGraw-Hill.

10

Univariate Analysis of Experimental Data

Using more advanced ANOVA models is often an art of leaving things out. At their simplest are models with one or more interaction effects deleted. We have already seen one example of this when we considered the main effects model for the DIALS data in the last chapter. In that case we chose between the simpler and the more complete (multiplicative) model after considering the results with different models. In this chapter we will consider data where prior knowledge affects our choice of a suitable model. Many of these models require few new concepts. In the last section of this chapter, however, we will consider complications that arise when some factors represent "random" effects. The issues raised there are more difficult and will require more extended comments. Let's start with some definitions.

10.1 Glossary of terms for ANOVA models

Aspects of designs

By designs, we refer to plans that are applied when data are collected. The choice of a design will impose necessary constraints on the choice of a model.

Complete design (also called **complete factorial design**). This is a design in which cases are included to represent all combinations of factor levels.

Incomplete design. This is a design in which some combination(s) of factor levels are not collected. This can arise out of choice (the researcher has no interest in certain combinations of factors) or necessity (certain combinations of factor levels were unavailable or logically impossible).

Aspects of models

By models, we refer to the set of effects specified in SYSTAT's GLM (MGLH) MODEL statement: the combination of main and interaction effects specified for the calculation of a given ANOVA.

Complete models. These are models which include main and interaction effects for all combinations of factors in a study. Note that, in our usage, a complete model can only be estimated if the data are collected in a complete design (see above).

Incomplete models. These are models in which some interactions among factors are not analyzed. Incomplete models can arise by choice (potentially estimable effects are left out of the model statement in analyzing a complete design) or by necessity (the study represents an incomplete design and so not all means pertinent to a given interaction effect can be estimated).

Saturated models. These are models in which all available degrees of freedom are used in accounting for the effects specified. In such a model there are as many means estimated as there are data points and there is no independent estimate of error variance. These models can be analyzed if 1) some terms are assumed to account for no systematic variance and thus can be used to obtain an estimate of error variance, or 2) we have a known error variance external to our data (presumably from prior research) we can test terms against.

Aspects of factors

By factors, we refer to the facets of a design which result in categorical variables in a model. The model for the GRAPHS data in Chapter 9 contained one factor: TYPE$. That for the DIALS data in Chapter 10 contained two: METHOD and BACK.

Treatment factors. These are factors whose levels describe a difference administered by the researcher in the course of an experiment. Examples are a factor whose levels represent the administration of different drugs or one whose levels represent the application of different instructional methods. The simplest treatment factor contains an experimental and control condition the experimenter uses to manipulate the presence or absence of a treatment.

Blocking factors. These are factors whose levels describe some characteristic of cases that was not under experimental control. Examples would be gender, age, geographical location, or time of treatment. Factors representing treatment versus blocking effects require no differences in the application of statistical models. However, the term blocking factor is often used more narrowly to refer to a factor which the experimenter desires to estimate as a simple main effect. We will see that this use does have implications for estimating models.

Crossed factors. These are two (or more) factors for which each level on one factor is tested at each level on the second factor(s)—that is, all cells (combinations of levels for the given factors) are both possible and represented in the data. Thus a complete design involves all crossed factors, but some incomplete designs may involve at least some completely crossed factors.

Nested factors. One factor is said to be nested in a second factor if each level on the first factor occurs on only one level of the second factor. Some examples are classrooms nested within schools (no classroom can exist in more than one school), cities nested within states, or resident physicians nested within training programs. There are two implications of this structure, both of which are characteristic of models involving nested factors:

1. A nested factor cannot yield a single estimate for its main effect and

2. No effect may be estimated for an interaction between a nested factor and the factor within which it is nested.

Fixed effects factor. This is a factor comprising an exhaustive set of levels. Examples would be a GENDER factor with two levels (MALE, FEMALE), or a FLUX factor with three levels (POSITIVE, NEGATIVE, NEUTRAL). Any new set of cases could be unambiguously assigned to one of the defined factor levels.

Random effects factor. This is a factor composed of specific levels which are a random sample of possible levels. Examples would be teachers in an educational study or randomly selected work teams in an industrial study or types of nouns in a verbal learning task.

Fixed and random effects factors require quite different handling in ANOVA analyses. Textbooks sometimes refer to the procedures which deal with these differences as "models" with designs containing only fixed effect factors called Model I, those with only random effects factors called Model II and those containing some combination of fixed and random effect factors called Model III or **mixed models**.

10.2 Analyzing designs with fixed effects factors

Our introduction to multi-way ANOVA in the previous chapter involved fixed effects factors. In the next major section of this chapter we will perform some of the same analyses discussed here, but using the procedures necessary for analyzing a "random effects" factor. At that time we will discuss the distinction and the limitations that derive from it.

Randomized block design

Snedecor and Cochran (1967) discuss a practical study of feed supplements to corn rations for pigs. The dependent variable was a measure of weight GAIN. Three different supplements were treated as factors with the amounts added to feed as levels: LYSINE (4 levels representing 0, .05, .10 and .15 percent), METHIOnine (3 levels representing 0, .025, and .05 percent), and PROTEIN (2 levels representing 12 and 14 percent soybean meal). A fourth factor, REPlication (2 levels), was included as well. The data are presented in Figure 10.1.

Design features

The REP factor in this study is called a blocking factor. A blocking factor is based on some intrinsic quality of the cases rather than the experimental treatment. The distinction between a factor created through blocking and one created through a formally controlled or manipulated treatment requires no changes in ANOVA procedures. Each may be modeled as main effect or in interaction with other factors.

Sometimes, as with REP in the present study, the term blocking factor has a narrower meaning, specifying not only a factor created in this way, but also one used to a particular purpose. For the FEED data, REP is a factor with no theoretical importance. The experimenter has included it to account for some miscellaneous but nevertheless systematic variance in the data (sometimes referred to as "controlling" or "stabilizing" the error variance in a study). Often these factors are time and/or space factors that could confound an experiment unless we included them. For example, research comparing new and old training techniques might run into a problem comparing productivity in newer more efficient factories and older less efficient ones; a psychological study using college students as subjects might find that performance deteriorates during the two weeks before semester exams; a comparison of fertilization techniques may be difficult due to variation in soil consistency among various plots that are to be used.

Figure 10.1
Data for a Study of Feed Supplements

CASE	REP	LYSINE	METHIO	PROTEIN	GAIN
1	1	1	1	1	1.11
2	2	1	1	1	0.97
3	1	1	2	1	1.09
4	2	1	2	1	0.99
5	1	1	3	1	0.85
6	2	1	3	1	1.21
7	1	1	1	2	1.52
8	2	1	1	2	1.45
9	1	1	2	2	1.27
10	2	1	2	2	1.22
11	1	1	3	2	1.67
12	2	1	3	2	1.24
13	1	2	1	1	1.30
14	2	2	1	1	1.00
15	1	2	2	1	1.03
16	2	2	2	1	1.21
17	1	2	3	1	1.12
18	2	2	3	1	0.96
19	1	2	1	2	1.55
20	2	2	1	2	1.53
21	1	2	2	2	1.24
22	2	2	2	2	1.34
23	1	2	3	2	1.76
24	2	2	3	2	1.27
25	1	3	1	1	1.22
26	2	3	1	1	1.13
27	1	3	2	1	1.34
28	2	3	2	1	1.41
29	1	3	3	1	1.34
30	2	3	3	1	1.19
31	1	3	1	2	1.38
32	2	3	1	2	1.08
33	1	3	2	2	1.40
34	2	3	2	2	1.21
35	1	3	3	2	1.46
36	2	3	3	2	1.39
37	1	4	1	1	1.19
38	2	4	1	1	1.03
39	1	4	2	1	1.36
40	2	4	2	1	1.16
41	1	4	3	1	1.46
42	2	4	3	1	1.03
43	1	4	1	2	0.80
44	2	4	1	2	1.29
45	1	4	2	2	1.42
46	2	4	2	2	1.39
47	1	4	3	2	1.62
48	2	4	3	2	1.27

This narrower use of a blocking factor also commonly leads to a decision to employ a **randomized block design**. Here the researcher, through knowledge of the field or creative intuition, foresees a factor's impact and creates a structured way to model its effect. Sets of cases are formed in equal numbers on the basis of the blocking factor, then equal numbers of the experimental treatment conditions (combinations of the other factor level conditions) are assigned at random to individual cases within each of the blocking levels. This creates equal sized groups for all possible combinations of factor levels, preserving the independence of all effects. In this way the analysis can involve a balanced investigation of all the main and interaction effects implicit in a multi-way design. If you look at the values across the REP and treatment factors in the FEED study, you will see that this is the case.

Choosing and analyzing a model

In Figure 10.2 we duplicate the original ANOVA that Snedecor and Cochran ran on these data.

The sources of all the calculated values in Figure 10.2 should be evident and will not be discussed. However the choice of terms in the model is of interest. First, note that the REP blocking factor has been specified solely as a main effect. We have followed Snedecor and Cochran in leaving out all the interactions involving the REP blocking factor. The blocking factor is a simple control for a nuisance factor. Assuming it is related to GAIN but its interactions with the other factors are nonexistent in the population, REP should extract a large sum of squares from the ERROR while the omitted interactions terms will leave large numbers of degrees of freedom in the ERROR term. Together these will diminish the mean square error and enhance the sensitivity of the *F* test on all the remaining effects which are of experimental interest.

Note that starting with this incomplete model merely assumes the absence of interactions between the blocking and treatment factors. To an extent the assumption is necessary for these data: With only 48 cases, estimating the complete model with all possible interactions would result in a saturated model—one with as many estimated means as degrees of freedom with nothing left over to provide an estimate of error. This is not uncommon in the use of blocking factors, as one prefers not to collect large sets of additional observations merely to control for a variable that has no theoretical significance and no expected interactions. However, later in our analysis, we will need to be sure to explore this assumption before we can be satisfied with our final model for these data.

Figure 10.2
Preliminary ANOVA

```
GLM
    USE FEED
    CATEGORY REP,LYSINE,METHIO,PROTEIN
    MODEL GAIN = CONSTANT+REP+LYSINE+METHIO+PROTEIN,
                +LYSINE*METHIO+LYSINE*PROTEIN+METHIO*PROTEIN,
                +METHIO*LYSINE*PROTEIN
    ESTIMATE
```

```
Categorical values encountered during processing are:
REP (2 levels)
        1,        2
LYSINE (4 levels)
        1,        2,        3,        4
METHIO (3 levels)
        1,        2,        3
PROTEIN (2 levels)
        1,        2


Dep Var: GAIN N: 48 Multiple R:  0.831 Squared multiple R:  0.690


                    Analysis of Variance
```

Source	Sum-of-Squares	DF	Mean-Square	F-Ratio	P
REP	0.133	1	0.133	4.854	0.038
LYSINE	0.043	3	0.014	0.518	0.674
METHIO	0.053	2	0.026	0.956	0.399
PROTEIN	0.536	1	0.536	19.492	0.000
LYSINE*METHIO	0.254	6	0.042	1.543	0.209
LYSINE*PROTEIN	0.240	3	0.080	2.911	0.056
METHIO*PROTEIN	0.082	2	0.041	1.495	0.245
METHIO*LYSINE *PROTEIN	0.068	6	0.011	0.415	0.861
Error	0.632	23	0.027		

Second, we need to begin evaluating the terms we have included in the model. Snedecor and Cochran suggest no prior expectations for the METHIONINE supplement; it was included perhaps for exploratory purposes. For this reason we should consider the four effects containing a METHIO term as multiple hypotheses. In looking at the table we hardly need to resort to a Bonferroni procedure in evaluating p values: none of the METHIO terms approaches even an unprotected level of significance. We should be able to reëstimate our model without including METHIO, thus saving substantial degrees of freedom.

In contrast, however, Snedecor and Cochran appear to expect a LYSINE*PROTEIN interaction. The active component of both the LYSINE and PROTEIN supplements consisted of a different type of protein. Hence it was expected that a linear effect for LYSINE effect would occur, but at only the lower PROTEIN level. At the higher PRO-TEIN level the maximum benefit of protein would have been reached, leaving no room for a further effect from the LYSINE. While the F for this effect is only marginally significant (p = .056), the expectation calls for a single degree of freedom test. Thus our new reëstimated model will include the LYSINE*PROTEIN effect and, by the conventions of model selection discussed in the previous chapter, also effects for the LYSINE and PROTEIN main effects.

Figure 10.3 presents the simplified model. You will note that the R-SQUARE estimate of explained variance dropped as the sum of squares due to the METHIO terms merged into the ERROR term. Nevertheless, the new analysis produces more sensitive F tests of the remaining effects due to the simultaneous merging of METHIO degrees of freedom into the ERROR term. The test on the LYSINE*PROTEIN interaction has now moved towards significance.

Checking assumptions

Figure 10.4 shows a residual plot from our second ANOVA. There is one low value which appears as an outlier at the bottom of the plot. Using the EDITOR to scan through the FEEDRES file RESIDUAL variable, we found the value to be for CASE=43. Its STUDENT value of -4.4 should occur only once in many thousands of cases, completely out of line for a data set comprising 48 cases. Reviewing the raw data in (Figure 10.1) we find GAIN=.80, the lowest in the study. Yet it occurs for a pig in the LYSINE=4 PROTEIN=2 cell of the design, one for which we might expect the highest GAIN. Small wonder that its value diverges from those of its cellmates.

What to do with the outlier? At the very least we should check its influence. Figure 10.5 shows a second re-estimate of the ANOVA, this time with the outlying case deleted with the SELECT facility. Our model shows a substantial improvement in every regard: its explained variance has climbed back up near to the level seen in the first overspecified model, and all effects in the model are discriminated more sharply than in either prior model. The new result would not change our conclusions about the study findings—the same effects show significance in both tables—except perhaps to strengthen our confidence in them.

Figure 10.3
First Reëstimated Model with METHIO Terms Removed

```
MGLH
    USE FEED
    CATEGORY REP,LYSINE,PROTEIN
    MODEL GAIN = CONSTANT+REP+LYSINE+PROTEIN+LYSINE*PROTEIN
    SAVE FEEDRES
    ESTIMATE
```

```
DEP VAR:   GAIN      N:   48     MULTIPLE R:   .683    SQUARED MULTIPLE R:   .466

                            ANALYSIS OF VARIANCE

    SOURCE    SUM-OF-SQUARES   DF   MEAN-SQUARE     F-RATIO      P

       REP            0.133    1        0.133         4.774    .035
    LYSINE            0.043    3        0.014          .509    .678
   PROTEIN            0.536    1        0.536        19.170    .000
   LYSINE*
   PROTEIN            0.240    3        0.080         2.863    .049

    ERROR            1.089   39        0.028
- - - - - - - - - - - - - - - - - - - - - - - - - - - - - - - - - - - - -
RESIDUALS HAVE BEEN SAVED


DURBIN-WATSON D STATISTIC        2.168
FIRST ORDER AUTOCORRELATION     -.085
```

There are those who argue that "data are data" and that no value produced under standard experimental practices should be altered. We think that if an outlier occurs, then the validity of the statistical analysis based on normal theory is in doubt. Keeping an outlier in an otherwise well behaved analysis is as bad as deleting an outlier to make the results look good and not informing readers of the change.

We also must ask, is this pig telling us something about the effects of LYSINE and PROTEIN feed supplements? Or was the result due to an unforeseen and totally extraneous issue? Could this pig have suffered from injury or disease during the study? Could it even have died before reaching the market? In short, is there good reason to think that this pig does not represent the population to which we wish to generalize our findings? A value as extreme as the present one would warrant an extended search for an influence of this kind. And finding one, we would feel justified in discarding the case from the statistical analysis.

Figure 10.4
Residual Plot for Reëstimated Model with METHIO Terms Deleted

```
BEGIN
PLOT RESIDUAL*ESTIMATE/SYMBOL=1,HEI=4IN,WID=4IN,YMIN=-.6,YMAX=.4
WRITE 'outside value'/HEI=.12IN,WID=.12IN,LOC=.5IN,.8IN
DRAW LINE / FROM=1.9IN,.8IN,TO=2.5IN,.25IN
END
```

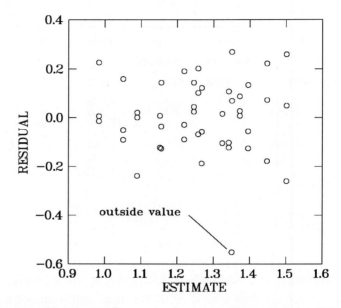

We do not recommend that you ignore such a case. For one, it is vital that a post hoc alteration of this kind be noted in the final report, alerting readers to the fact that the present results may not apply to some subset of the originally sampled population. Moreover, outliers can sometimes be informative in their own right. For instance, in the present climate of concern over side effects of food additives, one might well wonder why an animal in the most extreme condition cell should suffer an apparent failure to thrive. Do the most powerful treatments act (or interact) in potentially dangerous ways? Even from a simple economic standpoint this animal's experience could be a determining consideration. The loss of some animals due to overly powerful treatments could more than offset whatever advantage was gained in the better performance of the survivors. Results of this kind might suggest the need to collect more cases under the questioned conditions or even to replicate the study. We won't do the residual plot again for this reëstimated model. You can imagine it by looking at Figure 10.4 or, better, see it by doing it yourself.

Figure 10.5
Second Reëstimated Model—Outlier Deleted

```
SELECT GAIN>.8
CATEGORY REP,LYSINE,PROTEIN
MODEL GAIN = CONSTANT+REP+LYSINE+PROTEIN +LYSINE*PROTEIN
SAVE FEEDRES2 / MODEL
ESTIMATE
```

| DEP VAR: | GAIN | N: | 47 | MULTIPLE R: | .780 | SQUARED MULTIPLE R: | .608 |

ANALYSIS OF VARIANCE

SOURCE	SUM-OF-SQUARES	DF	MEAN-SQUARE	F-RATIO	P
REP	0.209	1	0.209	11.100	.002
LYSINE	0.059	3	0.020	1.045	.384
PROTEIN	0.671	1	0.671	35.633	.000
LYSINE*PROTEIN	0.188	3	0.063	3.334	.029
ERROR	0.716	38	0.019		

Analyzing patterns of means

Factorial studies with ordered factor levels invite single degree of freedom tests of trend. The LYSINE factor, for instance, uses three degrees of freedom in the numerator for its omnibus ANOVA table F value. The ordering of factor levels provides an opportunity for three single degree of freedom tests of trend.

In the absence of any interaction involving LYSINE, we could use a CONTRAST command to test for trend.:

```
HYPOTHESIS
EFFECT=LYSINE
CONTRAST=POLYNOMIAL / ORDER=1
TEST

HYPOTHESIS
EFFECT=LYSINE
CONTRAST=POLYNOMIAL / ORDER=2
TEST

HYPOTHESIS
EFFECT=LYSINE
CONTRAST=POLYNOMIAL / ORDER=3
TEST
```

As noted earlier, however, the experimenters expected a LYSINE*PROTEIN interaction: a linear effect for LYSINE but at only the lower PROTEIN level. The presence of a significant F for the LYSINE*METHIO interaction supports this view. Since our test involves an interaction effect we must use the SPECIFY command to compute **simple contrasts** among cell means. Simple contrasts compare cell means within only one level of a factor. For example, within level 1 of PROTEIN, we can contrast the four levels of LYSINE in a linear trend:

$$-3*LYSINE(1) -1*LYSINE(2) +1*LYSINE(3) + 3*LYSINE(4)$$

Figure 10.6 shows how to do this.

Figure 10.6
Linear Trend Test on LYSINE within First Level of PROTEIN

```
HYPOTHESIS
SPECIFY
-3*LYSINE[1]PROTEIN[1]-1*LYSINE[2]PROTEIN[1]+,
 1*LYSINE[3]PROTEIN[1]+3*LYSINE[4]PROTEIN[1]=0
TEST
```

HYPOTHESIS.

A MATRIX

	1	2	3	4	5
	0.000	0.000	6.000	4.000	2.000
	6	7	8	9	
	0.000	6.000	4.000	2.000	

NULL HYPOTHESIS VALUE FOR D

0.000

TEST OF HYPOTHESIS

SOURCE	SS	DF	MS	F	P
HYPOTHESIS	0.136	1	0.136	7.221	0.011
ERROR	0.716	38	0.019		

The higher order polynomials can be computed similarly. See the SYSTAT manual for further information.

Incomplete designs

In incomplete designs cases are not collected for all combinations of factor levels (cells). There are times when the phenomenon of interest forces the use of incomplete designs. For instance, a study of the age of cancer onset for factors "cancer type" and "gender" would find cases of both sexes for leukemia or lung cancer but not for cancer of the prostate. More often incomplete designs come about through informed choice. The experimenter simply does not collect cases for certain combinations of factors, giving up the ability to estimate some interaction effects but nevertheless reducing the total number of cases which need to be collected. Skilled use of experimental design insures that the set of cases that are collected will allow the estimation of all the effects that are of theoretical interest.

Latin squares

Latin squares are an extreme variation on the randomized block design. A Latin square deals with the problem of assigning levels on a treatment factor equally often across the levels on two or more blocking factors. It does so in a way that saves many degrees of freedom but results in a design for which only an additive main effects model can be estimated.

Figure 10.7 shows a Latin square design for a study with two blocking factors U and V (levels denoted by row and column numbers 1 to 4) and one treatment factor W (levels denoted by capital letters A to D), each factor comprising 4 levels. The left panel shows one of the standard Latin square layouts for use with 4-level factors as it might be selected from published tables such as Fisher and Yates (1953) or Cochran and Cox (1957). In common with published Latin squares, this matrix shows three factors and equal numbers of levels on all factors.

Before using this layout (pattern), we should permute the rows and columns randomly so that all possible permutations of the layout have an equal chance of being chosen for our actual study. The right panel of Figure 10.7 shows one possible permutation. All such permutations preserve the essential feature of the Latin square: all levels of the treatment factor appear equally often across the levels of the blocking factors

In the Latin square design, all two-way combinations of factors occur, but only for a balanced subset of levels on the third factor. That is, factor U levels 1-4 are each tested once under Factor V levels 1-4 (not just collectively for all levels of W) and similarly for U on W (not at all levels of V), and V on W (not at all levels of U).

Figure 10.8 shows the SYSTAT commands to produce a random Latin square. The DE-SIGN module generated the square and we saved it into a SYSTAT file. Retrieving and listing the file, we can see the layout for each replication listed as cases. We could have made several rows for each cell by adding the REPLICATES option.

Figure 10.7
A 4x4 Latin Square Design

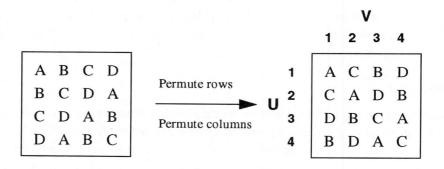

The trick to specifying a model and analyzing a Latin square study is that there is no trick. It is simply a 3-factor ANOVA for which you can analyze only main effects. For our 4x4 design, the model would be:

```
USE LATIN
CATEGORY X1,X2,X3
MODEL Y = CONSTANT+X1+X2+X3
ESTIMATE
```

Just as simply, all post hoc work analyzing patterns of means requires a straightforward use of the CONTRAST statement or standard multiple comparison procedures based on output from the estimated model. Investigating model assumptions will be somewhat curtailed. Checking residuals for normality and homogeneity proceeds as usual. You should be particularly alert to the presence of skewed residuals and a need for re-expression. These last can produce spurious interactions which are devilishly hard to track down in this design (outlined below) and can seriously weaken the power of this main effect model.

Figure 10.8
A Latin Square Design SYSTAT Program

```
DESIGN
SAVE LATIN
LATIN / LEVELS=4, SQUARE, RAND
USE LATIN
LIST / FORMAT=4,-1
```

```
Latin-Square Design:  4 Factors, Each With  4 Levels

            Factor 2
   Factor 1   1  2  3  4

      1      C  B  A  D
      2      B  C  D  A
      3      A  D  B  C
      4      D  A  C  B
The design matrix has been saved.


Variables in the SYSTAT Rectangular file are:
 RUN         X1              X2              X3
   Case number  RUN   X1   X2   X3
      1        1     4    1    4
      2        2     3    1    1
      3        3     4    3    3
      4        4     1    3    1
      5        5     1    4    4
      6        6     2    2    3
      7        7     2    4    1
      8        8     4    4    2
      9        9     4    2    1
     10       10     3    4    3
     11       11     2    1    2
     12       12     2    3    4
     13       13     1    2    2
     14       14     3    2    4
     15       15     1    1    3
     16       16     3    3    2
```

If you contemplate using a Latin square design, think seriously about the problem of missing interaction terms. One common misconception is that all of this elaborate randomization of factor levels yields a control—that the interactions get "cancelled out" in some mysterious way. Not true. The design simply balances the cells that are collected so that each estimated level mean reflects an average across all levels on each of the other factors taken separately, not their combinations. It in no way constrains individual case scores to fit this average.

There are three different places where interaction effects may be lurking in and around the Latin square:

1. Inside the estimated main effect terms as "aliases." Note that our U1 level in the design above was measured at only 4 of the 16 possible V*W combinations. What if these 4 just happened to be a synergistically powerful enhancer of the performance on the dependent measure? In such a case our estimated mean for level U1 would be high, not because of the U factor but because of the V*W interaction. In this sense the U effect and the potential V*W effect are completely overlapping and are said to be "aliases" for one another. The only way this possibility can be checked is by deviating from the Latin square design (see the next section).

2. In the ERROR term. As a more familiar possibility, consider what it might mean if our estimate for the U1 level mean was high but there appeared some very wide dispersion among the four V*W combinations on which it was based. This is the classic "lurking in the ERROR term" unestimated interaction. Our ANOVA procedure cannot estimate such an effect in a Latin square design due to the limited degrees of freedom. But you can use the graphical techniques to look for tell-tale patterns as described in the previous two chapters.

3. Outside the data. Finally, recall that the Latin square collects data on only a fraction of an implied complete factorial design. It is always possible that interactions in the phenomenon of interest do occur, but happen to do so in "cells" that were not collected. In this case there will be no ambiguity among aliased main and interaction effects, nor any noise weakening the sensitivity of your ERROR term. In fact you will not have the slightest indication that anything is wrong, until someone tries to replicate your study with a new square.

Fractional factorials

Somewhere between the randomized block and the Latin squares designs are the fractional factorials. These preserve the ability to analyze some of the simpler interactions but not the more complex ones. Fractional designs are useful in work with large numbers of factors where the numbers of cases needed for a complete factorial design would be prohibitively expensive to collect.

For instance, let us say that we get cold feet after doing the Latin square study above: we want to consider an interaction between the U blocking factor and the W treatment factor or perhaps we fear that a significant effect for factor V is merely an alias for an U*W interaction. This calls for expanding our Latin square design. Figure 10.9 shows how to do this.

Figure 10.9
Adding Cases to a Latin Square to Create a Fractional Factorial Design

Case number	RUN	X1	X2	X3
1	1	4	1	4
2	2	3	1	1
3	3	4	3	3
4	4	1	3	1
5	5	1	4	4
6	6	2	2	3
7	7	2	4	1
8	8	4	4	2
9	9	4	2	1
10	10	3	4	3
11	11	2	1	2
12	12	2	3	4
13	13	1	2	2
14	14	3	2	4
15	15	1	1	3
16	16	3	3	2
17	17	3	1	4
18	18	4	1	1
19	19	1	3	3
20	20	4	3	1
21	21	2	4	4
22	22	3	2	3
23	23	3	4	1
24	24	1	4	2
25	25	2	2	1
26	26	1	4	3
27	27	1	1	2
28	28	3	3	4
29	29	4	2	2
30	30	2	2	4
31	31	2	1	3
32	32	4	3	2

We have doubled the number of cells in order to provide information on the U(X1) by W(X3) interaction. To do this, we randomly permuted the V(X2) indices in the second group of cases such that none of the combinations duplicates the assignments in the first group. This yields 32 degrees of freedom, enough to estimate the following model:

```
MODEL Y = CONSTANT+X1+X2+X3+X1*X3
```

You can, of course, append cells to this design in order to test the other interactions as well. The upper limit is the fully factorial design, which includes 64 cells. At that point, you will have to have more than one subject per cell in order to get an error term, since there will be no interactions left to pool into the error. Finally, as with the Latin Square, you should not let the order in which you create the design dictate the order in which subjects are measured.

Incomplete designs due to missing data

Another common source of incomplete designs are those forced on the experimenter by circumstance—for example, the cancer study mentioned earlier where certain cancers do not occur in both sexes, or a study with observed levels (i.e., those created by blocking) and in which not all combinations were collected in the sample that happened to occur. For example, let's look at a two factor experiment that turned up the following numbers of cases per cell:

	A1	A2	A3	A4
B1	3	6	3	*
B2	2	3	4	3
B3	4	*	2	6

There are equal numbers of cases at each level of A and at each level of B, but two cells (A4B1 and A2B3) are empty. We cannot analyze an interaction of factors A and B because some of the data required for mean estimations are missing. If we tried to specify such a model, SYSTAT would object (unless you use the MEANS options of the MODEL statement). Yet if we are confident that there is no interaction between the two factors we can estimate an additive model and test hypotheses involving differences among level means with a CONTRAST statement:

```
MODEL Y = CONSTANT+A+B
ESTIMATE
HYPOTHESIS
EFFECT=A
CONTRAST
-2 -1 1 2
TEST
```

Just as with the planned incomplete designs above, however, you must stay alert to the confounding of main and interaction effects. For instance, finding a difference between A2 and A4 level means in our example could arise due to the imbalance of B1 and B3 cases if the two factors did have a tendency to interact. Unfortunately, despite the apparently adequate numbers of cases overall, the effort to estimate the full model,

```
MODEL dependent = CONSTANT + A + B + A*B
ESTIMATE
```

will result in an error message from SYSTAT; there are no cases with which to estimate the means for cells A2B3 and A4B1. In these situations we just have to make do with the model that can be estimated (or return to the field to get the missing cases).

This kind of problem most often arises in a study with many potential factors. In these, the data are so differentiated and cell frequencies so small that there is no cushion against the loss of even a few cases. The best way to get a grip on the situation is to use the TABLES module and TABULATE combinations of the factors that interest you the most. The resulting cell frequencies will tell you not only which models can be estimated (i.e., contain no cells empty of cases), but also which models can be estimated most reliably (i.e., provide cells with sufficient numbers of cases for adequate estimates of means). After that it up to you to choose which model, if any, provides the best trade-off between what is of interest and what is possible.

Take a look at the discussion of missing cells factorial designs in Chapter 10. We illustrate there how to use the MEANS model and the SPECIFY command to test hypotheses in missing cells designs. The tests based on the so-called "Type IV" sums of squares produced by these hypotheses can be useful in many instances as substitutes for the tests we do in fully factorial designs.

10.3 Analyzing designs with random effects factors

To keep to a familiar example, we will return to the Snedecor and Cochran FEED dataset treated at the beginning of this chapter. And for the present discussion we will assume a different interpretation for the REP factor. Let us say that it represents two different farms on which this study was conducted. Perhaps as researchers, we were concerned that the conditions on the two farms were not entirely comparable. We knew that one location kept young pigs isolated in carefully monitored feed lots while the other let them wander with older pigs in far more open pens. Past experience might tell us that the first farm tended to produce higher growth rates than the second and so indicate the need to control the extraneous variance due to this distinction in our study.

While REP is a simple two-level factor, it nevertheless can be viewed in two distinct ways. On one hand we might have chosen these two locations to represent the two unique and standard ways in which pigs are raised. On the other hand we might have chosen these two locations to represent merely two out of a much larger set of possible approaches to raising pigs.

An arcane difference of interest only to county agents you say? Perhaps, but the issue has a substantial effect on the data analyst's task. The distinction is that between viewing a factor as a fixed effect (where two farms represent all conditions of interest) or a random effect (where the farms represent just two out of a wider variety of conditions). And the sometimes difficult decision about whether effects are fixed or random leads to substantial differences in choosing appropriate statistical procedures.

A fixed effects factor is one made up of an exhaustive set of levels. In viewing REP in this way we are in effect saying that we could go to any farm where pigs are raised, inspect the facilities and determine that "Yep, pigs here are raised just as they were on the REP=1 (or REP=2) farm in the study we conducted." In other fields of research, examples of fixed effects levels might be male vs. female subjects, between an experimental group which received a treatment and a control group which did not, or among fresh, frozen and canned produce. For each example, selecting a new sample to replicate the study would present no difficulties; we could unambiguously classify each new study entity on one of the existing factor levels. This aspect allows us to assume that we have completely captured the range of the factor's possible effects. Any new sample of people or produce items would fall into the same set of levels, so that it can be our statistical expectation that the results would recur.

A random effects factor is one in which the studied levels represent a sample of possible levels. In viewing REP this way we are saying that our visits to new farms would result in judgments such as "This farm appears to have even looser standards of care than our REP=2 farm" or "This farm seems to be midway between our REP=1 and REP=2 farms since pigs start out in open pens but then are transferred to feed lots," and so on. In other research, examples might be distinction on the time of day in which sales are observed, randomly selected factories or work stations in a management study, differences due to individual people such as teachers in an educational study or research assistants in the implementation of an experiment, or verbs chosen from the dictionary in a verbal learning study. A complete sampling of all levels ranges from the impractical (e.g., applying even two experimental treatment levels across replications of all the possible five minute intervals in a sales day) to the impossible (e.g., each research assistant constitutes a unique level on the factor containing all possible associates one may have in a professional lifetime). In each of these examples, an effort to replicate the study with a new sample would result in new and different levels than seen in the original study. Here we are always uncertain about the degree of contrast contained in comparisons between the sampled levels. We must take this uncertainty into account when estimating the reliability of factor effects.

You will find that the presence of a random factor in a design introduces some major complications. Usually you will have little control over the responsibility to face up to these problems. For the most part, factors represent inherently fixed or random effects as outlined above. There are, however, occasions where you have some choice if you are willing to live with the limitations. If you have an inherently random effects factor, but are willing to limit your conclusion to just the particular conditions you have studied, then you may be justified in treating the factor as a fixed effect. For example, in the study above, let us say that methods of raising pigs do tend to vary a great deal from farm to farm, so that the farms we studied appear to be randomly selected levels on the set of possible REP levels. If we were concerned about only these two farms, if any conclusions we wished to draw applied to only these two farms, then we would have grounds to assume that our study had involved an exhaustive set of levels. The REP factor may be treated as a fixed factor in the analysis following the procedures in the first section of this chapter. But when we are using ANOVA procedures to generalize beyond the limitations of our present sample, the presence of a random factor cannot be finessed and there is need for more work and thought.

The most difficult aspect of dealing with random factors is that the presence of a random factor in a design affects not only tests on the random factor, but also tests on the other factors, whether fixed or random. This influence occurs due to differences in interaction terms in models containing just fixed effects factors versus models containing one or more random effects factors. In models containing only fixed effect factors, all interaction terms are also fixed effects. In models containing random effects, each interaction term involving a random effects element, whether or not the other elements represent fixed or random effects terms, is a random effect. And the presence of these random effect interaction terms introduces uncertainty (the possibility of varied findings in replications with new samples) that permeate the model.

A mixed model

Figure 10.10 shows a reanalysis of the study of feed supplements in which the REP factor is treated as a random factor and PROTEIN remains as a fixed factor. While we know that other factors are involved in a good model for these data, we analyze only these two for now to keep things simple. Beyond this, there are two essential differences in comparing this analysis to the one in the first section of this chapter: 1) the MODEL statement for the new ANOVA includes the interaction term involving the REP blocking factor and 2) there is a separate HYPOTHESIS sequence involving a new ERROR command which tests the PROTEIN effect in our model.

Figure 10.10
Computing *F*-tests with a Random Effects Factor

```
USE FEED
SELECT GAIN>.8
CATEGORY REP,PROTEIN
MODEL GAIN = CONSTANT+REP+PROTEIN+REP*PROTEIN
ESTIMATE
```

DEP VAR: GAIN   N: 47   MULTIPLE R: .694   SQUARED MULTIPLE R: .482

ANALYSIS OF VARIANCE

SOURCE	SUM-OF-SQUARES	DF	MEAN-SQUARE	F-RATIO	P
REP	0.210	1	0.210	9.554	0.003
PROTEIN	0.674	1	0.674	30.647	0.000
REP*PROTEIN	0.019	1	0.019	0.874	0.355
ERROR	0.945	43	0.022		

```
HYPOTHESIS
EFFECT PROTEIN
ERROR REP*PROTEIN
TEST
```

TEST FOR EFFECT CALLED:
                PROTEIN

TEST OF HYPOTHESIS

SOURCE	SS	DF	MS	F	P
HYPOTHESIS	0.674	1	0.674	35.085	0.106
ERROR	0.019	1	0.019		

The tests on the REP*PROTEIN and REP terms may be taken from the original ANO-VA table. Each of these effects is a random effect, and no other term in the model involves an interaction between one of these elements and a separate random effect. Thus the *F*-tests on these two effects are not premised on any more variability than they themselves introduce into the model. For this reason, the usual mean square ERROR term constitutes the denominator for the *F*-test, and this is the one that SYSTAT reports in the ANOVA table.

The test on the PROTEIN main effect, however, must be computed separately in a HYPOTHESIS sequence. You will recall from our earlier discussion of main and interaction effects that we do not interpret main effects for terms involved in interaction effects. The problem is even more severe when the interaction term is a random effect (i.e., involves an element due to a random effects factor). Since the REP*PROTEIN cell means are sampled rather than fixed, we are suddenly uncertain about just how much variability there really is among the REP*PROTEIN cell means. While on this occasion the REP*PROTEIN effect appears negligible, a replication of the study with new REP levels would certainly result in different level means. This in turn could well produce new REP*PROTEIN cell means and therefore a different estimate of the size of the REP*PROTEIN effect. Thus the negligible REP*PROTEIN interaction in the present data does not offer assurance of a similarly small effect in a replication with a new sample.

In fact, the more the level means for PROTEIN vary by levels of REP in our present results, the less likely it becomes that a replication at new ages would show comparable findings. For this reason, the variability of PROTEIN within levels of REP (the definition of a REP*PROTEIN interaction) constitutes the proper test for the reliability of the PROTEIN main effect. Thus, analyzed in a design containing a random effect, this fixed effect factor cannot be tested against the usual mean square ERROR, but should be tested against the mean square representing the interaction of the fixed effect with the random effect.

The HYPOTHESIS sequence in Figure 10.10 shows the simple way in which the test is performed. The ERROR command allows us to substitute the mean square REP*PROTEIN error in place of the default mean square ERROR. You can see that our conclusions for the study would be very different for the fixed and random effects views of REP. The fixed effect view (from the ANOVA table where experimental ERROR is the test mean square) shows a highly significant effect for PROTEIN, but the random effects view (from the HYPOTHESIS sequence where REP*PROTEIN is the test mean square) shows no significance ($p = .106$).

The difference in outcome arises not because the PROTEIN effect becomes smaller (it does not change) nor because the REP*PROTEIN effect is so large (as we have already seen, it is not even close to significant). Rather it arises because the random effects test is based on a denominator with only one degree of freedom. An F ratio based on 1 and 1 degrees of freedom must achieve a value of over 160 to achieve a probability lower than $p = .05$. As large as our PROTEIN effect is, it cannot overcome this obstacle.

We need not consider this the final answer, however. As discussed in the last chapter, analyzing multi-way ANOVAs for all possible main and interaction terms may involve a stepwise process in which more complex interactions are analyzed first and, where showing no significance, dropped from the model and so into the ERROR term. We will quickly see that this process—often called error pooling—is of particular value in analyzing models containing random effects factors.

For the FEED study we have seen that the REP*PROTEIN effect is not significant. Dropping it from the model we are left with a main effects model as estimated in Figure 10.11. For this model there are no interactions, and so the appropriate test of both main effects—the fixed effect for PROTEIN and the random effect for REP—is the common ERROR term. An in this case the benefit is obvious; with far more degrees of freedom the test of PROTEIN is much more sensitive and again appears very unlikely to have occurred by chance.

We must caution you that error pooling is a dangerous procedure when done on many terms. It can be like blind stepwise regression. Furthermore, if you do pool, it is best to describe the procedure in detail when you report your results. Then you and others can replicate your experiment and test the reasonableness of your pooling judgments. Pooling makes us uncomfortable, especially when it is done to favor one's hypothesis, but overfitting models by including terms which should be in the error term bothers us as well.

Figure 10.11
Testing a Random Effects Factor with Pooled Error Terms

```
GLM
   USE FEED
   CATEGORY REP,PROTEIN
   MODEL GAIN = CONSTANT+REP+PROTEIN
   ESTIMATE
```

```
DEP VAR:   GAIN   N:  47   MULTIPLE R:  .687   SQUARED MULTIPLE R:  .472


                      ANALYSIS OF VARIANCE

      SOURCE   SUM-OF-SQUARES   DF   MEAN-SQUARE    F-RATIO      P

         REP          0.207     1        0.207      9.457    0.004
     PROTEIN          0.669     1        0.669     30.520    0.000

       ERROR          0.964    44        0.022
```

Checking assumptions

The assumptions about errors for models with random effects are the same as for our previous discussions of fixed effects models. Thus no new residual procedures are involved. At the end of the next major section, where we consider more diverse models with random effects factors, we will elaborate on this point.

Comparing patterns of means

In this example our PROTEIN factor has only two levels and so the HYPOTHESIS is a single degree of freedom test. When a study involves a more differentiated factor we will want to perform the narrower and more explicit single degree of freedom F test as we described in our examples throughout this section of the book. The only difference for models with random factors is that each HYPOTHESIS sequence must specify the appropriate ERROR term for the effect on which the analysis is based.

Working with unequal numbers of cases

Similarly, our comments in previous chapters apply to applications with random effects factors. SYSTAT's least squares approach to ANOVA automatically produces valid results in many situations where some cells contain unequal numbers of cases. In fact, if you look at our work above, you will see that we have been working with such a study. We analyzed our FEED data set eliminating CASE=43, and so we produced a design involving unequal numbers of cases per cell. You can see that factor effects are not orthogonal, because the presence and absence of the REP*PROTEIN interaction term in the two models we estimated produces slightly different estimates for the REP and PROTEIN effects. But as long as we feel justified in assuming that the missing case is a result of random events unrelated to study procedures or questions, SYSTAT's estimates may be considered valid and the slight differences negligible.

Other mixed models

A simple rule of thumb for deriving an error term for fixed, random, and mixed models is:

> *The error term for a given effect is the set of interaction terms in which the given effect appears as an element and all other elements represent random effects. When no such interactions arise, choose mean square error.*

Specified in this way, the rule will lead you to an appropriate test whether your design involves all fixed effects, all random effects, or a mixture of fixed and random effects. Most textbooks refer to these three cases as "Model I, Model II and Model III" respectively. We find these designations to be confusing to users, implying more discontinuity among approaches and analysis than is actually the case. We will stick to the descriptive phrases.

Models in which all factors are fixed effects are straightforward. Since there are no random effect terms, the second sentence of the rule applies to all terms. For either main or interaction effects, the mean square error is the error term for F-tests. This is the error term SYSTAT uses in constructing the ANOVA table and by default in the HYPOTHESES sequences; you need not make any adjustments.

For models containing one or more random factors, Figure 10.12 will form a basis for our discussion. We have included all the entries required for analysis of up to four factors with up to two random effects. We had two purposes in mind in including it. The large number of possibilities will help you see and better understand the patterns which underlie the construction of error terms, the results of applying the simple two-sentence rule above. In addition, the table will later serve as a fully specified worksheet; by simply deleting rows and entries referring to factors which are not represented in a model, we can obtain a simplified version to correspond to our needs for less complex designs. We did not have in mind the presentation of a more rigorous derivation of the expectations listed in this table. For that we must refer you to an ANOVA textbook.

Figure 10.12
Worksheet for Error Terms in Models with Fixed and Random Effects
Two Random (a, b) and Two Fixed (C, D) Factors

			Expected Value							row for exact F or
test		effect		error term						[rows for pseudo F]
1	a	= a	+ ab					+ error		5
2	b	= b	+ ab					+ error		5
3	C	= C	+ aC	+ bC	+ abC			+ error		[6+8-11]
4	D	= D	+ aD	+ bD	+ abD			+ error		[7+9-12]
5	ab	= ab						+ error		16
6	aC	= aC	+ abC					+ error		11
7	aD	= aD	+ abD					+ error		12
8	bC	= bC	+ abC					+ error		11
9	bD	= bD	+ abD					+ error		12
10	CD	= CD	+ aCD	+ bCD	+ abCD			+ error		[13+14-15]
11	abC	= abC						+ error		16
12	abD	= abD						+ error		16
13	aCD	= aCD	+ abCD					+ error		15
14	bCD	= bCD	+ abCD					+ error		15
15	abCD	= abCD						+ error		16
16	error	=						+ error		

The first two columns provide simple reference terms for the following discussion: an identifying number and a simple coding of each possible term. For example row 10 contains elements pertaining to the factor C by factor D interaction term. The remaining columns reflect three aspects of each term's mean square. The first, "effect," contains the mean square unique to that term in the model; it is the mean square printed out in the ANOVA table. The next, "error term," reflects the proper test of the term's effect; it is the complete set of higher order interactions involving the given term and other terms referencing a random effect as defined by our rule earlier. The banner column, "expected value," is the total of these two columns; it is the sum of all the sources of variability that may be influencing the term in the given row of the table.

When we wish to test an effect, we need to form an *F* ratio in which a given term's "effect" is tested against its "error." However, the row entries, the specific terms we specified in our model, refer to the whole of the "expected value." Thus to test any given "effect" we must look for another row whose "expected value" contains precisely the elements in the "error" we desire.

An example with multiple random effects

Let's look one last time at the study of feed supplements, this time analyzing for REP, LYSINE and PROTEIN and assuming that LYSINE is a fixed effect and that both REP and PROTEIN are random effects (PROTEIN's rather limited levels of 12 and 14 percent soybean meal suggests that this might even be true). Our resulting model, Figure 10.13, is more complete than the one at the beginning of the chapter, involving all possible combinations of main and interaction effects as required in analyses containing random effects.

Figure 10.13
Model Preliminary to Testing Hypothesis with Multiple Random Factors

```
CATEGORY REP,LYSINE,PROTEIN
MODEL GAIN = CONSTANT+REP+LYSINE+PROTEIN+,
             REP*LYSINE+REP*PROTEIN+LYSINE*PROTEIN +,
             REP*LYSINE*PROTEIN
ESTIMATE
```

```
DEP VAR:    GAIN    N:   47    MULTIPLE R:  .813    SQUARED MULTIPLE R:  .660


                            ANALYSIS OF VARIANCE

    SOURCE    SUM-OF-SQUARES    DF   MEAN-SQUARE    F-RATIO      P

      REP            0.213      1        0.213     10.666      0.003
    LYSINE           0.061      3        0.020      1.025      0.395
   PROTEIN           0.677      1        0.677     33.852      0.000
    REP*
    LYSINE           0.039      3        0.013      0.658      0.584
    REP*
   PROTEIN           0.021      1        0.021      1.030      0.318
  LYSINE*
   PROTEIN           0.187      3        0.062      3.118      0.040
    REP*
  LYSINE*
   PROTEIN           0.031      3        0.010      0.519      0.672

    ERROR            0.620     31        0.020
```

To obtain tests for the 7 terms in this model, let's begin by paring down our random effects worksheet to match the present situation. Since we have two random effects (REP and PROTEIN) and one fixed effect (LYSINE), factors we need only those rows and elements that refer to factors "a," "b," and "C." Our worksheet is so reduced to:

test		effect	error term				row for test "error"
			Expected Value				
1	a	= a	+ ab			+ error	5
2	b	= b	+ ab			+ error	5
3	C	= C	+ aC	+ bC	+ abC	+ error	[6+8-11]
5	ab	= ab				+ error	16
6	aC	= aC	+ abC			+ error	11
8	bC	= bC	+ abC			+ error	11
11	abC	= abC				+ error	16
16	error	= error				+ error	

where a = REP, b = PROTEIN and C = LYSINE

Tests with exact *F* ratios

In models where only one or two factors are random, the search for an exact error term is generally an easy one. For example, our original worksheet shows that for 12 out of 15 possible effects there is another estimated effect (row of the worksheet) whose expected value corresponds to the given term's required error. Our simplified worksheet for the FEED2 data shows that for 6 out of 7 effects the needed term has been estimated. We will first deal with these easy situations, putting off until the next section such troublesome exceptions as the LYSINE main effect ("C" main effect, row 3).

From previous discussion, we know that the researchers went into the FEED study with the expectation of a LYSINE*PROTEIN interaction. More particularly, they expected a linear effect across the four levels of LYSINE at only the low level of PROTEIN. From our worksheet we see that the LYSINE*PROTEIN interaction (bc term) is appropriately tested on the REP*LYSINE*PROTEIN interaction term (abC term, row 11). Figure 10.14 shows two forms of this test.

Figure 10.14
Testing Hypotheses in Models with Multiple Random Factors

```
HYPOTHESIS
EFFECT LYSINE*PROTEIN
ERROR REP*LYSINE*PROTEIN
TEST
```

```
TEST FOR EFFECT CALLED:
                LYSINE
          BY
                PROTEIN

TEST OF HYPOTHESIS

        SOURCE    SS      DF      MS        F         P
    HYPOTHESIS   0.187     3     0.062     6.006     0.088
        ERROR    0.031     3     0.010
```

```
HYPOTHESIS
ERROR=REP*LYSINE*PROTEIN
SPECIFY
-3*LYSINE[1]PROTEIN[1]-1*LYSINE[2]PROTEIN[1]+,
 1*LYSINE[3]PROTEIN[1]+3*LYSINE[4]PROTEIN[1]=0
TEST
```

```
HYPOTHESIS.
A MATRIX
                    1         2         3         4         5
                  0.000     0.000     6.000     4.000     2.000

                    6         7         8         9        10
                  0.000     0.000     0.000     0.000     0.000

                   11        12        13        14        15
                  6.000     4.000     2.000     0.000     0.000

                   16
                  0.000

NULL HYPOTHESIS VALUE FOR D
                  0.000

TEST OF HYPOTHESIS

        SOURCE    SS      DF      MS        F         P
    HYPOTHESIS   0.136     1     0.136    13.096     0.036
        ERROR    0.031     3     0.010
```

The top panel shows how to obtain the omnibus F test that would be appropriate if we had no clear prior hypothesis. It answers the question, "Is there something going on with LYSINE*PROTEIN?" We use a HYPOTHESIS sequence with LYSINE*PROTEIN as the tested effect and REP*LYSINE*PROTEIN as the error. The answer in the printout appears to be that nothing very reliable is going on. The probability of a result this extreme in random data is about 9 in 100.

But since we have an explicit hypothesis, it is more appropriate to move directly to a one degree of freedom test as shown in the lower panel. Since our hypothesis involves an interaction effect we need to cast it with a SPECIFY statement. You can see the results of this contrast in the AMATRIX test in the bottom panel of Figure 10.14. Note that here too the appropriate error term for this test remains the REP*LYSINE*PROTEIN interaction term. The more refined hypothesis has proved more powerful, and we now see support for the researchers' expectations in a p value that is less than 1 in 20.

Tests with approximate *F* ratios

Unfortunately, and particularly as the number of random effects increases, you will also find many cases in which the error for a given term does not match the expected value for any other term. For example, look at our simplified worksheet for expected values in the FEED study. For the main effect of the fixed effect LYSINE (effect C, row 3) the error term matches no other row's expected value. For such terms, there is no error term to select!

Yet the desire to test for an effect of LYSINE is not entirely unwarranted here. If we had not had an explicit hypothesis for the LYSINE*PROTEIN interaction we might well have accepted the omnibus p of .088 as an indication of no significance and moved on to testing main effects.

For some of these cases we may be able to justify using a less than perfect expected value to make our test. For example, in an effort to test the C main effect (row 3), the expected value of the term aC (row 6) is almost what we need but for the lack of a bC element. If we can satisfy ourselves that the expected value for the bC element is negligible, then we will have grounds to make the assumption that the lack of the bC element in the aC expected value poses no threat to our test. We do this by testing the bC term (row 8) against its proper error term abC (row 11). Should we find no significant result, then we may construct an F ratio to test the main effect of C (row 3) using the expected value of aC (row 6) as our error term. In effect this preliminary test is just what we have done in our omnibus test of LYSINE*PROTEIN above. The remaining step would be to perform the test using LYSINE as the effect and REP*LYSINE as the error.

Another alternative is to pool error terms. This is the conventional stepwise procedure in which we first test more complex interaction terms against the experimental ERROR and after each test, assuming a finding of no reliable effect, reestimating the model with the tested term deleted. In this way the gradually accruing ERROR term becomes the appropriate test for the increasingly simpler effects, until finally we reach the term of interest. Again our original ANOVA table (where we find the REP*LYSINE*PROTEIN effect appropriately tested against the experimental error) and our HYPOTHESIS sequence for an omnibus test of the LYSINE*PROTEIN interaction has taken us through the first steps. The remaining steps would be to test REP*PROTEIN against REP*LYSINE*PROTEIN and then reestimate the model without the interactions. This would allow a test of LYSINE against the experimental ERROR—i.e., use the F and p values from the newly estimated ANOVA table.

The advantage of these strategies over the one discussed in the next section is that they allow us to construct conventional ANOVA F ratios. By pooling error terms to obtain a useful model we gain a way to refer directly to any effect and error that interests us. These can then be used with CONTRAST and SPECIFY statements to perform powerful comparisons among means.

The problem with these approaches is the reliance on a sequence of (i.e., multiple) tests. The statistical community has shown little consensus over the use of these strategies, and indeed you may well have come across a "never pool" edict in your reading or training. Early in this chapter we suggested that the use of these strategies at the very least requires you to make some effort to adjust your criterion p value in light of the number of hypotheses you are entertaining as you proceed. If you go this route, we recommend a Bonferroni procedure (dividing your criterion p by the number of preliminary tests you will make). But in any design containing more than two factors you will find that the adjustment makes it increasingly - and to some extent inappropriately - difficult to obtain significant findings on your effect of interest.

Tests with pseudo *F* ratios

The alternative is to construct a pseudo F (or quasi F) ratio with degrees of freedom adjusted in a procedure due to Satterthwaite (1946). To construct this test we calculate approximate F-ratios and degrees of freedom by hand using combinations of the available mean squares. Figure 10.15 provides a way to automate this hand work. It is a brief program that you can use with SYSTAT's BASIC module to obtain a pseudo F ratio for such situations. We have used it to obtain a test of the main effect of LYSINE for the FEED2 data.

Figure 10.15
Constructing an Approximate *F* Test When Exact Tests Cannot Be Obtained

```
BASIC
   REPEAT 1
   NOTE 'FIRST THE DATA'
   REM LYSINE
   LET NUM_MS = .02
   LET NUM_DF = 3
   REM REP*LYSINE
   LET D1_MS =  .013
   LET D1_DF =   3
   REM LYSINE*PROTEIN
   LET D2_MS =  .062
   LET D2_DF =   3
   REM REP*LYSINE*PROTEIN
   LET D3_MS =  .010
   LET D3_DF =   3
   LET F_RATIO = NUM_MS /  (D1_MS + D2_MS - D3_MS)
   LET DENOM_DF = DENOM_MS^2 / (D1_MS^2/D1_DF + D2_MS^2/D2_DF +,
                  D3_MS^2/D3_DF)
   LET P=1-FCF(F_RATIO,NUM_DF,DENOM_DF)
   LIST F_RATIO,NUM_DF,DENOM_DF,P
   RUN
```

		F_RATIO	NUM_DF	DENOM_DF	P
CASE	1	0.308	3.000	3.082	0.820

For those unused to seeing formulas in programmatic form, the last few lines of Figure 10.15 represent these calculations:

$$F\text{-}RATIO = \frac{MS\_B}{(MS\_aB + MS\_Bc - MS\_aBc)}$$

$$DF\_DENOM = \frac{(MS\_aB)^2}{DF\_aB} + \frac{(MS\_Bc)^2}{DF\_Bc} + \frac{(-MS\_aBc)^2}{DF\_aBc}$$

which is the form you will probably see in your statistics text. The logic? Well the expected value we need for the fixed effect B term is aB + Bc + aBc. If we simply used the sum of the aB and Bc expected values we would end up with

:

$$
\begin{array}{rcl}
\text{Ab} + & & \text{aBc} \\
& \text{Bc} + & \text{aBc} \\
\hline
\text{aB} + \text{Bc} + & & \text{2aBc}
\end{array}
$$

i.e., one too many aBc terms. Thus, subtracting the aBc expected value reduces our denominator to the appropriate range for a mean square to test the effect of B. If you look over our master worksheet you will see that we have indicated the terms that enter into the construction of these pseudo F-ratios and should be entered in the mean squares and degrees of freedom rows for D1, D2, and D3 in the program.

To evaluate the result, we use the upper tail of the cumulative F distribution (FCF) in SYSTAT BASIC. This function allows fractional degrees of freedom, as in our example where DF_DENOM=3.08. For the effect of LYSINE we need not bother, however, as an F less than 1 is significant in no section of anyone's table.

Checking assumptions

Ordinarily, we discuss how assumptions are checked before moving on to the kinds of hypothesis tests listed above. In discussing the analysis of the FEED data for random effects models we skipped this problem because the procedures and comments in our discussion of fixed effects models apply equally to imputed random effects models. For any set of estimated effects, the model we specify to obtain an estimate in the original ANOVA table will not differ whether effects are fixed or random. Only our procedures for testing effects will change. The residuals are identical.

Notes

Mixed models have received a lot of attention recently. New maximum likelihood procedures based on large sample theory are offered in BMDP5V and SAS® Proc Mixed. These procedures yield chi-squares instead of F statistics and are not suited for small samples. Nevertheless, there are designs and data for which they ought to be considered. The technical papers in this area are beyond the scope and audience for this book.

Further reading

Cochran and Cox (1957) is a classic in this field. More recent introductory treatments may be found in Box, Hunter and Hunter (1978), Milliken and Johnson (1983), and Neter, Wasserman and Kutner (1990). For social scientists involved in field research, the venerable Campbell and Stanley (1966) remains hard to beat. Kirby (1993) includes SYSTAT examples.

References

Box, G.E.P., Hunter, W.G., and Hunter, J.S. (1978). *Statistics for Experimenters: An Introduction to Design, Data Analysis, and Model Building.* New York: John Wiley & Sons, Inc.

Campbell, D.T., and Stanley, J.C. (1966). *Experimental and Quasi-experimental Designs for Research.* Chicago: Rand McNally.

Cochran, W.G., and Cox, G.M. (1957). *Experimental Designs.* New York: John Wiley & Sons.

Kirby, K.N. (1993). *Advanced Data Analysis with SYSTAT.* New York: Van Nostrand Reinhold.

Milliken, G.A., and Johnson, D.E. (1984). *Analysis of Messy data* (Vol. 1): *Designed Experiments.* New York: Van Nostrand-Reinhold Company.

Neter, J., Wasserman, W., and Kutner, M. (1990). *Applied Linear Statistical Models,* (3rd ed.). Homewood, IL: Richard E. Irwin, Inc.

Snedecor, G.W., and Cochran, W.G. (1967). *Statistical Methods* (6th ed.). Ames, IA: Iowa State University Press.

11

Analysis of Covariance

ANCOVA models are a hybrid of ANOVA and regression. As with both ANOVA and regression, ANCOVA models involve a quantitative dependent measure. On the independent variables side of the equation, ANCOVA models involve at least one categorical variable (factor) and continuous variable (covariate).

Figure 11.1 shows an example adapted from Huitema (1980) for an educational experiment on study instructions. Three groups of students each studied materials in a biology text. To keep things simple, we will confine our analysis to the first two groups. As denoted by the categorical variable INSTRUCT, one group was simply told to study everything (general) and a second was given the terms and concepts they were expected to master (specific). At the end of the allotted time all students were given the exam and their scores were recorded as the variable ACHIEVE.

This experiment involves a single factor, and Figure 11.2 shows a one-way ANOVA on ACHIEVE by INSTRUCT. The results are disappointing. The size of the error variance (MEAN SQUARE ERROR) is large relative to the size of the treatment. If you look back at the data in Figure 11.1, you will note that each group shows a wide array of scores, with some very low and very high scores occurring in each.

The experimenter might take one of three approaches in an effort to refine the analysis. One, the expensive approach, would be to collect additional subjects. The added degrees of freedom for the error term would, all other things being equal, produce a smaller mean square error and a more powerful test of the effect. Second, the experimenter might block the subjects on a factor which accounts for the wide variation within cells. For example, if males and females have very different achievement scores, adding gender to the design would allow us to focus on the effects within gender. This, too, is expensive because it usually involves adding subjects unless the subgroups are large already.

Figure 11.1
Instructional Methods Experiment

STUDENT	INSTRUCT$	INSTRUCT	APTITUDE	ACHIEVE
1	GENERAL	1.	29.	15.
2	GENERAL	1.	49.	19.
3	GENERAL	1.	48.	21.
4	GENERAL	1.	35.	27.
5	GENERAL	1.	53.	35.
6	GENERAL	1.	47.	39.
7	GENERAL	1.	46.	23.
8	GENERAL	1.	74.	38.
9	GENERAL	1.	72.	33.
10	GENERAL	1.	67.	50.
11	SPECIFIC	2.	22.	20.
12	SPECIFIC	2.	24.	34.
13	SPECIFIC	2.	49.	28.
14	SPECIFIC	2.	46.	35.
15	SPECIFIC	2.	52.	42.
16	SPECIFIC	2.	43.	44.
17	SPECIFIC	2.	64.	46.
18	SPECIFIC	2.	61.	47.
19	SPECIFIC	2.	55.	40.
20	SPECIFIC	2.	54.	54.

The third method is to use an additional quantitative variable, called a covariate, which is related to the heterogeneity within the groups. If this variable has a linear relation to the dependent measure *within groups*, it can be used to "soak up" some of the error variance and produce the desired reduction in the size of the error term. It is usually much cheaper to get one additional piece of information from each existing subject than it is to find, test, and query a whole new set of subjects.

The variable APTITUDE is a candidate for a covariate. In education, aptitude is viewed as a students' underlying ability to learn, acquired though a long history of familial and educational experiences. It is likely that different subjects in the experiment bring with them widely varying aptitudes for learning, and no matter how well or poorly they are instructed, their differential aptitude may produce the kinds of wide variability in performance seen in the ACHIEVE scores.

In earlier chapters we discussed how the sensitivity of an ANOVA model could be increased by adding a blocking variable: for example, the variable REP in the study of FEED. For the INSTRUCT data, however, APTITUDE is (presumably) a normally distributed continuous variable. It will use up only one degree of freedom in our model, yet work like a blocking variable to reduce the size of the mean square error.

Figure 11.2
Preliminary One-Way ANOVA

```
GLM
CATEGORY INSTRUCT
MODEL ACHIEVE = CONSTANT + INSTRUCT
ESTIMATE
```

```
Categorical values encountered during processing are:
INSTRUCT (2 levels)
         1,        2


Dep Var: ACHIEVE N: 20 Multiple R:  0.414 Squared multiple R:  0.171
o
                        Analysis of Variance

Source            Sum-of-Squares  DF  Mean-Square    F-Ratio       P

INSTRUCT               405.000     1    405.000       3.719      0.070

Error                 1960.000    18    108.889
```

11.1 Understanding an ANCOVA Model

Figure 11.3 shows the estimation of a model that includes the grouping variable (IN-STRUCT) and the covariate APTITUDE). Notice that the INSTRUCT effect is now highly significant ($p = .004$) and the coefficient for APTITUDE is also highly significant ($p = .001$).

Notice that the MODEL statement in Figure 11.3 looks like an additive two-way ANO-VA. The categorical INSTRUCT variable is handled just as in an ANOVA and produces a similar result. The APTITUDE term, however, shows two differences from a blocking variable in an ANOVA model. It is not included in the CATEGORY statement and the ANALYSIS OF VARIANCE table of results shows it to be estimated with only one degree of freedom despite its many distinct values.

Let's examine graphically what is being done here. Figure 11.4 shows a scatterplot displaying the relationships among the three variables included in this model. The dependent measure ACHIEVE is on the vertical axis, the quantitative independent APTITUDE is on the horizontal axis, and the categorical independent INSTRUCT is represented by showing each data point as the first letter of the subject's INSTRUCT$ group. The separate regression lines for each group and the 68 percent ellipses (one standard deviation) are also shown.

Figure 11.3
Specifying an ANCOVA Model

```
MODEL ACHIEVE = CONSTANT + INSTRUCT + APTITUDE
CATEGORY INSTRUCT
ESTIMATE
```

Categorical values encountered during processing are:
INSTRUCT (2 levels)
        1,   2

Dep Var: ACHIEVE N: 20 Multiple R: 0.760 Squared multiple R: 0.578

Analysis of Variance

Source	Sum-of-Squares	DF	Mean-Square	F-Ratio	P
INSTRUCT	641.424	1	641.424	10.915	0.004
APTITUDE	961.017	1	961.017	16.354	0.001
Error	998.983	17	58.764		

Figure 11.4
Display of an ANCOVA Model

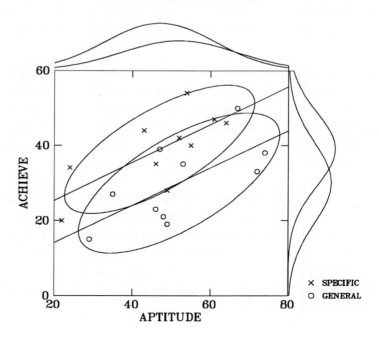

To the right of the frame in Figure 11.4 are two normal distributions centered at the means for the two INSTRUCT groups on the vertical ACHIEVE axis. Their spread is determined by the within groups standard deviations of ACHIEVE. These are the normal distributions on which the ordinary analysis of variance in Figure 11.2 is based. Notice that they are not well separated and the ANOVA is not significant.

Figure 11.5 shows how the analysis of covariance adjusts for the relation between ACHIEVE and APTITUDE within groups. We have plotted the residuals for the regression of ACHIEVE on APTITUDE within groups, centering each set of residuals at the least squares ACHIEVE means of the two groups. The new ellipses are based on the within groups standard deviations of ACHIEVE residuals and APTITUDE raw scores. Notice that the normal distributions on the right of the frame have smaller spread. These two distributions are significantly separated, according to the ANCOVA table in Figure 11.3.

11.2 Assumptions

ANCOVA analyses carry with them all of the usual assumptions of ANOVA procedures: errors that are normally distributed, homogeneous across groups, and independent of one another. These can all be investigated using the techniques described in the chapters on ANOVA and regression.

Homogeneity of slopes

There is one assumption that is unique to ANCOVA, called "homogeneity of slopes." If the slopes of the regression lines in Figure 11.4 looked substantially different, then our ANCOVA adjustment displayed in Figure 11.5 would be an inappropriate model. The ordinary ANCOVA model presumes, because there is no interaction term for APTITUDE*INSTRUCT, that the slopes are parallel. Figure 11.4 offers visual evidence that this assumption appears justified, but there is a formal statistical test of the parallelism hypothesis. You have seen its close relative in the ANOVA chapter: the test of significance of the interaction term. The upper panel of Figure 11.6 shows how to compute this test. We simply add the interaction to the model and recompute it.

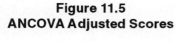

Figure 11.5
ANCOVA Adjusted Scores

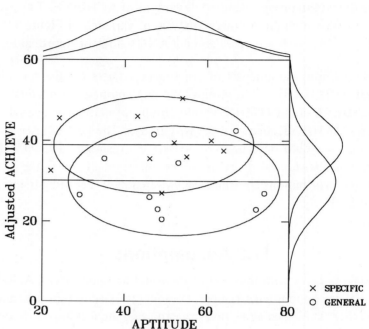

The results of this analysis indicate that the common slopes assumption is plausible. The interaction term is not significant ($p = .973$). What happened to the INSTRUCT effect? It's not significant now either. It turns out that we have created an artifact by the way we scored this information, so that the interaction has become highly correlated with the main effect for INSTRUCT. This artifact doesn't affect the test of the interaction, but it can lead to misinterpretation of the main effect if we happen to look at it.

Figure 11.6
The Separate Slopes Model

```
MODEL ACHIEVE = CONSTANT + INSTRUCT + APTITUDE,
                + INSTRUCT*APTITUDE
CATEGORY INSTRUCT
ESTIMATE
```

```
Categorical values encountered during processing are:
INSTRUCT (2 levels)
        1,      2


Dep Var: ACHIEVE N: 20 Multiple R:  0.760 Squared multiple R:  0.578


                       Analysis of Variance

Source              Sum-of-Squares   DF  Mean-Square    F-Ratio      P

INSTRUCT                   44.325     1       44.325      0.710    0.412
APTITUDE                  958.868     1      958.868     15.359    0.001
INSTRUCT*APTITUDE           0.071     1        0.071      0.001    0.973

Error                     998.912    16       62.432
```

```
LET APTS=APTITUDE-49.5
GLM
MODEL ACHIEVE = CONSTANT + INSTRUCT + APTS ,
                + INSTRUCT*APTS
CATEGORY INSTRUCT
ESTIMATE
```

```
Categorical values encountered during processing are:
INSTRUCT (2 levels)
        1,      2


Dep Var: ACHIEVE N: 20 Multiple R:  0.760 Squared multiple R:  0.578


                       Analysis of Variance

Source              Sum-of-Squares   DF  Mean-Square    F-Ratio      P

INSTRUCT                  641.495     1      641.495     10.275    0.006
APTS                      958.868     1      958.868     15.359    0.001
INSTRUCT*APTS               0.071     1        0.071      0.001    0.973

Error                     998.912    16       62.432
```

Basically, what we did by multiplying INSTRUCT and APTITUDE was to make a new variable whose values were large for all members of one INSTRUCT group and small for all members of the other. This means that INSTRUCT*APTITUDE and APTITUDE are highly correlated. This doesn't happen in the ordinary ANOVA with effects coding because both variables being multiplied are dummy variables centered at zero. The cure for this is to subtract the mean of the covariate out of the covariate. This doesn't affect the original analysis of covariance table but it does make the interpretation of the whole table for the homogeneity of slopes test more interpretable. The lower panel of Figure 11.6 shows this. Notice that the F value for INSTRUCT is now close to that of the regular ANCOVA in Figure 11.3.

What would happen if the interaction of the covariate and grouping variable were significant? We could stay with the interaction model in Figure 11.6. Some researchers, particularly those in nonexperimental fields, advocate this model. It is valid statistically, provided the usual regression assumptions are met. The problem with the interaction model lies in how to interpret the results. You may recall that in the regular factorial ANOVA, significant interactions precluded global statements about main effects. We had to make tests on and statements about separate *simple* effects instead. The problem is similar in ANCOVA. If the slopes were not parallel in our educational experiment, for example, we would have to say that the low achievers were differently affected by the treatments than the high achievers. The purpose of the ANCOVA would no longer be to reduce the size of the error term in a simple ANOVA, but rather to fit a multiplicative model to the data. Strictly speaking, this multiplicative model would no longer be termed an analysis of covariance, but rather an interaction regression model.

Nonzero slopes

Now suppose the regression coefficient for the covariate in the ANCOVA model were not significantly different from zero. What do we do in this case? This is a tricky question. It is not unlike the pooling question which we discussed in Section 10.3. From one point of view, the ANCOVA model would be overfitting because the ANOVA model would do as well. There is no point in using a covariate if the data look like Figure 11.5 to start with.

But what if they look like Figure 11.4 but there are not enough observations to make the covariate coefficient significant? In this case, we would be reluctant to give up the covariate model simply because the test of significance lacked power. Furthermore, you should not choose a covariate unless you have good theoretical reason to expect it would make a difference in the first place. It is unlikely that you would fail to find the covariate coefficient significant, but remember that a significant covariate coefficient is not an assumption for doing the analysis in the first place.

Equal covariate means

There is another condition that may seem like an assumption but is really something you hope for rather than a mathematical requirement. The assumption is that the means of the covariate across groups are equal in the population. Notice in Figure 11.4 that the normal curves at the top of the frame are not substantially separated.

If you randomly assigned subjects to treatments, it would be surprising if the groups significantly differed on the covariate. You can test the significance of the difference of means by using the model:

```
MODEL APTITUDE = CONSTANT + INSTRUCT
```

But significance is less important than substance. Even if we could get away with violating this assumption, we do not want the means on the covariate to be radically different, because mathematical extrapolation is precarious. Remember, we are taking the residuals from the pooled regressions and using them in an ANOVA. If the covariate means are substantially different, we are using linear regressions to predict group differences outside the bulk of the data. This is not only mathematically unstable but it can also lead to "counter-facts." This odd notion is rather simple. Imagine taking achievement and aptitude scores for chimpanzees (after all, they *can* put a pencil to paper) and using ANCOVA to equate their aptitude with that of humans in order to test differences in achievement between chimps and humans. The counter-fact in this peculiar approach is that a chimp could not have an aptitude score of 40, 30, or even 10 on this test, so equating scores by extrapolation is nonsensical.

Counter-facts can be historical ("If Hitler had not existed, would World War II have been fought?") semantic (pregnant males), or quantitative (chimps with 140 IQ's), and they can vary in degree of outrageousness. We should keep in mind that statistical adjustments, as in ANCOVA or causal modeling or partial correlations, can lead to philosophical problems.

Figure 11.7 summarizes graphically violations of the three types of conditions we have been covering under the Assumptions heading.

Figure 11.7
Inequality of Slopes, Zero Slopes, Inequality of Means

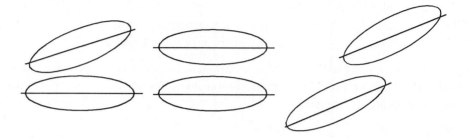

11.3 Extended techniques in ANCOVA

Obtaining adjusted means

The study of Instruction is designed as an experiment with subjects assigned at random to treatment groups. With random assignment we are justified in assuming that there were no systematic differences in achievement level from group to group prior to the experimental treatment. Over the long haul – many experiments or many subjects – this would be true in fact as well as in assumption. But for any single experiment with a limited number of subjects there is always some likelihood that subjects assigned to groups will have differed, perhaps even enough to obscure the effect of the experimental treatment. A covariate that is strongly related to the dependent variable within groups provides a way to assess such pre-experimental differences. The regression of the covariate on the dependent variable gives a way to predict the pre-treatment differences among groups on the dependent variable. The actual observed differences between groups on the dependent variable can then be adjusted for this prior estimated difference. In an ANCOVA model it is differences on these adjusted means that are compared and tested

SYSTAT makes it easy to simple to obtain adjusted means for the treatment groups. Simply type PRINT=LONG before you ESTIMATE your ANCOVA model. If you do, you will see that the adjusted mean for the GENERAL group is 28.745 and for the SPECIFIC group is 40.255. MGLH also prints standard errors for these means (2.444). Looking back at Figure 11.4, you can see that these adjusted means are computed by finding the intersection of each regression line with the vertical line drawn through the mean of the covariate on the bottom axis. Figure 11.5 shows this more clearly. The horizontal lines intersect the vertical axis at the respective least squares means. You can save these least squares means with the SAVE/ADJUSTED command in MGLH. This allows you to do other graphics or additional tabulations.

Multiple covariates

The use of multiple covariates is a straightforward extension. For any design, each continuous covariate is simply included as an additive term in the MODEL statement. The test for homogeneity of slopes requires testing all the interaction terms with both covariates. By adding a lot of covariates to a study, however, you risk interpretability of the outcome. It's hard enough to understand how the adjustment works for a single covariate. ANCOVA is not a panacea for large error terms and it is not a useful general method for "controlling nuisance variables."

Multifactor experiments

Multifactor ANCOVA is also a straightforward extension of what we have learned. Simply add the covariate(s) to the MODEL statement for the factorial design. For example, let's say that the study of instruction included an additional factor distinguishing study materials by contrasting the use of texts versus lectures. A complete ANOVA model with an interaction term for this design would be:

```
MODEL ACHIEVE = CONSTANT + ACHIEVE + FORMAT + ACHIEVE*FORMAT
```

The desired ANCOVA extension would be:

```
MODEL ACHIEVE = CONSTANT + ACHIEVE + FORMAT + ACHIEVE*FORMAT +,
                APTITUDE
```

Testing homogeneity of slopes is a bit more complicated. For a multi-way ANOVA, the interaction term should be tested for each effect. For example, if the experimenter had expectations involving the interaction term, the test for similar slopes should involve the complete ANOVA model plus the covariate plus the three-way interaction between the covariate and the two treatment factors:

```
MODEL ACHIEVE = CONSTANT + ACHIEVE + FORMAT + ACHIEVE*FORMAT +,
                APTITUDE + ACHIEVE*APTITUDE + FORMAT*APTITUDE +,
                ACHIEVE*FORMAT*APTITUDE
```

As you can see, most of the work in creating models of this kind involves issues of designing and interpreting the combinations of the categorical factors rather than any real complexity in adding the covariate. For a more detailed discussion of modeling and hypothesis testing with experimental data, see Chapter 11 where the analysis of experimental data is discussed at greater length. For example the use of CONTRAST statements to test main effect hypotheses, the use of AMATRIX statements to test hypotheses involving interactions, and the discussion post hoc multiple comparison procedures all apply to models involving an additive continuous covariate. Since the covariate is not specified in the CATEGORY statement it does not become part of the design matrix of dummy variables and so can effectively be ignored in specifying HYPOTHESES.

Using a covariate with MANOVA procedures

Here too the involvement of a continuous covariate requires no elaborate changes in the basic techniques developed for the basic underlying models. Some of the test statistics will be multivariate, but their significance levels should be interpreted as in this chapter. As in the earlier discussion of simple ANCOVA, the test for homogeneity should be evaluated. The interaction should be rejected and the simpler ANCOVA additive model should be estimated and interpreted only if the test shows a probability larger than the selected criterion.

Further reading

Huitema (1980) is the standard statistical text on analysis of covariance. Keppel (1991) provides a less technical summary. Cook and Campbell (1979) cover general issues in the analysis of field data where covariate adjustments may be required.

References

Cook, T.D. and Campbell, D.T. (1979). *Quasi-experimentation: Design and Analysis Issues for Field Settings.* Chicago: Rand McNally.

Huitema, B.E. (1980). *The Analysis of Covariance and Alternatives.* New York: John Wiley & Sons.

Keppel, G. (1991). *Design and Analysis: A Researcher's Handbook* (3rd ed.). Englewood Cliffs, NJ: Prentice-Hall.

12

Multivariate Analysis of Variance

Figure 12.1 shows some measures from a study of how day-care arrangements influence child development. The variable SETTING marks three groups: 1 for children cared for by their parents, 2 for those cared for by sitters, and 3 for those enrolled in group care nursery schools or day-care centers. The other variables are three measures of each child's social competence: a behavioral measure of skill seen during family dinnertime (DINNER), a second measure of skill in dealing with an unfamiliar adult in a laboratory session (STRANGER), and a third showing social problem solving skill in a cognitive test (PROBLEM).

These data represent a multivariate design – multiple dependent measures taken on the same set of subjects. The simplest form of multivariate analysis of variance (hereafter MANOVA) analyzes data of this kind. In the next chapter we will analyze a another kind of multivariate situation, repeated measures, in which a single kind of measure is taken a number of times on each subject – for example, opinion ratings taken before and then after a treatment intended to change attitudes. You may be aware that MANOVA analyses parallel a number of more advanced procedures including path analysis, structural modeling, factor analysis, and discriminant analysis. While it is possible to perform these kinds of analyses with SYSTAT's MGLH module, they are beyond the scope of the presentation and will not be treated in this chapter.

12.1 Purposes and requirements of MANOVA

Consider an analysis of the three dependent measures DINNER, STRANGER, and PROBLEM. A simple approach would be to perform a series of one-way ANOVAs on each of these and inspect the resulting differences in means over the three levels on the SETTING factor. The obvious advantage is that the complexities of MANOVA can be sidestepped.

Figure 12.1
DAYCARE Data

SETTING$	SETTING	DINNER	STRANGER	PROBLEM
PARENTS	1	676	529	16
PARENTS	1	625	144	9
PARENTS	1	900	784	64
PARENTS	1	900	289	81
PARENTS	1	729	1156	81
PARENTS	1	1024	64	4
PARENTS	1	16	625	9
PARENTS	1	1225	729	36
PARENTS	1	961	529	25
PARENTS	1	2209	625	81
PARENTS	1	1521	1024	64
PARENTS	1	1024	1089	100
PARENTS	1	625	100	49
PARENTS	1	1764	441	81
PARENTS	1	1444	841	64
PARENTS	1	2209	961	36
PARENTS	1	1764	841	100
PARENTS	1	1764	729	16
PARENTS	1	324	441	25
SITTER	2	1225	529	36
SITTER	2	1444	484	16
SITTER	2	2025	1089	100
SITTER	2	1296	625	49
SITTER	2	784	529	36
SITTER	2	1444	225	1
SITTER	2	1369	784	25
SITTER	2	900	361	16
SITTER	2	1764	289	49
SITTER	2	1936	729	64
CENTER	3	1369	900	64
CENTER	3	1521	961	25
CENTER	3	1936	676	64
CENTER	3	441	729	64
CENTER	3	1444	961	49
CENTER	3	961	1089	81
CENTER	3	1521	1024	49
CENTER	3	1936	676	100
CENTER	3	2116	961	100
CENTER	3	784	1024	81
CENTER	3	1849	1521	64
CENTER	3	1936	625	49
CENTER	3	441	576	64
CENTER	3	1024	529	36
CENTER	3	1849	1089	64
CENTER	3	1296	625	64
CENTER	3	841	1225	64
CENTER	3	1156	484	81
CENTER	3	1521	1024	100

There are disadvantages, however. First of all, a set of three one-way ANOVA tables on completely random data will yield at least one p value of less than or equal to .05 almost 15% of the time. One solution to this is familiar: simply use a Bonferroni procedure to establish a protected criterion p value. Since we contemplate 3 ANOVAs we would use .05/3 or $p = .0167$ as the level required to attribute a significant finding. This method lacks power, especially for larger numbers of variables, because it is designed to deal with a worst-case situation. For example, even if none of our separate tests show reliable group differences, there remains the possibility that a joint test using all the information obtained in all the dependent measures would find the groups to differ. This joint test is exactly what MANOVA procedures provide.

Second, with separate tests we cannot discern how many dimensions of variability we really are testing. Since our three measures are collected on a single set of subjects, there is a strong possibility of correlation among measures. If all three measures were perfectly correlated, then our three tests would be redundant; there would be only one underlying dimension of difference among children. If all three measures were independent, on the other hand, then each would represent a result on a distinct dimension. In real world situations, where the degree of correlation is somewhere between perfect and absent, we face questions that are often of prime theoretical interest: How many distinct underlying dimensions are actually represented; Which of the dependent variables are most involved in differences among groups? MANOVA procedures provide answers which the separate ANOVAs cannot.

12.2 Estimating and understanding a preliminary model

Figure 12.2 shows the commands to estimate the model and save the residuals. The output in the figure is for the standard MANOVA. We have added PRINT=LONG to reveal additional output, but we have eliminated some of the output (e.g. the test of the CONSTANT term) which we won't discuss and which is ordinarily not of interest.

The first part of the output shows the covariance and correlation matrices of the three variables within groups plus their means and standard errors within groups. The tests of MANOVA hypotheses follow.

Figure 12.2
MANOVA with Tests of Effects

```
ANOVA
USE DAYCARE
PRINT LONG
CATEGORY SETTING
SAVE DAYRES/RESID DATA
DEPEND DINNER,STRANGER,PROBLEM
ESTIMATE
```

```
Categorical values encountered during processing are:
SETTING (3 levels)
          1,         2,         3
Number of cases processed: 48
Residual covariance matrix  S
                     Y.X

                     DINNER     STRANGER     PROBLEM
   DINNER         287479.525
   STRANGER        46647.669    85193.843
   PROBLEM          5116.869     3323.431     749.802

Residual correlation matrix  R
                     Y.X

                     DINNER     STRANGER     PROBLEM
   DINNER             1.000
   STRANGER           0.298        1.000
   PROBLEM            0.349        0.416       1.000

----------------------------------------------------------------------

Least squares means.
SETTING     =1           N of Cases =       19.000

                   DINNER      STRANGER    PROBLEM
   LS. Mean        1142.316     628.474     49.526
   SE               123.006      66.962      6.282
----------------------------------------------------------------------

SETTING     =2           N of Cases =       10.000

                   DINNER      STRANGER    PROBLEM
   LS. Mean        1418.700     564.400     39.200
   SE               169.552      92.301      8.659
----------------------------------------------------------------------

SETTING     =3           N of Cases =       19.000

                   DINNER      STRANGER    PROBLEM
   LS. Mean        1365.368     878.895     66.474
   SE               123.006      66.962      6.282
----------------------------------------------------------------------
```

```
Test for effect called:      SETTING

Univariate F Tests

      Effect         SS        DF       MS            F           P

DINNER         687808.686     2    343904.343      1.196       0.312
  Error       1.29366E+07    45    287479.525

STRANGER       879394.074     2    439697.037      5.161       0.010
  Error       3833722.926    45     85193.843

PROBLEM          5526.593     2      2763.296      3.685       0.033
  Error         33741.074    45       749.802


Multivariate Test Statistics

            Wilks' Lambda =      0.723
              F-Statistic =      2.519   DF =   6,  86    Prob =      0.027

             Pillai Trace =      0.290
              F-Statistic =      2.488   DF =   6,  88    Prob =      0.029

   Hotelling-Lawley Trace =      0.364
              F-Statistic =      2.547   DF =   6,  84    Prob =      0.026

               THETA =  0.232 S =   2, M = 0.0, N = 20.5 Prob =      0.035

Test of Residual Roots

  Roots 1 through 2
    Chi-Square Statistic =      14.250      DF = 6

  Roots 2 through 2
    Chi-Square Statistic =       2.624      DF = 2

Canonical Correlations

                  1             2
                0.482         0.241
Dependent variable canonical coefficients standardized
by conditional (within groups) standard deviations

                  1             2
   DINNER       -0.341         0.980
   STRANGER      0.723         0.288
   PROBLEM       0.554        -0.424

Canonical loadings (correlations between conditional
dependent variables and dependent canonical factors)

                  1             2
   DINNER        0.068         0.918
   STRANGER      0.852         0.404
   PROBLEM       0.736         0.037
```

Test statistics

Let's focus on the test for the SETTING effect at the bottom of the output. First is a series of univariate tests. These are the same results that you would see if you were to perform a separate one-way ANOVA on each of the dependent variables separately. For each, the differences among means of SETTING groups are tested against the ERROR within groups on the dependent measure.

Second are the results for the multivariate tests: four separate statistics along with their associated p values. There is no single universally accepted procedure for multivariate hypothesis testing, but rather a number of different methods. Each responds to a different type of multivariate variation or dispersion in the scores. Let's consider each in turn. Our notation will be:

G :sum of squares and cross products matrix within groups (error)
H :sum of squares and cross products between groups (hypothesis)
T : sum of squares and cross products overall (total)

Also note that $\mathbf{T} = \mathbf{G} + \mathbf{H}$

Wilks lambda (Λ or W or likelihood ratio criterion)

For univariate tests, the F test statistic compares sum of squares between to sum of squares within to obtain a ratio that follows a known distribution in normal populations. For the multivariate case a parallel procedure forms the ratio of the determinant of **G** and of **T**. The mathematical derivation of a determinant is beyond the scope of this book, but you can think of it as a measure of the variability of the numbers in a matrix.

The statistic itself varies between 0 and 1 with smaller values denoting greater likelihood of significant group differences. The associated F statistic is an approximation due to Rao (1973). It is an exact F if the number of groups or variates is less than or equal to two. The power of this test is moderate in most situations (i.e., with varying numbers of dependents and degrees of correlation among them) when the assumptions of the MANOVA procedure are met. When conditions are not met it is moderately robust except in the presence of heteroscedasticity (nonhomogeneity, or difference variances/covariances in groups).

Pillai trace (V)

This statistic is formed from the sum of the diagonal elements of the inverse of **T** times **H**, or $T^{-1}H$. Like the determinant, the mathematical computation of the inverse is beyond the scope of this book. A matrix inverse functions like an ordinary (scalar) inverse. Multiplying by a matrix inverse is analogous to dividing by a number. The associated *F* statistic is an approximation that, like the others, is exact when the groups or variates are less than or equal to two.

Of the four tests, the Pillai trace has been found to be robust to the widest variety of violations of the MANOVA assumptions (i.e., multidimensional normality and homogeneity). In most situations, its power tends to be slightly less than that of the alternatives. In general, however, the differences in power is slight and, in view of its robustness, this test has much to recommend it.

Hotelling-Lawley trace (T)

This statistic is formed from the sum of the diagonal elements of the inverse of **G** times **H**, or $G^{-1}H$. The test is the most powerful of the alternatives in situations where the set of dependents reflect the presence of a number of relatively separate and uncorrelated dimensions. Like Wilks lambda, it is moderately robust to violations of assumptions on normality but not to homogeneity. The *F* statistic is an approximation like the others.

Theta (Roy's characteristic root statistic)

This statistic is the largest root criterion for Roy's union intersection test. This was the first widely used test statistic in MANOVA. Subsequent work with it and the alternatives above suggest that it is the least satisfactory for general use. In some circumstances it can be more powerful than the alternatives (e.g., when all dependents are highly correlated and tend to reflect the presence of a single underlying dimension), but more often it is by far the least powerful. More critically, it is the least robust to violations of any of the assumptions supporting MANOVA analysis.

A winner?

Although for this example there is not much difference, you will often see more disagreement in the significance levels of the various test statistics. Given that it is most robust to violations of equality (homogeneity) of covariances assumptions in MANOVA, and its power is not much worse than the other tests, we would recommend using the Pillai trace for most analyses. Only in circumstances where you are relatively certain that the group variation is concentrated in one dimension and the groups all share common variances and covariances among the dependent variables would we suggest you use theta instead.

"Seeing" a multivariate test

Why is it that the multivariate test of our model is significant while one of the three univariate tests is not? Are the multivariate tests some sort of "average" of the univariates? The simple answer to the latter question is "no." In fact, there will be times when the multivariate test will be significant when *none* of the univariate tests is. There even can be times when the multivariate test will not be significant when *all* the univariate tests are.

Figure 12.3 shows how. Both examples involve two groups and two variables we created with the SYSTAT normal random number generator. In the left graph, the two variables are highly correlated within groups and the centroids (means) of the groups are close together. The ANOVAs computed separately for each variable, represented by the normal curves at the edges of the plot, are not significant. The first canonical dimension is shown at the upper right corner of the frame. Notice that the groups are well separated when projected on this oblique best-discriminating axis. The MANOVA, represented by the curves on this oblique axis, is significant.

The right example shows how the multivariate test may not be significant even when the univariates are. The best discriminating axis for the multivariate test is shown at the upper left corner. The separation of the distributions on this axis is comparable to that for the two univariates at the borders. We lose a degree of freedom for the multivariate test, however, so it is less powerful than the univariate ones in this case. We paid a price for not knowing in advance which of the variates, or which linear combination of them, we wished to test alone. Admittedly, this is a rare example for two groups, but it is not uncommon for one or more univariate tests to be significant without a significant multivariate test when there are more than two variables and groups.

Figure 12.3
MANOVA Test Statistic Anomalies

Left: multivariate test significant, univariate tests not significant
Right: multivariate test not significant, univariate tests significant

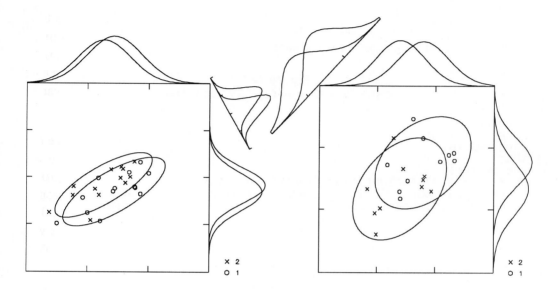

Estimating and evaluating components

Let's examine in more detail the variates (sometimes called components, canonical factors, or dimensions) that are the optimally weighted linear combinations of the original variables. For our analysis, two components have been estimated. There will always be one fewer components than the smaller of: a) the number of groups or b) the number of dependent variables.

The components are estimated in a sequence. The first maximizes the projected sum of squares between groups relative to the sum of squares within groups (i.e., the maximal separation among groups). The second is orthogonal (at right angles) to the first and maximizes projected separation of the groups, and so on.

Figure 12.4 shows these components for the DAYCARE data. We saved them into the file DAYCOMP.SYS by testing an HYPOTHESIS concerning SETTING. The printed output we get is similar to that in Figure 12.2.

We have added 95 percent confidence ellipses for the centroids of each group (ELM=.95) and have bordered the plot with normal curves so that we can examine the separation of the groups along each dimension. Notice that the first component, called FACTOR(1), shows the groups relatively separated, while the second does not. Keep in mind that MANOVA assumes that all the groups share a common pooled ellipse and the distributions on the margins have common spread (variance). To the extent that these are not all shaped similarly in Figure 12.4, this assumption is violated. We will examine this assumption more closely later.

Figure 12.4
Canonical Scores for DAYCARE Data

```
HYPOTHESIS
EFFECT=SETTING
SAVE  DAYCOMP
TEST
USE  DAYCOMP
PLOT  FACTOR(2)*FACTOR(1)/GROUP=GROUP,OVERLAY,
   ELM=.95,SYMBOL='P','S','C',XMIN=-3,XMAX=3,YMIN=-3,YMAX=3,
   DASH=1,7,10,LLAB='Parent','Sitter','Center',BORDER=NORM
```

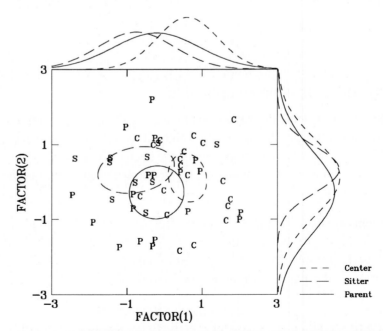

Now let's return to the output in Figure 12.2. First comes TEST OF RESIDUAL ROOTS. These tests are nested. The first tests the significance of group variation on both variates. It is, in fact, another multivariate significance test. The second chi-square tests the significance of group variation on the remaining components after the first. In this example there is only one, the second component. In keeping with what we see in Figure 12.5, the test tells us there is no significant group variation left after the first MANOVA dimension. When there are more groups or variates, there will be more chi-square tests. You can look for the first test which is not significant to determine the number of significant dimensions. These tests are correlated because they are nested, so you cannot take each one as a distinct test of the significance of each variate.

Next come the canonical correlations. Canonical correlations are like multiple correlations, except that the things being correlated are *both* linear combinations of variables. The multiple correlation is the correlation of a dependent variable with an optimal linear combination of independent variables. A canonical correlation is a correlation of an optimal linear combination of dependent variables (DINNER, STRANGER, PROBLEM) and another optimal linear combination of independent variables (SETTING1, SETTING2, SETTING3). There are two canonical correlations because there are two sets of variates. The plot in Figure 12.4 shows the two dependent variates which are based on the combination of DINNER, STRANGER, and PROBLEM. There will be as many canonical correlations as there are variates. They will descend in magnitude. Do not be surprised if you see large canonical correlations occasionally. Remember, MANOVA *optimizes* prediction, so if you use a lot of variables you will tend to get large correlations. The TEST OF RESIDUAL ROOTS will give you an idea of how many correlations are significant.

The remaining sections of the output show two aspects of the relation between the estimated components and the original variables. The section titled CANONICAL CO-EFFICIENTS shows the relative weights of original variables in the new estimated components.   For example, the first component variable is largely determined by PROBLEM and STRANGER with a small negative contribution from DINNER, while the second component involves the variance from DINNER and relatively less from PROBLEM or STRANGER. These coefficients have been standardized by the pooled within groups standard deviations so that different scales will not influence the interpretation of the coefficients. Because of this, they are interpreted the way we do standardized regression coefficients.

The section titled CANONICAL LOADINGS shows the relations of the estimated components to the original variables. These loadings are the correlations between the components and the original dependent variables. For example, the correlation of

PROBLEM with component 1 is .736 and the correlation of DINNER with component 2 is .918.

Contrasting the coefficients and loadings reveals "suppressor" or "moderator" relationships. Recall that in multiple regression it is possible to have a negative coefficient for a predictor variable which is positively correlated with the dependent variable. This occurs when the predictor variables are relatively highly correlated. It also makes it more complicated to interpret the regression equation. We have that situation here. Notice that the coefficient for DINNER on the first variate is -.341 yet the correlation between DINNER and this variate is only .068. Some have suggested that we ignore the coefficients altogether in characterizing the canonical variates and focus instead on the loadings. Blinders do not solve the problem, however. Each provides different information. The coefficients indicate how a component is created. The loadings show how it relates to its parts.

12.3 Residual analyses

The assumptions for MANOVA are similar to those for ANOVA. Residual analysis should focus on the key error assumptions: 1) Homogeneity, 2) Multinormality, 3) Independence.

Homogeneity. Instead of homogeneity of variance we must worry about homogeneity of variances *and* covariances. That is, within each group (cell) there is a matrix of variances and covariances among the dependent variables. For all groups, these matrices should be comparable. One way of seeing this is to plot a scatterplot matrix separately for each group. Figure 12.5 shows this for the three SETTINGs. We have added ellipses to enhance the scatterplots and detect systematic discrepancies.

We should be able to look across the plot and find comparable scatters of points. In addition, the normal curves in the diagonals of the SPLOMs should be comparable across the three groups. These samples are small, so we should be careful not to read too much into the differences in profiles in Figure 12.5. There do not appear to be any systematic things going on that would require, for example, logging or transforming the data or worrying about specific outliers.

Figure 12.5
SPLOM of Residuals

```
USE DAYCARE
LABEL SETTING/ 1='Parent',2='Sitter',3='Center'
SPLOM DINNER,STRANGER,PROBLEM/,
  GROUP=SETTING,DEN=NORM,ELL,DASH=1,7,10,OVERLAY
```

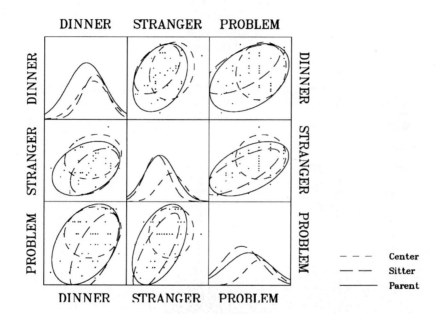

There are statistical tests for homogeneity of covariance matrices, generally based on the determinant of the sample covariance matrix. They are extensions of Box's and Bartlett's tests for homogeneity of variance and share many of their deficiencies. In general, these tests are so sensitive to non-normality (skewness, kurtosis, and outliers) that their usefulness is doubtful.

Multinormality. You will note that we SAVEd a file of residuals, DAYRES, when we estimated our preliminary model. When you USE this data set in any SYSTAT module, you will find that it contains ESTIMATEs and RESIDUALs for each of the dependent variables. The names are created with subscripts: ESTIMATE(1-3) and RE-SIDUAL(1-3). The subscripts follow the order of the variables you used in the MODEL statement.

We can pool the residuals and examine them for multinormality. Unfortunately, normality of each variable separately does not guarantee multinormality. It works the other way. Multinormality guarantees normality of each separate variable. Nevertheless, we should look at separate normal probability plots for each variable because a non-normal distribution on one separate (marginal) variable rules out the possibility of multinormality.

Figure 12.6
Plot of Residuals

```
USE DAYRES
PLOT RESIDUAL(3)*RESIDUAL(2)*RESIDUAL(1) / SPAN,DASH=1,7,10,
  GROUP=SETTING,OVERLAY,LLAB='Parent','Sitter','Center'
```

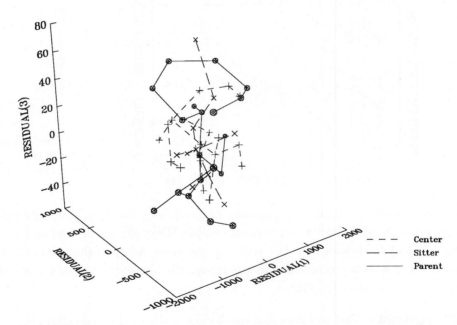

How do we view a multidimensional point cloud to assess it for multinormality? We would be looking for a watermelon shape in three dimensions and a hyper-melon in more! We could rotate a 3-D plot in the present example, because there are three dependent variables. Figure 12.6 shows a 3-D plot of the residuals. We've added a minimum spanning tree to connect the points and to highlight the separate groups. Despite these embellishments, it is difficult to judge the multinormality directly.

What we would like to do is slice this plot every possible way and see if every slice looks normal. This is impractical, of course, so the next best thing is to find some two-dimensional views which are most likely to reveal non-normality. One method is to compute the principal components of the residuals in the FACTOR module to identify multidimensional outliers.

The rationale for this is as follows. Components are weighted averages of the residuals. The first few components account for most of the variance in the residuals. These first components are most likely to be normal looking because most of the loadings are large and the components are, consequently, sums of a relatively larger number of variables. The central limit theorem tells us that this condition tends to produce normal variates. The last two components, on the other hand, account for the least variance. Typically, these last components involve a few high loadings on variables which are anomalous. By plotting the last two components we are more likely, on average, to encounter outliers and nonnormality. Figure 12.7 shows the procedure. Things look pretty clean and spherical.

Independence. The SERIES module can be used to examine the residuals for serial correlation, just as in ANOVA. If your cell counts are roughly equal, you should be especially attentive to serial correlations at the lag corresponding to the cell count. This would indicate that you might have lurking effects due to the way "early" subjects in each cell were treated relative to "later" subjects. Other patterns in the ACF plot can indicate other lurking variable possibilities.

12.4 Hypothesis testing

There are three basic strategies for more detailed analysis of MANOVA results. One way is to pursue single-degree-of-freedom contrasts on the independent variables (factors) of the multivariate model. The second is to examine effects on each dependent variable separately. The third is to compute contrasts on the dependent variables.

Figure 12.7
Plot of Last Component Scores of Residuals

```
FACTOR
USE DAYRES
SAVE FACRES/SCORES
MODEL RESIDUAL(1..3)
ESTIMATE/METHOD=PCA, NUMBER=3
USE FACRES
PLOT FACTOR(3)*FACTOR(2)/SY=1
```

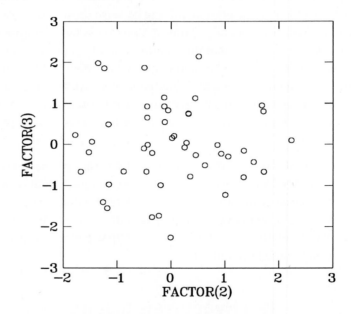

Single-degree-of-freedom contrasts. Some texts make single-degree-of-freedom contrasts sound abstruse, but with SYSTAT it is no more difficult to perform this kind of test on a multivariate model than it was on a univariate model in previous chapters of this section. For example, to express the hypothesis that social competence is adversely affected by institutional care, we might wish to predict a high outcome for parent and sitter children and a low outcome for center children. This would be expressed in a simple HYPOTHESIS sequence:

```
HYPOTHESIS
EFFECT SETTING
CONTRAST [1 1 -2]
TEST
```

The commands here are identical to those issued for a univariate model except for the presence of multiple dependents. By and large, the issues are also the same. You can read through the sections on single-degree-of-freedom tests, the CONTRAST statement (and SPECIFY and AMATRIX statements for models with more than one independent factor) to learn how to express more general hypotheses. The discussions of related issues – testing multiple hypotheses, dealing with unequal group sizes – will also apply. The one difference will be in the output. Our hypotheses will be tested by the multivariate F-tests and, if we set PRINT=LONG, we will always have access to the additional multivariate information (loadings of the dependents on the estimated variates and CHI-SQUARE tests) that can help discern just what effects (variates and dependents) are involved in the differences that we find.

Univariate tests. The second common strategy is to follow up a significant MANOVA result with tests on univariate models for each of the dependents taken separately. This is sometimes called a **protected F** procedure, analogous to Fisher's **least significant difference** post-hoc test. The preliminary multivariate F-test supposedly offers assurance that there is indeed "something going on" in the set of variables included in the model. In this way it "protects" against the possibility that a significant finding in one of a larger set of univariate models reflects simple chance variability. A more technical way to say this is that chance of "experimentwise error" is kept close to the nominal level of alpha (usually .05). Although some simulations have been done in support of this recommendation, the procedure does not necessarily maintain the nominal alpha level. You should be careful not to make too much of univariate F tests which are marginally significant.

There are some advantages to this approach. For example, we can interpret findings with reference to the variables collected rather than the more abstract underlying "variates," collect summary statistics such as means, and even work with multiple comparison procedures such as the Tukey HSD. There are, however, some flaws.

For one, the initial MANOVA indicates that there is something going on over all the data, but it does not assure that every subsequent univariate test is significant at its printed level of significance. If we have a small set of explicit hypotheses, we can use a Bonferroni procedure to select a new criterion p value that affords the appropriate level of protection. If our work is more exploratory, and we wish to test a number of possibilities, however, we are in deep water. The Bonferroni procedure will be overly conservative but there will be no real way to obtain a criterion p value which stays close to the alpha we desire. In such a case we are better off using the original multivariate output to gain insight about where effects are coming from.

For another, we sometimes may find that follow-up on a significant MANOVA will show no significant results on any of the set of univariate tests taken separately. This occurs because the MANOVA estimates an optimal weighting of dependents and uses information from all the data. At times it can be far more powerful than any of the univariate tests.

Finally, it is easy to get carried away with the individual results and lose track of the information that the original MANOVA provided – e.g., the knowledge that optimal group differences arise from combinations of dependents and that it is possible to discern which set of variables might provide a more parsimonious account of findings.

Contrasts on dependent variables. The third basic approach is to test hypotheses concerning linear combinations of the dependent variables. For example, do the measures of DINNER and STRANGER skills differ significantly by care setting? This is a double difference, like an interaction. The CMATRIX command in the HYPOTHESIS paragraph allows us to test contrasts on dependent variables in MANOVA similarly to the way we test contrasts on independent variables with the AMATRIX command.

Figure 12.8 shows how to test this hypothesis. Because it involves one degree of freedom, the F value is exact. We can conclude that DINNER and STRANGER are significantly different in the way they measure the differences between settings.

The CMATRIX command can be used to test the significance of any linear combinations of the dependent variables. As the SYSTAT manual illustrates, the number of rows in the CMATRIX determine the degrees of freedom for the test. As you will see in Section 13.3, it can play a role in testing the significance of trials effects in repeated measures ANOVA designs.

Figure 12.8
CMATRIX Contrast

```
HYPOTHESIS
CMATRIX [1 -1 0]
TEST
```

```
Hypothesis.

C Matrix

                    1           2           3
                    1.000      -1.000       0.0
Test of Hypothesis

        Source        SS        DF        MS              F            P

    Hypothesis  1.68114E+07     3   5603800.546        20.058       0.000
    Error       1.25720E+07    45   279378.030
```

12.5 Extensions

Factorial MANOVA

We might wonder whether social competence differs between boys and girls either overall (a main effect) or within sets of children who experience different forms of day-care (interaction of SETTING*SEX). The appropriate model now includes two independent variables, SETTING and SEX, and becomes parallel to a two-way ANOVA. Testing such a model requires no commands beyond those already discussed. For example, the following commands test the interaction and main effects:

```
ANOVA
USE CARE
CATEGORY SETTING,SEX
DEPENDENT DINNER,STRANGER,PROBLEM
ESTIMATE
```

Each hypothesis will produce different numbers of MANOVA components. The SETTING main effect will have 2 components, the SEX one, and the SETTING by SEX will have 2. Recall the rule: One fewer component than the number of dependents or the number of groups, whichever is smaller.

These will be global tests of the specified effects; the resulting multivariate output will allow you to discern if there is something going on at the level of the effect you specified. Naturally you can and usually should go beyond this to use CONTRAST, SPEC-IFY, or AMATRIX statements if you have more explicit hypotheses to test. Read through the discussion of these commands in the ANOVA section to see how differences among levels on a factor or among multi-factor cells of the design can be isolated and tested. Again, the output will be multivariate, but the interpretation of effects will be parallel.

Unbalanced groups and missing values

SYSTAT's use of a least squares approach to ANOVA permits simple ways for dealing with the imbalances: a few randomly missing cases can be ignored; systematic losses (or a sample which has group proportions out of line with those of the population of interest) can be corrected through reweighting with CONTRAST, SPECIFY, or AMATRIX statements in a HYPOTHESIS sequence. All of that discussion applies equally to MANOVA models. There is, however, a catch.

For ANOVA, the loss of any dependent value score results in the loss of that case from analysis. For MANOVA, the absence of a score on any one of the dependent measures results in the loss of the whole case from the analysis. Even an apparently minor scattering of missing values can easily produce a severe loss of cases for the overall model. With some messy data, we can easily find ourselves looking at empty groups or a model so depleted of information that no decent estimates of effects can be obtained.

This problem has no simple solution. You might think, for instance, that the model should make efficient use of the information available in each of the dependents taken separately – a "pairwise deletion" approach to estimating the model. SYSTAT offers no such option because the general linear model cannot produce valid tests under these circumstances. Beyond the obvious – going back into the field to recover the missing information or collect replacement cases – there are two options.

We can retreat back to separate ANOVA analyses and get the most information out of each of the dependents taken separately. You should look back to the opening paragraphs of this chapter, however, to recall what is lost in taking this approach: power in the absence of joint estimation and in the adjustments to criterion p values required when entertaining a long series of ANOVA tests; the possibility of finding a parsimonious explanation on a reduced set of underlying dimensions or better sense of which variables are most involved in differences that do arise.

Alternatively, we can "impute" missing values, that is, replace missing scores with some estimate of what they might have been had we obtained them. Common possibilities are the given dependent's grand mean for all the subjects, the average of means for the set of factor levels the case represents, or the mean for the case's group. The first uses the maximum number of cases to produce a estimated value that is stable but insensitive to any group differences; the last, conversely, produces the least stable value but one most likely to show group differences that occur in existing data. For a given data set you will have to look over the number of cases available for making an estimate at each given level and make a judgment about where the reasonable trade-off between stability and power will exist. In any case, you should decrement the error degrees of freedom by the number of missing values you estimated.

Imputing values also requires a sensible and conservative touch. Substitutions for more than a small percent of cases, especially if they are concentrated in a few cells of the design, is a simple exercise in self-deception. Statistical tests compare our sample to a theoretical distribution of as many perfectly independent values as are in our estimated model. Imputing values places nonindependent values into our estimated model and violates the assumptions of the test. Anything other than a very conservative use of this strategy distorts the comparison and destroys the validity of printed statistical tests.

Making use of components

In testing our hypotheses, MANOVA models estimate underlying components which combine the information in sets of dependents to discriminate maximally among groups. This seems like useful information, particularly if the given analysis is seen as a preliminary to building a more comprehensive model for study results. For instance, the measures DINNER, STRANGER, and PROBLEM were used in search for a better measure of how social competence differs among children experiencing differing daycare settings. Our MANOVA appeared to find commonality in STRANGER and PROBLEM and we might now wish to use that commonality (rather than diverse raw measures) in subsequent analyses.

We already have access to this new variable. We captured it when we SAVEd a file called DAYCOMP during the hypothesis sequence testing for the presence group differences in SETTING. The variable FACTOR(1) in this file is the particular weighted combination of DINNER, STRANGER, and PROBLEM that maximally discriminates among groups. We can merge this variable onto a file containing other information about the same children and use it to predict other child characteristics. For instance, do the social competence differences associated with different daycare experiences predict social competence in later school experience?

Further reading

Bock (1975) and Morrison (1976) are classical references on MANOVA. Harris (1985) is an elementary introduction to Morrison. Jobson (1992) is a useful recent text. Tabachnick and Fidell (1996) is accessible to non-statisticians and includes SYSTAT examples.

References

Bock, R.D. (1975). *Multivariate Statistical Methods in Behavioral Research*. New York: McGraw-Hill.

Harris, R.J. (1985). *A Primer of Multivariate Statistics* (2nd ed.). New York: Academic Press.

Jobson, J.D. (1992). *Applied Multivariate Data Analysis*. Vol. II: *Categorical and Multivariate Methods*. New York: Springer-Verlag.

Morrison, D.F. (1976). *Multivariate Statistical Methods* (2nd ed.). New York: McGraw-Hill.

Tabachnick B.G. and Fidell, L.S. (1996). *Using Multivariate Statistics* (3rd ed.). New York: HarperCollins.

13

Repeated Measures

The term "repeated measures" means that each subject or case is measured repeatedly. These are often called "within subjects" designs because the focus is on the way measurements vary within each subject. The designs we have seen in previous ANOVA chapters are "between subjects" because the focus is on the way measurements vary between blocks of different subjects The dependent variable(s) in repeated measures designs are often called "measures" and the occasions on which they are measured are often called "trials." Repeated measures designs are really a form of MANOVA, although they have not always been regarded that way. Traditionally, repeated measures designs have been treated like univariate split plot ANOVA designs. This approach requires an understanding of mixed models, which we discussed briefly in Section 10.3. We will contrast it with the multivariate approach in this chapter.

Let's look at some data. Supermarket produce comes in a variety of forms. You usually can choose fresh, frozen, or canned. Which is the most economical? We conducted a study to check. We sampled a dozen fruits and vegetables in a local supermarket and noted the price for a pound of each item fresh, frozen, or canned. The data we collected are in Figure 13.1 and Figure 13.2.

There are two forms of these data in these figures. The first is the multivariate layout, which is what we recommend for repeated measures. The second is a univariate layout, which suits the split plot approach. The first dataset we will call PRODUCE and the second, PRODUCE1. We will carry through our analysis on both datasets so that you can see the differences and similarities.

The advantage of the multivariate layout is that the MANOVA approach to repeated measures requires fewer assumptions about homogeneity of variance and covariance across trials and treatments. The details are beyond the scope of this book, but the benefits are worth the preference for MANOVA. The disadvantage of the MANOVA approach is that it will not work when there are fewer subjects than trials. This should rarely be a problem, but when it is, you will have to set up your data the other way.

For both layouts in Figure 13.1 and Figure 13.2, food NAME$ serves as "subjects." That is, the foods are repeatedly measured. TYPE$ is a grouping variable we will examine later in the chapter. The first analysis will concentrate on the trials to see whether there is a price difference in the preparation repeated measure (CANNED, FRESH, or FROZEN)

Figure 13.1
Data for the Study of Produce Costs - Multivariate Layout

CASE	NAME$	TYPE$	FRESH	FROZEN	CANNED
1	CARROTS	VEG	0.45	0.94	0.45
2	GREEN_BEANS	VEG	0.69	1.19	0.46
3	PEAS	VEG	0.99	0.99	0.51
4	CORN	VEG	0.42	0.99	0.43
5	LIMA_BEANS	VEG	0.69	1.26	0.78
6	SPINACH	VEG	2.38	0.99	0.62
7	POTATOES	VEG	0.35	0.99	0.43
8	SQUASH	VEG	0.38	0.72	0.55
9	CHERRIES	FRUIT	1.98	1.61	1.19
10	STRAWBERRIES	FRUIT	1.49	1.99	1.65
11	APPLES	FRUIT	0.50	1.40	1.05
12	PINEAPPLE	FRUIT	1.25	1.75	1.09
13	RASPBERRY	FRUIT	6.75	2.65	2.66
14	PEACH	FRUIT	2.49	1.58	0.85
15	BLACKBERRY	FRUIT	4.10	2.18	2.56
16	BLUEBERRY	FRUIT	6.50	2.39	2.29

13.1 Displaying the data

Let's look at the joint distributions of the three measures. Figure 13.3 (left) shows a SPLOM of the prices with histograms on the diagonals. Notice the positive skewness in the prices. We need to do a transformation before working with these data. A quick way to try the whole family of power transformations is to use the POW option of SPLOM:

```
SPLOM FRESH,FROZEN,CANNED / POW=.5
SPLOM FRESH,FROZEN,CANNED / LOG
SPLOM FRESH,FROZEN,CANNED / POW=-.5
SPLOM FRESH,FROZEN,CANNED / POW=-1
```

Figure 13.2
Data for the Study of Produce Costs - Univariate Layout

CASE	NAME$	TYPE$	PREP$	PRICE
1	CARROTS	VEG	FRESH	0.45
2	GREEN_BEANS	VEG	FRESH	0.69
3	PEAS	VEG	FRESH	0.99
4	CORN	VEG	FRESH	0.42
5	LIMA_BEANS	VEG	FRESH	0.69
6	SPINACH	VEG	FRESH	2.38
7	POTATOES	VEG	FRESH	0.35
8	SQUASH	VEG	FRESH	0.38
9	CHERRIES	FRUIT	FRESH	1.98
10	STRAWBERRIES	FRUIT	FRESH	1.49
11	APPLES	FRUIT	FRESH	0.50
12	PINEAPPLE	FRUIT	FRESH	1.25
13	RASPBERRY	FRUIT	FRESH	6.75
14	PEACH	FRUIT	FRESH	2.49
15	BLACKBERRY	FRUIT	FRESH	4.10
16	BLUEBERRY	FRUIT	FRESH	6.50
17	CARROTS	VEG	FROZEN	0.94
18	GREEN_BEANS	VEG	FROZEN	1.19
19	PEAS	VEG	FROZEN	0.99
20	CORN	VEG	FROZEN	0.99
21	LIMA_BEANS	VEG	FROZEN	1.26
22	SPINACH	VEG	FROZEN	0.99
23	POTATOES	VEG	FROZEN	0.99
24	SQUASH	VEG	FROZEN	0.72
25	CHERRIES	FRUIT	FROZEN	1.61
26	STRAWBERRIES	FRUIT	FROZEN	1.99
27	APPLES	FRUIT	FROZEN	1.40
28	PINEAPPLE	FRUIT	FROZEN	1.75
29	RASPBERRY	FRUIT	FROZEN	2.65
30	PEACH	FRUIT	FROZEN	1.58
31	BLACKBERRY	FRUIT	FROZEN	2.18
32	BLUEBERRY	FRUIT	FROZEN	2.39
33	CARROTS	VEG	CANNED	0.45
34	GREEN_BEANS	VEG	CANNED	0.46
35	PEAS	VEG	CANNED	0.51
36	CORN	VEG	CANNED	0.43
37	LIMA_BEANS	VEG	CANNED	0.78
38	SPINACH	VEG	CANNED	0.62
39	POTATOES	VEG	CANNED	0.43
40	SQUASH	VEG	CANNED	0.55
41	CHERRIES	FRUIT	CANNED	1.19
42	STRAWBERRIES	FRUIT	CANNED	1.63
43	APPLES	FRUIT	CANNED	1.05
44	PINEAPPLE	FRUIT	CANNED	1.09
45	RASPBERRY	FRUIT	CANNED	2.66
46	PEACH	FRUIT	CANNED	0.85
47	BLACKBERRY	FRUIT	CANNED	2.56
48	BLUEBERRY	FRUIT	CANNED	2.29

You can also observe these transformations on the fly with the popup graph tool in Version 6. The log transformation works quite well for these data, but the reciprocal (POW=-1) is not much different. The reciprocal of "dollars per pound" is "pounds per dollar." Both can be used to measure economy, and they will show us an important lesson about transformations.

Figure 13.3
SPLOM of Prices

```
USE PRODUCE
SPLOM CANNED,FROZEN,FRESH/DEN=HIST,SYMB=1

LET IFRESH=1/FRESH
LET IFROZEN=1/FROZEN
LET ICANNED=1/CANNED
SPLOM ICANNED,IFROZEN,IFRESH/DEN=HIST,SYMB=1
```

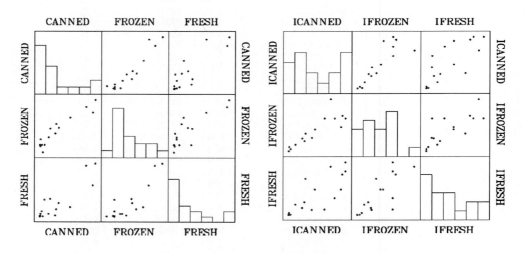

Figure 13.3 (right) shows the SPLOM of "pounds per dollar." We decided to create three new variables (LET IFRESH=1/FRESH, and so on) so that we can work with them throughout.

13.2 Constructing the model

We are ready to construct and estimate a repeated measures model for testing whether the prices differ among preparations. Basically, we have a profile of mean price for the three different types of food preparation, and our question is whether that profile is indistinguishable from a horizontal line. If it is approximately horizontal, then the means must not significantly differ. Because the repeated measures hypothesis is based on a test of this profile, it is often called "profile analysis."

Figure 13.4 shows this hypothesis graphically. The left panel shows the profile for dollars per pound and the right panel shows pounds per dollar. The horizontal line in each plot is positioned at the mean. Before relating these plots to our model, we should underscore the need for a transformation. If we did not plot the raw data as well as the profiles (as most published articles using ANOVA fail to do), we would not notice that the means on which the profile in the upper plot is based are not representative of the groups. The data are so skewed that the means are higher than the bulk of the data. Consequently, the apparently higher price of FRESH produce is an artifact of the skewness. Notice that FRESH turns out to be lower than CANNED, on average, in the right plot.

These data are a nice example of how failing to transform appropriately can lead to misleading statistical results. Many students ask, on first viewing transformations, how we can fiddle with the numbers. They wonder, for example, how we can take an understandable variable like "income" and change it into funny little numbers called "log of income." Some feel there is even something smarmy about this, that we are juggling the numbers to get results we want. "Pounds per dollar" makes as much sense as "dollars per pound." And it leads to more appropriate statistical conclusions about average costs. Paul Velleman (in the Data Desk manual) has provided another interesting example of a meaningful reciprocal transformation. "Miles per gallon" is often skewed for a sample of cars, while "gallons per mile," which is used more frequently in Europe as an economy measure, is not.

Let's lay this out as a MANOVA. The profile is simply the following model in GLM:

```
MODEL CANNED,FRESH,FROZEN = CONSTANT
```

The ANOVA procedure in SYSTAT fits this model with a simple DEPENDENT command. Figure 13.5 shows how this is done. We have added a NAME option to give the repeated measure a name (PREP).

Figure 13.4
Profile Plots of Dollars Per Pound and Pounds Per Dollar

```
BEGIN
DOT CANNED,FROZEN,FRESH/REPEAT,LINE,SIZE=0,
  YLAB='Dollars per Pound'
DEN CANNED,FROZEN,FRESH/REPEAT,DIT,AX=NONE,SC=NONE

BEGIN
DOT ICANNED,IFROZEN,IFRESH/REPEAT,LINE,SIZE=0,
  YLAB='Pounds per Dollar'
DEN ICANNED,IFROZEN,IFRESH/REPEAT,DIT,AX=NONE,SC=NONE
END
```

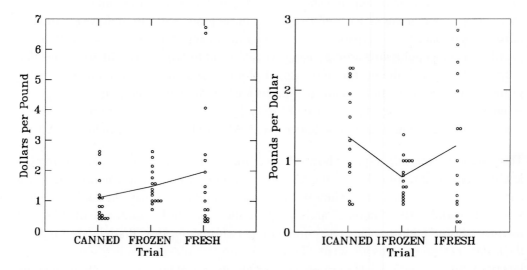

There are two tests of our hypothesis about trials (PREP) in Figure 13.5. The "Within Subjects" output is for a univariate repeated measures analysis. This analysis is based on a different model with more restrictive assumptions than the MANOVA approach.

Specifically, we must assume for the univariate model that the variances of the *differences* between all pairs of trials are homogeneous (the Huynh-Feldt condition). Some texts mistakenly say this assumption requires equal covariances between trials and equal variances within trials, but this so-called "compound symmetry" assumption is unnecessarily restrictive.

Figure 13.5
Repeated Measures as MANOVA

```
USE PRODUCE
LET ICANNED=1/CANNED
LET IFRESH=1/FRESH
LET IFROZEN=1/FROZEN
ANOVA
DEPENDENT ICANNED,IFRESH,IFROZEN / REPEAT,NAME='PREP'
ESTIMATE
```

```
Number of cases processed: 16
Dependent variable means

                      ICANNED      IFRESH      IFROZEN
                        1.339       1.209       0.776

-----------------------------------------------------------------------------

 Univariate and Multivariate Repeated Measures Analysis

Within Subjects
---------------

Source            SS        DF         MS        F       P      G-G     H-F

PREP             2.772       2        1.386     7.091   0.003   0.005   0.004
Error            5.865      30        0.195


Greenhouse-Geisser Epsilon:        0.8308
Huynh-Feldt Epsilon      :         0.9216
-----------------------------------------------------------------------------

 Multivariate Repeated Measures Analysis

Test of: PREP               Hypoth. DF  Error DF      F            P
   Wilks' Lambda=     0.424      2         14        9.494       0.002
   Pillai Trace =     0.576      2         14        9.494       0.002
   H-L Trace    =     1.356      2         14        9.494       0.002
```

The GREENHOUSE-GEISER epsilon is a term used to adjust the degrees of freedom when the compound symmetry assumption is not met. The HUYNH-FELDT epsilon adjusts when the less restrictive assumption is violated. The G-G and H-F probabilities in this section of the output are adjusted this way. For an analysis which meets the compound symmetry assumption, the G-G probability should not be much different from the usual one to the left. And if the more general sphericity assumption is met, the H-F probability should be similar to the one to the left. In summary, the H-F probability will tend to be more liberal than the G-G and it is the one you should trust because the compound symmetry assumption is not necessary for the univariate repeated measures analysis to be valid.

The multivariate analysis follows. This uses the same test statistics we discussed in the MANOVA chapter. The multivariate test assesses whether the vector (profile) in the right panel of Figure 13.4 is horizontal. This is functionally the same as the univariate approach, but the test statistics and assumptions differ. In the MANOVA test, the variances within trials and covariances between trials may differ.

Which should we choose and report – the univariate or multivariate analysis? This is a matter of some debate because there is not a simple answer. The univariate analysis will generally have more error degrees of freedom and thus more power than the multivariate approach. On the other hand, it requires the more restrictive Huynh-Feldt assumption. In general, if the H-F adjustment is not extreme (vastly different probability from the uncorrected one) and if the number of observations is relatively small compared to the number of trials, you should prefer the univariate approach. Otherwise, use the multivariate.

There is one remaining part of the output which we have not discussed. If you use PRINT=LONG before ESTIMATE, you will see "polynomial" contrasts in your output. These "orthogonal polynomials" are the same weights we used to compute post-hoc tests in factorial designs, but they are applied to the trials. With three trials (CANNED, FRESH, FROZEN) there are only two degrees of freedom for contrasts: linear and quadratic. The linear polynomial weights test for a linear increasing or decreasing trend across the three preparations. The quadratic polynomial weights cover a trend in which the middle preparation (FRESH) is higher or lower than the other two. See Figure 9.9 for examples of polynomial trend curves. Of course, the ordering of the dependent variables matters when you test for trend. We followed the ordering used in Figure 13.4. If you ask for the output, only the linear trend is significant. This finding fits our expectation from the right panel of Figure 13.4.

Figure 13.6 shows the output for the univariate data setup. We could use ANOVA to analyze this model as well, but we show a GLM setup to make the model explicit. Notice that NAME$ is explicitly included in the model. This design looks like a two-way ANOVA with no interaction. There is only one subject (NAME$) per cell, however, because only one fruit/vegetable is measured in each preparation condition (trial). An ANOVA with only one observation per cell seems strange, but it works fine if there is a valid error term. We are using in this case the NAME$ by PREP$ interaction for error and are thus assuming that it is normally distributed, independent, and homogeneous across cells. The last condition is another way of stating the compound symmetry assumption. Thus, the *F* test and associated probability are the same as in the univariate test of Figure 13.5.

We do not recommend that you follow this approach in general, however. Setting up your data as in the PRODUCE1 file will make your life more difficult with SYSTAT or other popular statistical packages. Statisticians prefer the data layout of the PRO-DUCE file for good reasons.

Figure 13.6
Repeated Measures ANOVA Model

```
GLM
USE PRODUCE1
LET IPRICE=1/PRICE
ORDER PREP$ / SORT='ICANNED','IFRESH','IFROZEN'
MODEL IPRICE = CONSTANT + PREP$ + NAME$
CATEGORY PREP$ NAME$
ESTIMATE
```

```
Categorical values encountered during processing are:
PREP$ (3 levels)
    FRESH, FROZEN, CANNED
NAME$ (16 levels)
   APPLES, BLACKBERRY, BLUEBERRY, CARROTS, CHERRIES, CORN, GREEN_BEANS,
   LIMA_BEANS, PEACH, PEAS, PINEAPPLE, POTATOES, RASPBERRY, SPINACH, SQUASH,
   STRAWBERRIES
Dep Var: IPRICE N: 48 Multiple R:  0.876 Squared multiple R:  0.767


                    Analysis of Variance

Source          Sum-of-Squares   DF  Mean-Square    F-Ratio       P

PREP$                    2.772    2       1.386       7.091     0.003
NAME$                   16.586   15       1.106       5.656     0.000

Error                    5.865   30       0.195
```

13.3 Factorial repeated measures

Now, let's enlarge our question to include whether preparation prices differ for fruits and vegetables in the same way. Figure 13.7 splits our profile plot in two – one for vegetables and one for fruits. We now have three repeated measures hypotheses. The first concerns differences between groups of "subjects" (vegetables versus fruits): are over-all costs of vegetables different from fruits? The second two concern differences within groups of subjects: do the different preparations vary in cost and does this pattern of variation differ between vegetables and fruits? In terms of Figure 13.7, these three questions amount to 1) are the two profiles at the same heights on the vertical scale? 2) are they both horizontal? and 3) are they parallel? In the Figure 13.8 output, these three questions are answered by the tests denoted by "TYPE$" (groups), "a" (trials), and "a*TYPE$" (groups by trials). You can label the trials factor if you wish by adding NAME='PREP' to the REPEAT option in GLM.

Figure 13.7
Profile Plots for Vegetables and Fruits Separately

```
USE PRODUCE1
LET IPRICE=1/PRICE
BEGIN
LINE IPRICE*PREP$/YLAB='Pounds per Dollar',GROUP=TYPE$
DEN IPRICE*PREP$/DIT,AX=NONE,SC=NONE,XLAB=' ',YLAB=' ',GROUP=TYPE$
END
```

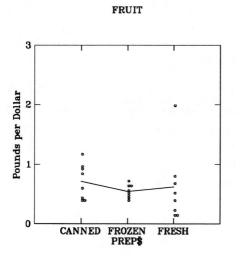 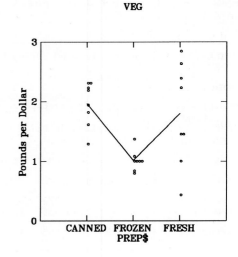

Figure 13.8 shows how this analysis is handled. It is an extension of the one-way repeated measures design in which we add a grouping variable to the right hand side of the MODEL. The assumptions concerning multivariate normality for the multivariate analysis and compound symmetry for the univariate apply to the factorial repeated measures model as well.

All three of our hypotheses are rejected at the conventional $p = .05$ level. This leads to some subtleties of interpretation. Since the profiles are not parallel, it is not reasonable to average them the way we did for our one-way analysis. For the same reason, the interpretation of the trials effect (PREP) should be limited. It is more reasonable to interpret the profile for vegetables and fruits separately.

Having said this, we must admit that the significance of this interaction is not earth-shattering ($p = .02$) and the profiles do not cross. If they did, then interpreting the main effect for trials would really be problematic. It is reasonable to say that for both fruits and vegetables, the preparations differ in cost. Also, fruits are in general more expensive than vegetables.

Notice that we followed an order of interpretation which is similar to that for ordinary factorial ANOVA. Look at the interactions first. If they are significant, be cautious about interpreting main effects because you are lumping together heterogeneous information. In this example, we went ahead and lumped because the significance of the interaction was marginal and the profiles did not cross.

Figure 13.8
Repeated Measures ANOVA Model

```
ANOVA
DEPENDENT ICANNED,IFRESH,IFROZEN /REPEAT,NAME=PREP
CATEGORY TYPE$
ESTIMATE
```

```
Categorical values encountered during processing are:
TYPE$ (2 levels)
    FRUIT, VEG
Number of cases processed: 16
Dependent variable means

                    ICANNED      IFRESH      IFROZEN
                     1.339        1.209        0.776

------------------------------------------------------------------------

Univariate and Multivariate Repeated Measures Analysis

Between Subjects
----------------
```

Source	SS	DF	MS	F	P
TYPE$	11.361	1	11.361	30.443	0.000
Error	5.225	14	0.373		

```
Within Subjects
---------------
```

Source	SS	DF	MS	F	P	G-G	H-F
PREP	2.772	2	1.386	8.841	0.001	0.005	0.003
PREP*TYPE$	1.474	2	0.737	4.701	0.017	0.034	0.028
Error	4.390	28	0.157				

```
Greenhouse-Geisser Epsilon:      0.6717
Huynh-Feldt Epsilon    :         0.7701
------------------------------------------------------------------------

Multivariate Repeated Measures Analysis
```

Test of: PREP		Hypoth. DF	Error DF	F	P
Wilks' Lambda=	0.211	2	13	24.280	0.000
Pillai Trace =	0.789	2	13	24.280	0.000
H-L Trace =	3.735	2	13	24.280	0.000

Test of: PREP*TYPE$		Hypoth. DF	Error DF	F	P
Wilks' Lambda=	0.360	2	13	11.568	0.001
Pillai Trace =	0.640	2	13	11.568	0.001
H-L Trace =	1.780	2	13	11.568	0.001

13.4 Multiple repeated measures

You can have designs which involve more than one repeated measure. In our example, we might wish to measure sweetness as well as price. For these types of designs, you should consult the SYSTAT manual or other ANOVA texts such as Neter and Wasserman.

Further reading

Neter, Wasserman and Kutner (1985) and Keppel (1991) discuss repeated measures. Jobson (1991) explains the multivariate approach somewhat more technically.

References

Jobson, J.D. (1991). *Applied Multivariate Data Analysis,* Vol I: *Regression and Experimental Design.* New York: Springer Verlag.

Keppel, G. (1991). *Design and Analysis: A Researcher's Handbook.* Englewood Cliffs, NJ: Prentice-Hall.

Neter, J., Wasserman, W., and Kutner, M. (1985). *Applied Linear Statistical Models,* (2nd ed.). Homewood, IL: Richard E. Irwin, Inc.

Part 4

Predicting Categorical Variables from Continuous Variables

Chapter 14: Regression with Categorical Dependent Variables

Chapter 15: Classification and Discriminant Analysis

14

Regression with Categorical Dependent Variables

Many university graduate departments have relied on undergraduate grades and admissions test scores to select graduate students. They have used these scores because many studies have shown that they predict performance early in graduate school. A more important question in using these criteria, however, is whether these scores predict success in obtaining a Ph.D. To explore this question, a department of psychology compared its admissions data over a ten year period to success in completing its graduate program.

Figure 14.1 contains data for a sample of 80 graduate students accepted into this department. The ADMIT data file contains the following information: Undergraduate grade point average on a 5 point scale (GPA); Graduate Record Examination Psychology Advanced Test score between 200-800 (GRE); whether a student completed a Ph.D. (PHD=1) or dropped out of the program (PHD=0).

Figure 14.1
Psychology Department Admissions Study

		GPA	GRE	PHD
CASE	1	4.17	600	0
CASE	2	4.82	630	0
CASE	3	4.40	640	0
CASE	4	4.42	610	0
CASE	5	4.91	650	0
CASE	6	4.45	640	0
CASE	7	4.53	590	0
CASE	8	4.56	520	0
CASE	9	3.77	800	0
CASE	10	4.24	540	0
CASE	11	3.77	410	0
CASE	12	4.51	580	0
CASE	13	4.02	560	0
CASE	14	4.67	560	0
CASE	15	4.64	570	0
CASE	16	4.66	580	0
CASE	17	4.68	560	0
CASE	18	4.82	630	0
CASE	19	4.38	680	0
CASE	20	4.57	600	0
CASE	21	4.61	560	0
CASE	22	4.36	530	0
CASE	23	4.73	510	0
CASE	24	5.00	640	0
CASE	25	4.02	700	0
CASE	26	4.36	670	0
CASE	27	4.26	560	0
CASE	28	4.90	650	0
CASE	29	4.76	600	0
CASE	30	4.32	560	0
CASE	31	4.25	580	0
CASE	32	4.27	660	0
CASE	33	4.78	570	0
CASE	34	4.02	550	0
CASE	35	4.21	580	0
CASE	36	4.31	580	0
CASE	37	4.32	530	0
CASE	38	4.30	660	0
CASE	39	3.91	580	0
CASE	40	4.36	530	0
CASE	41	4.14	470	0
CASE	42	4.05	570	0
CASE	43	4.67	625	0
CASE	44	4.56	540	0
CASE	45	4.50	500	0
CASE	46	4.66	590	0
CASE	47	4.90	670	0

	GPA	GRE	PHD
CASE 48	4.25	650	0
CASE 49	3.81	690	0
CASE 50	4.47	550	0
CASE 51	4.50	510	0
CASE 52	4.47	480	1
CASE 53	4.43	590	1
CASE 54	4.85	720	1
CASE 55	4.20	600	1
CASE 56	4.13	730	1
CASE 57	4.39	690	1
CASE 58	4.27	550	1
CASE 59	4.85	710	1
CASE 60	4.47	640	1
CASE 61	4.69	640	1
CASE 62	3.72	700	1
CASE 63	4.89	710	1
CASE 64	5.00	670	1
CASE 65	4.85	720	1
CASE 66	4.85	650	1
CASE 67	5.00	700	1
CASE 68	5.00	620	1
CASE 69	4.81	630	1
CASE 70	4.82	620	1
CASE 71	4.65	450	1
CASE 72	4.82	730	1
CASE 73	4.32	560	1
CASE 74	4.32	670	1
CASE 75	4.85	640	1
CASE 76	4.72	670	1
CASE 77	4.75	660	1
CASE 78	4.62	630	1
CASE 79	4.93	630	1
CASE 80	4.85	650	1

Let's plot PHD against GPA to see what a these data look like. Figure 14.2 shows a conventional scatterplot with the dependent variable on the vertical scale and an independent variable on the horizontal. Notice the horizontal strips of values. That's the kind of data this section is about: a categorical dependent and continuous independent variable(s).

Figure 14.2
Scatterplot of Ph.D. against Grade Point Average for 80 Students:
Psychology Department Admissions Study

```
USE ADMIT
CATEGORY PHD
LABEL PHD/0='No',1='Yes'
PLOT PHD * GPA / SYMBOL=1
```

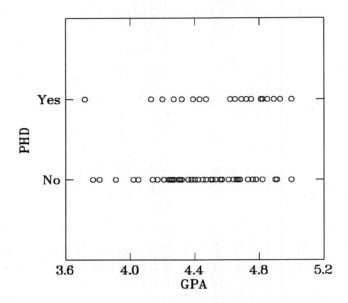

These data could be analyzed using some of the ANOVA methods described in Part 3. We are considering PHD, which is categorical, to be a *dependent* variable in this section, however. This distinction is crucial to the way we are going to pose questions and construct models to answer them.

14.1 Preliminary analysis

Let's examine these data to see if GPA or GRE can predict whether a student in the department is likely to complete a Ph.D. First, let's do a box plot (see Part III) on each variable separated by PHD.

Figure 14.3
Box Plots of Ph.D. against Independent Variables:
Psychology Department Admissions Study

BOX GRE*PHD/NOTCH
BOX GPA*PHD/NOTCH

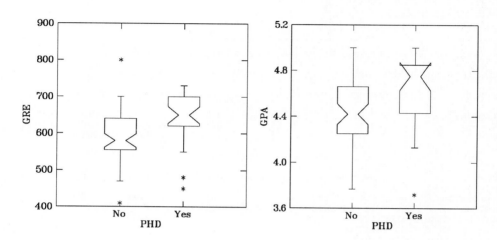

The group failing to get a Ph.D. appears to have a significantly lower median under-graduate GPA, because the notches around the medians do not overlap. The same is true for the GRE. Students failing to get a Ph.D. have significantly lower median GRE scores.

Constructing a linear model

How can we use these data to predict Ph.D.? One method would be to use the grades and test scores as predictors in a model equation. We could weight each predictor and add all of them up to get a prediction. The result would be a number closer to 0 (no Ph.D.) or 1 (Ph.D.). Here is this model:

$$PHD = B0 + B1*GPA + B2*GRE$$

In this model, B0 is a constant term and B1 and B2 are weights to apply to GPA and GRE in the prediction. You can compare this to similar linear models in the regression chapters.

Let's try to fit this model to the data.

Figure 14.4
Regression Analysis to Predict PHD:
Psychology Department Admissions Study

```
GLM
USE ADMIT
MODEL PHD = CONSTANT + GPA + GRE
SAVE RESID/RESID
ESTIMATE
```

```
Dep Var: PHD N: 80 Multiple R:  0.444 Squared multiple R:  0.197

Adjusted squared multiple R:  0.177    Standard error of estimate:     0.439

Effect         Coefficient    Std Error    Std Coef Tolerance    F    P(2 Tail)

CONSTANT          -2.715        0.753        0.0        .        13.019    0.001
GPA                0.400        0.155        0.267    0.967       6.620    0.012
GRE                0.002        0.001        0.310    0.967       8.901    0.004

                        Analysis of Variance

Source         Sum-of-Squares   DF  Mean-Square     F-Ratio       P

Regression          3.649        2     1.825         9.469       0.000
Residual           14.838       77     0.193
Durbin-Watson D Statistic     0.435
First Order Autocorrelation   0.775
Residuals have been saved.
```

The results appear encouraging. The *F*-ratio for the model is 9.469, associated with a probability of less than .001. The probabilities on the coefficients for GPA and GRE are both less than .05. In order to trust these probabilities, however, we have to assume that the residuals are normally distributed. Figure 14.5 shows plots of these residuals.

What's going on here? Usually in regression modeling, we see the residuals spread out in a single horizontal fuzzy band. Instead, we have two diagonal stripes. Furthermore, the stem-and-leaf plot is bimodal. This is because the dependent variable, PHD, has only two values. These residuals cannot be normally distributed. Thus, the use of the *F* distribution to assess the significance of this model or other ones with categorical dependent variables is invalid.

There is another problem with using this linear model to predict PHD, however. Let's do a stem-and-leaf diagram of the estimated values. Figure 14.6 shows the result.

Figure 14.5
Graphical Analysis of Residuals

```
USE RESID
PLOT RESIDUAL*ESTIMATE/SYMBOL=1
```

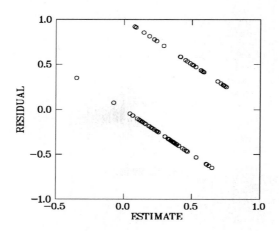

```
STATS
STEM RESIDUAL
```

```
Stem and Leaf Plot of variable:     RESIDUAL, N = 80
        Minimum:          -0.649
        Lower hinge:        -0.353
        Median:           -0.146
        Upper hinge:         0.415
        Maximum:            0.922

           -6    4210
           -5    33
           -4    666430
           -3 H 9888766543332200
           -2    544220
           -1 M 99886533321
           -0    9664
            0    7
            1
            2    456678
            3    14
            4 H 1112233789
            5    13488
            6
            7    067
            8    15
            9    12
```

Figure 14.6
Stem-and-Leaf Plot of Estimates from Regression:
Psychology Department Admissions Study

```
Stem and Leaf Plot of variable:    ESTIMATE, N = 80
      Minimum:        -0.348
      Lower hinge:       0.199
      Median:         0.367
      Upper hinge:       0.531
      Maximum:        0.751

        -3   4
  * * * Outside Values * * *
        -0   7
        -0
         0   4
         0   66789
         1   123334
         1 H 5688899
         2   0222344
         2   59
         3   00223334
         3 M 56678889
         4   01134
         4   566668
         5 H 01233
         5   6677888
         6   0124
         6   8
         7   12334
         7   5
```

We are getting a value of less than zero for two of the cases (at the top of the stem-and-leaf diagram). Does this mean that these two students are predicted to have less than no chance of getting a Ph.D.? Obviously not. We want a model which does not make predictions less than zero or greater than one. In fact, we don't want exactly zero or one predictions either, since we could not imagine grades and tests ever giving us a certain prediction of whether or not someone would complete a Ph.D.

14.2 The probit model

We have seen that the linear model we have been using has several problems in this context. Even if we give up the idea of using an F test on the results of fitting the model, it is still a poor representation of the data. To see why, let's consider a graph. The top plot in Figure 14.7 shows what a linear model for predicting PHD from GRE would look like.

Figure 14.7
Linear and Nonlinear Prediction of PHD from GRE:
Psychology Department Admissions Study

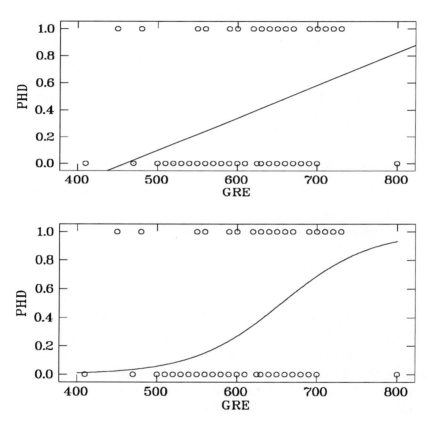

As we have noted before, the line in the top plot of Figure 14.7 continues above 1 and below 0. This means it not only gives us nonsensical predictions, but it also misses a lot of the real data. What we need is a line which comes closer to more of the data points. A curve which does not go above 1 or below 0 could come closer to these points. The bottom panel of Figure 14.7 shows such a curve.

This curve has another desirable property. Because it is bounded by 0 and 1, it can represent the probability of obtaining a Ph.D. given an applicant's GRE score. For example, the curve shows a student with a GRE score of 650 having an even chance of getting a Ph.D.

One of the best known probability curves is the **normal cumulative distribution function**. This probability curve is taken mathematically from the area under the normal "bell curve." In the NONLIN procedure of SYSTAT, the equation for fitting this curve is:

$$PHD = ZCF(CONSTANT + SLOPE*GRE)$$

In this equation, ZCF represents the normal cumulative distribution function. This function has the same shape as the S-curve in the lower part of Figure 14.7. The part inside the parentheses is just like a linear model: CONSTANT is a constant and SLOPE is a slope, or weight for GRE. We have, in other words, embedded a linear model in a nonlinear function called ZCF. Its inverse is often described as a **probit**, so we will call this a probit model.

Here is how to expand this model to two predictors, GPA and GRE:

$$PHD = ZCF(CONSTANT + SLOPE1*GPA + SLOPE2*GRE)$$

This model says "add the weighted predictor variables GPA and GRE and compute the cumulative distribution function for the resulting value."

The NONLIN module in SYSTAT can estimate nonlinear models. Figure 14.8 shows how to specify this MODEL in the NONLIN module. NONLIN estimates the parameters CONSTANT through SLOPE2 iteratively. We begin by choosing a value of 0 for each parameter (START=0,0,0). Then NONLIN uses these values to compute the ZCF function for each case. Then it sums the squared differences between the estimated value of PHD (on the curved function) and the observed value (0 or 1) across all cases. On each iteration, NONLIN adjusts the values of the parameters to reduce the size of this sum of squared differences. When it cannot reduce it further, NONLIN stops and prints out the final values of the parameters CONSTANT through SLOPE2.

Figure 14.8
Probit Model Prediction of PHD from GRE:
Psychology Department Admissions Study

```
NONLIN
USE ADMIT
MODEL PHD = ZCF(CONSTANT + SLOPE1*GPA,+ SLOPE2*GRE)
SAVE RESID / RESID
ESTIMATE / START=0,0,0
```

```
 Iteration
 No.     Loss        CONSTANT      SLOPE1        SLOPE2
  0 .200000D+02  .000000D+00  .000000D+00  .000000D+00
  1 .146351D+02 -.805931D+01  .100239D+01  .525357D-02
  2 .142529D+02 -.108477D+02  .126683D+01  .766905D-02
  3 .141836D+02 -.121245D+02  .136125D+01  .895000D-02
  4 .141687D+02 -.128030D+02  .141303D+01  .962059D-02
  5 .141655D+02 -.131455D+02  .144093D+01  .994652D-02
  6 .141648D+02 -.133107D+02  .145518D+01  .100981D-01
  7 .141647D+02 -.133882D+02  .146216D+01  .101670D-01
  8 .141646D+02 -.134240D+02  .146548D+01  .101982D-01
  9 .141646D+02 -.134404D+02  .146703D+01  .102123D-01
 10 .141646D+02 -.134479D+02  .146774D+01  .102187D-01
 11 .141646D+02 -.134513D+02  .146807D+01  .102216D-01
 12 .141646D+02 -.134528D+02  .146822D+01  .102229D-01
 13 .141646D+02 -.134536D+02  .146829D+01  .102235D-01
 14 .141646D+02 -.134539D+02  .146832D+01  .102237D-01
 15 .141646D+02 -.134540D+02  .146834D+01  .102239D-01

Dependent variable is PHD

    Source    Sum-of-Squares   DF   Mean-Square
 Regression        14.835       3      4.945
   Residual        14.165      77      0.184

     Total         29.000      80
Mean corrected     18.487      79

     Raw  R-square · (1-Residual/Total)     =       0.512
Mean corrected R**2 (1-Residual/Corrected)  =       0.234
     R(observed vs predicted) square        =       0.240

                                          Wald Confidence Interval
Parameter      Estimate     A.S.E.   Param/ASE   Lower < 95%> Upper
CONSTANT       -13.454       3.865     -3.481     -21.151     -5.758
SLOPE1           1.468       0.561      2.618       0.352      2.585
SLOPE2           0.010       0.003      2.983       0.003      0.017

Residuals have been saved.
```

We saved the residuals and predicted values from this model with the command SAVE
RESID. Figure 14.9 shows how to get a stem-and-leaf diagram of the estimated values.

Figure 14.9
Stem-and-leaf Diagram of PHD Predicted Values Using Probit Model:
Psychology Department Admissions Study

```
STATS
USE RESID
STEM ESTIMATE
```

```
Stem and Leaf Plot of variable:     ESTIMATE, N = 80
        Minimum:          0.000
        Lower hinge:         0.094
        Median:           0.276
        Upper hinge:         0.528
        Maximum:          0.861

        0    00222334444
        0  H 55557788899
        1    00112
        1    67899
        2    001234
        2  M 7788
        3    2344
        3    5679
        4    011
        4    789
        5  H 11222
        5    888
        6    00222
        6    556
        7    2
        7    6
        8    2344
        8    56
```

Now we see that the estimated values are all between 0 and 1.

14.3 The logit model

Another model produces results almost identical to the probit model we just reviewed. It is called the logit model:

$$PHD = LCF(CONSTANT + SLOPE1*GPA + SLOPE2*GRE)$$

Figure 14.10 shows both plotted in the same graph. We haven't labeled either curve because they are so close together.

Figure 14.10
Probit and Logit Curves

```
BEGIN
FPLOT Y=ZCF(X);,
    XMIN=-4,XMAX=4,YMIN=0,YMAX=1,AX=NONE,SC=NONE,TICK=INDENT
FPLOT Y=LCF(X*3.14159/SQR(3));,
    XMIN=-4,XMAX=4,YMIN=0,YMAX=1,XLAB='X',YLAB='P',TICK=INDENT
END
```

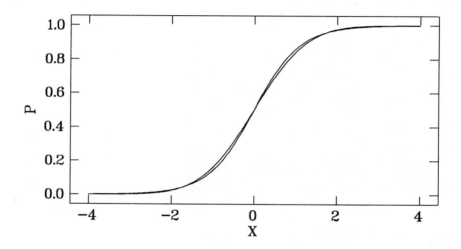

Figure 14.11 shows how to fit the logit model in NONLIN.

```
NONLIN
USE ADMIT
MODEL PHD=LCF(CONSTANT+SLOPE1*GPA+SLOPE2*GRE)
ESTIMATE
```

```
Variables in the SYSTAT Rectangular file are:
 GPA          GRE          PHD

 Iteration
 No.     Loss      CONSTANT      SLOPE1        SLOPE2
  0 .200000D+02 .000000D+00 .000000D+00 .000000D+00
  1 .146410D+02-.128608D+02 .159958D+01 .838348D-02
  2 .141802D+02-.180583D+02 .209925D+01 .128304D-01
  3 .141002D+02-.206721D+02 .231999D+01 .152589D-01
  4 .140873D+02-.219381D+02 .243560D+01 .163762D-01
  5 .140855D+02-.224660D+02 .248848D+01 .168093D-01
  6 .140852D+02-.226701D+02 .251063D+01 .169644D-01
  7 .140852D+02-.227470D+02 .251951D+01 .170191D-01
  8 .140852D+02-.227758D+02 .252298D+01 .170386D-01
  9 .140852D+02-.227866D+02 .252432D+01 .170456D-01
 10 .140852D+02-.227907D+02 .252484D+01 .170482D-01
 11 .140852D+02-.227922D+02 .252503D+01 .170491D-01
 12 .140852D+02-.227928D+02 .252511D+01 .170495D-01
 13 .140852D+02-.227930D+02 .252514D+01 .170496D-01
```

Dependent variable is PHD

Source	Sum-of-Squares	DF	Mean-Square
Regression	14.915	3	4.972
Residual	14.085	77	0.183
Total	29.000	80	
Mean corrected	18.487	79	

Raw R-square	(1-Residual/Total)	=	0.514
Mean corrected R**2	(1-Residual/Corrected)	=	0.238
R(observed vs predicted) square		=	0.244

Parameter	Estimate	A.S.E.	Param/ASE	Wald Confidence Interval Lower < 95%> Upper	
CONSTANT	-22.793	6.846	-3.329	-36.426	-9.160
SLOPE1	2.525	0.964	2.620	0.606	4.444
SLOPE2	0.017	0.006	2.848	0.005	0.029

If you save the residuals from this model, the predictions will be almost the same as for the probit. Why would we use a logistic function instead? Often, there is little reason to prefer one model over the other. The logit model generalizes more easily to multiple category designs, so some researchers prefer to use it for all categorical dependent variable models. It also has slightly "fatter" tails, so it fits extreme values better sometimes.

For binary dependent variables, however, you would have a hard time distinguishing the predictions made by the two models.

14.4 Maximum likelihood estimation

We computed the probit and logit regressions above using least squares as a loss function. That is, badness-of-fit was assessed by the sum of squared differences between the PHD values and the predicted curve at each value of the predictors. This method has some desirable features and it is simple, but it can fail to converge on the correct solution and has other problems. Usually we prefer to have **maximum likelihood estimates** of the parameters in the model.

A maximum likelihood estimate of a parameter is the population value for which the sample values are most likely. If we know the family of the population distribution, then we can substitute estimates of the parameter values to compute this likelihood and choose the value which has the greatest likelihood. Maximum likelihood estimates may not be "better" than least squares or other estimates in every respect, but they have one important advantage: they are **consistent**. That is, as the random sample size we use to compute the estimates increases, the estimates converge consistently toward the true parameter values. By choosing larger samples, then, we know we are getting more accurate estimates. And for very large samples, we also know that maximum likelihood estimates are normally distributed.

The SYSTAT manual illustrates how to do maximum likelihood estimation with NONLIN for the logit model. It involves specifying the negative of the log of the likelihood function in the LOSS statement. We will not spend time doing this on our example, except to say that the commands would look like this:

```
NONLIN
USE ADMIT
MODEL PHD=EXP(CONSTANT + SLOPE1*GPA + SLOPE2*GRE) /,
            (1 + EXP(CONSTANT+SLOPE1*GPA + SLOPE2*GRE))
LOSS = -(PHD*LOG(ESTIMATE) + (1-PHD)*LOG(1-ESTIMATE))
ESTIMATE / START=0,0,0,SCALE
```

SYSTAT has two procedures – PROBIT and LOGIT – which compute maximum likelihood estimates for these models much more efficiently. Figure 14.12 shows the results for PROBIT and Figure 14.13 shows them for LOGIT. We have omitted some more technical parts of the output. The sign reversals in the coefficients of the LOGIT output occur because this program codes the categories (PHD and NO PHD) opposite to the coding we used in NONLIN.

Figure 14.12
Maximum Likelihood Probit Model Prediction of PHD from GRE:
Psychology Department Admissions Study

```
PROBIT
USE ADMIT
MODEL PHD=CONSTANT+GPA+GRE
ESTIMATE
```

```
                          Binary Probit Analysis
                          ***********************


Dependent Variable:           PHD


Number Of Input Cases Processed:    80
Independent Variable Means

             Variable              Mean for D=0   Mean for D=1
  ============================================================
  1 CONSTANT                        1.0000000      1.0000000
  2    GPA                          4.4225490      4.6386207
  3    GRE                          590.49020      643.44828




  convergence achieved after    4 iterations.
   tol=         .100000E-02  % change in likelihood is        .619375E-06




Number Of Observations:   80
Number with Dummy = 0 :   51
Number with Dummy = 1 :   29
-2 times log likelihood ratio (chi squared) :   17.469
         with   2. degrees of freedom


Results of Estimation
*********************

Log Likelihood: -43.65299662332

          Parameter                Estimate    Standard Error  t-statistic
  ========================================================================
  1 CONSTANT                       -10.20896       2.673813      -3.8181
  2    GPA                          1.269561        .4975120      2.5518
  3    GRE                          .6686912E-02    .2309562E-02   2.8953
```

Figure 14.13
Maximum Likelihood Logit Model Prediction of PHD from GRE:
Psychology Department Admissions Study

```
LOGIT
USE ADMIT
MODEL PHD=CONSTANT+GPA+GRE
ESTIMATE
```

```
                    Multinomial Logit Analysis
                    ***************************


  Dependent Variable:        PHD


  Number Of Records Processed:    80

          Number of Choices in Each Category
          ===================================
             1        51
             2        29
  0                independent variable means
  =======================================================================


          Variable                 D =  1      D =  2

   1  CONSTANT                      1.000       1.000
   2     GPA                        4.423       4.639
   3     GRE                        590.5       643.4



  log likelihood at iteration   1 is  -55.451774
  log likelihood at iteration   2 is  -44.081946
  log likelihood at iteration   3 is  -43.457860
  log likelihood at iteration   4 is  -43.446836
  convergence achieved.


  Results of Estimation
  *********************

  Log Likelihood: -43.44683645539

          Parameter              Estimate   Standard Error t-statistic

  =======================================================================
   1  CONSTANT                    17.44466      4.778844      3.6504
   2     GPA                      -2.107042      .8509792     -2.4760
   3     GRE                      -.1185656E-01  .4247454E-02 -2.7915
```

Further reading

Aldrich and Nelson (1984) introduce logit and probit models to social scientists. Although binary statistical models have been around a long time, Cox (1970) is now a classic introductory reference. Finney (1971) is a detailed discussion of the probit model. Neter, Wasserman, and Kutner (1990) include probit and logit models in a general regression framework. McFadden (1982) discusses econometric applications.

References

Aldrich, J.H. and Nelson, F. (1984). *Linear Probability, Logit, and Probit models*. Beverly Hills: Sage Publications.

Cox, D.R. (1970). *The Analysis of Binary Data*. New York: Halsted Press.

Finney, D.J. (1971). *Probit Analysis*, (3rd ed.). London: Cambridge University Press.

McFadden, D. (1982). Qualitative response models. In W. Hildebrand (ed.), *Advances in econometrics*. London: Cambridge University Press.

Neter, J., Wasserman, W., and Kutner, M. (1990). *Applied Linear Statistical Models*, (3rd ed.). Homewood, IL: Richard E. Irwin, Inc.

15

Classification and Discriminant Analysis

When we have categorical dependent variables in a model, it is often because we are trying to classify cases: i.e. what group does someone or something belong to? For example, we might want to know whether someone with a GPA of 3.5 and an Advanced Psychology Test score of 600 is more like the group of graduate students successfully completing a Ph.D. or more like the group which fails. Or, we might want to know whether an object with a plastic handle and no concave surfaces is more like a wrench or a screwdriver.

Once we attempt to classify, our attention turns from parameters (coefficients) in a model to the consequences of classification. We now want to know what proportion of subjects will be classified correctly and what proportion incorrectly.

15.1 Classifying with the probit model

What would be the consequence of using our nonlinear probit model from the last chapter to admit students? "Percentage of variance accounted for" doesn't translate easily into "real people" units. Let's make a classification table which compares actual values of PHD (0 or 1) to values predicted by our model in the ADMIT dataset.

Figure 15.1 shows how to create classifications to tabulate. We have coded PREDICT to be 1 if there is better than a 50/50 chance that a person will get a Ph.D. according to the model. The variable ESTIMATE was produced by the NONLIN procedure. If ESTIMATE is less than .5 for a given student, then that student has less than a 50/50 chance of getting a Ph.D. according to the nonlinear model. We will tabulate the actual value of PHD against this estimated value to see how well we classified people.

Figure 15.1
Tabulating Observed against Predicted Values Using Probit Model:
Psychology Department Admissions Study

```
BASIC
USE RESID
SAVE RESID2
IF ESTIMATE<.5 THEN LET PREDICT=0
ELSE LET PREDICT=1
RUN
XTAB
USE RESID2
LABEL PHD,PREDICT / 0='No Ph.D.',1='Ph.D.'
TAB PHD*PREDICT
```

```
Frequencies
 PHD (rows) by PREDICT (columns)

           No Ph.D      Ph.D       Total
        +--------------------+
No Ph.D |    44          7  |        51
        |                   |
Ph.D    |    12         17  |        29
        +--------------------+
Total        56         24           80

Test statistic                Value       DF        Prob
  Pearson Chi-square          17.744     1.000      0.000
```

Notice the preponderance of No Ph.D. classifications. That is because our model is paying attention to the a priori 51/29 imbalance in the sample between Ph.D.s and No Ph.D.s. Our model is conservative. Out of 29 students who actually got their Ph.D.s, the model predicted that 12 wouldn't.

Classifying new data

To be safe, we kept aside another file of 80 students. This way, we could find out how well our function does with new cases. This new file is comparable to ADMIT (in fact, both were randomly sampled from a larger file of students). Figure 15.2 shows the result of applying or model to this new group of students.

Figure 15.2
Tabulating Observed against Predicted Values Using Probit Model on New
Sample of Students: Psychology Department Admissions Study

```
USE ADMIT2
LET ESTIMATE = ZCF(-13.454 + 1.468*GPA + .010*GRE)
LET PREDICT=1
IF ESTIMATE<.5 THEN LET PREDICT=0
LABEL PHD,PREDICT / 0='No Ph.D.',1='Ph.D.'
XTAB
TAB PHD*PREDICT
```

```
Frequencies
  PHD (rows) by PREDICT (columns)

              No Ph.D      Ph.D      Total
          +-------------------+
 No Ph.D  |     31         8  |       39
          |                   |
 Ph.D     |     28        13  |       41
          +-------------------+
 Total          59        21          80

Test statistic                  Value       DF      Prob
  Pearson Chi-square            1.294    1.000     0.255
```

The results could be better. We are classifying almost half the new students incorrectly. This is not unusual for this sort of thing. Many people get excited because a model fits some sample well, but they forget that it may not replicate to new data.

15.2 Classifying with Mahalanobis distances

We used the probit model to estimate a person's chance of getting a Ph.D. in this group of applicants. Then we used those estimates to place applicants into one of two categories: No Ph.D. (0) or Ph.D. (1). We found that the model did not do too well on a new sample of applicants.

We did not need to assume in the probit model that the errors are normally distributed because we did not use *F*-statistics to test goodness-of-fit. We simply assumed that each observation was independent of the others and that the underlying response function (probability of getting a Ph.D.) was that of a cumulative normal distribution.

If we know that the predictor variables are normally distributed within groups, however, we can use an alternative classification procedure called linear discriminant analysis

(Fisher, 1936). Before we present the method, however, we should warn you that the procedure requires you to *know* that the groups share a common covariance matrix and you must *know* what the covariance matrix values are. We have not found an example of discriminant analysis in the social sciences where this was true. The most appropriate applications we have found are in engineering, where a covariance matrix can be deduced from physical measurements. Discriminant analysis is used, for example, in automated vision systems for detecting objects on moving conveyer belts.

Nevertheless, we are going to perpetuate the abuse of the discriminant model by using our sample to derive this covariance matrix information so you can see how the results compare to the nonlinear models like probit and logit.

Why do we need to know the covariance matrix? We are going to use it to calculate **Mahalanobis distances** (developed by the Indian statistician Prasanta C. Mahalanobis). These distances are calculated between cases we want to classify and the center of each group in a multidimensional space. The closer a case is to the center of one group (relative to its distance to other groups), the more likely it is to be classified as belonging to that group. Figure 15.3 shows what we are doing.

The borders of this graph comprise the two predictors GPA and GRE. The two "hills" are centered at the mean values of the two groups (No Ph.D. and Ph.D.). Most of the data in each group are supposed to be under the highest part of each hill. The hills, in other words, represent mathematically the concentration of data values in the scatterplot beneath.

The shape of the hills was computed from a bivariate normal distribution using the covariance matrix averaged within groups. We've plotted this figure this way to show you that this model is like pie-in-the-sky if you use the information in the data below to compute the shape of these hills. As you can see, there is a lot of smoothing of the data going on and if one or two data values in the scatterplot influence unduly the shape of the hills above, you will have an unrepresentative model when you try to use it on new samples.

How do we classify a new case into one group or another? Look at the figure again. The "new case" could belong to one or the other group. It's more likely to belong to the closer group, however. The simple way to find how far this case is from the center of each group would be to take a direct walk from the new case to the center of each group in the data plot.

Figure 15.3
Observed Data and Normal Classification Model of Achieving Ph.D.

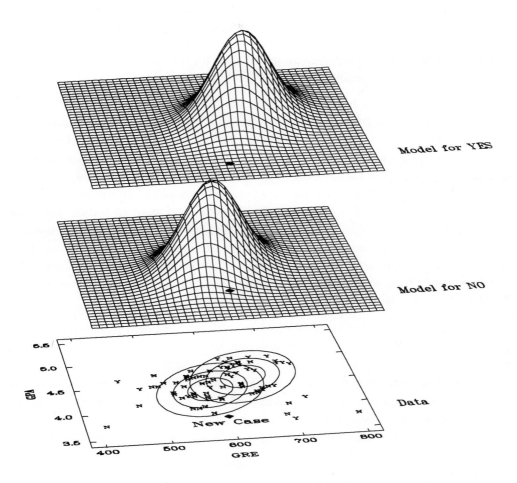

Instead of walking in sample data space below, however, we must climb the hills of our theoretical model above when using the normal classification model. In other words, we will use our theoretical model to calculate distances. The covariance matrix we used to draw the hills in the figure makes distances depend on the direction we are heading. The distance to a group is thus proportional to the *altitude* (not the horizontal distance) we must climb to get to the top of the corresponding hill.

Because these hills can be oblong in shape, it is possible to be quite far from the top of the hill as the crow flies, yet have little altitude to cover in a climb. Conversely, it is possible to be close to the center of the hill and have a steep climb to get to the top. Discriminant analysis adjusts for the covariance which causes these eccentricities in hill shape. That is why we need the covariance matrix in the first place.

So much for the geometric representation. What do the numbers look like? Figure 15.4 shows how to set up the problem with SYSTAT.

There's a lot to follow on this output. The counts and means per group are shown first. Next comes the pooled covariance matrix, computed by averaging the separate group covariance matrices, weighting by group size. The total covariance matrix ignores the groups. It includes variation due to the group separation. These are the same matrices found in the MANOVA output with PRINT=LONG. The between groups F matrix shows the F value for testing the difference between each pair of groups on all the variables (GPA and GRE). The Wilks lambda is for the multivariate test of dispersion among all the groups on all the variables, just as in MANOVA. Each case is classified by our model into the group whose classification function yields the largest score. Each function is like a regression equation. We compute the predicted value of each equation for a case's values on GPA and GRE and classify the case into the group whose function yields the largest value.

Next comes the separate F statistics for each variable and the classification matrix. The goodness of classification is comparable to that for the Probit model. We did a little worse with the No Ph.D. group and a little better with the Ph.D.. The jackknifed classification matrix is an attempt to approximate the kind of cross-validation we did with the Probit model on a new sample. It will tend to be somewhat optimistic, however, because it uses only information from the current sample, leaving out single cases to classify the remainder. There is no substitute for trying the model on new data.

Finally, the program prints the same information produced in a MANOVA by SYSTAT's MGLH (GLM and ANOVA). The multivariate test statistics show the groups are significantly different on GPA and GRE taken together. We'll come back to the remaining output shortly.

Figure 15.4
Linear Discriminant Model of Achieving Ph.D.

```
DISCRIM
USE ADMIT
PRINT LONG
MODEL PHD = GRE,GPA
ESTIMATE
```

```
Group frequencies
-----------------
                            1              2
  Frequencies              51             29

Group means
-----------
  GPA                   4.423          4.639
  GRE                 590.490        643.448

Pooled within covariance matrix  --  DF=      78
-------------------------------------------------
                         GPA            GRE
  GPA                  0.095
  GRE                  1.543       4512.409

Within correlation matrix
-------------------------
                         GPA            GRE
  GPA                  1.000
  GRE                  0.075          1.000

Total   covariance  matrix           -- DF=      79
-------------------------------------------------
                         GPA            GRE
  GPA                  0.104
  GRE                  4.201       5111.610

Total correlation matrix
------------------------
                         GPA            GRE
  GPA                  1.000
  GRE                  0.182          1.000

Between groups F-matrix  --  df =      2      77
------------------------------------------------
                           1              2
  1                      0.0
  2                      9.469          0.0

Wilks lambda
   Lambda =      0.8026    df =      2      1      78
   Approx. F=    9.4690    df =      2      77     prob =   0.0002

Classification functions
----------------------
                           1              2
  Constant            -133.910       -150.231
  GPA                   44.818         46.920
  GRE                    0.116          0.127
```

```
Classification matrix (cases in row categories classified into columns)
----------------------
                     1        2 %correct
    1               38       13      75
    2                7       22      76

        Total       45       35      75

Jackknifed classification matrix
--------------------------------
                     1        2 %correct
    1               37       14      73
    2                7       22      76

        Total       44       36      74

             Eigen       Canonical    Cumulative proportion
             values     correlations     of total dispersion
          ---------    ------------     ---------------------
             0.246          0.444              1.000

       Wilks  lambda=       0.803
           Approx.F=        9.469  DF=  2,      77  p-tail=  0.0002

     Pillai's trace=        0.197
           Approx.F=        9.469  DF=  2,      77  p-tail=  0.0002

Lawley-Hotelling trace=     0.246
           Approx.F=        9.469  DF=  2,      77  p-tail=  0.0002

Canonical discriminant functions
--------------------------------
                     1
Constant          -15.882
GPA                 2.064
GRE                 0.011

Canonical discriminant functions -- standardized by within variances
--------------------------------------------------------------------
                     1
GPA                 0.635
GRE                 0.727

Canonical scores of group means
-------------------------------
    1             -.369
    2              .649
```

Discriminating new data

To find out how well our probit model could classify new data, we used the probit equation to classify another 80 applicants to the same psychology department. Figure 15.5 shows us how to do this with the discriminant model.

Figure 15.5
Classifying a New Sample

```
DISCRIM
APPEND ADMIT ADMIT2
LET SAMPLE=1
IF CASE>80 THEN LET SAMPLE=0
WEIGHT = SAMPLE
MODEL GROUP = GPA,GRE
ESTIMATE
```

```
Classification of cases with zero weight or frequency
-----------------------------------------------------
                       1        2  %correct
    1                 21       18        54
    2                 12       29        71

        Total         33       47        63
```

SYSTAT allows us to fit a model on one set of scores and then use that model to compute estimates on another set of scores in the same file. First, we need to use the APPEND command to put both groups of students into one big file with 160 cases. Then we need to add a variable to the file in order to tell SYSTAT which sample of students a particular student came from. We've omitted other output already covered.

15.3 The linear discriminant function

We mentioned in the last section that the canonical coefficients are like a regression equation for computing distances up the hills. Let's look more closely at these coefficients. Figure 15.6 shows the plot underlying the surface in Figure 15.3. Superimposed on the bottom GRE axis are two normal distributions centered at the means for the two groups. The standard deviations of these normal distributions are computed within groups. The within-group standard deviation is the square root of the diagonal GRE variance element of the residual covariance matrix in Figure 15.4 (4512.409). The same is done for GPA, using square root of the within groups variance (.095) for the standard deviation and the group means for centering the normals.

Either of these variables separates the groups somewhat. The diagonal line underlying the two diagonal normal distributions represents a linear combination of these two variables. It is computed using the canonical discriminant functions in Figure 15.4. These are the same as the canonical coefficients produced by MGLH. Before applying these coefficients, the variables must be standardized by the within-group standard deviations. Finally, the dashed line perpendicular to this diagonal cuts the observations into two groups: those to the left and those to the right of the dashed line.

You can see that this new canonical variable and its perpendicular dashed line are an orthogonal (right-angle-preserving) rotation of the original axes. The separation of the two groups using normal distributions drawn on the rotated canonical variable is slightly better than that for either variable alone. To classify on the linear discriminant axis, make the mean on this new variable 0 (halfway between the two diagonal normal curves). Then add a scale along the diagonal running from negative to positive. If we do this, then any observations with negative scores on this diagonal scale will be classified into the No Ph.D. group (to the left of the dashed perpendicular bisector) and those with positive scores into the Ph.D. (to the right). All Y's to the left of the dashed line and N's to the right are misclassifications. Try rotating these axes any other way to get a better count of correctly classified cases (watch out for ties). The linear discriminant function is the best rotation.

Using this linear discriminant function variable, we get the same classifications we got with the Mahalanobis distance method. Before computers, this was the preferred method for classifying because the computations are simpler. We just use the equation:

$$F_Z = .635 * Z_{GPA} + .727 * Z_{GRE}$$

The two "Z" variables are the raw scores minus the overall mean divided by the within groups standard deviations. If F_Z is less than zero, classify No Ph.D., otherwise classify Ph.D.

As we mentioned, the Mahalanobis method and the linear discriminant function method are equivalent. This is somewhat evident in Figure 15.3. The intersection of the two hills is a straight line running from the northwest to the southeast corner in the same orientation as the dashed line in Figure 15.6. Any point to the left of this line will be closer to the top of the left hill and any point to the right will be closer to the top of the right hill.

Figure 15.6
The Linear Discriminant Function

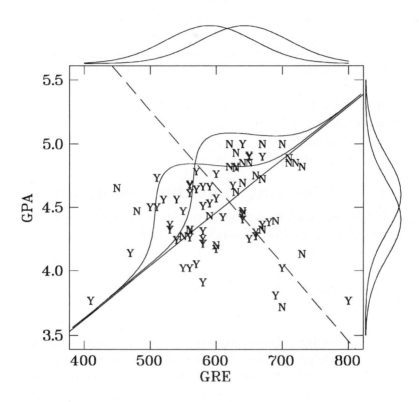

15.4 Prior probabilities

Our sample contained fewer Ph.D.s than No Ph.D.s. If we want to use our discriminant model to classify new cases and if we believe that this difference in sample sizes reflects proportions in the population, then we can adjust our formula to favor No Ph.D.s. In other words, we can make the *prior probabilities* (assuming we know nothing about GRE and GPA scores) favor a No Ph.D. classification. We can do this by adding the option

```
PRIORS=.625,.375
```

to the MODEL command. Do not be tempted to use this method as a way of improving your classification table. If the probabilities you choose do not reflect real population differences, then new samples will on average be classified *worse*. It would make sense in our case because we happen to know that more people in our department tend to drop out than stay for the Ph.D.

You might have guessed that the default setting is for prior probabilities to be equal (both .5). In Figure 15.6, this makes the dashed line run halfway between the means of the two groups on the discriminant axis. By changing the priors, we move this dashed line (the normal distributions stay in the same place).

If you use prior probabilities a lot, you should check the references further to see the role these probabilities play in Bayes' theorem. This theorem underlies classifications of the sort we have been doing.

15.5 Classifying more than two groups

The discriminant model generalizes to more than two groups. Imagine, for example, three hills in Figure 15.3. All the distances and classifications are computed in the same manner. The posterior probabilities for classifying cases are computed by comparing three distances rather than two. SYSTAT accommodates this model easily because the dependent variable in the MODEL statement is assumed to be categorical. All other commands are the same.

The multiple group (canonical) discriminant model yields more than one discriminant axis. For three groups, we get two sets of canonical discriminant coefficients. For four groups, we get three. If we have fewer variables than groups, then we get only as many sets as there are variables. The group classification function coefficients are handy for classifying new cases with the multiple group model. Simply multiply each coefficient times each variable and add in the constant. Then assign the case to the group whose set which yields the largest value.

Let's examine the OURWORLD example in the discriminant analysis chapter of the SYSTAT manual. We will use the birth rates and death rates of countries to predict the country groups used in the manual (Europe, Islamic, New World). Figure 15.7 shows a scatterplot and a 3-D density of these data . The density for the European group is so high that it must be clipped in the lower graph to reveal the other densities. Notice that the normal confidence ellipses for each group have a different shape. Because of this, we will ultimately need to apply a quadratic discrimant model to these data, because the linear model assumes all the ellipses represent the same within-groups distribution. First, however, we'll run the ordinary multiple groups discriminant analysis.

Figure 15.7
OURWORLD Dataset Plot of Death and Birth Rates

```
USE OURWORLD
PLOT DEATH_RT*BIRTH_RT/HEI=2IN,WID=4IN,
  YMIN=0,YMAX=30,XMIN=0,XMAX=60,GROUP=GROUP$,OVERLAY,ELLIPSE
```

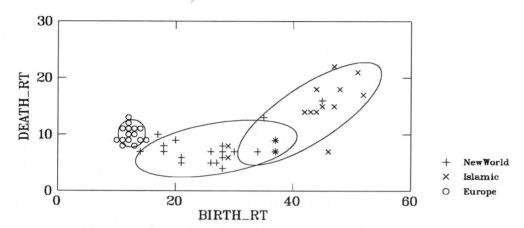

```
DEN  .*DEATH_RT*BIRTH_RT/NORM,GROUP=GROUP$,OVERLAY,
                HEI=2IN,WID=4IN,ALT=2IN,ZTICK=10,
                XMIN=0,XMAX=60,YMIN=0,YMAX=30,
                SURF=ZCUT,FILL=0,AX=CORNER,LEGEND=NONE
```

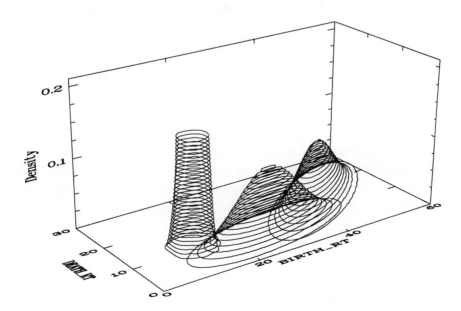

Figure 15.8 shows the quick-graph produced by SYSTAT for the two canonical discriminant factors. There are two canonical factors because we used only two predictors; even though we had three groups, there are really only two dimensions of variation among them. Compare Figure 15.8 to the upper plot in Figure 15.7. You need to flip FACTOR(2) to get the plots to correspond. Furthermore, the canonical plot is a slight rotation of the scatterplot in order to improve the discrimination. Finally, the canonical factors have been standardized by the pooled within-groups standard deviations; that is why the ellipses are fatter in Figure 15.8 than in Figure 15.7

To repeat, the radically differing ellipses in Figure 15.8 make it clear that the linear discriminant model is not appropriate for these data. You should always examine this quick-plot to be sure that the ellipses have the same shape and orientation within each group. If not, you should run the quadratic model and examine the test for equality of covariance matrices in the output. If the ellipses look different to you in the plot, then more than likely the test will be significant and you should be using A quadratic model.

We won't show the output for this ordinary linear discriminant analysis. It is similar to the one in the SYSTAT manual, except there are only two predictor variables. You should run the example yourself to see. Instead, we are going to examine this model further by classifying hypothetical cases in the scatterplot of Figure 15.7. We're going to do this so that you can see how the classification space is carved up by the linear discriminant model. After this, we will compute the quadratic model and show you the difference.

Figure 15.9 shows how to display the classification regions in the space of the original variables. We use SYSTAT BASIC to add cases to the dataset. We add $50 \times 50 = 2500$ cases. We also create a new variable INCLUDE and set its value to 1 for the cases in the original dataset and 0 for the additional cases. We set FREQ=INCLUDE below to exclude these new cases from the discriminant analysis but still calculate their predicted values for plotting. The LET statements in this program create index variables I and J so that we can cover the entire field of the plot with a lattice of X and Y coordinates. Rescaling these coordinates to the range of the data (0 to 60 for BIRTH_RT and 0 to 30 for DEATH_RT) will give us artificial values of these variables to classify using the model based on the real data.

Figure 15.8
Canonical Discriminant Plot

```
DISCRIM
USE OURWORLD
MODEL GROUP=BIRTH_RT DEATH_RT
ESTIMATE
```

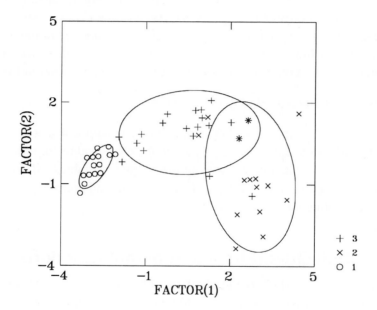

Canonical Scores Plot

The last section of the program selects only the artificial cases and uses a tiled bar chart to display the predicted values on the BIRTH_RT and DEATH_RT scales. Since there is only one data value at each I,J value, the height of each bar (in this case, the color or darkness of the tile representing each bar) stands for one of the three predicted groups. The resulting regions show how the model classifies new cases. In the multiple linear discriminant model, these boundaries are Voronoi tesselations over the group centroids (means). You may wish to look at examples of these tesselations in the SYSTAT manual (the VORONOI option) to see the resemblance.

The important thing to notice is that the cutting boundaries between groups are straight lines. Instead of one northwest-southeast cutting line between two groups, as in

Figure 15.6, there are three cutting lines between three groups. The model is based on the assumption that the "hills" for each group have the same orientation and shape and therefore intersect in straight lines when viewed from above. We will see in the next section that the quadratic model relaxes this assumption. By allowing the hills to have different heights, orientations, and shapes (although each is still assumed to be multivariate normal), the quadratic model allows curvilinear boundaries for classification.

We plotted this example on the original scatterplot space of the classifying variables because we wanted you to see the classification in the original space. This will not work with more than two classifying variables because we cannot visualize the classification regions in two dimensions. These regions become pyramidal polygons in three or more dimensions. An alternative is to plot these regions in the canonical plot shown in Figure 15.8. You might want to change the last command in Figure 15.9 to:

```
BAR PREDICTD*FACTOR(2)*FACTOR(1) / TILE, BTHICK=2
```

in order to see how the original variables map into the canonical space. The rectangle of predicted values looks like a parallelogram in the canonical factor space because the canonical factors are rotated composites of the original variables. If you were to use more than two predictors, you could modify the program in Figure 15.9 to include them as well before creating the prediction dataset.

15.6 Quadratic discriminant functions

As we have said, the world data clearly show different distributions for each group. Let's see how the quadratic model classifies the same data. Figure 15.10 uses the same artificial data we constructed for the linear model to fit a quadratic model. The only difference between the bottom commands in Figure 15.9 and those in Figure 15.10 is the MODEL statement. We have added a QUAD option to it to make the fitting quadratic. The resulting graph shows the classification regions. Now, few potential new cases would be classified as European (Group 1). The classification region is a small, nearly circular ellipse. The Islamic region (Group 2), on the other hand, resembles an hourglass. Finally, the New World region (Group 3) spans two areas. Paradoxically, the lower right corner of the plot is classified as New World because the height of the Islamic hill is lower than the New World hill in that area. For a similar reason, European countries are tightly bound in the circular classification region because the surrounding hill for New World countries is higher in the area outside the circle.

Figure 15.9
Linear Discriminant Function Classification Regions

```
BASIC
USE OURWORLD
REPEAT 2557
LET INCLUDE=1
IF CASE>57 THEN FOR
   LET I=INT((CASE-57)/50)
   LET J=(CASE-57)-50*I
   LET BIRTH_RT=60*I/50
   LET DEATH_RT=30*J/50
   LET INCLUDE=0
NEXT
SAVE WORLD
RUN
DISCRIM
USE WORLD
FREQ=INCLUDE
MODEL GROUP=BIRTH_RT DEATH_RT
SAVE JUNK / DATA DISTANCES
ESTIMATE
USE JUNK
SELECT CASE>57 AND BIRTH_RT>0 AND DEATH_RT>0
CAT PREDICTD
BAR   PREDICTD*DEATH_RT*BIRTH_RT/TILE,BTHICK=2,HEI=2IN,WID=4IN,
   YMIN=0,YMAX=30,XMIN=0,XMAX=60
```

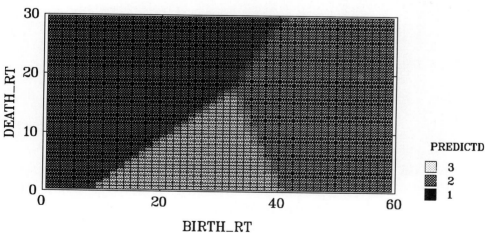

Compare Figure 15.10 to the lower graph in Figure 15.7. Notice that the European region cuts into the others because it is so concentrated in a small area. You can see from the output if you run the quadratic models that the fit is slightly better. Why not use the quadratic model all the time? Well, the number of parameters for the quadratic model is considerably larger than for the simple pooled linear model. As the manual explains, the quadratic model must include linear terms, quadratic terms, plus all the cross-products of the predictors as well. You pay a penalty for these extra parameters; it's the same kind of penalty you pay for fitting too many predictors in regression or ANOVA. The model is less likely to replicate on new data. In short, use the quadratic model only when you have lots of cases (say, 10 times groups times predictors) and when the fit is substantially better than the simple linear model.

Figure 15.10
Quadratic Discriminant Model Classification Regions

```
USE WORLD
FREQ=INCLUDE
MODEL GROUP=BIRTH_RT DEATH_RT / QUAD
SAVE JUNK / DATA DISTANCES
ESTIMATE
USE JUNK
SELECT CASE>57 AND BIRTH_RT>0 AND DEATH_RT>0
CAT PREDICTD
BAR  PREDICTD*DEATH_RT*BIRTH_RT/TILE,BTHICK=2,HEI=2IN,WID=4IN,
                        YMIN=0,YMAX=30,XMIN=0,XMAX=60
```

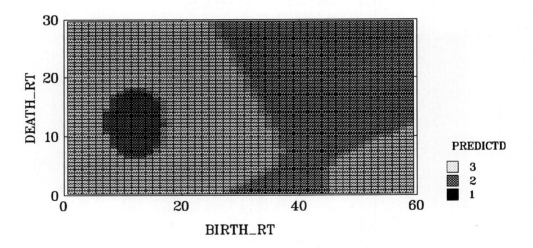

15.7 Nonparametric classification

Let's go back to our admissions data. We've been using a parametric model for classification because it seemed reasonable that GRE scores and GPAs are bivariate normally distributed. Often, however, this assumption is unreasonable. For these instances, there are discriminant models which base their classifications on sample data features rather than parametric distributions. These nonparametric discriminant models are not available in SYSTAT, but we can use the KERNEL option in SYGRAPH to classify cases graphically if we have only two classification variables.

Figure 15.11
Nonparametric Classification Model

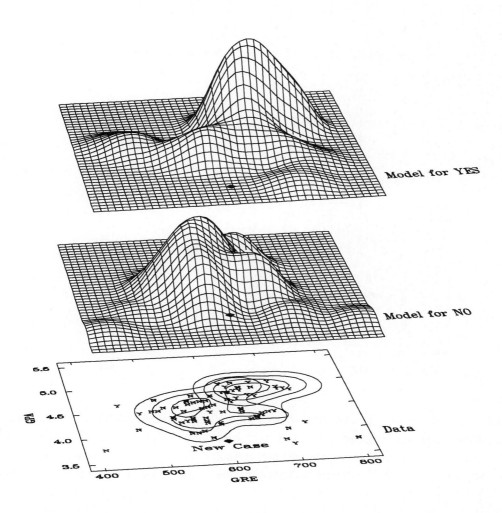

Figure 15.11 shows a nonparametric counterpart to Figure 15.3. The hills are now irregular, following the observed data more closely than the ellipsoidal model in Figure 15.3. The computations for classifying are similar to the normal discriminant model. Instead of Mahalanobis distances, however, we compute distance weighted by the contours for the two different groups. Figure 15.12 shows the two-dimensional view of the contours for both models. To find the distance of a new case to a group centroid, locate the value (or interpolate) from the nearest contour. We have not printed these values because the figure is small, but you can plot a larger version.

Figure 15.12
Nonparametric and Normal Classification Models

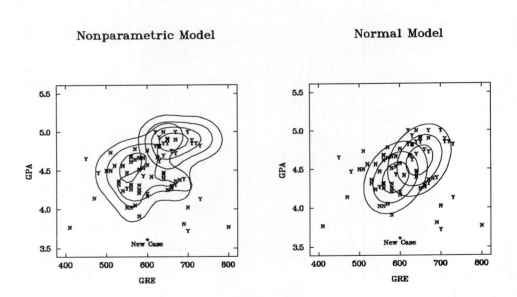

The point of this little demonstration is to show you graphically that the normal classification model can impose a structure which is quite different from that in the data themselves. Many psychologists assume variables like grade point averages and test scores are normally distributed because they are composites of many measurements. This is not necessarily true for subgroups, however, or for censored data like these. The full dataset from all the students in the department suggests that the distributions are different for the two groups and they are not normal.

15.8 Conclusion

We've analyzed the same data using both the probit and discriminant models. Which is better? In actual classifications, neither seems to do dramatically better on these data. Perhaps we should ask, "What's the difference?" Our question is complicated further by introducing the logistic model from the last chapter, which we said produces results almost indistinguishable from probit.

All three models can be used for classification. They rest on somewhat different assumptions, however. All three models require that each observation, or case, be independent from the others and that this independence is due to error variation common to all cases. The Fisher linear discriminant model has the additional requirement that the classifying variables be multinormally distributed within groups and that the distribution in each group is the same. The quadratic model relaxes the equality of covariances assumption but still requires multinormality. We called this a "pie in the sky" assumption because it is difficult to obtain in practice and difficult to verify when there are lots of classifying variables. We discussed testing for multinormality in the MANOVA chapter. All the procedures used there can be applied to the discriminant model to test assumptions. Press and Wilson (1978) compared the discriminant and logistic models for classification and found few substantial differences.

Notes

There is a problem with the range of scores on these tests in this sample. In the ten years covering these data, the psychology department sought students with high grades and GRE scores. This tended to restrict the range of scores in accepted students relative to the total pool of applicants. And that restriction reduced the available variation for predicting success in graduate school. Although the variation in GRE scores looks small in this sample as well, it is probably larger relative to the general pool of applicants.

The logit and probit models do not generalize easily to the multiple groups analysis. Judge et al. (1980) discuss these generalizations. SYSTAT's **multinomial logit** model is available for multiple groups, but the corresponding probit model does not appear in SYSTAT.

Klecka (1980) is a good introduction to discriminant models for social scientists. Lachenbruch's (1974, 1987) are excellent technical reviews. Goldstein and Dillon (1978) discuss discriminant models where the predictor variables are discrete.

References

Fisher, R.A. (1936). The use of multiple measurements in taxonomic problems. *Annals of Eugenics*, 7, 179-188.

Goldstein, M. and Dillon, W.R. (1978). *Discrete Discriminant Analysis*. New York: John Wiley & Sons.

Judge, G.G., Hill, R.C., Griffiths, W.E., Lutkepohl, H., and Tsoung-Chao, L. (1985). *The Theory and Practice of Econometrics* (2nd Ed.). New York: John Wiley & Sons.

Klecka , W.R. (1980). *Discriminant analysis*. Beverly Hills: Sage Publications.

Lachenbruch, P.A. (1975). *Discriminant Analysis*. New York: Hafner Press.

Lachenbruch, P.A. (1987). Discriminant analysis. In Kotz, S. and Johnson, N.L. (Eds.), *Encyclopedia of Statistical Sciences*, Vol. 2, 389-397.

Press, S. and Wilson, S. (1978). Choosing between logistic regression and discriminant analysis. *Journal of the American Statistical Association, 23*, 699-705.

Part 5

Analyzing Series

16

Regression on Time Series Data

Does prosperity foster innovation? Addressing this question almost inevitably involves historical data, whose observations are collected across time. Such measurements on a variable across time comprise a "time series." The regression and curve fitting methods we have studied so far are not usually appropriate for time series data because the observations in a series are usually dependent on previous observations. An ordinary regression model would fail to account for this interdependence. In this chapter, we will examine some time series and try some simple modifications of regression techniques to make them more appropriate for dealing with this type of data. Econometric modeling of time series goes beyond the scope of this book, but we can learn enough to handle simple models here.

To study innovation, we are going to examine applications to the U.S. Patent Office. Our measure of prosperity will be per-capita income. Figure 16.1 contains data on U.S. patent applications for new inventions plus related data since 1880. These data were compiled from several U.S. government sources, including Historical Statistics, Colonial Times to 1970 and the U.S. Statistical Abstract for years following 1970. To keep the numbers simple, we have scaled some of the variables and rounded to the nearest integer. POPULATN is the estimated or Census population in thousands. PATENT is number of patent applications. PATPOP is the number of patent applications per 100,000 population. GNP is the Gross National Product adjusted for 1970 dollars, and PERCAP is per-capita income in adjusted 1970 dollars.

Figure 16.1
Patents for New Inventions, GNP, and Related Economic Data for United States
Between 1880 and 1980 (PATENT)

YEAR	POPULATN	PATENT	PATPOP	GNP	PERCAP
1881	51542	24878	48	1000	194
1882	52821	30270	57	1030	194
1883	54100	33073	61	1060	195
1884	55379	34192	62	1090	196
1885	56658	34697	61	1120	197
1886	57938	35161	61	1150	198
1887	59217	34420	58	1180	199
1888	60496	34713	57	1210	200
1889	61775	39607	64	1250	202
1890	63056	39884	63	1310	207
1891	64361	39418	61	1350	209
1892	65666	29514	45	1430	217
1893	66970	37293	56	1380	206
1894	68275	36978	54	1260	184
1895	69580	39145	56	1390	199
1896	70885	42077	59	1330	187
1897	72189	45661	63	1460	202
1898	73494	33915	46	1540	209
1899	74799	38937	52	1740	232
1900	76094	39673	52	1870	245
1901	77584	43973	57	2070	266
1902	79163	48320	61	2160	272
1903	80632	49289	61	2290	284
1904	82166	51168	62	2290	278
1905	83822	54034	64	2510	299
1906	85450	55471	65	2870	335
1907	87008	57679	66	3040	349
1908	88710	60142	68	2770	312
1909	90490	64408	71	3340	369
1910	92407	63293	68	3530	382
1911	93863	67370	72	3580	381
1912	95335	68968	72	3940	413
1913	97225	68117	70	3960	407
1914	99111	67774	68	3860	389
1915	100546	67138	67	4000	397
1916	101961	68075	67	4830	473
1917	103268	67590	65	6040	584
1918	103208	57347	56	7640	740
1919	104514	76710	73	8400	803
1920	106461	81915	77	9150	859
1921	108538	87467	81	6960	641
1922	110049	83962	76	7410	673
1923	111947	76783	69	8510	760
1924	114109	87987	77	8470	742
1925	115829	80208	69	9310	803
1926	117397	81365	69	9700	826
1927	119035	87219	73	9490	797
1928	120509	87603	73	9700	804
1929	121767	89752	74	10310	846
1930	123077	89554	73	9040	734
1931	124040	79740	64	7580	611

YEAR	POPULATN	PATENT	PATPOP	GNP	PERCAP
1932	124840	67006	54	5800	464
1933	125579	56558	45	5560	442
1934	126374	56643	45	6510	515
1935	127250	58117	46	7220	567
1936	128053	62599	49	8250	644
1937	128825	65324	51	9040	701
1938	129825	66874	52	8470	652
1939	130880	64093	49	9050	691
1940	131954	60863	46	9970	755
1941	133121	52339	39	12450	935
1942	133920	45549	34	15790	1179
1943	134245	45493	34	19160	1427
1944	132885	54190	41	21010	1581
1945	132481	67846	51	21190	1599
1946	140054	81056	58	20850	1488
1947	143446	75443	53	23130	1612
1948	146093	68740	47	25760	1763
1949	148665	67592	45	25650	1725
1950	151235	67264	44	28480	1883
1951	153310	60438	39	32840	2142
1952	155687	64554	41	34550	2219
1953	158242	72284	46	36460	2304
1954	161164	77185	48	36480	2263
1955	164308	77188	47	39800	2422
1956	167306	74906	45	41920	2505
1957	170371	74197	44	44110	2589
1958	173320	77495	45	44730	2580
1959	176289	78594	45	48370	2743
1960	177135	79590	45	50370	2843
1961	179979	83100	46	52010	2889
1962	182992	85029	46	56030	3061
1963	185771	85724	46	59050	3178
1964	188483	87597	46	63240	3355
1965	191141	94632	50	68490	3583
1966	193526	88293	46	74990	3874
1967	195576	87872	45	79390	4059
1968	197457	93136	47	86420	4376
1969	199399	98386	49	93030	4665
1970	201385	102868	51	97280	4830
1971	203810	104566	51	100190	4916
1972	209284	98928	47	105950	5062
1973	211357	103695	49	111730	5286
1974	213342	102206	48	112720	5283
1975	215465	101014	47	111460	5173
1976	217563	102300	47	117430	5397
1977	219760	100900	46	123940	5640
1978	222095	100900	45	130180	5861
1979	224567	100500	45	133800	5958
1980	227236	104300	46	133440	5872

16.1 The ordinary least squares model

We are not going to regress PATENT on GNP to test our hypothesis. If you try this model (MODEL PATENT = CONSTANT + GNP) with the SYSTAT regression procedure, you will see a strong positive association between the two. Because population is increasing rapidly during this period, however, much of this association is explainable by population growth.

Figure 16.2
Plot of PATPOP against YEAR and PERCAP against YEAR

```
USE PATENT
LINE PATPOP * YEAR / XMIN=1850  XMAX=2000  XTICK=3  XFORMAT=0,
                     HEIGHT=2IN  WIDTH=4IN
LINE PERCAP * YEAR / XMIN=1850  XMAX=2000  XTICK=3  XFORMAT=0,
                     HEIGHT=2IN  WIDTH=4IN
```

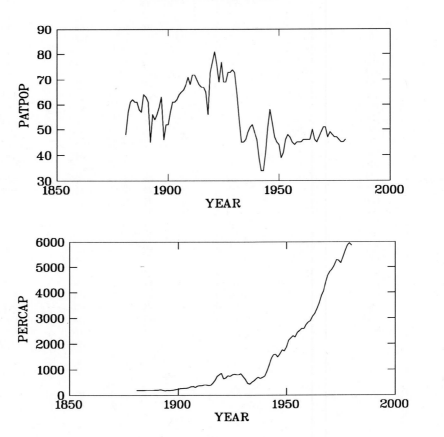

We are more interested in whether prosperity stimulates innovation at various levels of population. To examine this question, we want to use instead the normalized variables PATPOP and PERCAP, which adjust for population. Figure 16.2 contains the plots of PATPOP on YEAR and PERCAP on YEAR to show the data we are analyzing. Notice that per-capita income rises strongly during this 100 year period. Patent applications per 100,000 people fluctuate roughly between 40 and 80 during this same period.

Figure 16.3 shows the results of regressing PATPOP on PERCAP. There appears to be a significant association between patents per 100,000 and per-capita income, with a multiple correlation of .512. Oddly, the coefficient for PATPOP is negative now that we have normalized for population. Does per-capita income *suppress* patent applications?

Figure 16.3
Regression of PATPOP on PERCAP

```
REGRESS
   USE PATENT
   MODEL PATPOP = CONSTANT + PERCAP
   SAVE RESID / DATA   RESID
   ESTIMATE
```

```
Dep Var: PATPOP N: 100 Multiple R:  0.512 Squared multiple R:  0.262

Adjusted squared multiple R:  0.254     Standard error of estimate:      9.525

Effect          Coefficient    Std Error    Std Coef Tolerance     F   P(2 Tail)

CONSTANT           60.540         1.297        0.0        .   2178.403   0.000
PERCAP             -0.003         0.001       -0.512    1.000   34.744   0.000

                         Analysis of Variance

Source            Sum-of-Squares   DF   Mean-Square    F-Ratio      P

Regression           3152.044      1     3152.044      34.744     0.000
Residual             8890.706     98       90.721
Durbin-Watson D Statistic      0.267
First Order Autocorrelation    0.857
Residuals have been saved.
```

You can USE the file RESID.SYS, into which we saved the residuals from this analysis, to see how the usual regression assumptions are violated. Let's focus on one particular assumption, however: independence of residuals.

16.2 Examining residuals for autocorrelation

REGRESS prints two statistics when you request residuals. Both give us information about this independence assumption. The first, DURBIN-WATSON D, tells us whether the residuals are correlated with their previous residuals. That is, does a given residual's value correlate with the value of the previous residual in the series? If so, then the independence assumption required for hypothesis testing in the usual regression model is questionable. The second statistic, AUTOCORRELATION, is the sample correlation coefficient on which the DURBIN-WATSON D statistic is based. Unlike the sample autocorrelation, the DURBIN-WATSON statistic's significance values have been tabulated in many textbooks, so we can look in one of these tables to see whether the autocorrelation is significant for the size series we have. If there is little or no autocorrelation, this statistic is around 2, so the .267 value is quite small, suggesting we have a problem.

There is a more useful display in the SERIES module for examining autocorrelation. The DURBIN-WATSON statistic gives us information only on the first order autocorrelation. It is still possible that each residual might be dependent on the second prior residual, or the third, and so forth. We should examine all the possible autocorrelations of the residuals, or at least the first several.

The SERIES module contains a graphic display of all the autocorrelations for a series. The command for this display is ACF. What this command does is shift the series back by one year (or case) and then correlate the series with itself. This is the first-order autocorrelation (at LAG 1). Then it shifts it back a second time and correlates this twice-shifted series with the original. This produces the second-order autocorrelation (at LAG 2). And so on. Figure 16.4 contains this display.

Figure 16.4
Autocorrelation Plot of Residuals from Regression of PATPOP on PERCAP

```
SERIES
   USE RESID
   ACF RESIDUAL
```

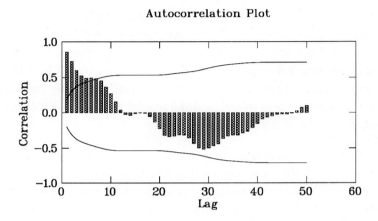

Autocorrelation Plot

The first four autocorrelations are substantial and significant. They lie outside the two-standard error confidence bound. Clearly, the assumption of independence of observations is violated in this analysis. There is little point in examining other regression diagnostics until we do something about these large autocorrelations.

16.3 Removing autocorrelation by differencing

One way to handle autocorrelations like this is to difference the data. We can do this by subtracting the previous value for each case from the current value. If each case in the series depends on variation in the previous case or cases, then differencing the cases can remove some of that variation.

There's another reason to consider differencing. Look again at the plots of PATPOP and PERCAP against YEAR in Figure 16.1. Notice there is a strong upward trend in PERCAP and a slight downward trend in PATPOP across the 100 years. Our regression has mostly measured trend and found that the two series have different trends. Differencing can help remove these trends before we do our regression.

Don't we *want* trend in our regression? Isn't there just noise left if we remove the trend? Not quite. Consider our original research question again. We are trying to relate prosperity to innovation. If we regressed PATPOP on PERCAP and found a large coefficient, it would be due almost entirely to trend. In fact, any variables which increased strongly from 1881 to 1980 would show a strong relationship in a regression: variables like the price of tea in China, the population of Great Britain, or the ever-changing estimates of the age of the Universe. None of these would be particularly interesting models because they would not be sensitive to decreases as well as increases in the same series. If we really feel that prosperity leads to innovation, then we should expect that relatively small positive and negative changes in prosperity would be followed by concomitant changes in innovation. Put another way, it would be really interesting if PATPOP followed the same pattern of fluctuations around its trend as PERCAP did around its own trend, perhaps with a year or two delay.

Let's use the SERIES module, then, to difference our data. Before we do so, however, notice that in Figure 16.1 the upward trend of PERCAP across years is curvilinear. To make the removal of trend by differencing comparable in both variables, we will first LOG the PERCAP variable. This will straighten it out and make the trend linear. The first seven commands in Figure 16.5 show these transformations.

Before we use these new differenced variables in a regression, however, let's check how they are related. First of all, let's look at the autocorrelation plots of both transformed variables. Figure 16.5 shows the ACFs for the logged and differenced PERCAP and differenced PATPOP. Notice the two SAVE commands. Each precedes the final transformation of the variable that we want saved into a file so we can do our regression later.

There is still a slightly significant autocorrelation remaining for PERCAP at LAG 1 and for PATPOP at LAG 8 (an 8 year cycle in changes in patent applications?). Before we think about further differencing, however, we should try our regression. It is the distribution of the regression residuals which is critical.

Figure 16.5
Autocorrelation Functions of Transformed PERCAP and PATPOP

```
SERIES
    USE PATENT
    LOG PERCAP
    SAVE PERCAP
    DIFFERENCE PERCAP
    SAVE PATPOP
    DIFFERENCE PATPOP
    ACF PERCAP
    ACF PATPOP
```

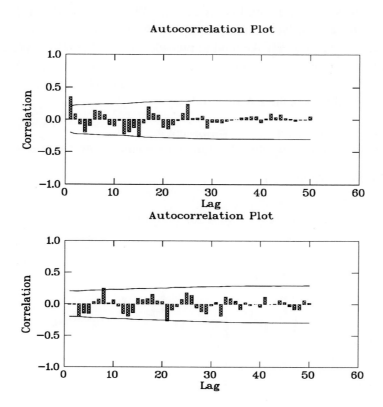

16.4 The cross correlation function

The SERIES module has another display for helping us with our regression. Regressing our transformed PATPOP onto transformed PERCAP will tell us whether there is a linear relation between changes in logged per-capita income and changes in patent applications during the same year. What if there is a lag in this relationship of a year or two? Perhaps changes in PERCAP don't influence PATPOP until a few years later. We will miss it if we examine only one regression. We should instead consider the correlation between the two series shifted once, twice, and so on. If there really is a delay (lag) of a year or two between changes in PERCAP and PATPOP, then we should be looking at the correlation between the PERCAP series and the PATPOP series shifted ahead one or two years.

The CCF (cross correlation) function in the SERIES module does this for us. Figure 16.6 shows the cross correlations between PERCAP and PATPOP for up to 7 years behind and ahead. Notice the peak in the function (.392) is at 2 years ahead, showing that changes in PERCAP tend to precede those in PATPOP. We are ready to try our regression on the transformed variables and examine the residuals. To do this, we need to lag the PERCAP variable by two years in the BASIC module. Figure 16.7 shows how to do this with the BASIC module.

Figure 16.6
Cross Correlation Function Plot of Differenced PERCAP and PATPOP

CCF PERCAP PATPOP

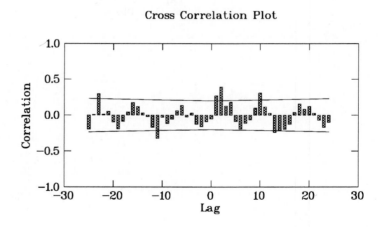

16.5 Fitting the identified model

We have finally identified our model, so let's prepare the data for the regression. We could use the SAVE command in the SERIES module to save the transformed values of PATPOP and PERCAP. It is simpler, however, to transform them again in the BA-SIC module rather than to merge several files. Figure 16.7 shows how to do this. Having transformed the variables, we must delete the first 3 cases because we lost one to differencing and two more to lagging.

Now we can USE the LPATENT file and regress differenced PATPOP (LPATPOP) on logged, differenced, and lagged PERCAP (LPERCAP). Figure 16.7 shows the results of this regression. Note that we have saved the residuals into a file RESID.SYS. The multiple correlation is .402, and the corresponding regression coefficient for LPER-CAP is 22.687, which is highly significant. The effect is not earth shattering, but we have shown that approximately sixteen percent of the variation in the differenced PAT-POP series can be accounted for by the lagged PERCAP variable.

Residual diagnostics

To check our regression assumptions again, we can plot the autocorrelation function of the residuals in the SERIES module. Figure 16.8 shows how to do this. No significant autocorrelations appear in the plot and there isn't even much regularity to the pattern of autocorrelations.

We still can't conclude that the residuals are independent, however. Now that we have invested in this model, it is worth subjecting the residuals to another test of independence. The RUNS test in the NPAR module can help us to find if there are any long runs of residuals above or below the forecast values. Since the residuals are still in time order, we simply USE the RESID file in the NPAR module and ask for RUNS. The second half of Figure 16.8 shows the results. There appear to be no significant runs in the residuals.

In ordinary least squares, we expect the residuals to be independent of the predictors. It is still possible in a time series regression that the residuals are correlated with the shifted predicted values. In other words, there may be seasonal or cyclical components in the residuals which correlate with the predictor series. To test this possibility, we should cross-correlate the residuals with the predictor (or predictors). Figure 16.9 shows this CCF plot. Again, we see nothing to worry about in this plot. None of the cross-correlations is large or significant.

Figure 16.7
Lagged Regression

```
BASIC
   USE PATENT
   LET LPATPOP = PATPOP - LAG(PATPOP)
   LET LPERCAP1 = LOG(PERCAP) - LOG(LAG(PERCAP))
   LET LPERCAP = LAG(LPERCAP1,2)
   IF CASE < 4 THEN DELETE
   SAVE LPATENT
   RUN
REGRESS
   USE LPATENT
   MODEL LPATPOP = CONSTANT + LPERCAP
   SAVE RESID2 / DATA  RESID
   ESTIMATE
```

```
Dep Var: LPATPOP N: 97 Multiple R:  0.402 Squared multiple R:  0.161

Adjusted squared multiple R:  0.152    Standard error of estimate:    4.495

Effect        Coefficient    Std Error    Std Coef Tolerance    t   P(2 Tail)

CONSTANT        -0.952         0.493        0.0        .      -1.930   0.057
LPERCAP         22.687         5.309        0.402    1.000     4.273   0.000

                         Analysis of Variance

Source          Sum-of-Squares   DF  Mean-Square    F-Ratio      P

Regression          368.969       1    368.969      18.259     0.000
Residual           1919.712      95     20.207
------------------------------------------------------------------------
Case      10 is an outlier      (Studentized Residual =      2.711)
Case      15 is an outlier      (Studentized Residual =     -3.483)
Case      35 is an outlier      (Studentized Residual =     -2.825)
Case      36 is an outlier      (Studentized Residual =      3.149)
Case      40 has large leverage (Leverage =      0.160)
Case      51 has large leverage (Leverage =      0.145)

Durbin-Watson D Statistic     2.317
First Order Autocorrelation  -0.160

Residuals have been saved.
```

Because we were warned about outliers and influence in Figure 16.7, we should plot the residuals against YEAR. Figure 16.10 shows three plots of STUDENT, LEVERAGE, and COOK against YEAR. These plots help us to see whether outlying observations occur in patterns. Despite the program warnings (often conservative), there is not much need for worry. The Cook's D values and leverages are relatively small. You can also PLOT LPATPOP*LPERCAP/INFLUENCE and examine the influence scatterplot. No observations are sufficient to influence the regression by as much as 0.1.

Figure 16.8
Autocorrelation Plot and Runs Test of Regression Residuals

```
SERIES
    USE RESID2
    ACF RESIDUAL
```

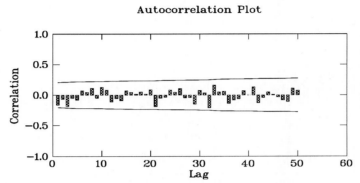

Autocorrelation Plot

```
NPAR
    USE RESID2
    RUNS RESIDUAL
```

Wald-Wolfowitz runs test using cutpoint =		0.0			Probability (2-tail)
Variable	Cases LE Cut	Cases GT Cut	Runs	Z	
RESIDUAL	43	54	41	-1.629	0.103

Figure 16.9
Cross Correlation Function Plot of Residuals against LAG2

```
SERIES
    USE RESID2
    CCF RESIDUAL LPERCAP
```

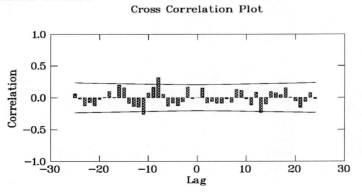

Cross Correlation Plot

Figure 16.10
Diagnostic Regression Plots against YEAR

```
USE RESID2
PLOT STUDENT * YEAR   / LINE,SIZE=0   XMIN=1880   XMAX=1980
PLOT COOK * YEAR      / LINE,SIZE=0   XMIN=1880   XMAX=1980
PLOT LEVERAGE * YEAR  / LINE,SIZE=0   XMIN=1880   XMAX=1980
```

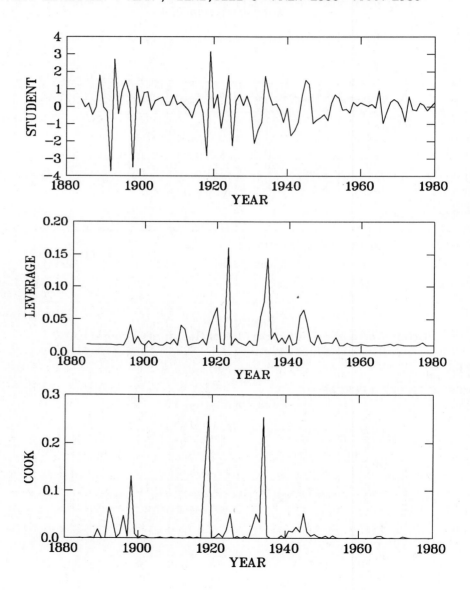

16.6 Conclusion

We have come a long way in attempting to answer our original question about innovation and prosperity. Careful time series work has required us to use the SERIES, REGRESS, and NPAR modules intensively. The analysis here is, if anything, simpler than most time series regressions. In any case, the results are worth the work because time series regression without attention to the autocorrelation problem is invalid. Let's review the strategy we followed.

First, we had to prepare the series to fit the assumptions of ordinary least squares regression modeling. To do this, we had to take into account trend and cyclical components by differencing the series. Because the PERCAP series had a nonlinear trend, we had to LOG it before differencing to remove trend. Incidentally, if a trend is truly quadratic, then differencing twice instead of logging and differencing will remove the trend entirely. If possible, however, you should avoid differencing data more than once. Interpretation of results becomes more difficult and there is a danger of injecting cyclical variation back into the series. If you try double differencing of the PERCAP data in theSERIES module (by typing the DIFFERENCE command twice), you will see that the doubly differenced series has greater variance at the end and stronger autocorrelations than our logged and differenced data.

Once we had series which showed essentially random ACF plots, we had to identify a regression model. At this point, our series were stationary because they did not contain trend, cyclical, or other nonrandom serial components. But we did not know how much of a lag to use in regressing PATPOP onto PERCAP. For this, we needed to do a CCF plot, which revealed a relatively large cross-correlation at a lag of two years (i.e. PERCAP leads PATPOP by two years, or PATPOP lags PERCAP by two years). We used the lag information to prepare the series in the BASIC module for regression with REGRESS.

Finally, we analyzed residuals from the regression. In ordinary least squares, we usually plot residuals against predictors and predicted values. While this can be useful in time series analysis, it is also important to plot residuals and influence statistics against time to see whether segments of the series are modeled differently from other segments. In addition, independence assumptions must be tested using ACF and CCF plots to be sure that cyclic and seasonal components are not affecting the distribution of errors.

This example only introduces the general problem of time series modeling. For more complex examples and multiple time series, you will have to consult an econometrics or statistical time series text. It is important to remember, however, that simple models are usually preferable to complex ones if the assumptions of the analysis are met. Our example could benefit from additional refinements, particularly involving the relative discontinuities in the series around the time of the Great Depression. It is possible, for example, to introduce dummy variables (as in the analysis of variance) to adjust for such discontinuities. The conclusions of our analysis would not change substantially, however. In the last U.S. century, relative changes in innovation tended to follow changes in prosperity.

This conclusion appears to contradict common sense. Doesn't innovation lead to new economic markets which, in turn, lead to increases in prosperity? Schmookler (1966) shows with a variety of historical economic data that this simplification is untrue. Surprisingly, Smookler found that invention follows economic trends rather than scientific developments: "When time series of investment (or capital goods output) and the number of capital goods inventions are compared for a single industry, both the long-term trend and the long swings exhibit great similarities, with the notable difference that lower turning points in major cycles or long swings generally occur in capital goods sales before they do in capital goods patents" (page 205). Smookler concluded that "(1) invention is largely an economic activity which, like other economic activities, is pursued for gain; (2) expected gain varies with expected sales of goods embodying the invention; and (3) expected sales of improved capital goods are largely determined by present capital goods sales" (page 206).

Notes

For further technical reading, consult Judge et al. (1982). Judge et al. (1985) is more advanced. Nerlove et al. (1979) present time series regression in a general econometric context. Brillinger (1975) and Hannan (1970) discuss multiple time series analysis. McDowall et al. (1980) cover problems with interrupted time series, such as our Depression series. Ostrom (1980) introduces time series analysis for social scientists.

References

Brillinger, D.R. (1975). *Time Series: Data Analysis and Theory.* New York: Holt, Rinehart and Winston.

Hannan, E.J. (1970). *Multiple Time Series.* New York: John Wiley & Sons.

Judge, G.G., Hill, R.C., Griffiths, W.E., Lutkepohl, H., and Tsoung-Chao, L. (1982). *Introduction to the Theory and Practice of Econometrics.* New York: John Wiley & Sons.

Judge, G.G., Hill, R.C., Griffiths, W.E., Lutkepohl, H., and Tsoung-Chao, L. (1985). *The Theory and Practice of Econometrics* (2nd ed.). New York: John Wiley & Sons.

McDowell, D., McCleary, R., Meidinger, E.E., and Hay, R.A., Jr. (1980). *Interrupted Time Series Analysis.* Beverly Hills: Sage Publications.

Nerlove, M., Grether, D.M., and Carvalho, J.L. (1979). *Analysis of Economic Time Series: A Synthesis.* New York: Academic Press.

Ostrom, C.W., Jr. (1980). *Time Seriea Analysis: Regression Techniques.* Beverly Hills: Sage Publications.

Smookler, J. (1966). *Invention and Economic Growth.* Cambridge: Harvard University Press.

17

Forecasting Using ARIMA Models

In Chapter 6 we discussed the special problems in regression modeling of time series data. This chapter introduces a special type of time series modeling—forecasting. In forecasting, we predict future events in a series from past events. If we were using regression, then forecasting would be like regressing a series on time. In fact some forecasting methods do just that, even though time itself is not an explanatory variable. Our focus in forecasting is less on understanding the variables explaining a series, however, than on making accurate predictions of future performance.

Figure 17.1 contains 99 weeks of the Dow Jones Industrial Average during 1985-1986 (closings to the nearest 5 points). Let's use the first half of the series to forecast the second.

17.1 The linear model

A linear regression of the Dow on Week (1-49) using SYSTAT yields the following equation: DOW = 1208 + 4.7*WEEK. Figure 17.3 shows the output of this regression

The first order autocorrelation of the residuals is .976. This means that after we remove the linear trend in the data, each week's residual can be predicted quite well from the previous week's residual. In other words, if the data are above the line one week, they are more likely to be above the line the next.

Figure 17.3 shows our linear fit extrapolated to the second half of the series. The model captures the increasing trend in the DOW.

Figure 17.1
99 Weeks in 1985 and 1986 of Dow Jones Industrial Average

DOW	WEEK	DOW	WEEK
1200	1	1580	51
1210	2	1615	52
1220	3	1650	53
1275	4	1690	54
1280	5	1710	55
1290	6	1695	56
1285	7	1750	57
1280	8	1780	58
1295	9	1790	59
1275	10	1815	60
1250	11	1740	61
1260	12	1790	62
1255	13	1850	63
1255	14	1845	64
1270	15	1780	65
1275	16	1785	66
1280	17	1760	67
1240	18	1825	68
1280	19	1860	69
1295	20	1870	70
1310	21	1880	71
1315	22	1870	72
1300	23	1860	73
1300	24	1870	74
1310	25	1880	75
1330	26	1905	76
1330	27	1815	77
1365	28	1775	78
1350	29	1810	79
1350	30	1800	80
1320	31	1785	81
1310	32	1855	82
1340	33	1885	83
1310	34	1890	84
1300	35	1900	85
1320	36	1910	86
1330	37	1760	87
1340	38	1770	88
1380	39	1780	89
1350	40	1785	90
1390	41	1790	91
1405	42	1840	92
1420	43	1835	93
1460	44	1880	94
1450	45	1890	95
1485	46	1880	96
1540	47	1895	97
1510	48	1910	98
1500	49	1910	99
1530	50		

Figure 17.2
Regression Predicting DOW from WEEK

```
USE DOW
GLM
SELECT CASE<50
MODEL DOW = CONSTANT+WEEK
SAVE RESID
ESTIMATE
```

Dep Var: DOW N: 49 Multiple R: 0.869 Squared multiple R: 0.756

Adjusted squared multiple R: 0.751   Standard error of estimate: 38.805

Effect	Coefficient	Std Error	Std Coef	Tolerance	t	P(2 Tail)
CONSTANT	1208.074	11.259	0.0	.	107.297	0.000
WEEK	4.730	0.392	0.869	1.000	12.067	0.000

Analysis of Variance

Source	Sum-of-Squares	DF	Mean-Square	F-Ratio	P
Regression	219263.880	1	219263.880	145.608	0.000
Residual	70774.895	47	1505.849		

Durbin-Watson D Statistic   0.031
First Order Autocorrelation   0.976

Residuals have been saved.

17.2 The Random Walk

While our linear regression forecasting model might have some uses (particularly if we were trying to sell someone stock during this period), there is a question whether the trend we are modeling can be fit by a "random walk." Many investors have been burned by assuming an upward or downward trend would continue forever. Let's see what happens if we make the Dow at one week a function of the Dow at the previous week plus random error. This model looks like this:

$$DOW_i = DOW_{i-1} + ERROR_i$$

Figure 17.3
Using Linear Regression Model from First Half of Series to Predict Second Half

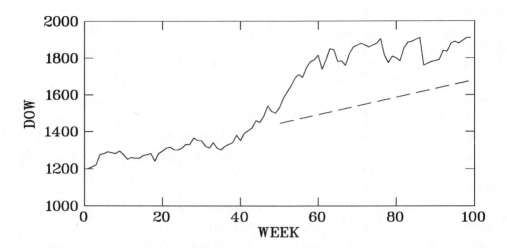

This model is called a random walk because it resembles the wandering of a pedestrian who flips a coin to decide whether to walk left or right on the next step (do not try this exercise in New York, Rome, or Chicago).

Now, let's see what happens when we *difference* a series generated by this model. We will subtract case i-1 from case i.

$$DOW_i - DOW_{i-1} = (DOW_{i-1} + ERROR_i) - DOW_{i-1} = ERROR_i$$

Differencing a random walk series produces a series of random errors, or "white noise." To give you an idea of how this looks, Figure 17.4 shows the differenced series and Figure 17.5 contains the autocorrelation function plots (ACF) for the original and differenced series (see Section 16.2 for further explanation of this plot). The ACF plot for the original series shows a strong relationship between each week's value and the previous week's (a correlation of .97). This carries through to the previous two weeks, three weeks, and so on.

Differencing removes this relationship throughout the series. Notice that there is no discernible pattern in the differenced series and that the ACF for the differenced series looks like the ACF of the random residuals for our final regression model in the previous chapter. Thus, while the upward trend looks significant by regression modeling on time, it is explainable as a random walk from a starting point, just like a coin flip.

You can use SERIES to model this random walk. Figure 17.6 shows the results. We are using ARIMA in SERIES, which computes estimates for parameters in equations which specify observations in a series as a function of previous observations. We differenced DOW first to produce a "stationary" series that does not wander. The P=1 means we are specifying one autoregressive parameter in the model (the weight to multiply times the previous observation in the series). The BACKCAST=30 means that the series is to be extended back 30 weeks before the first week using the fitted values to help smooth the estimates on each iteration. The FORECAST means that we wish forecasts to the end of the series. The ARIMA program must iterate to find a solution.

That the program came up with essentially zero as the autoregressive parameter confirms our suspicion that the DOW can be modeled with a random walk (which requires that the autoregressive parameter be 1). One the differencing is done, there is nothing left to model with this method. If you look back at the equation we used for the random walk model, you can see that it is equivalent to the following autoregressive model:

$$DOW_i = PHI* DOW_{i-1} + ERROR_i,$$

where PHI is a parameter (ϕ), whose value is 1. We call this an autoregressive model because we are regressing values in the series onto previous values.

Notice that the forecast based on the random walk model is less optimistic than that based on linear regression. The forecast values are horizontal. That is because the autoregressive model treats the trend as stochastic, or random. We will see later in this chapter how autoregressive and general ARIMA forecasts differ from linear and nonlinear regression forecasts. Later forecasts will look a little more glamorous. The ARIMA model can usually fit a fluctuating series with far fewer parameters.

On the other hand, the lack of "memory" in our random walk model is not wholly inappropriate to the subject of our forecast. Stock investors who think that stock trends contain enough information for intelligent investing are deceiving themselves. In general, we feel long term "charting" investment methods based solely on series data are worthless. Even more sophisticated models based on series data alone are more likely to increase forecast error variance than decrease it. We believe that for every success story on such models, there is another, less publicized, failure.

Figure 17.4
Plot of DOW and Differenced DOW

```
SERIES
USE DOW
TPLOT DOW
DIFFERENCE DOW
TPLOT DOW
```

Series Plot

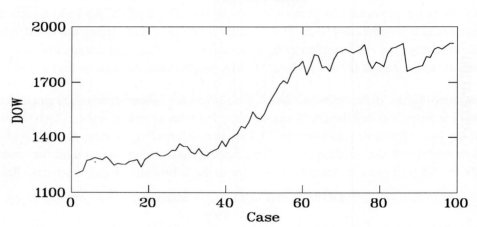

Series Plot

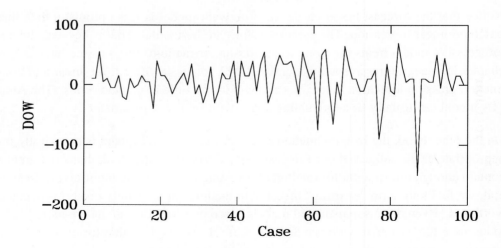

Figure 17.5
ACFs of DOW and Differenced DOW

ACF DOW
DIF DOW
ACF DOW

Autocorrelation Plot

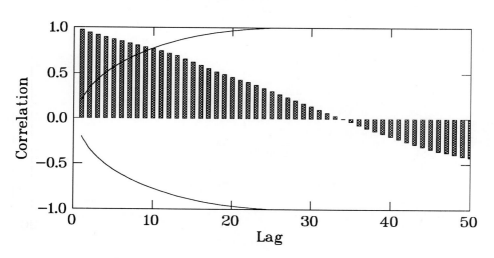

Autocorrelation Plot

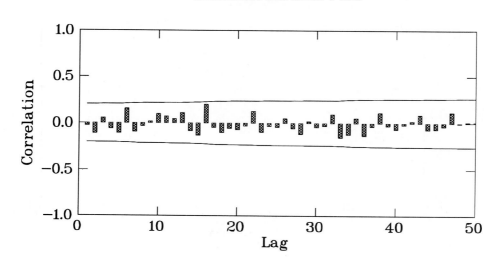

Figure 17.6
Autoregressive Forecast of DOW

```
SERIES
USE DOW
DIFFERENCE DOW
ARIMA DOW /P=1,BACKCAST=30,FORECAST=50..99
```

```
DOW copied from SYSTAT file into active work area


Series is transformed.
Iteration  Sum of Squares  Parameter values
     0        .1077105D+06    .100
     1        .1070893D+06    .024
     2        .1070893D+06    .024
Final value of MSE is      1104.013
Index  Type    Estimate        A.S.E.      Lower  <95%> Upper
  1     AR       0.024          0.102       -0.178       0.225

                    Forecast Values
  Period        Lower95      Forecast      Upper95
        51.     1465.590     1530.715     1595.839
        52.     1437.529     1530.732     1623.935
        53.     1416.114     1530.732     1645.350
                   (remaining forecasts omitted)
```

Series Plot

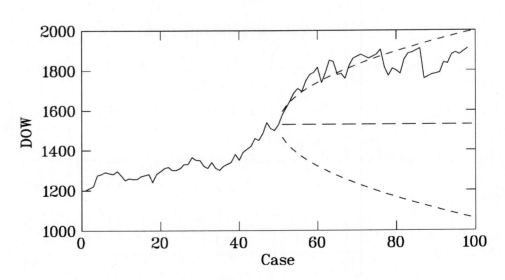

17.3 ARIMA forecasting

Although the random walk served as our introduction, we rarely try to forecast from random walk data. Otherwise, we could all be rich on the stock market. Nevertheless, we have seen the beginning of a strategy for forecasting with the ARIMA model. First, we must identify our model by looking at the ACF function. Next, we model the series by estimating parameters in the function we have identified. Finally, we diagnose the model, as in regression, by examining the residuals.

Stationarity

Before we can identify an ARIMA model, we have to be sure that the series we are examining is stationary. We'll give a technical definition in a minute, but the ordinary English meaning of the term isn't totally misleading. A stationary series is one which isn't going anywhere, locally or globally, in a systematic fashion. We require this because the ARIMA model decomposes a series into a few simple components based on local fluctuations in the series. A nonstationary series has additional components of variation which the ARIMA model will miss and, therefore, model incorrectly. Don't worry, however. If we are forecasting a nonstationary series, we can use some transformations to make the series stationary, do our ARIMA model, and then reverse the original transformations to get our forecasts.

A time series is stationary if the following three conditions are true:

1. The mean of the series is constant across time.

2. The variance of the series is constant across time.

3. The autocorrelations of the series depend only on difference in time points and not on the time period itself.

We can reasonably infer that these conditions are met if:

1. There is no general upward or downward trend in the series.

Remedy: Difference the data. In the SERIES module, use the DIFFERENCE command. We have seen in the series regression chapter and in the random walk model that differencing once removes linear trend. Differencing twice removes quadratic trend. For nonlinear trend, a nonlinear transformation prior to differencing (e.g. LOG or SQR) will usually do the trick.

2. The local fluctuation around the mean of the series is comparable at all time points.

Remedy: If the variance of the series is proportional to the mean level of the series and if the mean level of the series increases or decreases at a constant rate, then use the LOG transformation. This transformation will stabilize the variance and linearize the trend. A slightly less powerful transformation is the square root. You can try other power transformations (see the transformations in Chapter 22), but these two should serve most purposes.

3. There are no seasonal or cyclical fluctuations in the series and the ACF of the first half of the series is comparable to the ACF of the second half.

Remedy: Seasonally difference the data. In the SERIES module, type DIFFERENCE / LAG=*n* , where *n* is the seasonal period. The seasonal period can be found in the original series by counting the number of time periods from peak to peak or trough to trough. It can be found in the ACF by counting the periods between two successive peaks of positive or negative autocorrelation.

These suggested remedies should be done in the following order:

1. Stabilize the variance and/or linearize the trend via nonlinear transformations.

2. Examine the transformed series to see if the variance is stabilized and the trend is linear. In the SERIES module, you can use the following commands to check these conditions in a single plot.

```
SERIES
USE MYDATA
LOG SERIES
TREND SERIES
SQUARE SERIES
TPLOT SERIES
```

This plot will plot the squared variation around the mean of the series against time. If the trend has not been linearized and variance not stabilized by logging, the plot will show a trend in the plotted variance. Once you have confirmed the transformation worked, you can DIFFERENCE the series to remove trend instead of using the TREND command:

```
USE MYDATA
LOG SERIES
DIFFERENCE SERIES
```

3. Examine the transformed series and the ACF for any cyclical components. If you see them, then DIFFERENCE seasonally:

DIFFERENCE SERIES / LAG=4

The most frequent seasonal cycles involve 4 (quarterly business seasons), 7 (weekly calendar effects) and 12 (annual business cycles). In scientific data, other seasonal patterns exist (e.g. sunspots, migration).

Be careful not to difference the data too many times. You should really see wavy fluctuations in the series and the ACF should be wavy (not just a few spikes) before considering seasonal differencing. Figure 17.6 shows how we can introduce seasonal components into the DOW series by differencing twice: once with first differences and again with seasonal differences. Remember, the first difference of the series was a white noise process. Notice that the ACF now shows a pronounced negative autocorrelation spike (-.504) at lag 4.

Figure 17.7
Creating Seasonal Autocorrelation by Overdifferencing

```
USE DOW
DIFFERENCE DOW
DIFFERENCE DOW / LAG=4
ACF DOW
```

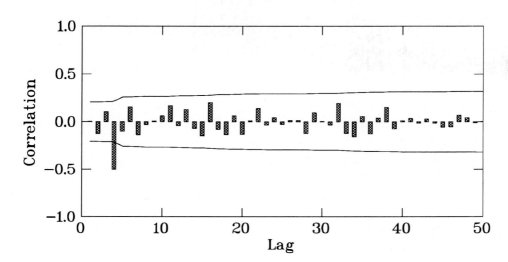

Autocorrelation Plot

17.4 Identifying the model

Once we know we have a stationary series, we are ready to identify the ARMA components of the model. This is the most difficult aspect of ARIMA modeling. We will use the autocorrelation function plot (ACF) and partial autocorrelation function plot (PACF) for this purpose. The PACF is similar to the ACF, except that each autocorrelation is computed after partialing out the effect of earlier autocorrelations, just as in the computation of ordinary partial correlations. We can cover only a few simple models within the scope of this book; you should consult the references for further examples.

Figure 17.8 contains a program in SYSTAT BASIC to compute several typical nonseasonal and seasonal stationary time series. Typical series produced by this program and their ACFs and PACFs are shown in Figure 17.9. Different values of PHI and THETA (positive and negative) have been chosen to show you the variety of series possible. You can adjust the values of the parameters PHI (ϕ) and THETA (θ) in this program to compute and plot other series. You can also use the RSEED command to compute additional random replications of the models. Finally, you can change the size of the series by modifying the REPEAT=99 statement to some other number. We strongly urge you to try this and run the program to get a feel for the vagaries of ARIMA models. Many books on ARIMA print theoretical ACF and PACF plots, but these can be quite different from the plots generated by real data on small samples.

One of the simplest stochastic models is the one we have already seen: the random walk. In the random walk, the autoregressive coefficient is 1. For most autoregressive series, however, this coefficient is less than 1 in absolute magnitude. If it were greater than 1, then the series would diverge because each new point in the series would tend to move away more from the mean of the series. The general first order autoregressive model looks like this:

$$Z_i = (1\text{-PHI})*\text{CONSTANT} + \text{PHI}*Z_{i-1} + \text{ERROR}_i$$

The CONSTANT in this model is not the mean level of the series. It is like the constant in a regression equation, namely, the constant amount to which variable effects are added to comprise the prediction for each case. From now on, we will omit the constant from our formulas to keep things simple, like this:

$$Z_i = \text{PHI}*Z_{i-1} + \text{ERROR}_i$$

Usually, differencing removes the constant anyway when we are making the series stationary, so you needn't worry about it. In a few cases where data have not been differenced, we must include the constant in our estimates. Make sure you add CONSTANT to the ARIMA command in SERIES for these cases. If the constant is not significant on the printout (it falls within two standard errors on either side) then you can omit it from the model and reestimate.

The first program in Figure 17.8 produces a first order autoregressive model using PHI = .8. This is labeled AR(1) in Figure 17.9. The **AR(1) model** is sometimes called a Markov process (after the Russian probabilist A. A. Markov). Any point in a Markov process is a function only of the previous point plus random error. Note that the series looks like the trace of a machine gun fired while moving from left to right. There are random gaps in the series as holder of the gun attempts to correct for being too high or low. When PHI is negative, on the other hand, the series becomes dense, fluctuating from high to low at almost every step. This is because PHI causes the current value in the series to compensate for the last by going high to low or low to high, rather than heading toward the mean of the series. In the AR(1) model, the ACF falls back from a large first order autocorrelation (roughly of the magnitude of PHI) to zero. The profile of this "falling back" is like an exponential decay, that is, inwardly curved. The PACF, on the other hand, has one spike at the first order autocorrelation.

The model in the above equation is called first order autoregressive because it involves influences from the first time period preceding the current period $(i - 1)$. If we expect direct influences on the current period from two periods back, then we need a second order autoregressive model:

$$Z_i = PHI1*Z_{i-1} + PHI2*Z_{i-2} + ERROR_i$$

This model is represented in the second row of Figure 17.9, labeled AR(2). In this example, PHI1 = .6 and PHI2 = -.6. You should try replacing these values with two positive or two negative values to see how this model can produce different results.

So far, we have been discussing autoregressive models, which regress current values in a series on previous values. There is a second type of stochastic time series model which is equally important, called a **moving average model** (MA). In moving average models, current values depend on the random errors of previous values. Moving average models, in other words, represent series which are cumulations of random shocks or disturbances.

The simplest moving average model is the first order:

$$Z_i = ERROR_i - THETA*ERROR_{i-1}$$

If this model represented a family's spending habits, for example, then whether every-one goes on a spending spree today (randomly overspending the family budget) depends on whether they went on one yesterday.

An MA(1) model is equivalent to an AR (infinity) model by expressing error terms in the MA model as functions of previous errors and current observations. Thus, MA models can substitute for AR models of relatively high order. This is one reason we have presented AR models only up to order 2. Higher order AR models are rare in practice.

The third row of Figure 17.9 shows a typical MA(1) model with THETA = -.8. The fourth row shows an MA(2) model, which is generated from the following formula:

$$Z_i = ERROR_i - THETA1*ERROR_{i-1} - THETA2*ERROR_{i-2}$$

In this example, THETA1 = -.8 and THETA2 = .8.

Sometimes we want to consider the possibility that a series is generated by a mixture of AR and MA terms. For example, we can mix AR(1) and MA(1):

$$Z_i = PHI*Z_{i-1} + ERROR_i - THETA*ERROR_{i-1}$$

The fifth row of Figure 17.9 shows the realization of this model. We have represented only one instance, with PHI = .8 and THETA = -.8. You should modify the program and try some others. By combining AR and MA models, we have a more general for-mulation called **ARMA**. An ARMA(1,0) model is equivalent to an AR(1) model and an ARMA(0,1) is equivalent to MA(1). The AR(1) and MA(1) mixed together is equiv-alent to an ARMA(1,1).

Finally, there are AR and MA series in which seasonal effects predominate. For exam-ple, a snow shovel manufacturer's sales are best predicted by the previous year's sales during the same season rather than by the prior season. For these series, we need to modify the AR and MA models to refer to terms that go back several points in the series to the previous season. For example, a **seasonal AR(1) model** with a four period season would look like this:

$$Z_i = PHI*Z_{i-4} + ERROR_i$$

and a seasonal MA(1) for the same seasonal period would look like this:

$$Z_i = ERROR_i - THETA*ERROR_{i-4}$$

A seasonal ARMA model, such as **SARMA(1,1)**, mixes these two.

The last three rows of Figure 17.9 show some typical seasonal models. Again, you should try varying the parameters in the simulation program of Figure 17.8 to see some other seasonal models. Most notable in the ACFs and PACFs of these seasonal models are spikes at the seasonal periods (in this case, multiples of 4). Other popular seasonal periods are 7 and 12, for weekly and annual cycles. You can modify the program in Figure 17.8 to produce other seasonal periods by increasing the LAG function to several more lags.

Figure 17.8
A SYSTAT Program to Generate Typical Time Series

```
BASIC
RSEED=13579
NOTE 'AUTOREGRESSIVE (1) PROCESS, ARMA(1,0)'
SAVE AR1
REPEAT 99
   let phi = .8
   let t = case
   let z = phi*lag(z,1) + zrn
   if case=1 then let z = zrn
run
NEW
NOTE 'AUTOREGRESSIVE 2 PROCESS, ARMA(2,0)'
SAVE AR2
REPEAT 99
   let phi1 = .6
   let phi2 = -.6
   let t = case
   let z = phi1*lag(z,1) + phi2*lag(z,2) + zrn
   if case=1 then let z = zrn
   if case=2 then let z = phi1*lag(z,1) + zrn
RUN
NEW
NOTE 'MOVING AVERAGE 1 PROCESS, ARMA(0,1)'
SAVE MA1
REPEAT 99
   let theta = -.8
   let t = case
   let u = zrn
   let z = u - theta*lag(u,1)
   if case=1 then let z = u
RUN
```

```
NEW
NOTE 'MOVING AVERAGE 2 PROCESS, ARMA(0,2)'
SAVE MA2
REPEAT 99
  let theta1 = -.8
  let theta2 = .8
  let t = case
  let u = zrn
  let z = u - theta1*lag(u,1) - theta2*lag(u,2)
  if case=1 then let z = u
  if case=2 then let z = u - theta1*lag(u,1)
RUN
NEW
NOTE 'AUTOREGRESSIVE MOVING AVERAGE (1,1) PROCESS, ARMA(1,1)'
SAVE ARMA11
REPEAT 99
  let phi = .8
  let theta = -.8
  let t = case
  let u = zrn
  let z = phi*lag(z,1) + u - theta*lag(u,1)
  if case=1 then let z = u
RUN
NEW
NOTE 'SEASONAL AUTOREGRESSIVE 1 PROCESS, ARMA(0,0)(1,0)'
SAVE SAR1
REPEAT 99
  let phi = -.8
  let t = case
  let z = phi*lag(z,4) + zrn
  if case<5 then let z = zrn
RUN
NEW
NOTE 'SEASONAL MOVING AVERAGE 1 PROCESS, ARMA(0,0)(0,1)'
SAVE SMA1
REPEAT 99
  let theta = .8
  let u = zrn
  let z = u - theta*lag(u,4)
  if case<5 then let z = u
RUN
NEW
NOTE 'SEASONAL AUTOREGRESSIVE MOVING AVERAGE  (1,1) PROCESS,
ARMA(0,0)(1,1)'
SAVE SARMA11
REPEAT 99
  let phi = -.8
  let theta = .8
  let u = zrn
  let z = phi*lag(z,4) + u - theta*lag(u,4)
  if case<5 then let z = u
RUN
```

By now you are glutted with ARMA models and may be wondering if ARMA identification is more art than science. There are computer programs which identify models automatically, but they look at only a few indicators in the ACF and PACF. Furthermore, many of these automatic programs have a difficult time recognizing stationarity and the need for transformations prior to model identification.

You are better off being aware of alternative plausible models by being forced to consider a number of ACFs and PACFs. If you wish to get more experience with model identification, you might even want to examine power spectrums of the series generated by the programs in Figure 17.8. These are explained further in Makridakis, Wheelwright, and McGee (1983) and can be computed easily in the SERIES module with the FOURIER command.

Keep one thing in mind: simplicity. We mentioned at the beginning of this chapter that the goal of forecasting is to get good forecasts. This process is aided by understanding real world factors which generate a series. But all other things being equal, simple models generate better forecasts with noisy data than complex models which overfit the data. The whole point of ARIMA modeling is to fit series with a few parameters. Remember the trade-off, for example, between AR(infinity) and MA(1). A similar trade-off exists between AR(1) and MA(infinity). In summary, if you cannot decide between a higher order and lower order model on the basis of plots, choose the lower order model.

Finally, we've covered AR, MA, and ARMA. Where's the ARIMA? The "I" in ARIMA stands for "integrated." If we needed to difference our series to produce stationarity before modeling, then the number of differencings (the order) is represented by the integration parameter. It is called "integrated" because the stationary series must be summed (the opposite of differencing) to yield the original series.

The most general model we can form, then is **ARIMA (P,D,Q)**. P stands for the order of the AR terms, D stands for the number of differences we computed to make the model stationary, and Q stands for the order of the MA terms. The seasonal model is ARIMA (PS,DS,QS), where the terms have similar meanings for seasonal effects. And, finally, we can have a multiplicative ARIMA model of the form (P,D,Q) (PS,DS,QS). This general model covers all the ones we have considered above. It also covers a number of other forecasting methods, such as several types of exponential smoothing. Many of the popular smoothing forecast methods can be expressed as moving average models or more general ARIMA models. You can consult the references for more information.

Figure 17.9
Series, ACFs, and PACFs for Stationary Nonseasonal and Seasonal Models

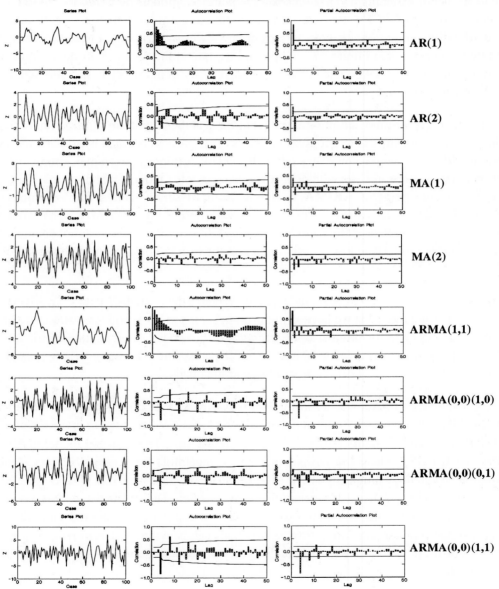

17.5 Estimating the ARIMA model

Once you have identified the general form of the ARIMA model you wish to estimate, you can use the ARIMA command in the SERIES module to compute the estimates. The options to the ARIMA command follow the nomenclature we have been using: P,Q, and PS,QS. One option that appears in SERIES and a number of other time series computer programs is called Backcasting. For shorter series, it is helpful to use the computed model to extend the series back in time so that there is not a sharp transition at the beginning of the series. On each iteration for computing the PHI and THETA estimates, backcasting is used to smooth the computation of estimates. You should generally choose BACK=n, where n is roughly a fourth to a third of a short series. If you are computing forecasts, then n should be at least as large as the number of forecasts you are computing ahead.

Testing assumptions

As in regression, it is important to test whether assumptions have been violated for your fitted model. The simplest test is to do an ACF plot of the residuals. The plot should appear as white noise. For seasonal models, the power spectrum should also appear random. You can examine this by using the FOURIER command on RESIDUALS of the model and then PLOTting them to see if there is any trend or pattern in the plot of Fourier components. Finally, you can DIFFERENCE the residuals. If they are truly white noise, then the first difference of the residuals should look like an MA(1) plot with THETA=1 (see Figure 17.9).

Forecasting

If you request FORECAST as an ARIMA option, you will get forecasts for several periods past the end of the series plus confidence intervals on the forecasts. The mathematics of the forecast intervals are beyond the scope of this book, but you should note that they get wider as the forecasts become more remote from the end of the series. This is as it should be, forcing us to take large extrapolations skeptically.

A GNP example

We need an example to save us from the perfect world of theory. Let's examine the GNP data from Chapter 6 to see if we can construct an ARIMA model to forecast. We begin with a plot of the series in Figure 17.10. Note that the series is increasing nonlinearly and that the variance does not seem to be constant across all parts of the series. This is a good candidate for a LOG transformation. After logging, we should replot the series and then examine the ACF. The second half of Figure 17.10 shows the logged series and it is substantially linear.

Figure 17.10
U.S. GNP and Logged GNP from 1881 to 1980

```
USE  PATENT
TPLOT GNP
LOG GNP
TPLOT GNP
```

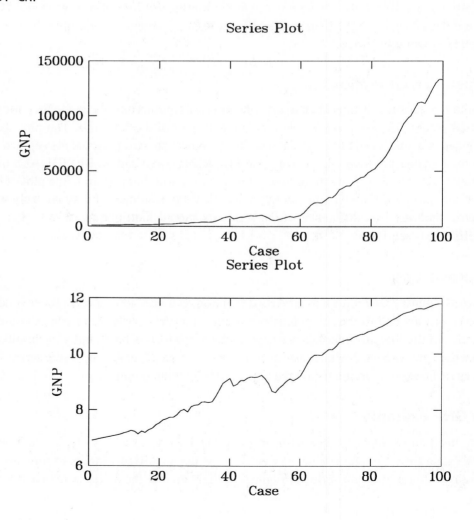

Figure 17.11 shows the ACF and PACF of the series. The large spike at the first lag in the PACF and the rapid tapering off of the first order ACF suggests an AR(1) model with a PHI coefficient somewhat smaller than the one we used in our theoretical plot in Figure 17.9. We will fit this model and ask for forecasts. Figure 17.12 shows this estimation. We have requested a constant term because the mean of the series is not zero after differencing. We might not need this parameter for good forecasts. You should try leaving it out to see how the results are affected. Note, however, that the estimate of the constant is significantly different from zero.

You can see how the forecasts are expressed in the original GNP units. SERIES keeps a record of the transformations and differencing while making the series stationary and then reverses these for the final forecast. Note, as well, how the confidence intervals increase dramatically as we reach ten years after the end of the observed series (1990).

Finally, we show the ACF of the residuals in Figure 17.13. There is a relatively large spike at lag 13, but it is isolated. Such spikes can occur randomly in an ACF. You can ask for more lags (e.g. ACF RESIDUAL / LAG=25), but you should not find any worrisome patterns.

A more ambitious, perhaps dubious example

Let's see what happens if we go out on a limb. We are going to try to predict what would have happened to U.S. Patent applications if the Great Depression had not happened. Unlike our analysis in the last chapter, we are not concerned with innovation per se but rather with extrapolating an observed series.

This goal is possibly dubious for two principal reasons. The first problem is that the model we propose may not be the "correct" ARIMA model even though its forecast appears plausible. Like many of the real datasets in this book, this interesting series does not fit the perfect examples you find in textbooks. The second problem is that, like all analyses of historical data, forecasting or "what if" statements involve "counterfacts." We would like to be able to make statements like "What would have happened if the Great Depression had not occurred?" or "Was slavery oppressive in comparison with today's standard of living among migrant farm workers?" In making these statements, we are being illogical, as if we were trying to describe talking fish or pregnant males. The best we can do is to make sure that the consequences of our conclusions are plausible. As we have noted, this problem lies at the heart of all causal modeling of nonexperimental data, including path analysis and structural equations.

Figure 17.11
ACF and PACF of Logged and Differenced GNP

DIF GNP
ACF GNP
PACF GNP

Autocorrelation Plot

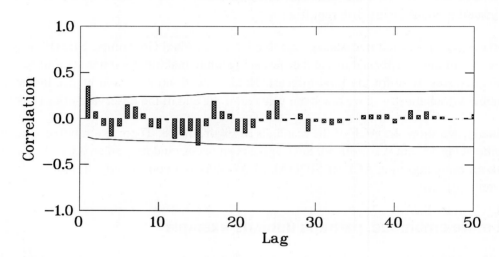

Partial Autocorrelation Plot

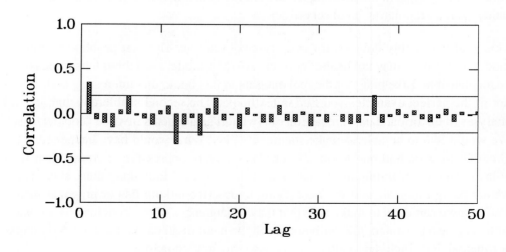

Figure 17.12
Estimation of AR(1) model for Logged GNP Series

```
SERIES
USE PATENT
LOG GNP
DIFFERENCE GNP
ACF GNP
PACF GNP
ARIMA GNP/P=1,CONSTANT,BACK=20,FORECAST=10
```

```
Iteration  Sum of Squares  Parameter values
     0        .6513199D+00   .000  .100
     1        .6185709D+00  -.013  .447
     2        .6161515D+00  -.008  .452
     3        .6091543D+00  -.002  .398
     4        .6076022D+00   .001  .351
     5        .6075585D+00   .000  .352
     6        .6075582D+00   .000  .352
     7        .6075582D+00   .000  .352
     8        .6075582D+00   .000  .352
     9        .6075582D+00   .000  .352
    10        .6075582D+00   .000  .352
Final value of MSE is       0.006
Index    Type    Estimate      A.S.E.        Lower  <95%> Upper
  1  CONSTANT     0.032        0.012         0.008        0.056
  2     AR        0.352        0.095         0.163        0.541
Asymptotic correlation matrix of parameters

                       1            2

            1        1.000
            2       -0.013        1.000


               Forecast Values
Period         Lower95       Forecast      Upper95
    101.      117874.617    137653.609    160751.437
    102.      110706.023    143698.281    186522.781
    103.      106467.281    150637.172    213131.734
    104.      103960.906    158143.953    240566.500
    105.      102547.867    166110.672    269071.969
    106.      101874.992    174510.516    298934.219
    107.      101737.320    183346.828    330420.156
    108.      102009.156    192634.984    363773.594
    109.      102610.187    202395.391    399218.625
    110.      103486.195    212650.750    436969.813
```

Figure 17.13
ACF of Residuals from ARIMA analysis of Logged GNP

ACF RESIDUAL

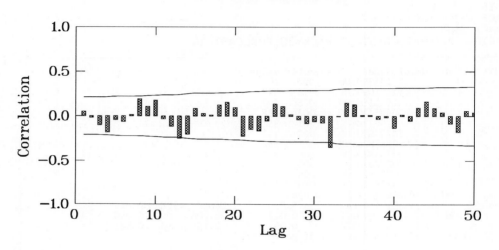

Figure 17.14 shows the plot of U.S. Patent applications by year. Note the sharp drop in applications after 1930. This is the point at which we will extrapolate our forecast. The entire series shows an obvious upward trend which we will have to remove by differencing. There does not appear to be a need for transformation, however, since the upward trend is not curvilinear and the variance appears relatively constant. Figure 17.15 shows the ACF and PACF for the undifferenced series. The trend component is so strong that the ACF does not drop steeply back to zero.

Figure 17.16 shows the ACF and PACF for the first differenced series. Now we see a cyclical pattern in the plots covering approximately 8 years. This pattern does not diminish quickly the way some of the sample plots in Figure 17.9 do. You might think this looks like an AR(2) process (see Figure 17.9), but notice the PACF does not show strong first and second order autocorrelations. Likewise, MA(2) can be cyclical, but it requires dominant autocorrelations in the PACF.

Although it is not conspicuous in the series, we think there is (multiyear) seasonal variation because the waves in the ACF and PACF do not decay. It is more evident later in the raw series, where almost every 8 years the patent applications take a downturn. We will not risk a causal explanation of this suggestion of a cycle, except to mention that business cycles in the GNP and other economic indicators are well established. In any case, we are going to risk overdifferencing by using seasonal (8 year) differencing on the series. The final panels of Figure 17.17 show the ACF and PACF for the seasonally differenced series.

Not surprisingly, we now see a spike in the ACF and PACF at lag 8, possibly induced by overdifferencing. Our model is still fairly simple, however. We will fit an ARIMA(0,1,0)(0,1,1) with a seasonal period of 8 years. Figure 17.18 shows this analysis. We did not fit a CONSTANT term to the data, although if you do, it will be slightly significant. Because the forecast is not substantially affected by the constant term, and because we are trying to minimize parameters, we left it out. Our model specifies that patent applications are a function of the previous year's applications and the eighth preceding year's, minus the error of the eighth preceding year's, plus random error. In ordinary English, you could describe it as a compensatory mechanism, in which 8 year peaks dampen subsequent applications.

Figure 17.14
Plot of U.S. Patent Applications by Year

```
USE  PATENT
TPLOT  PATENT
```

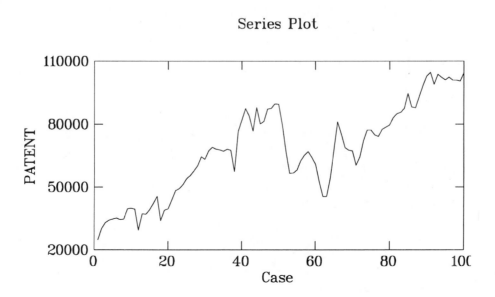

Figure 17.15
ACF and PACF of Patent Series

USE PATENT
ACF PATENT
PACF PATENT

Autocorrelation Plot

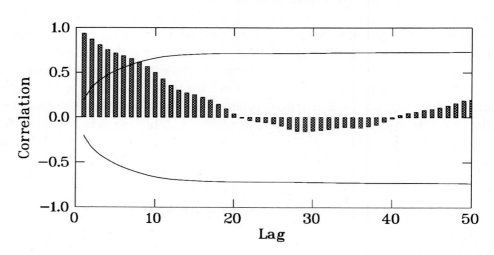

Partial Autocorrelation Plot

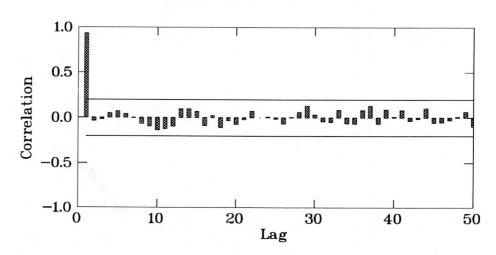

**Figure 17.16
ACF and PACF of Differenced Patent Series**

DIFFERENCE PATENT
ACF PATENT
PACF PATENT

Autocorrelation Plot

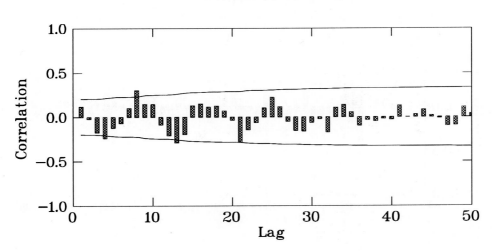

Partial Autocorrelation Plot

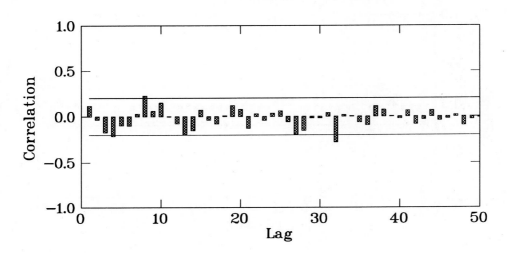

Figure 17.17
ACF and PACF of Seasonally Differenced Patent Series

```
DIFFERENCE PATENT / LAG=8
ACF PATENT
PACF PATENT
```

Autocorrelation Plot

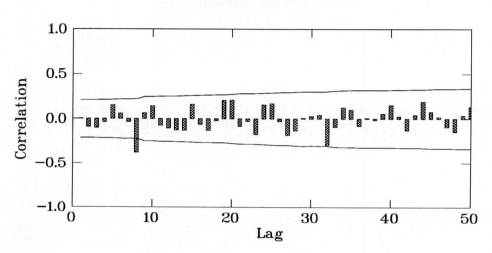

Partial Autocorrelation Plot

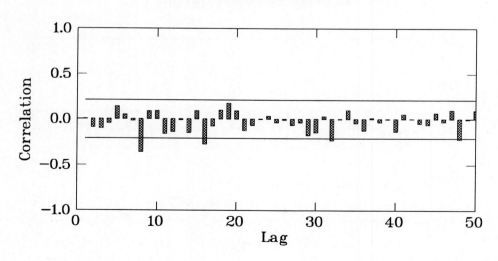

Figure 17.18
Estimating ARIMA(0,1,0)(0,1,1) Seasonal(8) Model

```
ARIMA PATENT / QS=1,SEASON=8,BACK=25,FORECAST=50..100
```

```
Iteration  Sum of Squares  Parameter values
    0          .3516575D+10    .100
    1          .3327942D+10    .190
    2          .2857784D+10    .593
    3          .2634184D+10    .847
    4          .2610959D+10    .865
    5          .2505951D+10    .933
    6          .2496049D+10    .939
    7          .2475262D+10    .947
    8          .2465005D+10    .953
    9          .2455294D+10    .959
   10          .2447963D+10    .966
   11          .2429240D+10    .973
   12          .2424456D+10    .984
Final value of MSE is  2.69384E+07
Index    Type   Estimate    A.S.E.      Lower  <95%> Upper
  1       SMA     0.984      0.006       0.973        0.995
```

Series Plot

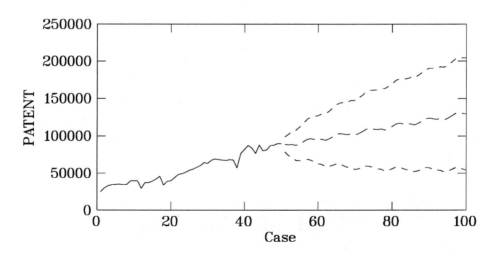

Now, our primary point of this chapter. Figure 17.18 shows a plot of our forecast. Notice how different the ARIMA forecast appears from an ordinary linear regression forecast. The local cyclical behavior has been incorporated into the forecast via a set of random terms. Not all ARIMA forecasts look like this. Some even look like straight lines. But ARIMA forecasts, unlike linear or polynomial ordinary regression forecasts, are responsive to local randomness and to observations in the series just before the beginning of the forecast period.

We will leave the diagnosis of this model up to you. If you plot the residuals from this model, they should appear as white noise. Let's look at one more plot, however. We mentioned before beginning this example that historical analyses can be dubious because of the risk of glaring "counterfacts." One check we can make is to see whether our forecast is plausible in terms of other relevant variables. In particular, does our forecast make sense when normalized by population? Figure 17.19 plots forecast patents per 100,000 population and the observed patents per 100,000 (PATPOP in the original dataset). Our forecasts are within the range of observed values at other time periods. It would appear that the country paid deeply for the Depression and it seems unlikely it could recover to the point it might have reached if patents applications had been uninterrupted by economic adversity. For theoretical background, see our discussion at the end of Chapter 6, which cites Smookler's work.

Figure 17.19
Plot of Observed and Forecast Patents per 100,000 Population

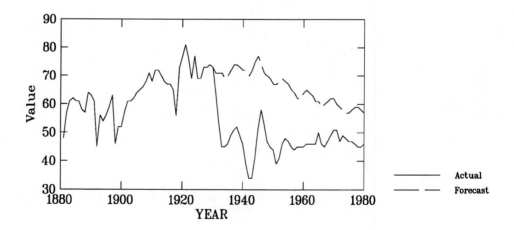

Notes

We must qualify our conclusions about the patent forecast not only because of the dubious assumptions we mentioned but also because it is an unusual way to approach the problem. To pursue the problem further would take us beyond the scope of this book, but we should point out that econometric modeling of this series would have to include explicit terms for the relative interruption of the series by the Depression. Furthermore, if we were treating this strictly as a forecast, we should exclude the post-1930 data from our analysis. We included this to illustrate the seasonal variation, which is in large measure due to the second half of the series.

Box and Jenkins (1976) is the classic introduction to the ARIMA model. McCleary and Hay (1980), Cleary and Levenbach (1982), Nelson (1973), and Vandaele (1983) are much more applied introductions. Makridakis, Wheelwright and McGee (1983) is a compendium of forecasting techniques.

References

Box, G.E.P. and Jenkins, G.M. (1976). *Time Series Analysis: Forecasting and Control* (Rev.Ed.). San Francisco: Holden-Day, Inc.

Cleary, J.P. and Levenbach, H. (1982). *The Professional Forecaster: The Forecasting Process through Data Analysis*. Belmont, CA: Wadsworth, Inc.

Makridakis, S., Wheelwright, S.C., and McGee, V.E. (1983). *Forecasting: Methods and Applications* (2nd ed.). New York: John Wiley & Sons.

McCleary, R., and Hay, R.A. Jr. (1980). *Applied Time Series Analysis for the Social Sciences*. Beverly Hills, CA: Sage Publications.

Nelson, C.R. (1973). *Applied Time Series Analysis for Managerial Forecasting*. San Francisco: Holden-Day, Inc.

Vandaele, W. (1983). *Applied Time Series and Box-Jenkins Models*. New York: Academic Press, Inc.

18

Finding Patterns in Time Series

We have shown that prediction models on time series require a different set of tools than those for cross-sectional data. The same is true for detecting patterns in time series. In this chapter, we will discuss some smoothing techniques for getting rid of noise in a series and a method called Fourier analysis for detecting cyclical and other patterns.

Figure 18.1 shows instantaneous rates of neural firing by a single ganglion cell in an anesthesized cat's retina stimulated over a period of approximately seven seconds. The data were taken from a series of experiments by Michael Levine and Laura Frishman (Levine, Frishman, & Enroth-Cugell, 1987). The original data from which these were derived comprised the times of occurrence in milliseconds of individual neural impulses (spikes) over the seven second interval. The variable called RATE in Figure 18.1 was computed by taking the reciprocal of the differences between consecutive spike times (Shapley, 1971).

The stimulus in these experiments consisted of two filtered light-emitting diodes (LEDs), one green and one red. The light beams from these LEDs were focused directly on the center of the receptive field of the cells being recorded. The intensity of the LEDs was controlled by varying the width of current pulses delivered every five milliseconds. One of the beams was sinusoidally modulated at 1.96 Hz. In other words, the retina was stimulated by a beam that smoothly varied from bright to dim approximately twice a second. We are going to analyze these data for purposes quite different from those in the original study, since it focused on other aspects of these data. Nevertheless, we would expect that if the measured ganglion cell is responding linearly to this input, it should output pulses in a sinusoidal pattern with approximately two cycles per second.

Figure 18.1
Single Cell Firing Rate in Cat Retina Cell

#	RATE	TIME	#	RATE	TIME	#	RATE	TIME	#	RATE	TIME	#	RATE	TIME
1	34.483	0.027	51	21.739	1.386	101	45.455	2.744	151	30.303	4.102	204	55.556	5.542
2	35.714	0.054	52	20.833	1.413	102	40.000	2.771	152	32.258	4.130	205	50.000	5.569
3	52.632	0.082	53	27.027	1.440	103	37.037	2.798	153	52.632	4.157	206	83.333	5.597
4	71.429	0.109	54	19.231	1.467	104	33.333	2.825	154	43.478	4.184	207	55.556	5.624
5	40.000	0.136	55	50.000	1.494	105	32.258	2.853	155	45.455	4.211	208	58.824	5.651
6	58.824	0.163	56	38.462	1.521	106	37.037	2.880	156	41.667	4.238	209	58.824	5.678
7	47.619	0.190	57	32.258	1.549	107	76.923	2.907	157	43.478	4.265	210	90.909	5.705
8	45.455	0.217	58	22.222	1.576	108	45.455	2.934	158	52.632	4.293	211	47.619	5.732
9	62.500	0.245	59	34.483	1.603	109	37.037	2.961	159	40.000	4.320	212	58.824	5.760
10	38.462	0.272	60	37.037	1.630	110	35.714	2.988	160	30.303	4.347	213	43.478	5.787
11	41.667	0.299	61	40.000	1.657	111	40.000	3.016	161	19.608	4.374	214	40.000	5.814
12	38.462	0.326	62	58.824	1.684	112	66.667	3.043	162	30.303	4.401	15	34.483	5.841
13	37.037	0.353	63	25.000	1.712	113	76.923	3.070	163	32.258	4.428	216	52.632	5.868
14	35.714	0.380	64	50.000	1.739	114	34.483	3.097	164	27.027	4.456	217	34.483	5.895
15	33.333	0.408	65	41.667	1.766	115	62.500	3.124	165	9.901	4.483	218	50.000	5.923
16	62.500	0.435	66	40.000	1.793	116	45.455	3.151	166	21.277	4.510	219	50.000	5.950
17	27.027	0.462	67	23.810	1.820	117	41.667	3.179	167	37.037	4.537	220	30.303	5.977
18	52.632	0.489	68	25.000	1.847	118	43.478	3.206	168	40.000	4.564	221	33.333	6.004
19	32.258	0.516	69	17.857	1.875	119	45.455	3.233	169	29.412	4.591	222	58.824	6.031
20	31.250	0.543	70	27.778	1.9022	120	38.462	3.260	170	37.037	4.619	223	40.000	6.058
21	35.714	0.571	71	21.277	1.929	121	55.556	3.287	171	30.303	4.646	224	58.824	6.086
22	71.429	0.598	72	37.037	1.956	122	62.500	3.314	172	25.641	4.673	225	35.714	6.113
23	38.462	0.625	73	29.412	1.983	123	41.667	3.342	173	28.571	4.700	226	58.824	6.140
24	62.500	0.652	74	45.455	2.010	124	37.037	3.369	174	33.333	4.727	227	47.619	6.167
25	58.824	0.679	75	37.037	2.038	125	41.667	3.396	175	52.632	4.754	228	40.000	6.194
26	37.037	0.706	76	50.000	2.065	126	50.000	3.423	176	27.778	4.782	229	34.483	6.221
27	50.000	0.734	77	33.333	2.092	127	28.571	3.450	177	43.478	4.809	230	35.714	6.249
28	50.000	0.761	78	45.455	2.119	128	32.258	3.478	178	21.739	4.836	231	52.632	6.276
29	66.667	0.788	79	38.462	2.146	129	24.390	3.505	179	25.000	4.863	232	71.429	6.303
30	47.619	0.815	80	50.000	2.173	130	40.000	3.532	180	31.250	4.890	233	58.824	6.330
31	29.412	0.842	81	43.478	2.201	131	27.778	3.559	181	66.667	4.917	234	52.632	6.357
32	33.333	0.869	82	41.667	2.228	132	43.478	3.586	182	27.027	4.945	235	52.632	6.384
33	58.824	0.897	83	71.429	2.255	133	52.632	3.613	183	38.462	4.972	236	41.667	6.412
34	37.037	0.924	84	35.714	2.282	134	62.500	3.641	184	43.478	4.999	237	32.258	6.439
35	28.571	0.951	85	35.714	2.309	135	43.478	3.668	185	32.258	5.026	238	34.483	6.466
36	18.182	0.978	86	21.739	2.336	136	58.824	3.695	186	43.478	5.053	239	17.544	6.493
37	28.571	1.005	87	17.241	2.364	137	34.483	3.722	187	41.667	5.080	240	19.608	6.520
38	23.810	1.032	88	29.412	2.391	138	35.714	3.749	188	58.824	5.108	241	41.667	6.547
39	35.714	1.060	89	31.250	2.418	139	45.455	3.776	189	43.478	5.135	242	29.412	6.575
40	52.632	1.087	90	37.037	2.445	140	58.824	3.804	190	47.619	5.162	243	55.556	6.602
41	41.667	1.114	91	41.667	2.472	141	50.000	3.831	191	55.556	5.189	244	38.462	6.629
42	43.478	1.141	92	32.258	2.499	142	31.250	3.858	192	43.478	5.216	245	41.667	6.656
43	32.258	1.168	93	43.478	2.527	143	33.333	3.885	193	40.000	5.243	246	45.455	6.683
44	43.478	1.195	94	37.037	2.554	144	55.556	3.912	194	33.333	5.271	247	41.667	6.710
45	27.778	1.223	95	37.037	2.581	145	28.571	3.939	195	23.256	5.298	248	40.000	6.738
46	38.462	1.250	96	55.556	2.608	146	45.455	3.967	196	28.571	5.325	249	38.462	6.765
47	76.923	1.277	97	90.909	2.635	147	32.258	3.994	197	27.778	5.352	250	38.462	6.792
48	33.333	1.304	98	37.037	2.662	148	25.641	4.021	198	28.571	5.379	251	40.000	6.819
49	31.250	1.331	99	41.667	2.690	149	27.778	4.048	199	45.455	5.406	252	50.000	6.846
50	28.571	1.358	100	45.455	2.717	150	16.393	4.075	200	33.333	5.434	253	52.632	6.873
									201	47.619	5.461	254	55.556	6.901
									202	27.027	5.488	255	35.714	6.928
									203	34.483	5.515	256	43.478	6.955

Figure 18.2 shows the plot of RATE against TIME. It is difficult to discern a wavelike pattern in this plot. We need a method for getting rid of some of the random error. In the rest of this chapter, we will explore several approaches to this problem.

Figure 18.2
Plot of Instantaneous RATE against TIME

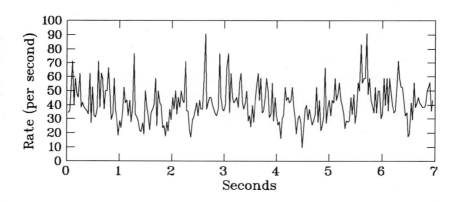

18.1 Running window smoothers

Running Means

If the random error around the sine wave we are seeking is additive and its expected value is 0, then averaging across points in the time series will tend to cancel out the error and leave the sines. Take two points in a series, for example:

$$X_i = SIN(T_i) + ERROR_i$$
$$X_{i+1} = SIN(T_{i+1}) + ERROR_{i+1}$$

Averaging these two points will yield the following smooth (Si)

$$S_i = [SIN(T_i) + SIN(T_{i+1})]/2 + [ERROR_i + ERROR_{i+1}]/2$$

Since we expect the errors to average to zero over the long run, then this procedure is likely to smooth the points to the average value of the sines in the "window" we have chosen. In this example, our window is of length 2 because we averaged 2 points to get each smoothed point.

There is a trade-off, however. We want our window to be wide (longer than 2) so that the errors will be more likely to cancel. If we choose too many points, however, we will average out model variation as well because the sine wave is changing as T (or time) changes In the extreme, we could choose a window as long as the series itself and thus average all the errors as well as the sine terms. In that case, we would end up with only one smoothed point, the mean of the series.

Figure 18.3 shows six different running smooths on our data performed in the SERIES module using the SMOOTH command. The first (MEAN=3) makes the second point in the series the average of the first three, the third point the average of the second, third, and fourth, and so on. The second smoother (MEAN=5) averages the first 5 points, then points 2 through 6, then 3 through 7, and so on.

These running smooths of means are sometimes called **filters** because they remove noise or other features from the series. The width of the filter mainly (but not exclusively) determines the type of variation which is removed. For example, MEAN=3 averages errors across adjacent triples, and tends to remove single outliers, or jitters. MEAN=10 averages more points and thus tends to smooth out bumps or jitters consisting of several points. Thus, longer windows tend to be **low pass filters** because they allow low frequency variation (no jitters) to pass through after smoothing. When you turn down the treble on your hi-fi, you are using a low pass filter because you are suppressing high frequency sounds.

Each filter leaves some points at the beginning or end of the series unsmoothed. If the filter is of length n, where n is even, then we lose $n/2$ points at the beginning and end. If n is odd, as in some of the examples in Figure 18.3, then we lose $n/2 - 1$ points at either end. Notice, for example, that for MEAN=13 the first and last 6 points of the series are unsmoothed. There are several approaches to this problem. A simple one is to pad the series on both ends with estimated values before smoothing. Picking values can be problematic, however. We could extrapolate beyond the series by following the trend at those points or by inserting the mean of the series. Another approach would be to use shorter length filters at the ends of the series. This is closer to the approach we will take.

Figure 18.3
Running Means Smooths on RATE Data

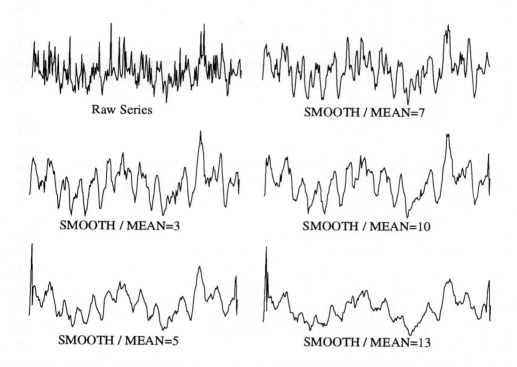

Compound mean smoothers

None of the smoothings in Figure 18.3 are particularly satisfying, although the longer smooths begin to reveal the sinusoidal pattern. We may smooth these smoothed data again, however, to get rid of further irregularities. For example, the

```
SMOOTH / MEAN=7
```

example appears to reveal a two cycle per second waveform but it still has too much high frequency jitter or error. If we combine this with shorter length smoothers, we should be able to average out the jitters around the wave.

Figure 18.4 shows the result of three successive smooths on the retina data. This result fits closely what we are seeking. Notice there are about two smooth waves per second, indicating that the ganglion cell is outputting the same sinusoidal pattern as the LED's are inputting.

Figure 18.4
MEAN 3/5/7 Smooth on RATE Data

```
SMOOTH / MEAN=7
SMOOTH / MEAN=5
SMOOTH / MEAN=3
```

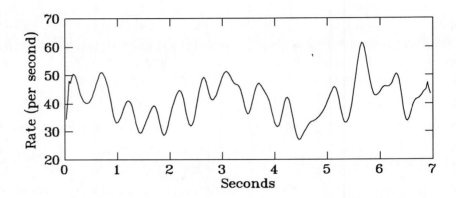

You can use the SMOOTH and TPLOT commands in the SERIES module to decide when to stop smoothing. It does not matter in what order you do the smooths because means of sums are the same as sums of means (more about that in the next section on smoothing with weights). Because shorter windows can smooth closer to the end points, however, it is better to begin with the longer and finish up with the shortest length smooths. If your final smooth is MEAN=2 or MEAN=3, then there is little need to extend the series to smooth the end points.

Smoothing with symmetric weights

Running means smoothers weight each point in the mean window equally. In other words, each smoothed point is the mean of an equally weighted number of points in the raw series on either side of it. Sometimes we want to weight points near the smoothed point more than those far away. In fact, that is what we did when we used the mean

7-5-3 compound smoother on these data in Figure 18.4. Let's take a simple example, smoothing with MEAN=3 twice:

SMOOTH / MEAN=3

$$S_1 = (X_1 + X_2 + X_3)/3$$
$$S_2 = (X_2 + X_3 + X_4)/3$$
$$S_3 = (X_4 + X_5 + X_6)/3$$
$$\cdots$$

SMOOTH / MEAN=3

$$S_1 = (S_1 + S_2 + S_3) = (X_1 + 2X_2 + 3X_3 + 2X_4 + X_5)/9$$

Our mean 3-3 compound smoother is thus equivalent to smoothing with a single window having weights 1,2,3,2,1. (SYSTAT divides these weights by their sum before smoothing, so you do not have to use fractions.) You can confirm this on the retina data. If you want to do a lot of tallying, you can also confirm that the mean 7-5-3 smoothing we did in Figure 18.4 is the same as a single smooth with the following weights:

SMOOTH RATE / WT=1,3,6,9,12,14,15,14,12,9,6,3,1

Running weights can describe any linear smoother. A popular one, called "Hanning," is the following:

SMOOTH RATE / WT=1,2,1

You can use the same algebra we use above to convince yourself that this is equivalent to a compound 2-2 mean smoother:

SMOOTH RATE / MEAN=2
SMOOTH RATE / MEAN=2

The Hanning smoother takes out single outliers in a series.

Smoothing with asymmetric weights

In Section 17.5, we mentioned that running smoothers can be used to forecast future cases. Many forecasters do this by weighting points ahead of the smoothed point (future points) zero. They do this for two reasons: they don't have the future values (unless they're prophets), and they are dealing with a different error structure than the one we have described. You should review the forecasting chapter to understand other time series error structures In the typical forecasting case, the process is moving average, e.g.:

$$X_i = ERROR_i - THETA*ERROR_{i-1}$$

In this case, averaging previous cases produces a smoothed value (forecast) based on the current level of the series. By weighting past cases less and less, the moving average smooths out recent disturbances. To forecast beyond the end of a series, smoothed values themselves are successively smoothed.

The following command, for example, weights the three previous points in a linearly descending sum. The middle point in the weighting window is the one being forecast:

SMOOTH / WT=1,2,3,0,0,0,0

For the fourth point in a series (the first point we can smooth by this window), the smoothed point would be:

$$S_1 = X_1 + 2X_2 + 3X_3$$

Exponential smoothing is another past-weighting scheme. The weights decrease exponentially as they apply to earlier points in the series. Here is a typical set of exponential weights for five points back:

SMOOTH / WT=.082,.1024,.128,.16,.2,0,0,0,0,0,0

These asymmetrical smoothers are less appropriate for the retina data because we are assuming the errors around the sine wave are not autocorrelated. Asymmetrical smoothers are used frequently in financial modeling, however. You can read more about their application in the forecasting chapter and in Makridakis, Wheelwright and McGee (1983). SYSTAT has a separate command (EXPO) for exponential smoothing which computes these weights automatically.

Running medians

Means are efficient and unbiased estimators of the center of a normal distribution. If we think that the errors we are trying to smooth out are not normally distributed, then running means may not be the most appropriate smoothers. Sometimes errors, for example, are based on contaminated distributions which occasionally generate extreme outliers. One way to pay less attention to these outliers is to use running medians instead of means.

First, let's check to see if this is the case with our retina data. We can plot the residuals of the mean 7-5-3 smooth to see if they look normal. Figure 18.5 shows how to do this. There do appear to be outliers. These are large positive values which are due to relatively intense bursts of neural firings. You can see in Figure 18.1 that several adjacent firings yield instantaneous rates of over 70 firings per second. Clearly, the residuals are not normally distributed. You can do a normal probability plot to confirm this. Before we proceed to median smoothers, however, we should mention that logging the RATE variable would be in order. We will leave it as an exercise for you to rerun the smooths and other analyses in this chapter using the LOG(RATE).

Figure 18.6 shows a compound median smooth on the retina data, known as 4-2-5-3H. This consists of the following smooths:

```
SMOOTH RATE / MEDIAN=4
SMOOTH RATE / MEDIAN=2
SMOOTH RATE / MEDIAN=5
SMOOTH RATE / MEDIAN=3
SMOOTH RATE / WT=1,2,1
```

The final smooth is Hanning, which takes out single spikes or jitters in the median smoothed series. The results are quite similar to our 7-5-3 mean smooth, indicating that the outliers are not having a worrisome effect on the results. This is in part due to our using a long smoothing window, which reduces the effect of one or two outliers.

Running medians should be used with care because they can smooth out "real" features in a series. Especially with wide filters, you can end up with smooths having runs of the same value   That is why it is desirable to combine them with running means to smooth out the smooth and also to compare them carefully to the results of running means before accepting results You should also examine residuals to running medians carefully. If the residuals contain systematic components lost in the smoothing, one remedy is to smooth the residuals and add the residual smooth back into the main smooth and smooth the result (Velleman and Hoaglin, 1985). Finally, if the residuals to running means look normal, you should not consider running medians.

Figure 18.5
Residuals from Mean 7-5-3 Smooth of Retina Data

```
USE RETINA
SMOOTH RATE/MEAN=7
SMOOTH RATE/MEAN=5
SAVE TEMP
SMOOTH RATE/MEAN=3
MERGE RETINA TEMP
LET RESIDUAL=RATE-SMOOTH
STATS
STEM RESIDUAL
```

```
Stem and Leaf Plot of variable:    RESIDUAL, N = 256
         Minimum:        -17.294
         Lower hinge:      -7.230
         Median:          -1.822
         Upper hinge:      5.619
         Maximum:         41.615

        -1    766
        -1    5554444
        -1    33333322222222
        -1    1111110000000000000
        -0    999999888888888
        -0  H 777777766666666666666
        -0    55555544444444444444
        -0    333333333333333332222222222
        -0  M 11111111111111100000000000000
         0    000000011111111111
         0    22222223333333
         0  H 4455555555
         0    6666777777
         0    88888888999
         1    0001111
         1    22222333
         1    4455
         1    66667
         1    8889
         2    00
         2    23
         2    4
     * * * Outside Values * * *
         2    5599
         3    127
         4    1
```

Figure 18.6
Running Medians (4-2-5-3H) Smooth of RATE

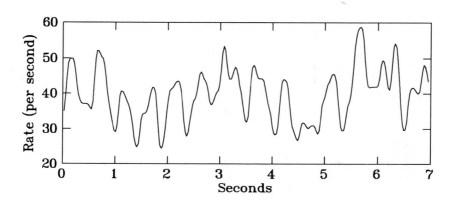

Locally weighted (LOWESS) smoothing

SYSTAT has a procedure that lies between running means and running medians in its responsiveness to outliers. It is less likely than running means to be pulled astray by single or multiple outliers but it is also less likely than running medians to produce over-smoothed plateaus. This procedure was developed by Bill Cleveland at Bell Labs. It is usually applied to smoothing scatterplots, but it also works nicely on time series data.

LOWESS is a locally weighted least squares algorithm. Each point in a series is predicted by a weighted combination of points to its right and left in a regression equation. More distant points are weighted less than close ones. For data regularly spaced on the X axis (i.e. equally spaced time series data like these), this procedure is not unlike symmetric exponentially weighted smoothing.

Instead of choosing a window size in number of data items, we choose a "tautness" criterion (F). F is the proportion of the data contained by the window. If F is near 1, the resulting smooth is very taught (little high frequency variation). If F is near 0, more high frequency variation passes through. F, in other words, is roughly related to the frequency of the filter. For our purposes, we set $F = .05$ to allow the 2Hz waves to appear in the smooth, namely:

```
SMOOTH RATE / LOWESS=.05
```

Figure 18.7 shows the result. As you can see, it is similar to the others. We prefer LOWESS to other time series smoothers because it is generally more robust. Another way to produce Figure 18.7 directly with SYGRAPH is to use the command:

```
PLOT RATE*TIME / SMOOTH=LOWESS,TENSION=.05
```

Figure 18.7
LOWESS Smooth of RATE from Retina Data

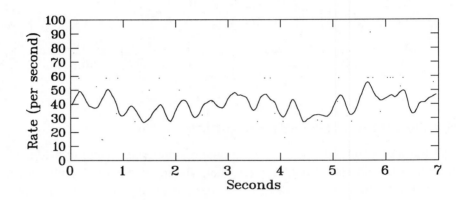

18.2 Identifying cyclical variation: The Fourier transform

As we have seen, the length of filters has something to do with the number of peaks and troughs left in the smoothed series. If data really are periodic, then we could benefit from a technique for finding the number of cycles in a series and then choose a filter to reveal them. The **fast Fourier transform** allows us to do this.

The Fourier transform represents a series by a sum of sine and cosine waves of different frequencies. Instead of going into the algebra of the Fourier transform, let's look at some pictures. Figure 18.8 shows several waveforms which have been added together. In the first column, for example, we have at the top a full cycle of a sine wave. Underneath it is a full cycle of a cosine wave. The sum of these two waves is directly underneath. Notice that wherever the sine and cosine are high, the sum is high, and wherever low, the sum is low. They also can cancel each other out in places. The second column shows two more sine and cosine waves added to this sum. On the top is the summed wave from the bottom of the first column. Below that is a two-cycle sine wave, then a two-cycle cosine wave. The sum at the bottom follows the general shape of the last sum, but it now has local variation produced by the higher frequency. Finally, we add three-cycle sine and cosine waves to this sum and produce a summation with even more local variation.

Figure 18.8
Summing Sine and Cosine Waves to Produce Series

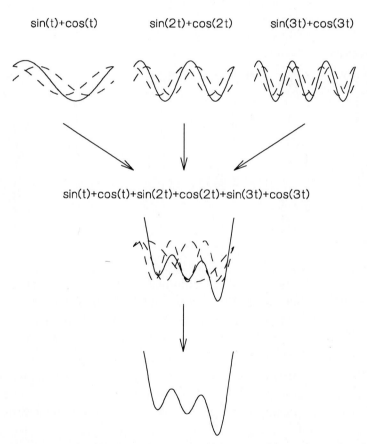

Following this summation process, we can model any finite series with the sum of sine and cosine waves at different frequencies. In Figure 18.8, we weighted each wave equally, but it is possible to weight them with unequal Fourier coefficients to produce more irregularly appearing series. Let's try decomposing the retina data into a set of regular waves. Figure 18.9 shows how to do this and the result.

Figure 18.9
Fourier Decomposition of RATE Data

```
SERIES
USE RETINA
FOURIER RATE
```

```
RATE copied from SYSTAT file into active work area



Fourier components of RATE

Index Frequency      Real   Imaginary   Magnitude    Phase   Periodogram
   1 0.0           41.147      0.0        41.147      0.0     866860.000
   2 0.00391        0.890      0.562       1.052      0.563      566.894
   3 0.00781        1.480      1.891       2.401      0.907     2952.101
   4 0.01172       -1.118     -1.707       2.041      0.991     2131.882
   5 0.01563        0.020     -0.977       0.977     -1.550      488.857
   6 0.01953        0.224     -0.416       0.473     -1.077      114.439
   7 0.02344       -0.003     -0.114       0.114      1.546        6.646
   8 0.02734        0.754      0.368       0.839      0.454      360.074
   9 0.03125       -0.378      0.224       0.440     -0.535       98.900
  10 0.03516        0.240     -0.210       0.319     -0.718       52.195
  11 0.03906        1.387     -0.799       1.601     -0.522     1312.096
  12 0.04297        1.600      0.793       1.786      0.460     1633.752
  13 0.04687       -0.478      0.528       0.712     -0.834      259.706
  14 0.05078        0.358      0.250       0.437      0.609       97.679
  15 0.05469       -1.821     -2.417       3.026      0.925     4689.591
```

Look at the REAL and IMAGINARY columns. These are the coefficients used to weight the cosine and sine waves. They are called REAL and IMAGINARY for certain mathematical reasons having to do with exponential functions, but we can think of them simply as cosine and sine coefficients respectively. The first (41.147) weights a wave of zero cycles, namely a straight line. It means that the overall height of the series is 41.147. When the Fourier decomposition is used on electrical data, this is called the **DC level** because it represents the mean level of voltage in the wave. The second pair (.890 and .562) weight a cosine and sine wave of one cycle through the series. The third (1.480 and 1.891) weight a cosine and sine wave of two cycles. And so on. The program prints the first 15 coefficients, but you can ask for all of them by typing

```
FOURIER RATE / LAG=256.
```

If our series consists of a systematic portion plus white noise, then we should be able to model it with a relatively small number of Fourier components. How do we find how many to retain? Let's concentrate on pairs of sine and cosine waves at the same frequency. We want to find the frequency at which the REAL and IMAGINARY coefficients for the sines and cosines become relatively small. The column called MAGNITUDE is the square root of the sum of squared REAL and IMAGINARY coefficients. If MAGNITUDE is small, then neither the sine nor cosine coefficient can be very large. You can see this happening after the fourth or fifth component, but there is another increase around the 15th.

The easiest way to evaluate trends in MAGNITUDE is to plot it. The plot we are going to produce is called a periodogram. It plots squared magnitude against frequency. The SERIES module automatically replaces a variable with its MAGNITUDE when you do the Fourier transform. To produce the periodogram, we square the MAGNITUDE values.

With these data, the DC level is so large relative to the other coefficients that the plot is hard to discern. All the higher order coefficients lie in a straight line. When this happens, it helps to log the periodogram to get better definition. Do not log a periodogram unless you have trouble getting adequate resolution. Also, do not confuse logging the periodogram with logging the data. We are logging the periodogram simply to be able to view the graph more easily. Figure 18.10 shows the result. We produced it with the Quick Graph facility by tapping YPOWER down to zero, which is the equivalent of log-transforming the vertical axis. You can get the same result by adding SQUARE and LOG after the FOURIER command. See Section Figure 18.11 for an example.

This plot is sufficient for recognizing two relative peaks at 2 and 14 cycles over the series. These peaks occur at the third and fifteenth case, but since the first case in the plot corresponds to DC level, we should subtract one to figure the cycle number.

We can construct a more meaningful plot with SYGRAPH by making a more useful base scale. By dividing the case (index) number by 6.955, the length of the series in seconds, we have a cycles per second scale. We have truncated the plot at 3 cycles per second, so that you can see two relative peaks at around a third of a cycle per second and 2 cycles per second. These peaks are the same ones we observed in Figure 18.10 at cases 2 and 14.

Figure 18.10
Quick Graph Log Periodogram of RATE

```
USE RETINA
FOURIER RATE
(tap,tap,tap ...)
```

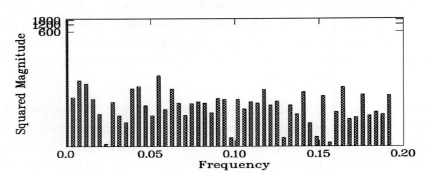

Figure 18.11
Log Periodogram of RATE

```
SERIES
USE RETINA
FOURIER RATE
SQUARE RATE
SAVE TEMP
LOG RATE
USE TEMP
LET CPS=CASE/6.955
PLOT TRANSF*CPS /LINE,SIZE=0,HEI=1.5IN,WID=4IN,
               YLAB='Logged Squared Magnitude',
               XLAB='Cycles per Second', XMIN=0,XMAX=3
```

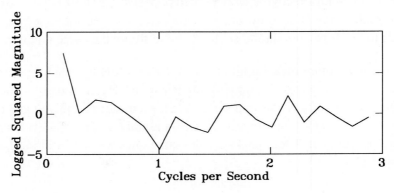

Power spectra

You may hear some people talking about power spectra. Luminaries at cocktail parties often do. In our context, however, the periodogram is an estimate of the power spectrum of the process underlying these data. For a given process, the power spectrum is a representation of the relative contributions of different frequencies (points on the spectrum) ignoring error. We can get a closer approximation to the power spectrum for these data by smoothing the periodogram itself. It may seem strange to be smoothing something that is not the data, but we are trying to discern where most of the power in this series lies.

Figure 18.12
Plotting Smoothed Periodogram to Estimate Power Spectrum

```
USE RETINA
LOG RATE
FOURIER RATE
SQUARE RATE
LOG RATE
SMOOTH RATE/MEAN=5
SAVE TEMP
SMOOTH RATE/MEAN=5
USE TEMP
LET CPS=CASE/6.955
PLOT SMOOTH * CPS /LINE,SIZE=0 HEI=1.5IN, WID=4IN,
                  YLAB='Logged Squared Magnitude',
                  XLAB='Cycles per Second'
```

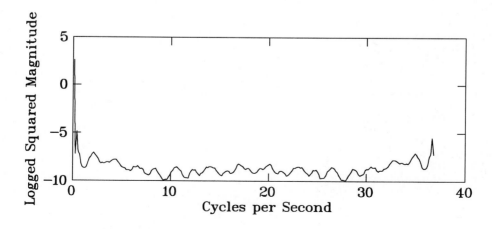

Figure 18.12 smooths the above periodogram by applying the 5 mean smoother twice. We repeat the computer instructions for the Fourier analysis in case you have lost your place. Unlike before, we are now transforming the original series by logging it. Fourier analysis is particularly sensitive to high variance. If the data are not logged when they should be, then higher frequency components will be required to fit the sinusoidal pattern and the spectrum will not taper off at the high end.

Figure 18.13
Smoothing with Selected Fourier Components

```
SERIES
USE RETINA
SAVE TEMP
FOURIER RATE
BASIC
USE TEMP
SAVE FOUR5
IF CASE>5 THEN FOR
   LET REAL=0
   LET IMAG=0
NEXT
RUN
USE TEMP
SAVE FOUR15
IF CASE>15 THEN FOR
   LET REAL=0
   LET IMAG=0
NEXT
RUN
SERIES
USE FOUR5
SAVE TEMP5
FOURIER REAL,IMAG
USE FOUR15
SAVE TEMP15
FOURIER REAL,IMAG
BASIC
USE RETINA,TEMP5
SAVE TEMP
LET SMOOTH5=REAL
RUN
USE TEMP,TEMP15
SAVE FOURIER
LET SMOOTH15=REAL
LET RESIDUAL=RATE-SMOOTH15
LET SINE=SMOOTH15-SMOOTH5
RUN
```

Smoothing using Fourier components

We now have the tools to construct yet another smoother. We have (almost) seen two peaks in the spectrum of this series—one at a third of a cycle per second and one at around 2. Why not reassemble the Fourier components near these values and see what results? We will use the DATA module to zero out the Fourier coefficients at frequencies we consider nonessential. Figure 18.13 shows how to do this. We save the REAL and IMAGINARY coefficients into a temporary file. Then we zero coefficients beyond the fifth pair in the first run and beyond the 15th in the second. Then we USE these zeroed coefficients in the SERIES module and perform the inverse Fourier transform on them. This converts them back to a REAL series. We merge this series with the original data and plot its values against TIME. While merging, we also calculate and add RESIDUAL to the file for testing assumptions.

Figure 18.14 shows the plot of our Fourier smoothed data. The high frequency component (2 cycles a second) varies around a low frequency component of roughly one cycle per every 3 seconds. We can examine this higher frequency component directly by subtracting the 3 cycle trend from it, which we did in making the SINE variable in the last step of the DATA module. Figure 18.15 shows this final plot.

Figure 18.14
Plot of Low and High Frequency Fourier Components of RATE against TIME

```
USE FOURIER
PLOT SMOOTH5,SMOOTH15*TIME/LINE,SIZE=0,
 HEIGHT=1.5IN,WIDTH=4IN,
 YLAB='Rate (per Second),
 XLAB='Seconds'
```

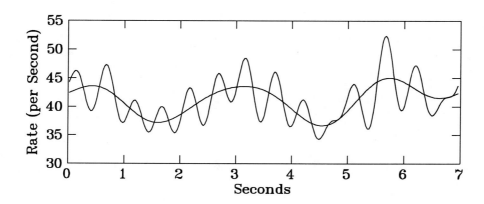

Figure 18.15
Plot of Filtered 1.96 Hz Component of RATE against Time

```
USE FOURIER
PLOT SINE*TIME/LINE,SIZE=0,HEIGHT=1.5IN,WIDTH=4IN,
 YLAB='Deviation from Fundamental Rate,XLAB='Seconds'
```

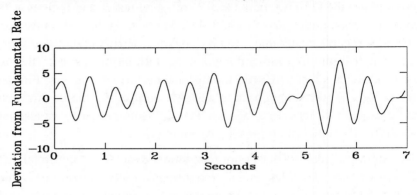

Finally, we analyze the residuals from the smoothed 14 cycle curve. Figure 18.16 shows the ACF of RESIDUAL. Plot and compare this to the ACF on RATE, which shows a substantial autocorrelation due to the cycles. Figure 18.16, by contrast, shows only white noise. If you STEM RESIDUAL, you will see the need for logging the data before doing the Fourier analysis. We leave it to you to complete this as an exercise.

Figure 18.16
ACF of Residuals from Fourier Analysis

```
USE FOURIER
ACF RESIDUAL
```

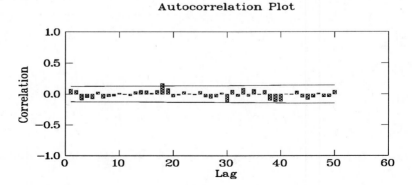

18.3 Finding patterns in multivariate data

We wish we could present a simple way to find common features in several series simultaneously. Unfortunately, the problems we discussed in regression on time series data all apply here. Of course, you can do Fourier analyses separately on several series and compare components. And you can transform several series to white noise before using principal components or factor analysis. If multiple series are spectrally correlated, however, you cannot use ordinary principal components or factor analysis. Brillinger (1975) discusses principal components on multivariate time series, but this goes beyond the scope of this book.

Notes

We did one sneaky thing in demonstrating Fourier analysis. The fast Fourier transform which SYSTAT uses to compute Fourier components requires that the length of a series be a power of two (i.e. 2,4,8,16,32,64,128,256,512 ...). Our series was exactly 256 in length. If a series is not one of these lengths, then the FOURIER command truncates it to the next lowest power. If your series is just short of a power of 2, this truncation can be drastic. In such cases, you can extend the series to the next power of 2 by padding it on the end with zeros in the DATA module. This introduces "leakage" into the series, however. In other words, extra Fourier components will appear as artifacts. To mitigate this problem, you can prepare the series for Fourier analysis by tapering it. The TAPER command in SYSTAT smooths the end values so that fluctuations at the end of the series will not be picked up in the Fourier transform.

The most readable introductions to Fourier analysis are Brigham's (1974) and Bloomfield's (1976) books. Makridakis, Wheelwright and McGee (1983), Chapter 3 is a good source for learning about smoothing. Velleman and Hoaglin (1985) discuss median smoothers.

References

Bloomfield, P. (1976). *Fourier Analysis of Time Series: An Introduction.* New York: John Wiley & Sons.

Brigham, E.O. (1974). *The Fast Fourier Transform.* Englewood Cliffs, NJ: Prentice-Hall.

Brillinger, D.R. (1975). *Time Series: Data Analysis and Theory.* New York: Holt, Rinehart & Winston.

Levine, M.W., Frishman, L.J., and Enroth-Cugell, C. (1987). Interactions between the rod and the cone pathways in the cat retina. *Vision Research, 27,* 1093-1104.

Makridakis, S., Wheelwright, S.C., and McGee, V.E. (1983). *Forecasting: Methods and Applications* (2nd ed.). New York: John Wiley & Sons.

Shapley, R. (1971). Fluctuations of the impulse rate in *Limulus* eccentric cells. *Journal of General Physiology, 57,* 539-557.

Velleman P. and Hoaglin D. (1985). *The ABC's of EDA.* Boston: Wadsworth.

Part 6

Finding Groups and Patterns

Chapter 19: Cluster Analysis

Chapter 20: Principal Components and Factor Analysis

Chapter 21: Multidimensional Scaling

19

Cluster Analysis

It's not hard to get a divorce nowadays. Many do. Not long ago, however, states required specific reasons for divorce. These ranged from relatively innocuous grounds such as "incompatibility" to bemusing ones such as "loathsome diseases" to quite serious ones like "attempted homicide." Figure 19.1 lists 14 of the most prevalent grounds for divorce in 1971. The variable labels should be self-explanatory except, perhaps, for DESERT (desertion), SUPPORT (lack of support), PREGNANT (pregnancy at wedding), DRUGS (drug and/or alcohol abuse), and CONTRACT (fraudulent contract). We have coded these grounds with 1's and 0's to indicate presence or absence. The STATE$ variable contains the official U.S. Postal two-letter state abbreviations. The source is Long (1971).

Suppose we want to identify which grounds for divorce frequently co-occur across states. We might expect to see health, morals, and criminal grounds grouping together in three clusters. On the other hand, we might want to see how different states group together. Perhaps there is a cluster of southern states, another of coastal states, and so on. In each of these state clusters, we might expect to see similar shared values or profiles of grounds for divorce. We will begin by clustering grounds.

Cluster analysis comprises several methods for clumping objects into categories. All the cluster methods attempt to place two or more objects which are similar across a set of attributes into a single cluster or category among several alternatives. There are two basic ways to accomplish this. **Hierarchical methods** produce families of clusters which contain other clusters which contain other clusters, and so on. In hierarchical models, the smallest clusters contained by other clusters are the objects themselves. **Nonhierarchical methods** produce discrete or overlapping clusters which contain only objects. SYSTAT offers several types of hierarchical methods under the JOIN command and one type of nonhierarchical method under the KMEANS command. Let's examine first the hierarchical methods, which are more popular.

Figure 19.1
Grounds for Divorce in United States in 1971

ADULTERY	CRUELTY	DESERT	SUPPORT	FELONY	IMPOTENT	PREGNANT	DRUGS	CONTRACT	INSANE	BIGAMY	SEPARATE	STATE$
1	1	1	1	1	1	0	1	0	0	0	0	AK
1	1	1	1	1	0	1	1	0	0	0	0	AL
1	1	1	1	1	0	1	1	0	0	1	1	AR
1	1	1	1	1	0	0	1	0	0	0	1	AZ
0	0	0	0	0	0	0	0	0	1	0	0	CA
1	1	1	1	0	1	0	1	0	0	0	0	CO
1	1	1	0	1	0	0	1	1	0	0	0	CT
1	1	1	1	1	0	0	1	0	0	1	1	DE
1	1	1	0	0	1	0	1	0	0	1	1	FL
1	1	1	0	1	1	1	1	1	0	0	0	GA
1	1	1	1	1	0	0	1	0	0	0	1	HI
1	1	1	0	1	0	1	1	0	0	0	0	IA
1	1	1	1	1	0	0	1	0	0	0	1	ID
1	1	1	0	1	1	0	1	0	0	1	0	IL
1	1	1	1	1	1	0	1	0	0	0	0	IN
1	1	1	0	1	0	0	1	1	0	0	0	KS
1	1	1	0	1	1	1	1	1	0	0	1	KY
1	0	0	0	1	0	0	0	0	0	0	1	LA
1	1	1	1	1	1	0	1	0	0	0	0	MA
1	0	1	0	1	1	0	0	0	0	0	1	MD
1	1	1	1	0	1	0	1	0	0	0	1	ME
1	1	1	1	1	1	0	1	0	0	0	0	MI
1	1	1	0	1	1	0	1	0	0	0	0	MN
1	1	1	0	1	1	1	1	0	0	1	0	MO
1	1	1	0	1	1	1	1	0	0	1	0	MS
1	1	1	1	1	0	0	1	0	0	0	0	MT
1	1	1	1	1	1	0	1	0	0	0	0	NB
1	0	0	0	0	1	1	0	0	0	0	1	NC
1	1	1	1	1	0	0	1	0	0	0	0	ND
1	1	1	1	1	1	0	1	0	0	0	0	NH
1	1	1	0	0	0	0	0	0	0	0	0	NJ
1	1	1	1	1	1	1	1	0	0	0	0	NM
1	1	1	1	1	1	0	1	0	0	0	1	NV
1	1	1	0	1	0	0	0	0	0	0	1	NY
1	1	1	0	1	1	0	1	1	0	1	0	OH
1	1	1	0	1	1	1	1	1	0	0	0	OK
1	1	1	0	1	1	0	1	0	0	0	0	OR
1	1	1	0	1	1	0	0	1	0	1	0	PA
1	1	1	1	1	1	0	1	0	0	0	1	RI
1	1	1	0	0	0	0	1	0	0	0	1	SC
1	1	1	1	1	0	0	1	0	0	0	0	SD
1	1	1	1	1	1	1	1	0	0	1	0	TN
1	1	1	0	1	0	0	1	0	0	0	1	TX
1	1	1	1	1	1	0	1	0	0	0	0	UT
1	0	1	0	1	1	1	0	0	0	0	0	VA
1	1	1	1	1	0	0	0	0	0	0	1	VT
1	1	1	1	1	1	0	1	1	0	0	1	WA
1	1	1	1	1	0	0	1	0	0	0	1	WI
1	1	1	0	1	0	0	1	0	0	0	1	WV
1	1	1	1	1	1	1	1	0	0	0	0	WY

19.1 Hierarchical methods

A simple method for producing hierarchical clusters involves joining objects (grounds) sequentially according to similarity. The first step is to join the two most similar grounds and call this a cluster. Then find the next two closest objects and join them. If one of these objects is already in a cluster, then bring the other object into its cluster. Otherwise, make another cluster. And so on. In this process, objects will be joined to objects, objects to clusters, and clusters to clusters. Figure 19.2 shows how SYSTAT implements this procedure, called single linkage cluster analysis (see the Linkage Methods subsection below for more information).

The display printed by SYSTAT looks like a sideways tree. This tree shows the order in which objects (grounds) were joined from left to right. Notice that CRUELTY and DESERT and ADULTERY were the first to join. Moving from the left, we can see that these joined DRUGS in a single cluster and then FELONY. These five grounds form a relatively distinct cluster because they do not join another object or cluster until they meet SUPPORT at the right-hand side of the tree.

Another cluster is evident below this one in the tree. This cluster comprises PREG-NANT, INSANE, CONTRACT, and BIGAMY. Notice that neither IMPOTENT nor SEPARATE joins in the other clusters until quite late (to the right in the tree).

Notice that the process of finding clusters in trees is somewhat subjective. On the left there are as many clusters as objects and on the right there is only one. If you cut the tree with a vertical line corresponding to some joining distance, you will get some number of clusters in between. The trick is to find a cutting point such that a few clusters contain most of the objects. Your eye, in effect, must cluster the tree.

Distance measures

The DISTANCE scale below the tree shows the joining distance at each branch. For example, FELONY is joined to the (DRUGS, CRUELTY, DESERT, ADULTERY) cluster at approximately a distance of .35. What is this distance? The program calls it normalized EUCLIDEAN. For binary data like this (1's and 0's), it amounts to the square root of the average number of disagreements (1-0 or 0-1) between grounds within states. For CRUELTY and DESERT, there are 2 disagreements, so the distance is the square root of 2/50, which is .2. In general, normalized Euclidean distance is the root mean square discrepancy between objects across attributes.

Figure 19.2
Single Linkage Cluster Analysis of U.S. Grounds for Divorce
Euclidean Distance

```
CLUSTER
USE DIVORCE
JOIN / COLUMNS
```

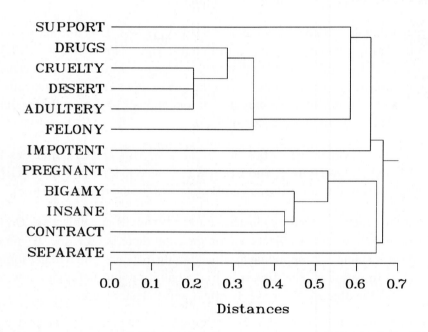

We need a distance metric in order to decide which objects are closest, but what does this Euclidean distance mean? For example, if two grounds occur in no states, should we say they are similarly treated? And what about two grounds which could occur in every state? Are they similar? The Euclidean distance metric says they are. It pays attention to the pattern of agreements and disagreements, but it is also influenced by the size of the disagreements.

There are other distances and quasi-distances which we can use in clustering. You should read Section 23.4 to learn about other distance measures. For example, we could use a measure which ignores overall level of disagreements and responds only to pattern. One minus the Pearson correlation is such a measure. The Pearson correlation measures the association between two variables (objects) after standardizing the scales on which the variables are measured. Try adding DISTANCE=PEARSON to the commands in Figure 19.2 to see the effect of standardizing scales. You can also examine other distance measures in the CORR module and pass the computed triangular matrix to the CLUSTER module to compare results. For binary data like these, there are some special similarity coefficients (S2-S6) which can be used to form distance measures.

Linkage methods

So far, we have been looking at the effect of different distances on cluster solutions. The joining method we have used is always to join objects or clusters which are closest to each other. This is easy to do with objects; just examine the distance between them. But how do we decide how close two clusters or a cluster and an object are? We need a linkage method (amalgamation rule) to decide how to aggregate distances in these cases.

In the **single linkage method**, two clusters are joined according to the closest two points in each cluster. Thus, the distance between a point and a cluster is taken to be the distance of a point to the nearest point in the cluster. The distance between two clusters is taken to be the distance between the nearest two points from each cluster. Single linkage (sometimes called the MIN method) can produce long, stringy clusters because clusters tend to join at nearest linkage points:

Another method which produces more globular clusters is complete linkage. The **complete linkage method** defines the joining distance between a point and a cluster as the largest distance between the point and another point in the cluster. Similarly, the joining distance between two clusters is the largest distance between two points, one in each cluster. Complete linkage clustering (sometimes called the MAX method) tends to produce globular, compact clusters because clusters cannot join unless their most distant members are relatively close to each other.

Single and complete linkage are two extremes in a continuum of linkage methods. They are popular, in part, because they are guaranteed to produce cluster trees with monotonically increasing joining distances. That is, if a cluster is joined to another cluster, its joining distance will be larger than the distance between any two objects or clusters in either of the two being joined. There are other widely used amalgamation methods included in SYSTAT which do not have this property.

The **centroid method** has an intuitively appealing definition of joining distance. Simply average all the objects in each cluster. Then compute the distance between these averages (centroids). **Ward's linkage** is modeled after analysis of variance (ANOVA). It minimizes the within-cluster sum of squares relative to the between-cluster sum of squares at each level of joining. Ward's method is best suited to clusters with equal number of cases. Otherwise, it tends to join clusters with a smaller number of cases first.

Two methods work with all the pairwise distances between clusters. The **average method** averages all the pairwise distances, producing a mean distance. This method tends to produce clusters with similar variance on each variable. The **median method** computes the median distance instead of the average.

Figure 19.3 shows how these linkage methods compare on a simple two-dimensional (two-variable) dataset. The curves show the boundaries separating the clusters for a two-cluster solution by each linkage method. These are the partitions occurring at the *last* join in the tree to the right of each frame. None of the solutions in these figures is completely satisfying, since we picked the numbers to exploit differences between the methods. With strong and compact cluster structure (completely separated blobs), all the linkage methods would result in the same clustering. In this figure you can see that the single linkage clusters tend to be longer than the complete ones. The other methods tend to be a compromise between these two extremes.

Now let's look at an alternative to single linkage on real data. Figure 19.4 shows a complete linkage clustering for the divorce data. For these data, SUPPORT moves over to the other cluster (see Figure 19.2). Actually, both clusterings reveal that SUPPORT, IMPOTENT, and SEPARATE do not cluster well with the other variables. We really have two relatively tight clusters (DRUGS, FELONY, CRUELTY, DESERT, ADULTERY) and (PREGNANT, BIGAMY, CONTRACT, INSANE) against the background of the other variables.

Figure 19.3
Different Linkage Methods Produce Different Clusterings

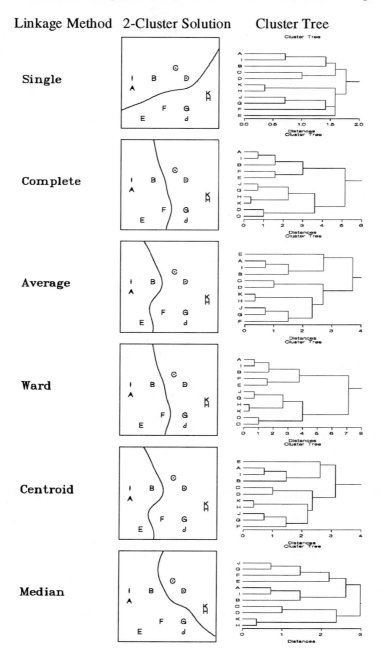

Figure 19.4
Complete Linkage Cluster Analysis of U.S. Grounds for Divorce
Euclidean Distance

```
CLUSTER
USE DIVORCE
JOIN / COLUMNS,LINKAGE=COMPLETE
```

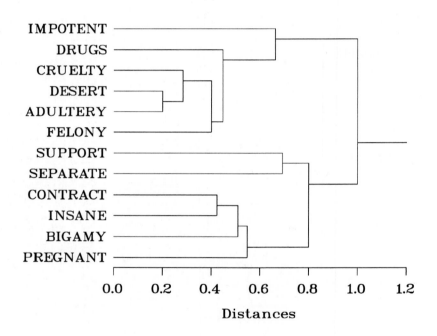

Cluster Tree

19.2 Nonhierarchical (overlapping) methods

Sometimes we know in advance how many clusters a dataset should contain. In these cases, we can search for the best partition into *k* clusters using some distance measure. This partition does not depend on what grouping might be best for *k - 1* or *k + 1* clusters. Nonhierarchical clustering methods thus do not merge clusters in a stepwise fashion. Instead, they search for a "best" separation into *k* groups among all the objects. One of the simplest of these nonhierarchical methods is called ***k*-means clustering**.

Let's examine this method on a new dataset. Those of you who own cars probably know about the *Consumer Reports* data: cylinders, miles per gallon, frequency of repair . . . all the things a sensible car buyer should know. We're going to classify cars a little differently. Figure 19.5 shows performance data on a select group of cars from the enthusiast magazine *Car and Driver*. ACCEL represents seconds to 60 mph, BRAKE is braking distance in feet from 60 mph, SLALOM is speed through a zig-zag slalom course, MPG is miles-per-gallon (of less interest to buyers of some of these cars), and SPEED is top speed in miles-per-hour. The dataset has been sorted on ACCEL. Some of the cars are labeled ambiguously. The Porsche 911T is really the 911 Turbo. The Mazda RX-7T is a turbo as well. The BMW 635 is *not* the M6. And the Sentra is a Nissan SE.

Figure 19.5
Performance of Selected Cars

ACCEL	BRAKE	SLALOM	MPG	SPEED	NAME$
5.0	245.0	61.3	17.0	153.0	Porsche911T
5.2	252.0	64.3	10.0	173.0	Countach
5.3	242.0	61.9	12.0	181.0	Testarossa
5.8	243.0	62.6	19.0	154.0	Corvette
6.6	266.0	63.0	16.7	150.0	CamaroIROC
6.6	259.0	64.8	19.2	145.0	MazdaRX-7T
6.7	289.0	65.3	15.5	148.0	MustangGT
6.7	255.0	64.2	20.0	120.0	ShelbyGLH-S
7.0	267.0	57.8	14.5	145.0	Mercedes560
7.5	246.0	62.4	22.0	137.0	Mercedes300
7.6	271.0	59.8	21.0	124.0	Saab9000
7.9	259.0	61.7	19.0	130.0	ToyotaSupra
8.0	267.0	63.1	21.1	126.0	FieroGT
8.3	256.0	59.3	20.0	132.0	Audi5000Q
8.5	263.0	59.9	17.5	131.0	BMW635
8.7	287.0	64.2	35.0	115.0	CivicCRX
9.0	249.0	61.9	28.0	122.0	BMW325es
9.1	268.0	54.6	17.0	119.0	BMW735i
9.3	258.0	64.1	24.5	129.0	AcuraLegend
9.7	295.0	58.6	18.5	120.0	Bonneville
10.3	246.0	63.8	24.0	115.0	Pulsar
10.8	287.0	60.8	25.0	100.0	VWFoxGL
11.7	317.0	59.4	19.8	115.0	Sable
12.9	300.0	61.2	31.5	92.0	Hyundai
13.0	253.0	62.3	27.0	95.0	ChevyNova
13.3	264.0	60.7	27.0	100.0	SentraSE

How many clusters should we expect in these data? We might begin by looking for sport versus basic transportation. In this case, $k = 2$ and we want to separate all the cars into two groups. The k-means algorithm attempts to place cars into clusters such that, over all cars, the Euclidean distance of each car to its cluster center is as small as possible. If only one clustering variable were used, this would mean that a one-way analysis of variance (ANOVA) between the two car clusters would be as significant as possible.

This goal of reducing overall error of misclassification based on distances to cluster centers would require an enormous amount of computation. As a compromise, the *k*-means algorithm begins by splitting the cars into *k* groups on the variable with the largest variance. From this initial state, the algorithm then attempts to move points from one to another cluster in order to reduce classification error (total distance of points from cluster centers). This process continues until the error cannot be reduced further.

The *k*-means algorithm has several disadvantages (Fisher and Van Ness, 1971). First, *k*-means might not find the optimum split even for perfectly clustered data. This is because the selection of seed cases for the initial clustering is somewhat *ad hoc*. The iterative procedure, as well, does not examine all possible partitions. Second, adding duplicates of already existing cases to a file can change a *k*-means clustering.

Since Euclidean distance is used to compute classification error, it is essential that variables be on comparable scales to prevent one or more variables from unduly influencing the outcome. We discuss this problem further in Section 23.2. Our car data clearly show different scales, so we STANDARDIZEd the data before clustering.

Notice that the clustering in Figure 19.6 distinguishes small and large cars (not sporty vs. basic). The first cluster appears to be a blend of high-performance and luxury cars. The second cluster is relatively inexpensive small cars. Finally, notice that the summary statistics show SLALOM contributing little to the discrimination ($F=.603$). Let's look for three clusters which might separate the high-performance and luxury cars. Figure 19.7 shows this.

The first cluster is now sports cars except for the Mercedes 300, BMW 325 and Acura Legend. These three sedans are well-known for their sporty handling, however. The second cluster includes the small cars. The third cluster now includes the luxury cars with relatively less maneuverability but higher speed. Notice that the Bonneville moved to the third cluster of larger sedans. The three cluster solution is not simply a splitting of the two cluster solution.

Figure 19.6
Two-Group *K*-means Clustering of Selected Cars

```
CLUSTER
USE CARS
STANDARDIZE / SD
IDVAR=NAME$
KMEANS / NUMBER=2
```

```
Distance metric is Euclidean distance
k-means splitting cases into 2 groups
Summary statistics for 1 clusters
```

	Variable	Minimum	Mean	Maximum	St.Dev.
	ACCEL	-1.45	0.00	2.01	1.00
	BRAKE	-1.21	-0.00	2.65	1.00
	SLALOM	-2.85	-0.00	1.48	1.00
	MPG	-1.89	0.00	2.47	1.00
	SPEED	-1.69	0.00	2.31	1.00

```
Summary statistics for all cases
```

Variable	Between SS	DF	Within SS	DF	F-Ratio
ACCEL	14.371	1	10.629	24	32.451
BRAKE	10.300	1	14.700	24	16.816
SLALOM	3.863	1	21.137	24	4.386
MPG	6.375	1	18.625	24	8.214
SPEED	11.993	1	13.007	24	22.129
** TOTAL **	46.902	5	78.098	120	

```
-------------------------------------------------------------------
Cluster 1 of 2 contains 18 cases
     Members                                  Statistics
```

Case	Distance	Variable	Minimum	Mean	Maximum	St.Dev.
Porsche911T	0.63	ACCEL	-1.45	-0.50	0.76	0.62
Countach	1.11	BRAKE	-1.21	-0.42	1.21	0.62
Testarossa	1.12	SLALOM	-1.56	0.26	1.48	0.84
Corvette	0.52	MPG	-1.89	-0.33	1.25	0.77
CamaroIROC	0.38	SPEED	-0.66	0.45	2.31	0.81
MazdaRX-7T	0.49					
MustangGT	0.97					
ShelbyGLH-S	0.55					
Mercedes560	0.92					
Mercedes300	0.36					
Saab9000	0.66					
ToyotaSupra	0.25					
FieroGT	0.44					
Audi5000Q	0.60					
BMW635	0.55					
BMW325es	0.88					
AcuraLegend	0.69					
Pulsar	0.93					

```
-------------------------------------------------------------------
Cluster 2 of 2 contains 8 cases
     Members                                  Statistics
```

Case	Distance	Variable	Minimum	Mean	Maximum	St.Dev.
CivicCRX	1.16	ACCEL	0.09	1.12	2.01	0.77
BMW735i	1.33	BRAKE	-0.65	0.94	2.65	1.08
Bonneville	0.75	SLALOM	-2.85	-0.58	1.03	1.15
VWFoxGL	0.20	MPG	-0.67	0.74	2.47	1.11
Sable	0.90	SPEED	-1.69	-1.02	-0.43	0.51
Hyundai	0.78					
ChevyNova	0.92					
SentraSE	0.65					

Cluster Profile Plots

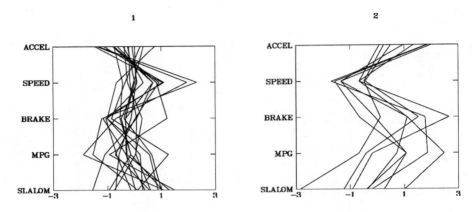

19.3 Clustering rows (cases) or columns (variables)

You can cluster rows or columns of a matrix with SYSTAT. The JOIN command offers this as an option and the KMEANS command can work on a TRANSPOSEd matrix. If you are clustering on Euclidean distances, you may want to standardize your data before using the JOIN or KMEANS commands. Some variable clustering methods (e.g. Tryon and Bailey, 1970) are based on factor analysis, but it is usually easier to compute distances directly on a transposed matrix and then operate directly on the distances as JOIN/COLUMNS does.

SYSTAT offers a MATRIX joining procedure which simultaneously joins rows and columns. The clustering display shows the data matrix and the tree for rows as well as columns. Figure 19.8 shows the two-way joining of the CARS data. The display enables us to perceive joint variation. For example, the Testarossa-Countach cluster is based on similar values for all variables except SLALOM performance (where the Countach excels). The BMW735i stands out for doing poorly on the SLALOM. It is a heavy car tuned to high speed maneuvering (above 100 mph) but is not particularly agile at low speeds. A cure for its problems is to install an M6 engine, a Quaife differential, and Dinan suspension (contact Wilkinson or Leo Franchi at Midwest Motorsport for further information).

Figure 19.7
Three-Group *K*-means Clustering of Selected Cars

KMEANS / NUMBER=3

```
Distance metric is Euclidean distance
k-means splitting cases into 3 groups
Summary statistics for 1 clusters
                          | Variable    Minimum     Mean   Maximum   St.Dev.
                          | ACCEL        -1.45      0.00      2.01      1.00
                          | BRAKE        -1.21     -0.00      2.65      1.00
                          | SLALOM       -2.85     -0.00      1.48      1.00
                          | MPG          -1.89      0.00      2.47      1.00
                          | SPEED        -1.69      0.00      2.31      1.00
Summary statistics for all cases
  Variable      Between SS   DF   Within SS   DF    F-Ratio
  ACCEL            16.090     2      8.910     23    20.768
  BRAKE             4.757     2     20.243     23     2.703
  SLALOM           16.192     2      8.808     23    21.143
  MPG              16.878     2      8.122     23    23.897
  SPEED            14.068     2     10.932     23    14.798
  ** TOTAL **      67.985    10     57.015    115
---------------------------------------------------------------------
Cluster 1 of 3 contains 11 cases
      Members                                   Statistics
    Case      Distance  | Variable    Minimum     Mean   Maximum   St.Dev.
  Porsche911T    0.52   | ACCEL        -1.45     -0.84     -0.20     0.44
  Countach       0.85   | BRAKE        -1.21     -0.46      1.21     0.71
  Testarossa     0.93   | SLALOM       -0.14      0.60      1.48     0.54
  Corvette       0.40   | MPG          -1.89     -0.60      0.20     0.65
  CamaroIROC     0.23   | SPEED        -0.43      0.78      2.31     0.84
  MazdaRX-7T     0.34   |
  MustangGT      0.86   |
  ShelbyGLH-S    0.61   |
  Mercedes300    0.53   |
  ToyotaSupra    0.52   |
  FieroGT        0.63   |
---------------------------------------------------------------------
Cluster 2 of 3 contains 8 cases
      Members                                   Statistics
    Case      Distance  | Variable    Minimum     Mean   Maximum   St.Dev.
  CivicCRX       0.90   | ACCEL         0.09      1.02      2.01     0.80
  BMW325es       0.63   | BRAKE        -1.01      0.13      1.77     1.05
  AcuraLegend    0.69   | SLALOM       -0.39      0.29      1.03     0.60
  Pulsar         0.66   | MPG           0.55      1.20      2.47     0.66
  VWFoxGL        0.59   | SPEED        -1.69     -0.95     -0.03     0.61
  Hyundai        0.96   |
  ChevyNova      0.59   |
  SentraSE       0.58   |
---------------------------------------------------------------------
Cluster 3 of 3 contains 7 cases
      Members                                   Statistics
    Case      Distance  | Variable    Minimum     Mean   Maximum   St.Dev.
  Mercedes560    0.64   | ACCEL        -0.62      0.15      1.34     0.65
  Saab9000       0.42   | BRAKE        -0.49      0.58      2.65     1.11
  Audi5000Q      0.54   | SLALOM       -2.85     -1.28     -0.71     0.75
  BMW635         0.43   | MPG          -1.10     -0.44      0.03     0.38
  BMW735i        0.76   | SPEED        -0.66     -0.14      0.69     0.46
  Bonneville     0.47   |
  Sable          1.11   |
```

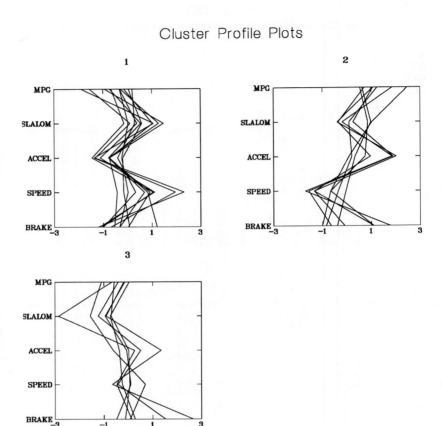

Cluster Profile Plots

19.4 Special problems in clustering

As you can see, clustering can be a subjective, exploratory procedure. Unlike discriminant analysis, we do not have a training sample or prior knowledge of the distributions we are working with. This makes a lot of users wary of using clustering, despite the obvious benefits in identifying outliers in data and searching for structure. Several problems in clustering are particularly troublesome: 1) deciding on the best clustering procedure for a dataset, 2) deciding on the number of clusters and 3) deciding whether a solution is "significant." These problems are related, since we cannot decide on the number of clusters if there are no significant clusters in the data. And we cannot decide if there are really clusters present unless we use the best clustering method. Nevertheless, it is easier to consider them separately.

Figure 19.8
Joint Clustering of Cars Data

```
USE CARS
STANDARDIZE / SD
IDVAR NAME$
JOIN ACCEL,BRAKE,SLALOM,MPG,SPEED / MATRIX
```

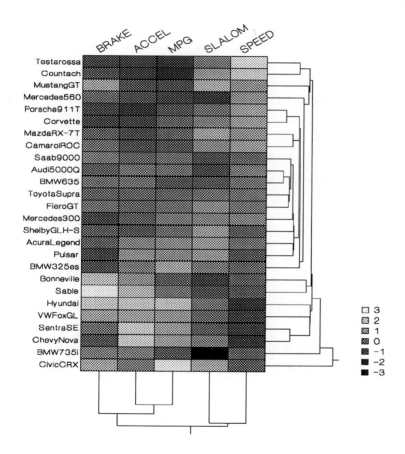

Permuted Data Matrix

Deciding on the best clustering procedure

Fisher and Van Ness (1971) wrote an important, albeit restrictive, review article in which they defined standards of "admissibility" against which clustering procedures could be assessed. For example, one criterion was convexity: a convex cluster contains cases which are a weighted average of other cases in a cluster. Another criterion was perfect clustering: if a clustering exists such that all distances within clusters are less than all distances between clusters, an admissible clustering procedure should discover it.

Many popular methods of clustering, such as k-means and Ward's method, failed Fisher and Van Ness' tests. On the other hand, these same methods did better than some of Fisher and Van Ness' "admissible" procedures in some Monte Carlo studies using hypothetical datasets (Milligan, 1980, 1981). Since many of these random datasets shared similar multivariate normal structures, it is hard to generalize about "best" methods. Nevertheless, the Monte Carlo studies and theoretical work suggest the following methods are better for the following cluster structures:

Cluster Structure	Clustering Method
globular (spherical) equal variance equal size	Ward's or Average Linkage
globular unequal variance unequal size	Complete Linkage
elongated unequal variance unequal size	Single Linkage
large (many objects) globular equal variance equal size	k-means

If you have no idea what to expect in your data, you should probably use several methods to get different views. If you try different linkage methods and get radically different clusterings, your data are unlikely to contain highly separated, compact, globular clusters. The converse is not always true, however. You cannot assume that you have highly separated clusters simply because different methods yield the same clusters.

Deciding on the number of clusters

No satisfactory general method has been developed for deciding how many clusters exist in a dataset of unknown structure. Several different approaches can be used on the same data. You can graph the data if you have only a few clustering variables or if you use a dimension reducing technique. Or, you can compute goodness-of-fit indices to models for k clusters and compare these indices across different values of k.

Graphical methods

Graphical methods can reveal clusters if you can manage to reduce dimensionality enough to see them. You can do pairwise plots of clustering variables in a SPLOM if you have only a few. For three variables, you can rotate plots in SYSTAT. For more than a few variables, you will have to reduce dimensionality in order to see clusters on joint variables. Principal components and factor analysis, because they are linear models, usually are not as useful for this purpose. Multidimensional scaling, on the other hand, tends to be more effective in reducing dimensions for viewing clusters. Figure 19.9 shows a scatterplot of the two-dimensional multidimensional scaling solution on the standardized cars dataset used to illustrate k-means clustering above. We TRANSPOSEd the dataset and then computed Euclidean distances in the CORR module. After merging the MDS configuration with the car names, we plotted the result. See Figure 21.7 for the commands to produce a similar graph.

Figure 19.9 reveals less clustering than we might imagine from the k-means output. We have outlined each cluster on the scatterplot to show how the clusters were selected using the method illustrated in Figure 21.7. Although the clusters are relatively convex (none penetrates another), they are not as compact and discrete as they could be. Instead, there appears to be a rather even distribution of points through the space.

Figure 19.9
Two-dimensional MDS solution for Cars Dataset

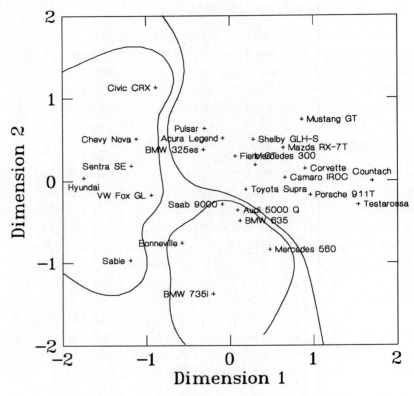

Goodness-of-fit

No goodness-of-fit index can determine the optimal number of clusters in all datasets with a high degree of power. The reason is that the notion of a cluster is diffuse. Clusters may be convex shaped (lines connecting edges of a cluster all pass through the cluster) or they may wrap around themselves. Clusters may be separable by planes, or hyperplanes, or may be nested within each other. They may be globular or long, and so forth. No goodness-of-fit measure is uniformly powerful against all of these alternatives.

You can see, for example, that the F-statistics in the k-means output above are all highly significant. We can see the cars are well separated by the clustering, but do they form *clusters* in the same sense as we would call chairs one cluster and tables another?

If we could assume that the clusters were from multivariate normal distributions, then one way to identify the number of clusters would be to compute a sum of squares within clusters for different numbers of clusters. Hartigan (1975) suggests one possible index involving a ratio of mean squares:

$$F = (SS_k/SS_{k+1} - 1)(m - k + 1)$$

where m is the number of variables, k is the number of clusters, and SS_k is the within cluster sum of squares across all clustering variables. Although this index is called F, it is not distributed as Fisher's F statistic if the variables on which the sums of squares are computed were also used to perform the clustering. This problem is similar to that of the pseudo F statistics reported in popular stepwise regression programs.

If this ratio is above 10 or so, then we should consider that $k+1$ clusters is plausible instead of k. Applying this test for two vs. three car clusters, for example, yields:

$$SS_2 = 10.329 + 14.219 + 24.387 + 16.456 + 13.497 = 78.888$$
$$SS_3 = 9.485 + 15.070 + 8.841 + 14.184 + 12.186 = 59.766$$
$$F = (78.888/59.766 - 1)(5 - 2 + 1) = 1.28$$

There appears to be little evidence for choosing three clusters over two. In fact, there appears to be little evidence favoring two clusters over one. The sum of squares within groups for one group is

$$SS_1 = 26 + 26 + 26 + 26 + 26$$

(remember, we standardized the variables over 26 cars). So,

$$F = (130/78.888 - 1)(5 - 1 + 1) = 3.24$$

Keep in mind that this method is only useful if the data are normally distributed or at least globular. You can read about further methods for computing goodness-of-fit in hierarchical clustering in Milligan and Cooper (1985). None of the computed indices did well across a variety of datasets. Aldenderfer and Blashfield (1984) review other types of indices, including a plot of within cluster joining distance against k for a hierarchical clustering. Peck, Fisher, and Van Ness (1989) present a rigorously developed criterion for special clustering problems, but it is not available in SYSTAT or other popular packages.

Deciding whether a solution is "significant"

As we mentioned earlier, the question of whether a clustering is "significant" is related to the question concerning the optimal number of clusters. Again, we may compute a goodness-of-fit index such as Hartigan's k-means F test above. If we cannot find a large value of the index for any value of k, then we should be cautious in concluding there are clusters.

Everitt (1980), Duda and Hart (1973), and others introduce and review the various tests of significance for clustering. The problem with all these tests is that the null hypothesis is ill defined, a problem shared with the parallel literature in multidimensional scaling. What is a random clustering?

Although we cannot construct a universally acceptable test statistic, we can get some idea of what clusters on random data look like. First of all, let's make some random data corresponding to the grounds for divorce dataset. We can use SYSTAT BASIC to create a uniform distribution of 1's and 0's on 12 variables and 50 cases.

```
BASIC
SAVE RANDOM
RSEED=13579
REPEAT 50
LET DRUGS=INT(2*URN)
LET BIGAMY=INT(2*URN)
        etc.
```

Now let's cluster these random data:

```
CLUSTER
USE RANDOM
JOIN / COLUMNS,LINKAGE = SINGLE
JOIN / COLUMNS,LINKAGE = COMPLETE
```

Figure 19.10 shows the results of these two cluster analyses. Although the single linkage tree doesn't appear to show clear clusters, the complete linkage tree seems to reveal two clusters. The only thing we have to protect ourselves in this instance is some knowledge of the data. In the real dataset, we can see that the complete linkage clusters correspond roughly to criminal and personal/contractual grounds. As with other multivariate statistical methods, there is no substitute for knowing what to expect in the data. Variable names can seduce you if you roam post-hoc through an analysis.

The main indicator of uniform randomness in this clustering is the length of the branches. Notice that there are no tightly bound clusters in either tree. When you examine any tree, look for binding at the ends of the branches, not near the root.

Figure 19.10
Single and Complete Linkage Cluster Analyses
of Uniform Random Data using Divorce Variable Names

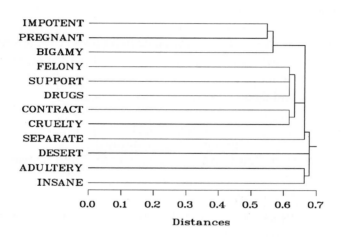

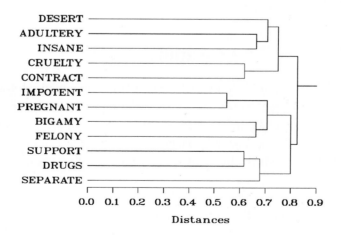

To assess *k*-means clustering, we constructed a random dataset corresponding to the cars dataset. Using the FACTOR and DATA modules, we generated normally distributed random variables with the same total covariance matrix as in the real CARS data. This procedure is described in the SYSTAT manual. Figure 19.11 shows the global test for clusters on each variable. Notice every one is significant. If we did a multidimensional scaling of these data, we would find that KMEANS has carved out three sections of a single watermelon flying through space.

It is not difficult to feed CLUSTER random data in SYSTAT. We strongly advise you to do so in order to chasten yourself whenever you get the temptation to wax poetic about the meaning of your clusters. Remember this: try several different cluster methods, try random data, and then replicate, replicate, replicate.

Figure 19.11
***K*-means Cluster Analysis**
of Normal Random Data Using Car Variable Names

```
SUMMARY STATISTICS FOR    3 CLUSTERS

   VARIABLE      BETWEEN SS  DF   WITHIN SS  DF      F-RATIO        PROB

     ACCEL          17.743    2      7.257   23       28.118       0.000
     BRAKE           7.789    2     17.211   23        5.204       0.014
    SLALOM          19.062    2      5.938   23       36.920       0.000
       MPG          11.227    2     13.773   23        9.375       0.001
     SPEED          13.604    2     11.396   23       13.729       0.000
```

19.5 Additive trees

Additive trees (Sattath and Tversky, 1977) is a clustering method which resembles joining trees but is different in the way joins are computed. Although this procedure has been available in special purpose software since the late 1970's, additive trees clustering has not appeared in any widely used statistical package before SYSTAT. This is unfortunate because additive trees clustering often produces better fits to data than other joining methods.

An additive tree is a directed graph whose path lengths represent distance between objects. Ordinary cluster trees represent distances between objects as the distance between their parent nodes. All objects within a given cluster are thus taken to be the same distance to some other object not in that cluster. For additive trees, on the other hand, the distance between any two objects is found by tracing the shortest path between them on the tree. In Figure 19.12, for example, the distance between HEAD-ACHE and CHEST is shorter than that between FEVER and CHEST.

The computation of the tree goes beyond the scope of this book. In very rough terms, it is a cross between joining and multidimensional scaling (MDS). Branches are joined iteratively by examining tetrads of objects (groups of four) over the entire similarity matrix. After the joins are completed, branch lengths are computed by least squares estimation. Each branch is expanded or contracted so that the sum of the squared discrepancies between the length of the branches and the scaled distances in the original data matrix is as small as possible. In common with MDS, additive trees require a symmetric matrix of similarity/dissimilarity data.   We have used the SYMPTOMS data from the Section 21.1 to illustrate additive trees. Figure 19.12 shows the resulting tree.

Notice that there is no distance scale on the tree. That is because distances are calculated by tracing along branches instead of by measuring against a common scale. For similar reasons, the tree is ragged edged. Tightly clustered objects are recognized as clusters by their having short branches.

If your data are directly measured similarities or dissimilarities between objects, you should consider using additive trees instead of the conventional hierarchical joining methods. The method is especially useful if you intend to use MDS as a spatial representation. Additive trees can represent your data without the metric assumptions required by MDS. You can read more about these assumptions in the MDS chapter.

Figure 19.12
Additive Tree for Symptoms Data

CLUSTER
USE SYMPTOMS
ADD FEVER..SNEEZE

Additive Tree

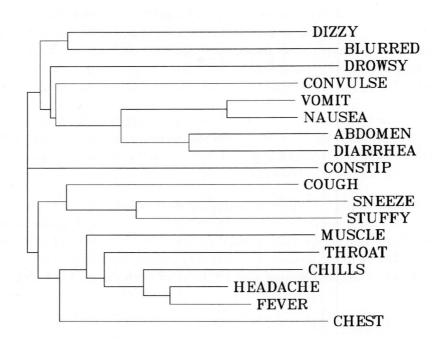

19.6 Conclusion

As we have seen, there are three major types of cluster analysis available in SYSTAT: hierarchical, nonhierarchical, and additive trees. For all three, there are several steps you must consider.

First, you need to consider whether to cluster cases or variables. This is a substantive question, but remember that similarities/dissimilarities can be computed for either cases or variables. There is nothing in the algorithms to prevent you from doing one or the other. You can read more about this in Chapter 23.

Second, you must decide what distance (similarity) method to apply unless the data are similarities or dissimilarities already. Chapter 23 discusses these issues further.

Third, you need to choose a cluster method. Choose hierarchical methods if you: 1) have no idea how many clusters to expect and 2) are interested in a tree structure relating the objects. The non-hierarchical *k*-means clustering is useful in contexts where you might consider an ANOVA or discriminant analysis but you do not know the grouping variable. Finally, consider additive trees if your data are similarities (or dissimilarities) and you would plan to use multidimensional scaling otherwise.

Notes

The cluster literature is enormous and scattered across diverse fields. Several texts are useful guide-books, however. Jardine and Sibson (1971) and Anderberg (1973) are somewhat dated introductions. Hartigan (1975) is a readable statistical discussion of a wide variety of cluster models. Everitt (1980) and Aldenderfer and Blashfield (1984) are more recent introductions. Kaufman and Rousseeuw (1990) present interesting recent methods for displaying cluster results. Gordon (1987) reviews a variety of hierarchical methods.

References

Aldenderfer, M.S. and Blashfield, R.K. (1984). *Cluster Analysis*. Beverly Hills, CA: Sage Publications.

Anderberg (1973). *Cluster Analysis for Applications*. New York: Academic Press.

Duda, R.O. and Hart, P.E. (1973). *Pattern Classification and Scene Analysis*. New York: John Wiley & Sons.

Everitt, B.S. (1980). *Cluster Analysis*, (2nd ed.). London: Heineman Educational Books Ltd.

Fisher, L., and Van Ness, J.W. (1971). Admissible clustering procedures. *Biometrika, 58*, 91-104.

Gordon, A.D. (1987). A review of hierarchical classification. *Journal of the Royal Statistical Society, Series A, 150*, 119-137.

Hartigan, J.A. (1975). *Clustering Algorithms*. New York: John Wiley & Sons.

Jardine, N., and Sibson, R. (1971). *Mathematical Taxonomy*. New York: John Wiley & Sons, Inc.

Kaufman, L., and Rousseeuw, P.J. (1990). *Finding Groups in Data: An Introduction to Cluster Analysis*. New York: John Wiley & Sons, Inc.

Long, L.H. (Ed.) *The World Almanac*. New York: Doubleday, 1971.

Milligan, G.W. (1980). An examination of the effect of six types of error perturbation on fifteen clustering algorithms. *Psychometrika, 45*, 325-342.

Milligan, G.W. (1981). A review of Monte Carlo tests of cluster analysis. *Multivariate Behavioral Research, 16*, 379-407.

Milligan, G.W. and Cooper, M.C. (1985). An examination of procedures for determining the number of clusters in a data set. *Psychometrika, 50*, 159-179.

Peck, R., Fisher, L., and Van Ness, J. (1989). Approximate confidence intervals for the number of clusters. *Journal of the American Statistical Association, 84*, 184-191.

Sattath, S., and Tversky, A. (1977). Additive similarity trees. *Psychometrika, 42*, 319-345.

Tryon, R.C. and Bailey, D.E. (1970). *Cluster Analysis*. New York: McGraw-Hill.

20

Principal Components and Factor Analysis

Are there types of crimes? We frequently hear about personal and property crimes, but do crimes occur in these patterns? Figure 20.1 shows FBI reported crimes for the U.S. in one year per 100,000 population (U.S. Statistical Abstract, 1980). The data are listed in the source as representing two basic types of crime in the U.S.: violent crime (MURDER, RAPE, ROBBERY, and ASSAULT) and crimes against property (BURGLARY, LARCENY, and AUTOTHFT).

There are many ways to summarize these data. We can note that the murder rate is high in Nevada, that New Yorkers experience a lot of robbery, or that people in Massachusetts spend more than their fair share of time replacing their cars. On the other hand there are similarities in the information contained in different variables. The three states high in MURDER, ROBBERY, or AUTOTHFT also tend to be high on each of these three crimes. It seems possible that something in common to all 7 kinds of crimes, perhaps a single crime index, may distinguish among states. Alternatively, the two general headings under which the data were reported—violent crimes and crimes against property—may summarize the differences among states.

Principal components and factor analysis produce summary variables. We will discuss the differences between the two procedures later in this chapter. For now, you can assume that principal components are exact combinations of the observed variables, while factors are combinations of hypothetical variables which cannot be observed directly. If this confuses you, take comfort in knowing that most computer users of these two procedures don't know the difference either.

Figure 20.1
CRIME80 Data

STATE$	MURDER	RAPE	ROBBERY	ASSAULT	BURGLARY	LARCENY	AUTOTHFT	REGION
ME	2.8	12.9	30.8	147	1183	2772	219	1
NH	2.5	17.3	42.0	118	1313	2877	310	1
VT	2.2	29.1	38.9	109	1527	2988	295	1
MA	4.1	27.3	235.5	334	1740	2686	1052	1
RI	4.4	17.1	118.6	268	1716	2964	844	1
CT	4.7	21.6	218.0	168	1701	3090	679	1
NY	12.7	30.9	641.3	345	2062	3060	760	2
NJ	6.9	30.7	303.7	263	1878	3189	730	2
PA	6.8	23.0	177.9	156	1039	1916	418	2
OH	8.1	34.3	223.7	232	1466	3040	427	3
IN	8.9	33.1	141.4	194	1313	2807	432	3
IL	10.6	26.9	217.0	240	1243	3039	499	3
MI	10.2	46.6	244.0	339	1741	3710	585	3
WI	2.9	17.9	70.7	94	1079	3291	245	3
MN	2.6	23.2	99.1	103	1246	3030	296	4
IA	2.2	14.3	54.9	129	1080	3219	248	4
MO	11.1	32.6	223.6	287	1669	2795	415	4
ND	1.2	9.5	7.7	36	486	2242	179	4
SD	0.7	12.5	20.1	94	693	2255	169	4
NB	4.4	23.2	82.2	115	915	2922	244	4
KS	6.9	31.5	113.1	238	1521	3196	272	4
DE	6.9	24.2	137.0	307	1631	4216	455	5
MD	9.5	40.1	392.7	410	1698	3629	451	5
VA	8.6	27.4	120.1	151	1203	2882	228	5
WV	7.1	15.8	48.5	112	738	1430	200	5
NC	10.6	22.7	82.3	339	1423	2546	216	5
SC	11.4	37.5	118.1	493	1670	2803	306	5
GA	13.8	44.3	197.6	300	1699	2977	372	5
FL	14.5	56.9	355.5	557	2507	4434	477	5
KY	8.8	19.2	95.2	143	1041	1876	251	6
TN	10.8	37.4	180.6	229	1501	2175	363	6
AL	13.2	30.0	132.1	273	1527	2642	316	6
MS	14.5	24.6	81.0	222	1179	1718	178	6
AR	9.2	26.7	80.9	218	1119	2170	187	6
LA	15.7	44.5	197.0	408	1524	2888	376	6
OK	10.0	36.3	104.9	268	1693	2521	420	6
TX	16.9	47.3	208.5	278	1853	3181	558	6
MT	4.0	21.0	34.0	164	951	3530	322	7
ID	3.1	22.4	46.8	241	1239	2993	237	7
WY	6.2	28.6	44.4	313	904	3345	345	7
CO	6.9	52.5	160.1	309	2031	4326	448	7
NM	13.1	43.3	127.9	431	1493	3521	351	7
AZ	10.3	45.2	193.6	402	2155	4891	473	7
UT	3.8	27.7	80.2	192	1322	3922	324	7
NV	20.0	67.2	460.6	366	2907	4346	678	7
WA	5.1	52.7	135.1	271	1862	4193	396	8
OR	5.1	41.5	152.4	291	1748	4088	360	8
CA	14.5	58.2	384.2	437	2317	3880	743	8
AK	9.7	62.5	90.0	317	1386	3728	617	8
HI	8.7	34.7	190.2	66	1847	4723	612	8

20.1 Principal components

Definitions using only two crimes

Before we compute the principal components of our crimes, let's try to understand what these statistical things are. We'll compute the principal components of just two variables: BURGLARY and ASSAULT. Figure 20.2 shows how to do this. We are computing principal components on the covariance matrix just as we do in regression. The diagonal elements of this matrix are the variances of ASSAULT (13606.923) and BURGLARY (213397.800). The off-diagonal element is the covariance between BURGLARY and ASSAULT (36921.411).

Figure 20.3 is a graphical representation of the analysis we performed. Let's use it to interpret the numbers in Figure 20.2. First of all, we have drawn several lines on the scatterplot. If you use REGRESS on these data, you can confirm that the two regression lines

$$BURGLARY=816.3+2.713*ASSAULT \; and$$
$$ASSAULT=-8.421+.173*BURGLARY$$

are different. Because the former line regresses toward the mean of BURGLARY and the latter toward the mean of ASSAULT, they form a sideways "X" on the scatterplot. The first principal component (F_1) is half-way between the two regression lines. The second (F_2) is perpendicular to the first. We have shown the equations for these two components in the figure. The coefficients for these equations are taken from the FACTOR SCORE COEFFICIENTS in Figure 20.2. Like the regression lines, the components are linear combinations of the variables. Unlike the regression lines, however, they are combinations of *both* variables. And unlike regression lines, they don't regress toward anything. Instead, F_1 passes through the widest scatter and F_2 passes through what's left. These components summarize the data as well as the original variables.

Why bother to make a new set of variables (components) which look like a simple rotation of the original ones? The reason we go to this trouble is that F_1 now describes most of the variance in the data. The amount of variance it describes is shown in the first **eigenvalue**, or **latent root** (220002.5453). The amount of variance the second component describes is shown in the second eigenvalue (7002.1772). Notice that the sum of these two numbers is the same as the sum of the variances of the original variables (13606.9229+213397.7996). Thus, F_1 has larger variance than either BURGLARY or ASSAULT alone. It summarizes the variation in the data better than either crime variable. As the output shows, nearly 97 percent of the total variance in the two variables is accounted for by the first component. The scatterplot shows this graphically. F_1 passes through the longest axis of the data. Only about 3 percent of the variance is left to describe by F_2.

Figure 20.2
Principal Components of BURGLARY and ASSAULT

```
FACTOR
USE CRIME80
MODEL BURGLARY,ASSAULT
ESTIMATE / COVA
```

```
Latent Roots (Eigenvalues)
                            1            2
                     220002.545    7002.177

Component loadings
                            1            2

     BURGLARY          461.715      -14.735
     ASSAULT            82.595       82.371

Variance Explained by Components
                            1            2

                     220002.545    7002.177

Percent of Total Variance Explained
                            1            2

                        96.915        3.085

Coefficients for Standardized Factor Scores
                            1            2

     BURGLARY            0.002       -0.002
     ASSAULT             0.000        0.012

Standardized scores have been saved.
```

Figure 20.3
Plot of Principal Components of BURGLARY and ASSAULT

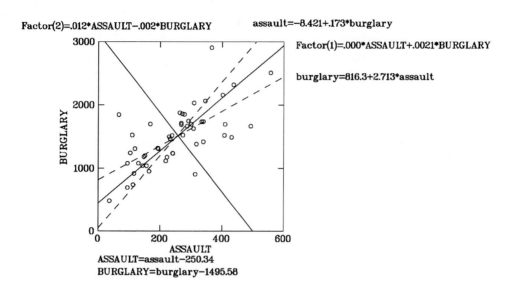

Our new component variables have no name. We could name F_1 "ASSAULT+BUR-GLARY" and F_2 "ASSAULT-BURGLARY", but this would be something of a misnomer. Any names will misrepresent, but we generally end up naming components or factors after the variables containing them. You can see now that component analysis is circular. We have gained insight, presumably, by summarizing things, but the summaries depend on the definitions of the things we started with. Some users confuse the naming with the concepts and believe that components are "real things" that take on a life of their own. We always have to remember that they are simply linear combinations of the original variables.

The last feature of the output we must note are the LOADINGS. These are the covariances of the original variables with the components. The covariance between F_1 and ASSAULT, for example, is 82.5946. If you USE the SCORES.SYS file containing the component scores, for example, you can merge these scores with the original data and compute this covariance in the CORR module. Incidentally, if you graph the scores in SCORES.SYS, the scatterplot will look just like observing Figure 20.3 after tilting your head about 40 degrees to the left. After all, the components are simply a rotation of the original axes about 40 degrees.

Graphical analysis

Grabbing a bunch of data and immediately factoring is the way most of the users who do components and factor analysis proceed. Let's try to restrain our impulses and look at the distribution of these variables before we factor them. Figure 20.4 shows a scatterplot matrix of the variables we want to factor. We used the SPLOM command to draw this scatterplot matrix. Each respective square shows the scatterplot between the row and column variable. The lower left plot, for example, shows the scatter of AU-TOTHEFT on the vertical axis against MURDER on the horizontal.

Notice that the histograms are generally skewed positive. Furthermore, each cell tends to look like a funnel or megaphone. The variables appear **heteroscedastic** (different variances at different scale values). This is because the data are counts of crimes per 100,000 people. Standardized counts are usually positively skewed and often can be normalized by a square root transformation (see Section 22.2). We will do this transformation with the LET ()=SQR(@) aggregate function. We could also use the Quick Plot tools to transform the SPLOM on the fly by setting XPOWER to .5.

Figure 20.5 shows the scatterplot matrix of these transformed data. Notice that the point clouds look more elliptic and the histograms are more normally distributed. Some variables, such as ROBBERY, have been dramatically changed.

Why do we worry about things looking normal? Some analysts will tell you that principal components analysis does not require normality in the variables. Don't believe them. Principal components analysis is a linear procedure like least squares regression. It is susceptible to outliers and non-normal distributions in the same way. Even if you are not interested in significance testing, we recommend that you inspect the SPLOM of your variables for normality. You will get different components, even different *numbers* of components, for non-normal data.

Deciding how many components to request

The common first question is "How many underlying components are needed?" Two rules of thumb are often used in evaluating components when we use a correlation matrix as input: (1) an eigenvalue greater than 1 is taken as evidence that a component accounts for an appreciable portion of the variance in the data (because the variance of standardized variables is 1 and we want to explain at least as much variance as any original variable); (2) the presence of at least three variables with component loadings greater than + or - .3 supports the notion that a component has some interpretable generality. These are both rules of thumb, however. Neither has a basis in statistical theory, but they are practical and popular.

Figure 20.4
Scatterplot Matrix of CRIME Data

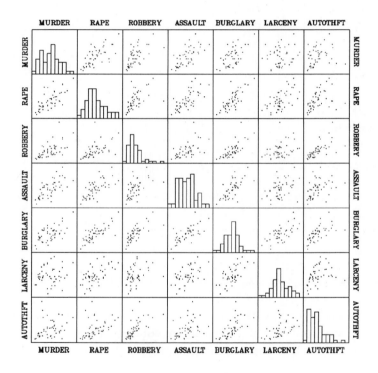

The eigenvalue-greater-than-one rule does provide some sense of external reference—it is equivalent to the amount of variance each original variable might carry if all variables in the analysis were equal and separate carriers of information on a common scale, but using it rigidly is unwise. What if the second component carried an eigenvalue of 1.001 and the third .999? Would we really want to distinguish between the relative merits of two such similar values? At the very least we will need to look at the eigenvalues for the entire sequence of components to see if we can spot a place where there is a relatively large interval between values that may help mark the transition.

Figure 20.5
Scatterplot Matrix of Square-Rooted CRIME Data

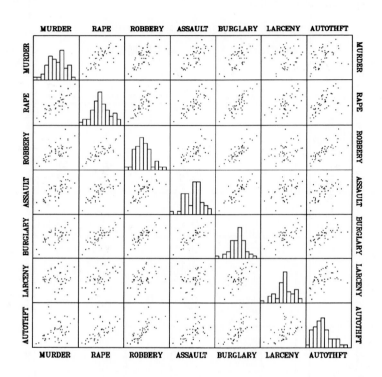

One common visual aid to this inspection is the construction of a "scree" plot; we simply plot eigenvalues (roots) against their index numbers. SYSTAT provides this plot automatically when you compute components. Figure 20.6 shows a scree plot for the transformed CRIME data. We are looking for an "elbow," a point at which the plot changes from a steep to a flat slope, which shows only marginally more explained variance for each additional component retained. This elbow appears in this figure at index 2, suggesting that we have only 1 meaningful dimension in our data. There is a suggestion of a break at 4, however, which could indicate 3 dimensions. We will compromise and retain two components for further analysis. Scree plots do not usually show clean breaks, and the judgment about effective dimensionality is difficult.

Figure 20.6
Scree Plot of Eigenvalues for Square Rooted CRIME Data

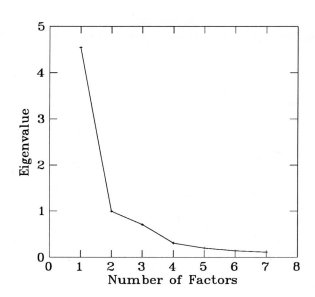

Principal components on the crime variables

Now let's look at the principal components of the crime variables. When more than two variables are involved, the first component passes through the axis with the most variance (like the long axis of a cucumber, for example), the second component passes through the next most major axis perpendicular to the first, and so on. In this way, we hope to summarize the variance on all the crime variables using just a few components. We hope that the last few components, as in the ASSAULT-BURGLARY example, will contain a negligible portion of the variance.

We are going to factor the correlation instead of the covariance matrix. Doing this is equivalent to standardizing all the variables before computing covariances. By standardizing, we are equating the influence of variables on different scales and letting the covariation alone determine the major axes. Using the correlation matrix makes sense when our variables are on different scales and we wish to adjust for these differences.

We do this in regression when we examine standardized regression coefficients. Furthermore, when we input correlations instead of covariances, the LOADINGS are the correlations between the original variables and the components (because covariances between standardized variables are correlations). This makes the components easier to interpret on a common metric. Figure 20.7 shows our analysis.

Figure 20.7
Principal Components Analysis on Square-Rooted CRIME Data

```
FACTOR
USE CRIME80
LET (MURDER..AUTOTHFT)=SQR(@)
MODEL MURDER..AUTOTHFT
ESTIMATE / NUMBER=2
```

Latent Roots (Eigenvalues)					
	1	2	3	4	5
	4.541	0.994	0.702	0.306	0.200
	6	7			
	0.142	0.115			

Component loadings		
	1	2
MURDER	0.744	0.602
RAPE	0.880	0.066
ROBBERY	0.868	0.069
ASSAULT	0.824	0.258
BURGLARY	0.928	-0.148
LARCENY	0.617	-0.657
AUTOTHFT	0.734	-0.322

Variance Explained by Components		
	1	2
	4.541	0.994

Percent of Total Variance Explained		
	1	2
	64.873	14.205

Interpreting factor plots

Once components have been computed, the task is to understand the relations among variables contributing to components. SYSTAT generated a factor loadings plot automatically so that you can see the loadings displayed in a graph.

Figure 20.8
Plot of First Two Components of Transformed Crime Data

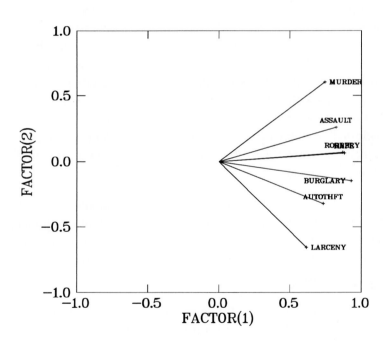

Factor Loadings Plot

The factor loadings plot treats the component loading matrix as data with components as "variables" and variables as "cases." You should not confuse this plot with the SCORE plot in Figure 20.11. The program produces a scatterplot for each of all possible pairs of components. Notice that RAPE and ROBBERY overlap, because their loadings are nearly identical.

One key feature of the plot is the distance a variable lies out, in any direction, away from the origin. The greater this distance, the greater the proportion of the variable's variance that is captured by the plotted components. A second feature is the proximity of a variable to one or another axis of the plot. The closer to an axis, the more a variable's explained variance overlaps with the component represented by the axis

Rotating components

The first component of our transformed crime data appears to be a global index of crime, while the second is ambiguous. At times this emphasis on a strong first factor will be what you want from your analysis. For our analysis, where we are interested in distinguishing between violent crimes and crimes against property, this does not seem desirable. Since all of the variables load more strongly on the first component than the second, neither component can help us make this distinction. The first contains too much of everything to have any narrower meaning, the second contains too little of anything to have much force. We would prefer to have two components that are each more clearly identified with subsets of our original variables and that together show a more equitable sharing of explained variance. The issue may also arise in the other direction: the original solution may portray clusters of variables comprising separate components when you want a view that focuses on some central source of variance in just one or a few components.

The desire for these kinds of variations on a principal components is often termed a search for a **simple structure**. For these occasions, principal components solutions can be rotated to aid this search. As we saw in Figure 20.11, principal components involve a rotation in the space of the data in the first place. Now we want to rotate further in the plane (space) represented by the components.

Changing the orientation of the axes can be useful. For example we could arrange it so that the MURDER variable falls on the positive end of FACTOR(2). Murder will now have the highest loading on the second component, and this component will now have a meaning closer to that contained in the variance associated with this variable. The only potential problem is that this, or any other particular twist, has implications for the loadings of all other variables on both of our components. In our mental exercise for instance, LARCENY would now lie close to the positive pole of FACTOR(1) giving this component a meaning closely associated with this variable's meaning. Rotation procedures attempt to work on the entire pattern of loadings. While in a mathematical sense the placing of axes is arbitrary, the alternatives can make interpretation of the relations among components and original variables easier.

Principal components procedures deal with the variance of individual cases on variables. Rotation procedures, however, treat the component loadings matrix as "data" and work on the variability of the loadings. For instance, loadings on our first component range from .929 for BURGLARY to .617 for LARCENY and have a mean, standard deviation and all the other qualities of variables. Changing the orientation of the axes so that the first axis passes through LARCENY would increase LARCENY's loading and simultaneously pull the axis farther away from its old association with ROBBERY and so decrease ROBBERY's loading. The joint result would be a first component that has a larger range of variability and one that is more clearly distinguished in terms of these two variables. Considered across all of the loadings in the FACTOR(1) column, maximizing variability will tend to distinguish variables in this way.

SYSTAT offers five rotation options:

- **Varimax.** Works to maximize the variance of loadings down through columns of the component loadings matrix. In most applications it tends to distribute the primary loadings of different variables across more different components, resulting in a more equal distribution of the total explained variance across the set of components. Identification of components with particular subsets of original variables tends to be clarified, but interpretation of components with respect to one another tends to be obscured.

- **Quartamax.** Works to maximize the variance of loadings across rows of the component loading matrix. In most applications it tends to concentrate loadings on a strong first or "general" factor. Interpretation of components with respect to one another tends to be clarified, but identification of components with particular subsets of variables tends to be obscured.

- **Equamax**. A compromise that works to maximize simultaneously the variance of loadings across rows and down through columns of the component loadings matrix. In most applications it tends to create a view that lies somewhere the Varimax and Quartamax rotations.

- **Orthomax.** The orthomax method is a compromise, represented on a continuum by a gamma parameter, between Quartamax (when gamma = 0) and Varimax (when gamma = 1).

- **Oblimin.** This is an oblique rotation method. After rotation, the axes are no longer orthogonal (at right angles to each other) and the interpretations of the axes become interrelated.

Our original solution already tended to show all variables loading on a strong first factor. Moreover, with only two components of interest, there are few grounds for "maximizing variability across rows" of the component loading matrix. A Quartamax rotation would be redundant with our original view of loadings. To display a contrasting view, Figure 20.9 shows the application of a VARIMAX rotation to the CRIME80T dataset along with the COMPONENT LOADINGS and FACTOR PLOT of the new view. We have omitted the parts of the output which duplicate Figure 20.8.

We have added one other command to our input. The SORT option causes SYSTAT to sort the loadings from largest to smallest so that variables with similar loadings will appear together.

As you see in the figure, the configuration of variables is the same as in our prior solution. Only the orientation of this structure to the plot axes has shifted—about 45 degrees counterclockwise and transposed. From the plot and the loadings from which it derives, we also see the two common results of the Varimax rotation. First, a few variables, BURGLARY LARCENY and AUTOTHFT, are now closer to and so load more highly on the second component than the first component. The solution is "simplified" in the sense that the second component may now be understood as close in meaning to crimes of property as captured by these variables in their original form. Second, the total explained variance is now more equally distributed across the components.

On data with more variables and more potentially interesting components, the effects of different rotations will be more varied. It is entirely acceptable to try all three out and select the one that offers the kind of simplification that best suits your needs. Remember, however, that the "correctness" of the selection you make stems not from any mathematical features of the analysis, but from your judgment based on your knowledge about the phenomenon you are measuring. And remember that the whole process is circular. The factors or components you find are not "real things" out there waiting to be discovered. They are associations among variables for which you are providing names.

Figure 20.9
Varimax Rotation of First Two Components

```
FACTOR
USE CRIME80
MODEL MURDER..AUTOTHFT
ESTIMATE / SORT  NUMBER=2   ROTATE=VARIMAX
```

Latent Roots (Eigenvalues)

	1	2	3	4	5
	4.541	0.994	0.702	0.306	0.200
	6	7			
	0.142	0.115			

Component loadings

	1	2
BURGLARY	0.928	-0.148
RAPE	0.880	0.066
ROBBERY	0.868	0.069
ASSAULT	0.824	0.258
MURDER	0.744	0.602
AUTOTHFT	0.734	-0.322
LARCENY	0.617	-0.657

Variance Explained by Components

	1	2
	4.541	0.994

Percent of Total Variance Explained

	1	2
	64.873	14.205

Rotated Loading Matrix (VARIMAX, Gamma =   1.0000)

	1	2
MURDER	0.957	0.012
ASSAULT	0.798	0.328
RAPE	0.719	0.512
ROBBERY	0.712	0.501
BURGLARY	0.619	0.707
LARCENY	0.055	0.899
AUTOTHFT	0.359	0.717

"Variance" Explained by Rotated Components

	1	2
	3.093	2.443

Percent of Total Variance Explained

	1	2
	44.181	34.897

Factor Loadings Plot

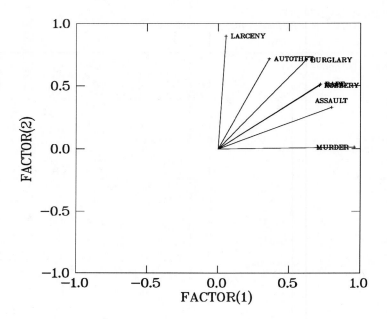

Component scores

A component expresses a linear combination of original variables. Component scores are the values attributed to individual cases on this new variable. For example, the first component (the index of violent crime) might be entered into a regression to predict severity of legislative penalties, the conviction rate and the severity of sentencing in courts, the average length of time served in prison, etc. Now that we have obtained a set of components we like, we can get the scores that derive from them by doing the principal components analysis one last time as you see in Figure 20.10. We have omitted parts of the output which duplicate earlier figures.

Figure 20.10
Computing Component Scores

```
SAVE  SCORES  /  SCORES,DATA
ESTIMATE  /  NUMBER=2   ROTATE=VARIMAX   SORT
```

```
Coefficients for Standardized Factor Scores

                      1            2

     MURDER         0.513       -0.361
     ASSAULT        0.305       -0.084
     RAPE           0.191        0.073
     ROBBERY        0.192        0.068
     BURGLARY       0.062        0.245
     LARCENY       -0.318        0.595
     AUTOTHFT      -0.082        0.352

Standardized scores have been saved.
```

The FACTOR SCORE COEFFICIENTS are used to compute the scores on the components. If we were working with unrotated components, the FACTOR SCORE CO-EFFICIENTS would have a simple interpretation, they would be the COMPONENT LOADINGS divided by their respective EIGENVALUES. With rotated components, the computation is less direct and beyond the scope of this chapter. In either case, the result is a weight that reflects a variable's contribution to a component. These weights can be applied to the values in the original data to obtain the FACTOR SCORES for each case. SYSTAT does this automatically and saves the data into the file you specified in the SAVE statement.

Figure 20.11 shows how to plot the computed scores. We have given our factors names that reflect our interpretation—VIOLENT for FACTOR(1) and PROPERTY for FACTOR(2). Finally, we reversed the components' signs. This last step stems from the analysis shown for the original CRIME data in the FACTOR chapter of the SYSTAT manual (pre Version 4). There as here it highlights the correspondence between crime and the geographical map of the United States.

Figure 20.11
Plotting Component Scores

```
USE SCORES
LET VIOLENT = -FACTOR(1)
LET PROPERTY = -FACTOR(2)
PLOT VIOLENT * PROPERTY / LABEL=STATE$
```

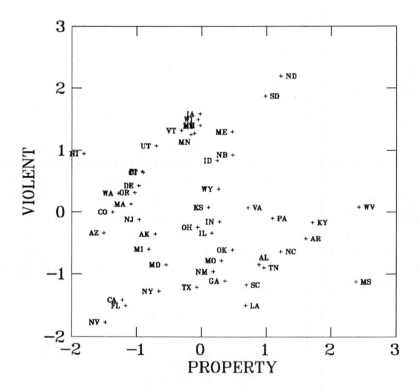

The spatial pattern still appears with southern states high in violent crimes and western states high in property crime. Compared to the 1970 results in the SYSTAT manual (pre Version 4), however, the separation of these types is less clear for areas of the country which tended to have the most 1980 crime. For instance, some states with high 1970 rates of property crime have also become those with relatively high 1980 rates of violent crime as well—e.g., California, Nevada, and even Hawaii have moved substantially towards the "bad" lower left quadrant; Florida and New York have shifted to more extreme positions in this section of the plot. The effects of urbanization and increased migration, mentioned as a possibility in the interpretation of the 1970 results, seem even more plausible. At the opposite extreme—towards the upper right, we see two thin shoots of cases representing the rural north with low violent crime and the rural south with low property crime.

Figure 20.12 shows how these scores fit on the map. We have merged the US file that comes with SYSTAT and the scores. We standardized LABLAT and LABLON in the US file so that the locations of the center of each state cover roughly the same range as our factor scores.   Then we used the VECTOR option of PLOT (VECTOR=LABLON,LABLAT) to locate the vectors on the center of each state. Now we can see how much the factor solution based on correlations among state crime patterns deviates from a geographical model. Notice that most of the badness of fit is on the PROPERTY crime dimension, since the vectors are mostly horizontal. No amount of rescaling of the latitudes or longitudes changes this overall pattern. We could use a similar graphical method to record the changes between 1970 and 1980.

Figure 20.12
Component Scores Plotted against State Locations

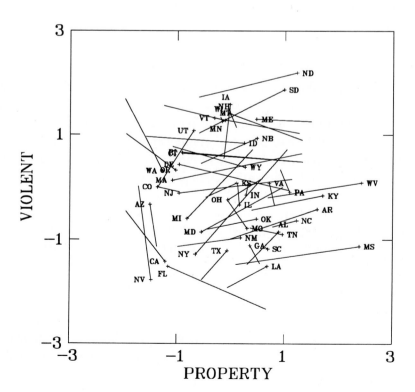

Unit weight scores

Components computed with score coefficients are optimal in the sample. That is, they have the greatest variance of all possible orthogonal components. In new samples, components computed from the weights taken from a different sample do not have this property. If you are using a principal components analysis to construct a scale for use on future samples, you should consider using unit weights for scoring the components. To do this, simply weight a variable 1 if its loading is greater than, say, .5, -1 if it is less than -.5, and 0 otherwise. Components computed this way will, under most conditions, account for more of the total variance in the new sample than traditionally scored components.

Principal components vs. MDS

Chapter 21 has an example of an analysis of the same data by both principal components and MDS. The results diverge, even though both are spatial models of the same variation. The end of Chapter 23 contains additional examples of how principal components (and factor analysis) and MDS can differ.

20.2 Factor analysis

In the SYSTAT manual, Wilkinson (1990) argues that factor analysis results rarely differ from principal components. This does not mean, however, that the two models are identical or even substitutes for one another in every situation. In fact, factor analysis can be considered the *reverse* of principal components in one respect. Namely, in the principal components model, unobserved variables (components) are functions of observed variables, while in the factor model, observed variables are functions of unobserved variables (factors).

Factor analysis has been favored by many psychologists, we think, because of two advantages. First, the factor model is consistent with **classical test theory** in psychology and education. Classical test theory is based on the idea that measured test scores are a function of true abilities plus random error. Thus, a factor can be regarded in a psychological context as the representation of a "true" general level of intelligence or some other ability. From this point of view, it is not surprising that factor analysis emerged from the intelligence testing movement in psychology. Second, factor analyses generally can summarize variables in fewer dimensions than can principal components.

The factor model

If factors are linear combinations of *unobserved* variables, what are these variables? They are theoretical, or latent variables estimated by the factor analyst, who assumes that they have normal distributions and common variances (**communalities**). The part not estimated is specific variance (**specificities**), which acts like random error in a regression model.

Imagine a regression equation in which the predictor variables (**factors**) are not directly observed. These predictor variables are to be combined in an additive equation with regression weights (**patterns**) for each factor. The simplest example is the single factor model Spearman devised almost a century ago. Spearman assumed that he could account for the correlations among a group of mental ability tests by the use of a single factor. He overlooked the possibility that other data structures could account for the correlations as well; high intercorrelations do not necessarily imply a single underlying factor. Each test was assumed to be an approximate measure of a single general intelligence factor called *g*. The remaining variation in each test was assumed to be due to random error. Spearman's factor (regression) equation for each test therefore had a single predictor variable (*g*) and its associated coefficient. In Spearman's model, the partial correlations among the observed tests (partialling out the effect of *g*) were assumed to be zero.

More recent factor models due to Thurstone and others contain more than one explanatory factor. Multiple factor models thus contain more than one predictor variable in each regression equation. The fundamental factor relation holds in these models as well: the partial correlations among the observed variables, with the factors partialled, are zero in the population.

Estimation of the factor model

The factor model's attractive theoretical properties are not matched by a simple, closed form for computing estimates as in the regression case. The problem is that measures on the theoretical factors are not available to the researcher. They must be inferred from the observed patterns in the data and there is no unique set of scores on these factors which fit the model.

Two approaches to the estimation problem are now popular. Both are iterative, terminating when changes in estimated values are negligible. And both are susceptible to incorrect or degenerate solutions under certain circumstances. The first, least squares, uses a decomposition similar to the one for principal components. The second method, maximum likelihood, is based on maximum likelihood theory.

The least squares method amounts to a factoring of a modified correlation (or covariance) matrix. The diagonal elements (variances in a covariance matrix or 1's in a correlation matrix) are replaced by "shrunk" values. Typical shrunk values for a correlation matrix are the largest absolute correlations in the corresponding row/column or the squared multiple correlation of each variable with the others. For a covariance matrix, the values can be scaled to correlations before factoring and rescaled after. Since the factor model specifies that observed variances are due to communalities plus specificities, shrunk values are intended to approximate the communalities. After repeated factorings, the diagonal elements of the factored matrix tend to converge on the communalities themselves.

We recommend the maximum likelihood method because it converges more surely and is usually faster. It also provides maximum likelihood estimates which allow testing of hypotheses. Figure 20.13 shows a factor analysis of our crime data using SYSTAT. Notice that the results are similar to our components analysis.

Wilkinson asserted in the original SYSTAT manual that "principal component and common factor solutions for real data rarely differ enough to matter." This generated an acerbic article by Borgatta, Kercher, and Stull (1986) and a refutation by Wilkinson (1989) which revealed a mathematical flaw in their artificial example. Subsequently, Velicer and Jackson (1990) discussed in detail the issues behind this debate; a whole issue of *Multivariate Behavioral Research* was devoted to their article and replies and rejoinders. In this entire time, no one has supplied *real data* to refute Wilkinson's original claim. Judge for yourself on the CRIME data and then try both methods on other data. See if you can find any example where the difference in results would be large enough to affect a scientific theory or practical policy.

Special problems in factoring

Although the factoring of the square root crime data looks similar to the principal components method, some differences are revealing. Notice that the communality for MURDER is 1.0. This implies that MURDER contains no specific error, i.e. it perfectly represents a latent factor. This circumstance is called a **Heywood case**. In these instances, unconstrained iterations can allow communalities greater than 1.0, an impossibility in the model.

Figure 20.13
Factor Analysis of Transformed CRIME Data

```
FACTOR
   USE CRIME80
   MODEL MURDER..AUTOTHFT
   ESTIMATE / METHOD=MLA   NUMBER=2   ROTATE=VARIMAX   SORT
```

Initial Communality Estimates

	1	2	3	4	5
	0.758	0.781	0.777	0.628	0.818
	6	7			
	0.623	0.629			

Iterative Maximum Likelihood Factor Analysis: Convergence = 0.001000.

Iteration Number	Maximum Change in SQRT(uniqueness)	Negative log of Likelihood
1	0.614297	0.886377
2	0.431731	0.668293
3	0.108710	0.600624
4	0.030748	0.594157
5	0.001252	0.594126
6	0.000633	0.594118

Final Communality Estimates

	1	2	3	4	5
	1.000	0.732	0.709	0.627	0.920
	6	7			
	0.568	0.547			

Canonical Correlations

	1	2
	1.000	0.960

Factor pattern

	1	2
MURDER	1.000	-0.000
RAPE	0.707	0.482
ROBBERY	0.665	0.516
ASSAULT	0.692	0.386
BURGLARY	0.590	0.756
LARCENY	0.125	0.743
AUTOTHFT	0.327	0.663

```
Variance Explained by Factors

                       1            2

                    2.892        2.212


Percent of Total Variance Explained

                       1            2

                   41.307       31.596

Rotated Pattern Matrix ( VARIMAX, Gamma =        1.0000)

                       1            2

   MURDER          0.998        0.060
   RAPE            0.677        0.524
   ROBBERY         0.633        0.555
   ASSAULT         0.667        0.427
   BURGLARY        0.544        0.790
   LARCENY         0.080        0.749
   AUTOTHFT        0.287        0.682

"Variance" Explained by Rotated Factors

                       1            2

                    2.684        2.419

Percent of Total Variance Explained

                       1            2

                   38.339       34.564

Percent of Common Variance Explained

                       1            2

                   52.589       47.411
```

Factor Loadings Plot

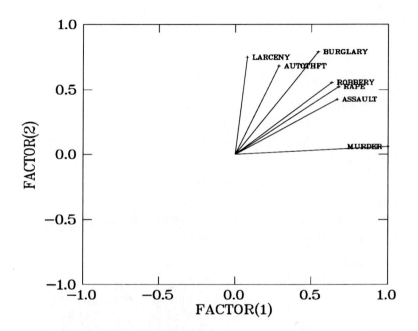

Heywood cases often indicate over-factoring. They can usually be eliminated by choosing fewer factors (in this case 1). Another approach, taken automatically by SYS-TAT in this example, is to constrain the communality to be 1.0 and iterate until the other communalities converge. A third approach is to eliminate the variable causing the Heywood case. None of these solutions is entirely satisfactory. An ultimate solution, of course, would be to revert to principal components, which do not have this problem.

Other indeterminacies exist in factor analysis. In addition to the score problem, discussed below, there are also identification problems. For some matrices, it is possible to have an infinite number of solutions which fit the same factor model perfectly. Wilkinson (1989) discusses these indeterminacies.

Factor scores

No unique set of factor scores can be computed to fit the factor model. As the SYSTAT manual points out, many programs compute "regression" estimates of factor scores, but if you save these scores and correlate them, they will not reproduce the correlation matrix of the factors the way component scores do, nor will they correlate with the observed variables as specified in the model. If you need scores, then try unit weights or switch to components. The clearest presentation of this problem is in Steiger and Schonemann (1978).

20.3 Conclusion

When should you use principal components and when factors? Some will tell you there is only one answer, and that answer depends on which model they endorse. We take a more pragmatic view. Both, after all, are simply mathematical models which yield different information.

If you are interested in summarizing multivariate information into linear composites and computing scores on those composites, then use components. Although there are formulas for computing casewise scores on common factors, we believe they involve too many theoretical ambiguities to be of much use.

If, on the other hand, you wish to decompose a correlation or covariance matrix into a few factors , then consider factor analysis. You will tend to get fewer factors than components and their structure *may* be simpler to interpret. If anyone tries to tell you that factors are more "scientific" or "accurate" or "meaningful" than components, however, don't believe it. Mathematically, it is just as reasonable to consider factors as approximations to components as the other way around. The differences between factors and components on real data are not large enough to justify the controversy over this issue.

Notes

Jolliffe (1986) is a good general introduction to principal components analysis. Harmon (1976) is a classic reference on factor analysis. Mulaik (1972) is one of the best factor analysis books and a favorite of ours, but it is out of print. Gorsuch (1983) is a recent useful introduction.

References

Borgatta, E.F., Kercher, K., and Stull, D.E. (1986). A cautionary note on the use of principal components analysis. *Sociological Methods & Research, 17,* 460-464.

Gorsuch, R. L. (1983). *Factor Analysis (2nd Ed.).* Hillsdale, NJ: Lawrence Erlbaum.

Harman, H.H. (1976). *Modern Factor Analysis. 3rd. Ed.* Chicago: University of Chicago Press.

Jolliffe, I.T. (1986). *Principal Component Analysis.* New York: Springer-Verlag.

Mulaik, S.A. (1972). *The Foundations of Factor Analysis.* New York: McGraw-Hill.

Steiger, J.H., and Schonemann, P.H. (1978). A history of factor indeterminacy. In S. Shye (Ed.), *Theory Construction and Data Analysis in the Behavioral Sciences: A Volume in Honor of Louis Guttman.* San Francisco, CA: Jossey-Bass.

Velicer, W.F. and Jackson, D.N. (1990). Component analysis versus common factor analysis: Some issues in selecting an appropriate procedure. *Multivariate Behavioral Research, 25,* 1-28.

Widaman, K.F. (1993). Common factor analysis versus principal component analysis Differential bias in representing model parameters? *Multivariate Behavioral Research, 28,* 263-311.

Wilkinson, L. (1989). A cautionary note on the use of factor analysis. *Sociological Methods & Research, 20,* 449-459.

Wilkinson, L. (1990). *SYSTAT: The System for Statistics.* Evanston, IL: SYSTAT, Inc.

21
Multidimensional Scaling

What kind of symptoms tend to comprise illness syndromes? For example, if you have a stuffy nose, are you likely to sneeze, or have a fever, or a sore throat? Do headache, nausea, and diarrhea tend to occur together when you get sick? To examine this question, we took the Merck manual (Merck, 1985), chose 18 representative symptoms, and tallied how many times they occurred together in 50 different diseases involving a wide range of human body systems. Figure 21.1 shows this tally. The data are symmetric because each symptom is represented by a column and a row in the matrix. The numbers on the diagonal are the number of times each symptom occurs across all the 50 diseases, while the rest of the values show the coöccurrence of pairs of symptoms. For example, fever occurred in 21 diseases, diarrhea occurred in 9, and both occurred together in 2 diseases. The names of the variables are self-explanatory, except for CONSTIP (constipation), STUFFY (stuffy nose), CHEST (chest pains), BLURRED (blurred vision), THROAT (sore throat), ABDOMEN (abdominal pains), and MUSCLE (muscle pain).

There are several ways to analyze these data so that symptoms coöccurring frequently will be shown together in the same display. Multidimensional scaling, or smallest space analysis, is a particularly effective method for making such a display. Let's use a mental exercise to see how it works.

First, write the name of each symptom on one of 18 poker chips. Next, place all 18 chips on a table. Now look at the matrix in Figure 21.1 and find the two symptoms occurring most frequently together. NAUSEA and VOMIT occur together in 10 of the 50 diseases and HEADACHE and FEVER occur together likewise. Now place those poker chips near each other in two pairs. In Figure 21.2, these symptoms have been assigned letters for identification. NAUSEA is D and VOMIT is N, and HEADACHE is G and FEVER is A. Thus, D-N and G-A should be two poker chip pairs.

Figure 21.1
Tally of Coöccurrences of Symptoms for 50 Typical Diseases

```
BASIC
   SAVE SYMPTOMS
   TYPE=SIMILARITY
   INPUT FEVER DIARRHEA CONSTIP NAUSEA STUFFY CHEST,
         HEADACHE BLURRED THROAT ABDOMEN CHILLS MUSCLE,
         DROWSY VOMIT CONVULSE COUGH DIZZY SNEEZE
   RUN

21
 2  9
 1  2  3
 2  4  0 14
 3  0  0  0  8
 3  0  0  0  0  4
10  2  2  4  0  3 21
 1  0  0  2  0  0  2  5
 6  0  1  0  2  2  5  0  8
 3  7  1  5  0  0  2  0  0  9
 7  1  2  0  0  3  8  0  4  1  9
 4  1  1  0  0  1  6  0  2  1  4  8
 0  2  0  1  0  1  2  0  0  1  0  0  4
 3  5  0 10  0  0  4  1  0  5  1  1  1 14
 2  0  1  4  0  1  4  1  1  0  1  0  1  5  9
 3  0  0  1  2  2  3  0  3  0  3  3  0  1  1  8
 3  0  0  4  1  0  5  2  0  0  0  1  1  1  2  0  9
 1  0  0  1  4  0  0  0  0  0  0  0  0  1  1  2  0  5
~
```

Now our task becomes more complicated. We must rearrange all the rest of the poker chips so that pairs with frequently coöccurring symptoms are near each other and those having no coöccurrences are far apart. As you pursue this exercise, you will begin to realize that you cannot arrange all of the chips so that all of the distances between them follow the numbers in Figure 21.1 (0 far apart, to 10 close together).

Imagine our best effort in getting the distances between the chips to fit the numbers in this fashion. Every time we move one chip, we affect 17 distances of that chip to the remaining symptoms. The total number of distances we must think about is 153, the number of pairwise coöccurrences in Figure 21.1.

To find out how successful we were in representing the numbers in Figure 21.1 with a configuration of poker chips, we can measure with a ruler all the distances between the chips and plot them against the corresponding numbers in the figure. In a good solution to the problem, we should have a scatterplot which is smoothly decreasing, namely, a swarm of points showing large distances corresponding to infrequent coöccurrence (dissimilarity) in the upper left of the plot and small distances to frequent coöccurrence (similarity) at the lower right. The part of Figure 21.2 called "SHEPARD DIAGRAM" (named after Roger Shepard) shows this scatterplot for SYSTAT's solution to the problem. The numbers you see in the plot are overlapping asterisks. Notice that the plot of distances against similarities (fitted distances against observed data) appears curved rather than a straight line. This often happens in multidimensional scaling solutions. Remember, we have required only that smaller distances correspond to greater similarities, not that they be a linear function of the similarities.

How does the computer do this task? First, it begins by computing initial estimates of where the poker chips should be placed. It then calculates the data for a Shepard diagram. Next, it fits a curve through the points in the diagram. It then calculates small movements for each chip. After moving the chips slightly, it recalculates the Shepard diagram, fits a curve again, and checks to see if there has been any improvement in the fit of distances to dissimilarities. If the fit has improved, then it repeats this process. It stops when it cannot improve the fit in the Shepard diagram by moving the chips.

The number called KRUSKAL STRESS (named after Joseph Kruskal) in Figure 21.2 is a measure of how badly the curve fits all the points in the SHEPARD DIAGRAM. It is closely related to MEAN SQUARE ERROR in regression; the bigger the STRESS, the more the distances are estimated badly by the data. Therefore, we are looking for s small STRESS in a good solution. Finally, SYSTAT prints the configuration of points (poker chips). The second graph is a plot of this configuration.

21.1 Checking the fit of the solution

How do we know that the computer has found the "right" solution? We don't. Although a lot of technical details have been left out of our description, it should be clear to you that multidimensional scaling involves a "trial and error" approach to estimation which is more like nonlinear regression than procedures such as principal components or ordinary least squares. Nevertheless, there are a number of ways to cross check the solution.

Figure 21.2
Two-Dimensional Scaling of Disease Symptoms

```
MDS
    USE SYMPTOMS
    MODEL FEVER..SNEEZE
    SAVE MDSRES / RESIDUALS
    ESTIMATE
```

```
Monotonic Multidimensional Scaling
The data are analyzed as similarities
Minimizing Kruskal STRESS (form 1) in 2 dimensions

Iteration       STRESS
---------       ------
      0        0.271553
      1        0.227769
      2        0.205173
      3        0.192560
      4        0.184142
      5        0.177353
      6        0.170046
      7        0.161750
      8        0.154572
      9        0.149059
     10        0.144972
     11        0.141827
     12        0.139068
     13        0.136579
     14        0.134276
     15        0.132056
     16        0.129878
     17        0.127705
     18        0.125630
     19        0.123748
     20        0.122091
     21        0.120642
Stress of final configuration is: 0.12064
Proportion of variance (RSQ) is: 0.90827
```

```
Coordinates in 2 dimensions
Variable        Dimension
--------        ---------
                   1      2
  FEVER          .01    .25
  DIARRHEA      1.10   -.45
  CONSTIP       1.18    .63
  NAUSEA         .38   -.56
  STUFFY       -1.37    .27
  CHEST         -.37    .72
  HEADACHE       .13    .17
  BLURRED       -.69  -1.07
  THROAT        -.33   1.14
  ABDOMEN       1.17   -.25
  CHILLS         .18    .73
  MUSCLE         .45    .94
  DROWSY         .25  -1.26
  VOMIT          .45   -.48
  CONVULSE      -.12   -.28
  COUGH         -.67    .51
  DIZZY         -.34   -.56
  SNEEZE       -1.40   -.44
Root mean squared residuals for each point

Variable         Residual
FEVER           0.21614
DIARRHEA        0.09996
CONSTIP         0.10287
NAUSEA          0.14000
STUFFY          0.17599
CHEST           0.24019
HEADACHE        0.18490
BLURRED         0.19739
THROAT          0.16230
ABDOMEN         0.13736
CHILLS          0.11497
MUSCLE          0.17814
DROWSY          0.24368
VOMIT           0.14666
CONVULSE        0.16134
COUGH           0.17018
DIZZY           0.19657
SNEEZE          0.20344
Residuals have been saved.
```

Shepard Diagram

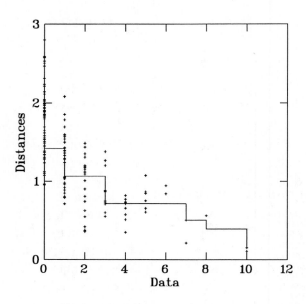

Configuration

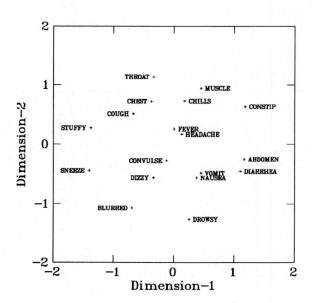

Stress

The statistic which summarizes how well dissimilarities (or similarities) are fit by distances is called STRESS. Some methodologists advise that STRESS ought to be below .1 in a "good" solution. The distribution of STRESS depends on the number of points and the number of dimensions, however, so it is not possible to give such a global criterion.

Stenson and Knoll (1969), Spence and Olgilvie (1973), Levene (1978), and others have performed Monte Carlo simulations to see what STRESS would look like for random data for various numbers of points in each of several dimensions. You can refer to the tables they provide to determine whether a solution is random. There is a serious problem with using these tables this way, however. On the one hand, you will have difficulty rejecting the null hypothesis of complete randomness for small datasets, such as judgments of the perceptions of 7 colors, which is known theoretically and empirically to require only two dimensions. On the other hand, you will find that almost any larger number of points you scale will have STRESS lower than the tables show for random data (even at $\alpha = .05$). The null hypothesis of complete randomness leaves too many alternative hypotheses untested. Should we generate random dissimilarities or add random noise to a spatial configuration? Should we use uniform or normal random distributions? And even if we reject some null hypothesis, our solution may still be practically worthless. Spence (1974) discusses many of these problems. Ramsay (1978) offers a computational solution to this hypothesis testing problem based on normal distribution theory, but it requires fairly rigid assumptions and is less practical on large datasets.

You can get a sense of how random data scale by using SYSTAT to create some random samples. Figure 21.3 shows a simple way to create a file of random dissimilarities you can scale directly in MDS. We selected 18 points in 2 dimensions for the simulation to correspond to the disease data. Although we are generating a rectangular matrix, we are going to use only the lower triangular elements by setting TYPE=SIMILARITY. If you use the RSEED command to set a new random number seed, you can repeat this step enough times to replicate the Monte Carlo studies. More importantly, you will be able to see how all aspects of the output look with random data, not just STRESS.

The scary thing is the lower panel of Figure 21.3. Notice how reasonable the plot looks. Throw some labels into this picture and we could be making solemn pronouncements about national health care. The same problem occurs in exploratory factor analysis. It's a cinch to read meaning into any factor plot. People do every day, deceiving themselves and others. There is no substitute for having theoretical expectations before jumping into the interpretation of a plot.

There's additional (albeit slight) protection here if you are careful: the Shepard diagram. Although there are tables and theoretical studies on the distribution of the STRESS statistic under certain kinds of randomness, there is no substitute for looking at Shepard diagrams of random data. In Figure 21.3, the variance of the residuals is equal to or larger than the "variance" of the fitted "curve." Furthermore, if we scaled the random data in higher dimensions, this situation would not radically improve with random data. Figure 21.9 shows a plot of STRESS versus dimensionality for the symptom data. You might want to make this plot for random data and see the difference.

Figure 21.3
Scaling Random Data

```
BASIC
    NEW
    RSEED=12345
    REPEAT 18
    DIM X(18)
    FOR I=1 TO CASE
        LET X(I)=URN
    NEXT
    RUN
    TYPE=SIMILARITY
    SAVE RANDOM
    RUN
MDS
    USE RANDOM
    MODEL X(1..18)
    ESTIMATE
```

```
Monotonic Multidimensional Scaling
The data are analyzed as similarities
Minimizing Kruskal STRESS (form 1) in 2 dimensions

Iteration        STRESS
---------        ------
     0          0.360867
     1          0.314267
     2          0.304696
     3          0.300770
     4          0.297652
     5          0.295688
     6          0.294376
     7          0.293333
     8          0.292387
     9          0.291473
    10          0.290541
    11          0.289588
    12          0.288690
    13          0.287950
    14          0.287406
    15          0.287006
    16          0.286701
Stress of final configuration is: 0.28670
Proportion of variance (RSQ) is: 0.43907

Coordinates in 2 dimensions
Variable             Dimension
--------             ---------
                        1     2
  X(1)            -.40 -1.22
  X(2)             .10   .99
  X(3)             .14   .05
  X(4)           -1.17  -.35
  X(5)            -.68  -.62
  X(6)            -.13   .63
  X(7)             .46   .52
  X(8)            1.03   .56
  X(9)            1.11  -.96
 X(10)            -.49   .25
 X(11)            -.69   .05
 X(12)             .54  -.33
 X(13)             .26  -.70
 X(14)             .67   .97
 X(15)            -.66  1.12
 X(16)            1.08  -.15
 X(17)           -1.24   .20
 X(18)             .06 -1.01
```

Shepard Diagram

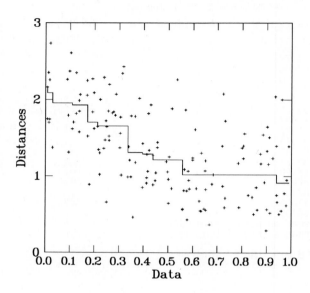

Configuration

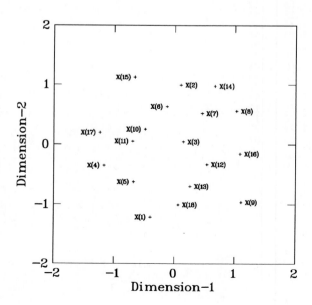

The Shepard diagram

Relying on STRESS to judge the quality of MDS solutions is like looking at correlation coefficients without examining scatterplots. A single statistic cannot summarize the complexity of a scatterplot or Shepard diagram. Outliers (for example, a few large distances) can influence the STRESS value considerably. The Shepard diagram will let you see this.

Figure 21.4 shows an MDS solution with a STRESS of zero. We devised this example to show you why you should look at the Shepard diagram before examining STRESS. We deliberately constructed this starting configuration to mislead the program into a "degenerate" solution. You can detect this by looking at the Shepard diagram. Notice that the fitted function relating distances to dissimilarities is "L" shaped. Instead of smoothly relating the fitted and observed values, this function breaks sharply on the 6th value. All the distances are tied except for one, not a satisfying fit to data with many distinct values. You can see another zero-stress solution by leaving out the CONFIG-URATION paragraph and rescaling the example. Neither solution is more "correct" in a monotonic sense since both have a stress of zero. The second is more satisfying, how-ever, because it fits the data with more distinct distances. Any time you observe a Shep-ard diagram with only a few sharp steps, you should be suspicious of the solution, regardless of the STRESS value. If this happens, you can try the REGRESSION=LIN-EAR option of MDS to force the function in the Shepard diagram to be along a straight line rather than a curve. Borg (1985) provides other examples of degenerate MDS so-lutions.

Identifying badly fitting points

SYSTAT offers a unique way to examine the Shepard diagram more closely in order to identify points which fit poorly in the number of dimensions selected. If you type SHEPARD=2 before the SCALE command, you will get two Shepard diagrams. One shows distances labeled by the first point in each pair and the other shows the same plot of distances labeled by the second. In addition, the fitted regression line predicting dis-tances from dissimilarities is marked in each plot with an asterisk so you can recognize outliers. This double plot is not shown here, but it can be useful for identifying points which do not scale well in the number of dimensions you have chosen.

Figure 21.4
A Degenerate Multidimensional Scaling Solution

```
BASIC
    SAVE POINTS
    INPUT A B C D
    TYPE=DISSIMILARITY
    DIAGONAL ABSENT
    RUN
     4
     3 2
     6 5 1
     ~
MDS
    USE POINTS
    MODEL A..D
    CONFIGURATION [ 5      0;
                    0      3;
                    0     -3;
                   -5      0]
    ESTIMATE
```

```
Monotonic Multidimensional Scaling
The data are analyzed as dissimilarities
Minimizing Kruskal STRESS (form 1) in 2 dimensions

Initial configuration
     5.00      .00
      .00     3.00
      .00    -3.00
    -5.00      .00

Iteration      STRESS
---------      ------
    0        0.008880
    1        0.006162
Stress of final configuration is: 0.00616
Proportion of variance (RSQ) is: 0.99929

Coordinates in 2 dimensions
Variable        Dimension
--------        ---------
                   1      2
    A            1.22     .00
    B             .00     .72
    C             .00    -.72
    D           -1.21     .00
```

Shepard Diagram

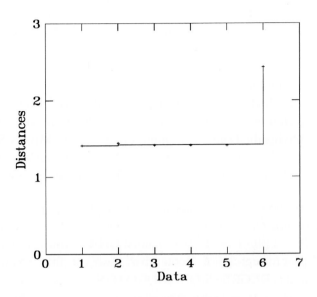

Configuration

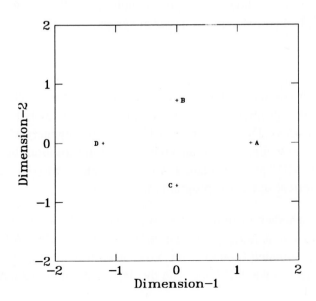

Another way to identify badly fitting points is to save the residuals from the Shepard diagram by typing SAVE MYFILE / RESIDUAL before the SCALE command. When you select this option, SYSTAT prints root-mean-squared residuals. For each point in the configuration, these are badness-of-fit summed over all other points. Alternatively, you can think of these numbers as contributions to the STRESS statistic. Any point with a relatively large root mean square residual value is not being modeled well by the scaling. For "good" solutions based on at least 15 points, you should expect these values to be lumpy in the middle with two tails. Badly fitting points will appear in the upper tail in a stem-and-leaf diagram, perhaps excluded as "OUTSIDE VALUES." Figure 21.5 shows a stem-and-leaf diagram of the contributions to stress for the medical data. We saved the residuals and then imported the ROOT MEAN SQUARED RESIDUALS from the output into a SYSTAT file. Notice the values are fairly normal looking, indicating that no symptom fits the two-dimensional solution too poorly.

You can also analyze the saved residuals using many of the graphical methods we discussed in the regression chapters. If you plot DIST against DATA, you will get the Shepard diagram. If you plot RESIDUAL against DHAT, you will get something like the usual residual plot in regression. Remember, however, that if you use monotonic regression (the default is REGRESSION=MONOTONIC) instead of linear (REGRESSION=LINEAR), there will be many zero residuals because the fitted values are allowed to step monotonically through the data values. Provided you have at least 15 points or so, the residuals should be approximately normally distributed overall. Remember, each residual corresponds to a *pair* of symptoms.

Local minima

Because MDS is an iterative technique, it is not guaranteed to reach the correct solution. Sometimes MDS programs may stop at a high stress value before reaching a solution with a lower stress. This problem is different from "degenerate" solutions, which can have the same or smaller stress than a more satisfying solution. Instead, local minima occur when the MDS program cannot move points enough to reduce stress substantially. In a metaphorical sense, the program hits a blind alley.

One way to check whether a solution you have found is a local minimum is to rescale your data with a different starting configuration. Normally, SYSTAT begins with its own configuration estimated from the data. You can modify this by using the CONFIGURATION command as we did above with the degenerate point example.

Figure 21.5
Stem-and-Leaf Plot of Contribution to Stress Statistic and Scatterplot Using Contribution as Symbol Size

```
MDS
    USE SYMPTOMS
    SAVE SYMPRES / RESID
    MODEL FEVER..SNEEZE
    ESTIMATE
```

```
Stem and Leaf Plot of variable:     RESIDUAL, N = 18
        Minimum:        0.100
        Lower hinge:        0.140
        Median:         0.173
        Upper hinge:        0.197
        Maximum:        0.244

        0   9
        1   01
        1   3
        1 H 44
        1 M 66777
        1 H 899
        2   01
        2
        2   44
```

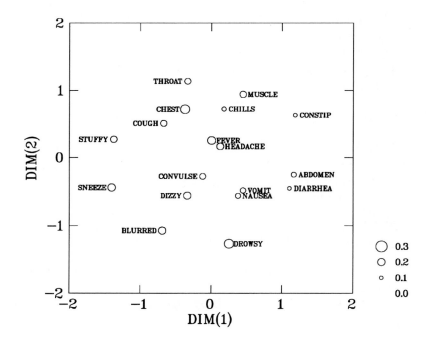

Another check on the solution is to use a completely different program to represent similarities between objects. As we have seen in the cluster analysis chapter, the CLUSTER module produces a tree of similarities by joining the two closest objects, the next two closest objects (or clusters), and so forth. Figure 21.6 shows the CLUSTER solution on the symptom data in Figure 21.1. Notice that VOMIT-NAUSEA and HEADACHE-FEVER are linked early in the cluster analysis and are close together in the MDS.

Figure 21.6
Cluster Analysis of Symptom Data

```
CLUSTER
    USE SYMPTOMS
    JOIN FEVER..SNEEZE / LINKAGE=COMPLETE
```

Cluster Tree

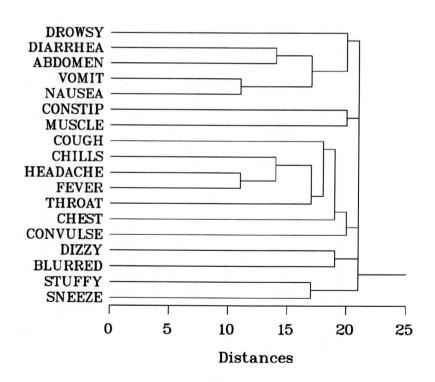

Distances

We can relate the entire cluster tree to the multidimensional scaling configuration by circling the objects which are joined at each stage in the tree. This is called a Wroclaw diagram (Sneath & Sokal, 1973). Figure 21.7 shows how to do this for all symptoms occurring at least 4 times together. It is a rather lengthy SYSTAT program, but keep in mind that researchers wanting to do this have had to have an artist draw them by hand.

The program begins by saving the variable names as labels (using TRANSPOSE) and then merging them back into the data file. Then the MDS and CLUSTER solutions are saved into files and merged themselves. Finally, a set of indicator variables are created, each denoting cluster membership for each object. We then contour around these indicator variables which have only two values, 0 or 1. By setting ZMAX=1 and ZTICK=2, we are insuring only one contour will be drawn at a height of .5, since the INVERSE smoothing does not get above a height of 1. With other data, you might have to fiddle with TENSION to get the contours where you want to see them. The benefit of all this work is that you get contours where they belong according to the density of the objects in the clusters rather than by an artist's eye.

21.2 Interpreting multidimensional scalings

That we used cluster analysis to check the multidimensional scaling does not mean that we should always look for clusters of points in interpreting our results. Nor should we necessarily look for meaningful axes in the configuration. Some researchers who are familiar with principal components or factor analysis expect to rotate multidimensional scaling solutions and search for "factors." This misses the point of the method.

Louis Guttman (who developed smallest space analysis, which SYSTAT offers in the METHOD=GUTTMAN option), and Roger Shepard (who produced the first multidimensional scaling program) have both demonstrated the usefulness of looking for "structures" rather than "factors" in multidimensional scaling solutions. Krumhansel (1979) has shown, for example, that the perception of musical pitch can be represented by a conical spiral of notes in three-dimensional space. Guttman has designed studies whose facets order variables in lines, circles, cones, cylinders, and other geometric figures. The configuration of symptoms above, for example, is most easily viewed as three pie-shaped sectors comprising somatic, respiratory, and neurological symptoms. Wilkinson, Gimble, and Koepke (1982) validated this structure for both medical self-diagnoses and symptom coöccurrences. Figure 21.8 shows this arrangement with the sectors labeled at the periphery of the scaling.

Figure 21.7
Cluster Analysis Results Superimposed on Multidimensional Scaling

```
USE SYMPTOMS
TRANSPOSE
SAVE TEMP
RUN
MERGE SYMPTOMS TEMP(LABEL$)
MDS
SAVE MDSCONF / CONFIG
MODEL FEVER..SNEEZE
ESTIMATE
CLUSTER
IDVAR LABEL$
SAVE CLUSCONF / NUMBER=4
JOIN FEVER..SNEEZE / LINK=COMPLETE
MERGE MDSCONF CLUSCONF
LET C1=0
LET C2=0
LET C3=0
LET C4=0
IF CLUSTER=1 THEN LET C1=1
IF CLUSTER=2 THEN LET C2=1
IF CLUSTER=3 THEN LET C3=1
IF CLUSTER=4 THEN LET C4=1
BEGIN
PLOT C1*DIM(2)*DIM(1)/
CONTOUR,ZMIN=0,ZMAX=1,ZTICK=2,ZPIP=0,SMOOTH=INVS,
    TENSION=.1,AXES=0,SCALE=0
PLOT C2*DIM(2)*DIM(1)/
CONTOUR,ZMIN=0,ZMAX=1,ZTICK=2,ZPIP=0,SMOOTH=INVS,
    TENSION=.1,AXES=0,SCALE=0
PLOT C3*DIM(2)*DIM(1)/
CONTOUR,ZMIN=0,ZMAX=1,ZTICK=2,ZPIP=0,SMOOTH=INVS,
    TENSION=.1,AXES=0,SCALE=0
PLOT C4*DIM(2)*DIM(1)/
CONTOUR,ZMIN=0,ZMAX=1,ZTICK=2,ZPIP=0,SMOOTH=INVS,
    TENSION=.1,AXES=0,SCALE=0
PLOT DIM(2)*DIM(1)/LABEL=LABEL$
END
```

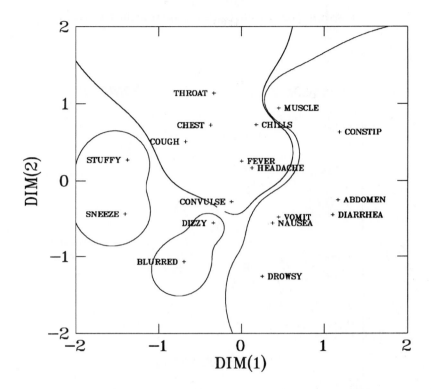

Some multidimensional scaling solutions can be elucidated by labeling axes or dimensions. It is usually best to search for nonorthogonal axes, since there is no intrinsic meaning to the principal axes of a scaling solution. In fact, the flexibility of the function relating dissimilarities/similarities to distances in the Shepard Diagram often means that orthogonal factors or principal components can be represented parsimoniously in scaling spaces of fewer dimensions. Rosenberg, Nelson, and Vivekananthan (1968) represented a well-known three-dimensional factor structure of implicit personality theory (Evaluation-Potency-Activity) in a two-dimensional MDS. Furthermore, these authors used multiple regression to fit external ratings of the scaled objects to the axes in the scaling space. Kruskal and Wish (1978) and Shepard (1978) give many other examples of data structures which can be found in multidimensional scaling solutions.

Figure 21.8
Symptom Sectors in Multidimensional Scaling

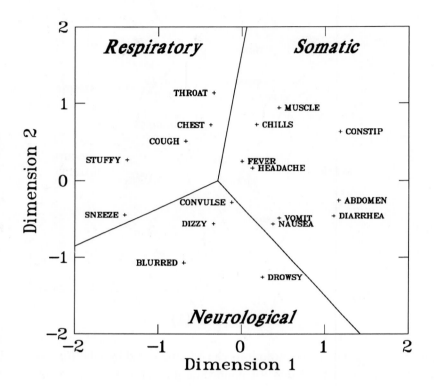

21.3 How many dimensions should you choose?

So far, we have scaled data only in 2 dimensions. The SYSTAT MDS program will allow you to choose between 1 and 5 dimensions. Deciding how many dimensions to scale can be problematic.

One method derived from the "scree" plot in factor analysis is to plot the stress statistic for a scaling in each dimension on a vertical axis against the dimension numbers on the horizontal axis. We ran the symptoms scaling five times, adding a statement DIMENSION=1 to DIMENSION=5. Then we entered the final stress value for each scaling into a SYSTAT file and plotted it. Figure 21.9 shows this plot. In FACTOR scree plots, we choose the number of factors (based on eigenvalues) to be one to the left of the elbow. In MDS, we choose the number of dimensions (based on STRESS) at the elbow itself. There does appear to be an elbow at 2 dimensions.

This method does not work well with real data, however. Typically, the plot looks more rounded, and it is difficult to decide.

Figure 21.9
Stress vs. Dimension for Symptom Data

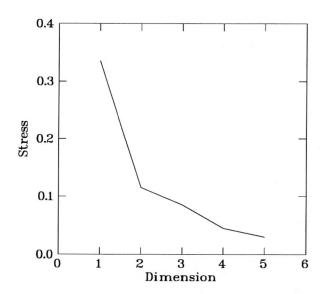

Spence and Graef (1974) computed tables of stress for varying numbers of points and dimensions. Unlike the Monte Carlo studies which generated random dissimilarities (as we did in Figure 21.3), these studies used points in known dimensionality and added random error to the dissimilarities between points. Thus, these results provide one way to judge the dimensionality of a given set of data. Our symptom data are most likely two-dimensional, according to their tables. Isaac and Poor (1974) offer additional tables for determining dimensionality.

21.4 The relation between multidimensional scaling and principal components

Multidimensional scaling need not begin with a symmetric matrix. You can use the SYSTAT CORR module to compute correlations or Euclidean distances on a set of variables and then scale the resulting triangular matrix with MDS. With this approach, you can compare multidimensional scaling to principal components on the same data.

Recall that multidimensional scaling represents the elements of a triangular matrix by distances between points in a space. The principal components decomposition represents the same elements by the cosines of angles between vectors in a space. Under some simplifying linear assumptions beyond the scope of this book, the two procedures can be shown to be mathematical reparameterizations of each other. In general, they reveal different facets of the same geometric structures, but nonmetric multidimensional scaling is more flexible (relaxed) because its relation to the data need be only monotonic.

If you use correlations as the measure of similarity between variables (objects), then multidimensional scaling and principal components solutions will frequently coincide. Many of the simple structures clearly visible in low dimensions via multidimensional scaling will be completely obscured by principal components or factor analyses, however. Here is an example.

Figure 21.10 shows data reported by Suchman in Stouffer et al. (1952). They denote whether or not World War II soldiers reported certain physiological reactions following combat. The names of the variables should be self explanatory, except for POUNDING (pounding heart), and SINKING (a sinking feeling in the stomach). The variable COUNT is the number of soldiers in the survey reporting the given combination of symptoms. For example, there are 512 possible patterns, of which only 52 actually occurred. Six soldiers reported no symptoms, and 2 had POUNDING, SHAKING, STIFF, and BOWELS. At the end of the list, 6 soldiers reported all symptoms.

Figure 21.10
Combat Symptom Data

POUNDING	SINKING	SHAKING	NAUSEOUS	STIFF	FAINT	VOMIT	BOWELS	URINE	COUNT
0	0	0	0	0	0	0	0	0	6
1	0	1	0	1	0	0	1	0	2
0	0	0	0	0	0	1	0	0	1
0	0	0	0	0	1	0	0	0	1
0	0	0	1	0	1	0	0	0	1
0	1	0	0	1	0	0	0	0	1
1	0	0	0	0	0	0	0	0	7
1	0	1	0	0	0	0	0	0	1
1	0	0	1	0	0	0	0	0	1
1	0	0	0	1	0	0	0	0	1
1	0	0	0	0	0	1	0	0	1
1	0	0	0	0	0	0	1	0	1
0	1	0	0	0	0	0	0	0	1
1	1	0	0	0	1	0	0	0	1
1	1	0	0	0	0	0	0	0	7
1	1	0	1	0	0	0	0	0	2
1	1	0	1	0	1	0	0	0	1
0	1	0	0	1	0	0	0	0	1
1	1	0	0	1	0	1	0	0	1
1	1	0	1	0	0	1	0	0	1
1	1	0	1	0	0	1	1	0	1
1	1	0	1	0	0	1	1	1	1
0	1	1	0	0	0	0	0	0	1
1	1	1	0	0	0	0	0	0	3
1	1	1	0	1	0	0	0	0	3
1	1	1	0	0	1	0	0	0	1
1	1	1	1	0	0	0	0	0	2
1	1	0	1	0	1	0	0	0	2
1	1	1	1	0	1	0	0	0	1
1	1	1	1	0	0	1	0	0	2
1	1	0	1	1	0	0	0	0	2
0	1	1	1	1	0	0	0	0	1
1	1	1	1	1	0	0	0	0	2
0	1	0	1	1	0	1	0	0	1
1	1	0	1	1	0	1	0	0	1
1	0	1	1	1	0	0	0	0	1
1	1	1	0	1	1	0	0	0	1
1	1	1	1	1	1	0	0	0	6
1	1	1	1	1	1	0	1	0	1
1	1	1	1	1	1	0	0	1	1
1	0	1	1	1	0	1	0	0	1
1	1	1	1	1	0	1	0	0	1
1	1	0	1	0	1	1	0	0	1
1	1	1	1	0	1	1	0	0	1
1	1	1	0	1	1	1	0	0	1
1	0	0	1	1	1	1	0	0	1
1	0	1	1	1	1	1	0	0	1
1	1	1	1	1	1	1	0	0	5
1	1	0	1	1	1	1	1	0	1
1	1	1	1	1	1	1	1	0	7
1	1	1	1	1	1	0	1	1	1
1	1	1	1	1	1	1	1	1	6

Figure 21.11 shows how to scale these data in two dimensions. First, we use the CORR module to compute Euclidean distances between the variables (which is the same as counting the number of disagreements in the soldiers' reports). Then we use the MDS module to scale the matrix we saved.

Figure 21.11
Scaling Combat Data with MDS

```
CORR
    USE COMBAT
    SAVE COMB
    FREQ=COUNT
    EUCLIDEAN POUNDING..URINE
MDS
    USE COMB
    MODEL POUNDING..URINE
    ESTIMATE
```

```
Monotonic Multidimensional Scaling
The data are analyzed as dissimilarities
Minimizing Kruskal STRESS (form 1) in 2 dimensions

Iteration      STRESS
---------      ------
    0         0.043737
    1         0.037156
    2         0.033275
    3         0.030911
    4         0.029333
Stress of final configuration is: 0.02933
Proportion of variance (RSQ) is: 0.99556

Coordinates in 2 dimensions
Variable           Dimension
--------           ---------
                    1      2
  POUNDING        1.52    .25
  SINKING         1.18    .02
  SHAKING          .28   -.64
  NAUSEOUS         .40    .30
  STIFF            .11   -.47
  FAINT           -.26   -.02
  VOMIT           -.58    .56
  BOWELS         -1.19    .08
  URINE          -1.46   -.08
```

Shepard Diagram

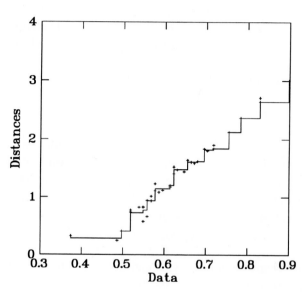

Configuration

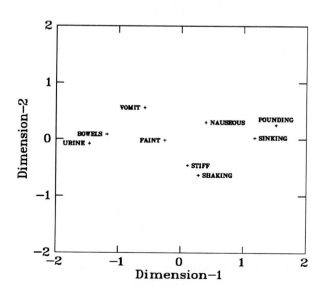

Notice that the symptoms scale in almost a straight line. We don't even need the second dimension to represent the variation in the original data. This is because the data comprise a **Guttman simplex**. A simplex is a single scale representing, in this case, severity of symptoms. If you are interested, you might want to take a look at the original ordering of symptoms produced by Suchman in the original reference. Without a computer, he sorted the data into the same order revealed in the multidimensional scaling.

What happens if we do a principal components analysis on the same data? Figure 21.12 shows how to set up the problem. We let the FACTOR module compute Pearson correlations and then the principal components.

FACTOR has missed the simple scale ordering the symptoms. In fact, a simplex scale cannot be represented by a single principal component or common factor because components and factors represent angles between vectors rather than distances between points. If you look carefully, the scale is distributed evenly across the components. In fact, it is distributed all the way up through five components. Rotating the components will not help this problem because the total variation is in many dimensions.

Principal components and factor analysis can conceal other simple patterns as well. Many researchers routinely factor data and find 5, 10, or even 16 factors which could much more simply be described with one or two simple scales. You should consider using MDS to analyze data before you do a principal components or factor analysis or even more complex latent variable structural modeling. That way, you can be alert to the possibility that the model you are choosing is not the most parsimonious one for describing the data.

The end of Chapter 23 discusses these issues and presents other types of data structures. That summary reveals other examples of where MDS and principal components analysis coincide.

21.5 Collecting data for multidimensional scaling

As we have seen, you can scale direct or derived distances, providing your assumptions are appropriate. To understand the impact of some of these assumptions when you compute derived distances, you should read Section 23.4.

There are many ways to collect similarities or dissimilarities directly. The simplest method is to ask subjects to evaluate every pair of objects on a numerical scale (e.g.

1=similar ... 7=different). Confusions among objects can be regarded as a measure of similarity. Sometimes confusions depend on order of presentation, as in the Rothkopf (1957) data on Morse codes analyzed by Shepard (1963) and in the SYSTAT manual. In these cases, pairs can be averaged to get one index of confusion for each pair.

Figure 21.12
Principal Components Analysis of Combat Data

```
FACTOR
    USE COMBAT
    FREQ=COUNT
    MODEL POUNDING..URINE
    ESTIMATE / NUMBER=2 SORT
```

Latent Roots (Eigenvalues)					
	1	2	3	4	5
	3.370	1.111	0.975	0.876	0.761
	6	7	8	9	
	0.608	0.493	0.427	0.379	

Component loadings		
	1	2
NAUSEOUS	0.722	0.164
FAINT	0.721	0.077
STIFF	0.692	0.221
SHAKING	0.664	0.373
BOWELS	0.651	-0.576
VOMIT	0.614	-0.150
URINE	0.541	-0.590
SINKING	0.474	0.433
POUNDING	0.301	0.020

Variance Explained by Components		
	1	2
	3.370	1.111

Percent of Total Variance Explained		
	1	2
	37.440	12.345

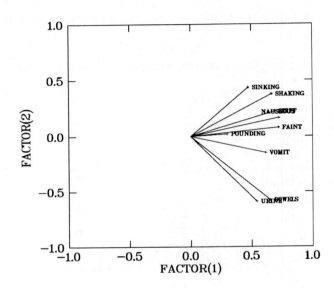

Factor Loadings Plot

Coombs (1964) and Kruskal and Wish (1978) present several other contexts in which proximities or similarities can be obtained for multidimensional scaling. Communications between cities, colonies, or individuals can be regarded as proximity measures, for example. Open field associations of primates (number of contacts or duration of contacts among individuals) comprise proximities. The scaling of these associational data can often reveal social networks. coöccurrences (as in the symptom data in this chapter) can be found in numerous social and physical systems.

With many objects, presenting all possible pairs may be tedious or impossible. Since MDS can adapt to missing data (by leaving missing values out of the STRESS calculation), incomplete data collection schemes can be used. Care must be taken to cover the range of distances needed in the Shepard diagram, however. If only long distances are deleted, only local structure will be preserved. Graef and Spence (1979) discuss some of these issues.

Finally, large designs can be accommodated by averaging data over subjects. With enough subjects, for example, you can get similarity information by counting the coöccurrences of objects in sorted piles. Subjects need only be asked to sort objects into piles of similar objects. Even the number of piles may vary. Rosenberg and Kim (1975) discuss this type of procedure.

21.6 Assumptions

When multidimensional scaling was first developed in the early 1960's, it was sometimes viewed as a magical technique for turning non-numerical information into numerical scales—for uncovering hidden multidimensional structures in rank order data. Beals, Krantz and Tversky (1968) dampened some of this enthusiasm with a paper on the mathematical assumptions of multidimensional scaling. Much of their paper focused on the definition of a **metric**, a mathematical condition required for the type of spatial model employed in MDS. Tversky (1977) illustrated these assumptions with practical examples. A metric requires the following:

1. $d_{ij} = d_{ji}$

2. $d_{ij} = 0$ if and only if $i = j$

3. $d_{ij} =< d_{ik} + d_{jk}$,

where d_{ij} is a distance between objects i and j.

For objects to be scaled in a Euclidean space, we must have a metric on the data we are scaling. Consider some counterexamples. If I am asked the distance from Evanston to Chicago, I might reply differently if I imagine myself in Evanston or in Chicago at a certain time of day because commuting time may influence my judgment of distance. Psychological distance may not be symmetrical. If I am asked how similar Miami is to Havana, I might reply "very similar." And Havana to Moscow? Very similar? How about Miami and Moscow? Psychological judgments may be "framed," notes Tversky, such that similarity comparisons may not be based on conditions which can be embedded in a single metric space.

These caveats apply to other types of data as well. If we measure distance using gasoline consumption in a trucking fleet, distances will not be symmetric (uphill uses more gas than downhill). If we measure proximity by adjacency in a serial list of objects, sequence may influence its value.

How do we know if metric assumptions are appropriate for a given set of data? In many cases, the solution is logical. We must think carefully about the process generating the data. Some authors have proposed diagnostic statistics to distinguish the appropriateness of spatial vs. network models for a given dataset. Pruzansky, Tversky, and Carroll (1982) suggest that negative skewness of distances and greater than .6 proportion of elongated triangles (triads of distances) indicate that a network model is more appropriate than a spatial. If so, the ADDTREE clustering model in SYSTAT can be used instead of MDS. Tversky and Hutchinson (1986) provide additional diagnostics.

Other scaling models

We have no room left to discuss several important MDS models. One is **individual differences MDS,** presented in Carroll and Chang (1970) and elsewhere. These models allow one to scale several triangular matrices simultaneously, yielding a composite space solution and a set of individual weights fitted to each separate matrix. Carroll and Chang's INDSCAL model is especially useful for fitting multi-subject designs. It is illustrated in the SYSTAT Version 6 manual.

Unfolding is a scaling model in which only a subset of distances are fit: namely, those between one set of objects and another. Coombs (1964) discusses applications of this model to preference and attitude scaling. It is also discussed in the Version 6 manual.

Notes

SYSTAT offers another method for fitting the points called METHOD=GUTTMAN (named after Louis Guttman). The GUTTMAN method uses a COEFFICIENT OF ALIENATION which is based on the distances permuted to the rank order of the original similarities. It takes longer to compute than the default KRUSKAL method, but Monte Carlo studies have shown (e.g. Lingoes and Roskam, 1973) it is more likely to find a correct solution in many cases.

There are several popular texts on multidimensional scaling. Shepard, Romney, and Nerlove (1972) is a classic two-volume contributed collection. Kruskal and Wish (1978) is the best brief introduction. Schiffman, Reynolds and Young (1981) is MDS program-oriented with a somewhat narrow applied focus. Borg (1981) is the best comprehensive text because it covers the basics as well as important diagnostic and confirmatory issues. Borg will teach you how to avoid the many pitfalls in using MDS. Davison (1983) is a relatively limited mathematical treatment, but a useful extra reference.

References

Beals, R., Krantz, D.H., and Tversky, A. (1968). Foundations of multidimensional scaling. *Psychological Review, 75*, 127-142.

Borg (1981). *Anwendunsorientierte Multidimensional Skalierung*. Berlin: Springer-Verlag.

Carroll, J.D. and Chang, J.J. (1970). Analysis of individual differences in multidimensional scaling via an N-way generalization of 'Eckart-Young' decomposition. *Psychometrika, 35*, 283-319.

Coombs, C.H. (1964). *A Theory of Data*. New York: John Wiley & Sons, Inc.

Davison, M.L. (1983). *Multidimensional Scaling*. New York: John Wiley & Sons, Inc.

Graef, J., and Spence, I. (1979). Using distance information in the design of large multidimensional scaling experiments. *Psychological Bulletin, 86*, 60-66.

Isaac, P.D. and Poor, D. (1974). On the determination of appropriate dimensionality in data with error. *Psychometrika, 39*, 91-109.

Krumhansl, C.L. (1979). The psychological representation of musical pitch in a tonal context. *Cognitive Psychology, 11*, 346-374.

Kruskal, J.B., and Wish, M. (1978). *Multidimensional Scaling*. Beverly Hills: Sage Publications, Inc.

Levine, D. (1978). A Monte Carlo study of Kruskal's variance based measure of stress. *Psychometrika, 43*, 307-316.

Lingoes, J.E. and Roskam, E.E. (1973). A mathematical and empirical comparison of two multidimensional scaling algorithms. *Psychometrika, 38*, Monograph Supplement.

Pruzansky, S., Tversky, A., and Carroll, J.D. (1982). Spatial versus tree representations of proximity data. *Psychometrika, 47*, 3-19.

Ramsay, J.O. (1978). Confidence regions for multidimensional scaling analysis. *Psychometrika, 43*, 241-266.

Rosenberg, S. and Kim, M.P. (1975). The method of sorting as a data-gathering procedure in multivariate research. *Multivariate Behavioral Research, 10*, 489-502.

Rosenberg, S., Nelson, C., and Vivekananthan, P.S. (1968). A multidimensional approach to the structure of personality impressions. *Journal of Personality and Social Psychology, 9*, 283-294.

Rothkopf, E.Z. (1957). A measure of stimulus similarity and errors in some paired associate learning tasks. *Journal of Experimental Psychology, 53,* 94-101.

Shepard, R.N. (1963). Analysis of proximities as a technique for the study of information processing in man. *Human Factors, 5,* 33-48.

Shepard, R. N. (1978). The circumplex and related topological manifolds in the study of perception. In Shye, S. (ed.), *Theory Construction and Data Analysis in the Behavioral Sciences.* San Francisco, CA: Jossey-Bass, Inc., 29-80.

Shepard, R.N., Romney, A.K., Nerlove, S. (eds.) (1972). *Multidimensional Scaling: Theory and Applications in the Behavioral Sciences.* New York: Seminar Press.

Shiffman, S.S., Reynolds, M.L., and Young, F.W. (1981). *Introduction to Multidimensional Scaling: Theory, Methods, and Applications.* New York: Academic Press.

Sneath, P.H.A. and Sokal, R.R. (1973). *Numerical Taxonomy.* San Francisco: W.H. Freeman and Company.

Spence, I. (1974) On random rankings studies in nonmetric scaling. *Psychometrika, 39,* 267-268.

Spence, I., and Graef, J. (1974). The determination of the underlying dimensionality of an empirically obtained matrix of proximities. *Multivariate Behavioral Research, 9,* 331-342.

Spence, I., and Olgilvie, J.C. (1973). A table of expected stress values for random rankings in nonmetric multidimensional scaling. *Multivariate Behavioral Research, 8,* 511-518.

Stenson, H.H. and Knoll, R.L. (1969). Goodness of fit for random rankings in Kruskal's nonmetric scaling procedure. *Psychological Bulletin, 71,* 122-126.

Tversky, A. (1977). Features of similarity. *Psychological Review, 84,* 327-352.

Tversky, A., and Hutchinson, J.W. (1986). Nearest neighbor analysis of psychological spaces. *Psychological Review, 93,* 3-22.

Wilkinson, L.,Gimbel, B. R., and Koepke, D. (1982). Configural self diagnosis. In Hirschberg, N. (Ed.). *Applied Multivariate Models in the Social Sciences.* Hillsdale, NJ: Lawrence Erlbaum.

Part 7

Special Topics

Part 7

Special Topics

Chapter 12: Transformations

Chapter 13: Similarity, Dissimilarity, and Distance

Chapter 14: Graphics

22

Transformations

Transformations (sometimes called reëxpressions) can simplify interpretation of statistical results and improve subsequent analysis. The simpler the model, the more readily we can interpret it. For example, a nonlinear relationship between an independent and the dependent variable can often be transformed into a straight-line relationship. Or, skewed residuals from a model may be made to look like a normal distribution through a simple transformation. Or, nonconstant variance in residuals can be made more uniform. Transformations themselves are not the goal of data analysis. They are means which can help you understand the information in your data more easily or meet the assumptions necessary to do statistical inference.

This chapter will deal mostly with data having positive values. There are two reasons for this. First, most problems requiring transformations occur with positive data like counts and proportions. Second, transforming negative and zero values is a non-trivial task which gets beyond the scope of this book. The one exception here is for correlations, which can be negative. We will discuss a simple transformation for correlations.

We'll begin with the problem of standardizing a variable to a selected location and scale. Then we'll discuss transformations to make a variable look normally distributed, or at least lumpy in the middle and symmetric. Then we'll cover the more general issue of transforming data so a linear model can be used, if that is possible. Finally, we'll describe a specific method for normalizing variances.

22.1 Standardizing a variable

Figure 22.3 shows DIT density plots of the male life expectancy variable from the world data in Chapter 24. The bottom density shows the raw data, which range from 40 to 75. The middle plot shows the same density after standardizing male life expectancy to have mean = 0 and standard deviation = 1. This was done by the SYSTAT command:

```
STANDARDIZE MALE / SD
```

The top plot shows the same density after standardizing so that the range of the data is 1. This was done by the SYSTAT command:

```
STANDARDIZE MALE / RANGE
```

All three plots are the same, except for the scale at the bottom of each. Some think that "standardizing" changes the shape of the data, perhaps because the transformed values, or **z-scores** (mean = 0, SD = 1) are associated with the normal distribution. Another reason for this mistaken belief may be that the shape of histograms is sensitive to the scale, so that people who look at typical histograms of their data before and after standardizing them may think something changed about the distribution because the histograms look different. Figure 24.35 in Chapter 24 shows this phenomenon. In any case, keep in mind that standardizing changes nothing but the scale on which the data are measured.

Why do people standardize data, then? There are several reasons. Social scientists often standardize data in order to compare measurements across groups. For example, an educator who grades "on the curve" wants to equate average test difficulty and range of difficulty for two different classes or tests. For example, a teacher may give the same test two different years and decide that the difference in average performance between the two classes is a nuisance. Under pressure to give roughly the same number of A's, B's, C's, and D's each year, the teacher standardizes the grades and then cuts the distribution at the same places each year. This method penalizes an outstanding class (and helps a poor class) but the procedure has a consistency about it that makes it attractive. Our experience teaching suggests that most teachers and professors tend to grade "on the curve" across years, although some may do it rather informally without resort to a computer. This is true, in our experience, even when other factors, such as grade inflation, contribute to a long-term trend in grades.

Another form of grading "on the curve" is to equate tests. That is, if a teacher gives three tests during a semester, he or she may decide to standardize each test and then average the standard scores. This gives each test equal weight in determining the final grade. Like standardizing across groups, this procedure involves inequities. Nevertheless, it prevents a single extremely difficult test passed by only one or two students, for example, from determining almost the entire final grade. Modern test theory (underlying, for example, the ACT's, College Boards, and Graduate Record tests) involves much more sophisticated methods of test equating, but this simple form of standardizing is still used widely.

Figure 22.1
Standardizing a Variable

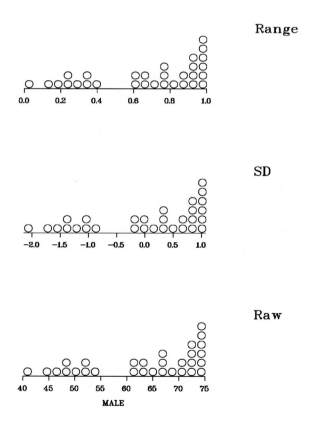

There is another type of standardizing (called "normalizing") that is illustrated in Figure 22.2. It really belongs in the next section of this chapter, but we'll discuss it here as a preview and to illustrate what some may think standardizing actually does (which it doesn't). This is a form of the **rankit transformation**.

First, we sort MALE. Next we calculate the rankits. These are taken from the inverse normal distribution function (ZIF) of the fractiles of the data: (CASE-.5)/N. Other fractiles could be computed, such as CASE/(N+1), but the smallest value may not be zero and the largest may not be 1. Then we rescale the numbers with the mean (63.333) and standard deviation (10.864).

The lower part of Figure 22.2 shows the histogram for our normalized data with a kernel overlaid. The kernel looks like a bell curve. If you did a probability plot (PPLOT) of these transformed values, it would show a straight line. That is not surprising, because the transformation used to produce the vertical scale of a PPLOT is the same as in Figure 22.2.

Stigler (1986) discusses the role that this transformation played in Francis Galton's theories on heredity. More than a century later, Galton's "statistical scale" continues to influence psychometrics and contemporary discussions of IQ (Herrnstein & Murray, 1994; Fienberg, Devlin, Resnick & Roeder, 1995).

22.2 Transforming a variable to look normal

If a variable is normally distributed, then we can use classical distributions like z, t, and F to make various inferences about the population mean and other parameters. Even if we are not making inferences, simple description using statistics like the mean (sample average) make more sense when the data are symmetric and lumpy in the middle. These reasons are why we seek transformations for data that look skewed to the left or right.

Figure 22.2
Normalizing a Variable

```
USE WORLD
SORT MALE
LET RMALE=63.333+10.864*ZIF((CASE-.5)/30)
BEGIN
DEN RMALE/HIST,XMIN=0,XMAX=100,BARS=15,YMAX=10
DEN RMALE/KERN,XMIN=0,XMAX=100,BARS=15,YMAX=10,AX=0,SC=0
END
```

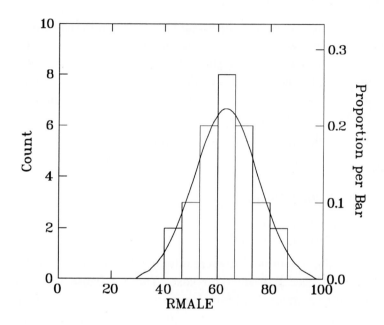

The ladder of powers

Tukey (1977) introduced an ordering of transformations from higher to lower powers which he called the **ladder of power transformations**. Figure 22.3 summarizes this ladder. The histogram labeled "xpow=1" (third down from the top) is sampled from a normal distribution and rescaled to have all positive values. The histograms at the bottom of the figure can be transformed to normality by one of the methods in the ladder, assuming the lowest values of the data are near zero. Let's look at them in more detail.

At the top of the ladder in the figure is a **cubic transformation**. In SYSTAT:

```
LET YNEW = Y^3
```

Next is the **quadratic transformation**:

```
LET YNEW = Y^2
```

These will transform histograms like the top two into ones like the third, namely a normal. The next transformation is "no transformation" because a value to the first power is itself.

The next lower on the ladder is the **square root transformation**:

```
LET YNEW = SQR(Y), or
LET YNEW = Y^.5
```

It will transform a positively skewed histogram, like the fourth one shown, into a normal. The square root of a variable is a common transformation for counts: the number of items produced in a manufacturing study, the number of bar-presses in animal research, or the number of tumor sites in a medical study. The square root does the opposite of the square. It shrinks the larger values much more than smaller values and reduces the right-hand tail of the frequency distribution.

The next one down is the **logarithmic transformation**:

```
LET YNEW =  LOG(Y)
```

If you prefer log to the base 10, use

```
LET YNEW = L10(Y), or
LET YNEW = LOG(Y)/LOG(10)
```

It's counterintuitive, but common statistical inferential procedures don't care whether you log to the base 10, base 2, or any other base. That's because logs turn multiplicative effects into additive effects, and different bases affect only the additive constant. Adding a constant value to your data (as in the linear transformation) does not change results for hypothesis tests. Also, if you're wondering how a logarithm can be equivalent to a power of zero (well, the neighborhood of zero), Tukey and Mosteller (1977) explain this in detail. Otherwise, trust us, it works.

The logarithmic transformation is frequently applied to growth data because growth is often proportional to the size of the population. That is, the percentage change is constant. Common data for a log transform are population growth, economic data, or death rates as a function of age. As a reshaping transform, logs are more powerful than square roots, shrinking the right-hand tail of the frequency distribution even more than the square root.

Logging is common in economics, where taking logs of both the independent and dependent variables has important theoretical implications for analysis of economic production functions. It implies a constant relationship between the percentage rate of change, called constant marginal elasticity, in the independent and dependent variables, for small changes.

Next come the **reciprocal transformations**:

```
LET YNEW = -1/Y^.5, and
LET YNEW = -1/Y
```

We've omitted higher powers in the denominator because you can see that the simple inverse (-1/Y) already transforms an extremely skewed distribution. The negative sign preserves the original order of the values, but it is not necessary as long as you keep in mind the direction of the relationship with other variables.

To find the appropriate transformation, plot a variable then compare your histogram to the histograms in Figure 22.3. In the middle column, you will find the appropriate transformation that makes the variable look Normal. Version 6 includes a popup graph tool that allows you to examine these transformations in real time. Just tap the button and the data replot themselves. This helps you hunt for a transformation visually and then code the value of the power for further analysis. It's not a video game, but it's worth a few giggles.

The arcsine transformation for proportions and percents

Proportions range between zero and one, producing a truncated distribution, nonconstant variance, and skewness when the mean is not near .5. Batches of proportions look like the leftmost histograms in the lower panel of Figure 22.3. When the population proportion is .5, a histogram of a batch of sample proportions looks like the normal histogram (pow=1). When the population proportion is near zero, sample histograms look positively skewed (e.g. pow=-1) and when it is near one, sample histograms look negatively skewed (e.g. pow=3).

The arcsine transformation stabilizes the variance and spreads the tails of the distribution. The arcsine transformation doesn't have a parameter to worry about (like power), so you can simply apply it with the command:

```
LET YNEW = 2*ASN(SQR(P))
```

where P is a proportion. Percentages can be converted to proportions by dividing by 100. Another name for this transformation is the angular or the inverse sine transformation.

If you have access to the original data from which the proportions were calculated, an improved arcsine transformation due to Freeman and Tukey (1950) is:

```
LET YNEW = .5*(ASN(SQR(X/(N+1)))+ASN(SQR((X+1)/(N+1))))
```

where X/N = P, a proportion.

Fisher's *z* transformation for correlation coefficients

Correlations range between -1 and 1, producing a truncated distribution, nonconstant variance, and skewness when the mean is not near .0. Batches of correlations look like the leftmost histograms in the lower panel of Figure 22.3. When the population correlation is 0, sample histograms look like the normal histogram (pow = 1). When the population correlation is near -1, sample histograms look positively skewed (pow = -1) and when it is near +1, sample histograms are negatively skewed (pow = 3).

Fisher's z transformation normalizes them in a transformation without extra parameters:

```
LET YNEW = ATH(R)
```

The function used is called the arc hyperbolic tangent. You should use this transformation regularly when doing statistical analyses on a batch of correlations. If the correlations are not skewed, the transformation will leave the shape unchanged. Otherwise, it will straighten out the skewness. This transformation will work adequately for other correlations derived from the Pearson, such as Spearman. It is even satisfactory for others which aren't, provided they range between -1 and +1.

Figure 22.3
Ladder of Power Transformations

Power P	SYSTAT BASIC	Name	Notes
P	Y^P	power	DOWN: shorten upper tail.
⋮	⋮	⋮	⋮
3	Y^3	Cube	Not commonly used.
2	Y^2	Square	The highest commonly used power.
—> 1	Y^1	Original data	No transformation.
1/2	Y^(1/2)	Square root	Commonly used for counts.
"0"	LOG(Y)	Logarithm	Commonly used for financial data.
-1/2	-1/Y^(1/2)	Reciprocal root	The minus sign preserves order.
-1	-1/Y	Reciprocal	Lowest commonly used power.
-2	-1/Y^2	Reciprocal square	
⋮	⋮	⋮	⋮
– P	-1/Y^P	Reciprocal power	UP: shorten lower tail.

Original Data   Transformed Data

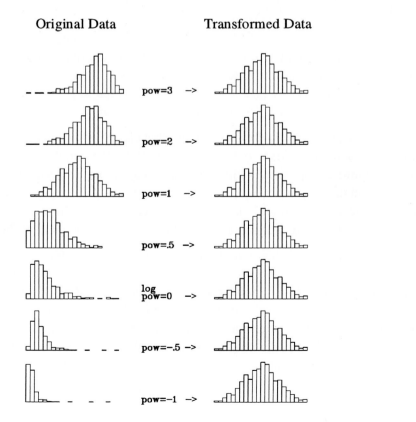

22.3 Transformations to linearize

Certain nonlinear functions can be made into linear ones by a simple transformation. For example, the function:

$$y = ax^b \varepsilon$$

can be linearized with a log function on both sides of the equation:

$$\log y = \log a + b \log x + \log \varepsilon$$

Now the parameters are different, but the function is linear and we can analyze it with a linear model routine. If data are generated with linearizable functions like this, then we can simplify things with a transformation.

Another example is the function:

$$y = b \log x + \varepsilon$$

By transforming x with a log, we can fit a curvilinear plot with a straight line.

The trick is to know whether this is plausible. In many fields, you will not have prior knowledge of the nonlinear function so you will have to use a scatterplot of the data or the residuals to help find a suitable transformation. The left column of Figure 22.4 gives some examples of how nonlinear relationships appear. We added a rough smoother to the plots (i.e. DWLS) to make the curvature clearer.

The first thing to notice in the figure about this class of functions is whether the error is multiplicative or additive. In the top three plots on the left, the errors are multiplicative; the points fan out to the right, so the residuals are **heteroscedastic**. In the bottom two plots on the left, the errors are additive; the points are homogeneous about the regression line, so the residuals are **homoscedastic**. The top three plots are representative of the first type of equation above and the last two are typical of the second.

Now, the text next to each plot indicates the transformation which produces the plot on the right. The multiplicative models respond to a log-log transformation and the additive models respond to a nonlinear transformation on x only. The particular transformation chosen depends on the shape of the curved line in the left plot. When you're exploring this kind of scatterplot to figure out a transformation, it's a good idea to use DWLS or LOWESS to fit a rough smoother so that you can concentrate on these two key points: 1) are the residuals heteroscedastic? and 2) what is the type of curvature (log, square, square root, inverse)? Note that each plot on the right looks like a good candidate for a linear model. We superimposed the regression line to make that clearer.

Figure 22.4
Transformations on Scatterplots

Original Data   Transformed Data

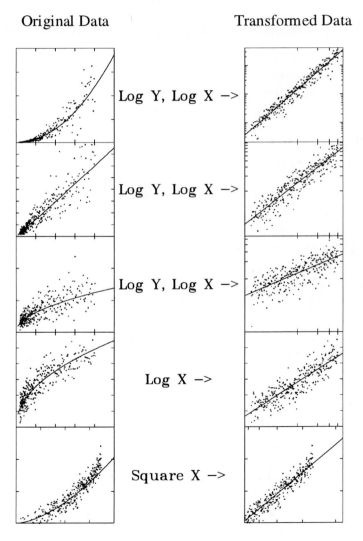

What do we do if we have more than one predictor? Our suggestion is to do pairwise scatterplots of *y* with each predictor (e.g. with SPLOMs).   If every one is heterosce-

dastic, consider logging all the variables. Otherwise, try logs on some and other transformations on the others. In the end, the most important final diagnostic tool is the
residuals plot. If you did everything right, the residuals of fit to the the transformed
data will look normally distributed and homogeneous across the predicted values.

22.4 Transformations for constant variance

For hypothesis testing in ANOVA, we require that the data have constant variance as
in regression. Heteroscedasticity can bias F-tests and produce artifactual (scale dependent) higher-order interactions. This makes the model more complex and harder to interpret. Correction of heteroscedasticity may permit a simpler interpretation at the level
of main effects or lower-order interactions.

Is heteroscedasticity present?

Heteroscedasticity in ANOVA is most easily seen in box plots. In the box plots, we
would like to see all boxes and all whiskers of about the same width. If some are substantially larger than others, then the data may be heteroscedastic. Figure 22.5 shows
a grouped box plot of the food data from Chapter 14. We have plotted the two-way
design of preparation (canned, fresh, frozen) by type of food (vegetable, fruit). The
boxes vary considerably across conditions. We should consider a transformation.

Figure 22.5
Food Dataset
Box Plot of PRICE by PREP by TYPE

```
USE  PRODUCE1
BOX  PRICE*PREP$  /  GROUP=TYPE$
```

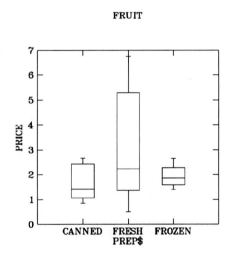

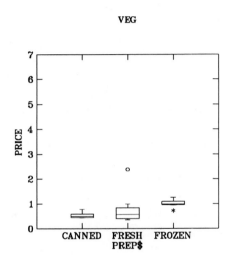

Which transformation?

A tool called a **spread-versus-level plot** can guide us to a transformation to remove heteroscedasticity. To use this tool, we must assume that the variance (or, more generally, the spread) changes with the level. A typical relationship is that the spread gets wider as the values of the variable become larger. If we remove the relationship between the level and the spread, then we have removed the heteroscedasticity. To see the relationship we can plot a measure of the level against a measure of spread.

Suppose, for example, we assume that the standard deviation of a variable is proportional to its mean. Then if we plot the logarithm of the mean against the logarithm of the standard deviation we should obtain a line. (For the mathematical derivation of why this is so, see the notes at the end of this chapter.)

The use of a spread-versus-level plot has four steps. First, find the level and spread of each of the groups. Second, plot the logarithm of the level against the logarithm of the spread. Third, if the plot looks linear, find the slope of the best fitting line. Finally, if b

is the slope of the spread-versus-level plot, then $P = 1 - b$ is an estimate of the power transformation which stabilizes the spread. As with other power transformations, if $P = 0$, use logarithms. (The family of power transformations is presented in Figure 22.3.)

Figure 22.6
Spread vs. Level Plot of Food Dataset

```
STATS
    USE PRODUCE1
    SAVE PROD / AG
    BY PREP$,TYPE$
    STATISTICS PRICE / MEAN,SD
    USE PROD
    LET LMEAN = LOG(ME1PRICE)
    LET LSD=LOG(SD1PRICE)
    PLOT LSD*LMEAN / SMOOTH=LINEAR,SHORT,XMIN=-3,XMAX=3,YMIN=-3,YMAX=3
```

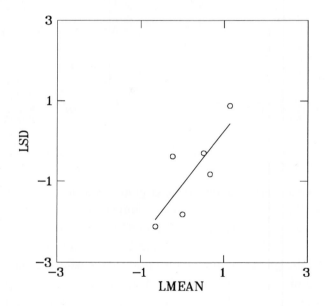

Figure 22.6 shows how to do this plot in SYSTAT. There are a few things to review. The AG option to SAVE in STATS saves the statistics in an aggregate format so that the mean and standard deviation can be on the same record. We do the calculations by both factors in the design (BY PREP$,TYPE$). The reason for the funny names for the means and standard deviations (ME1PRICE, SD1PRICE) is that the AG format allows many variables on the same record. The SYSTAT manual contains other examples of this convention. We then log the statistics and do the plot. The scales are fixed in order

to make the physical slope the same as the numerical. We've omitted the STATS output to save space.

Since the spread-versus-level plot in Figure 22.6 shows that the log of the mean and the log of the standard deviation are linearly related, we can use the slope of the line to find an estimate of the appropriate power transformation, P. Figure 22.7 gives the regression used to estimate the slope. Using the formula P = 1 - b and the estimate b = 1.337 from Figure 22.7, we find that P = -.337. As with other power transformations, if P = 0, use logarithms.

Figure 22.7
Computing Slope for Spread vs. Level Plot of Food Dataset

```
GLM
    MODEL LSD = CONSTANT + LMEAN
    ESTIMATE
```

The output is:

```
Dep Var: LSD N: 6 Multiple R:  0.796 Squared multiple R:  0.633

Adjusted squared multiple R:  0.542    Standard error of estimate:      0.739

Effect         Coefficient    Std Error    Std Coef Tolerance    t    P(2 Tail)

CONSTANT          -1.088         0.326        0.0         .      -3.339    0.029
LMEAN              1.337         0.508        0.796      1.000    2.629    0.058

                        Analysis of Variance

Source         Sum-of-Squares    DF   Mean-Square    F-Ratio    P

Regression          3.774        1       3.774        6.913     0.058
Residual            2.183        4       0.546
```

Regression transformations can also be found using spread-versus-level plots. Since regression variables are continuous, you will have to sort your data on a variable that is related to the heteroscedasticity. Heteroscedastic variances appear in many circumstances. One common circumstance occurs when they are related to some measure of the "size" of the cases; good candidates are variables that measure quantities like weight, height, income, expenses, production, population, speed, or other variables where the ratio of the smallest to the largest case is 1-to-100 or more. Then divide the sorted data into equal sized groups, as a rule of thumb at least 6 and preferably 8-10 groups. The remaining steps are identical to those we followed in the ANOVA example above. It is not always possible to find a transformation that stabilizes the variance of a regression model. A better alternative approach, weighted least squares, is presented in Section 6.4.

Keep several cautions in mind as you use spread-versus-level plots. First, they do not give you a transformation to correct all forms of heteroscedasticity. They work only when you can find some measure of spread (e.g. variance, standard deviation, interquartile range) which is proportional to some measure of level (e.g. mean, median). This is a common form of heteroscedasticity, but it is not the only form. See Judge et al. (1985, Chapter 11) for further discussion. Second, if the data in the spread-versus-level plot do not form a straight line, you may not be using the correct measure of spread. Try a different one. Third, means and measures based on them (e.g. variance, standard deviation) are sensitive to outliers. Correct outliers before you estimate the transformation. Finally, see Emerson (1991), Emerson and Strenio (1983) and Emerson and Stoto (1983) for other examples of the use of spread-versus-level plots in exploratory data analysis.

In addition to the spread-versus-level plot, several rules of thumb can help you choose a transformation. First, if the sample means seem approximately proportional to the variances, then a square root transformation often makes the variance constant. Second, if the sample means seem to be proportional to the standard deviation or to the range of each sample, then the log transform may be an effective way to stabilize the variance. Always check the results of the transformation. You will often need to try several transformations before deciding which is best.

In analysis of variance, you occasionally find that your data are from normally distributed populations but the variance is not constant. This is a serious problem because any transformation to make the variance homoscedastic also makes the data nonnormal. This is part of the Behrens-Fisher problem, and solutions to it are beyond the scope of this book. See Scheffe (1970) and Lee and Gurland (1975) for more information.

22.5 Conclusion

First, look at plots. Scatterplots, box plots, SPLOMS, and residuals plots reveal nonlinearity, while normal probability plots show non-normality. In both cases, the histogram and the ladder of power transformations (Figure 22.3) can be used to select a transformation. Scatterplots, especially residuals plots, also reveal heteroscedasticity. Spread-versus-level plots can help find a transformation to correct it.

Transformations have the greatest impact when the data deviate from a straight line in smooth envelopes. In addition, the minimum value should be near zero, and the ratio of the minimum value to the maximum value should be at least 2- or 3-to-1 before a transformation makes much difference. Sometimes you may want to subtract a constant from all values to increase this ratio. Under the best circumstances, interpretability may be improved and you may gain up to about 10% in explained variance by using the transformed data over the untransformed variables. On the other hand, irregular or multimodal data often cannot be fixed by a transformation. Furthermore, outliers and other pathological problems with your data can make the plots misleading or difficult to interpret. Clear up these problems before you try any transformations.

It is important to keep transformations in perspective. They are not a panacea for all the ills of your data. Draper and Smith caution:

> ...keep in mind that there is no guarantee that use of transformations will necessarily be better than analyzing the data on the original scale; much depends on the data. The effectiveness of a transformation is best assessed by trying it on the data and then checking the fit of the model and the resulting pattern of residuals (1981, p. 239).

Notes

Which transformation?

Here is a more mathematical discussion of why, when we assume the mean is proportional to the standard deviation, we actually plot the log of the mean against the log of the standard deviation. Mathematically our assumption of proportionality can be expressed as:

$$\text{mean} = c \, (\text{standard deviation})^b$$

Taking logarithms of both sides we obtain:

$$\log(\text{mean}) = \log(c) + b \log(\text{standard deviation})$$

If we let $Y = \log(\text{mean})$, $k = \log(c)$ and $X = \log(\text{standard deviation})$ we have:

$$Y = k + bX$$

This is the equation for a straight line. Thus, the logarithm of the mean is linearly related to the logarithm of the standard deviation. If you would like more mathematical details, see Emerson and Strenio (1983, especially Section 3D).

Further reading

Excellent discussions of the practice of transformation are in Mosteller and Tukey (1977), Tukey (1977), and Velleman and Hoaglin (1981). These books use the word "reëxpression" in place of transformation. A variety of more complex transformations are discussed in Atkinson (1985).

References

Atkinson, A. C. (1985). *Plots, Transformations, and Regression.* New York: Oxford University Press.

Box, G. E. P. & Cox, D. R. (1964). An analysis of transformations. *Journal of the Royal Statistical Society, Series B, 26*, 211-252.

Draper, N. & Smith, H. (1981). *Applied Regression Analysis* (2nd ed.). New York: John Wiley & Sons.

Emerson, J.D. (1991). Introduction to transformation. In D. C. Hoaglin, F. Mosteller & J. W. Tukey (Eds.), *Fundamentals of Exploratory Analysis of Variance* (pp. 365-400). New York: John Wiley & Sons.

Emerson, J. D. & Stoto, M. A. (1983). Transforming data. In D. C. Hoaglin, F. Mosteller & J. W. Tukey (Eds.), *Understanding robust and exploratory data analysis* (pp. 97-128). New York: John Wiley & Sons.

Emerson, J. D. & Strenio, J. (1983). Boxplots and batch comparison. In D. C. Hoaglin, F. Mosteller & J. W. Tukey (Eds.), *Understanding robust and exploratory data analysis* (pp. 58-96). New York: John Wiley & Sons.

Fienberg, S.E., Devlin, B., Resnick, D.P., and Roeder, K. (1995). *Heritability, IQ, and Life Outcomes.* New York: Springer Verlag.

Freeman, M. F. & Tukey, J. W. (1954). Transformations related to the angular and the square root. *Annals of Mathematical Statistics, 21*, 607-611.

Herrnstein, R.J. and Murray, C. (1994). *The Bell Curve: Intelligence and Class Structure in American Life.* New York: The Free Press.

Judge, G. G., Griffiths, W. E., Hill, R. C. & Lee, T. (1985). *The Theory and Practice of Econometrics* (2nd ed.). New York: John Wiley & Sons.

Lee, A. F. S. & Gurland, J. (1975). Size and power of tests for equality of means of two normal populations with unequal variances. *Journal of the American Statistical Association, 70,* 933-941.

Mosteller, F., & Tukey, J. W. (1977). *Data Analysis and Regression.* Reading, MA: Addison-Wesley.

Scheffe, H. (1970). Practical solutions for the Behrens-Fisher problem. *Journal of the American Statistical Association, 65,* 1501-1508.

Stigler, S.M. (1986). *The History of Statistics: The Measurement of Uncertainty Before 1900.* Cambridge: Harvard University Press.

Tukey, J. W. (1977). *Exploratory Data Analysis.* Reading, MA: Addison-Wesley.

Velleman, P. F. & Hoaglin, D. C. (1981). *Applications, Basics, and Computing of Exploratory Data Analysis.* Boston: Duxbury.

23

Similarity, Dissimilarity, and Distance

The last section of this book concerns three procedures: principal components analysis, cluster analysis, and multidimensional scaling. The mathematical foundations of these methods and the kinds of output they produce often make them appear very different from one another. Indeed, from these two perspectives they are quite distinct. For a data analyst, however, these procedures are similar in the forms of data they analyze and the kinds of questions they can help answer. Our goal in the this chapter will be to highlight these similarities and to give you some basic tools for creating and managing the data you will enter into these procedures. At the conclusion we will discuss some criteria for selecting the procedure that will best suit a given problem you may wish to analyze, and we will show you how different data structures are decomposed by these methods.

In the first section we will show the relation between a standard "variables-by-cases" rectangular file of the kind analyzed in most SYSTAT modules and the kind of "triangular" file analyzed in the procedures of this part of the book. In this section we will also point out some of the alternative ways that triangular files can be assembled, either indirectly from a given rectangular data set, or directly through data collection.

In a second section we will discuss how similarity may be measured. Understanding the issues can help you to avoid the inappropriate use of principal components and factor analyses. A third section covers dissimilarity and distance.

Finally, we discuss how measures of similarity respond to different data structures. Classical statistical procedures assume a flat file structure, with rows of independent observations on columns of variables. We discuss alternative data structures which are decomposed differently by multidimensional scaling, principal components, and cluster analysis.

23.1 Forms and sources of data

Characteristics of triangular files

Figure 23.1 contains performance data for five sporty cars. The data have been selected from various reviews in *Car and Driver* magazine. The variables are horsepower, torque, curb weight, rear axle ratio, and 0-60 mph acceleration.

Figure 23.1
Data and Correlation Matrix, Performance Data

HP	TORQUE	RATIO	WEIGHT	SIXTY	LABEL$
650	330	4.66	1950	3.6	Ferrari333
132	129	3.55	2190	8.4	Neon
370	422	3.08	3420	5.9	Mustang
170	167	4.45	3080	7.7	Saab900
240	225	3.15	3145	5.4	BMWM3

```
CORR
USE CARS
PEARSON HP..SIXTY
```

```
Pearson correlation matrix

                   HP       TORQUE      RATIO      WEIGHT      SIXTY
   HP           1.000
   TORQUE       0.717      1.000
   RATIO        0.403     -0.175      1.000
   WEIGHT      -0.381      0.262     -0.564      1.000
   SIXTY       -0.905     -0.685     -0.191      0.168      1.000

Number of observations: 5
```

For rectangular data like these, the rows usually represent objects of some sort. The columns usually represent attributes of the objects. Data in this form are said to be "row contingent" because once we know one value in a given row we have an expectation for other values in that row.

Many statistical procedures begin with data collected this way. For example, we might compute a matrix of correlation coefficients for our car data, as is shown at the bottom of Figure 23.1, and look among the 6 resulting coefficients to see whether horsepower and torque are related.

Two things happened when we moved from the usual "rectangular" to a "triangular" form of data. First, we collapsed one aspect of the information. The row (cars) information disappeared in order to provide the new view of column (attributes) information. Note that the triangular matrix contains no information about the *size* of the data base on which it was assembled—the resulting matrix would have the same basic form whether it came out of an analysis of 5 cars or 1,000. Second, our new triangular file contains data that are different from the ratings we started with. Each value is an measure of association that shows how strongly the information described by each original attribute follows the information in each of the other attributes.

Sources of triangular files

From columns of a rectangular file

We have already discussed the most common source of a triangular matrix. A rectangular file of variables and cases is the standard in most areas of data analysis. Figure 23.2 shows a display of the change we impose in moving from one form to the other.

Figure 23.2
Rectangular to Triangular Matrix

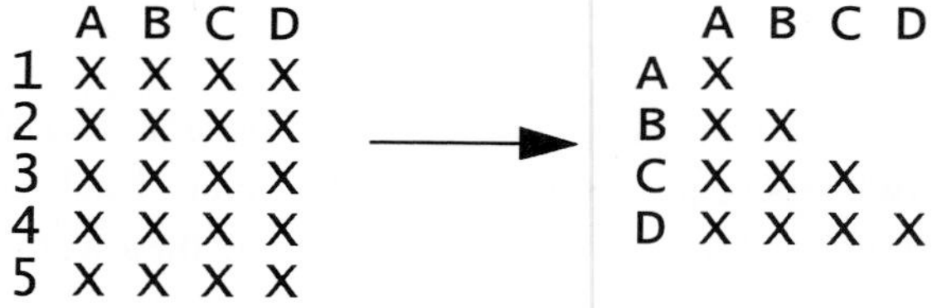

```
      A B C D                A B C D
  1   X X X X            A   X
  2   X X X X            B   X X
  3   X X X X    ⟶       C   X X X
  4   X X X X            D   X X X X
  5   X X X X
```

While this transformation is familiar, let's widen our understanding of the possibilities a bit. For example, there is no necessity for the data that start out in rows and columns to be the kinds of "objects" and "attributes" described above. One common example is a set of ratings in which a set of different objects are compared on a single attribute but by a number of different judges. The SYSTAT manual provides an example in the NPAR chapter where 20 women are ranked on mothering skill by each of 13 judges. In this situation a judge's ranking for one mother has a necessary consequence for his ranking for the others (once he gives out a 1, the average of all the others will be lower than the overall average rank, for example). Here it is the judgments of each judge that are distinct from those of the other judges. To be set up for a gamma rank correlation matrix, the judges must be entered as rows and the mothers as columns.

From rows of a rectangular file

To go a step further let's consider the cars example again. While we computed a correlation matrix for "attributes," it seems more likely that we would to want to know something about the associations among the "objects" (cars). Does a Neon perform like a Saab900? Can we rank order the cars over all the variables together?

Since SYSTAT performs correlations on columns, we need to TRANSPOSE our data. Figure 23.2 shows how this works.

Figure 23.3
Transposed Rectangular to Triangular Matrix

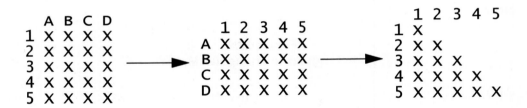

Notice that now the "case" information is preserved but the "variable" information is lost. Figure 23.4 shows this sequence for our CARS data. Exchanging rows and columns does nothing to change the constraints on how the data were collected. The data are still "car contingent," the cars are still the objects, even if the information is now stored by columns.

Figure 23.4
Correlation Matrix on Transposed CARS Data

```
USE CARS
TRANSPOSE
LIST / FORMAT=8,2
CORR
PEARSON
```

```
    * Case ID * Ferrari3    Neon  Mustang  Saab900    BMWM3
HP             650.00    132.00   370.00   170.00   240.00
TORQUE         330.00    129.00   422.00   167.00   225.00
RATIO            4.66      3.55     3.08     4.45     3.15
WEIGHT        1950.00   2190.00  3420.00  3080.00  3145.00
SIXTY            3.60      8.40     5.90     7.70     5.40

Pearson correlation matrix

            Ferrari333      Neon    Mustang    Saab900      BMWM3
Ferrari333       1.000
Neon             0.961     1.000
Mustang          0.973     0.997     1.000
Saab900          0.960     1.000     0.997      1.000
BMWM3            0.966     1.000     0.999      1.000      1.000

Number of observations: 5
```

Direct assessment of similarity

An alternate source of a triangular matrix is to collect similarity information directly. For example, we could find a group of "gearheads" at a local bar or race track and ask them to rate our five cars for similarity in performance. Or, we could put them on a race track for one lap and measure the distance between each pair of cars after the first crosses the finish line (although this matrix of pairwise distances would have only one underlying dimension). The value we assign to each comparison can be entered into a triangular matrix that has the same form as the correlation matrix computed on the transposed CARS data.

Chapter 21 on multidimensional scaling covers a variety of procedures for collecting similarity and dissimilarity data directly. Outside of psychology, these data can be found in tables of intercity distances, degrees of interaction among pairs of catalysts, and counts of genetic coincidences among species.

23.2 Standardizing data

Up to now, we have been computing our correlations on raw data. If we use raw scores for calculating similarity or distance measures, then variables with larger average absolute values (e.g. curb weight) will dominate others with smaller values (e.g. 0-60 time and gear ratio) in the calculations.

To make the influence of attributes or variables comparable, we can standardize them before calculating similarity or dissimilarity measures across them. To see how this makes a difference Figure 23.5 shows the result of standardizing before transposing.

Figure 23.5
Standardizing and Transposing Data

```
USE CARS
STANDARDIZE
TRANSPOSE
LIST FERRARI333..BMWM3 / FORMAT=8,2
CORR
PEARSON
```

```
    * Case ID * Ferrari3    Neon   Mustang  Saab900    BMWM3
   HP              1.61    -0.86     0.28    -0.68     -0.35
   TORQUE          0.63    -1.04     1.39    -0.73     -0.25
   RATIO           1.20    -0.31    -0.95     0.91     -0.85
   WEIGHT         -1.25    -0.88     1.03     0.50      0.60
   SIXTY          -1.36     1.15    -0.16     0.79     -0.42

Pearson correlation matrix

                 Ferrari333       Neon     Mustang     Saab900       BMWM3
   Ferrari333       1.000
   Neon            -0.511       1.000
   Mustang         -0.223      -0.551      1.000
   Saab900         -0.513       0.633     -0.644       1.000
   BMWM3           -0.579      -0.355      0.736      -0.114       1.000

Number of observations: 5
```

You *could* use a similar procedure to compute the correlations among performance measures after standardizing within cars. Simply transpose the matrix, standardize the cases, transpose it back and compute the correlations. Why don't we do this all the time before computing correlations? The answer is that when doing correlations among the columns of a file, we usually assume a flat file format in which the cases vary comparably. That is, we assume that none of the cases are multivariate outliers. For nonsampled data in which this is not true, we might want to consider standardizing rows before computing correlations across columns. Finally, some analysts standardize rows *and* columns. This is called double centering (and double scaling) a matrix.

Figure 23.6 shows the result of standardizing. Notice that standardizing makes comparisons across the profiles relative. The differences in the car profiles now tell us how the cars differ relatively on each attribute and comparably across all attributes.

Figure 23.6
Parallel Coordinate Plots of Raw and Standardized Car Data

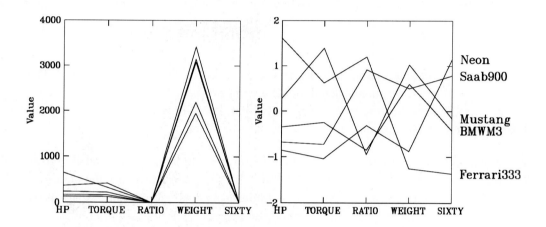

23.3 Similarity

As Figure 23.6 shows, our cars differ in two ways: they have different variability across attributes and they have different overall elevations or levels of attributes. Correlations are influenced by shape, but not by levels. Measures of mean differences across attributes are influenced by levels, but not by shape. Some methodologists describe correlations as poor measures of profile similarity because they only respond to shape. Measures are neither bad nor good in themselves, however. They summarize different aspects of data and are useful in different contexts.

We need to examine further how correlations measure similarity among profiles and, more generally, how other measures of similarity function. Cronbach and Gleser (1953), Sneath and Sokal (1973), and Clifford and Stephenson (1975) discuss these issues in more detail.

The Pearson correlation coefficient

The Pearson correlation coefficient between two profiles i and j (r_{ij}) is the mean product of the standardized profiles (z-scores). Some authors present an unnecessarily complicated formula for computing this coefficient. Our verbal description is all you need to remember. First, standardize profile i. To do this, you subtract the mean (level) of the profile across attributes and divide by the standard deviation (variability) of the profile across attributes. Then do the same for profile j. Finally, multiply the respective standardized values and average the products. As in computing mean square error for ANOVA, however, we lose a degree of freedom by standardizing. Thus, our average is computed by dividing by N - 1 rather than N:

$$r_{ij} = \Sigma\ z_i z_j / (N - 1)$$

Now, how did our calculations affect differences in profile level and variability? They were removed when we standardized the ith and jth profiles, subtracting the mean (level) and dividing by the standard deviation (variability). Thus, the Pearson correlation coefficient pays attention only to profile shapes.

As an exercise, try computing similarities of states using their crime statistics in the CRIME dataset. First, you need to TRANSPOSE the dataset to make the states columns. Then you can use the PEARSON command in CORR to compute Pearson correlations between states. With this method, two states with similar patterns of crime will appear similar even when their overall levels and variability of crime are different (e.g. California and Georgia).

The same issues apply if we are correlating variables instead of cases. For example, we might be interested in computing similarities of crimes (rather than states). To do this, we would use the PEARSON command on the file directly (no TRANSPOSE). Here, similar patterns across states would result in two crimes having a high correlation even when they have different means and standard deviations (e.g. MURDER and ASSAULT).

Other similarity and correlation coefficients

The Pearson correlation coefficient measures the linear association between two variables or cases. Other correlation coefficients respond to nonlinear association as well. "Nonparametric" coefficients such as Spearman's rho, Kendall's tau-b, and Goodman-Kruskal Gamma are invariant under rank transformations of the data. If you find that variables you are considering are not linearly related (after examining pairwise scatterplots or SPLOMS) then one of these nonmetric coefficients may be more useful than the Pearson correlation. The same issues concerning variability and level influencing the similarity apply to these coefficients as well. You can read more about these nonmetric coefficients in Chapter 2.

Cross products and covariances

The CORR module in SYSTAT can compute cross products between variables using the SSCP command. As we have seen, part of the computation of the Pearson correlation involves cross products on standardize values. SSCP computes products after subtracting out means (levels) but does not divide by standard deviations (variability). This means that SSCP measures of similarity will be influenced by variability between profiles. The COVAR command in CORR produces similar information, because covariances are cross products divided by $N - 1$, where N is the number of objects over which the measure is computed.

Cross products and covariances can be useful when you wish to pay attention to variability in profiles. Variability per se will not induce large covariances. Rather, similar profiles with large variability will be drawn together, and dissimilar profiles with large variability will be repelled. In this regard, covariances act like difference amplifiers relative to correlations.

Similarity measures for binary data

Any of the coefficients we have discussed can be computed on binary data, but there are several which apply solely to binary data. Various binary similarity measures differ on how they treat ignored (or zero) values.

The upper part of Figure 23.7 shows a schematic table of possible ratings for two cars. The letters in the cells represent the counts for each combination. Car i and car j were rated "1" a times, for example.

Figure 23.7
Similarity Measures for Binary Data

		J	
		1	0
I	1	a	b
	0	c	d

S2: a/(a+b+c+d)
S3: a/(a+b+c)
S4: (a+d)/(a+b+c+d)
S5: a/{a+2(b+c)}
S6: (a+d)/{a+2(b+c)+d}

The CORR module of SYSTAT contains the five similarity coefficients shown in the lower part of Figure 23.7. Each of these coefficients can have widely different values for the same data. S4 and S6, for example, include ignored values (0,0) in the numerator and thus count them as agreements. They would be suitable for data where the joint lack of an attribute (or failing to rate objects positively) is as much evidence of similarity as joint presence. S6 gives more weight to disagreements (0,1 and 1,0) than does S4, so disagreements reduce its magnitude more. S4, incidentally, is equivalent to one minus normalized squared Euclidean distance for binary data (see below). This means that you will get the same structures from binary data with S4 similarities or Euclidean distances in the MDS or CLUSTER modules. S3 and S5, on the other hand, exclude ignored values (0,0). They would be more suitable when we wish to consider ignored values as missing data. S5 gives more weight to disagreements than does S3, so disagreements reduce its magnitude more than S3's. Finally, S2 falls between these two extremes. Ignored values (0,0) *penalize* the coefficient as much as disagreements.

Which coefficient is right for your data? As with the others in this chapter, the answer to this question depends on your goals, your analysis, and your data. The techniques which depend on similarity coefficients (e.g. cluster analysis, multidimensional scaling) simply map your data into a geometric or hierarchical representation. One or another coefficient will emphasize a different structure in your data. It is up to you to decide which structure you wish to reveal.

23.4 Dissimilarity

We have been discussing similarity measures. Sometimes, we want to represent relations by *dissimilarity* instead. In a trivial sense, dissimilarities are the opposites of similarities, so we can transform similarities into dissimilarities by multiplying by -1 or inverting them:

$$d_{ij} = -s_{ij}$$
$$d_{ij} = 1/s_{ij} \qquad (s > 0)$$

Some dissimilarity measures are produced by these types of transformations of similarity measures. Some of the references we cited in the Similarity section discuss these formulas. We want to focus on a particular class of dissimilarity measure, however: distances. We use the term "distance metric" for a measure on objects which satisfies the following three conditions:

1.　　$d_{ij} => 0$; $d_{ii}=0$; $d_{jj}=0$

2.　　$d_{ij} = d_{ji}$

3.　　$d_{ij} <= d_{ik} + d_{jk}$

The last condition is often called the "triangle inequality" because i, j, and k are easily seen as points on the vertices of a triangle. We usually measure distances in our three-dimensional physical world in a way which is consistent with these three rules. Sometimes, however, directly measured or derived dissimilarity data fail to meet these conditions. In these cases, we cannot appropriately call them distances and should not represent them in a metric spatial model such as multidimensional scaling.

Euclidean distances

Several methods for deriving dissimilarities from rectangular matrices produce metric distances. The most popular is Euclidean distance, which follows our three rules when applied to real data. Euclidean distances are root squared differences. In order to keep the size of the numbers reasonable for large profiles, the SYSTAT CORR module uses normalized Euclidean distances, namely, root *mean* squared distances. For correlations, we standardized profiles i and j and computed cross products before meaning. For Euclidean distances, we do not compute products of standardized profiles, but rather square *differences* between profiles i and j before meaning and rooting. If we did standardize the profiles, then Euclidean distances would be an inverse transformation of Pearson correlations. Thus, the dissimilarity measure

$$d_{ij} = 1 - r_{ij}$$

is proportional to the Euclidean distance between i and j if the ith and jth profiles are standardized. The results of a cluster analysis or multidimensional scaling using either of these measures would be identical. If our profiles are not standardized, however, substantial differences between Euclidean distances and Pearson correlations can occur.

Non-Euclidean distances

There are many other measures which qualify as distance metrics. For our purposes, we will consider one simple one: the city block metric. This distance measure is simply the sum of the absolute differences between profiles.

City block and Euclidean distance differ in a simple way. Suppose we ask a pedestrian and a crow to measure the distance from Times Square to Gracie Mansion in New York City. The crow would fly diagonally northeast while the pedestrian would have to walk east and north along fixed streets and avenues. Thus, city block distance weights each leg of the trip (absolute value of profile difference) equally, while Euclidean distance emphasizes larger legs (profile differences) relative to smaller because it is squaring the discrepancies before summing them.

The CORR module has a command called CITY for computing these distances. As with Euclidean distances, SYSTAT normalizes the distances by dividing by the number of objects in the profile over which the discrepancies were computed.

23.5 Data structures and models

Cluster analysis, multidimensional scaling, and principal components all provide different views of the same data. Each interacts differently with different data structures. Researchers who have a pet procedure (say, factor analysis or MDS) and run their data exclusively through that procedure often fail to detect these simple patterns and end up reporting artifacts.

We have assembled in Figure 23.8 a set of illustrations showing these differences. The top row shows typical data matrices in shaded format. This shading resembles the output found in the JOIN/MATRIX option of the CLUSTER module. Larger absolute numerical values correspond to darker shades. The rows and columns of these matrices have been permuted to reveal the structures of interest. We assume the columns and rows have been standardized to comparable scales. You can often detect these patterns directly by standardizing your data and running them through JOIN/MATRIX, but not always. Sometimes it is necessary to examine the pattern of correlations and MDS and principal components output to be sure.

The second row shows the correlation matrices corresponding to each of these data types. They are shaded similarly, with solid black indicating a correlation of 1 and white indicating 0. The diagonal stripes in the BAND correlation matrix denote negative correlations.

The remaining rows show the analyses of the data. Since our data contain a tiny amount of noise, the solutions are not perfectly regular. The third row shows two-dimensional multidimensional scaling solutions based on these correlation matrices as similarity data input. The fourth row shows the same thing for principal components, and the final row, cluster analysis. The columns of the original data matrices, or row/columns of the correlation matrices, have been labeled with the first ten letters of the alphabet. For the cluster trees, the branches are in alphabetical order from top to bottom. Note that these are clusters of variables, not cases.

Figure 23.8
Data Structures

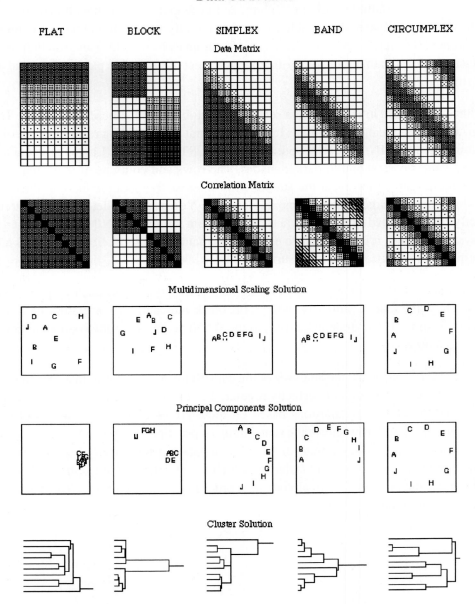

Flat data structures

We use the term **flat** to describe the horizontal orientation of the data values. Do not confuse this term with the descriptor "flat file," which simply describes a rectangular data file in general. This data structure is frequently analyzed via popular statistical procedures.

Notice that this structure produces an equi-correlation matrix. That is, all the values off the diagonal are comparable. If the correlations are large, as in this example, then the structure resembles what Spearman sought in his concept of a single intelligence factor (see Chapter 20 on factor analysis). If all the correlations are very small, then the matrix is essentially noise.

The single factor structure of this example is confirmed in the principal components plot: all the loadings are on a single dimension. The principal components or factor representation is parsimonious for this data structure.

The same cannot be said for the MDS plot. It is essentially noise because MDS attempts to scale the inverses of the correlations (dissimilarities) as distances between points. Since all the correlations are comparable, the structure cannot fit in as few as two dimensions. MDS is not a parsimonious representation for these data.

Finally, the cluster tree is noisy as well. There are no clear clusters of variables in these data, so all branches join near the right of the tree.

Block data structures

Block data structures are frequently encountered in experiments or cross-sectional data from different groups. Figure 23.8 shows a special case of this structure: the blocks of variables in the columns are statistically independent. This is revealed in the pattern found in the correlation matrix below. The correlations show a staircase pattern. Correlation matrices with this pattern have been described as "multitrait-multimethod" matrices (Campbell and Fiske, 1959) in psychology.

The principal components solution captures the block structure among variables well. Since there are two independent blocks, the loadings fall along two axes separated approximately 90 degrees. Thurstone called this type of pattern a "simple structure."

As with the flat structure, MDS fails to represent this simple structure parsimoniously. The blocks do appear as fairly tight clusters, but MDS attempts to fit all the correlations and is "confused" by the noisy variation in the within-cluster correlations.

Finally, the cluster solution shows two clear clusters. They join at the far right of the tree to produce the last cluster. The cluster solution, like the principal components one, is a parsimonious representation of these data.

Simplex data structures

This structure has been known in the social sciences as the **simplex** (Guttman, 1944). It also underlies unidimensional scales in other fields. In educational testing and psychology it is related to the **latent trait** (e.g. Lazarsfeld and Henry, 1968; Rasch, 1960; Lord & Novick, 1968; Bock, 1975; Goodman, 1978). In probability and statistics, it is related to a **Markov process** (e.g. Anderson, 1960). Morrison (1976) discusses other examples. In all these cases, the underlying structure is one dimensional, a simple scale. The structure arises when the variables (columns) are ordered on a scale, such as time, complexity, space, ability, intensity, etc., and when the observations (rows) can be ordered on the same scale.

Notice that the correlation matrix has a simple banded pattern. Variables near each other are correlated highly and those at the extremes are correlated near zero. You can often detect this structure by computing the correlation matrix and running it through the JOIN/MATRIX option of CLUSTER.

The MDS solution is almost perfectly one dimensional. There is a slight bending at the extremes because of noise when we scale it in two dimensions, but with simplexes it is often a good idea to scale in two dimensions anyway to see if the bending is extreme or other than a slight horseshoe shape like this. MDS is clearly a parsimonious spatial representation for these data.

The principal components (or factor analysis) solutions of simplex structures are generally confusing. In this example, the data align on the edge of a semicircle, suggesting two dimensions when only one is needed to reproduce the structure. When there are more variables, the dimensionality of the principal components or factor solutions increases. For some simplex data, there can be almost as many principal components or factors as there are variables. In short, simplexes are easily disguised in principal components or factor solutions, and multiple factor solutions are frequently published where the author fails to recognize this unidimensional structure (e.g. Adkins, 1973). In these cases, higher dimensional factors are simply artifacts.

The cluster solution, if we try to search for clusters, is similarly misleading. Notice that the cluster structure simply shows each variable joining the last in turn, allowing for some noise in our data. In fact, the shape of the cluster structure is reminiscent of the original data. This is because SYSTAT sorts the branches according to similarity between the objects they represent.

Band data structures

This structure, like the simplex, pops up in various fields. Thurstone (1927) proposed a model of comparative judgments which involved this type of scale. Coombs and Avrunin (1977a,b) presented a similar model for preferences. Coombs, Dawes, and Tversky (1970) described several other varieties of this single peaked response function. Like the simplex, it is intrinsically one-dimensional. While the simplex has a monotonically increasing function relating rows and columns, the band structure has a single peaked function relating them. Figure 23.9 shows how five variables align on simplex and band scales. You can discern these two structures by running your eye down the columns of the SIMPLEX and BAND matrices in the figures and noticing how the intensity (darkness) of the values increases and decreases.

Band structure matrices occur in preference data. If objects are ordered along the rows of a matrix and judges along the columns, for example, then the dark areas of the matrix depict which objects are preferred by each judge. The also occur with spectrographic data. The rows represent points along a spectrum and the columns represent objects which differ in their spectral sensitivity.

Notice that the correlation matrices of simplex and band structure data are quite similar. The only difference is that the correlations in the band structure matrix run from large positive along the diagonal to large negative in the corners. For the simplex, they run from large positive to zero on the corners. The circumplex correlation matrix seems similar also, but these correlations run from large positive on the diagonal to zero and back to large positive in the corners.

The MDS solution is the same for the simplex and band datasets, even though the correlation matrices are somewhat different. This is because the rank orders of the correlations in the cells of both correlation matrices are the same, even though some of those in the band correlation matrix are negative. For simplex, the correlations are scaled between 0 and 1, while for band, they are scaled between -1 and 1. Nonmetric MDS pays attention only to the rank order of the correlations.

Figure 23.9
Simplex and Band Data Scales

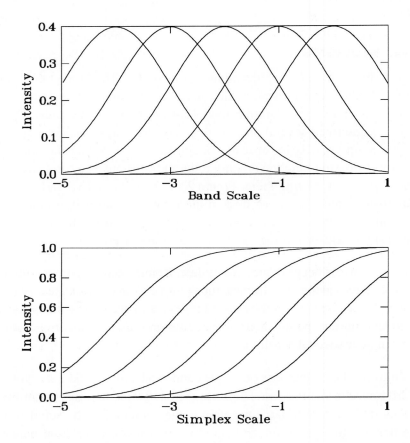

The principal components solutions are comparable after a 90 degree rotation. As with the simplex model, however, the components (or factors) conceal the essentially one-dimensional layout of the data.

Finally, the cluster analysis follows the shape of the original data matrix, although clusters are not discernible because they are not present in the data. The single peaked form is apparent in the triangular layout. As with the simplex cluster tree, this pattern will not be discernible with other cluster programs because only SYSTAT sorts the branches according to similarity.

Circumplex data structures

Guttman (1954) called this structure a circumplex because it represents a circular ordering. Many multivariate circular statistics involve this type of data structure. The SYSTAT manual MDS chapter contains an example involving color perception. LaForge and Suszek (1951), found this structure in personality ratings, which became known popularly as the Leary Interpersonal Circle (Timothy Leary's nonpharmacological contribution to personality psychology).

The correlation matrix shows a cyclic pattern moving from the diagonal to the off-diagonal corners. This reflects the barber-pole pattern in the original data. Both the principal components and MDS solutions reproduce this circular pattern perfectly. The cluster solution, on the other hand, is noisy and not of any use.

23.6 Conclusion

The outline of this book might lead you to suspect that doing data analysis is a matter of identifying what type of variables you have (*nominal, ordinal, interval, ratio*) and then finding the appropriate statistical procedure for analyzing them. Indeed, there are some "artificial intelligence" programs and statistics packages which ask you a few questions about your data and then spit out recommended analyses. If you have "ordinal" variables, for example, these packages won't let you do so-called "interval" analyses.

This methodological nonsense, promulgated by uncritical disciples of Stevens (1946), was debunked in the early 1950's in an entertaining note by Frederick Lord (1953). If statistical methodology could be pigeonholed into stereotypes of Stevens' measurement categories as easily as some introductory statistics texts suggest, there would be no statisticians left in the world. Most statistical procedures developed since the early 1950's, including the entire field of robust statistics, do not fit Stevens' typologies. Velleman and Wilkinson (1993) discuss the history of this issue and its relevance to computer software.

Furthermore, we have seen in this chapter that widely accepted methods, such as MDS and factor and cluster analysis, can conceal important structures in your data if used uncritically. We cannot emphasize too strongly the relevance of Figure 23.8. This is only a *sample* of the types of data structures which can be concealed in thoughtless analyses based on inappropriate models. If nothing else, we hope you remember the following. If someone approaches you touting a nifty new procedure – hierarchical linear modeling, latent variable causal modeling, catastrophe theory, qualitative analysis, chaos theory – without knowing or at least looking at your data first, *run*. And don't look back. With methodological friends like that, you won't need enemies. Data do not exist to show off new statistical methods. Statistical methods are for exploring and learning about data.

Notes

The methodological issues discussed in this chapter are not found in most statistics books. The classic book by Coombs (1964) is out of print, but it is worth locating in a library if you want to pursue these issues more thoroughly. Jacoby (1990) summarizes some of these issues in briefer form.

References

Adkins, D. (1973). A simpler structure of the American Psychological Association. *American Psychologist, 28*, 47-54.

Anderson, T.W. (1960). Some stochastic process models for intelligence test scores. In K.J. Arrow et al. (eds.), *Mathematical Methods in the Social Sciences*. Stanford, CA: Stanford University Press, 205-220.

Bock, R.D. (1975). *Multivariate Statistical Methods in Behavioral Research*. New York: McGraw-Hill.

Campbell, D.T., and Fiske, D.W. (1959). Convergent and discriminant validation by the multitrait-multimethod matrix. *Psychological Bulletin, 56*, 81-105.

Clifford, H. and Stephenson, W. (1975). *An Introduction to Numerical Taxonomy*. New York: Academic Press.

Coombs, C.H. (1964). *A Theory of Data*. New York: John Wiley & Sons, Inc.

Coombs, C.H., and Avrunin, G.S. (1977a). A theorem on single-peaked preference functions in one dimension. *Journal of Mathematical Psychology, 16*, 261-266.

Coombs, C.H., and Avrunin, G.S. (1977b). Single-Peaked functions and the theory of preference. *Psychological Review, 84*, 216-230.

Coombs, C. H., Dawes, R.M., and Tversky, A. (1970). *Mathematical Psychology: An Elementary Introduction.* Englewood Cliffs, NJ: Prentice-Hall, Inc.

Cronbach, L. and Gleser, G. (1953). Assessing similarity between profiles. *Psychological Bulletin, 50*, 456-473.

Goodman, L.A. (1978). *Analyzing Qualitative/Categorical Data.* Cambridge, MA: Abt Books.

Guttman, L. (1944). A basis for scaling qualitative data. *Americal Sociological Review*, 139-150.

Guttman, L. (1954). A new approach to factor analysis: The radex. In P.F. Lazarsfeld (ed.), *Mathematical thinking in the social sciences.* New York: Free Press.

Jacoby, W.G. (1990). *Data Theory and Dimensional Analysis.* Beverly Hills: Sage Publications. Inc.

Lazarsfeld, P.F. and Henry, N.W. (1968). *Latent Structure Analysis.* Boston: Houghton Mifflin.

Lord, F.(1953). On the statistical treatment of football numbers. *American Psychologist, 8*, 750-751.

Lord, F., and Novick, M.R. (1968). *Statistical Theories of Mental Test Scores.* Reading, MA: Addison-Wesley.

Morrison, D.F. (1976). *Multivariate Statistical Methods.* New York: McGraw-Hill.

Rasch, G. (1960). *Probabilistic Models for some Intelligence and Attainment Tests.* Copenhagen: The Danish Institute for Educational Research.

Sneath, P. and Sokal, R. (1973). *Numerical Taxonomy.* San Francisco: W.H. Freeman.

Stevens, S. S. (1946). On the theory of scales of measurement. *Science, 103*, 677-680.

Thurstone, L.L. (1927). A law of comparative judgment. *Psychological Review, 34*, 273-286.

Velleman, P.F., and Wilkinson, L. (1993). Nominal, ordinal, interval, and ratio typologies are misleading for classifying statistical methodology. *The American Statistician, 47*, 65-72.

24

Graphics

We've used a lot of graphs in this book, but we haven't discussed graphs *per se*. That is, what do you do when the goal of the analysis is to display the data as a graph. This chapter is a brief addition to the SYSTAT manual's discussion of cognition, plus some pointers on creating graphs with the programming system in SYSTAT. We cannot cover all the presentation graphs in SYSTAT itself. There isn't even room here to cover all the options of particular graph types. Instead, we intend to give you examples which illustrate methods which are not obvious in the SYSTAT manual and which can guide you toward exploring the capabilities of the graphics programming system.

We will begin with a section on the psychology of graphics. This section is intended as a supplement to the SYSTAT manual discussion, "Cognitive Science and Graphic Design." Then the following sections will cover typical graphs for the types of variables on which the major parts of this book are based: categorical, continuous, and mixed categorical-continuous. Finally, we will cover more advanced graphs and programming methods.

We have deliberately included several fairly complex programs. Only a few SYSTAT users have fully explored the graphics programming capabilities of SYSTAT. They have produced graphs which look entirely different from the ones in the manual. The graphs in this chapter may give you some ideas for some yourself.

Figure 24.1 contains data on birth rates, death rates, male and female life expectancies, type of government and a measure of urbanization for selected countries. These U.N. data are adapted from the OURWORLD dataset in the SYSTAT manual. We will use them for a number of the graphs in this chapter.

Figure 24.1.
World Health Statistics

COUNTRY$	BIRTH	DEATH	MALE	FEMALE	GOV$	URBAN$
Finland	13	10	71	80	Democracy	city
France	14	9	73	82	Democracy	city
Spain	11	8	75	82	Democracy	city
UK	14	11	73	79	Democracy	city
Italy	10	9	74	81	Democracy	city
Sweden	13	11	75	81	Democracy	city
Hungary	12	13	67	75	OneParty	city
Germany	11	11	72	79	Democracy	city
Gambia	48	18	46	50	Democracy	rural
Iraq	46	7	66	68	OneParty	city
Ethiopia	45	15	49	52	Military	rural
Guinea	47	22	40	44	Military	rural
Mali	51	21	45	47	OneParty	rural
Libya	37	7	65	70	Military	city
Somalia	47	15	53	54	OneParty	rural
Sudan	44	14	51	55	Democracy	rural
Turkey	29	8	64	67	Military	city
Algeria	37	9	61	64	OneParty	city
Yemen	52	17	48	49	Military	rural
Argentina	20	9	67	74	Democracy	city
Barbados	18	8	73	77	OneParty	city
Bolivia	35	13	52	56	Democracy	city
Brazil	26	7	62	68	Democracy	city
Canada	14	7	74	81	Democracy	city
Chile	21	6	70	77	Military	city
CostaRica	28	4	74	79	Democracy	city
Ecuador	30	7	64	68	Democracy	city
Jamaica	21	5	75	79	OneParty	city
Haiti	45	16	52	55	Military	rural
Trinidad	28	6	69	74	Democracy	city

24.1 Psychology and Graphics

Before we try some graphs, let's review some of the basic issues in graphing. Wilkinson summarized in the SYSTAT manual some principles of cognition bearing on the design of graphs. If you haven't read that chapter, you might want to do so before reading this. Here, under the heading of a few popular slogans (not), are some additional issues. We're playing devil's advocate to make a point.

A Picture is not worth a 1000 words

The "1000 word picture" shibboleth continues to appear in discussions of graphic design, graphic user interfaces (GUI's), and scientific visualization. Favorite "straw man" examples are presentations of a table of numbers alongside a graph of the same data, or a listing of a complex computer program next to a flowchart or object diagram. In fact, this popular notion doesn't fit common sense, and there is no sound psychological theory to support it.

Common sensical? Don't we feel pictures are richer, deeper, more packed with content, than words? Many of us do, and that is a result of our culture, individual differences, and even our religion. The Shema in the Bible, "Hear, O Israel, The Lord our God is One," has elicited more commentary and conveys more "meaning" than the Sistine Chapel ceiling. Judaism isn't the only religion of words. Islam's visual arts are abstract and subservient to the verbal text of the Q'uran.

How about psychology? Well, it turns out that research indicates that the processing of sounds and verbal information is at least as complex as the processing of visual images. Visual stimuli are encoded by the sensory system in ways that can be modelled by a Fourier decomposition similar to what we discussed in Chapter 18. The same appears to be true for sounds. Visual and aural signals, by the time they reach the cortex, are multidimensional. Those who have said that vision is multidimensional and hearing is unidimensional, or that vision is parallel and hearing is serial are not laboratory psychologists. As for words input visually, current research indicates that reading is a parallel process as well.

For our purposes, we simply need to keep in mind that a graph has its uses. Sometimes it is better to convey our information in a graph, sometimes in numbers or words. It depends on our purpose, our hearers/viewers, and the data themselves. There are no absolutes.

The mind is not a video camera

The mind is many things, but it is not a device to hold pictures. Visual information is not stored more permanently, reliably, or efficiently than other information. Visual data may indeed by stored differently than verbal, but it is clearly not stored as pictures. There is considerable abstraction and compression before visual information is retained. And when visual information is retrieved, it is reconstructed from components which can cause significant distortion of the original scene.

If the visual system were a video camera, we could assume that the most detailed graph could be remembered forever. Eyewitness testimony tells us otherwise. Instead, we need to design graphs differently when they are to be remembered after a quick viewing than when they are to be analyzed at leisure (Wilkinson and McConathy, 1992).

The eye is not the royal road to the brain

Because computer interfaces are primarily visual nowadays, many are fond of invoking cognitive psychology to justify this status quo. We are constantly told by some computer interface designers that visual interfaces are "closer" to the way people think and feel than command interfaces, that graphs and icons are easier to understand than numbers and words. In fact, the eye is one road to the brain, but there are many others which are equally "effective." Which pathway works best for a particular purpose can vary from individual to individual.

Much of the current thinking about graphics being the best way to communicate with the brain derives from a popularization of 1970's cognitive psychology. It is commonly noted that cognitive psychologists overthrew a dominant paradigm underlying empirical psychology: behaviorism. This is only partly true, but more important for our purposes is another paradigm that even some cognitivists *think* they overthrew: individual differences. The measures and methodologies cognitive researchers used (reaction times, errors, protocol analysis, between subjects designs) and their subjects (mostly college sophomores) tended to mask individual differences in performance and strategies. Psychologists are once again noticing that people vary in the way they process information. This is not just a "left brain/right brain" issue, for that too is an oversimplification. Innate and learned strategies make some of us prefer graphical input while others prefer linguistic, numerical, or even sound and tactile input. We need to be aware of this when we present data or design computer interfaces.

Less is not more

Edward Tufte, in a pioneering book on graphic design (Tufte, 1983), introduced a clever index called the "data-ink ratio." At least one computer program now includes this index as a feature. The less ink needed to display variation in data, according to Tufte, the better. Figure 24.2 shows an example of this principle: Tufte's redesign of Tukey's box plot. The lower panel of the figure shows a Tukey schematic plot of birth rates for selected countries. The plot directly above, which looks like horizontal lines with a dot in the middle, is Tufte's revision. The dot marks the median; only the whiskers are drawn. Tufte uses white space (taking advantage of figure/ground contrast) to mark the central 50 percent of the data.

Tufte evidently did not consider important that Tukey's central box gives visual weight to the middle 50% of the data. He is correct in pointing out that the box plot is intrinsically one-dimensional. In his desire to simplify, however, Tufte removed a valuable redundant cue that was intended to give weight to the center. Tufte's plot contains the same essential information but conveys a different message.

This is a well-known principle of cognitive psychology. Redundant relevant cues (up to a point) enhance learning. Only irrelevant cues that vary in such a way as to elicit incorrect hypotheses, impede performance. Tufte undoubtedly has the latter in mind when he assails "chart junk." But the data-ink ratio alone is not a useful criterion for judging the effectiveness of graphs.

If anything, the box plot could use some additional features because it does not reveal bimodality and other distributional anomalies. The dot-box plot, shown at the top of the figure, helps with this problem. Its data-ink ratio might be considered high because it contains a separate symbol for every data value as well as the ink needed for the box plot. But the components are additive. The box gives us the (approximate) quartiles *and* the dots give us the data.

Can *irrelevant* cues be harmless? Yes, if they can be ignored. The psychologist Ian Spence (1990) conducted a series of experiments in which he tested the effects of irrelevant cues in graphical perception. He created 3D "chart junk" versions of ordinary 2D bar charts and found that subjects could easily ignore irrelevant 3D cues to judge rapidly and correctly the quantitative information. In short, "chart junk" may be ugly, but it does not necessarily interfere with or bias judgments. Tufte has a fine eye for good design and we tend to prefer the kind of quantitative graphs he does. But this is a matter of aesthetics, not psychology.

Figure 24.2.
Variations on the Box Plot

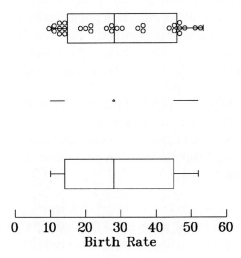

24.2 Graphing categorical variables

The following examples, from simple to complex, show how to display one or more categorical variables in a single plot. The graphical elements we will feature in this section are bars, lines, pyramids, dots, and tiles. These graphs are all alternatives to tables of numbers, such as frequency tables and cross-tabs. We will add options succesively so that you can see how complex graphs are built from simpler components.

One categorical variable

Figure 24.3 shows a bar graph of the counts of number of countries in each type of government category. Notice that SYSTAT automatically produces the vertical count axis when only one variable is supplied. Since the variable GOV$ has character values, these are displayed on the horizontal axis, slanted to avoid collisions. If your variable is numeric rather than character, you can use the LABEL command to add value labels for the categories.

Figure 24.3
Bar Graph of Types of Government

BAR GOV$

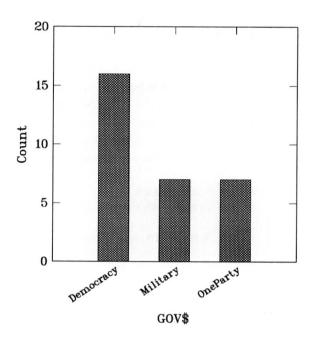

Figure 24.4
Bar Graph with Error Bars

BAR GOV$/SERROR=.95,FILL=.5,YMAX=25,HEI=2IN,WID=3IN

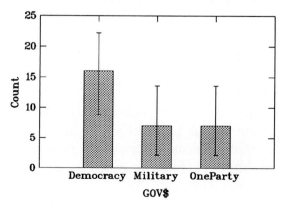

Figure 24.4 shows a bar graph of the counts of number of countries in each type of government category. We have added standard error bars (SERROR=.95) to give us an idea of the variability in the counts that we would expect to see in repeated samplings of data from a population (countries of the world) with these proportions in the government categories. We picked .95 to specify a 95 percent confidence interval on the counts. Incidentally, the sampling theory for these data might be dubious, since we are dealing with a finite population of countries of the world. With the way countries come and go nowadays, however, the theory might be less smarmy than it first appears! Finally, we reduced the fill gradient to .5 in order to let the error bars show through, and we modifies the height and width of the graph to save room. Often with bar graphs, you might want to change the **aspect ratio** (ratio of the physical height to width) this way in order to handle more categories on the horizontal (X) axis.

Figure 24.5
Line Graph with Error Bars

```
LINE GOV$/SERROR=.95,YMAX=25,HEI=2IN,WID=3IN
```

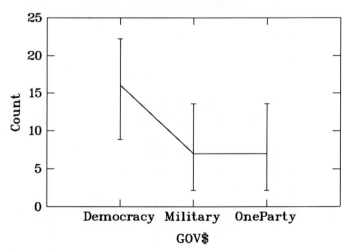

Figure 24.5 shows the same data with lines instead of bars. Why use lines? Lines emphasize slope, and therefore change from category to category. If this is of interest, rather than the absolute value of the counts, then you might want to consider lines. You can also use pies, dots, pyramids, or profiles to display the same data. Simply substitute PIE, DOT, PYRAMID, or PROFILE for LINE.

Two categorical variables

Now let's consider two variables instead of one. If we were tabulating data, we would produce a cross-tab of the two variables, showing the counts of each combination of values in the data. Figure 24.6 shows a pyramid graph representing type of government and the measure of urbanization against each other. The heights of the pyramids represent the counts in each cell. Notice that the command includes a leading period (.) to represent the count. If we had left this out, we would have gotten a pyramid plot of the values of GOV$ against URBAN$ rather than the counts of their combinations. We didn't need this for the one-way plots above because there was no ambiguity in the command, although it would have done no harm to insert a period there as well (e.g. BAR .*GOV$).

If you want to experiment, you can try other types of 3-D categorical plots by substituting BAR, LINE, DOT, or PROFILE for PYRAMID.

Figure 24.6
Pyramid Plot of Two Variables

PYRAMID .*GOV$*URBAN$

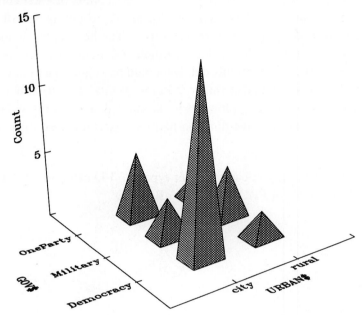

Figure 24.6 has several problems. The counts are not easily discernable from the single scale and the tall bar in the foreground obscures the others. Figure 24.7 adds several enhancements to solve these problems. First, we changed the axes to "CORNER" so that we could put grids on each plane. Also, we used XREV to reverse the URBAN$ categories on the X axis. This pushed the tall pyramid to the right. You can add YREV to do the same on the Y axis for GOV$ and it would have pushed the pyramid to the rear corner. You can also accomplish the same result by reordering the categories with the ORDER command. See the SYSTAT manual for how to do this.

Figure 24.7
Enhanced Pyramid Plot of Two Variables

PYRAMID .*GOV$*URBAN$/XGRID,YGRID,ZGRID,AX=CORNER,XREV

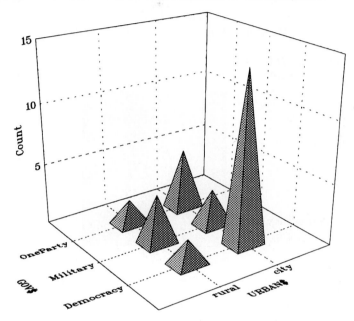

Three dimensional plots may look pretty, but they have serious disadvantages. First of all, perspective is a serious distorter of information. As the SYSTAT manual pointed out in the Cognitive Science and Graphics chapter, many perceptual illusions are grounded in the mechanisms of 3-D perspective processing. Most 3-D graphs can be represented in two dimensions by adding shading, color, or fill textures. Figure 24.8 shows an example for our data. As an alternative to the 3-D pyramid plot of Figure 24.7, this **mosaic plot** represents the counts by shades of color (gray in this book). Try it on your color monitor or printer to see how the colors map to counts.

We have made several modifications to crate a unique kind of graph. First, we eliminated axes (AX=0) because the labels do a sufficient job of delineating the table. Second, we used BTHICK=2 to make the tiles twice as thick as normal so that the entire area is filled. Finally, we labeled the X and Y axes to make the plot more informative.

The SYSTAT option for making a mosaic is TILE. This option means to represent the third dimension with color or fill in two dimensions. It works as well for surfaces as for bars. See the Continuous Variable section below for examples.

Figure 24.8
Mosaic (TILE) Plot of Two Variables

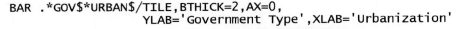

BAR .*GOV$*URBAN$/TILE,BTHICK=2,AX=0,
                  YLAB='Government Type',XLAB='Urbanization'

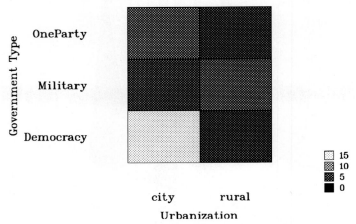

Figure 24.9 shows another way to represent this crossing of categorical variables. This **dual plot** takes advantage of the binary nature of the URBAN$ variable to place two separate bar charts back-to-back. Another, perhaps more appropriate name for this kind of graph is a **mirror plot**. This name reflects the antisymmetry in the plot, which make it easier to detect differences in counts across the categories between groups. Incidentally, you can substitute LINE, DOT, PROFILE, etc. for BAR as in earlier graphs.

As in earlier plots, we have made several modifications to the default form of this plot. First, we transposed the plot so that the bars are horizontal (just personal preference). Second, we added a label for X variable and a grid for the counts (YGRID). Notice that references to X and Y in the SYSTAT command are to the *roles* of the variables, not their physical position. Thus, we use YGRID to grid COUNT, even though the grids are vertical after transposing. The same principal applies to the X label. You may think TRANSPOSE this way: do everything you have to do to make a graph look the way you want it. Then add TRANSPOSE. Everything will transpose appropriately without having to modify your options.

Figure 24.9
Dual Bar Graph

```
BAR GOV$/DUAL=URBAN$,TRANSP,YGRID,XLAB='Government Type'
```

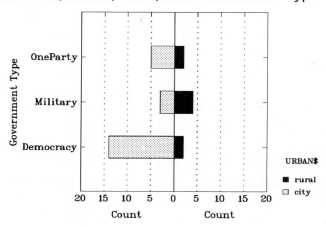

If there are more than two grouping categories, you cannot use a DUAL plot. Figure 24.10 shows how to make a **grouped bar graph**. The GROUP option, coupled with OVERLAY, makes side-by-side bars (instead of the DUAL back-to-back ones).

Figure 24.10
Grouped Bar Graph

```
BAR GOV$/GROUP=URBAN$,OVERLAY,
        YGRID,XLAB='Government Type',HEI=2IN,WID=3IN
```

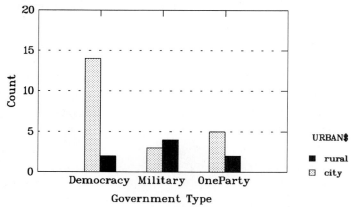

If you do not use the OVERLAY option with GROUP, you will get separate bar graphs for each group. We won't show this but encourage you to try.

Sometimes it helps to represent variation in a circle instead of a rectangle. A circle can represent more categories because there is more room to avoid collisions. Also, a circle can have meaning for some kinds of data. In his younger, non-pharmacokinetic years, the psychologist Timothy Leary worked on a circular theory of interpersonal behavior. There are no "ends" to Leary's scale. Geophysical and metereological data sometimes fit a circular arrangement as well. If you can order categories so that direction is meaningful, a polar chart makes sense. Figure 24.11 shows such a chart for our GOV\$ variable. This is not the best example of a polar categorical chart, but we used the same data so that you can compare the result to the bar chart in Figure 24.3. This type of graph is sometimes called a **spider diagram**. Our spider is a bit lazy and asymmetrical in this case, but you get the idea. Notice that the count variable is represented by distance from the center of the circle. We've added grids to make the indexing clearer. Incidentally, resist the temptation to add other grouping variables to this chart, modify the height and width separately, and otherwise produce chart-junk out of this command. SYSTAT will obey your orders, but you will forfeit your license to use it.

Figure 24.11
Polar Line Graph (Spider Diagram)

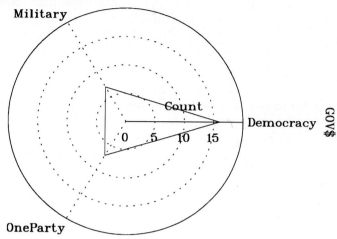

24.3 Graphing continuous variables

Continuous variables are represented graphically on continuous scales. The scales for counts in our category plots could take only integer values and the categories themselves were placed at fixed intervals on their own scales. Continuous scales, on the other hand, can represent a data item at any position along the scale. They represent, in other words, a bounded subset of the real numbers. The graphical objects for representing continuous variables are typically points, curves, and surfaces rather than dots, bars, and pyramids. As in the last section, we will proceed from the simple to the complex.

One continuous variable

Figure 24.12 shows histograms of male and female life expectancies. Notice, by the way, that SYSTAT produces automatically a separate graph for each variable requested. Histograms look like bar charts because they make use of the same graphical elements (bars!). The only difference is that the variable along which the bars are arrayed is continuous rather than categorical. Each bar touches, instead of being separated, because the data are divided into adjacent "bins" before making the bars. Usually, these bins have equal widths, although you may wish to try gap histograms (see the SYSTAT manual) on these same variables to see what unequal width bars look like in a histogram. You can control the bin widths before or after plotting the graph by using the BARS option. The popup graphics tool lets you try this in real time. See Figure 24.35 below for further information on how bar widths affect the appearance of a histogram. Also, try the other densities (DOT, DIT, FUZZYGRAM, etc.) in place of the histograms of Figure 24.12.

Figure 24.12
Simple Histograms of Male and Female Life Expectancies

DEN MALE,FEMALE / HIST

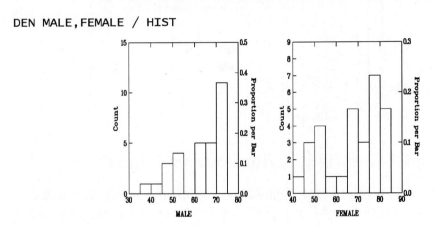

Two continuous variables

There are other density displays available for a single continuous variable. See Figure 24.34 for a summary of the ones available in SYSTAT. Let's move to two variable displays. Figure 24.13 shows a three dimensional histogram. The two base variables are MALE and FEMALE life expectancies. We've added XGRID, YGRID, ZGRID and corner axes to anchor the bars visibly. As with the last figure, try some of the other 3-D densities (KERNEL, NORMAL, etc.) in this figure.

The histogram shows the two variables are substantially correlated because the histogram is narrow and long along the diagonal axis. The following figures will display these two variables in a simple scatterplot to see another view of this relationship.

Figure 24.13
Three dimensional Histogram of Male and Female Life Expectancies

```
DEN  .*MALE*FEMALE/HIST,AX=CORNER,XGRID,YGRID,ZGRID
```

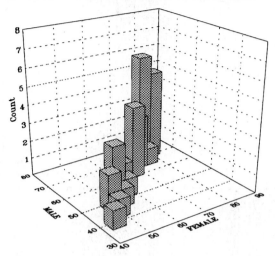

Figure 24.14 is a **scatterplot** of MALE and FEMALE life expectancies. Each case in the dataset is represented by a point in the plot. We have added box plots to the border of the scatterplot to show the densities at the margins. (See Figure 8.4 for an explanation of the meaning of box plots.) These box plots reveal the skewness in the data - most of the countries are concentrated at the higher life expectancy end of the scale, with a few outlying countries at the other end. Incidentally, you might want to try bordering with DIT, STRIPE or KERNEL densities instead of BOX.

We also added limits to the scales (with XMIN, YMIN, etc.) to keep them the same on the vertical and horizontal axes. Otherwise, SYSTAT chooses scales so that the numbers are nice and the frame is filled.

Figure 24.14
Scatterplot with Border Densities

`PLOT FEMALE*MALE/BORDER=BOX,XMIN=30,XMAX=90,YMIN=30,YMAX=90`

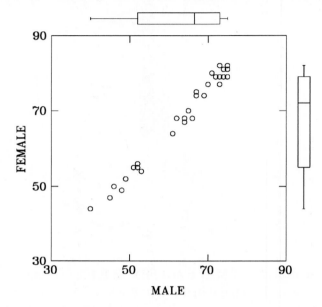

Three or more continuous variables

To accommodate more than two continuous variables, we have to use an additional scale (in three dimensions) or employ some other attribute such as size or symbol type. Before we try a three dimensional perspective plot, however, we should look at several methods for displaying three or more variables in a two dimensional plot. Three dimensional plots are sexy, but two dimensional plots often are easier to interpret and contain fewer visual illusions.

Let's start by adding another variable to Figure 24.14 by using symbol size. We added box plots on the border as in the previous graph and used BIRTH rates to control size. Notice that we decided to move the legend inside the frame to show you how this feature works. Ordinarily, we would want the legend outside of the frame to avoid covering data. Notice that the large circles predominate in the lower left, showing that high birth rates are associated with lower life expectancies among these countries.

Figure 24.15
Scatterplot with Symbol Size Proportional to Birth Rates

```
PLOT FEMALE*MALE/SIZE=BIRTH,BORDER=BOX,XMIN=30,XMAX=90,
          YMIN=30, YMAX=90, HEI=4IN,WID=4IN,LEGEND=3IN,.25IN
```

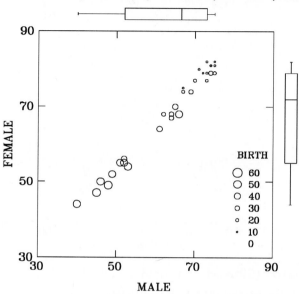

Figure 24.16 shows another way of representing a third variable in a two dimensional plot. We **overlay** two variables on the same vertical scale (assuming they are measured on comparable scales), using different symbols for each variable. In addition, we added a running **mode smoother**, which is one of our favorite exploratory smoothing methods. It has several advantages. First, it follows the data concentration, appearing only where there are relatively more data points. This feature helps reveal discontinuities in the data and tends to prevent unwarranted extrapolations. Second, the modal smoother allows for two predictions at one "x" (horizontal scale) value when there are two concentrations of data in that region. This is not evident in the Figure 24.16 because there is only one curve for each group, but you can see an example in the SYSTAT manual. Third, the modal smoother is quite resistant to outliers and other sampling anomalies. It follows the data concentration but does not get distracted by single points at the left and right edges of the plot, like LOWESS or other smoothers. Finally, the running mode, like LOWESS, is excellent for detecting nonlinearities. We can clearly see in Figure 24.16 that the downward trend in both variables is not linear.

Figure 24.16
Overlay Scatterplot with Running Mode Smother

PLOT BIRTH,DEATH*FEMALE/ OVERLAY,SMOO=MODE

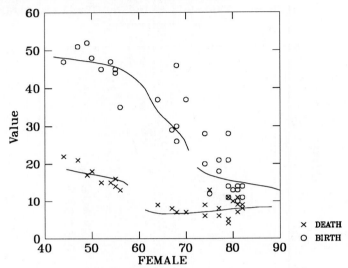

The **scatterplot matrix** (SPLOM) is a popular method for representing more than two variables in a two dimensional graph. It offers pairwise scatterplots in a tightly bound display. Axes are omitted because the main purpose of the display is to discover patterns, not quantify single values. Figure 24.17 shows a SPLOM of our demographic variables with two dimensional **kernel densities** superimposed. These densities are the objects used for the running mode smoother that we just saw in Figure 24.16. They are computed by finding the contours enclosing a constant level of density among points. That is, everywhere along a kernel contour, there should be a comparable concentration of data points in the local neighborhood. The default SYSTAT setting for the contour (.68) tends to place it toward the edge of point clouds. Set this way, it tends to enclose approximately 68 percent of the data points. This is the same setting used for EL-LIPSE, which is based on a normal distribution (see the SYSTAT manual). You can change this setting by adding KERNEL=#, where # is a value between 0 and 1.

We added two other options. The first, HALF, makes only half a SPLOM (since the other half is a symmetric reflection). The second, DENS=KERNEL, places kernel densities on the diagonal instead of the default histograms (you can try other densities here). This is convenient for comparing them to the contours.

Figure 24.17
Scatterplot Matrix (SPLOM) with Kernel Densities

`SPLOM BIRTH,DEATH,MALE,FEMALE/KERN,HALF,DENS=KERNEL`

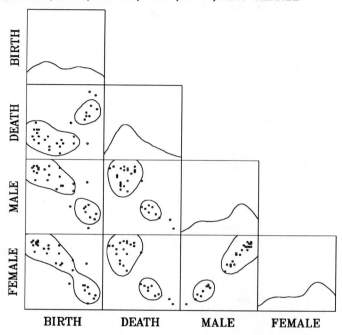

Figure 24.18 shows a grouped SPLOM. We have overlaid two SPLOMS, one for UR-BANized countries and another for rural countries. SYSTAT will overlay as many groups as are denoted in your grouping variable(s). SYSTAT distinguishes the sub-groups by dashed vs. solid lines here. We used the DASH option to choose ones we like. Notice that we get separate densities and clouds for each group. There are clear differences in these demographic variables by urbanization.

This graph belongs in the next section because it involves a categorical variable (UR-BAN) and several continuous variables. We're putting it here, however, so that you can compare it more easily with the previous SPLOM in Figure 24.17. Incidentally, the grouping variable for these overlaid plots can have more than two categories and you may even overlay two grouping variables. Good luck interpreting them.

Figure 24.18
Overlaid SPLOM with Kernel Densities

```
SPLOM BIRTH,DEATH,MALE,FEMALE/KERN,HALF, DENS=KERNEL,
GROUP=URBAN$,OVERLAY, DASH=1,10
```

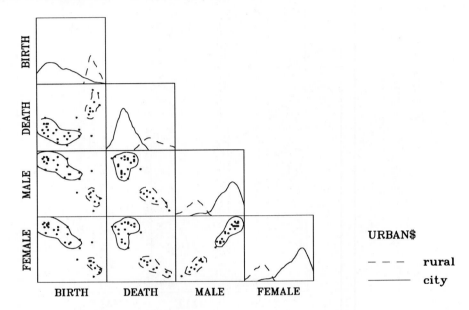

Figure 24.19 shows our promised 3-D plot. We did two plots to show you different rep-resentations. The left plot contains a **distance weighted least squares** (DWLS) smoother. This smoother is available in two or three dimensions. It computes the height of the surface at a selected point by regressing on the height of nearby data points. This regression is weighted by the distance of data points to the selected point. Data points far from the selected point contribute little to the prediction and data points near contribute the most.

We reversed the X and Y axes in order to make the surface face the viewer. The same could be accomplished by rotating the graph 180 degrees with the popup graph tool. The spikes in the right plot show a different method for representing the relationship of female life expectancies to birth and death rates. While the surface hides the points, the spikes show every point and hint at a possible surface. Neither representation is suffi-cient. Finally, we used the LOC option to put the graphs side-by-side. You should use this option to reposition graphs in general.

Figure 24.19
Three Dimensional Scatterplots with DWLS Smoother and Spikes

```
BEGIN
  PLOT FEMALE*BIRTH*DEATH/XREV,YREV,HEI=4IN,WID=2IN,
                         SMOOTH=DWLS,LOC=-2IN,0
  PLOT FEMALE*BIRTH*DEATH/XREV,YREV,HEI=4IN,WID=2IN,
                         SPIKE,LOC=2IN,0
END
```

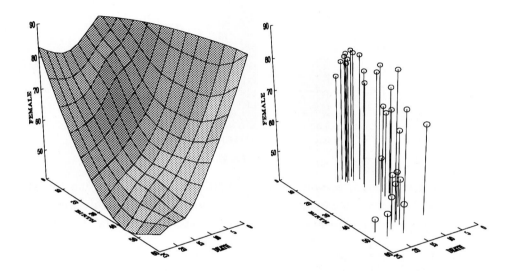

24.4 Graphing categorical and continuous variables

SYSTAT offers a variety of methods for displaying mixed categorical and continuous variables in a single graph. You can simulate many of these with other graphics systems. Let's begin with the simplest examples, which involve one categorical and one continuous variable.

One categorical and one continuous variable

Figure 24.20 shows a two variable bar graph. At first glance, it would seem to be the same type of graph as Figure 24.3. The earlier bar graphs we have seen dealt with counts rather than averages of a second variable, however. In Figure 24.20, the height of the bars represents the average BIRTH rate for each GOV$ category.

Figure 24.20
Two Variable Bar Graph

```
BAR BIRTH*GOV$ / HEI=2IN,WID=3IN
```

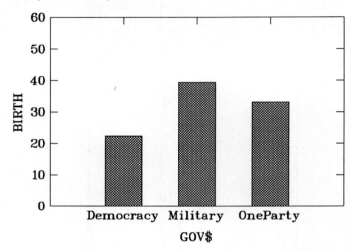

Figure 24.21shows the data on which Figure 24.20 is based. Including the dots allows us to see the scatter of points around each bar. This type of graph is rarely seen, perhaps because researchers seldom want to reveal the messiness of their data!

We've used BEGIN-END to overlay two graphs. Notice that we used AX=0 and SC=0 to suppress axis and scale printing for the overlay. It wouldn't show anyway, but why waste resources? We set FILL=0 in order to let the points show through the bars.

Figure 24.21
BAR-DOT Graph

```
BEGIN
  BAR BIRTH*GOV$/HEI=2IN,WID=3IN,FILL=0,
                XLAB='Government Type', YLAB='Birth Rate'
  PLOT BIRTH*GOV$/HEI=2IN,WID=3IN,AX=0,SC=0
END
```

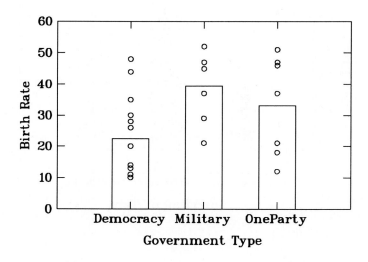

Figure 24.22 is an interesting variation on the previous figure. This is a true DOT plot, in which overlapping dots sidestep each other. The result is a symmetrical pile of dots. Medical researchers have made this plot popular. It's been rediscovered many times. See, for example, Box, Hunter & Hunter (1978, p. 65), and Hoaglin, Mosteller & Tukey (1991, p. 167). This plot could be overlaid on bars instead of using the PLOT command, as in Figure 24.21.

Figure 24.22
DOT Plot

```
DEN BIRTH*GOV$/DOT,HEI=2IN,WID=3IN,
            XLAB='Government Type', YLAB='Birth Rate
```

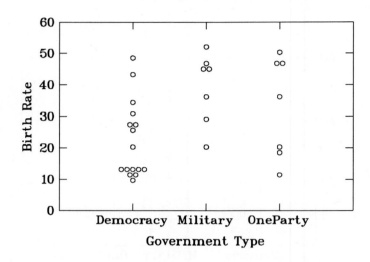

Two categorical and one continuous variables

Figure 24.23 contains an additional categorical variable. We have split the dots by the values of URBAN\$. SYSTAT automatically offsets these dots so they do not overlap within a category. There's little to say about this plot except that we specified the symbols explicitly (SYMBOL=1,2) to make clear the groups. SYSTAT generalizes the notion of the dot plot to any symbol plus colors and fills. Notice, incidentally, that we had to use OVERLAY to get a single graph with a legend. Otherwise, we would have gotten two separate dot plots.

Figure 24.23
DOT Plot by Groups

```
DEN BIRTH*GOV$/DOT,HEI=2IN,WID=3IN,
              XLAB='Government Type', YLAB='Birth Rate',
              GROUP=URBAN$,OVER,SYMBOL=1,2
```

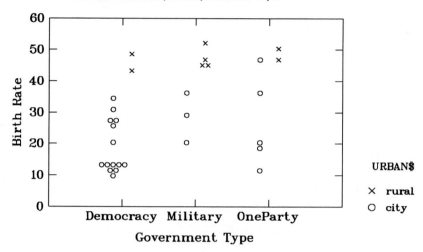

Figure 24.24 carries our theme to one more variation. This DOX plot combines the features of a box plot density with the dot plot. The disadvantage of box plots is that they do not reveal bi- (or multi-) modality and other local features. The disadvantage of dot plots is that they do not show the median and quartiles of the data. Putting them together combines the best of both displays.

Figure 24.24
DOX (DOT plus BOX) Plot

```
DEN BIRTH*GOV$/DOX,HEI=2IN,WID=3IN,
            XLAB='Government Type',YLAB='Birth Rate',
            GROUP=URBAN$,OVER,SYMB=1,2
```

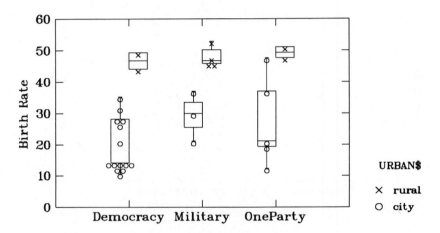

Figure 24.25 moves to three dimensions to accomodate a third variable. As in other three dimensional examples, we added grids to the axes and specified corner axes. If bars hide other bars, you may need to reverse axes or rotate the plot to correct the problem.

Figure 24.25
Three Dimensional Bar Graph

```
BAR  DEATH*GOV$*URBAN$/XGRID,YGRID,ZGRID,AX=CORNER,
                  YLAB='Government Type',XLAB='Urbanization'
```

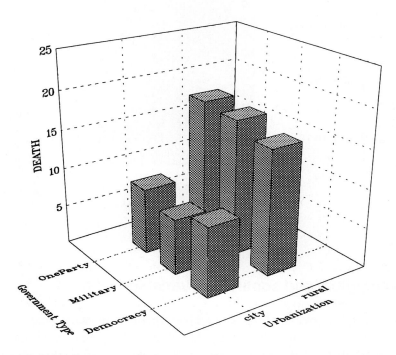

When 3-D bars collide, it is often better to fall back to two dimensions. Figure 24.26 shows a mosaic plot of the same data used for Figure 24.25. This plot is similar to Figure 24.8, which involved only two variables and cells representing counts. Once again, we used BTHICK=2 to make the bars fill the entire space. AX=0 tells SYSTAT not to draw the axes.

Figure 24.26
Mosaic Plot

BAR DEATH*GOV$*URBAN$/TILE,BTHICK=2,AX=0
YLAB='Government Type',XLAB='Urbanization'

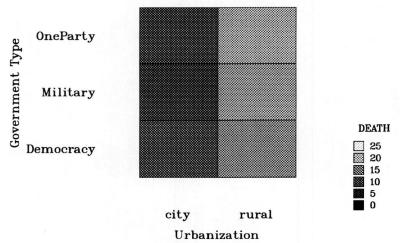

Many categorical and continuous variables

Figure 24.27 displays two continuous variables against one categorical variable. You may wish to try some of the other categorical plot models, such as PYRAMID, DOT, LINE, and PROFILE, on this same graph. You can also try more than two continuous variables on the same bar graph.

Figure 24.27
Overlay Bar Graph

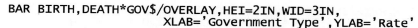

```
BAR BIRTH,DEATH*GOV$/OVERLAY,HEI=2IN,WID=3IN,
              XLAB='Government Type',YLAB='Rate'
```

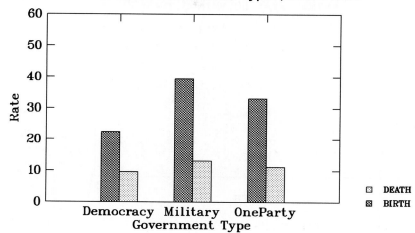

Figure 24.28 shows a grouped scatterplot containing four variables: two continuous and two categorical variables. The two categorical variables (URBAN$ and GOV$) have been combined in a single legend . We chose the symbols explicitly to represent the three values of GOV$ and the fill patterns to represent the two values of URBAN$. See the SYSTAT manual for other choices of symbols and fill patterns.

Note we resized the plot so that a rate difference of one point is the same physical distance on both axes of the plot. This makes the graph **isotropic**. When both axes are rates or share a common metric, it is usually a good idea to make units physically comparable in both directions by changing the physical **aspect ratio** (ratio of vertical to horizontal size) of the plot and setting the axis limits (YMIN, YMAX, etc.) appropriately.

Finally, note that the graph shows the predominance of rural countries among the high death rate/high birth rate cases. See Figure 24.32 for more detail on these data.

Figure 24.28
Grouped Scatterplot

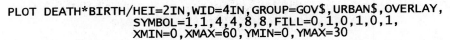

```
PLOT DEATH*BIRTH/HEI=2IN,WID=4IN,GROUP=GOV$,URBAN$,OVERLAY,
              SYMBOL=1,1,4,4,8,8,FILL=0,1,0,1,0,1,
              XMIN=0,XMAX=60,YMIN=0,YMAX=30
```

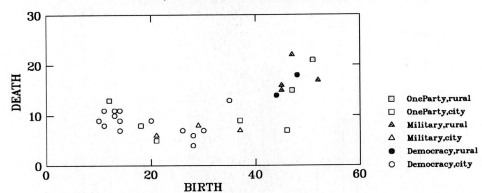

Figure 24.29 shows a graph popular among demographers. The usual data for this type of graph is ages of males and females in a particular population. We have used UR-BAN$ instead of gender as the dual, separating variable and BIRTH rate instead of age. The back-to-back nature of this graph makes it easy to detect asymmetries. SYSTAT's DUAL option allows you to construct this type of back-to-back display for any rectangular 2-D graph it produces. Finally, note that we transposed the graph to fit the conventions of the age-sex pyramid display.

Many age-sex pyramid graphs are really bar graphs rather than histograms. If your data are already aggregated into age groups, you can use SYSTAT's BAR procedure to create the same graph (e.g. BAR AGE*GROUP/DUAL=SEX). In Figure 24.29, SYSTAT did the aggregation automatically with its histogram binning routines.

Figure 24.29
Population Pyramid (DUAL Histogram)

```
DENSITY BIRTH/HIST,HEI=2IN,WID=3IN,XLAB='Birth Rate',DUAL=URBAN$,
          TRANSPOSE,FILL=.1,.9
```

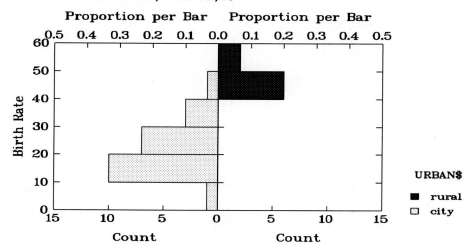

Figure 24.30 shows another approach to the population pyramid. Instead of the usual histograms, we use kernel densities of BIRTH rates for the two URBAN$ groups (urban, rural). This time, we kept the plot horizontal so you could see the difference. The concentration of BIRTH rates is clearly higher for the rural group of countries. The same pattern was clear in Figure 24.29. Notice how we used the DASH option to differentiate the two kernels in the legend.

We hope that when you see a published population pyramid you will now recognize that it is a special case of a much more general mirrored graph. Try using DUAL for other data and graph types. We think you will begin to appreciate its advantages when you want to make symmetrical comparisons.

Figure 24.30
Mirrored Kernel (DUAL Density)

```
DENSITY BIRTH/KERNEL,HEI=2IN,WID=3IN,XLAB='Birth Rate',DUAL=URBAN$,
                DASH=1,10
```

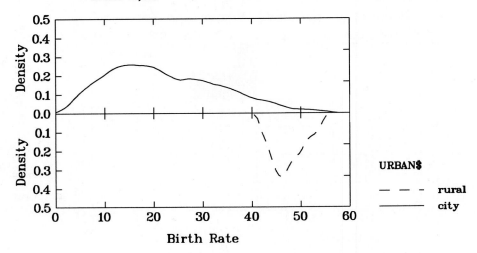

Finally, Figure 24.31 shows a **quantile-quantile plot** grouped by URBAN$. The Q-Q plot displays the sorted values of one variable against those of another. If the two variables are distributed similarly, the plot should fall close to a diagonal straight line. We include this plot to encourage you to consider grouping any plot you might otherwise produce separately for groups. Superimposing the plots with the OVERLAY option allows you to compare trends in the same data area.

Figure 24.31
Quantile-Quantile Plot

```
QPLOT BIRTH*DEATH/GROUP=URBAN$,OVERLAY
```

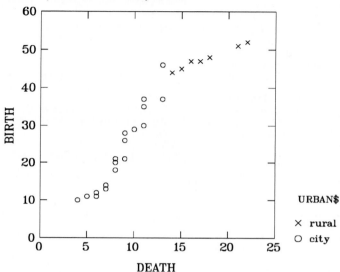

24.5 Enhancing scatterplots

This section deals with more advanced topics for continuous variables. We want to show you how to enhance ordinary scatterplots to reveal trends and other structures. At the same time, we'll illustrate more advanced SYSTAT graphics capabilities.

If you regress death rates on birth rates in REGRESSION (MGLH), you will find a highly significant regression coefficient for this relationship. Higher death rates are linearly associated with higher birth rates. This makes sense: societies with higher death rates need to replenish their population more to grow.

It's also a misrepresentation of the data. The panels of Figure 24.32 show a scatterplot of this relationship. This figure contains a wealth of information. Let's review the parts of the script that produced it.

Figure 24.32.
Kernel Densities on Scatterplots

```
BEGIN
REM LOWER PANEL
PLOT DEATH*BIRTH/HEI=3IN,WID=6IN,
                XMIN=0,XMAX=60,YMIN=0,YMAX=30,XTICK=6,
                SYMBOL=1,SIZE=.5,LABEL=COUNTRY$,SMOO=MODE,KERNEL=.8
DRAW LINE /FROM=0,0,TO=3IN,3IN,DASH=11
WRITE 'Zero Population Growth'/,
                HEI=.1IN,WID=.1IN,ANGLE=45,LOC=1.5IN,1.6IN
REM UPPER PANEL
PLOT DEATH*BIRTH/HEI=3IN,WID=6IN,LOC=0,4IN,
                XMIN=0,XMAX=60,YMIN=0,YMAX=30,XTICK=6,
                SYMBOL=1,SIZE=.5,LABEL=COUNTRY$,SMOO=MODE
DEN .*DEATH*BIRTH/HEI=3IN,WID=6IN,LOC=0,4IN,
                XMIN=0,XMAX=60,YMIN=0,YMAX=30,XTICK=6,
                KERNEL,CONTOUR,ZTICK=10,ZPIP=0,AX=0,SC=0
END
```

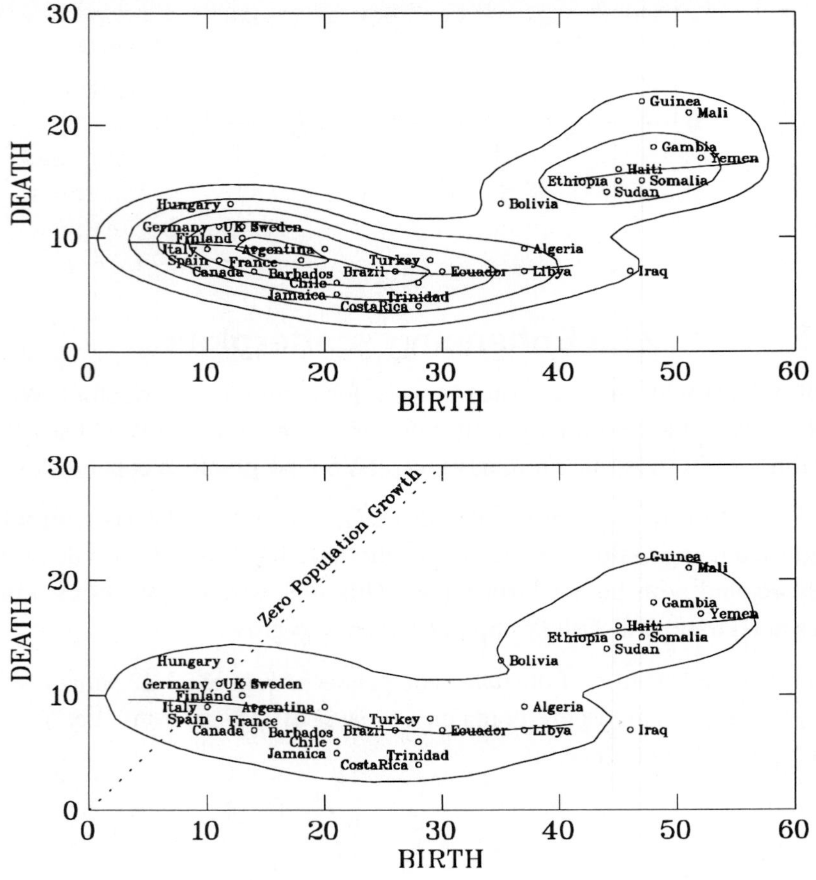

The size of the figure, specifically the **aspect ratio** of the axes, was chosen to keep the scales comparable (using HEIGHT=3IN, WIDTH=6IN). Thus, the Zero Population Growth line is at 45 degrees. Countries to the left of the line are losing population, and those to the right are gaining.

The kernel contour is a method of representing the density of the points by a smooth curve. This curve is computed by finding the points on a surface that all have the same altitude. In both panels, we are looking down on this surface, so the graph is like a topological map. We can see two hills (clusters) in the data, one comprising more developed countries, and the other, less developed.

The surface itself is a weighted averaging of points in a given neighborhood. The more points in the neighborhood, the higher the density estimate and the higher the hill. The weighting is done by a function which looks like an upside down "U" centered at each averaging point. Thus, points farther from the averaging point are given less weight. Those close to the point are given more weight, so wherever there are lots of points near an averaging point on the surface, the surface will be relatively higher. We will see more of this technique, called **kernel density estimation**, in the next section. We chose the option KERNEL=.8 in the lower panel to make the curve enclose more points. The default value for KERNEL is .5. The value specifies the proportion of the volume under the hill within the bounds of the kernel contour. In the upper panel, we have superimposed a 3D kernel density on the scatterplot to show more contours.

Notice the syntax of the DENSITY command. The initial period (.) is required as a place holder because it represents the implied height computed by the density operation. Since the entire density is contoured, the KERN option takes no number, as it did in the bottom panel of Figure 24.32. In short, the KERNEL plot option allows you to specify the level of the one contour (bottom panel), but the KERNEL density option produces a whole set of contours (top panel), so there is no need for a number.

Finally, there is a modal regression smoother that can be used to predict death rates from birth rates. Notice that the regression line has broken into two pieces. This follows the ridge of the kernel smooth hill. Both methods are based on the same mathematics, so this is not surprising. The modal smoother is our favorite exploratory smoother because it has this quality of splitting when needed. For each value of X, it is possible to have more than one value of predicted Y. If the data are approximately bivariate normal, like an elliptical cloud, then the modal smoother will resemble a single straight line. When not, the modal smoother will pick up curvilinearity *and* multimodality (2 lines). None of the other popular smoothers have this quality.

When you think about it, the modal (conditional mode) smoother is not so strange. The **conditional mean** smoother is in the SMOOTH=MEAN option to PLOT. This smoother displays the mean on Y of all points in a neighborhood of X. The **conditional median** smoother is in the SMOOTH=MEDIAN option. This displays the median Y value for all points in a neighborhood of X. Finally, the **conditional mode** smoother is in SMOOTH=MODE. It works like the others, but when there are two modes on Y in the neighborhood of X (or at least two hills at almost the same altitude) then two lines are displayed. The calculations are rather complex, but the result is simple to interpret. Incidentally, the conditional linear smoother is SMOOTH=LINEAR. This is ordinary linear regression, but you can think of it as a conditional mean smoother where the overall curve is constrained to be a straight line. The advantage of a linear smoother is that it is simple and easy to communicate. It is completely described by a slope and intercept, as we saw in Chapter 4. Our strategy is to try SMOOTH=MODE, and if it looks like a straight line, switch to SMOOTH=LINEAR. That is clearly inappropriate here, so we settled for the mode.

Figure 24.32 is a good example of a graph which may be more useful than a parametric statistical analysis. We could try to model the distribution in the figure, but it is probably better just to look at it. We can extend this analysis to a multivariate context. Figure 24.33 gives some examples. In the lower panel, we have made the size of the symbol in the plot proportional to the difference between male and female life expectancies. We standardized this difference by average life expectancy. The LTITLE option, by the way, is for a Legend Title. Try to find it in the index to the SYSTAT manual. In the larger OURWORLD file in SYSTAT, there are several countries where males tend to outlive females. Can you devise a graph to reveal the size *and* direction of the difference in those cases?

The upper panel shows the same difference in life expectancy information displayed as a contour overlay. We first made a new variable to represent a standardized difference in male and female life expectancies. The standardization of DIFF by total life expectancy in each country removes the influence of level of life expectancy from the statistic. We used distance weighted least squares to smooth the DIFF scores (SMOOTH=DWLS) and then contoured this surface over the scatterplot of death rates against birth rates. The contours indicate that females tend to outlive males more in countries where the birth rates are lower relative to death rates, not surprisingly. We tend to prefer the lower panel graph in this figure because it displays the raw data values of DIFF better and lets the viewer discern the relationship.

Figure 24.33.
Representing a Third Variable by Smoothing vs. Size

```
LET DIFF=ABS(FEMALE-MALE)/(FEMALE+MALE)
BEGIN
REM LOWER PANEL
PLOT DEATH*BIRTH/HEI=3IN,WID=6IN,SIZE=DIFF,
                 YMIN=0,YMAX=30,XMIN=0,XMAX=60,
                 XLAB='Birth Rate',YLAB='Death Rate',
                 LTITLE='Difference'
REM UPPER PANEL
PLOT DIFF*DEATH*BIRTH/HEI=3IN,WID=6IN,LOC=0,4IN,
                 SMOOTH=DWLS,CONTOUR,
                 YMIN=0,YMAX=30,XMIN=0,XMAX=60,
                 XLAB='Birth Rate',YLAB='Death Rate',
                 ZTICK=10,ZPIP=0,SYMBOL=1,ZFORMAT=2
END
```

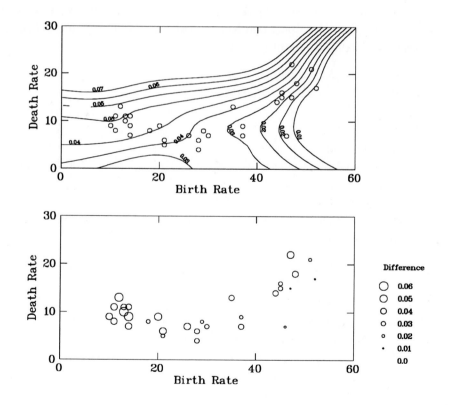

24.6 Densities

SYSTAT offers many ways to represent a density in 1, 2, or 3 dimensions. Densities (including histograms) represent the concentration of data in local regions of a scale. We encourage you to experiment on the same data to learn how each method highlights a different aspect of data density. Figure 24.34 shows the 1, 2, and 3D densities available in SYSTAT for the male life expectancy data. The 1D densities in the bottom row are useful for bordering scatterplots (e.g. PLOT ... / BORDER=STRIPE). They are also especially suited for grouped density displays (e.g. DENSITY RAIN*REGION$/ DOX). The 2D densities in the middle row yield the traditional density vertical scale. The 3D densities in the top row require a leading period (.) in the DENSITY command to represent the density axis. Otherwise, you would get a grouped density plot.

Choosing among the densities is a matter of personal taste, although we tend to prefer DIT, BOX, and DOX 1D densities, and KERN and HIST among 2 and 3D densities. The GAP density is useful for identifying outliers.

Figure 24.34.
Densities in SYSTAT

```
BEGIN
REM LOWER PANEL
DEN MALE/HEI=1IN,WID=1IN,LOC=0,0,AX=1,SC=0,STICK=OUT,STRIPE
DEN MALE/HEI=1IN,WID=1IN,LOC=1IN,0,AX=1,SC=0,STICK=OUT,JITTER
DEN MALE/HEI=1IN,WID=1IN,LOC=2IN,0,AX=1,SC=0,STICK=OUT,BOX
DEN MALE/HEI=1IN,WID=1IN,LOC=3IN,0,AX=1,SC=0,STICK=OUT,DOX
DEN MALE/HEI=1IN,WID=1IN,LOC=4IN,0,AX=1,SC=0,STICK=OUT,DOT
DEN MALE/HEI=1IN,WID=1IN,LOC=5IN,0,AX=1,SC=0,STICK=OUT,DIT
REM MIDDLE PANEL
DEN MALE/HEI=1IN,WID=1IN,LOC=0,1IN,AX=1,SC=0,STICK=OUT,NORM
DEN MALE/HEI=1IN,WID=1IN,LOC=1IN,1IN,AX=1,SC=0,STICK=OUT,KERN
DEN MALE/HEI=1IN,WID=1IN,LOC=2IN,1IN,AX=1,SC=0,STICK=OUT,POLY
DEN MALE/HEI=1IN,WID=1IN,LOC=3IN,1IN,AX=1,SC=0,STICK=OUT,HIST
DEN MALE/HEI=1IN,WID=1IN,LOC=4IN,1IN,AX=1,SC=0,STICK=OUT,FUZZY
DEN MALE/HEI=1IN,WID=1IN,LOC=5IN,1IN,AX=1,SC=0,STICK=OUT,GAP
REM UPPER PANEL
DEN .*MALE*FEMALE/HEI=1IN,WID=1IN,ALT=1IN,
                 LOC=0,2.5IN,AX=13,SC=0,STICK=OUT,NORM,CUT=10
DEN .*MALE*FEMALE/HEI=1IN,WID=1IN,ALT=1IN,
                 LOC=1.5IN,2.5IN,AX=13,SC=0,STICK=OUT,KERN,CUT=10
DEN .*MALE*FEMALE/HEI=1IN,WID=1IN,ALT=1IN,
                 LOC=3.0IN,2.5IN,AX=13,SC=0,STICK=OUT,POLY
DEN .*MALE*FEMALE/HEI=1IN,WID=1IN,ALT=1IN,
                 LOC=4.5IN,2.5IN,AX=13,SC=0,STICK=OUT,HIST
END
```

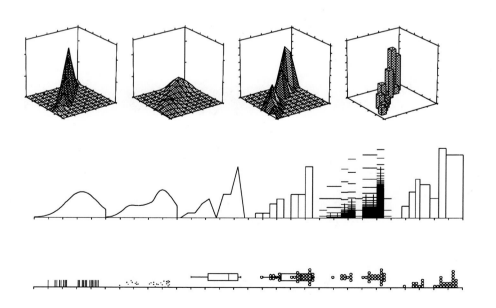

We are so used to histograms for our density displays that we tend to forget how much they can distort data and how primitive they really are. Figure 24.35 is an exercise to show how much histograms change in appearance when we change the number of bars or the cutpoints between bars. We've included all the commands, repetitious as they are, so that you can examine the individual graphs and see how to overlay graphs with the LOC option.

The bottom set of histograms is based on BARS=10, but we have shifted the scale by a few years in each panel. Simply by shifting the cutpoints, we produce histograms that vary considerably. The next row shows what happens when we vary the number of bars from 10 to 15. The differences are almost as dramatic as those from shifting scales. Finally, the top row shows what happens when we change TENSION for the KERNEL density. The only noticeable effect is that the higher tensions tend to mask the slight bimodality of the distribution. The default tension computed by SYSTAT exposes this bimodality, however. The main point we want to make is that, in general, kernel densities will better reveal the shape of a distribution than histograms. Use histograms if you wish to make categorical mental calculations rather than shape judgments (such as the count of countries where people die between 50 and 60). Otherwise, use kernels. If you *really* want to count, use stem-and-leaf diagrams or dit plots (see Figure 24.37).

Figure 24.35.
Densities with Varying Bars, Cutpoints, and Tensions

```
BEGIN
REM BOTTOM ROW
DEN MALE/XMIN=0,XMAX=100,BARS=10,HEI=1IN,WID=1IN,
        LOC=0,0,YMAX=35,SC=0
DEN MALE/XMIN=2,XMAX=102,BARS=10,HEI=1IN,WID=1IN,
        LOC=1IN,0,YMAX=35,SC=0
DEN MALE/XMIN=3,XMAX=103,BARS=10,HEI=1IN,WID=1IN,
        LOC=2IN,0,YMAX=35,SC=0
DEN MALE/XMIN=5,XMAX=105,BARS=10,HEI=1IN,WID=1IN,
        LOC=3IN,0,YMAX=35,SC=0
DEN MALE/XMIN=7,XMAX=107,BARS=10,HEI=1IN,WID=1IN,
        LOC=4IN,0,YMAX=35,SC=0
DEN MALE/XMIN=9,XMAX=109,BARS=10,HEI=1IN,WID=1IN,
        LOC=5IN,0,YMAX=35,SC=0
REM MIDDLE ROW
DEN MALE/XMIN=0,XMAX=100,BARS=10,HEI=1IN,WID=1IN,
        LOC=0,1IN,YMAX=35,SC=0
DEN MALE/XMIN=0,XMAX=100,BARS=11,HEI=1IN,WID=1IN,
        LOC=1IN,1IN,YMAX=35,SC=0
DEN MALE/XMIN=0,XMAX=100,BARS=12,HEI=1IN,WID=1IN,
        LOC=2IN,1IN,YMAX=35,SC=0
DEN MALE/XMIN=0,XMAX=100,BARS=13,HEI=1IN,WID=1IN,
        LOC=3IN,1IN,YMAX=35,SC=0
DEN MALE/XMIN=0,XMAX=100,BARS=14,HEI=1IN,WID=1IN,
        LOC=4IN,1IN,YMAX=35,SC=0
DEN MALE/XMIN=0,XMAX=100,BARS=15,HEI=1IN,WID=1IN,
        LOC=5IN,1IN,YMAX=35,SC=0
REM UPPER ROW
DEN MALE/XMIN=0,XMAX=100,HEI=1IN,WID=1IN,
        LOC=0,2IN,YMAX=35,SC=0,KERN,TENS=.35,AX=4
DEN MALE/XMIN=0,XMAX=100,HEI=1IN,WID=1IN,
        LOC=1IN,2IN,YMAX=35,SC=0,KERN,TENS=.40,AX=4
DEN MALE/XMIN=0,XMAX=100,HEI=1IN,WID=1IN,
        LOC=2IN,2IN,YMAX=35,SC=0,KERN,TENS=.45,AX=4
DEN MALE/XMIN=0,XMAX=100,HEI=1IN,WID=1IN,
        LOC=3IN,2IN,YMAX=35,SC=0,KERN,TENS=.50,AX=4
DEN MALE/XMIN=0,XMAX=100,HEI=1IN,WID=1IN,
        LOC=4IN,2IN,YMAX=35,SC=0,KERN,TENS=.55,AX=4
DEN MALE/XMIN=0,XMAX=100,HEI=1IN,WID=1IN,
        LOC=5IN,2IN,YMAX=35,SC=0,KERN,TENS=.60,AX=4
END
```

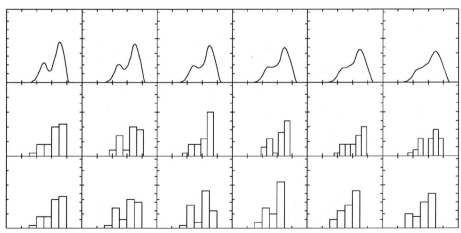

Figure 24.36 shows another example of the type of kernel used in Figure 24.32. We have bordered the plot with kernels (in the second PLOT command) to show how the marginal distributions at the edges relate to the joint distribution in the plot. To see how this kernel density looks in 3D, examine the second plot from the left in the top row of Figure 24.34. Also, try the different density options in a scatterplot matrix (SPLOM) to see how they appear across a range of variables.

Figure 24.36.
Joint Density of Life Expectancies

```
BEGIN
DEN  .*MALE*FEMALE/YMIN=30,YMAX=100,XMIN=30,XMAX=100,
                  KERN,CONTOUR,CUT=60,ZTICK=5,ZFORMAT=1,
                  YLAB='Male Life Expectancy',
                  XLAB='Female Life Expectancy'
PLOT   MALE*FEMALE/YMIN=30,YMAX=100,XMIN=30,XMAX=100,
                  BORDER=KERN,AX=0,SC=0,SYMBOL=1,SIZE=.5
END
```

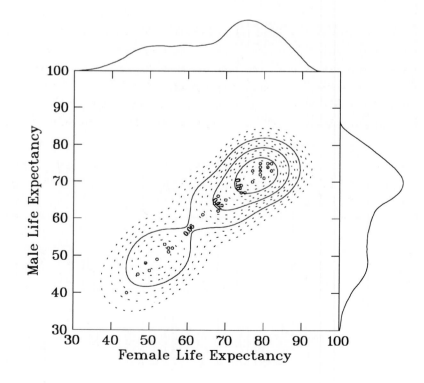

Notice here, as in the last example, that we specified the axis ranges explicitly. It's a safe idea to do this with overlays to be sure things fit, although SYSTAT takes care of it anyway. If you set the ranges for any overlay, be sure to set them the same for all overlays between BEGIN and END. SYSTAT Version 6 uses the same data range for every graph of a variable, whether the display is a histogram, scatterplot, or whatever. This makes overlays and bordering work without fiddling.

24.7 Aggregations

Histograms, bar charts, line graphs, and other aggregate displays were designed before computers offered a way to graph data *and* aggregates at the same time. Now that dot and dit plots can be displayed in any resolution, there is little excuse for using these older methods on fewer than a hundred thousand cases. This section will present several examples of how to enhance aggregate plots to communicate the distribution of data as well as the summaries.

Figure 24.37 shows a density on the Food Price data of Chapter 14. The symbols for Fruits and Vegetables (F,V) have been used to build a dit density for the whole sample. A kernel overlay helps smooth the result visually. You need to do some fiddling with SIZE to make these kinds of plots work, since the height of the dit plot is determined by the size of the symbols. By using letters to represent subgroups, we have created a type of stem-and-leaf diagram in which the leaves have been replaced by non-numeric characters. You may wish to try other ways to differentiate subgroups in DIT and DOT plots (color, fill, symbol).

If you are interested in the shape of the separate distributions rather than the pooled, try a back-to-back mirrored density (with the DUAL option). Or, if there are more groups, try overlaying kernels.

Figure 24.37.
DIT Density AND Kernel of Food Prices

```
USE PRODUCE1
BEGIN
DEN PRICE/DIT,SYMBOL=TYPE$,SIZE=3,AX=0,SC=0
DEN PRICE/KERNEL
END
```

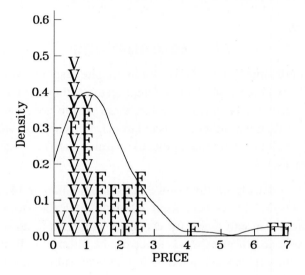

Figure 24.38 shows the classic line plots seen in 99 percent of the graphs accompanying ANOVAs in published articles. The lower plot is typical of the ones in psychology journals. The upper plot adds standard error bars, a favorite among scientific journals. We'll exaggerate to make our point: using these plots is a form of lying. Why do people like them? They are beloved because they conceal the messiness of the data behind them. The error bars are by definition symmetric, even though the data on which they are computed may not be. Outliers are concealed. Everything is tidy.

It is easy to modify these plots without losing the essential summary information. Simply add dots of the data to the plots. For many data, dot-box plots with connecting lines are even better, because they show the medians and interquartile range as well as the means. Figure 24.39 is an example of this type of modification. We have overlaid DOT densities on the line plots, leaving the lines to connect the means.

Figure 24.38.
Two-way Line Plots of Food Prices

```
LET IPRICE=1/PRICE
BEGIN
DOT  IPRICE*PREP$/GROUP=TYPE$,OVER,LINE,
              HEI=2IN,WID=3IN,SYMBOL=4,5,SIZE=2
LINE IPRICE*PREP$/GROUP=TYPE$,OVER,DASH=1,10,SERROR,
              HEI=2IN,WID=3IN,LOC=0,3IN
END
```

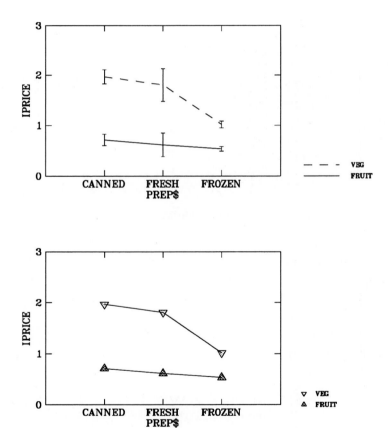

Figure 24.39.
Two-way Data Plots of Food Prices

```
BEGIN
DEN  IPRICE*PREP$/DOT,SYMBOL=TYPE$,SIZE=2,HEI=2IN,WID=3IN
LINE IPRICE*PREP$/GROUP=TYPE$,OVER,DASH=1,7,HEI=2IN,WID=3IN
DEN  IPRICE*PREP$/DOX,GROUP=TYPE$,OVER,LEGEND=NONE,
               HEI=2IN,WID=3IN,LOC=0,3IN
LINE IPRICE*PREP$/GROUP=TYPE$,OVER,DASH=1,7,
               HEI=2IN,WID=3IN,LOC=0,3IN
END
```

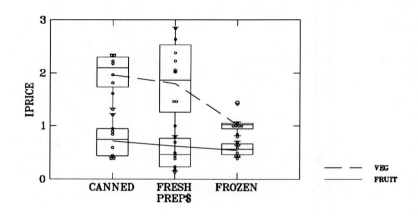

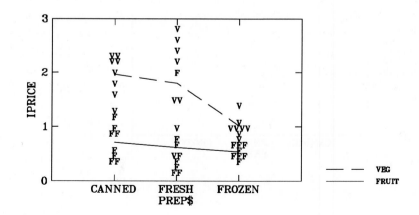

Bar charts are the most abused of all aggregate displays. They make sense for data which are already aggregated or consist of only one positive number per bar. Otherwise, a dot or line plot is almost always better. Scientists sometimes like bar charts with error bars, similar to the line chart at the top of Figure 24.38. These, too, can be improved by superimposing the actual data. Figure 24.40 shows how to do this with the PLOT command.

Figure 24.40 illustrates an aspect of SYSTAT's design that puzzles some people who encounter it in a graphing package for the first time. In SYSTAT, axes *always* cover the range of the data on which the graph is based, regardless of the contents of the frame (bar, cloud, line, etc.). This prevents you from making a misleading graph. In a bar chart, the vertical axis is based on the full range of data points making up each bar. If you try to raise the heights of the bars by cutting the vertical range, you may get a warning message that some points have been excluded. The guiding principle of SYGRAPH is that graphs are consistently connected to data. This is a fundamental principle of good statistical graphics which is easily forgotten in a world of freehand drawing/charting packages.

What if you want the bars higher? If the bars are particularly low in the frame, as in the lower panel of Figure 24.40, it is probably a sign of positive skewness in the data; you need a transformation to produce symmetry. The upper panel shows how the inverse transformation of prices (pounds per dollar instead of dollars per pound) raises the height of the bars.

In the same vein, SYSTAT makes it difficult to embed a smoother based on one set of points in a frame containing another. What you see inside the frame is what you get - for smoothers, confidence ellipses, etc. If you want to violate this principle, feel free to customize the axis limits and physical dimensions of overlaid components between BEGIN/END. By using AXES=0, SCALES=0, you can customize just about anything. Be sure to add annotation that the graph is not what it seems, however.

Figure 24.40.
Bar Plots of Food Prices

```
BEGIN
BAR   PRICE*PREP$ /FILL=0,AX=0,SC=0,HEI=2IN,WID=3IN
PLOT  PRICE*PREP$ /SYMBOL=1,HEI=2IN,WID=3IN
BAR   IPRICE*PREP$/FILL=0,AX=0,SC=0,HEI=2IN,WID=3IN,LOC=0,3IN
PLOT  IPRICE*PREP$/SYMBOL=1,HEI=2IN,WID=3IN,LOC=0,3IN
END
```

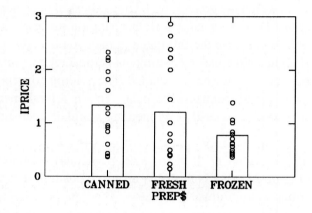

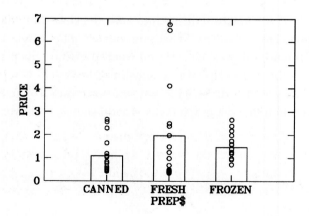

24.8 Maps

We could do a whole chapter on maps, but this book is reaching the outer limit of its binding and we want to save some trees. We'll simply finish with a 3-D graph containing a map to show you how map coordinates carry through all the elements of a SYSTAT plot. Figure 24.41 plots winter temperatures from the US dataset in the SYSTAT manual on top of a map of the US.

The program in the figure first draws the map on the XY facet. In 3-D, the XY facet is on the floor of the graph. We set the height, width, and altitude explicitly so that each facet of the graph (the map, the contour, and the surface) will match correctly. We chose a stereographic projection for the map. You can fiddle with others, if you like. The important thing is that the same projection must be used for each component of the graph. This is why SYSTAT includes PROJECTION as an option to almost all its graphs. Maps and graphs can be blended with no extra effort. Finally, we use WINTER temperatures to determine the fill density for each state. The darker fills in the southern states indicate higher average winter temperatures.

The next part of the graph is created by the first PLOT command. This is the set of WINTER temperature contours on the surface of the map. SMOOTH=INVS specifies **inverse distance averaging** (Shepardizing), which tends to make surfaces flat at the edges rather than steep (as with DWLS). To compute a point on the contour surface, inverse smoothing averages Winter temperatures of all the states, weighting more distant points less. By contrast, DWLS uses a weighted regression equation of state temperatures rather than an average to compute its estimated surface points. We use AX=0 and SC=0 for the contours because we do not want a new set of axes to be drawn over the ones from the 3-D surface we plot next. Also, we use ZPIP=12 to create more dotted contour lines to emphasize the surface. ZTICK controls the number of solid contours in a plot, and ZPIP controls dashed contours. Finally, SIZE=0 masks the points themselves. We don't want points plotted for the states.

The surface itself is plotted with the next command. Notice that we again use the PROJ=STEREO option to make the surface fit the curved domain. AX=SPOON makes the axes look like a soup spoon, with the handle for the vertical axis. Notice that the map projection causes the axes to curve automatically. All the different projections and coordinate systems do this to axes in SYSTAT.

Incidentally, the surface floats above the map because this plot creates a 3-D graph, unlike the map and contour plots, which create 2-D graphs. The surface and axes match the orientation of the map and contours because we kept the dimensions of the whole

graph constant (3IN). Thus, FACET=XY places all two dimensional graphics components (the map and the contour) at the bottom floor of the 3-D graph.

Figure 24.41.
US Winter Temperatures

```
BEGIN
FACET=XY
MAP/FILL=WINTER,PROJ=STEREO,HEI=3IN,WID=3IN,ALT=3IN,LEGEND=NONE
PLOT WINTER*LABLAT*LABLON/PROJ=STEREO,SMOO=INVS,CONTOUR,AX=0,SC=0,
  HEI=3IN,WID=3IN,ALT=3IN,SIZE=0,ZPIP=12
PLOT WINTER*LABLAT*LABLON/PROJ=STEREO,SMOO=INVS,SIZE=0,AX=SPOON,
  HEI=3IN,WID=3IN,ALT=3IN,ZLAB='Winter
Temperatures',XLAB='Longitude',
  YLAB='Latitude',SURFACE=FILL
END
```

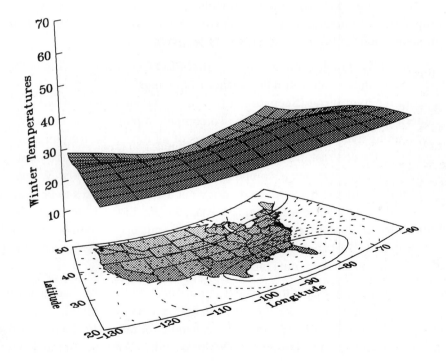

24.9 Conclusion

As we said earlier, we haven't space to cover all the graphs available in SYSTAT. We encourage you to experiment with the system using the examples we gave you in this chapter. The design philosophy behind SYSTAT graphics is orthogonality: wherever an option is available (coordinates, projections, transpose, dual, groups, etc.), it ought to be available everywhere (unless the result is nonsense or impossible). This is why we encourage you to construct a graph to your liking and then try, for example, polar coordinates. The results may surprise you or they may look like a familiar graph.

When an option is incompatible with or meaningless on a particular graph, SYSTAT may simply ignore your request. A smoother won't work on a bar graph, for example. You cannot lose by asking, however, so feel free to click or type options which interest you. Send us your most horrendous examples and we might put one in the next edition.

Further reading

In addition to the Cleveland citations in the SYSTAT manual and Cleveland (1993), Wainer and Thissen (1981) and Everitt (1978) are useful introductions to graphical methods in statistics. Tufte (1983, 1990) covers graphic design in two classic books. Wilkinson (1992) surveys graphical methods for medical research. Box, Hunter and Hunter (1978) is an excellent example of the intelligent and creative use of graphics in engineering statistics, especially for a 1970's vintage book. It uses dot plots and numerous other graph types not ordinarily seen in technical sources to show data and illustrate assumptions.

References

Box, G.E.P., Hunter, W.G., and Hunter, J.S. (1978). *Statistics for Experimenters*. New York: John Wiley & Sons.

Cleveland (1993). *Visualizing Data*. Summit, NJ: Hobart Press.

Everitt, B. (1978). *Graphical Techniques for Multivariate Data*. London: Heinemann.

Hoaglin, D.C., Mosteller, F., and Tukey, J.W. (1991). *Fundamentals of Exploratory Analysis of Variance*. New York: John Wiley & Sons.

Spence, I. (1990). Visual psychophysics of simple graphical elements. *Journal of Experimental Psychology: Human Performance and Perception, 16,* 683-692.

Tufte, E. (1983). *The Visual Display of Quantitative Information.* Cheshire, CT: Graphics Press.

Tufte, E. (1990). *Envisioning Data.* Cheshire, CT: Graphics Press.

Wainer, H. and Thissen, D. (1981). Graphical data analysis. *Annual Review of Psychology, 32,* 191-241.

Wilkinson, L. (1992). Graphical displays. *Statistical Methods in Medical Research. 1,* 3-25..

Wilkinson, L. and McConathy, D. (1990). Memory for graphs. In *Proceedings of the Section on Statistical Graphics.* Alexandria, VA: American Statistical Association.

Index